MECHANISMS OF ADAPTIVE BEHAVIOR

Clark Hull at the American Psychological Association meeting, 1936.
(Photograph courtesy of Ruth Hull Low)

Mechanisms of Adaptive Behavior

*Clark L. Hull's Theoretical Papers,
with Commentary*

Abram Amsel

and

Michael E. Rashotte

NEW YORK
COLUMBIA UNIVERSITY PRESS
1984

Library of Congress Cataloging in Publication Data

Hull, Clark Leonard, 1884–1952.
   Mechanisms of adaptive behavior.

   Consists of Clark L. Hull's 21 papers from Psychological review, 1929–1950, with introductory matter.
   Includes bibliographies and index.
   1. Conditioned response—Addresses, essays, lectures.
2. Learning, Psychology of—Addresses, essays, lectures.
3. Behaviorism (Psychology)—Addresses, essays, lectures.
I. Amsel, Abram.   II. Rashotte, Michael E.   II. Title
BF319.H833   1984   150.19'434   84-7608
ISBN 0-231-05792-X

Columbia University Press
New York   Guildford, Surrey
Copyright © 1984 Columbia University Press
All rights reserved

Printed in the United States of America

Clothbound editions of Columbia University Press books are Smyth-sewn and
printed on permanent and durable acid-free paper.

Table of Contents

Chronological Listing of Hull's *Psychological Review* Papers

(Hull is sole author of all but Papers 17 and 18, where multiple authorship is noted. In our commentaries, we will often refer to these papers by using the numerals designating the order of their appearance.)

Preface

THE IDEA for this book came to us several years ago when we prepared a history of learning theory in America with special reference to Clark Hull's contributions (Amsel & Rashotte, 1977). We became aware at that time of the fact that for every major American learning theorist except Hull a volume of collected papers was available. Hull's special place in American psychology seemed reason enough to correct this omission. But an even better reason is that, as we shall document in our commentaries, the portrayal of Hull as a "Traditional Learning Theorist" in recent discussions has focused almost entirely on his book, *Principles of Behavior* (1943; see Koch, 1954 for an intensive analysis of the *Principles*). It is our conviction that although the *Principles* represents the best of Hull's contributions to formal theory in psychology, Hull's theoretical papers published in the *Psychological Review* from 1929 to 1950 provide a much truer picture of what will be his lasting influence. The centenary of Hull's birth, 1984, seemed a fitting time to collect these papers in a single volume—and we couldn't resist adding our commentaries.

The *Psychological Review* papers, together with Hull's books and experimental articles, comprise his published work in learning theory. (He made other early and important contributions, including his *Psychological Monograph* on concept formation and his books on hypnosis and aptitude testing.) But in addition to these published sources, Hull left an extensive amount of additional material, most of it unpublished, and these working papers provide a clear window on the origins of and influences on his published work.

One source, Hull's private "Idea Books," were kept by him from the time he was in high school until about two weeks before his death. Passages from these Idea Books have been published (Ammons, 1962; Hays, 1962), and the entire collection is said to run to 73 volumes (Hays, 1962). The collection is held at the Sterling Memorial Library of Yale University. We have employed excerpts from the published Idea-Books material in this volume.

Another source of unpublished material are Hull's memoranda, written between 1936 and 1945. These comprise several hundred typed pages, include informative discussions of many key concepts that appeared in his published work, and contain interesting analyses of topics that would undoubtedly have found their way into the unwritten third volume of his planned three-volume series. That volume was intended to deal with behavior in social settings. The memoranda include, for example, discussions of Freudian concepts applied to personality and to culture; of symbolism, magic, and religion; and of language and cooperative behavior in humans and animals. Hull wrote these memoranda for his seminars at the Institute of Human Relations at Yale. They demonstrate the breadth of Hull's interests in psychological science and reflect his role in the Institute. The memoranda are available in the libraries of the University of Iowa, the University of North Carolina, Chapel Hill, and at Yale University. There are four volumes, bound under the titles "Hull's Psychological Seminars, 1938–1939," "Notices and Abstracts of Proceedings," "Psychological Seminar Memoranda, 1939–1944," and "Research Memorandum Concerning the Empirical Determination of the Form of Certain Basic Molar-Behavioral Equations and the Values of their Associated Constants, 1945."

Hull's voluminous correspondence provides another, more personal source of information about his work and his motivation for it. We have quoted from some of Hull's letters in our commentaries. The correspondence he maintained is staggering in its amount. Most of it that is available to scholars at the present time is in the Manuscripts and Archives section of the Sterling Memorial Library at Yale University, and in the Archives of the History of American Psychology at the University of Akron, Akron, Ohio. The Archives at Akron hold collections of the private papers of many psychologists, and Hull's letters are found in several. The most massive correspondence is in the papers of Kenneth W. Spence. The Hull-Spence correspondence began in 1935 and continued until near the time of Hull's death in 1952. It contains hundreds of letters, and this correspondence may be unique in all of science—certainly in psychology—in documenting the development of a theoretical approach. The continuing intellectual interaction between these two men provides the best justification for characterizing the resulting theoretical approach, particularly of the later years, as the "Hull-Spence system."

A definitive biography of Clark Hull, emphasizing his role in twentieth-century psychology, would include materials from all these sources. We have not begun to undertake such a task in this volume.

We are indebted to a number of people and institutions. Marion White McPherson and John Popplestone, directors of the Archives of the History of American Psychology at the University of Akron, were particularly helpful and gracious hosts during a visit by MER to the Archives. Mr. John Miller, Jr., librarian in charge of the Archives at the Bierce Library, University of Akron, cheerfully facilitated the search and retrieval of pertinent documents during that visit. Ludy T. Benjamin made several very helpful suggestions about the project and sources of documents. Patricia L. Bodak, Reference Archivist in the Manuscripts and Archives section of the Yale University Library, was most cooperative in providing catalogue entries of the Hull holdings under her supervision. Joseph H. Grosslight, a participant in Hull's classes at Yale, encouraged the project in several material ways and provided a student's perspective on Hull. Financial support for travel both to the Archives at Akron and to Austin, Texas was provided to MER by grants from The Florida State University President's Fund and by the Southern Regional Education Board in Atlanta, Georgia.

We are indebted to Mrs. Ruth Hull Low and Dr. Richard H. Hull for permission from Hull's estate to reprint excerpts from his private correspondence, to Professor Janet T. Spence for permission to use portions of Kenneth Spence's letters to Hull, and to the Archives of the History of American Psychology for easy access to that correspondence. The twenty-one theoretical papers that we reprint in Section 4 are now materials in the public domain. The source of those reprinted works is credited in the text. The Archives of the History of American Psychology kindly made available to us reprints of several of Hull's papers which we used in the production of Section 4 of this book. We thank them also for their help in this regard. Reprints were also provided by Professors J. S. Brown, M. R. Denny, F. A. Logan, N. E. Miller, and B. J. Underwood.

The manuscript was typed through several revisions with great care and patience by Debra Brock and Cindy Smoke at Florida State University, and by Marguerite Ponder at the University of Texas, who painstakingly put the typed manuscript into its final form and aided in the preparation of the reference list.

Finally, we are very grateful to Professors M. E. Bitterman, G. R. Grice, and F. A. Logan for critical readings of the entire commentary; to Columbia University Press for seeing the historical value in the project; and to Susan Koscielniak and David Diefendorf for guiding us gently to its conclusion.

In any jointly authored work the order of authorship has to be resolved. This volume represents a case of truly collaborative work extending over several years in which order of authorship was never discussed. We both viewed this project as a chance to continue some historical research which we had found surprisingly enjoyable in the mid-1970s (Amsel & Rashotte, 1977). We also saw in it a chance to raise historical awareness not only about Hull's learning theory but about others in the first part of this century as well. We had fun doing it and we learned a lot. We hope our colleagues and their students will find the result stimulating. When we were finally forced to it, MER insisted that the order of authorship should reflect proximity of intellectual kinship. Of course, Clark Hull is the prime author of this volume.

A.A.

M.E.R.

MECHANISMS OF ADAPTIVE BEHAVIOR

Introduction

A Brief Professional Biography

Clark Leonard Hull was born in Akron, New York, on May 24, 1884, and died in New Haven, Connecticut, on May 10, 1952. He earned the Bachelor's degree from the University of Michigan in 1913, and the Master's (in 1915) and Doctor's (in 1918) degrees in experimental psychology from the University of Wisconsin. At the time of his doctorate, Hull was 34 years old. His graduate work was done primarily under the direction of Professors Joseph Jastrow, Daniel Starch, and Vivian A. C. Henmon. Two years before receiving the doctorate, Hull recorded some of his earliest career plans in his private "Idea Books" (Ammons, 1962, p. 814). "It seems," he wrote, "that the greatest need in the science at present is to create an *experimental* and a *scientific* knowledge of higher mental processes." He planned to become the "supreme authority" in the psychology of abstraction, concept formation and, possibly, reasoning—to "both know the literature and create the literature on the subject." His doctoral dissertation was entitled "Quantitative Aspects of the Evolution of Concepts" and it was published in the *Psychological Monographs* series (Hull, 1920).

Throughout his life, Hull was afflicted by a variety of health problems and his relatively late entry into the field was another threat to his long-range goal. For example, he wrote in 1930, at the age of 46, "Sometimes I have been depressed and discouraged in my hope to achieve a major contribution to the theory of knowledge by the fact of my age. Recently, however, the examination of the ages at which several of the great critics have produced their best works has shown that I have by no means reason to be depressed. The list is as follows: Hobbes, 63; Spinoza, 45; Leibnitz, 68; Locke, 58; Berkeley, 25; Hume, 28; Kant, 57" (Ammons, 1962, p. 836). He was right. The record of his scholarly accomplishments over the remaining 22 years of his life, when he suffered from increasing health problems, is remarkable.

As he had hoped, Hull enjoyed a productive and successful career in psychology which continued right up to the time of his death. His scientific standing was recognized by election to membership in a number of societies, includ-

SECTION 1. INTRODUCTION

ing the American Academy of Arts and Sciences (1935) and the National Academy of Sciences (1936). He was awarded the Warren Medal of the Society of Experimental Psychologists in 1945. He was elected President of the American Psychological Association for 1935–36. A frequently cited measure of his influence is that during the decade 1941–1950 approximately 40 percent of all experimental articles published in the *Journal of Experimental Psychology* and the *Journal of Comparative and Physiological Psychology* included references to his work (Spence, 1952). Today Hull seems best remembered for one theoretical book on learning theory, *Principles of Behavior* (1943). On the occasion of the centenary of Hull's birth, it seems appropriate to recognize his broader contributions to the problem of adaptive behavior. The present volume brings together in one place, and provides a modern commentary on, a more representative, but today less well-known, portion of his work on this problem. We reprint here the twenty-one theoretical articles he published in the *Psychological Review* between 1929 and 1950. The impetus for these papers, and their relation to Hull's other major contributions, are evident in the following biographical notes.

In the first decade or so after receiving his doctorate Hull stayed in the Psychology department at the University of Wisconsin where he rose through the academic ranks from Instructor to Assistant Professor in 1920, to Associate Professor in 1922 and, finally, to Professor and Director of the Laboratory in 1925. During these years, he worked intensively on a variety of projects including the effects of tobacco smoking on mental and motor efficiency (Hull, 1924), the improvement of vocational guidance through more scientific aptitude testing (Hull, 1928), and the scientific basis of hypnosis (Hull, 1933; see Triplet, 1982). He was frequently aided in some of this work by his wife, Bertha Iutzi Hull, who coauthored one paper with him (Hull & Hull, 1919). He designed and constructed complex machines, including one, used in the project on aptitude testing, that automatically computed correlations (Hull, 1925a,b). Indeed, Hull was fascinated by the idea of using the logic of machine design in his scientific attack on the problem of higher mental processes and much of his subsequent work in learning theory reflects this general orientation, including the form of the theory for which he is best known. An extended passage in his Idea Books dated March 1, 1926 (Ammons, 1962, pp. 820ff) captures this aspect of his thinking and identifies many important themes that emerged in his later work:

> It has struck me many times of late that the human organism is one of the most extraordinary machines—and yet a machine. And it has struck me more than once that so far as the thinking processes go, a machine could be built which would

2

SECTION 1. INTRODUCTION

do every essential thing that the body does (except growth) as far as concerns thinking, etc. And since to think through the essentials of such a mechanism would probably be the best way of analyzing out the essential requirements of thinking, responding to abstract relations among things, and so on, I may as well play with the idea, making assumptions as frugally as possible and of such a nature as are known probably to be true. In cases where I have to make a fundamentally new assumption this will be some presumption that some such new action of the nervous system is to be sought for, i.e., some organic mechanism must exist of that general nature. This will be a good start for all kinds of researches to check up the various hypotheses. In fact the whole thing can probably be reduced to a mathematical formula and it is not inconceivable that an automaton might be constructed on the analogy of the nervous system which could learn and through experience acquire a considerable degree of intelligence by first coming into contact with an environment.

He outlined a variety of principles that would guide the design of such a machine, many of which anticipate emphases in his later work. For example, he proposed that energies impinging on the machine should result in relatively weak random movements governed by a generalized tendency toward continuation if the stimulus energy were noxious and termination if it were "satisfying." The parts of the machine should be autonomous to some degree, but subject to various hierarchies of control originating in other parts of the system. For him, Pavlov's conditioning identified the principle by which an event in one subsystem could come to influence functioning in remote parts of the machine, and Thorndike's Law of Effect the principle whereby originally random movements could be selected and be linked as responses to specific stimulus patterns. The design of the machine should allow for common reactions to stimuli with sensory similarity, for the learning of common reactions to stimuli with quite different sensory qualities, and for the possibility of differential responding to minute differences in stimulus pattern.

In concluding this passage written in 1926, Hull briefly considered how the problem-solving behavior of Kohler's apes (Kohler, 1925) could be approached in these mechanistic terms and then closed with the following comment which proved to be thematic for his future work.

> The more I think of this notion of small unitary stimulus-response units, attached to *parts* of stimulus patterns, and these units being aggregated into larger and larger units always operating on the same general principle, the more and more impressive become the enormous possibilities for economy.
>
> It shows how originally the basic units may have been acquired by pure trial and error. But with these small units available the element of trial and error becomes enormously reduced.

3

Section 1. Introduction

> It would almost seem that along with this there must also go a kind of hierarchy of facilitating tendencies. *This must be thought out.* (Ammons, 1962, p. 822, italics in original.)

In 1929, Hull left the University of Wisconsin to accept the position of Research Professor of Psychology at the Institute of Psychology (later the Institute of Human Relations) at Yale University where he remained for the rest of his career. On the occasion of his arrival at Yale, at 45 years of age, Hull reviewed his past work and the outlook for the future in an entry in his Idea Books dated, "New Haven. September 16, 1929." The opening sentence declares that he had reached a turning point in his scientific career: "I have torn myself from the associations of fifteen years, to make a new start in my scientific life" (Ammons, 1962, p. 826). He went on to describe his scientific work as having three parts: the work on hypnosis and suggestion, already underway for eight years; the work on aptitude tests, which he viewed as having great practical significance and which he intended to pursue at Yale but did not do; and, finally, the work on higher thought processes, which was his original interest as an undergraduate at the University of Michigan and the topic of his dissertation. Significantly, he noted that his work at Michigan included the construction of a "logic machine," and his additional comments on the role of machines and machine imagery in his work provide an important perspective on this aspect of his thinking. He wrote:

> It is rather striking, as revealing the characteristic nature of my talent, that the two major scientific projects of my life should be associated with the design of an exceedingly complex automatic machine. The thing which has given me as much prominence as any one thing so far except perhaps the book on testing, has been the correlation machine. This was a truly great task and it may very well be that I shall never again do anything which equals it as an achievement. It is probably significant that this machine is woven into the very fabric of my scheme for vocational guidance. No doubt this connection of extremely complex automatic machines with ambitious psychological projects and programs is a trifle grotesque, though no one seems to notice this very much except myself.
>
> Just as the correlation machine has been intimately associated with the testing program, so it appears that the design and construction of automatic psychical machines will be intimately associated with my attempts to work out my program involving the higher mental processes. . . . I am pretty certain to be criticized and called a trifle insane at the very least. But whatever genius I have quite evidently lies in this direction. I can do no less than make the best of it—let the tendency have free rein and go as far as it possibly can. I will let things go on to their perfectly logical conclusion. It may lead to real insight into the higher mental processes. In any case it is a true *gedanken* experiment yielding all kinds of

4

SECTION 1. INTRODUCTION

novel points of view and probably novel insights at least into the implications of a mechanistic psychology. It may possibly serve as the final *reductio ad absurdum* of a mechanistic psychology. If it does, well and good. But even if this should take place, it may at the same time result in such a development in psychic machines displaying an utterly new and different order of automaticity that mechanical engineering of automatic machines will be revolutionized to a degree similar to the introduction of steam engines and electricity. (Ammons, 1962, p. 828–29.)

As Research Professor, Hull had no formal teaching assignment at Yale, but he engaged in graduate instruction through a weekly seminar that attracted graduate students and personnel of the Institute for discussion of a variety of issues in behavior theory. (Notes prepared for these seminars comprise much of Hull's *Psychological Memoranda,* to which we referred in the Preface.)

By Hull's own account, "The Institute of Human Relations was a loose organization of behavioral scientists from various fields, mostly psychologists, sociologists, and cultural anthropologists, assembled at Yale by James R. Angell, Robert M. Hutchins, Milton C. Winternitz, and later by Mark A. May, for the purpose of making a unified, i.e., integrated, contribution to the social (behavioral) sciences" (Hull, 1952b, pp. 155–56). The conceptual framework for this unified contribution was provided by Hull's theoretical system. His role in the Institute is a topic for discussion elsewhere. Here we note simply that Hull's influence is evident in several important publications authored by personnel at the Institute (e.g., *Frustration and Aggression,* 1939, by Dollard, Doob, Miller, Mowrer & Sears; *Social Learning and Imitation,* 1941, by Miller & Dollard; *Personality and Psychotherapy,* 1950, by Dollard & Miller). From a contemporary perspective, the undertaking at the Institute in the 1930s and 1940s is similar in spirit to E. O. Wilson's efforts to provide a "new synthesis" of biological, psychological, and sociological sciences under the rubric of *Sociobiology* (Wilson, 1975).

Even before going to Yale, Hull planned to prepare a *"magnum opus"* on the scientific analysis of higher mental processes. The earliest titles Hull considered for his work, listed in his Idea Books in 1928 (Ammons, 1962, pp. 824–25), indicate this intended focus and the mechanistic emphasis.

Psychology of the Thinking Process
Mechanisms of Thought
Mechanisms of Mind
Mental Mechanisms
Mechanisms of Mental Life
Psychology from the Standpoint of a Mechanist

SECTION 1. INTRODUCTION

In 1930, Hull's Idea Books refer to the great philosophers—Hume, Locke, Kant, and Hobbes—who had attempted to construct a theory of knowledge, thought, and reason on the basis of conscious experience but who, in Hull's eyes, had failed. He planned to attack the same problem using the opposite strategy. He wrote, "I shall invert the whole historical system. I shall start with action—habit—and proceed to deduce all the rest, including conscious experience, from action, i.e., habit" (Ammons, 1962, p. 837). In fact, he had settled on *Habit* as the title for his *opus,* but that title was preempted by Knight Dunlap (1932). In an Idea Book entry dated January 17, 1937 (Ammons, 1962, p. 864), Hull documented these facts and listed new possibilities for the title:

Principles of Behavior
Behavior
Science of Behavior
Adaptive Behavior
Introduction to Behavior
Introduction to the Theory of Behavior
Introduction to the Study of Behavior
Psychology of Habit
Principles of Habit
Habit: An Introduction to Behavior
Behavior as Habit

Hull's plans for the magnum opus finally jelled as a projected three-volume work. The plan was ambitious and straightforward (Hull, 1952a, pp. 1–2). The first volume was mainly intended to present a set of formal axioms that constituted a logical system (or machine design) from which hypotheses about mammalian adaptive behavior could be deduced. This volume, which Hull completed in his 58th year, appeared in 1943 and was titled *Principles of Behavior: An Introduction to Behavior Theory.* The second volume was to illustrate the ability of such a system to generate fruitful hypotheses and deductions for the behavior of animals in nonsocial settings. The intended orientation of this volume was toward specific instances of adaptive behavior such as maze learning and problem solving. It was completed in Hull's 68th year and appeared shortly following his death, in 1952, titled *A Behavior System: An Introduction to Behavior Theory Concerning the Individual Organism.* The third volume, which was to have applied the system to some elementary phenomena of social mammalian behavior, was, of course, never completed. Of it, Hull said in his autobiography that he felt it would have been the most important part of his system for civilization in general (Hull, 1952b, p. 162).

Section 1. Introduction

In his methodical fashion, Hull conceived a unique strategy in the writing of these volumes. His Idea Books indicate that as early as 1928 he set out to write a series of carefully thought through theoretical articles that were to provide the basis for his major work, and he approached them with the utmost seriousness. The Idea Book entry of March 15, 1930, summarizes the strategy.

> The series of articles on theory which I propose to write will probably require the greatest acuity of mind of anything I have ever attempted. In all probability it will require three or four years to develop them—probably a dozen or sixteen, or even twenty, articles in all. If the task can be completed in good shape it ought to be of tremendous significance. It will, in effect, be the real basis for my *magnum opus*. After the articles have appeared and received such criticism as they may attract, I shall be in a position to organize the whole into a unified exposition with the crudities of first expression filed away, i.e., smoothed off, transitional logic supplied, and possibly experimental material in place. . . .
>
> I am led to hope that it will be a sufficiently original performance in what really amounts to mechanical design to be fairly impressive (Ammons, 1962, p.833).

As it turned out, Hull published twenty-one theoretical papers and two brief notes in learning theory between 1929 and 1950, all in the *Psychological Review*.

Why Reprint the Papers?

We have reprinted all of Hull's papers on learning theory in Section 4 of this volume. We think there are at least three important reasons for making them readily accessible. First, for most workers in the field of animal learning and motivation in recent years, Hull's contribution to the understanding of adaptive behavior is identified with the *Principles*. However, *Principles*, the most formal and abstract side of his work, published in 1943, represents only a part of Hull's contribution and, notwithstanding his plan, the 1943 book is in no sense a refinement or a restatement of the substance of Hull's articles in the *Review* between 1929 and 1943. (Portions of the second volume, *A Behavior System*, 1952, come a little closer to being such a refinement.) The Papers are more functionalist and diagrammatic, with representations of states, processes, and their interconnections. They were strongly and directly influenced by Darwinian Theory, Pavlovian and Thorndikian conditioning, and Gestalt psychology, and dealt with far more complex mechanisms than did the *Principles*. They also represent, better than his books do, his orienting attitudes and what we expect will be his long-term influence on the science of psychology. In this expectation, we are in agreement with Koch (1954):

7

Section 1. Introduction

There *is* a sense in which it is fruitful to look for core components of Hull's *approach* to theory. But this is not in the direction of *postulates*. It is in the direction of his orienting attitudes, and the various guiding ideas, explanatory mechanisms, scattered hypotheses which *look towards* theory, that function in some way in the many "derivations" and pre-theoretical analyses he has put forward. The evaluation of which of the orienting attitudes of a theorist like Hull are both feasible and fruitful is a matter of great moment for the future development of the field. Also of great importance would be the isolation and further development of those pre-theoretical hypotheses which, in one context or another, appear to contain promising explanatory potential. In this connection, it must be remembered that the fertility of such mechanisms as r_G, certain applications of S_D, various of the concrete roles imputed to proprioceptive stimulation, mechanisms such as *secondary* and *indirect* generalization, the habit family hierarchy, etc., is independent of their "derivability" from the postulates of *Pr.B. {Principles of Behavior}*, or any alternate set that Hull has put forward. Their possible fertility is also independent of any commitment to *exclusively* peripheral or S-R variables for the analysis of behavior. It is likely that such materials are much closer to anything that may be considered the *core* of Hull's *approach* than are the postulates of *Pr.B.* It is also clear that a search for core components of this order can go only a short way via any analysis restricted to *Pr.B.*, but rather must be based on the entire range of Hull's writings. (p. 96)

A search of the *Science Citation Index* for the decade of the 1970s makes the point that this other side of Hull's work is little known and appreciated (even as history) in contemporary behavior theory. What it shows is that in these ten years, the largest total number of references to any of the twenty-one Papers was to the one on stimulus intensity dynamism published in 1949—29 references in ten years. Table 1 gives the overall picture. The mean number of references to these twenty-one Papers over the ten-year period was 6.7; the median was 5. In any one of the last five years, the median and modal number of references to all the Papers was zero. On the other hand, references to Hull's *Principles* averaged over 40 per year in the ten-year period without any sign of decline. Citations of *A Behavior System* have remained remarkably steady at about 15 per year over the decade. While, as we have indicated, that book is closer in style and in content to the Papers than is the *Principles,* the scope and sweep of Hull's career in learning theory is best captured in the Papers.

Second, it seemed appropriate to collect Hull's papers in learning theory in one volume if for no other reason than that he is the only major learning theorist for whom such a collection is not available. (The exception to this is Guthrie, but he didn't write many theoretical papers. His theory was in his books.) We became acutely aware of this fact when, a few years ago, we pre-

8

Section 1. Introduction

Table 1. References in the 1970s to Hull's *Psychological Review* Papers*

	Total Citations 1970–1979	*Citations by Year* 79	78	77	76	75	70–74
A functional interpretation of the conditioned reflex (1929)	7	2	1	0	1	1	2
Simple trial-and-error learning: a study in psychological theory (1930)	3	0	0	1	0	0	2
Knowledge and purpose as habit mechanisms (1930)	20	3	1	1	1	3	11
Goal attraction and directing ideas conceived as habit phenomena (1931)	13	5	2	1	0	1	4
The goal-gradient hypothesis and maze learning (1932)	12	0	1	2	2	0	7
The concept of the habit family hierarchy and maze learning. Part I (1934)	5	0	0	1	0	0	4
The concept of the habit family hierarchy and maze learning. Part II (1934)	2	0	0	0	0	0	2
The mechanism of assembly of behavior segments in novel segments suitable for problem solution (1935)	1	0	0	1	0	0	0
The conflicting psychologies of learning— A way out (1935)	7	0	0	0	3	1	3
A comment on Dr. Adams' note on method (1937)†							
Mind, mechanism, and adaptive behavior (1937)	5	0	0	3	0	0	2
The goal-gradient hypothesis applied to some field-force problems in the behavior of young children (1938)	6	0	0	1	2	0	3
The problem of stimulus equivalence in behavior theory (1939)	0	0	0	0	0	0	0
The problem of intervening variables in molar behavior theory (1943)	3	0	0	0	0	0	3
A postscript on intervening variables (1943)†							
The place of innate individual and species differences in a natural science theory of behavior (1945)	9	1	1	2	1	2	2
The discrimination of stimulus configurations and the hypothesis of afferent neural interaction (1945)	1	0	0	0	0	0	1
The problem of primary stimulus generalization (1947)	6	0	0	0	1	0	5

9

Table 1. *(Continued)*

	Total Citations 1970–1979	Citations by Year					
		79	78	77	76	75	70–74
A proposed quantification of habit strength (1947)	0	0	0	0	0	0	0
Characteristics of dispersions based on the pooled momentary reaction potentials ($S^{\dot{E}}R$) of a group (1948)	0	0	0	0	0	0	0
Stimulus intensity dynamism (V) and stimulus generalization (1949)	29	3	0	1	0	2	23
Behavior postulates and corollaries—1949 (1950)	3	0	0	0	2	0	1
Simple qualitative discrimination learning (1950)	9	2	1	0	0	0	6
References in the 1970s to Hull's Books on Learning Theory							
Mathematico-deductive theory of rote learning (1940)	16	2	0	1	2	2	9
Principles of behavior (1943)	423	44	24	55	40	44	216
Essentials of behavior (1951)	29	1	2	3	1	3	19
A behavior system (1952)	158	13	9	15	16	16	89

*The citation counts in this table were made by reference to the *Cumulative Science Citation Index* for the years 1970–74 and to the *Science Citation Index* for individual years between 1975 and 1979. Citations under the name C. L. Hull, only, were counted. The citation counts presented here are indicative of Hull's recent influence but they are not exhaustive of his citations in the scientific literature. For example, we have ignored citations that involved incomplete or typographical errors (e.g., C. Hull; C.K. Hull) and have not included citations in the *Social Sciences Citation Index,* which appear to overlap somewhat with citations in the *Science Citation Index.*

†These are brief addenda to the papers with which they are coupled.

pared a history of S-R learning theory with particular reference to Hull's contributions (Amsel & Rashotte, 1977). It was brought home in another way at a European conference where this state of affairs drew a complaint from a leading Soviet Pavlovian. He wanted at first to know where he could find a volume of Hull's collected papers. When told that such a volume did not exist, he was unbelieving: "How can it be," he asked, "that no one in America has assembled a volume of the papers of such an important scientist?" The reply was polite and evasive, but one was tempted to reply that in Soviet terms Hull had become something of a "nonperson" in the American psychology of the 1960s and

Section 1. Introduction

1970s; that there had been an informal consensus, based almost exclusively on the approach represented by the *Principles,* that the enterprise had failed and that there was little left to salvage; that general, systematic theories of conditioning and learning were premature and actually counterproductive. Such a reply would have been difficult for a Russian—and particularly a Pavlovian—to credit.

Finally, in recent years the term "Traditional Learning Theory" has emerged as something of an epithet, and in many instances of its use, TLT can be taken as synonymous with Hull's *Principles of Behavior.* Indeed, in a recent book, Dickinson (1980) characterizes Hull (along with Guthrie, Mowrer, and Skinner) as a "behavior analyst" rather than as a "learning theorist." The "animal-learning establishment" and "the old stimulus-response paradigm" have been attacked by a succession of "born-again" cognitivists (e.g., Bolles, 1975; Dickinson, 1980; Honig, 1978) who advocate changes in learning theory that are generally less parsimonious, more mentalistic, and more structuralist. Indeed, in the recent cognitive treatments of animal learning (e.g., Dickinson & Boakes, 1979; Hulse, Fowler, & Honig, 1978), almost no mention is made of Hull's pre-*Principles* work, the earliest of which addressed such concepts as goal attraction, purpose, and directing ideas. We have here an example of how great men and women of science often come to be known for restricted portions of their work—in Hull's case the *Principles*—while substantial portions of other important facets of their work are "rediscovered" in a more modern context. This is, perhaps, inevitable; but, still, there should be an attempt to keep the historical record alive and straight. We hope the present collection of Hull's papers, along with our commentary, will help clear up such misconceptions.

The remainder of this volume is organized into four sections. Section 2 describes the intellectual climate in which Hull worked. Section 3 is a detailed commentary from a contemporary perspective on the Papers grouped under topical headings, and more generally on Hull's contribution to psychological theory; Section 4 presents in chronological order Hull's twenty-one *Psychological Review* papers; and Section 5 is a Postscript in which we provide some closing comments on the decline of Hull's influence in the contemporary psychology of learning, and the portions of Hull's work that remain influential.

11

The Intellectual Climate

IN ORDER to gain perspective on Hull's papers, particularly the earlier ones, let us examine the dominant influences in experimental psychology at that time.

Evolutionary Theory

By the turn of the century, Darwin's theory of evolution had already stimulated important research efforts in the comparative study of animal intelligence by George Romanes (1883), C. Lloyd Morgan (1894), Willard Small (1900, 1901), Edward L. Thorndike (1911), John B. Watson (1914), and others. This work suggested that intelligent or adaptive behavior of animals results from the operation of relatively simple mechanisms provided by the species' evolutionary history and activated by the animal's life experiences. Very simple creatures seemed incapable of profiting much from experience, and relied very heavily on their genetic endowment for adaptation to changing conditions. Animals with more complex nervous systems, and particularly mammals, seemed capable of extraordinary feats of learning which allowed them to adapt and survive and radiate into new environments.

Hull's preoccupation with the concepts of natural selection and adaptation are not generally recognized or understood by recent commentators on Traditional Learning Theory, particularly the "neo-Darwinians."[1] The publication of

1. Even Kendler (1981, p. 162), whose intellectual upbringing was Hullian, writes: "Perhaps the future will prove, if it has not already been demonstrated, that theoretical psychologists, such as Hull (1943) and Lewin (1935), made a strategic error when they sought conceptual guidance from the physical theories of Newton and Galileo rather than from Darwin." In the case of Hull, it is perhaps not without meaning that Kendler cites *Principles* specifically. Our discussion has already suggested that this would not be an entirely apt characterization of the Hull of the Papers or *A Behavior System*. Indeed, it would appear to us to be not entirely accurate for the Hull of *Principles*, in the sense that, whereas the Newtonian influence was there and perhaps predominated, the Darwinian influence was certainly not absent. Early in the book (pp. 17–19) in sections headed "Organismic Need, Activity, and Survival" and "The Organic Basis for Adaptive Behavior," Hull explicitly acknowledges his indebtedness to Darwin and ends on this note (p. 19): "A closely related task [to isolating the basic laws by which environmental and internal stimuli bring about behavior] is to understand why the behavior so mediated is so generally adaptive, i.e., successful in the sense of reducing needs and facilitating survival."

SECTION 2. THE INTELLECTUAL CLIMATE

Darwin's *The Origin of Species* (1859) and *The Expression of the Emotions in Man and Animals* (1872) made it necessary to think of organisms against a background of evolution and to consider both organismic structure and function in terms of survival: the organism is sensitive to stimulation from its external and internal environments, and acts to eliminate need states which threaten survival. Hull's first Paper on the conditioned reflex in 1929 pursued this Darwinian theme; his APA presidential address, *Mind, Mechanism and Adaptive Behavior*, refers to Darwin in the first sentence; and the emphasis on adaptiveness runs throughout his writings, to the final chapter of *A Behavior System* in 1952, where, in passing on the torch, his final admonition is that any set of principles that comprises a viable behavior theory must take into account automatic and adaptive responses of organisms. Hull believed that once the laws of learning and their relation to innate behavior were discovered, they would be found to be similar in all mammalian species and that individual and species differences could be handled as parametric variations. He formalized this view in his paper on "innate individual and species differences" (Paper 14). Experiments in classical and instrumental conditioning he viewed as the *basic* laboratory methods for investigating the adaptive mechanisms *that depend on learning*.

Hull's strong biological-evolutionary orientation has not been generally appreciated in present-day discussions of the generality ("biological boundaries," "constraints") of learning and its relation to the biological makeup of animals (e.g., Bolles, 1975; Hinde & Stevenson-Hinde, 1973; Seligman & Hager, 1972; Shettleworth, 1972). An exception is the excellent characterization of Darwin's influence on Hull's theorizing in a recent textbook on learning (Fantino & Logan, 1979, pp. 25–26):

> In seeking a physicalistic model with which to account for apparent purpose, Hull turned to Darwin. Darwin, too, had faced the problem of finding a physical explanation for an apparently purposeful phenomenon. Organic change across generations appeared to serve an adaptive purpose. Darwin had successfully devised a physical account of the adaptations produced in organic evolution, and his account focused on the mechanism of natural selection. Determined to do the same for ontogenetic changes in behavior, Hull borrowed Darwin's model. Perhaps phylogenetic change could provide a useful analogue for the explanation of ontogenetic change. Note that Hull was *not* using evolutionary principles to explain behavioral change. He was instead extending the evolutionary *model* of change, that is, the logic of evolutionary change, into a different realm—the realm of behavioral ontogeny. Accordingly, Hull was to devise a mechanism by which certain responses were selected out of an existing pool of behavior (as genetic characters that facilitate reproduction success are selected from a much larger gene pool). The selected elements were then maintained to the relative exclusion of others.

14

SECTION 2. THE INTELLECTUAL CLIMATE

Darwin's mechanism of selection was reproductive success. Hull chose as his selecting mechanism *response-contingent reinforcement*—that is, stimulus consequences dependent for their occurrence upon the emission of a particular response.

To begin, Hull, like Darwin, needed *variability*. Any process of selection is predicated upon an existing range of elements from which to select. Moreover, the flexibility possible in the selection process depends on the amount of variability among elements. Since behavior appeared to be extremely flexible, Hull assumed extreme variability. This assumption was contained in his notion of the *behavioral tendency*. A given stimulus does not simply evoke a single specific response. Rather, the stimulus sets up a behavioral tendency [or habit-family hierarchy] consistent with the occurrence of a whole range of individual responses. Any one of these responses might be produced at a given time by the stimulus in question. Each individual response in the set has, moreover, a particular probability of occurrence. This probability represents that element's initial *reaction potential*. That response which is most adaptive will be selected out (by reinforcement) and will, therefore, have the greatest reaction potential. Of all the responses possible, given a particular behavioral tendency, the one with the greatest reaction potential will be the one that actually occurs. Each response has a measurable reaction potential, and by determining the factors that contribute to reaction potential, it is possible to assign a probability value to the occurrence of any response in any situation—in effect, to predict behavior. This was Hull's task, and his theory essentially addressed interactions among factors contributing to reaction potential.

There is, finally, another link between Darwin and Hull that is rarely acknowledged and that was probably not recognized even by Hull. Ghiselin (1969) has argued that Darwin's theoretical style was heavily committed to the use of the hypothetico-deductive method. In this sense, Hull's well-known advocacy of this style of theory makes him the most Darwinian of the classical and modern learning theorists.

Early Experimental Psychology

In addition to Darwin's influence, several other lines of thought from abroad were woven into American psychology in Hull's time, and all of these influences are reflected in his work. The most general of these was an air of optimism about a scientific approach to its subject matter which stemmed from the earlier work of Helmholtz, Fechner, Wundt, and other European pioneers in the study of sensory processes and psychophysics. Laboratories of experimental psychology were established at many universities in America beginning in the late nineteenth century (Boring, 1957), and early in the twentieth century the behavioristic approach which represented for many the essence of an objective science

15

SECTION 2. THE INTELLECTUAL CLIMATE

of psychology was aggressively advocated by Edward L. Thorndike, John B. Watson, Walter S. Hunter, and others.

Thorndike's (1898, 1911, 1932) work provided an orientation, methodology, and conceptual framework that fostered the growth of psychology. Influenced greatly by Darwin, he took the position that the analysis of human "mental" functioning would be furthered by comparative studies in which the origin of "mental life" was traced down through the phylum. The following statement of Thorndike's position in 1913 became a hallmark of the S-R approach that flourished later in America and emphasized the study of animal learning.

> The complexities of human learning will in the end be best understood if at first we avoid them, examining rather the behavior of the lower animals as they learn to meet certain situations in changed, and more remunerative, ways. (Thorndike, 1913, p. 6)

His own research program, which included extensive experimental work with various species of animals and humans was marked by methodological innovations that greatly influenced subsequent laboratory studies of learning. In cats and dogs, for example, Thorndike studied the learning of arbitrary responses such as pulling a loop or depressing a lever that mechanically unlatched a cage door and led to food. But he also studied more natural responses such as fur-licking or scratching in cats. He attempted to measure performance objectively and he presented the outcome of his experiments in a quantitative fashion.

Perhaps Thorndike's most significant contribution to S-R theories of learning was his conceptualization of associative processes. The results of his laboratory studies, and his general deterministic orientation, led him to propose that learning involves the development of associations between situations (S) and responses (R) and that associations form according to certain "laws," including the famous Law of Effect. He regarded the total behavior of an organism as resulting from both learned and unlearned S-R connections. The biological makeup of each organism determined its unlearned reactions to various situations, and the experiences of each organism determined which learned connections would be formed between situations and responses. The position of a species in the phylum was thought by Thorndike to be positively correlated with the number of acquired associations of which it was capable. Bitterman (1969) has commented more fully on Thorndike's influence on comparative psychology.

Watson's influential views on the nature of psychology, as expressed in his books *Psychology from the Standpoint of a Behaviorist* (1919) and *Behaviorism* (1924), provided a particularly visible example of the mechanistic approach. Hull's re-

16

action to Watson's books, and to the views adopted by some of Watson's followers, is interesting for what it reveals of Hull's dispassionate attitude toward scientific theory:

> Personally, while inclined to be sympathetic with Watson's views concerning the futility of introspection and the general views of objectivity, I felt very uncertain about many of his dogmatic claims. In this connection I recall the semi-fanatical ardor with which, at that time, some young people, including a few relatively ignorant undergraduates, would espouse the Watsonian cause with statements such as, "Behaviorism has made a greater contribution to science than has been produced by psychology in its entire previous history." This attitude on the part of some precipitated equally violent opposing claims. The zeal of both sides took on a fanaticism more characteristic of religion than of science. (Hull, 1952b, p. 154)

Freudian Determinism

A second influence from abroad was Freud's deterministic view of behavior which claimed to show that even the "unintentional" behavior of humans has identifiable antecedents. Freud's views also emphasized the centrality of learning and motivation as determinants of behavior.

Freud's influence on Hull is rarely made explicit in the Papers or elsewhere in Hull's published works. The flavor of Hull's attitude towards Freud's work is captured in the following passage from one of the *Psychological Seminar Memoranda, 1939–1940*. This memorandum, dated April 23, 1940, was the basis for a seminar discussion conducted by Hull on the behavioristic analysis of some of Freud's theorizing:

> Whatever anyone may think of Freud's views, no one can deny that he concerned himself with a large number of exceedingly vital problems. The student should neither take Freud's views as gospel nor reject them because he may find them distasteful—science judges questions on the basis of evidence rather than on the ground of "wishful" thinking. In this seminar Freud's views will be taken as a point of departure for a tentative behavioristic analysis of the problems involved.
>
> From your casual reading of Freud, would you say that he developed a formal theoretical system with definitions, postulates, theorems, etc.? The careful reading of Freud will show, nevertheless, that there is a good deal of logical structure in his writings—more than at first meets the eye. Moreover, Freud was absolutely deterministic, which probably saved him from many a pitfall in the mazes of psychopathology. It is greatly to be regretted that no sympathetic student of Freud with a taste for systematization has yet exhibited the structure of his theory in formal detail. Such a work would greatly aid the enterprise which we are about to undertake. It seems hardly credible that several sciences of behavior such as the

17

> Pavlovian reflexology, American behaviorism, and psychoanalytic theory can go
> on developing independent of each other without an integration which will be
> more comprehensive than any one alone. (p. 118)

Hull reveals in his autobiography that, several years before he conducted this seminar, Freud's writings were already occupying a significant place in the Institute of Human Relations at Yale. In the following passage, Hull describes the way his own theoretical ideas, when combined with Freud's, became a framework for an integrative approach in the social sciences.

> The influence of these [Hull's] ideas was brought to bear on the Institute and
> related personnel quite definitely in 1936, when several of us, including Neal E.
> Miller, John Dollard, and O. H. Mowrer, ran an open seminar specifically con-
> cerned with the essential identities lying in conditioned reflexes and behavior laws
> generally on the one hand, and, on the other, in the phenomena considered by
> Freud and his psychoanalytic associates. I prepared the agenda and Mowrer pre-
> pared abstracts of the significant parts of the discussions. These were mimeo-
> graphed and sent out widely after each meeting. Much interest was aroused,
> sometimes as many as seventy people attending. For the first time in the six-year
> history of the Institute of Human Relations its personnel were induced to assem-
> ble for a serious discussion of the integration of the social sciences. In addition,
> Miller spent vast amounts of time explaining the system to members individually.
> (Hull, 1952b, p. 156)

Several years later, Dollard and Miller published a book entitled *Personality and Psychotherapy* (1950) which provided a stimulus-response analysis of neurotic behavior and of Freudian psychotherapeutic strategies. The book was dedicated "To Freud and Pavlov and their students."

Russian Reflexology

A third influence, particularly consistent with the mechanist bias in ex-perimental psychology, was Pavlov's (English translations 1927, 1928) work on salivary conditioning in dogs, and Bekhterev's (1913) studies of the condition-ing of motor reactions. These provided evidence that simple learning, at least, might involve the formation of reflexlike connections between neural correlates of stimuli and responses. Pavlov in particular took the hard-line position in his writings that adaptive behavior originated in these mechanistic processes. That emphasis corresponded very well with the stimulus-response, trial-and-error-learning approach to adaptive behavior developed by Thorndike.

Pavlov's approach to the study of learning was in many respects similar to Thorndike's. A strict determinist who rejected mentalism in favor of the view that behavior is lawfully determined by an organism's inherited and acquired reflexes, Pavlov devised innovative experimental procedures for the study of learning which influence laboratory research to the present day. In extrapolating findings from dogs to other animals, including humans, Pavlov viewed his work as being pertinent to the understanding of adaptive behavior, and invoked the Darwinian principle of evolutionary continuity. He made no sharp distinction between humans and other animals, attributing the adaptive advantages of humans to the evolution of a language capacity ("the second signal system"), and not to mentalistic capabilities (Pavlov, 1955, pp. 35, 262). Finally, his conceptualization of behavior in terms of reflex units, in which a given stimulus evokes a given response, was very similar to Thorndike's S-R proposals and, like Thorndike, he undertook a vigorous program of research into how learned associations are formed.

The essence of Pavlov's approach is revealed in a quote from his famous *Lectures*, published in English in 1927:

> Every material system can exist as an entity only so long as its internal forces, attraction, cohesion, etc., balance the external forces acting upon it. This is true for an ordinary stone just as much as for the most complex chemical substances; and its truth should be recognized also for the animal organism. Being a definite circumscribed material system, it can only continue to exist so long as it is in continuous equilibrium with the forces external to it: so soon as this equilibrium is seriously disturbed the organism will cease to exist as the entity it was. Reflexes are the elemental units in the mechanism of perpetual equilibration. (Pavlov, 1927, p.8)

Obviously, the developing S-R psychology of learning in the United States could not have found a better conceptual ally, and Pavlov's impressive experimental evidence about conditioned reflexes made the alliance even more desirable.

Pavlov's approach to the study of learned associations differed from Thorndike's in two principal respects. The first was of relatively little direct consequence in the development of S-R learning theory: unlike Thorndike, Pavlov used his behavioral findings to construct a neurophysiological theory of the functioning of the cerebral hemispheres, and particularly the neocortex. American psychologists never embraced the quasiphysiological aspects of Pavlov's theorizing and he publicly chastized them for failing to emphasize the physiological implications of conditioned reflex experiments (Pavlov, 1932). While his criticism fell on deaf ears, Spence (1961, pp. 1187ff) noted one often-neglected contribution of Pavlov's theorizing to the development of theoretical psychology in the United States. He pointed out that Pavlov demonstrated how a program of behavioral research could provide the basis for developing and testing hypotheses about speculative theoretical concepts. In Pavlov's case, the hypotheses were about physiological terms and behavioral data guided the development of a theory of cortical functioning. Theorists such as Hull and Spence tested hypotheses about theoretical terms that had no necessary physiological referents. Spence commented that in some limited respect, at least, it would be appropriate to regard Hull-Spence theory as neo-Pavlovian.

The second difference between Pavlov and Thorndike concerned the details of their procedures for studying the formation of associations, and this proved to be very important in the development of learning theory. Whereas Thorndike arranged repeated sequences of situations, responses, and "effects" to strengthen situation-response associations, Pavlov arranged repeated pairings of stimuli. In some arrangements, the CS came to elicit salivation and this was taken as evidence that an excitatory association had been established between the CS and the UR, the salivary motor center. In other arrangements, the CS came to suppress salivation and even to induce drowsiness and sleep, and this was taken as evidence that the CS evoked an inhibitory state.

The situation-response-effect procedure of Thorndike laid stress on different variables in the formation of associations from those of Pavlov's stimulus-stimulus procedure. This led some later theorists to propose that different learning processes were involved in the two cases, and learning theories divided on the issue of the nature and number of learning processes (see Hilgard & Marquis, 1940). Pavlov himself expressed the view in one of his famous Wednesday meetings that Thorndike's procedures established associations that were not fundamentally different from associations formed in experiments on conditioned reflexes, although he thought the associations formed in Thorndike's experiments were more permanent than those established with conditioned reflex procedures (Pavlov, 1955, p.582).

Gestalt Theory

The fourth European influence was less congenial to the mechanist bias. Gestalt psychology (Koffka, 1925; Kohler, 1929; Wertheimer, 1912) maintained that, at least in organisms with complex nervous systems, molar perceptual processes, rather than the reflex units of S-R psychology, governed adaptive behavior. Insight, reasoning, and other modes of adjustment to environmental change were thought to originate in such primary processes. In contrast to this Gestalt position, Thorndike, Watson, and Lloyd Morgan had been particularly strongly opposed to any view that cognitive functioning, represented by processes such as insight and reasoning, was influential in adaptation. The experimental evidence of the time seemed not to favor such processes, although that evidence was open to criticism on the grounds that the experimental arrangements were too simple and artificial to allow those processes to be revealed (e.g., Hobhouse, 1915). Well-publicized cases in which supposed cognitive functioning in animals was debunked, such as in the German horse "Clever Hans" (Pfungst, 1911), contributed to the air of suspicion about cognition in animals.

Despite the prevailing negative attitude towards "mental" processes in mechanistic American psychology, Hull became interested in the Gestalt approach while he was on the faculty at the University of Wisconsin, and he actually attempted to study with Koffka in Germany. His autobiography includes an account of his early experiences with Gestalt theory, and of its impact on his theoretical views:

> I early made an attempt to secure a foreign fellowship to go to Germany and study with Kurt Koffka, but without success. As an alternative I conceived the idea of bringing Koffka to the University of Wisconsin for a year. This move, while very expensive, was successful. When Koffka finally arrived [for the academic year 1926–27], his personal charm captured everyone. However, his expository approach was strikingly negative. At least half of his time was spent in attacking Watson. I listened to his lectures with great interest. While I found myself in general agreement with his criticisms of behaviorism, I came to the conclusion not that the Gestalt view was sound but rather that Watson had not made out as clear a case for behaviorism as the facts warranted. Instead of converting me to *Gestalttheorie,* the result was a belated conversion to a kind of neobehaviorism—a behaviorism mainly concerned with the determinism of the quantitative laws of behavior and their deductive systematization. (Hull, 1952b, p.154)

Conflict between Gestalt views and reflex-oriented American thought was aggravated by the emigration to America of Wolfgang Kohler, Kurt Koffka, Kurt Lewin, and Max Wertheimer, leaders of Gestalt psychology in Germany who had fallen under the political pressures of the times (see Sokal, 1984). Edward C. Tolman, an American, constructed a kind of blend of the behavioristic approach and Gestalt theory that proved to be very influential and quite frequently troublesome for S-R theory. Personal and published interactions between proponents of the S-R and Gestalt approaches flavored much of American psychology between 1920 and 1950. These interactions were particularly strong and frequent between the adherents to Hull's approach and the "Gestalters" since they differed on such fundamental issues as the very form that a theory of adaptive behavior should take, as well as on the units of analysis. Many of Hull's papers reprinted later in this volume reflect his own concerns about *Gestalttheorie* and, as our commentaries will show, Hull's private correspondence in the 1930s and 1940s indicates in yet another way that Gestalt ideas provided the major counterforce which his developing theoretical system confronted. In this respect, it is interesting to note that the Skinnerian approach, which has been such a significant force in American learning psychology, had little apparent influence on Hull's work beyond providing a methodology (the "Skinner-box," which Hull is reputed to have named) for some experimental work in his laboratory.

The tone of relations between Hullians and the Gestalt psychologists is reflected in the following excerpt from a letter Hull wrote to his associate Kenneth W. Spence, dated May 20, 1941. In the letter Hull described his recent experiences at a meeting of the "Psychological Session" of the Philosophical Society held at Philadelphia. Kohler and Tolman were among the participants, and Hull described a postsession discussion which is a vignette of the personal side of the behaviorist-versus-Gestalt conflict that had been underway for many years.

> Following Tolman's address which was the event of the meeting, an informal reception was given at which beer and assorted sandwiches were served. At about the time the reception was over I succeeded in gathering several people, including Kohler, [Karl] Zener, Kohler's assistant, and Tolman, around in a circle talking shop. Then of course we had to get out, and someone proposed that we find a beer joint and drink beer. So we all went down two or three blocks, found a table, and sat down to talk shop. I managed to sit beside Kohler and had quite a long talk with him. I spent some time working on him, as I did on Zener there at Athens [Ohio, at the 1941 meeting of the Midwestern Psychological Association], trying to persuade him that it would be better for the prestige of psychology if we did less fighting and cleared up, so far as possible at least, the pseudo-differences which stand between us. He countered with the suggestion that the behaviorists had been the ones who had been doing the attacking. I was naturally somewhat astonished at this remark, and he called my attention to that old article written years ago by Professor [E. S.] Robinson, which appeared in the *New Republic* [in November 1929]. You may remember it; Robbie entitled his article, "The Little German Band." It was a good take-off on the Gestalters of course, but as a piece of criticism it was about nil. Apparently those boys are still writhing under the gibes that Robbie threw at them. I was so slow on the up-take that I neglected to point out to Kohler that in the first place Robbie was not a behaviorist, and in the second place he had written (as I recall it) a similar article in the same magazine, giving a take-off on the behaviorists. Am I right about this? Kohler then went on and made a remark something like this: "Also, I have heard it said that a professor in one of the prominent eastern universities is accustomed,

whenever he refers to the Gestalt psychologists, to call them, 'those goddamned Gestalters.' " I must confess that my face was pretty red. The whole crowd gave me a good horse laugh, and of course I had it coming to me. There again my uptake was so slow that it didn't occur to me to tell them that I always smile when I use that expression, which, it seems to me, does make a difference. Then Kohler went on to complain that you had made some dirty cracks at them. He mentioned some remark which I understood him to say you had made at the Dartmouth meeting, probably not in a set paper but in some discussion following a paper, to the effect that the behavioristic approach to some particular problem was the *scientific* approach, implying that the alternative Gestalt approach was *not* scientific. Of course I knew nothing about this particular event, and very likely you yourself have forgotten it if it ever took place. He seemed to be blaming me more or less for these sharp things which you sometimes have said about the Gestalters. I came back, however, with the remark that if he had known the sharp things which I had persuaded you *not* to publish he wouldn't blame me for the things you had published. Then as a final blow-off, *apropos* of the general argument that I was putting forward to the effect that scientific matters should be settled on a scientific and logical basis rather than by some kind of warfare, he came out with this remark: he said that he was willing to discuss most things in a logical and scientific manner, but when people try to make man out to be a kind of slot machine, then he would fight. And when he said the word "fight," he brought his fist down on the table with a resounding smack, and he did not smile when he said it, either. That is the crack of which I wrote to you the other day. This was such an astonishing remark that I wanted to get some further reactions on the subject, and tried to obtain a general discussion among the people at the table on the point. In order to do this I pointed out to him that even though a person did feel like fighting about such a matter, the fighting wouldn't settle it and was really futile so far as the scientific status of the thing was concerned. At that point he began telling me about the trouble he had had with the Nazis in Germany and commented on how stupid the English had been not to prepare for war, and so on. This seemed, and still seems to me to be, utterly irrelevant to the logical question involved, though as a psychological proposition I can understand how a man's scientific wires might get crossed through emotional upsets in his personal life. Actually one would hardly expect a thoroughgoing scientist to do a thing like that, but Kohler clearly did it on that occasion. Upon the whole, it was not a very impressive demonstration of either scientific or philosophical poise.

Just one final word. While talking to Kohler in the rather mellow mood over the beer that night in Philadelphia, he told me he expected to ask his graduate students to read a number of my theoretical studies. As a result I sent him, when I returned to New Haven, a complete bound copy of my theoretical reprints, and [M.] Haire wrote me the other day, in his bread-and-butter letter, that the reprints were being read extensively at Swarthmore. It seems to me a small miracle that a man like Kohler would ask his students to read anything written by an American, and especially one who is inclined to behavioristic views.

SECTION 2. THE INTELLECTUAL CLIMATE

Hull's Synthesis

Hull's special contribution was to merge the legacies of Darwin, Thorndike, Pavlov, Watson, and to some extent Freud, into a single theoretical position that was intended to provide an account of the ordinary forms of mammalian adaptive behavior, including behaviors that appeared to the Gestalt psychologists and others to involve relatively complex cognitive functioning. As we shall see in his papers and stress in our commentaries, it was more in the Papers, and particularly in the earlier ones, than in his books that all of these emphases came together.

SECTION 3

Commentaries on Papers

Pavlovian Beginnings

1. A functional interpretation of the conditioned reflex. (1929)

IN THIS first of his papers in learning theory, working toward the master plan of his magnum opus, Hull shows how the excitatory and inhibitory processes of Pavlovian conditioning might, together, provide what he called an "automatic trial-and-error mechanism" that could mediate "blindly but beautifully, the adjustment of the organism to a complex environment." Written shortly after the appearance of Pavlov's lectures in English translation (Pavlov, 1927, 1928), this article is essentially an elaboration of ideas sketched in Pavlov's (1927) first lecture on the biological significance of conditioned reflexes. Although the most extensive recent review of work on this same topic (Hollis, 1982) makes no reference to Hull's paper, it, along with his subsequent chapter in Murchison's handbook which summarizes Pavlovian facts and theory (Hull, 1934), was particularly important in bringing the functional implications of the conditioned reflex to the attention of Western psychologists (see Skinner, 1981). (The chapter is not reprinted here, but it would be interesting reading for those who lump Hull with Traditional Learning Theorists who are said to claim equal associability of all stimuli and responses.) It is appropriate, perhaps, that this first of Hull's papers in learning theory should attempt an account of the biological-adaptive significance of Pavlovian processes. So much of Hull's subsequent work was devoted to refining this attempt and to defining a rational means of deciding when that attempt was successful.

The paper considers four main mechanisms that involve an interplay between Pavlovian excitation and inhibition. As we shall see, these mechanisms can be regarded as themes that occur again and again in many of Hull's subse-

25

quent writings. In every case, excitatory learning, which occurs first, functions as "a tentative trial, or first approximation aspect of an adaptive process." Inhibitory learning, which builds on the excitatory, provides "the selective, corrective, or precision-insuring aspect" of the mechanism.

The first mechanism is *redintegration / experimental extinction.* The term "redintegration," no longer in use, was popularized by H. L. Hollingworth (1928) who used it to describe the fact that when several sensory elements have occurred jointly in a compound stimulus, a single element may be sufficient to evoke the response appropriate to the whole compound. This may occur because each element is capable of reinstating a neural representation of the entire compound, a process similar to what has recently been termed "within-compound associations" (e.g., Rescorla & Durlach, 1981). Hull made a simpler and more direct interpretation, which, it turns out, is not supported by more recent data on stimulus selection in Pavlovian conditioning: each element, he thought, tends "independently and indiscriminately" to acquire the ability to evoke the conditioned response. In Hull's view, redintegration had obvious adaptive advantages, but it was likely to be disadvantageous as well because the conditioned animal would react "inappropriately" when it encountered stimulus elements which had happened only by chance to be present in the compound. However, an adaptive advantage would be ensured by the "corrective" action of inhibition which, in this case, was produced by experimental extinction. The idea is that chance stimuli will occur frequently in the absence of the US and, therefore, will become inhibitory in relation to the conditioned response. The net result is that, initially, this two-part mechanism will promote conditioning to all stimuli present on a trial but, eventually, will ensure that only the relevant stimuli will evoke the response.

The second bipartite mechanism, *patterned stimuli / conditioned inhibition,* has the property of mediating the organism's ability to respond to differences in the pattern of stimulation. In the discussion of this mechanism, Hull noted that a simple algebraic model of associative summation would subserve adaptive behavior in many situations—for example, when two danger signals are present it is to the organism's probable advantage to take greater evasive action than when only one signal is present. However, adaptive behavior often depends on the ability to respond to differential *patterns* of the same stimulus elements. Hull presented an experimental example from Pavlov's laboratory in which a dog learned to salivate when one sequence of four stimuli was followed by the US, but not when the same four stimuli were presented in a different sequence without the US. Hull proposed that inhibition operates to suppress responding to the nonreinforced *pattern* in the manner of extinction training, and cited the case of Pavlovian conditioned inhibition as a special case of learning to respond differentially to patterns.

The third mechanism, *irradiation / differential inhibition,* explains the case in which excitatory conditioning to one stimulus makes it possible for stimuli with similar properties, but not involved in the conditioning procedure, also to have the ability to evoke the conditioned response. This process, called "irradiation" by Pavlov and "stimulus generalization" in much of the subsequent American literature, has important advantages for adaptive behavior. In particular, it allows the animal to respond appropriately when minor variations in an excitatory stimulus occur from one occasion to another. However, inhibition is necessary to correct the tendency to respond to stimuli that differ too greatly from the original and, here, Hull cited Pavlovian differential conditioning as the experimental instance of this process.

The fourth mechanism, *the anticipatory tendency / inhibition of delay,* pertains to the timing of behavior. Hull commented that the tendency for conditioned responses to anticipate the US has obvious adaptive advantages, particularly when the US inflicts injury, but that in many circumstances it is important that the animal time the occurrence of its anticipatory response rather precisely. Here, again, inhibition serves the corrective function, as illustrated by Pavlov's demonstrations of inhibition of delay.

Finally, Hull posed a dilemma for conditioned-reflex mechanisms in the form of a problem that theorists have confronted ever since. The case is one in which the animal learns to respond to a predictive signal (CS) for an aversive event (US) in such a way that it *prevents* the aversive event from occurring. By means of the stimulus-substitution principle, the conditioned-reflex account can deal with the fact that a CS-US pairing results in the CS evoking an "avoidance" response. But, by definition, once successful avoidance has been conditioned, the process of experimental extinction should set in and avoidance behavior should deteriorate. The dilemma is that failures to avoid would not be to the organism's adaptive advantage, and the fact is that avoidance behavior seems not to show the kind of deterioration that would be predicted by the conditioned reflex account. Hull suggested that the extinction process might be inoperative or, simply, retarded in the case of avoidance learning, but he recognized that the former suggestion was inadequate and that the latter suggestion was highly tentative. As we have indicated, the "dilemma" of avoidance learning has been the source of continuing theoretical activity (see Overmier, 1979, for a recent review).

Section 3. Commentaries on Papers

Many of the ideas in this paper surface in later portions of Hull's work. The tendency of all stimuli present to become conditioned when the US occurs (the first mechanism) is the subject of an extended analysis of the role played by "background" stimuli in discrimination learning (Paper 21). The analysis of learning to respond to patterns of stimuli (the second mechanism) receives a particularly detailed treatment in the *Principles* (Chapter 19) and in Paper 15 on "afferent neural interaction." Stimulus generalization (the third mechanism) was also a major issue in *Principles* (Chapter 12) and in Papers 12, 16, 19, and 21. The tendency for conditioned responses to become anticipatory (the fourth mechanism) is the basis of Hull's well-known *fractional anticipatory goal response* (r_G-s_G), which proved to be so important in his analyses of purpose, foresight, and other "cognitive" processes (Papers 3 and 4, in particular). All of these are subjects for later commentary. It seems most appropriate in the remainder of this commentary to touch on Hull's early strategy and guiding ideas.

First, a comment on style. Compared with his later ones, in this first paper Hull simply accepts Pavlov's phenomena, terminology, and the conditioning paradigm. He also accepts the theoretical language of excitation and inhibition as "given" mechanisms of adaptation. The formalism and the attempts at derivation characteristic of subsequent papers is absent. The paper is not, however, slavishly Pavlovian, and this too is notable. For example, like other American psychologists, Hull did not take seriously Pavlov's neurological speculations about excitation and inhibition, and he applauded Hollingworth's attempt to take a more comprehensive view of excitatory learning as reflected in the concept of "redintegration." A few years later, in 1935, in an S-R analysis of "problem solution" (Paper 8), Hull explicitly rejected the idea that his work included a strict application of Pavlovian reflexology. In a footnote, he wrote:

> In order to correct a frequent misunderstanding, due presumably to the wide dissemination of the views of J. B. Watson, the writer wishes to make it quite clear that neither here nor in any previous publications has he assumed that the more complex forms of behavior are synthesized from reflexes which play the role of building blocks. This may or may not be true. His working hypothesis is, rather, that the *principles of action* discovered in conditioned reflex experiments are also operative in the higher behavioral processes. The compound adjective in the expression, "conditioned-reflex principles," accordingly refers to the locus of *discovery* of the principles rather than to their locus of *operation*. (pp. 227–28)

A theme that is touched on repeatedly in this first of Hull's papers in learning theory concerns the relation between Pavlovian conditioned reflexes and the trial-

28

and-error learning which is usually thought to characterize Thorndikian experiments. The issue is raised, for example, when Hull appeals to the conditioned reflex as an "automatic trial-and-error mechanism" in adaptive behavior; we now know it is also germane to the resolution of the avoidance "dilemma" posed at the end of the paper. The history of this issue in Hull's writings, and in learning theory in general, has been reviewed by Coleman and Gormezano (1979). We note here only that Hull's S-R framework led him to the monistic view that both types of conditioning result in stimulus-response connections, and in all versions of the theory those connections were assumed to be learned according to the same principle. The principle of reinforcement for which Hull became best known, in the form of the special hypothesis of *need-reduction,* took shape over the decade following publication of his first paper, is advanced specifically in his review of Thorndike's book *Fundamentals of Learning* (Hull, 1935), and is part of the definition of habit strength in the *Principles* and their first revision in 1950 (Paper 20). By the time he published *Essentials* a year later, and in *A Behavior System* a year after that, Hull had changed the postulate on primary reinforcement from "diminution . . . of a need" to "diminution in the motivational stimulus (S_D or s_G). The *principle of reinforcement* as a *necessary* condition for formation of an association was not a part of Hull's earliest theorizing in learning.

Hull's preoccupation with adaptive behavior extended to the last chapter of his last book, *A Behavior System* (1952a, pp. 347–50). Here, he listed eight examples of "adaptive automatic behavior mechanisms," and this was not intended to be an exhaustive list. These eight mechanisms can be compared with the original views Hull expressed in the 1929 paper, but most of all they underline for the last time his enduring concern with mechanisms of adaptive behavior. The mechanisms are: (1) unlearned stimulus-response connections or reflexes, (2) the ability to learn, (3) anticipatory defense reactions, (4) negative response learning (i.e., the process by which acts that provide no reduction in drive stimulation are eliminated), (5) trial-and-error learning, (6) discrimination learning, (7) the traces of stimuli which persist in a decaying fashion after the physical stimulus ceases and which enter into associations with responses, and (8) the directive properties of the fractional antedating goal reaction which allow for foresight, knowledge, expectancy and purpose. Even today, this list provides a reasonable starting point for developing a mechanistic theory of adaptive behavior. In fact, there seems to be a growing interest in combining ecological, ethological, and psychological approaches in a new attack on this prob-

29

Section 3. Commentaries on Papers

lem (e.g., Houston, 1980; Kamil & Sargent, 1981; Shettleworth, 1984). Some parts of that work which are concerned with Pavlovian mechanisms of adaptive behavior (e.g., Booth, 1980; Buzsaki, 1982; Garcia, Hawkins & Rusiniak, 1974; Hollis, 1982; Rashotte, O'Connell & Beidler, 1982; Williams, 1981), are, in particular, a continuation of the spirit of Hull's first *Psychological Review* paper.

A Primer in Deductive Method

2. Simple trial and error learning: A study in psychological theory. (1930)

The subtitle indicates the focus of the paper; it provides a primer on the mechanics of explanation and prediction by theories in psychology, a theme to which Hull returned often. The argument is that satisfactory explanation is not achieved simply by labeling a known phenomenon as an instance of a more general principle (e.g., conservation of energy), or as a putative case of the influence of a stimulus-response, Gestalt, or other mechanism. Such "explanations" are superficial. Instead, Hull maintained, a far deeper understanding is achieved by employing a deductive strategy, which has the important feature that it can yield new predictions whose accuracy can be tested in the laboratory, thereby providing an objective means of checking on the correctness of the "explanation." This is the view of scientific theory expounded by the philosopher Karl Popper (e.g., 1962). In Hull's case it is obviously connected with his long-time interest in devising machine models of psychological processes.

Hull's analysis of "simple" trial-and-error learning illustrates the nature of his theoretical strategy and provides the first of several so-called *miniature theoretical systems* that were worked out in the Papers. The case of trial-and-error learning considered here is the sort studied by Thorndike in his problem boxes, in which the animal is reinforced by food, say, when it performs the correct response, but experiences no special outcome following incorrect responses. Hull's first step was to describe 12 key characteristics of behavior in these situations (Part II). Then, by weaving together a series of explicit assumptions about the variables which cause behaviors to be strengthened and weakened, and some simple mathematical rules of logic, he showed how those 12 behavioral characteristics could be deduced (Parts III and IV), and new predictions made (Part VI). In a sense, the choice of a Thorndikian behavioral example is less important than the *approach* to the problem that is being illustrated. Whereas the example was from Thorndike, the assumptions and mechanisms were based on Pavlov, a fact which comments on the weak distinction he and others made between Pavlovian and Thorndikian conditioning at that time.

This paper also fired the opening shot in what turned out to be a prolonged conflict between Hull and his supporters on the one hand, and the advocates of a learning theory based on Gestalt principles on the other. The general case Hull argued was that the deductive method provides a sound means for comparing the merits of different theoretical approaches. He noted in particular that the Gestalt psychologists, Wolfgang Kohler and Kurt Koffka, had offered "painstaking" criticism of S-R theory's theoretical constructs. To them, and to critics of any other persuasion, he issued a "friendly invitation" to state their theoretical principles in a precise form and to use the deductive method to explain, and to make new predictions about, the simple case of trial-and-error learning he had analyzed. Hull anticipated four possible outcomes of such an exercise and interpreted each of them as follows. If no deductions were forthcoming, it would imply immaturity or possible inadequacy in the alternative theoretical approaches. If, however, a deduction were made that used the equivalent of recognized S-R principles, it would indicate that the alternative approach was not distinctive. Third, should a different theoretical approach yield a deduction identical to that based on S-R principles, the theoretical parallelism would be, in Hull's words, "mutually illuminating to all parties to the discussion." Finally, should a different prediction be made from the alternative theory, the dispute could be settled by an appropriate laboratory test.

The history of learning theory indicates that the proponents of other theoretical positions were not greatly influenced by Hull's "invitation." There were some attempts at direct comparisons of different theories, notably in Tolman's presidential address to the American Psychological Association (Tolman, 1938), Spence's analysis of learning theories (1942) and, much later, in the exhaustive analysis of learning theories coauthored by Estes, Koch, MacCorquodale, Meehl, Mueller, Schoenfeld, and Verplank (1954).

Hull did not, of course, succeed in having the deductive strategy embraced by all psychological theorists. Instead, the Gestalt theorists and others remained more inclined to point out difficulties in the Hullian system and to present a string of interesting behavioral phenomena that they believed could not be deduced from S-R principles. Purposive behavior, discontinuity (insight) in learning, and transposition in discrimination learning stand as prime examples. Thus thwarted, Hull and his associates followed a counterstrategy. They set out to show that S-R theory could provide *in principle* analyses of supposedly intractable behavioral phenomena and, most important, they attempted to establish the superiority of S-R theory by predicting (and sometimes demonstrating) limiting conditions for the phenomena in question. Notable examples are Neal Miller's analysis of foresight (Miller, 1935), and Spence's treatments of transposition

Section 3. Deductive Primer

(Spence, 1936, 1937) and gradual versus sudden solution in discrimination learning (Spence, 1938). This counterstrategy proved to be very influential and undoubtedly contributed to the dominance of the Hullian approach in the 1940s and 1950s.

In the final section of this paper, Hull addresses the possibility of constructing machines that display psychic characteristics and comments on the potential of such machines for modern society. As we noted in Section 1, Hull's affinity for machinery and for machine-models of psychological processes surfaced early in his career, and it is an interest he maintained throughout his lifetime. In addition to the work by Hull and Baernstein (1929) cited in this paper, there followed attempts to construct actual devices that exhibit the adaptive characteristics of the conditioned reflex (Baernstein & Hull, 1931; Krueger & Hull, 1931). Hull comments in the closing paragraph of this paper on trial-and-error learning that an S-R theory should provide a favorable climate for the development of "psychic" devices, such as the computers and robots that had their greatest development after Hull's death.

The fact is, however, that much of the work in information processing and artificial intelligence reflects the influence of machines—computers and robots—on modern "cognitive science" rather than any influence that S-R psychology had on the development of the machines. As we point out later in discussing the habit-family hierarchy papers, however, many of the simpler statements of contingency made by the cognitivists in this field are not distinguishable in substance from their S-R theory counterparts. The fact of the matter seems to be that, in his use of machine models in his work, Hull was doing in the 1930s something very much like what is being done today with computer analogies. Of course, he was forced to use the machine imagery of his time, as we are of our time. But the styles of approach are not very different, and this will be worth keeping in mind when this field of work begins to reconstruct its history.

33

S-R Analyses of "Cognitive" Processes

3. Knowledge and purpose as habit mechanisms. (1930)

4. Goal attraction and directing ideas conceived as habit phenomena. (1931)

These are the first of Hull's papers to explore the consequences for S-R theory of assuming that adaptive behavior is controlled jointly by external stimuli *and* by a variety of internal stimuli. These papers provide a rich supply of S-R mechanisms designed to supplant traditional mentalistic processes as the causes of behavior. The four mentalistic processes identified in the titles—knowledge, purpose, attraction by future goals, and directing ideas—provided the vehicle for Hull's analysis. But the specific subject matter is less important than the principles devised for its analysis. In fact, these principles rank among the most significant contributions to S-R theory, and, as we shall see, to learning theory in general, and Hull employed them repeatedly in his later work. They are the basis both for S-R accounts by others of complex processes (e.g., Berlyne, 1960, 1965; Dollard & Miller, 1950; Maltzman, 1955; Miller & Dollard, 1941; Mowrer, 1960b; Osgood, 1953), for the Pavlovian mediational models of instrumental performance (e.g., Amsel, 1958; Logan, 1960; Mowrer, 1960a; Spence, 1956), and arguably for contemporary two-process theory (Gray, 1975; Rescorla & Solomon, 1967; Trapold & Overmier, 1972).

The underlying theme in these papers was the application of S-R language not just to the relations of observable stimuli to behavior, but also as a characterization of the theoretical substrate, those hidden sources of behavioral control that are typically assigned to mentalistic entities. Of course, Watson's behaviorism had attempted a stimulus-response account of processes such as thoughts and feelings (e.g., Watson, 1930), but this was the later, doctrinaire Watson whose simple reflexology and strident style invited caricature and easy dismissal by critics. Hull's approach was more sophisticated and much more in the spirit of the earlier Watson (1913, 1919), whose behaviorism was a simple extension of pragmatic functionalism, and who, as Amsel (1982) has pointed out, was comfortable with the use of stimulus and response as intermediary constructs

34

representing the emotions (e.g., Watson & Rayner, 1920). Hull's proposal for extending S-R concepts to complex behaviors involved the identification of an array of unobservable stimuli that could enter into associative relations with responses and thereby, along with observable external stimuli, exert control over behavior.

The most important of the unobservable stimuli in Hull's analysis derive from a venerable concept in physiology—feedback stimulation (kinesthesis) produced when a response is executed. In his analysis of *Knowledge* in Paper 3, Hull exploited the idea that such stimulation could be produced not only by overt but also by covert responses. For him, an animal's knowledge of its world is, to use a modern term, "encoded" in response chains. The idea was simple and entirely appropriate for an S-R theory, as it was based on that universally accepted premise of response-produced stimulation.

Hull begins with the assumption that external stimuli generate distinctive reactions in receptive organisms. Sequences of stimuli that occur repeatedly, and therefore are not likely to be random events, generate a sequence of responses that may become chained together by means of response-produced stimulation. The feedback stimulus from each response forms an associative linkage with the next response in the series. Once established, these chain linkages make it possible for the entire response sequence to "run off," *even in the absence of the external stimulus sequence,* provided that at least one external stimulus initiates a response in the chain. These relatively autonomous response chains constitute a kind of replica of external stimulus events and, in terms of S-R theory, provide a mechanism for the organism's knowledge of the world it has experienced.

These response chains constituting "knowledge" are not, of course, at the observable level. To conceptualize their covert nature, Hull appealed to the experimental observations of Thorndike and others that instrumental responses tend to diminish in strength to a point at which they are just capable of producing an effective consequence. When their sole function is to generate the chaining stimuli, which in turn generate later responses in the chain and finally the adaptive response, these responses may become entirely unobservable. Hull called these stimulus-producing responses *pure-stimulus acts.* His analysis envisioned the instigating stimulus (S1) evoking an unobservable sequence of responses and response-produced stimuli that represent a series of previous experiences. And, depending on the circumstances, it might be possible to bypass early elements in the series so that only those response-produced stimuli that occur late in the chain evoke observable (i.e., instrumental) responses. In terms of its immediate antecedents, the importance of response-produced (kinesthetic) cues in sequential habits and the idea of short-circuiting can be found a decade earlier in Watson (1919) (see Amsel, 1982).

In the analysis of *goal attraction* (Paper 4), Hull proposed yet another source of response-produced stimulation which turned out to be one of the most important mechanisms in S-R theory. In that analysis, he explored the implications of assuming that Pavlovian conditioned responses are concurrently evoked by the stimuli, more specifically the persisting drive stimuli (S_D) that control instrumental response sequences. His argument was that, just as a CS precedes the biologically significant US-UR event in Pavlov's experiment, so these persisting stimuli precede the biologically significant consequences (S_D-R_G) of successful instrumental response sequences. Accordingly, these persisting stimuli would function as Pavlovian CSs *as well as* evoking the instrumental response directly.

Hull characterized the "nonconflicting components" of such mediating Pavlovian CRs as "fractional anticipatory goal responses" to underscore two of their important characteristics. One is the assumed morphological similarity between the CR and at least some portion of the response evoked by the stimulus at the goal (i.e., "fractional"). The other is that like other CRs, they antedate the UR or goal response (i.e., "anticipatory"). A crucial third assumption was that these Pavlovian CRs generate feedback stimulation; hence the symbolic representation of the fractional anticipatory goal response, "r_G-s_G." Once the persisting stimuli of the class S_D evoke the conditioned r_G-s_G in an instrumental response sequence, s_G, like other response-produced, directing stimuli, becomes associated with the responses in the sequence. The upshot was an analysis of goal anticipation and its control over behavior leading to that goal, all within the framework of S-R theory. This theoretical strategy gave Hull considerable leverage in analyzing instances of goal-directed behavior that were a favorite topic for Tolman and other Gestalt-oriented theorists (e.g., Tolman, 1932).

In Paper 3, Hull had attributed *purpose* in behavior to associations involving an implicit "persisting stimulus" that occurs unchanged throughout the response sequence evoked by the changing world stimulation. He gave as examples stimuli arising from the knitting of the brow while solving a puzzle, or interoceptive stimulation arising from an organism's deprivation condition. In Paper 4, he emphasized the role played by stimuli from deprivation in bringing r_G-s_G into existence. In fact, in the 1931 paper he substituted for "persisting stimulation" the r_G-s_G concept as the mechanism underlying purpose.

Hull's assumption that adaptive behavior is jointly controlled by stimula-

36

tion arising from three sources—external stimuli, response-produced stimuli, and stimuli generated by the state of the animal (e.g., deprivation)—required that the theory provide rules by which these sources of control combine to generate observed performance. He favored a simple summation rule: the strengths of all S-R associations acting at a given moment were combined and the response with the highest total strength occurred. Important supplemental assumptions were needed about the strength of S-R associations at different distances from the goal and about the contribution made by individual stimuli with multiple response associations. These latter assumptions anticipate later more detailed expositions of the *goal gradient hypothesis* (Papers 5 and 11) and the *habit family hierarchy* (Papers 6 and 7). Taken together, these ideas allowed Hull to offer an *in principle* S-R account of many features of complex behavior. For example, he was able to explain why unnecessary steps in problem solving are ultimately eliminated with training rather than being "stamped in" as a simple application of Thorndike's law of effect would require. This account of "short-circuiting," as he termed it, is a good example of the sophisticated nature of Hull's analysis, and it stands in rather sharp contrast to other S-R behavioristic treatments at the time and since.

In these early papers, Hull did not take the position, as he did later in the *Principles,* that reinforcement is necessary for the formation of an S-R association, and we find here many references to association by sheer temporal contiguity between S and R, a characteristic of the earlier treatments of Watson and Guthrie.

From the perspective of the early 1930s, these two papers constitute a quantum leap in sophistication of S-R theory. Yet the advance was achieved at the cost of assigning behavioral control to unseen sources of stimulation. Hull was as hard-headed about psychology as anyone, so how could he justify this move toward the unobserved? The answer lies in three factors. First, he believed that these unseen events control behavior precisely as observed events do. Accordingly, such an analysis required no new principles beyond those that existed for observable events. Second, he believed that maze learning provided an excellent laboratory model of the reflex chains he assumed to underly complex processes. Consequently, through an experimental and theoretical analysis of maze learning he expected to arrive at a thorough understanding of the principles governing the action of reflex chains. In fact, the next several papers in the series were concerned with this problem. Finally, he believed that adherence to strict deductive logic (Paper 2) would guard against reckless application of these

37

principles. The logic of the approach seemed impeccable and the extension of S-R reasoning was very creative. It is understandable, then, that many behaviorists were influenced by the publication of these papers.

From the perspective of the 1970s and 1980s and the focus on cognitive processes, these papers might have been expected to retain at least historical interest. Our compilation of references to Hull's papers (Table 1) shows that this has not been the case. As we have indicated, the theoretical ideas first described in these articles stimulated several influential S-R accounts of complex processes. But, with the advent of information processing approaches to such problems in the 1960s, the nature of the enterprise began to be questioned. Was it the job of the psychologist to explain behavior? Or was it rather his/her job to examine cognitive processes by making inferences from behavior? In the words of Dickinson (1979, p. 553), who favors the latter view, "Behavior is but a spade to disinter thought."

All this aside, these early papers make contact with current associative research and point to some issues that may turn out to be important for understanding the determinants of complex behavior. One issue is Hull's emphasis on the role of stimulus compounds in the control of behavior. At each point in the response sequences he considered, Hull envisioned a simultaneous compound of stimuli arising from external, response-produced and interoceptive sources. In the light of recent experimental results, Hull's understanding of associative learning in stimulus compounds is primitive. For example, he assumed that all elements in a compound are independently conditioned and that performance is determined by the summed associative strengths of these elements. Recent research on blocking indicates that stimuli in a compound do not condition independently of their previous associative history (e.g., Kamin, 1968; Mackintosh, 1975; Rescorla & Wagner, 1972), and that a simple summation rule does not encompass all instances of conditioning to compound CSs involving simultaneously occurring elements (e.g., Rescorla, 1973). That Hull himself was well aware of this latter point is indicated by his discussion of stimulus patterning in Pavlov's experiments (Paper 1, and also Paper 15).[1] And we have reason to be modest about our understanding of associative learning in stimulus compounds many years after Hull's attempts to do so. For example, we are far

1. Anderson (1976), in his book *Language, Memory, and Thought*, writes: "As an empirical aside, animals can apparently be conditioned to respond to patterns (see Rescorla & Wagner, 1972). This fact has been a sore point for S-R theories." If this was a "sore point" for Hull, he did not, to extend the metaphor, avoid touching it, but attempted to treat it from his earliest writings until his last book in 1952.

from having a complete account of stimulus patterning and little is known about the relative amounts of control exerted by external and internal sources of stimuli in a compound (Adam, 1967; Bykov, 1957). The intriguing possibility that there is bias toward control by certain of these stimulus sources over others in compounds (e.g., Razran, 1961) certainly deserves special experimental attention.

The *successive* nature of the stimulus compounds in Hull's analyses identifies yet another problem that would repay our research efforts. If there is ever to be a successful S-R account of complex behavior sequences, it is likely to include the kind of control depicted in Hull's diagrams, in Paper 4 say, where a chain of responses is evoked by a succession of *compound stimuli* involving simultaneously occurring elements. The nature of associations formed when *single* stimuli are presented sequentially prior to a US, a far simpler case, has become a problem of interest in the West relatively recently (e.g., Baker, 1968; Kehoe & Gormezano, 1980; Wickens, 1965). It remains to be seen whether theoretical analysis of even this simpler case will require the complex Hull-like associative structure seen as necessary by some Soviet Pavlovian theorists (e.g., Asratyan, 1976; Rudenko, 1974).

Whatever the eventual outcome, such work should make it easier for us to see Hull's analyses in historical perspective. Hull's schematic diagrams convey an impression of order and stereotypy in stimulus compounds that is not likely to be justified in specific cases of problem solving, perhaps not even in the prototypical case of maze learning. Consider, for example, his portrayal of the environment as discrete, successive-stimulus compounds that control successive responses in the series. One problem here is that, as training progresses, the timing of responses and the composition of the stimulus compounds on which they depend is likely to change as performance becomes increasingly skilled. At the very least, this will be true for response-produced stimuli. What would be needed for Hull's applications is an understanding of how *variability* in the composition and the timing of stimulus compounds (particularly early in training) influences associative learning. A solution to this question is likely to be some years away. Furthermore, Hull's reliance on response-produced stimuli in his analysis of chained responding poses some troublesome problems. For example, Lashley (1951) argued that the speed of neural transmission prohibits proprioceptive feedback stimulation from being a significant source of control in rapidly executed response chains, such as the playing of an arpeggio on the piano. Perhaps more significantly, Taub & Berman (1968) have demonstrated experimentally that monkeys are capable of performing a previously learned motor task and can learn new skilled responses despite surgical deafferentation of their limbs. The role of proprioceptive and kinesthetic feedback in the control of behavior remains to be clarified; and many of these problems would be solved if the response-produced feedback stimulation—the pure-stimulus act, the r_G-s_G—were regarded as central rather than peripheral. Such considerations affect, and are addressed by, theoretical positions more recent than Hull's (e.g., Konorski, 1967; Mowrer, 1960a; Rescorla & Solomon, 1967).

Another emphasis found in Paper 4 is the subject of recent and current interest. The r_G-s_G mechanism is the clear forerunner of work on the mediation of instrumental performances by Pavlovian CRs (e.g., Amsel, 1958, 1967; Logan, 1960; Mowrer, 1960a,b; Overmier & Lawry, 1979; Rescorla & Solomon, 1968; Spence, 1956). In fact, Spence's (1956) version of Hullian theory assigned major importance to this mechanism in simple instrumental learning, and Amsel (1958) significantly extended the theory's scope by introducing the idea that aversive emotional goal reactions evoked by nonreward can occur in anticipatory form. He proposed that r_G-s_G be used as a general term to symbolize a class of anticipatory goal responses, and the members of this class be r_R-s_R (reward at the goal), r_F-s_F (aversive "frustrative" reaction evoked by nonreward at the goal), and r_P-s_P (aversive reaction by exteroceptive "painful" stimulation at the goal).[2] Amsel's conceptualization of r_F-s_F proved to be particularly important in allowing Hull-Spence theory to deal with otherwise troublesome phenomena related to partial reinforcement, extinction, and contrast effects (see Rashotte, 1979b for a review).

Parenthetically, we draw attention to Hull's account of extinction in Paper 4 (Part V). The extinction-induced disintegration of goal-directed response chains is attributed to the change of stimulus conditions that occurs when r_G-s_G is removed from the stimulus complex. This stimulus-change account of extinction anticipates the main feature of Skinner's (1950) and Capaldi's (1967) treatment of extinction. However, as we have stated, it clearly could not deal with the range of partial reinforcement effects that began to appear in the literature several years later (e.g., Humphreys, 1939; Skinner, 1938). The theories of Amsel and of Capaldi (e.g., Amsel, 1967; Capaldi, 1967), in particular, let Hullian theory cope with these phenomena.

In the light of some of the more recent discussions of "classical incentive motivation theory" (e.g., Bindra, 1972; Bolles, 1972), it is interesting to note that r_G-s_G has, in this early treatment, a purely *directive* function. This is not

---

2. Mowrer's (1960a) terms for these latter three forms of anticipatory responses are *hope, disappointment,* and *fear*—to which he added *relief,* so that *hope* is to *disappointment* as *relief* is to *fear.*

40

the kind of incentive or goal-anticipation that energizes habits through a motivational process (Spence's later K factor, introduced by Hull, 1950b). It has none of the properties of general drive. It is precisely the kind of directive goal expectancy mechanism Bolles (1975) found absent in Hullian theory 40 years later, despite the fact that, in the meantime, Hull's intellectual descendants (e.g., Amsel, 1958, 1962, 1967; Logan, 1960; Mowrer, 1960a,b) had depended heavily on the directive (stimulus) properties of incentive in their theorizing. It is curious that several recent accounts of incentive motivation either ignore completely Hull's contribution or cite only his *Principles* (1943), in which the role of r_G-s_G is mentioned just once in a terminal note and plays no role in the body of the theory.

While Hull's r_G-s_G has encouraged research and theory, the concept has not been without problems. Perhaps the main difficulty is that it depends on Pavlovian conditioning of r_G to a sequence of very complex stimuli that precede the goal. The uncertainties surrounding Pavlovian conditioning to successive compound stimuli we have noted above make it difficult to be precise about the status of r_G at various points in a stimulus-response series, not to mention at the various stages of training. Furthermore, there has never been a comprehensive attempt to bring r_G-s_G theory into line with the new information about "blocking," "overshadowing," and other forms of stimulus selection in compound CSs. Uncertainties about such fundamental points as these allow a certain looseness in the concept that is particularly nettlesome to some critics—for example, Razran (1971, p.205) has commented that r_G-s_G should be termed the "intervening fractional anticipatory do-alls and sense-alls." Perhaps because of difficulties such as these, an entire line of work on the Pavlovian mediation of instrumental performance omits any discussion of the details of the assumed Pavlovian infrastructure of baseline instrumental performances (Overmier & Lawry, 1979; Rescorla & Solomon, 1967). The more recently discovered phenomenon of autoshaping has been interpreted as a case of the *direct* evocation of instrumental responses by Pavlovian CSs (e.g., Brown & Jenkins, 1968; Hearst & Jenkins, 1974; Locurto, Terrace & Gibbon, 1981). Thus, while it seems that Hull was on the right track when he emphasized Pavlovian influences on the performance of instrumental responses, that influence may be more complex than he understood it to be.

A point of interest about Hull's r_G-s_G concept is its relation to phenomena dubbed the "misbehavior of organisms" which has aroused some interest in operant circles (Boakes, Poli, Lockwood & Goodall, 1978; Breland & Breland, 1961). The essence of these phenomena is that a chain of behaviors that should be executed smoothly to produce reinforcement suffers disruption from the anticipatory intrusion of goal-like behaviors. One much cited example is the difficulty hungry raccoons experience in carrying small discs from one side of a room to the other to obtain food reward. As training proceeds, they begin to respond as though the discs *are* the food (e.g., they rub them together as if they are washing the food items before eating them). These intruding responses delay completion of the response that is instrumental in obtaining food. In the present papers, Hull envisioned the r_G-s_G mechanism as an instance of the intrusion of goal-responses at early points in goal-directed behavior sequences. Curiously, the "misbehavior" literature had made little or no reference to Hull's mechanism despite the fact that he noted certain instances of maladaptive behavior that seem symptomatic of anticipation of the goal. For example, he cited *ejaculatio praecox* during sexual activity as one such instance (Paper 3). Apparently, what is one man's misbehavior is another's fractional anticipatory goal response.

Skinner has recently contributed some interesting history on this point. During a visit to Skinner's laboratory in 1937, Hull noted that some features of the performances he observed there suggested the anticipatory intrusion of goal responses into the instrumental response sequence. Skinner comments that on these grounds Hull may have been the first to identify "misbehavior" and to suggest the probable Pavlovian basis for it (Skinner, 1977, p. 1007).

The S-R analysis of complex behavior offered in these papers never formed the basis for the tightly reasoned deductions for which Hull hoped. He employed the deductive strategy most fully in the *Principles,* which was specifically intended *not* to deal with complex behaviors; consequently, most of the ideas described in these two papers played no role in that book. The ideas do reappear two decades later in *A Behavior System,* a book devoted to more complex phenomena. However, this last book of Hull's is more a prospectus for a deductive approach to complex behaviors than a well-honed series of deductions. The problem seems to have been twofold. Data sufficient to provide precise quantitative principles for such deductions were lacking, and the sheer number of factors involved and the nature of their interactions made a formal deductive strategy virtually unworkable. These problems appear to remain for current information-processing approaches to complex behavior.

A legitimate question that arises, then, is: Can a detailed analysis of stimulus conditions and response characteristics be combined with associative logic to generate an effective account of complex learning? The current popularity of cognitive, information-processing approaches to language, memory, thinking, and their relationship to complex behavior certainly constitutes a strong nega-

SECTION 3. COGNITIVE PROCESSES

tive vote on this possibility. Writing on the subject "Cognitive Science" in the Centennial issue of *Science*, Herbert A. Simon (1980), who was obviously alluding to Skinner's behaviorism but could have been referring to Hull's S-R analyses of purpose, directing ideas, foresight, and knowledge, says the following:

> Over the past quarter-century, no development in the social sciences has been more radical than the evolution—often referred to as the information processing revolution—in our way of understanding the processes of human thinking. Behaviorism was suited to the predominantly positivist and operationalist views of the methodology and philosophy of science, and seemed to provide some guarantee against metaphysical "mentalistic" explanations of human behavior. The price paid for these qualities was to confine experimental psychology to relatively simple memory and learning experiments, and to a preoccupation with laboratory rats rather than humans engaged in complex thinking and problem-solving tasks.
>
> A quarter-century later, the picture has changed radically. Experimental psychology has achieved a new sophistication and a new confidence both in studying with precision simple, fundamental mental processes (for example, reaction times and short-term memory capacities), and in bringing into the laboratory professional-level cognitive tasks like chess playing, solving mathematics or physics problems, understanding natural language or making medical diagnoses. Moreover, the analysis and explanation of all of these diverse sorts of processes had been brought within a general paradigm, the information processing paradigm—without loss of operationality, and with a great gain in precision and rigor. (p.76)

From Simon's perspective, this is a perfectly reasonable statement. Indeed it conveys a remarkably similar point of view to a statement made some years ago by a "behaviorist" in a section headed "Will S-R versus cognitive arguments persist?" in an essay on neo-Hullian behaviorism (Amsel, 1965).[3]

> . . . The major overlap of interests between cognitive theorists and S-R theorists of the Hullian inclination has been in "expectancy" as a mediating mechanism. This boils down to a difference between a *conditioning-expectancy* and a *cognitive-expectancy* model. Stimulus-response conditioning-expectancy theory is r_G theory, and the advantage of this kind of theory over the cognitive-expectancy variety is that the conditioning model has definite rules and limits of operation established by the findings of conditioning experiments. . . . On the other hand, the cognitive-expectancy language has been a language of common sense. Such a language is difficult . . . to apply rigidly to lower animals operating in simple situations or to humans operating at prearticulate or subarticulate levels. The result has been that the cognitive theorists, generally speaking, have left the lower-level learning phenomena to the stimulus-response psychologists and have moved on to

3. This paper was a revision and extension of a paper for a *Symposium in Learning Theory* presented at the AAAS Meeting in December 1958 in Washington, D.C.

tackle more complex human behavior, usually involving language—a level of behavior for which their kind of theorizing was always more appropriate.

. . . The new cognitive psychology is a different animal: It is an attempt to describe cognitive processes in the language of the computer and information theory. It speaks not [like Tolman] of demands, appetites, expectancies, and readinesses but rather of inputs, outputs, and channel capacities. "Plans" have replaced cognitive maps, but the plan seems a more exclusively human phenomenon. In place of means-ends-readinesses, and sign-Gestalt-expectations, there are bits and chunks of information to be "processed" by the organism. The new cognitivists and structuralists are questioning the vitality of stimulus-response psychology in much the same way that the Gestaltists and older cognitivists did twenty years ago. There are, however, at least two important differences: (1) The current challenge is, at least, at a level more appropriate to the language of the challenger; the earlier challenges were not. (2) The new cognitivists carry with them a more powerful, analytical language than did the old. . . . (pp. 201–2)

In this statement there was a recognition that cognitive psychology (as opposed to S-R, *not* behaviorism) already, in 1965 (the article was originally written for an AAAS symposium in December 1958), meant something different than it had to Tolman. The question was not whether there should be a "cognitive science" but rather whether there was any longer a common ground of observation between the stimulus-response and cognitive approaches. Amsel's view then was that "we do not really need to choose between stimulus-response and cognitive approaches to the study of behavior, but that each is a more appropriate description for some particular level of observation" (p. 203). This was essentially the position of Mandler (1962) at that time, in an article entitled "From Association to Structure," and something along very much the same lines has been recognized recently by Wickelgren (1979). Perhaps S-R behavioristic theory oversteps the bounds of its heuristic value when it is applied to complex behavioral phenomena. (Recent work from the Harvard laboratory on "symbolic communication" and "self-awareness" in the pigeon indicate that at least some behaviorists are not yet willing "to-give-up-the-ship" [Epstein, Lanza, & Skinner, 1980, 1981].) Perhaps S-R theory has its place at certain phylogenetic levels and at certain early (and perhaps very late) stages of development in humans and nonhuman mammals (e.g., Amsel & Stanton, 1980). The care and precision with which Hull argued the S-R case over 50 years ago in these two papers can help illuminate the advantages and limitations of the approach.

The Goal Gradient
and Habit-Family Hierarchy

5. The goal gradient hypothesis and maze learning. (1932)

6. The concept of the habit-family hierarchy and maze learning: Part I. (1934)

7. The concept of the habit-family hierarchy and maze learning: Part II. (1934)

8. The mechanism of the assembly of behavior segments in novel combinations suitable for problem solution. (1935)

11. The goal-gradient hypothesis applied to some 'field-force' problems in the behavior of young children. (1938)

In addition to their main foci on the Pavlovian fractional anticipatory goal response and on trial-and-error learning, Papers 1 through 4 included brief references to a variety of mechanisms that seemed to Hull necessary for a complete S-R account of complex behaviors. Papers 5 through 8 and Paper 11 present in detail Hull's thinking about the nature of two of these adaptive mechanisms, and include a discussion of their application to some specific behavioral phenomena. The mechanisms are the *goal gradient hypothesis* and the *habit-family hierarchy*. Our commentary begins by identifying briefly three of Hull's continuing preoccupations which the discussion of these mechanisms clearly reflect: Gestalt psychology, Darwinian adaptation, and quantification.

SECTION 3. COMMENTARIES ON PAPERS

The competition with Gestalt psychology is revealed particularly in the last two papers in which Hull applies his S-R principles to problem-solving (Umweg) tasks and to the study of conflicting valences that had been the province of Gestalt theory, and more specifically of Lewinian field theory—hence the single quotes around 'field force' in the title of the 1938 paper. Hull wanted to show in a context other than simple maze learning that an analysis in terms of "conditioning principles" could make more and better specific predictions than could one in field-theory terms, even when, as he says (Paper 11, footnote 17), the assumptions both start with are the same. Needless to say, the hostilities between Hull and his followers and the Gestalters, to which we have referred in our general comments in Section 2, were not lessened by these extensions of S-R theory to the domain of field-theory phenomena.

We were struck again as we read these papers by the profound influence of Darwin on Hull's theorizing, and by the recent resurgence of Darwinian thinking in learning theory. Almost 40 years after these articles of Hull, Staddon and Simmelhag (1971), in a very influential paper, seemed to have resuscitated the spirit, if not the letter, of the goal-gradient hypothesis and the habit-family concept in their application of evolutionary-adaptive principles to operant behavior. They appear to do this quite unknowingly, for their only mention of Hull, obviously in reference to the *Principles,* is in statements such as: "Little remains of the impressive edifice erected by Hull and his followers on this base [of the Law of Effect]. . . . Hullian theory has proven effective neither in the elucidation of complex cases nor as an aid to the discovery of new phenomena" (p. 16).

Staddon and Simmelhag's references to interim and terminal activities as depending on "states," as being interrelated in strength, and as depending on properties of the reinforcer evoke all kinds of early-thirties Hullian imagery (a) of r_G-s_G: ". . . the stimulus . . . most predictive of reinforcement comes to control a state or mood . . . appropriate to that reinforcer" (p. 34); and (b) of the goal-gradient principle: ". . . [the] strength . . . of activities during the interim period is *directly related* to the strength of the terminal response" (p. 35). In their discussion of variation and the essentially selective properties of reinforcement—" . . . only the *disappearance* of behaviors being attributable to the effects of reinforcement" (p. 23)—Staddon and Simmelhag's treatment comes close to the habit-family hierarchy concept which, for Hull, is made up at any given moment of learned and unlearned associations to the environment. Beyond these specifics, we are struck by the similarity of the general argument in the two cases, based as they both are on the application to the behavior of the individual organism of Darwinian evolutionary principles of adaptiveness and

46

SECTION 3. GOAL GRADIENT—HABIT HIERARCHY

survival. This similarity, as we have indicated, is in our eyes as beholders; the Staddon and Simmelhag article makes no reference to it.

A noteworthy feature of all five papers in this section is Hull's obvious desire to sow the seeds of a future quantitative learning theory. Throughout he provides hypothetical numbers designating strengths of reaction tendencies, and carries out arithmetic and algebraic manipulation as examples of the kind of science of behavior he obviously foresees. It is all highly conjectural, of course, and many of the paradoxical predictions he derives in, for example, the "field force" paper, appear to depend almost entirely on his intuitions, which are then confirmed by choosing numbers (excitatory strengths) that make it come out right arithmetically. Some ten years later, Hull was to make a more serious attempt at quantification of habit strength and excitatory potential in a series of experimental and methodological studies with Felsinger, Gladstone, and Yamaguchi (see, for example, Papers 17 and 18). We will comment at greater length on this aspect of Hull's theorizing, an aspect he came to feel was perhaps the most important, in later sections.

Now, some more specific comments to provide background for the reading of the papers:

Paper 5

In its simple versions, S-R theory seemed unable to deal with a variety of phenomena in maze-learning. For example, rats tend to choose the shorter of two paths to a goal, but this behavior cannot be derived from Thorndike's "Laws." These laws simply asserted that S-R connections are strengthened as a result of simple frequency of occurrence and by positive outcomes (Laws of Exercise and Effect, respectively), and there was no mechanism by which a short-path response could dominate if these other factors were equally strong for both responses. This state of affairs encouraged other than S-R theoretical approaches to maze learning. In particular, the cognitive-Gestalt view was often employed to account for behavior of humans and animals in problem-solving situations, in which the observed performances seemed too "rational" to be determined by mechanistic S-R processes. In Paper 5, Hull described a goal-gradient mechanism that allowed S-R theory to fare much better in the arena of maze-learning, and it provided him with theoretical leverage on a number of other problems as well. Characteristic of Hull's approach, the goal-gradient mechanism made detailed predictions about the fine grain of behavior in maze-learning situations, and exposed one of the weaknesses of the Gestalt view.

The goal-gradient hypothesis asserts that the strength of an S-R connection

47

is directly related to the closeness in time or space of the S-R event to the goal reaction. Hull attempted to specify a first approximation to the exact shape of the gradient and thereby to achieve precise deductions of specific phenomena. He rejected a number of simple possibilities because they yielded incorrect deductions, and proposed that the gradient was a positively accelerated logarithmically shaped curve that increased up to the point at which the goal object occurred. This proposal was consistent with data from an extensive experiment by one of Tolman's students (Yoshioka, 1929) on the rat's tendency to choose the shorter of two paths leading to a goal. By means of this hypothesis, Hull was able to show how it is that rats come to choose the shorter path, and to demonstrate that the elimination of entries into blind pathways in the maze and the order of the elimination of blinds were special cases of this phenomenon. Furthermore, he offered a number of new and testable predictions about maze learning. This additional predictive power gave Hull's theoretical approach an advantage over those offered by his competitors.

By the time he wrote *Principles,* Hull's thinking had evolved to considering the goal gradient "a secondary phenomenon [derived] from Perin's gradient of reinforcement acting in conjunction with the principle of secondary reinforcement" (Hull, 1943, p. 143). Indeed, Hull anticipated that this might be the case in a footnote (p. 42) of his next paper on the habit-family hierarchy (Paper 6). The gradient of reinforcement was a purely temporal gradient extending to about 30 seconds in Perin's (1943) experiment using a "Skinner box" with pellets delivered after 0, 2, 5, 10, 20, or 30 seconds following a single response. The goal gradient was more extended in time and maintained the meaning Hull had given it in his early papers. A few years later, Perkins (1947) showed that the secondary reinforcement in delayed reward learning could be proprioceptive, and Grice (1948) showed that if differential secondary reinforcement from these proprioceptive cues were eliminated, the temporal gradient of reinforcement was much steeper, and that little learning occurred with delays longer than 5 seconds. (A more complete account of the evolution of the gradient of reinforcement from the goal gradient, and the experimental shortening and steepening of the gradient of reinforcement can be found in Kimble, 1961).

Papers 6 and 7

The responses that comprise goal-directed behavior sequences are remarkably flexible. For example, rats readily select an alternative path to the goal when their preferred pathway is blocked. In this case, as in others involving flexibility in learned behavior sequences, a simple version of S-R theory encounters difficulty because it focuses primarily on factors involved in the learning of the dominant S-R associative tendency. In Papers 6 and 7, Hull attempted to improve the situation by outlining the workings of two "compound" habit mechanisms that involve multiple associative tendencies, and a hybrid mechanism comprised of these two, the "habit-family hierarchy." These mechanisms provided a significant advance for S-R theory in analyses of the more complex behavioral phenomena which, at times, had seemed to be the exclusive province of Gestalt theory.

Hull distinguished between two types of compound habit mechanisms. A *divergent* habit mechanism is characterized by a set of independent excitatory response tendencies that can be visualized as radiating out in a fan-shaped pattern from a single stimulus. These response tendencies are in competition in the sense that they cannot be executed by the organism simultaneously. They may be thought of as providing the organism with the equivalent of a set of learned "strategies" for dealing with a given stimulus situation. The divergent mechanism would be exemplified by multiple response tendencies activated by stimuli at the choice point of a maze.

The second, *convergent,* habit mechanism is the case in which several independent stimuli have the same excitatory tendency to evoke a given response. These excitatory tendencies can be visualized as a fan-shaped pattern emanating from the multiple stimulus sources and converging on a single response. Hull proposed that the functional equivalence of stimuli and the mediation of identical behaviors across very different stimulus conditions could be understood in terms of this associative mechanism. In Paper 6, for example, he showed how Shipley's (1935) experiment on finger withdrawal represents a case of mediation of behavior by a convergent habit process.

The mechanism Hull called habit-family hierarchy is an ingenious combination of the convergent and divergent mechanisms. The prototypical habit-family hierarchy originates from a single stimulus situation that is portrayed as activating a set of mutually exclusive response sequences by means of the divergent habit mechanism. These response sequences could differ from each other in their qualitative properties and/or in the time necessary for their completion. However, by means of response-produced stimuli these response sequences ultimately generate a set of different stimulus conditions all of which have the same excitatory tendency. That is, each sequence ends in the same final "goal response," thereby allowing a set of different response-produced stimuli to have excitatory tendencies to evoke a single response. In this way, the habit-family hierarchy terminates in a convergence of habit.

Hull noted that the most obvious example of a habit-family hierarchy is the set of alternative locomotor response sequences that lead to the same spatially localized goal in a maze. However, he thought that the mechanism had applications far beyond these cases, that it provided a basis for a physical theory of knowledge. In modern terms a habit-family hierarchy might be said to represent the animal's "encoded" knowledge about specific response "strategies" that will be successful in a given setting. It even seems to embody a kind of "parallel processing," which is highly regarded in the present-day design of machines in the context of work in artificial intelligence. The neocognitivists who seem most critical of "behaviorism," by which they often mean "S-R psychology" (see Amsel, 1982), even those who work in fields most removed from actual behavior, such as computer-based cognitive theory (e.g., artificial intelligence), often come dangerously close to S-R behavioristic conceptualization, at least of the early Hullian variety. In their work on production systems, Newell and Simon (1972) show that not only are productions set off by appropriate matching of condition with the data structure (like Rs set off by Ss), but that the data structure and conditions are importantly defined by the "feedback" from productions (like all the little Ss in Hull's analysis of knowledge). Further, the "principle of adaptation" reads as follows: "Other things equal the subject will adopt that production system that more closely attains his goals" (Newell, 1973). Production systems can thus be viewed not only in the spirit of an S-R theory of knowledge, but even of S-R *reinforcement* theory.[4]

Of some historical and contemporary interest is the proposal in Paper 6 (Part IV) that, when one member response in a habit hierarchy results in the attainment of a goal in an objectively novel situation, the learning that results is transferred without further practice to the other member responses in that hierarchy. The basis of this transfer is the r_G-s_G mechanism: because each response sequence in the hierarchy results in the same goal response as every other, the r_G-s_G that invades one response in the hierarchy will provide the same goal-specific stimulating conditions for all others. Thus, if r_G-s_G were conditioned to a novel exteroceptive stimulus during the execcution of one response sequence, that novel stimulus condition would, through the mediational action of r_G-s_G, also activate the other sequences in the hierarchy. In this way, Hull provided in S-R associative theory a mechanism for adaptive functioning in new situations that does not require the *de novo* learning of each and every association— a requirement, for example, that is often characterized by Chomskian psycholinguists as a fatal flaw in Skinner's analysis of language learning. (Hull later devoted an entire article, Paper 12, to this problem of "stimulus equivalence.")

---

4. We are indebted to Professor Allan R. Wagner for bringing this to our attention.

SECTION 3. GOAL GRADIENT—HABIT HIERARCHY

Much later, in the *Principles,* Hull, who was now treating simpler learning phenomena, introduced the concept of "secondary stimulus generalization" (1943, pp. 191–94) which, as a transfer mechanism, is conceptually identical to the 1934 version but without the necessary intervention of r_G-s_G. More recently, something closer to Hull's early treatment has been employed to deal with transfer of the controlling properties of anticipatory frustration (r_F-s_F) from one external stimulus context to another, and here the term "mediated generalization" is used (e.g., Amsel, 1967; Kruse & Overmier, 1982; Rashotte & Amsel, 1968; Ross, 1964). Of course, it was transfer phenomena of this sort that had, in Hull's day, appeared to fall outside the scope of S-R theory, and that cognitive theorists to this day take to be one of the major weaknesses of the "behaviorist" approach to learning (see the earlier example of Chomsky versus Skinner on language learning).

Papers 6 and 7 include derivations of other aspects of maze-learning and offer especially detailed predictions about the elimination of entries into blind alleys during the early stages of learning. To accomplish these deductions Hull provided a complex blend of the ideas outlined here and in earlier papers. The Pavlovian emphasis in Hull's theory is apparent in many of these analyses. Perhaps the most obvious is his appeal to Pavlovian inhibition and disinhibition as processes that influence maze performance when pathways are blocked by the experimenter or are not used by the animal for long periods of time.

As an historical aside, Hull's "frustration hypothesis," which is a feature of these and the following papers, is an inhibitory mechanism identified with Pavlov's internal inhibition; it bears no resemblance to the later extensions of Hullian theory to encompass the concept of frustration (Amsel, 1958; Brown & Farber, 1951). For Hull, frustration was the simple equivalent of extinction, and could be produced either by the absence or the blocking of a goal event. For Brown and Farber, frustration is a drive state produced by conflicting excitatory tendencies; it has no inhibitory (or as Hull had it, internal inhibitory) component. For Amsel (1967), primary frustration has drive and drive stimulus properties, and its conditioned or anticipatory form has, in addition to drive and drive stimulus, suppressive properties. In the latter case, the anticipatory frustration that promotes extinction is a competing excitatory tendency and bears no conceptual resemblance to Pavlovian internal inhibition.

Papers 8 and 11

These papers apply S-R analyses to several instances of complex problem-solving behavior that had appeared to be the purview of Gestalt theory. For example, Paper 8 deals with W. Kohler's observations of tool-use by chimpanzees, and with N.R.F. Maier's experiments on reasoning in rats. Paper 11 is concerned with a number of phenomena exhibited by nonverbal organisms (especially young children or retarded persons) that had already been subjected to Gestalt analysis by K. Lewin. Hull's analysis of these problems drew heavily on mechanisms outlined in earlier papers, particularly the goal-gradient hypothesis (Paper 5), the habit-family hierarchy (Papers 6 and 7), and the Pavlovian principle of stimulus patterning (Paper 1; also Paper 15). These analyses sparkle with ingenuity and, in typical Hullian fashion, provide several predictions about the fine grain of performance in experiments not yet conducted. The overall impression conveyed in these papers is that Hull's version of S-R theory had an excellent chance not only of equalling Gestalt Theory as an explanation of the more complex phenomena, but even of besting it by predicting features of performance in greater detail. Readers knowledgeable in the history of learning theory will recognize in these papers many themes which later became influential. One prominent example in Paper 11 is Hull's account of conflict behavior in terms of the interactions between goal-gradients of opposite valence. In this he was greatly influenced by Kurt Lewin's famous life-space field-force diagrams with their opposing (positive and negative) valences and tensions (see Lewin, 1931). Hull's paper and Lewin's work were the forerunners of N. E. Miller's (1944) elegant theory of conflict and of J. S. Brown's important experiments which provided the empirical support for the slopes of the approach and avoidance gradients and for the effect on them of level of motivation (e.g., Brown, 1942a,b).[5] The concepts of compatibility and incompatibility of response tendencies and of stable and unstable equilibrium in the latter case go back to a general psychology textbook by Smith and Guthrie (1923).[6]

While the Papers in the series discussed here are brilliant in many respects, for the modern reader they raise once again the nagging question of whether

5. An interesting historical sidelight is that Hull chaired a session on *Conflict and Frustration* at the 1937 meeting of the American Psychological Association in Minneapolis. Four papers from Yale on various aspects of S-R conflict theory were presented by C.I. Hovland, R.R. Sears, N.E. Miller, and O.H. Mowrer. The abstracts of these papers indicate that they addressed experimentally, with both human and animal subjects, deductions from goal-gradient and other S-R analyses of Lewinian and Freudian descriptions of consequences of conflict such as "leaving the field" and "regression." Obviously the subject of conflict was very much a feature of Hull's seminars at the time, even though, because of its complexity, it was to play no part in the *Principles* on which Hull was then beginning to work.

6. In an historical note to his chapter "Behavior in Space" in *A Behavior System*, Hull commented that his derivations of the "barrier problem" in Paper 11 were defective in that he did not include in the account the afferent-neural-interaction and the stimulus-patterning principles.

Section 3. Goal Gradient—Habit Hierarchy

an analytical S-R account of complex behaviors is viable. To explain the instances of complex behavior described in these papers, Hull invoked a large number of associative mechanisms including r_G-s_G, the goal gradient, the habit-family hierarchy, "patterning" of the elements that comprise stimulus compounds, forward and backward connections, disinhibition, summation of excitatory tendencies, and so on. The sheer number of individual associative bonds, and the problem of quantifying their individual and combined momentary status to predict behavior is mind-boggling. To paraphrase Guthrie's famous comment about Tolman's theory, Hull's analyses (e.g., p. 243, Figure 2) would seem to leave the animal buried in a morass of associative tendencies. Hull's analysis was unwieldy and subject to many uncertainties in specific application, as Hull himself noted frequently. As a case in point, the analytical diagrams Hull provided in these papers were always acknowledged to be simplified. The habit-family hierarchy, for example, suffers from the almost insurmountable complexity that the individual links in the response sequences are themselves probably comprised of habit family hierarchies (Paper 7, Section X).

There is still no agreement on the optimal level of analysis for complex behaviors. On this point, it may be worth remarking that some constructs used in other theoretical approaches bear more than a passing resemblance to the main concept in this series of Hull's papers, the habit-family hierarchy. For example, as Berlyne (1965) has pointed out, a habit-family hierarchy turned sideways closely resembles the tree-diagrams and the associative-cluster concept used in some analyses of human semantic memory; the idea of nerve-nets invoked in some neural theories of learning and performance is analogous, if not homologous, to habit hierarchies (e.g., Hebb, 1949); and, as we have already indicated, Staddon and Simmelhag's (1971) treatment of adaptive behavior contains a version of the same idea.

At bottom, then, we think the problems encountered by Hull's analysis of complex behavior are not unique to this early, and generally overlooked, portion of Hullian theory. Rather, the detail and logical rigor that characterized Hull's approach helped identify some fundamental problems inherent in the analysis of complex behavior, whoever attempts such an analysis.

The Beginning of Formalism

9. The conflicting psychologies of learning—A way out. (1935)

9a. A comment on Dr. Adams' note on method. (1937)

10. Mind, mechanism and adaptive behavior. (1937)

For Hull, Issac Newton's *Principia* provided the model of how a scientific field advances by formal and quantitative statements within a hypothetico-deductive methodology. Following this natural sciences model, the behavioral scientist elaborates a set of postulates, or first principles, and uses them as premises in deducing, by rigorous logic, inferences or theorems about behavioral phenomena. The postulates are statements derived from available empirical evidence, shrewd guesses about the processes underlying behavior.[7] They involve hypothetical entities (intervening variables) invented by the theorist to organize thinking about the relationships among experimental manipulations and measurements (independent and dependent variables) related to behavioral phenomena of interest. The theory can be evaluated by translating the deductions from the theory into experimental operations and seeing how it fares in the laboratory.

7. Bergmann and Spence (1941, p.7), referring specifically to the Hull et al. monograph, *Mathematico-Deductive Theory of Rote Learning,* point out that Hull's theorizing was not hypothetico-deductive in the sense of "a formal language system developed as a consequence of a basic set of relations (called postulates or implicit definitions) between otherwise undefined terms." This statement also foreshadowed Spence's reaction to the formality of the *Principles*. In the foreword to its seventh printing, Spence makes reference to his article with Bergmann as an analysis which shows that Hull's postulates were not of the hypothetico-deductive kind. "They did not begin with a set of purely formal (i.e., undefined) terms that have no other meaning than that provided by a set of implicit definitions (axioms). . . . Rather Hull began with operationally defined experimental variables in terms of which he introduced his theoretical constructs. Thus an examination of the postulates in the *Principles* will show that they are statements of functional relationships linking the intervening variables to the experimental variables and to each other" (pp. xv–xvi). In his teaching at Iowa, Spence often referred to the form of the theory in *Principles* as being of the logical- (or empirical-) construct variety, and to the postulates as being "guessed-at laws."

Section 3. Beginning of Formalism

Papers 9 and 10 were especially devoted to illustrating the nature of this theoretical approach in psychology (Paper 9a is a brief rejoinder to a note of D. K. Adams which was critical of all the undefined terms in Paper 9. Hull replied, essentially, that the materials in his paper were largely illustrative and that he realized that there were weaknesses in definition.) These papers extend the strategy begun in Paper 2 in which so-called "miniature theoretical systems" are developed for specific problem areas. In Paper 2, Hull had presented a rather elementary application of the deductive approach to the problem of trial-and-error learning. The present papers represent more mature applications of the approach to rote learning in humans (Paper 9) and to the problem of complex adaptive behavior (Paper 10). The former paper was the basis for the monograph, *Mathematico-Deductive Theory of Rote Learning* (Hull, Hovland, Ross, Hall, Perkins & Fitch, 1940). The latter paper is Hull's presidential address to the American Psychological Association, delivered September 4, 1936, in Hanover, New Hampshire.

These Papers clearly anticipate the formal characteristics of the *Principles*. There is little reason to summarize here the extensive favorable and unfavorable critical comment which this aspect of Hull's theorizing attracted. Instead, we will excerpt three passages from Hull's private correspondence which relate to the matter of theoretical style in psychology. These excerpts provide some historical perspective on the approach outlined in Papers 9 and 10.

The first letter was written by Hull in response to a letter from one of his former students, St. Clair A. Switzer. The letter is dated September 27, 1934, and it describes a public discussion between Tolman and Neal E. Miller at the 1934 meeting of the American Psychological Association in New York City. The substance of the interchange concerned the relative abilities of sign-Gestalt theory and conditioned reflex principles to account for an experiment on foresight in rats (Miller, 1935; Tolman, 1932). The point of interest here is not the substantive detail of that discussion (for a summary, see Rashotte, 1979a), but Hull's perception of his own theoretical style and of Tolman's. Also noteworthy is Hull's account of his agreement with Richard M. Elliott, the editor of the influential Century Psychology Series, to write a theoretical book which appeared nine years later as *Principles of Behavior*. Hull describes how this undertaking would require important changes in his research program and the rapid publication of some more *Psychological Review* papers, including those presently under discussion (Papers 9 and 10).

> The Tolman-Miller horn entangling episode which you mention in your letter came off according to schedule. Tolman was on the job and Miller made contact with

55

him almost immediately, it would appear, and had a long conversation with him before I met him. After a certain amount of preliminary conversation it was arranged to have a bull session with him and a very selected group of others to look on. I think this took place on the afternoon of the second day of the meetings. Professor [Harvey] Carr was chairman and a kind of referee for the cock fight—if you will pardon my mixing my metaphors. This was a real honest-to-goodness showdown. As we had expected, Tolman turned out to be very frank and good-natured about everything. Miller and I tried our best to be so also, though I fear we may have been somewhat more aggressive than Tolman was. The upshot of the bull session was that it became fairly obvious to everyone, I think, that the various things which we have been suspecting about Tolman's anthropomorphism and his lack of logical rigor were well substantiated. This bull session must have lasted close to three hours. The next day the papers were read, and meanwhile rumors of the probability of a lively controversy seemed to have spread around somewhat, and there was quite a crowd on hand. Tolman's paper came first, and he began by saying that he wanted to change the title of it from stating that his experiment could not be explained on conditioned reflex principles to stating that *he* (Tolman) could not explain it on conditioned reflex principles. He added that he understood that Mr. Miller would do that in the paper which was to follow his. He then presented his paper, after which Miller, with suitable introductory material connecting with Tolman's remarks, proceeded to do a very fine piece of exposition. Miller's experiment was illustrated with excellent lantern slides, and upon the whole it was an exceedingly effective presentation of a very fine experiment. Following this there was a general discussion of both papers, in which Thorndike also took part. Miller was able to hand back in a very snappy but wholly courteous manner our stock retorts to the various stock objections which came up almost immediately. After that Tolman made two fairly long speeches, and at last I myself got into the thing and spoke twice also. The upshot of the whole thing was that Tolman practically admitted that he had never seriously attempted to make logical deductions for his system, claiming for it little more than that it suggested to him a large number of interesting experiments. He seemed to be distinctly on the defensive, and said he thought he had a right to go on thinking in that way if he found it satisfying and if it suggested lots of interesting experiments to perform. I of course admitted quite freely that his experiments had been very ingenious but emphasized the distinction between the merit of fertility which might be possessed by a mere point of view and the merit of truth which must be possessed by a theory if it shall be entitled to any status in science as a theory. The whole thing went off with the utmost good nature on the part of everyone, and I believe the crowd found the discussion most stimulating and enlightening. I myself got a number of new slants on things. Partly as a result of this episode I have written a new theoretical article during the week just past, in which I attempt to explain in some formal detail the famous Tolman-Honzik "insight" maze experiment which Tolman claimed in his Ithaca [New York, at a meeting of the Gestalt psychologists at Cornell University] paper could not be explained

Section 3. Beginning of Formalism

on conditioned reflex principles. I expect to use this manuscript as the basis for my first informal seminar this year.

I should tell you that partly as a result of the Tolman affair in New York, both sessions of which were taken in by [Richard M.] Elliott of [the University of] Minnesota, I permitted myself to be persuaded to undertake the writing of a book presenting my theoretical views in psychology, for the Appleton-Century series. This means that while I shall continue with the conditioned reflex experimental work, the choice of experiments will be largely such as will be likely to throw light on the truth or falsity of my various postulates. I shall accordingly not do a great deal of work of a simple exploratory nature, as was my general intention when you left. It is going to be a terrific task, but one which is most fascinating. This means that I shall get after these numerous theoretical manuscripts which are now floating around, polish them up, and feed them in to the *Psychological Review* as rapidly as possible.

In describing his "miniature theoretical systems" in Papers 9 and 10, Hull made unflattering evaluations of less rigorous forms of psychological theory, and he did not hesitate to name names. Gestalt psychology was often singled out as an example of weakness in theoretical form. The Gestalt group argued superiority for their approach on several grounds, particularly on matters of breadth. This controversy focused on issues that were—and still are—important in arguments about theoretical style in psychology. The arguments are captured in a colorful way by Hull's description of an incident at the 1939 meeting of the Society of Experimental Psychologists at Princeton University. The description is in a letter dated April 11, 1939, which Hull wrote to his principal confidante and associate, Kenneth W. Spence. Spence, himself, had already made influential S-R analyses of discrimination learning and transposition, the latter previously very much the province of Gestalt psychology (Spence, 1936, 1937). The relevant portion of that letter is reproduced here.

Just before noon on the second day of the Princeton meeting it came Wertheimer's turn to report experimental work. It seems that that theoretical study of yours in which you derived the phenomena of discrimination learning, transposition, etc., is simply burning those Gestalt people up. You have heard, I am sure, about how much disturbed Krechevsky and Wertheimer have been about the matter. Well, Wertheimer was mumbling along under his mustache, telling about some experiments which he had performed on children some twenty-five or thirty years ago (by his own admission), and I was sitting there dozing contentedly, when it suddenly dawned on me that he was talking about you, and more or less indirectly about me. Presently he turned to me and said that the conclusion of his investigation was that your principles applied to his problem (which was not discrimination learning but discrimination of children under verbal instruction)

57

broke down. He then proceeded to lambaste the construction of miniature systems. Since these meetings are extremely informal and lots of discussion is encouraged, I naturally rose to the occasion and proceeded to look into the matter. The poor old chap was in a rather bad state because he had been claiming that he could deduce from his system the outcome of his experiments which were in agreement with fact, whereas according to your system there was a disagreement with fact. I proceeded to inquire rather meticulously as to how large a system he had. Naturally, of course, he gave nothing but evasive answers. The point of the whole thing was that he was claiming to have made deductions, yet he was unable to give either the number of postulates or the number of the theorems in his system. When I first began talking with him I understood him to be saying that he did not approve of small systems. I asked him how he could have a big system before he had a small system, inasmuch as theorems had to be derived one at a time. To make a long story short, we had very much of an argument for some minutes. The whole thing was, of course, extremely futile. I had a quiet conversation with Wertheimer afterwards, when it appeared that these Gestalt people have grossly misunderstood the meaning of my use of the expression "miniature systems." They assume (without any warrant from me, I am sure) that I mean by "miniature system" a system which is arbitrarily restricted from becoming a large system. The whole thing is utterly absurd, of course, but that's the way they interpret the expression. They try to get some color for this interpretation by stating that the type of postulates which we use are of the kind which necessarily limits the application to a very restricted field.

Of course what they say about our postulates is true in a certain sense. For example, when we take the principles of generalization and association, those principles naturally do not apply to the solar system and to astrophysics and to other cosmic processes. They believe apparently, on the other hand, that their own postulates do cover such a widespread range of phenomena. Now of course I at least would have no objections to having postulates that would apply to the solar system if at the same time they really applied to the running of rats in a maze. The trouble is that I have been unable as yet to develop anything which looks like a system which would be as comprehensive as they would like. My considered opinion is that while it is probably true that some of their concepts, such as field, etc., are of such a nature that you could subsume the solar system under them, they are so vague when formulated in that way that you could not deduce anything rigorously from them so far as behavior is concerned. This, of course, brings out the real issue—namely, that they are claiming to have a logical system when in plain fact they have no logical system; to put the thing in other words, if they would formulate their postulates in such a way that it would be possible to deduce anything rigorously regarding animal behavior, it would become evident at once that their systems are no more general than are ours.

It is, however, becoming very evident that our vigorous logical attacks on these problems is making them extremely uneasy, and they are distinctly on the defensive, saying one moment that it is too early to attempt such systematizations as we are attempting, and at the next moment that they have already developed such systems, only on a much larger and more comprehensive scale. This last is what burns me up. It seems to me that the conflict at this point is hardly any more a question of science, but becomes almost a moral matter: They are simply claiming things and pretending things which are not so.

In another letter written at that time, Hull sent essentially the same comments to Wertheimer.

The "miniature system" papers also made reference to the positivistic attitude in psychology which maintained that theory was unnecessary, even detrimental, for progress in science. Later, Skinner (1950) elaborated this position in the framework of his own experimental work in his famous paper, "Are theories of learning necessary?" In view of the importance of positivistic thinking in recent years, it is interesting to read the following extended comment by Hull on the relation between the strict positivist approach and his own hypothetico-deductive theorizing. The comment is found in a letter dated April 11, 1939, from Hull to Frank Geldard of the University of Virginia. Geldard had delivered a paper on theory and positivism to a meeting Hull attended of the Southern Society for Philosophy and Psychology at Duke University. Hull's comment on Geldard's paper provides an elegant plea for coexistence of theoretical and positivistic approaches in psychology (cf. Feyerabend, 1970). We think the points are worth repeating in the 1980s because in the contemporary climate of antibehaviorism, *even among learning theorists,* this basic distinction is often not recognized. It should be noted that subsequent correspondence between Geldard and Hull continued the discussion of Geldard's paper. Hull to Geldard:

It has always seemed to me that Karl Pearson's position on the nature of scientific theory (or explanation) was a little inconsistent and perhaps even self-contradictory, though it may be that with a certain amount of recasting this appearance would vanish. For example, as I understood your paper, you were saying substantially this:

(1) Explanation of all sorts of systematic theory (including mathematical physics, relativity, quantum theory, etc.) is nothing whatever, in so far as it agrees with the facts, except description.

(2) Description is the proper job of science and is of the greatest value.

(3) Systematic scientific theory at its best is a waste of time and at its worst is positively dangerous.

It seems to me that as indicated by the above brief summary you are putting yourself into a kind of dilemma which consists of saying in the same breath that you approve of description, disapprove of systematic theory, and yet are insisting that the two things are the same.

Perhaps you are wondering how I myself would solve this dilemma? My answer would be that in the first place I regard both purely explorational experimental work and the development of theoretical constructs as valuable. It seems to me that theoretical work is only vicious when it becomes metaphysical in the sense that the theorems implied by the postulates of a system are of such a nature that they cannot be tested experimentally. This surely is completely vicious. And surely when you are attacking systematic theory you ought not to attribute to testable systematic structures the evils characteristic of medieval theology. However, I do not recall that you did this in your paper. My recollection is that your chief objection to systematic theory was that it tended to blind people to certain possibilities which were not included in the theoretical structure. This is, of course, quite true. On the other hand, you seem to forget that a genuine theoretical structure may raise exceedingly significant questions which a person with no theoretical background would never see. The point is that theory, while possibly blinding an investigator to some things, leads him to see many other things. You might conclude from this statement that theory blinds a person to as many things as it leads him to see, and therefore that at best the theoretical structure leaves the number of novel insights about where it would be in any case, and that the labor involved in developing the system would consequently be a pure loss. This, I think, would be a serious mistake. And this, I believe, is the thing which critics of the theoretical approach most commonly make. The mistake is to judge a theoretical approach as if *all* of the scientists should confine themselves to that approach only. Actually it seems to me that an ideal combination is for a relatively small number of people with suitable training to work rather intensively on the theoretical side, for a large number of other people to have a working understanding of the theoretical structures but to let their experimental work be guided in part by purely explorational experimental investigation and in part by the theoretical constructs produced by themselves and the other theorists, and for a large number of other workers to pay little attention to theoretical matters but, on the other hand, to confine their research activities to sheer explorational work uninfluenced by theoretical considerations. This, of course, is actually what is happening. In my opinion the present arrangement is just about ideal. You see, by the present arrangement you have the advantage of *both* procedures. Accordingly it seems a little unfair to attack the theoretical approach as if the theorists were advocating that it be the only approach. I believe no theorist has ever advocated such a thing; I myself explicitly avoided such implications in my article entitled, "The Conflicting Psychologies of Learning—A Way Out."

Hull's formal theoretical approach had great appeal in the abstract; in practice the difficulties proved overwhelming. First of all, the systematic gathering of empirical evidence about learning—not to say behavioral phenomena in general—began only late in the nineteenth century, and the experimental methods in the earlier work were often crude and overcomplex. Consequently, when Hull was developing his approach about fifty years ago, the empirical base on which he started was very weak and he relied on "shrewd conjectures" in the formulation of his postulates. Second, the absence of a sound empirical data-base for the known phenomena of learning made it difficult for Hull to be as meaningfully quantitative as he would have liked. Nevertheless in the *Principles* and later (e.g., Papers 17 and 18), he went through the motions of quantifying habit strength and excitatory potential, apparently to provide some direction for later, better efforts. Finally, Hull's overall theoretical objective, to state the principles that allow deductions of "the range of ordinary mammalian behavior" was extremely ambitious for the 1940s (indeed, the objective proved unattainable in the 1970s). But Hull realized, and stated often (e.g., in Paper 2, Section V, and early in *A Behavior System,* 1952), that in so young a science as psychology the integrity of any postulate set could not survive for very long.

The rigorous deductive approach as a way of achieving scientific advances in psychology has not been influential in recent years. Instead, we seem to have endorsed the model of scientific progress described in Kuhn's (1962) *The Structure of Scientific Revolutions,* in which science is viewed as progressing through a series of "revolutionary" changes in theoretical orientation and subject matter that are brought about by the publication of anomolous findings or even simply by the proposal of a new approach to a problem.[8] Karl Popper, the philosopher of science, has argued eloquently against a Kuhnian view of scientific progress (e.g., Popper, 1959, 1962, 1970; see Lakatos & Musgrave, 1970). Popper insists in a most impressive way that scientific progress is made through the testing of rigorously derived deductions from formal theoretical statements. Hull's work represents perhaps the major example of the Popperian approach in psychology. Formulating precise postulates and arranging rigorous tests of deductions is difficult scientific work, and Kuhn is probably correct in arguing that it is rarely done. In his view, most of us are engaged in "normal science," uncritically accepting the conceptual *status quo* and going about our research by conducting experiments that are unlikely to yield results damaging to the prevailing "paradigm." The papers that we have discussed in this section indicate that Hull would have endorsed Popper's trenchant comment on Kuhn's characterization: "normal scientists" have simply been badly trained in the ways of doing science (Popper, 1970, p.52). Indeed, the last two paragraphs of Spence's foreword to the seventh printing of the *Principles* (circa 1960) encapsulate Hull's feelings about his theoretical approach:

8. It is our opinion that this Kuhnian emphasis has created a strong bias towards a kind of historical revisionism in psychology in which a prior scientific era is inaccurately portrayed and oversimplified to justify "revolution." Much of the writing on Traditional Learning Theory in recent times stands as a prime example. (See our later discussion of this issue under General Lawfulness.)

SECTION 3. COMMENTARIES ON PAPERS

In bringing these comments to a close one further and most important characteristic of Hull's theorizing should be emphasized, namely its provisional character.
Hull understood well both the tentative and incomplete nature of the empirical
foundations on which he had dared to go ahead and also the very great likelihood
that the principles he put forward would be found to be defective in one respect
or another. He was not afraid of being wrong, for he knew that science is to some
extent a trial and error process in which errors as well as successes will occur. He
deplored vagueness and attempted to make his own theory as precise and clear as
possible, partly as a means of detecting errors quickly and thus hastening a correct
formulation.

Finally, no one knew better than he the enormity of the task he was undertaking or appreciated more the limited progress that would be made in his lifetime. His hope was that the younger generation of psychologists would be stimulated by this beginning to engage in the kind of research and theory necessary
to attain the goal he sought, a behavioral science at the level of development achieved
by the physical sciences in the age of Galileo and Newton. . . .

However as one of us wrote a few years later, when invited to forecast the
future of Hullian neobehaviorism:

So far as I can see, Hullian theory is already many kinds of things, each to some
degree influenced by Hull's *Principles of Behavior* (1943) and later systematic developments (Hull, 1950, 1951); but influenced to an even greater degree by the
very important theoretical and experimental writings in the thirties and early for-
ties of Hull and people whose views were then close to his (most notably N. E.
Miller, Mowrer, and Spence, but also others such as J. S. Brown, Dollard, Hovland, and Sears, to mention a few). Hull's 1943 theory and the 1949 revision
were realtively unified treatments of simple, nonintentional learning (classical
conditioning and simple, instrumental learning) and are still among the most
completely integrated theories we have. However, even in Hull's own late work,
particularly in his book, *A Behavior System* (1952), completed just before his death,
there is an indication that he was returning to some of the interests, evident in
his earlier papers, which he had shelved temporarily to concentrate on a rigorous
analysis of classical and instrumental conditioning. As Spence (1952) has pointed
out, he regarded such an analysis of conditioning as basic to an understanding of
more complex behavior and had gone through a period of being greatly influenced
by formal considerations. In many respects, Hull's theorizing in the thirties, which
employed a conditioning-model approach to more complex instrumental behavior,
is more like Hullian theory today than in his 1943 theory (Amsel, 1965, pp.
191–92).

And later in the same paper:

It seems rather obvious that Hullian theory is less unified than it was ten years
ago, and that it was less unified then than it was in 1943. This is not surprising:
the 1943 treatment dealt, after all, mainly with classical and instrumental con-

ditioning. The current Hull-Spence approach, on the other hand, is a collection of separate but related treatments of various behavioral phenomena, having descriptive language and the more basic conceptions in common. The beginnings of this return to interests in a wider range of phenomena were already apparent in Hull's last book (1952). Here, the separate chapters, each representing a behavioral problem area, could not be derived in a strict fashion from the set of postulates at the beginning and what was said or implied in one chapter might be contradicted in another. (For example, in Chapter 5, on the antedating goal response [Hull, 1952, p.128] there is, in the treatment of delay of reinforcement, an apparent return to $H = f(w)$, which had been abandoned earlier.)

As the Hullian type of approach is applied to an ever wider range of phenomena the theoretical forays will be more restricted than Hull's, but based on more specific evidence. The relatively broad coverage of behavior envisioned by Hull in the last chapter of *Behavior System* is likely to be reduced to experimental operations in small pieces; and tighter, more data-bound generalizations will emerge, on the order of Spence's recent theorizing. When this kind of theoretical activity has organized separate problem areas and has gained reasonable predictive control over them, there will be a movement toward integration and greater theoretical unity. This, at least, is the present writer's guess (Amsel, 1965, pp. 193–94).

As any knowledgeable reader of this volume will know, this forecast of Amsel's—like most forecasts—would not appear to represent what is going on in learning theory almost two decades later. There are still pockets of theorizing in the formal Hullian style, perhaps the best example being Logan's recent Hybrid Theory of Conditioning (Logan, 1977, 1979), but the "movement toward integration and greater theoretical unity" has certainly not occurred, either for a Hull-style theory or any other. While cognitive theory has returned as a force in animal learning, it is not yet an integrated or cohesive movement except as its adherents close ranks against Traditional Learning Theorists, whose members appear to include not only (but certainly) Hull, but *all* learning theorists (including Tolman) whose work antedates 1970. Were Hull alive today he might find it necessary to revive his crusade against the imprecision of a cognitive approach. On the other hand, he might think the battle irretrievably lost.

Properties of the Stimulus

12. The problem of stimulus equivalence in behavior theory. (1939)

15. The discrimination of stimulus configurations and the hypothesis of afferent neural interaction. (1945)

16. The problem of primary stimulus generalization. (1947)

19. Stimulus intensity dynamism (V) and stimulus generalization. (1949)

21. Simple qualitative discrimination learning. (1950)

These five papers can be said to define the concept of "stimulus" in Hull's S-R psychology. The initial paper in the group (Paper 12) is clearly one of those that Hull published in the *Review* with the intention of drawing critical comment before including its ideas in the *Principles*. It addresses the definition of "stimulus" and the conceptualization of stimulus equivalence in terms of S-R theory. The remaining papers are of post-*Principles* vintage and they have a different character. Five other post-*Principles* papers, discussed in the next four commentaries, deal mainly with formal and methodological considerations.

Paper 15, on the discrimination of stimulus configurations, is an attempt to defend and expand upon important parts of the *Principles*.

Paper 16 is a response to Lashley and Wade's (1946) attack on the idea Hull had endorsed that stimulus generalization is independent of experience and, therefore, can be considered as a fundamental process in a theoretical account of learning, a process he characterized as "A primary social science law" in a later, more popular treatment of the subject (Hull, 1950).

Paper 19 is a conceptualization of stimulus intensity effects within the context

64

of Hull's theory, with particular emphasis on the way this variable influences stimulus generalization.

Finally, Paper 21, the last one Hull published in the *Review*, is a theoretical account of discrimination learning. It is largely Hull's elaboration of Spence's theory of discrimination learning (Spence, 1936, 1937). In some ways, this last paper characterizes Hull-Spence theory well because it blends Spence's theoretical analysis with Hull's more mature behavior theory. Paper 21 appeared, substantially unchanged, as a chapter in Hull's final book, *A Behavior System*.

Many of the issues addressed in these papers are of interest in contemporary theory and research. Our commentary addresses five main themes in this group of papers.

Definition of the Stimulus

In earlier papers, particularly Papers 9 and 10 in which the formal postulate format was used, Hull had made the distinction between a source of stimulus energies that impinge upon the organism (the stimulus object) and the functional stimulus, which is the process initiated in the nervous system by stimulus energies (the stimulus trace). Paper 12 contains a more extended analysis of the stimulus. Here, Hull distinguished among "stimulus objects" (things capable of giving off energy that can stimulate a sense organ), "potential stimuli" (the entire range of energies that can be given off by a stimulus object), the "stimulus" (one of the potential stimuli which actually makes contact with an organism's sensory apparatus) and, finally, the "stimulus trace" (a physiological reaction initiated in the organism by the stimulus and persisting, in a decaying fashion, for some time after the stimulus is removed). It is the stimulus trace which enters into association with reactions.

The all-important functional role assigned to the stimulus trace in this analysis would seem to be one reason for Hull's heavy emphasis on the physiology of sensory systems in his subsequent treatment of "stimulus" in chapter 3 of *Principles*. In that treatment, Hull also included and extended the Pavlovian idea that the properties of a given stimulus trace are themselves modified by the presence of other stimulus traces concurrently present in the nervous system. This latter idea was called the hypothesis of afferent neural interaction. It figured prominently in the *Principles* and is the subject of Paper 15, which will be discussed later in this commentary. Together, the two principles of "stimulus trace" and "afferent neural interaction" comprised the first two postulates in Hull's formal theoretical system.

Section 3. Commentaries on Papers

Hull's physiological analysis of the stimulus (and of other constructs in his theory, such as "drive") was, as we indicate in our commentary on Paper 13, the subject of perhaps the sharpest disagreement on matters of theoretical strategy between him and Spence. Their correspondence (see next commentary, *Scientific Method, 1941*) on the occasion of the publication of the *Principles* illustrates this difference of opinion.

In the late 1950s, Sigmund Koch commented on trends over several decades in the science of psychology as he abstracted them from chapters in his edited volumes titled *Psychology: A Study of a Science* (Koch, 1959). Koch detected a major shift away from a prevailing practice among behaviorists of conceptualizing the stimulus in terms of physical energies measured by pointer readings. Instead, he foresaw that the organism's perceptual-psychological interpretations of physical energies would have to be included in a successful treatment of stimulus in behavior theory. In one sense, Koch's expectation was realized in later conditioning theories that emphasized attentional processes (e.g., Lovejoy, 1968; Sutherland & Mackintosh, 1971). However, attention theories have not proved durable and there is far from a consensus about the definition of stimulus in current associative theories. For example, in the Rescorla-Wagner model of associative learning, the functional stimulus is seen as isomorphic with the experimental manipulations that define it. Gormezano's (e.g., 1972) analysis of conditioning assigns a major role to physiological, Hull-like stimulus traces. Wagner (1981), in his recent S.O.P. theory, portrays the stimulus in a trace-decay mode and formulates precise rules that govern temporal changes in the state of elements in a "node," an intervening variable which is responsive to experimentally defined stimulus events. The point is that many or most features of the stimulus trace, the functional stimulus for Pavlov and Hull, can be found in recent theories of associative learning. It would not be surprising if the stimulus-trace concept proves to be durable, especially as we become more and more informed by studies of the neural and molecular basis of habituation and conditioning (see Kandel & Schwartz, 1982, for a recent review).

In view of these recent developments, it is interesting to look back to a statement about "attention" made by Hull in a letter to Spence. The letter comments on Lashley's (1942) attack on the "continuity" interpretation of discrimination learning for which Spence was primarily responsible. Hull to Spence, July 2, 1942:

> I expect with some confidence that sooner or later we must really do something much beyond what we have yet done, in order to meet [Lashley's] objection based on the subjective phenomenon of attention. I myself have no doubt whatever that

this is a genuine phenomenon in human adaptive behavior, and is not an illusion. I have some tentative ideas as to the S-R mechanism which may mediate this— probably some kind of perseverational or trace effect in combination with anticipatory goal reactions and their perseveration. However, this will need to be made explicit, and it might very well come out in the controversy which seems to impend. I doubt some whether this mechanism is a very potent one, and that it plays a very great role in ordinary animal learning. Nevertheless, it probably does play some role, and as such it is up to us to elaborate it if we can. The reason I think it does not play a very great role is that we have been able to get along for a long time without paying any attention to it at all.

Three Basic Principles of Stimulus Function

1. *Stimulus generalization.* Like Pavlov, Hull viewed stimulus generalization as a basic property of the mammalian nervous system and identified it as a "primitive assumption" or postulate in his theory. For example, in the papers we are considering, detailed assumptions about the generalization process were the basis for Hull's treatment of stimulus equivalence (Paper 12) and discrimination learning (Paper 21). It is understandable, then, that Lashley and Wade's (1946) attack on stimulus generalization as a primary process should provoke a vigorous rejoinder from Hull (Paper 16).

Lashley and Wade asserted that generalization gradients could be obtained only from organisms that had a history of differential experience with stimuli on the stimulus dimension tested. In Paper 16, Hull reviewed the known facts about generalization gradients obtained after training with a single stimulus value, progressed to an itemized listing of Lashley and Wade's objections to the traditional interpretation of these facts (including substantive quotes from correspondence with Lashley about the issues), and concluded with a detailed examination of the merits of the Lashley-Wade case, which he found insubstantial.

Of course, both Hull and Lashley were constrained in their arguments by the limited nature of the data available to them. The 1950s and 1960s saw an explosion of research on stimulus generalization which can be thought to have begun with Guttman & Kalish's (1956) highly successful use of operant procedures to obtain gradients of generalization from individual animals. As it turned out, these more adequate data supported Hull's rejection of the Lashley and Wade position (see Honig & Urcioli, 1981, for a review). In any event, at the time he wrote Paper 16 Hull was convinced that he was on the right track and he continued to treat generalization as a fundamental mechanism in his behavior theory.

SECTION 3. COMMENTARIES ON PAPERS

2. *Stimulus intensity dynamism.* The principle of stimulus intensity dynamism acknowledges the outcome of several investigations which indicated that the strength of a reaction is positively related to the intensity of the stimulus which evokes it. Paper 19 announced that this principle would be a basic element in Hull's formal theory and, indeed, the principle appeared as a postulate in subsequent statements of the system (Hull, 1951, 1952a).

Earlier, in our biographical comments, we noted that Paper 19 was cited more frequently during the 1970s than any of the other papers. These citations largely reflect the empirical content of the stimulus intensity dynamism principle, not its systematic status. What makes the paper particularly visible for today's audience is that it was the first to state the principle clearly, and to show how it could influence the generalization gradients of stimuli on a dimension of intensity: when conditioning is accomplished with a weak stimulus, generalization testing with more intense stimuli on the same stimulus dimension can be expected to yield a relatively flat gradient; when conditioning is to a stimulus of high intensity and testing is with less intense stimuli, the gradient should show a steeper decline. Thus gradients of stimulus *intensity* generalization should not be symmetrical about a midpoint of stimulus intensity. Hull saw this influence of stimulus intensity as being particularly important for that part of his theoretical program which was concerned with identifying the quantitative details of generalization gradients under a variety of circumstances.

A number of investigators who could at the time have been classed as Hullians (Logan, 1954; Mowrer & Lamoreaux, 1951; Perkins, 1953) quickly concluded that stimulus intensity dynamism (V) was not a primary principle but could be deduced from a principle of generalization of inhibition from background stimuli during intertrial intervals. Given that the background intensity is weak (often zero), and that these stimuli are not reinforced, they generate inhibition which generalizes to the active, reinforced stimulus. The more intense the active stimulus, the weaker the generalization of inhibition to it; hence the dynamism effect. This position on V was disconfirmed by an experiment (Grice, Masters, & Kohfeld, 1966) in which the CS in eyeblink conditioning was a shift from one stimulus intensity to another in a within-subjects design. All intensities served as background and as active stimuli. Significant stimulus intensity effects were obtained which were *independent of the absolute intensity* but depended upon the amount of stimulus change. This result amounted to a new interpretation of the effect of V, and it corroborated an earlier study (Grice & Hunter, 1964) which showed that the intensity effect was greatly increased if the subject was exposed in the experiment to more than one stimulus intensity.

68

Section 3. Stimulus Properties

3. *Afferent neural interaction.* In his treatment of the stimulus in *Principles,* Hull included and extended the Pavlovian idea that the properties of a given stimulus trace are themselves modified by the presence of other stimulus traces currently present in the nervous system. This idea, known as the hypothesis of afferent neural interaction, served as a postulate in all versions of Hull's formal system. It is addressed again in Paper 15 on the discrimination of stimulus configurations, published two years after *Principles,* and figured prominently in Hull's analysis of discrimination learning (Paper 21), both of which papers we will discuss later. (An interesting historical sidelight is that in and after the revised 1949 postulates [Paper 20] it was referred to as "Afferent *Stimulus* Interactions," undoubtedly as a defensive reaction to criticisms by Spence and others of the neurologizing in the *Principles.*)

It was a departure for Hull to devote a *Review* article to a topic he had already considered in depth, and the circumstances leading to the publication of this fifteenth paper are, therefore, interesting. In correspondence during 1941 while *Principles* was being written, Hull and Spence discussed afferent neural interaction in relation to Gestalt ideas about interactions among brain fields activated by sensory events. An excerpt from a letter to Spence from Hull dated May 20, 1941, is particularly informative here:

> I have been under the rather strong impression that my afferent-interaction hypothesis is actually a very close parallel to a view held by Kohler. When I talked to him in Philadelphia I asked him specifically about the matter. After talking it over he agreed that it was rather close, though when I pointed out how the hypothesis would explain such a matter as external inhibition he shook his head and said he had never made that application of it, though he seemed to be inclined to agree that the theorem followed all right from the hypothesis. When I asked him specifically what he had been in the habit of calling the equivalent of this hypothesis, he said he called it "dependent part qualities." This expression, I take it, is probably a literal translation of some German expression, since it doesn't seem to make much sense in English. Perhaps one might interpret this as meaning that in terms of his theory of parallels between receptor discharges and conscious qualities the conscious qualities resulting from the stimulation of a part of a stimulus compound are dependent on the other stimuli which are entering the nervous system at the same time. This, of course, would be practically identical with what I mean by afferent interaction. When I asked him to give me a reference in which he had elaborated his views on this matter he told me to read his last published work on *Dynamics in Psychology.* As soon as I returned from Philadelphia I ordered the book, and have since read it over rather hastily. I agree with you that there is very little in this book that I would take exception to, except his implicit assumption that consciousness is a completely reliable indicator of what is going on in the nervous system.

SECTION 3. COMMENTARIES ON PAPERS

Spence urged Hull to write a *Psychological Review* paper on these ideas before the book was published, but Hull declined because time was needed to finish the book. As it turned out, however, the section of *Principles* concerned with afferent neural interaction, particularly as it applied to the learning of Gestalt-like discriminations between different patterns of stimuli, was not as successful as Hull had hoped. Therefore, as a sort of postscript to the *Principles*, Hull prepared the article on afferent neural interaction (Paper 15), which, according to a letter to Spence dated July 20, 1944, was intended as "a somewhat simplified account of my theory of patterning, exploiting the hypothesis of afferent neural interaction. This article is being written mainly because I have found by trial that most people are quite unable to understand what I have tried to say in my chapter on the subject in *Principles of Behavior.*" In fact, Paper 15 was assembled from several *Psychological Memoranda* Hull had prepared between 1941 and 1943, as he acknowledged in a footnote to the paper.

Despite its derivative background, Paper 15 contained a proposal for a new experimental methodology that would measure the amount of afferent interaction. The procedure was based on Pavlov's concept of external inhibition and involved measuring the degree of response decrement that followed presentation of novel stimuli of known physical intensity in a standard training situation. Hull hoped that this procedure would reveal general quantitative features of afferent neural interaction. To our knowledge the procedure was never applied in the way Hull recommended. It may, however, still be a useful means of obtaining information about sensory interactions in some well-defined experimental situations.

Our remaining discussion of Hull's treatment of the stimulus will deal rather specifically with the historical background for and the contemporary relevance of Papers 12, 15, and 21. (For Papers 16 and 19 we have already provided such material in some detail.)

Stimulus Equivalence

Paper 12 on stimulus equivalence asks, from the S-R perspective, how it can come about that responses, on occasion, can be evoked by stimuli to which they have never been directly conditioned. The paper begins with a brief review of empirical data on primary stimulus generalization and offers some theoretical speculation about the ways generalization gradients interact. With these ideas as the foundation, and with his formal logical method as the guide, several detailed predictions are deduced about the conditions under which stimulus

70

equivalence should occur when it is mediated by primary stimulus generalization. For example, a response should be evoked by a stimulus to which it has never been conditioned when it is the recipient of subthreshold associative strengths generalized from two conditioned stimuli at opposite ends of a stimulus continuum. This prediction requires the twin assumptions that associative tendencies must exceed some threshold value in order to affect behavior, and that generalized associative tendencies summate. Both assumptions provided S-R theory with considerable leverage in conceptualizing stimulus function.

Paper 12 also described how stimulus equivalence could be mediated across stimuli whose features are so different as to preclude simple stimulus generalization. Here, Hull employed another important S-R principle, secondary generalization, which can occur when a set of stimuli all have associative connections with a common response. Given this state of affairs, the effect of conditioning of a new response to one of these stimuli is to make the other stimuli in the set functionally equivalent to the first because the common response to which all stimuli are conditioned serves a mediating role. This idea was   and is—a powerful basis for flexible and adaptive stimulus function within the mechanistic logic of S-R theory.

The stimulus equivalence paper provided another point of contact between the Gestalt and S-R approaches. Hull's comments in this paper on Gestalt theory were mild in comparison to some in earlier papers, yet the Hull-Spence correspondence indicates they evoked a reaction from Kohler. Hull to Spence, April 11, 1939:

> [Kohler] criticised me for implying in the last paragraph of my last study, on stimulus equivalence, that the Gestalters would insist on introducing a perceptual or conscious element between the stimulus and ordinary adaptive reactions. He finally admitted, however, that Lewin did insist on such an introduction. For his part he claims that he uses consciousness merely as an indirect guide to the structure of the nervous system, and if he succeeds in developing a complete physiology of the nervous system he would expect to derive behavior from the original stimuli as a purely physical process, and would make no reference whatever to consciousness or experience. I wish to heaven some of these people would make a few such simple statements as that in print. It would certainly clear the air a good deal.

Discrimination Learning with Stimulus Configurations

In many of Hull's earlier papers, and in Spence's influential papers on discrimination learning and transposition, it seemed possible to analyze the prob-

71

lems under discussion without considering the difficult problem of "patterning" of stimuli. Whenever multiple stimulus sources were thought to influence behavior, the assumption was made that the associative response strengths to the individual stimuli combined in an algebraic fashion to yield a net behavior tendency. Papers 3 and 4, which identified multiple internal and external stimulus sources acting jointly to determine purposive behavior are cases in point. However, even in the first of the Papers, Hull had noted that this assumption alone would not account adequately for much adaptive behavior which seemed to be controlled by prevailing patterns of stimulation. Accordingly, his analysis of patterning in the *Principles,* and again in Paper 15, is an important part of his mechanistic approach to adaptive behavior.

The problem of patterning is well illustrated in a discrimination where two stimuli, A and B, are always followed by food when presented individually, but never when presented simultaneously. The fact that animals learn to respond to A and B separately, but withhold the response to the AB compound, was known from Pavlov's work. It raises an apparently insurmountable problem for theories which assume that individual stimuli acquire associative linkages, and that the net associative value of a compound is the sum of the individual associations.

Hull's solution involved the application of the principle of afferent neural interaction. If, as this principle asserted, the neural stimulus trace activated by a given source of physical energy is modified by the presence of other stimulus traces simultaneously present in the nervous system, then the AB compound cannot be considered the simple sum of A and B. Instead, AB should be comprised of modified versions of A and B whose resemblance to the individually presented stimuli can, in principle, be understood in terms of stimulus generalization. Since the modified A and B stimuli are nonreinforced on AB− trials, and the original A or B stimuli are reinforced, the animal can learn the discrimination on the basis of ordinary associative mechanisms. This discrimination should be a relatively difficult one, however, as it involves differential conditioning to very similar stimuli. A study of patterning in dogs, carried out under Hull's direction by Woodbury (1943), produced excellent quantitative data which confirmed Hull's analysis.

The problem of patterning is by no means of historical interest only. For example, a recent popular model of associative learning (Rescorla & Wagner, 1972) assumes that the associative value of a compound stimulus, such as AB in the example given above, will be the sum of the associative strengths of the individual stimulus elements that comprise the compound. Of course, it is just

Section 3. Stimulus Properties

this assumption that is inadequate to account for learning of the A+, B+, AB− discrimination we have outlined. Attempts to deal with cases like this in the context of the Rescorla-Wagner model have assumed that A and B, when together, form a "unique stimulus" which can enter into the association (e.g., Rescorla, 1973). Of course, Hull's solution was logically different because it asserted that the two stimuli remained as separable entities in the compound but that the properties of each were modified by the presence of the other. At the present time, the theoretical and experimental analysis of stimulus patterning remains inconclusive.

Hull's analysis of stimulus configurations provides yet another instance in which his creative assumptions made it possible for S-R psychology to account for a phenomenon that seemed to involve Gestalt-like perceptual processes. Paper 15 speaks to some of the reactions Hull's analysis drew, but even within Hullian circles the analysis was controversial. Hull had refined his analysis in a series of presentations to his associates at the Institute for Human Relations before *Principles* was published. A controversy following one of these presentations is described in the extended passages we now quote from letters in the Hull-Spence correspondence. The letters are concerned with the reactions of one of Hull's associates, O. H. Mowrer, to the analysis of patterning. These passages make a particularly good illustration of the importance Hull attached to patterning in a theory of adaptive behavior, and they show the value he placed on analyzing complex phenomena into their component parts. The circumstances leading to Hull's letter to Mowrer are given in this excerpt of a letter from Hull to Spence, February 3, 1943:

> Some days ago I gave a talk before the Monday night group here at the Institute, in which I attempted to make a quasi-popular presentation of my theory of stimulus patterning. Mowrer came down from Cambridge to attend the session, and afterwards he told me that he was terribly disappointed, and felt that I had fallen from grace; that I had given up the behavioristic position and that he regarded himself as the only remaining orthodox member of the Institute group. Since his train did not return to Cambridge until three in the morning, he was forced to stay around here until then. Apparently he spent part of the time drinking beer with Whiting and Dollard, and arguing about this business of patterning. Along about one o'clock that morning he sat down and wrote me a long letter, in which he expressed, among other things, what I have indicated above. A few days later I replied to his letter and sent him a somewhat revised version of a portion of my talk. I enclose herewith a carbon copy of my letter to him, which I thought you might find of interest.

73

SECTION 3. COMMENTARIES ON PAPERS

Hull's reply to Mowrer, dated January 26, 1943:

Thanks very much for your letter of one o'clock last Tuesday morning. I have read it with both interest and profit, I am sure. There are one or two things, however, which I venture to call to your attention.

In an early paragraph you remark: ". . . I happen still not to believe that you have been essentially wrong in the past, and I therefore can't believe you are essentially right in the present." I assume that you imply by this that in the past I have been opposed to the idea of patterning. If that is your meaning it is a very serious error. It happens that I am not talking about a subjective state or attitude on my part. Nearly fourteen years ago, to be specific, on about the 15th of April, 1929, I wrote an article for the *Psychological Review* in which is contained the following paragraph:

Even so, innumerable life situations arise where the simple addition or subtraction of the potencies of the several components of a stimulus complex is not adequate. In many situations a particular combination or pattern of stimulus components (either simultaneous or temporally extended) is the very essence of the stimulus. To change a single minute component of certain stimuli will completely change the nature of the appropriate response. A telegram is an example of such a patterned stimulus complex. If a single letter in it be changed, the reaction of the receiver may be made either one of joy or of despair. [A functional interpretation of the conditioned reflex, *Psychological Review* (1929), 36:503.]

So you see that the general belief in the genuineness of stimulus compounds as distinguished from the components is not at all new.

Secondly, I would point out to you that the postulates from which you derive the business of patterning are also not new; on the contrary, every single one of them comes from Pavlov. Moreover, in my opinion the Gestalt people, unless they use substantially the same postulates, will find it quite impossible to derive in any detail the behavior of Woodbury's dogs [see our previous reference].

In this connection I am taking the liberty of enclosing a somewhat revised version of the memorandum I distributed at the meeting which you attended. In this memorandum I venture to call your attention to the footnote on page 4, which gives a direct quotation from Pavlov. There are three or four other passages in Pavlov which are about equally explicit in regard to this matter.

In view of the above considerations, I don't quite see why you should take the view that I am inconsistent with my former beliefs. I have always had a strong belief in the Pavlovian empirical findings, and for many years at least I have had a deep-seated conviction of the genuineness of the patterning phenomena as such. It is only recently, however, that I have been able to *derive* the patterning phenomena from other Pavlovian principles. This, it seems to me, is a distinct advantage, because otherwise the principle of patterning appears superficially to be a kind of contradiction, or to stand in opposition to the ordinary conditioning principles as viewed by a person who has a rather inadequate and naive attitude toward those conditioning principles. Specifically, I am of the opinion that the so-called false analysis which I give on page 3 is almost exactly the kind of analy-

74

sis which a hostile Gestalt attempt to reduce the behavioristic principles to an absurdity would take. Moreover, I am afraid that if you yourself, when in the mood in which you wrote your letter to me, should attempt to derive the Woodbury phenomena (and patterning phenomena in general) you would wind up with substantially the same logical sequence as is contained in the "False Analysis." I do not think that you can really laugh this off, as you seem to have done in your conversation with Whiting, as reported in your letter.

. . . I should tell you that in some of the specific drive situations I am convinced that one absolutely needs the interaction hypothesis and the patterning phenomena which it ultimately generates with learning, in order to explain them. A case in point is that study on motivation which I published some years ago and which Dr. Leeper repeated shortly after with essentially concordant results. This experiment involved the necessity of the animal learning to turn to the right around a rectangle for food in case he was hungry, and turning to the left around the other side of the same rectangle for water, in case he was thirsty. Now according to my analysis, the only thing which enables the organism to distinguish which way he should turn is the presence of a drive stimulus. For a long time Spence held the view that the drive stimulus alone was a sufficient cue to make the animal turn to the right on hunger days, and to the left on thirst days; that also was my own view when I wrote the article, I regret to say. However, consider this: if the animal has a right-turning habit conditioned to the thirst state or the thirst stimulus, irrespective of the other stimuli operating at the same time, then it would follow that when the animal found himself in a state of hunger, in his cage on a later occasion, he would immediately begin turning around to the right indefinitely, and when thirsty but not hungry, he would begin turning around to the left continuously, no matter where he happened to be. I think these considerations will show you that the organism simply must be conditioned to the various stimuli in combination. Fortunately it is not necessary to scrap any of the legitimate conditioned reflex principles in order to handle this thing, as I think I have shown in the memorandum which I enclose.

Simple Discrimination Learning

Paper 21, the last one Hull published in the *Review*, addresses the problem of simple discrimination learning. Hull, in a footnote to the paper, characterized it as largely an elaboration of Spence's famous theory of discrimination learning (Spence, 1936, 1937); however, the paper turns out to have some novel and important theoretical features. We comment on three aspects of Hull's analysis.

1. *The role of background stimuli.* Hull devoted a sizable part of this paper to consideration of the role played by "incidental" or "static" stimuli in simple cases of what he called qualitative discrimination learning. The specific data he

analyzed were collected in his laboratory with a discrete-trials procedure. Initially, rats learned to push open a door containing a white card (S1) in order to obtain food reward. Then, in discrimination training, rewarded trials (S1+) were intermixed irregularly among trials on which a black card (S2−) was present and the animal was not rewarded. At the beginning of discrimination training the rat responded more or less equivalently to the white and black cards, but eventually the animals learned to respond strongly to white and very weakly to black. In modern jargon, this kind of training is often called a "go–no go" discrimination.

Hull pointed out that the two discriminative stimuli used in this kind of experiment should be thought of as occurring against a background of "incidental" or "static" stimuli (now often called "contextual" stimuli) such as general cues from the apparatus and stimulation arising from the animal's own body (e.g., from its movements, deprivation state, etc.). Hull designated these background stimuli as S3. The important role assigned to these background stimuli in Hull's analysis is based on two assumptions. First, S3 is assumed to be functionally equivalent to S1 and S2, and is therefore capable of acquiring excitatory or inhibitory associative connections on the basis of reinforcements or nonreinforcements, respectively. Second, on S1 and S2 trials, S3 acts jointly with the discriminative stimuli to determine response strength. That is, discrimination trials involve two compound stimuli, S1+S3 (reinforced) versus S2+S3 (nonreinforced). The role played by afferent neural interaction in these compounds was not included in this paper, possibly as a means of keeping the analysis simple; but a more complete treatment of discrimination learning in *A Behavior System* includes some discussion of afferent neural interaction and of stimulus intensity dynamism in simple discriminations. In any event, Hull made the point that the role of background stimuli in combination with the discriminative stimuli must be considered in a theoretical treatment of discrimination learning.

Drawing on these two assumptions, and on the usual assumption that a reinforced trial yields an increment in the strength of an excitatory tendency while a nonreinforced trial yields an increment in the strength of an inhibitory tendency, Hull was able to account for two features of the data in his illustrative experiment. First, he noted that when the black card (S2) was initially introduced in discrimination training the animals responded to it very strongly, apparently showing virtually complete generalization from the white card (S1) to S2. Hull proposed that this apparently exceptional amount of generalization could be understood as the influence of a strongly excitatory S3 combining with the relatively weak excitatory strength which the negative S2 would have as a

SECTION 3. STIMULUS PROPERTIES

result of generalization from the previously reinforced S1. Of course, the reason the background-stimulus (S3) would be excitatory at the beginning of discrimination training is that it had participated as a stimulus element in the S1 + S3 stimulus compound present on reward trials given prior to discrimination training. Hull also noted that this same line of reasoning would account for the fact that a variety of experiments (summarized in Paper 12) had shown relatively strong responding to all stimuli along the generalization continuum on the first test trial, but that subsequent trials yielded more steeply sloping gradients.

The second aspect of the discrimination data to which S3 pertains is that the strength of responding to S1 on reinforced trials declined somewhat when the discrimination was formed. Hull envisioned this result as being primarily a consequence of the original excitatory tendency of S3 being offset by the growth in an inhibitory process to S3 as a result of the nonreinforced S2 + S3 trials (in this experiment the ratio of nonreinforced to reinforced trials was high; see Hull, 1952a, footnote on p.67): responding to S1 would be expected to decline somewhat as the net associative value of the co-occurring S3 is neutralized.

Hull's treatment of background stimuli in discrimination learning and, by clear implication, in all conditioning procedures includes many general emphases found in today's learning theories. Increasingly, in the past decade or so, theoretical analyses of conditioning assign an important role to background stimuli. The impetus for this recent emphasis was a series of findings in experiments on Pavlovian conditioning reported in the late 1960s which showed, for example, that the acquisition of associative strength to a stimulus will be affected by the prevailing associative status of other stimuli with which it is presented in a compound on conditioning trials (e.g., Kamin, 1968, 1969; see LoLordo, 1979, for a review). Findings such as these have unleashed a spate of theories designed to deal with stimulus compounding and the role of background stimuli in associative learning (e.g., Gibbon & Balsam, 1981; Jenkins, Barnes & Barrera, 1981; Mackintosh, 1975; Rescorla & Wagner, 1972; Wagner, 1976, 1978, 1981). These recent theories incorporate the many changes in thinking about the conditions of associative learning and stimulus processing that have occurred since Hull's time. Some comparisons between the most influential of these, the Rescorla-Wagner theory, and Hull's treatments of background stimuli will provide some basis for estimating how much change has occurred.

(1) While both Hull and Rescorla and Wagner agree that the stimuli function as separable entities in a stimulus compound (allowing for afferent neural interaction in Hull's case), Rescorla and Wagner assume that the stimuli in a compound compete for a fixed amount of associative strength; Hull assumed

77

that the stimulus elements acquire associative strength independently. It would seem from today's perspective that Hull's assumption was wrong.

(2) Rescorla and Wagner assume that a stimulus can have only one associative tendency which can assume positive (excitatory) or negative (inhibitory) values; Hull and most other theorists assume that multiple associative tendencies can be acquired by individual stimuli, including simultaneous excitatory and inhibitory tendencies which summate algebraically to yield a net associative strength. The prominence of this multiple-tendency assumption in some recent associative theories (Pearce & Hall, 1980; Wagner, 1981) can be regarded as a return to Hull's view.

(3) The Rescorla-Wagner analysis of simple discrimination learning indicates that the background stimuli will remain excitatory after extended discrimination training (Rescorla & Wagner, 1972); Hull asserts that the background cues will be neutralized (i.e., will have a net associative value of zero). A kind of intermediate view, favored by attention theorists such as Sutherland and Mackintosh (1971), is that irrelevant background cues lose control because they are not attended to, even though they may continue to have substantial associative strength.

2. *Inhibition.* There is a fiction created by modern Pavlovian—one might better say Konorskian (1967)—theorists, and nurtured by neocognitive theorists of conditioning that American learning theory has neglected the concept of inhibition. Halliday (1979, p.6) writes:

> The feature of Konorski's work, which probably contributed to its unpopularity in America, was its concern with processes of inhibition. . . . [There was a] general distaste for the concept of inhibition [that] needs no further documentation. . . . Of course, reactive and conditioned inhibition were familiar terms in the context of Hullian theory, but they had always aroused disquiet and were tolerated largely because of Hull's immense prestige; by the early 1950s these concepts were under heavy attack as the weakest part of the Hullian edifice.

Halliday's statement makes reference to Skinner's (1938) view that the inhibition concept is unnecessary; but Skinner is perhaps the only major learning theorist in America who took such a stance. Indeed prominent Skinnerians (Guttman, 1959; Hanson, 1959; Hearst, 1968; Terrace, 1972) do not follow Skinner in this regard and employ an inhibition concept very close to Spence's in their account of such phenomena as stimulus control and peak shift in discrimination learning.

Another learning theorist who much later spoke out against the necessity for an inhibition concept in accounts of extinction, discrimination learning, and response suppression is Amsel (1962, 1972). His treatment of prediscrimination influences on discrimination learning is in terms of anticipatory reward and frustration and the related approach and avoidance tendencies, both excitatory. This account is closer to Miller's (1944) than to Spence's or Hull's, although Spence did refer interchangeably to reinforcement versus frustration and excitation versus inhibition; and his statements were often about competing excitatory tendencies and could readily have been cast in terms of approach and avoidance. Inhibition was, nevertheless, an indispensable part of Hull-Spence theory. In any case, if one states that the Hull-Spence inhibition theory was "under heavy attack," one cannot also maintain that the Hullians showed a "general distaste for the concept of inhibition."

Spence's famous discrimination learning papers (1936, 1937, 1942) were argued *entirely* on the basis of gradients of excitation and inhibition. His elegant theory of transposition could not have been developed without reference to a negative (inhibitory) generalization gradient. There is in Spence's treatment a clear distinction between a principle of excitation or reinforcement and one of inhibition or frustration. Indeed, it would have been perverse of theorists who worked in the wake of Sherrington and Pavlov to favor excitatory to the exclusion of inhibitory mechanisms. Hull's treatment of discrimination learning in 1950 was characterized by him in a footnote as "essentially an elaboration of the writer's interpretation of Spence's extension and formalization . . . of Pavlov's analysis . . . of discrimination learning."

3. *Relation to Spence's Theory.* There are these differences between Hull's and Spence's treatments of discrimination learning:

(1) Spence's gradients were positively accelerated or sigmoidal whereas Hull favored the negatively accelerated form, a disagreement which figures prominently in the Hull-Spence correspondence in the 1940s in which Hull invoked in support of his preference Hovland's (1937a,b) generalization experiments.

(2) Hull, as we have seen, formally conceptualizes the role in discrimination learning of "incidental or static stimuli" (S3), whereas Spence refers more specifically to stimuli related to original position preferences.

(3) Hull's treatment is somewhat more generalized, more formal and mathematical (the ordinates of the figures are expressed as units of reaction potential [$S^E R$] in the style of the earlier papers on quantification), whereas Spence's deals more with particular, albeit hypothetical, cases.

(4) Hull's treatment of inhibition contains no reference to reactive inhibition (I_R) but goes directly to *conditioned inhibition* ($S^I R$), and is conceptually

79

similar both to Pavlov's differential (internal) inhibition and to modern uses of conditioned inhibition when they are based on differential conditioning (e.g., Rescorla, 1969). This is somewhat different from Spence's use of inhibition, which as we have indicated was not a conditioned inhibition concept in the same sense.

All told, Hull's papers on the stimulus constitute an impressive attempt to deal with very difficult problems that persist to the present time. Taken together, these papers show Hull in peak form trying to make data and theoretical ideas come together in the most meaningful way possible.

Scientific Method, 1941

13. The problem of intervening variables in molar behavior theory. (1943)

13a. A postscript concerning intervening variables. (1943)

The nine theoretical papers and one brief note that Hull published in the *Psychological Review* from the time of appearance of the *Principles* until his death—from 1943 to 1952—were either elaborations of portions of the *Principles* or drafts of chapters of his final book, *A Behavior System.* Four of these papers make up the bulk of the previous section, and they deal with properties of stimulation—afferent neural interaction, generalization, dynamism, and discrimination. The five others are somewhat more diverse, but they are all attempts to characterize and to formalize intermediary constructs. Many if not most of our earlier comments on Papers 9 and 10 apply, perhaps with increased force, to these latter papers.

This paper on intervening variables was part of a symposium on Psychology and Scientific Method at the University of Chicago in 1941 in which Hull participated with E. Brunswik and K. Lewin. In it Hull is at some pains to defend the position on which the then forthcoming *Principles* would be based: that natural science lawfulness can be a characteristic of the study of behavior, and that the intervening variable approach which he was formalizing is the appropriate mechanism for arriving at such lawfulness at a molar level.

The interchanges among the three participants reveal the richness and the turmoil of a developing but difficult science. Hull's summary of the three positions is that he and Lewin are *in principle* strict determinists, whereas Brunswik is something less than this. The uncertainties in behavioral lawfulness, according to Hull, are of the same order as in physics, albeit the number of variables may be greater and the variety of boundary conditions therefore more diverse in the case of behavior.

In the course of this brief paper Hull provides glimpses of his position on several of the issues that are of perennial concern to psychologists.

1. While he was in 1943 a molar theorist in the Newtonian mold, he was

not committed to the future of molar or (as he called it in a footnote) "coarse-grained" theorizing. He appeared to regard the intervening variable approach as a temporary theoretical strategy, referring to such variables as "interior conditions . . . which cannot be subjected to observation and measurement." In a few years, he would be attempting to show that if not observable, they could at least be subjected to a kind of quantification (see Papers 17 and 18). It does seem clear, however, that Hull could envisage a time when advances in neuroanatomy and physiology would make possible more fine-grained, molecular theories of behavior.

2. Related to the first point is Hull's stance on arriving at quantitative molar laws through what he calls "sagacious pooling of the data." Hull's defense of statistical methods appears to be not so much a matter of statistical inference as of averaging to balance out chance variability (which he attributes to molecularity, "the random spontaneous firing of the individual nerve cells") as a way of arriving at those molecular laws. This chance variability of conditions was formalized by Hull in the concept of behavioral oscillation (S^OR). It takes various forms in his writing. In *Mathematico-Deductive Theory of Rote Learning* (Hull et al., 1940), it represents a chance oscillation of the reaction threshold. In this paper in 1943, it is referred to as "the oscillation (O) of habit strength" (footnote, p. 276), while in *Principles* and later it is an inhibitory oscillation of reaction potential ($S\dot{E}R$). In the *Principles* oscillation is of strictly Gaussian form, whereas in the 1949 postulates and corollaries (Hull, 1950) the distribution is said to deviate slightly from this normal probability form, being more leptokurtic (based on data from Yamaguchi, Hull, Felsinger, & Gladstone, 1948), and this is carried through in the *Essentials* (1951) and in *A Behavior System* (1952). Hull is often criticized for developing a set of postulates and theorems on the basis of very little data, but his treatment of variability shows him to be meticulous in this regard when he had the data.

The cryptic little paper (13a) that is a postcript to Paper 13 is a quick apology to Tolman. The reason for it can be found in Hull's own words at the end of a long letter from him to Spence dated July 14, 1943.

> You may remember that you wrote me some months ago, after seeing my symposium manuscript, that I had treated Tolman's system very badly in my diagram of it [in Paper 13]. In this connection you will, I think, be interested to know that a couple of weeks ago I received a very strongly worded letter from Tolman, in which he told me in an astonishingly vigorous manner that he was thoroughly peeved at two things: first, the fact that I had not credited him with the invention and introduction into psychology of the concepts of molar behavior and symbolic constructs, and second, that I had misrepresented his system in a gross manner in my diagram in the symposium paper.

SECTION 3. SCIENTIFIC METHOD

I must confess that the violence of his reaction quite astonished me. I had always supposed him to be an exceedingly mild and amiable person. His letter was anything but that. I am sure that he had genuine grievance in the case of the diagram, so I immediately wrote a note acknowledging the fault, and sent it to Langfeld, who is going to publish it in the September issue of the *Review*. A galley proof of this note has already come in. Secondly, I got on long distance telephone and reached the Appleton-Century people and arranged with them to make two changes in the book. Fortunately the plates for the preface had not yet been cast, and the plates for the chapter where I discussed molar theory *may* not have been cast. In any case I sent in appropriate changes for both places, with the assurance that the preface would be changed and that a terminal note in the chapter might possibly be inserted. This whole thing I found extremely painful, but I have done everything possible to rectify matters. I sent copies of the proposed changes to Tolman, and he was reasonably appreciative, I think. I certainly hope so, because these matters of priority are awful messy and I would do almost anything to escape being involved in a controversy of that sort.

A word about the use of the term "molar" that appears in the title of Paper 13 and throughout the text. When Hull used the term, he obviously thought himself in agreement with Tolman, who, in his "A new formula for behaviorism" (Tolman, 1922), argues for a "nonphysiological behaviorism" and cites the similar views of Holt, de Laguna, Kantor, and others. The argument was with Watson, who was seen to favor observation at the level of "muscle contractions" and "gland secretions." The early behaviorists apparently wanted to distance themselves from Watson, at least in this respect: they favored a behaviorism separate from—in the sense of not wholly dependent upon—physiology. This was Hull's view also, although in the *Principles,* terms like "afferent neural interaction" and the little s and r in S-s^{H}r-R suggested otherwise. Criticisms of Hull's molecularity were addressed mainly against his speculative neurophysiologizing (Leeper, 1944; Ritchie, 1944). Ritchie, for example, refers to Hull's "molecular bias" (p. 641) and his "[regression] to a muscle-twitch *peripheralism*" (p. 642). In a critique of the afferent-neural-interaction principle, he says ". . . for the molar psychologist there is no problem of stimulus patterning. The compound of the two buzzers is a different physical object from either of them taken separately . . ." (p. 643). There is also the suggestion that classical conditioning is molecular and maze learning is molar. In these senses the distinction becomes one of an analytical versus a nonanalytical (Gestalt) approach, or one of complexity of the learning paradigm. These are not acceptable meanings of the molecular-molar distinction in Tolman's (1922) sense, and against these charges Hull could maintain his position of being a molar theorist.

Hull's theoretical style did not, however, exclude neurological speculation. Of course, this neurology is primitive by today's standards, but Hull freely made guesses about the neurological basis for many of his constructs, for example, primary need and innate behavior tendencies (*Principles,* Chapters 3, 4, 5). In contrast, Spence was less prone to neurophysiological speculation and more in favor of abstract theorizing; and the portions of Hull-Spence theory for which Spence was responsible made little reference to physiology. An excerpt from a letter from Spence to Hull dated September 8, 1943, makes this plain. The letter was written on the eve of publication of *Principles:*

> I received the autographed copy of your book and appreciated very much the little note in the front of the book. . . . On the whole I think that it reads fairly well although I do think that some of those earlier chapters on sensory processes could have been almost eliminated when you gave up the notion of writing a primer.
>
> I shall await with interest the reaction of the reviewers. As I have indicated several times, I feel quite sure that most of the people who read the book will completely miss the point and will go off into picayunish criticisms of some of the neurophysiological "notions" that you have elaborated. This, of course, represents our old difference in viewpoint. I have always been very unhappy about the fact that you have been inclined to throw in hypotheses as to the mediational mechanisms underlying the abstract mathematical concepts. I can just see the critics bemoaning the extent to which you hypostatize little things inside the brain. In other words I fear that you will have the non-physiologically minded people jumping on your theorizing as being nothing but neurophysiological speculation and the physiologically minded people for having made what from their point of view would be naive neurophysiological speculation. To me, of course, the meat of the discussion is the framework of mathematical theory (constructs and postulate relations) and I would have been much happier if the whole discussion had been kept on a very abstract level.

In a conciliatory reply, Hull commented on the role that physiological suggestions would play in the second theoretical volume *(A Behavior System)* which he had already begun to prepare, and described his motivation for including physiological material in *Principles.* Hull to Spence, September 21, 1943:

> Thanks much for your remarks about the new book. I think that I am following out your preference substantially in the writing of the second volume, as I think you will find little or nothing of the objectionable physiological nature in the Chapter II [a draft of the second chapter of the new volume which Spence already had]. The same, I think, will be true in all of the others. I simply take these equations and go on from there, paying no attention whatever to the physiological suggestions which I sprinkled more or less throughout the first volume. I am, of course, not very much concerned with what the reviewers say; what I am interested in is what the graduate students say. Those are the boys who will decide the matter. . . . As you know, my motive in introducing the sub-molar physiological suggestions was the hope that it would make it somewhat easier for rel-

84

atively naive graduate students to secure a sense of reality from the theory, which many people have difficulty in doing from the mere inspection of equations.

Spence, like Skinner in his experimental analysis of behavior, took the position that neurophysiological speculations detracted from the goal of the theorist, which, for Spence, was to arrive at mathematically stated laws of behavior. Hull seemed by his speculation to encourage neurophysiological investigations of learning, and this at a time when, with the impetus from a new collaboration with Gustav Bergmann, Spence had become involved in writings on operationism and methodological behaviorism (Bergmann & Spence, 1941; Spence, 1944, 1948). In a foreword to the seventh printing of the *Principles* (circa 1960), Spence points out that Hull was criticized by "the Tolman camp" (Leeper, 1944) and by Skinner for not being molar enough—for his excessive neurologizing. As Spence says, this was a reflection of Hull's desire to see his theory linked eventually to neurophysiology on the one hand and to the social sciences on the other. The current style in which learning theory, physiological psychology, and developmental psychobiology seem to be drawing ever closer together would seem closer to Hull's style—and, as Amsel (1982) points out, to the earlier Watson (1913, 1914, 1919)—than to Spence's or Skinner's.

General Lawfulness

14. The place of innate and species differences in a natural science theory of behavior. (1945)

Our commentary on this little paper will appear to be disproportionately lengthy. The reason for this is that there are several more recent treatments of "individual and species differences"—some of them very influential—that should be discussed in connection with Hull's.

The Background

This paper, published just two years after the *Principles,* appears to be a softening of the admonition (Hull, 1943, p. 27) that a "prophylaxis against anthropomorphic subjectivism . . . [is] to regard . . . the behaving organism as a completely self-maintaining robot." This exhortation to objectivism was sometimes taken as a denial of individual and species differences in the search for general lawfulness, and the 1945 paper, followed in the 1950, 1951, and 1952 versions of the theory by a postulate on individual differences was, we think, Hull's attempt to set this part of the record straight.

In a letter to Spence, dated July 20, 1944, Hull confesses that he wrote this paper and the one on afferent neural interaction as a respite from his work on two chapters of *A Behavior System* (Hull, 1952a):

> Ever since January I have been working very hard, trying to write what I originally regarded as Chapter VII of my new book. I found, however, as I worked on it that it tended to become very long, and it has now broken into two portions. The first portion will be concerned with compound heterogeneous trial and error; the second portion will be Chapter VIII and will be called something like, "Compound Homogeneous and Mixed Trial and Error."
>
> I have found these two chapters to be terribly difficult. The difficulty lies in the fact that we have so many experimental data and I have been trying to find a set of equations and constants which, when adapted to the various experimental conditions, would yield all of the experimental results of all the different experiments without any changes. I still think this can be done and I have already attained a considerable approximation to this end, though by no means one which satisfies me. The thing got so bad that I began to have digestive difficulty, so I had to give up the work for a time. As a kind of alternative I have written two

articles, a brief one of about a dozen manuscript pages in which I attempted to exploit my hypothesis as to the nature of innate individual and species differences. This manuscript has already been sent to Langfeld [the editor of the *Psychological Review*]. This afternoon Miss Hays has just completed the typing of a second short article in which I attempt to give a somewhat simplified account of my theory of patterning, exploiting the hypothesis of afferent neural interaction [see our commentary, "Properties of the Stimulus"].

Hull took the position that, across mammals at least, individual and species differences should be conceptualized as empirical constants in the general equations of learning theory. This reflected his Newtonian view that there is indeed some generality in the laws across species; however, as in other sciences, general laws of learning are idealizations, and the specific application of these laws are subject to the influences of a complex of interacting parameters related to individual and species differences.

Hull's preoccupation with individual and species differences that led to the 1945 paper is documented in a letter he wrote to Spence on April 15, 1943. Hull refers to a talk he gave to the medical and technical staff at Rockland State Hospital which seems to have sensitized him to the problem of comparative research in psychopathology:

I have been particularly interested in the opportunities of a joint theoretical and experimental analysis of the effects of insulin and electrical shock treatments which are given to certain types of very severe psychosis. In many cases they report substantial improvement and sometimes even complete recovery. Because of the extreme complexity of the phenomena of the factors operating in human maladjustments I should like to see these insulin and electric shock treatments applied to dogs and rats, say, and then follow up with (1) a detailed study of the learning processes of various types by these animals, after which (2) the brains would be subjected to a microscopic examination.[9]

This question of what happens in a situation of this kind presents some exceedingly fascinating theoretical problems. You and I, I suppose, assume that all behavior, both normal and pathological, occurs according to exactly the same fundamental laws; just as we assume (or at least I assume) that the learning of rats, dogs, chimpanzees, and humans, both young and old, operates according to exactly the same fundamental laws. If we think of these laws as written out in the form of equations, what change, if any, in these equations is responsible for the change in the resulting behavior after shock treatment, for example? If one is to be consistent, the only way I can account for the striking differences which result in the details of learning is that certain of the constants in the equations change

9. Note that this letter was written just a few months before the one of September 21, 1943 (p. 84) in which Hull promised Spence that he would pay "no attention whatever to . . . physiological suggestions" in his preparation of *A Behavior System*.

their value, while the general form of the equation remains the same. This, you will recall, is just what happens in the case of the familiar equation or law stating the acceleration of a falling object under the influence of gravity, the parameters in this case being the value of g and the value of t. In this equation, you will remember of course, the value of g is very different in different parts of the world; most elementary textbooks in physics give a table showing the value of g for Buenos Aires, Paris, London, Washington, and other well known portions of the world. It strikes me that following this analogy, animals which find discrimination easy may have a different exponent which determines the shape of the gradient of generalization, than the animals which find discrimination difficult. This, of course, is highly speculative, but it is exactly the kind of thing which we must face if we are going to consider the problem of individual differences realistically from a theoretical point of view. Needless to say, this approach is enormously different from that of our factor analysis friends at Chicago.

As is evident from the species he mentions, Hull was interested in mammalian behavior. He was in no sense a true comparative psychologist, although his review of conditioned reflexes in Murchison's *Handbook of General Experimental Psychology* (Hull, 1934) was, for its time, a thoroughgoing catalog of conditioning in all the species that had been studied. "Rats, dogs, chimpanzees, and humans, both young and old" were the animals in the experiments with which he was mainly concerned. Really general laws of mammalian behavior had to have a way of dealing with individual differences.

"The Snark Was a Boojum" Revisited

A few years later, Frank A. Beach (1950) sounded a note of concern that in America's most prestigious journal devoted to comparative psychology the percentage of papers involving *Rattus norvegicus* had increased from about 10 percent in 1911 to about 70 percent in 1948. During these years about 50 percent of the articles in this journal were on conditioning and learning, so the charge that the study of learning in America was tending towards the study of a single species was documented. Bitterman (1965) later reported that the 1948 percentage remained unchanged in the decade 1948–1958.

How did this state of affairs come about? And what is its significance for Hull's behaviorism and for learning theory in general? The answer to the first question has several parts. For one thing, neither Thorndike (1898) nor Watson (1914), who included the study of a wide range of species in a variety of tasks in their early work, found convincing evidence for species differences in what they regarded as the basic learning process. For another, while Pavlov worked almost exclusively with dogs, he was obviously persuaded that the laws of conditioning he was uncovering were applicable to a wide variety of species. Finally, the work of Willard S. Small (1901) on maze learning in the rat had shown that this rodent was easily bred in the laboratory, was readily available in large numbers, and that its maintenance involved relatively little cost. As Miles pointed out in reviewing the literature (1930), the rat's physical characteristics (size, mobility, etc.) made it an easy preparation for behavioral experiments. Consequently, in the absence of data indicating species differences in learning, the rat was chosen by many investigators in the United States as the laboratory animal of convenience. As these pages make clear, however, Hull and his students at Yale seemed almost indifferent about which mammal they worked with; certainly humans were the subjects as often as were rats, dogs were used in several experiments, and Spence's seminal work in discrimination learning was with chimpanzees.

As to the significance of Beach's statistic, and its use in current writings about learning theory, we think these points should be made. First of all, there is no denying that rats were the preferred subject in research published in the single comparative journal Beach surveyed. But, broadening the perspective, one is led to ask whether the *influential* developments in learning theory in the first half of this century were mostly rat-based. The answer must be negative. As we have noted, the influential early experimental work that provided the foundation for learning theory involved many species of animals. In the period 1911 to 1958, in addition to the seminal work of Pavlov and Thorndike with dogs and other animals, there are many examples of this kind: Watson and Rayner's (1920) conditioning of fear in the human infant; Thorndike's (e.g., 1932) studies of learning in humans; Tinklepaugh's (1928) work on memory in chimpanzees; Guthrie and Horton's (1946) studies of learning by cats in a puzzle box; Spence's (1936, 1937) work on discrimination learning in chimpanzees; Harlow's (e.g., 1949) researches on learning sets in monkeys; Ferster and Skinner's (1957) studies of reinforcement schedules in pigeons; and Solomon's experiments on avoidance learning in dogs (e.g., Solomon & Wynne, 1953). And did the rat "take over" in 1960 and beyond? We think not. In this more recent period, theoretically influential research has been done with humans (e.g., Spence's, 1966, work on eyelid conditioning); dogs (e.g., Rescorla's, 1966, truly-random control studies and the learned-helplessness work of Overmier & Seligman, 1967); pigeons (e.g., Brown & Jenkins', 1968, report of autoshaping; Staddon & Simmelhag's, 1971, study of superstition; Herrnstein's, 1970, work on the matching law); chickens (e.g., Hess's, 1964, studies of imprinting); and rabbits (work on associative learning by Gormezano, e.g., Gormezano, Kehoe,

& Marshall, 1983, and Wagner, 1978). Whereas most investigators have tended to concentrate on a single species of animal, Bitterman, Gonzalez and others (see later section on "constraints") have studied associative learning in a number of vertebrate and, more recently, invertebrate species. To be sure, the rat has had its place of influence during these times but, in our opinion, it was and is simply wrong to imply that ours is a field whose key ideas are based exclusively on the study of the rat.

History of Learning Theory According to Neisser

The kind of divisive polemics we are opposing is exemplified by the following comments of Ulrich Neisser who is arguing for a change in direction in the study of human memory:

> Not long ago, learning theory dominated almost the whole of experimental psychology (at least in America). It set the problems, prescribed the methods, defined the range of permissible hypotheses, and seemed generalizable to every aspect of life. Its intellectual leaders wrote books with titles like *Principles of Behavior* and *The Behavior of Organisms,* and their broad claims were backed up by hundreds of experiments. To be sure, the experimental subjects were almost always white rats; a few skeptics wondered whether it was quite safe to generalize from "animals" to humans, but hardly anyone doubted that at least animal behavior was being investigated in a scientifically fruitful way. The most influential philosophers of the time produced accounts of scientific method—hypothesis testing, manipulation of variables, and the like—that justified the learning theorists at every step. There was dispute about whether Hull, Spence, Skinner, or (as an outside possibility) Tolman was closest to ultimate truth, but not much about the merit of their common enterprise.
>
> Today, learning theory has been almost completely swept away. Not entirely, perhaps: with the mainland of animal behavior lost to their foes, a behaviorist remnant is holding out on well-defended islands like "behavior modification" or "behavior therapy." They still sound confident, but they are watching the straits with an anxious eye. There are even a few stalwarts fighting rearguard actions in the rat laboratories, putting out research reports that the triumphant majority don't bother to read. Nevertheless, the battle is essentially over, and it was surprisingly brief. What happened?
>
> The fundamental blow was struck by a small group of scientists who called themselves "ethologists," not psychologists, and who were not concerned with learning theory at all. They wanted to know how animals really behaved in natural environments. They were not so much interested in hypotheses as in the animals themselves. Wasps, herring gulls, ducklings, and jackdaws are a curious base on which to build a scientific revolution, but one occurred. The work of the ethologists showed that the concepts and methods of learning theory were simply

90

Section 3. General Lawfulness

irrelevant to the understanding of natural behavior. Every species seems to have a different set of learning abilities, and to respond to different sorts of variables. Even in a single species or a single organism, patterns of behavior vary drastically with changes in the gross environment, with fluctuations in hormone levels, with stages of maturation. Given these facts, notions like "conditioning," "reinforcement," "extinction," and "generalization" require constant reinterpretation if they are to survive at all. The very distinction between what is learned and what is innate has become uncertain. Even the laboratory rat has turned on his old friends (rats are apparently treacherous after all) by exhibiting a kind of learning that none of the old models could accommodate: a food aversion acquired on a single trial with a reinforcement delay of many hours. (Neisser, 1978, pp. 10–12)[10]

Neisser prefaced this passage with the comment that memory researchers would do well to pay attention to the history of learning theory because of the lessons it holds for them. But what they are offered here is little more than a caricature of our field. Perhaps the worst part is that "historical" summaries such as this—and Neisser is not alone as a reading of some recent texts in animal learning will show—are taught to graduate students and students newly come to psychology who deserve a far better deal in scholarship. Pressure to conform to the popular Kuhnian analysis of science makes these caricatures highly attractive to teachers, textbook writers, and polemicists who are eager to find a "paradigm shift" in our past. Stephen Brush (1974) once asked whether the history of science should be rated "X," put off-limits for the young, so that students will learn a pat, "fictionalized" history. We obviously think that students should have knowledge of their field's history as a protection against such "fictionalization." The remaining comments in this section are presented in juxtaposition with Neisser's rather extreme views.

Comparative Psychology and Constraints

In his writings, Bitterman (1975) has distinguished two general views of a comparative psychology of learning. One view advocated by Bitterman himself derives from Thorndike, and this is the position that modern experimental techniques should be employed to evaluate the possibility of commonality of learning processes across species. Bitterman and his colleagues, following Thorndike's example, have produced a wealth of data on the performance of fishes, reptilians, birds, and rodents in experiments on probability learning, successive-reversal learning, and reinforcement schedules (see Bitterman, 1960, 1965,

---

10. We are indebted to Professor Darryl Bruce for bringing this passage to our attention and for discussions of the problem it raises.

91

1975 for reviews). His more recent work has been concerned with associative learning in an invertebrate species, the honeybee (Couvillon & Bitterman, 1980, 1982). The similarities and differences across species demonstrated in this work constitutes perhaps the major body of experimental data we have on cross-species comparisons of learning processes under comparable laboratory conditions. Even more recently, comparative work in learning has been in the form of ontogenetic investigation, mainly, so far, in the rat (e.g., Amsel & Stanton, 1980; Spear & Campbell, 1979).

The second view Bitterman distinguishes is more closely tied to ethology, and the emphasis here is on how species are differentially adapted through evolutionary processes for interactions with their environment. According to this emphasis, learning is "constrained" by organismic variables. Bitterman (1975, p. 700) points out that we are led by the most extreme form of this position to the understanding that "each instance of learning must be treated as a specialized capability shaped by selective pressures and understandable only by reference to ethology—that there are no general laws of learning at all." The influence of species-specificity on learning has attracted many adherents not only from the ranks of the ethologists and biologists interested in animal behavior, but also from psychologists with backgrounds in learning theory. In America, a number of discoveries fueled interest in "constraints on learning" positions. These and others were reported in two volumes of collected papers titled *Biological Boundaries of Learning* (Hinde & Stevenson-Hinde, 1973) and *Constraints on Learning* (Seligman & Hager, 1972). The phenomena adduced as inimical to traditional views of learning come from diverse sources.

One of the most striking discoveries (Neisser's one example) was the long-delay conditioning of taste to "illness," the work of John Garcia, a student of Tolman, and others (early references are Garcia & Koelling, 1966; Smith & Roll, 1967). This work on poison-avoidance and food-preference learning has resulted in increased emphasis on the specificity of cue-to-consequence relationships. It had been well known for years that rats form associations readily between some feature of poisons and the postingestional consequence generally classed as "illness." They subsequently avoid such poisons and are neophobic, being hesitant to take new, strange foods. The association can be formed, often in a single trial, even though the illness ("UR") follows the taste ("CS") by hours rather than the minutes or seconds of Pavlov's laboratory, or the fractions of a second in some American preparations. The original work of Garcia, J. C. Smith, and others on learned aversions used X-irradiation as the US. Later work has more frequently involved injections of lithium chloride. Associations between taste

92

and electric shock, on the other hand, appear to be more difficult to form, as do associations between visual stimuli or even visual aspects of the poisoned food or liquid and lithium-induced illness. However, there is evidence that the apparent difficulty of conditioning with at least some pairs of these stimuli may arise from a lack of sensitivity in the testing procedure, rather than from a lack of associability (e.g., Willner, 1978). (It is not usually pointed out in this regard that Pavlov appeared to have little difficulty conditioning associations in dogs between extroceptive CSs and gastrointestinal URs). The long-delay feature of this work calls into question not only the generality of the principle of contiguity in conditioning, but also the cues-consequences relationships, the assumption, if it ever was held generally, of equipotentiality of cues in conditioning. The term used nowadays for the latter is "selective association," which calls to mind an earlier "Principle of Selective Association" which stated that "only those drive stimuli which are themselves reduced become connected to a rewarded response" (Kendler, 1946, p. 217; see also Amsel, 1949; Levine, 1953)— clearly, even then, not a principle of equipotentiality of stimuli. A careful reading of Hull's (1934) chapter in Murchison's *Handbook* on the conditioned reflex should convince the reader that in the early 1930s, at least, Hull, for one, did not believe that all CSs were equipotential for conditioning of all responses. And Neisser to the contrary notwithstanding, the long-delay feature and the rapidity of taste-aversion conditioning (and conditioning between a buzzer and shock for that matter) can certainly be handled with the "empirical constant" approach Hull recommended in his letter to Spence in 1943 and in this paper in 1945.

We have already mentioned another phenomenon, observed by Keller and Marian Breland (1961), which has taken on considerable importance in the "constraints" camp. The have found in training animals for public performances that reinforcement does not always seem to have the desired effect on the response just preceding it. For example, raccoons trained to get food by dropping coins into a "piggy-bank" container will not, after some number of trials, drop the coins directly into the box but will hold onto them and rub them together. The animal is presumably hungry, and the intrusion of this behavior is disconcerting to trainers employing reinforcement in an operant setting—so disconcerting that the Brelands termed this and similar behavior in other species "misbehavior." Raccoons rub food before eating it in much the same way they do coins. As we have said, Hull referred to such effects as anticipatory intrusions of the goal response into the instrumental sequence, and he would not have thought of such phenomena as representing "misbehavior" against his early theorizing.

SECTION 3. COMMENTARIES ON PAPERS

Another piece of evidence against general laws of learning that emerged out of a traditional Skinnerian laboratory is the now well-known phenomenon of autoshaping (Brown & Jenkins, 1968; Locurto, Terrace & Gibbon, 1981). The pigeon, for example, does not need to be shaped to peck a lighted key to get grain out of a food hopper. Simply pairing keylight and food delivery in a Pavlovian mode, with no peck-food contingency, will cause the bird to peck the lighted key. And what is more, the *form* of the peck will "correspond" to the nature of the reinforcer, so that if keylight is followed by food, the animal will appear to eat the key; if keylight is followed by water, it will appear to drink the key. A Hullian sees in this a dramatic materialization of the fractional anticipatory goal response, which seems very much related to the "misbehaviors" studied by the Brelands. For the "constraints" people, however, autoshaping is another example of species-typical behavior that defies "traditional" (or general) explanation.

It is difficult to argue with the notion that there are species differences in learning and that they may not be as tractable to mathematical treatment as Hull hoped. But the ethologically oriented investigators of learning and its "constraints" (to perpetuate an unfortunate term) have done little that is truly comparative. The work on taste-aversion is preponderantly with rats, and pigeons are the animals of choice in the vast majority of autoshaping studies.

Preparedness as an Explanation

An influential attempt to provide a metatheoretical statement of the "constraints" position was made by Seligman (1970). The gist of his proposal is that organisms are more or less "prepared" by evolution to form associations between various CSs and USs, between various responses and various outcomes. "Relative preparedness" is defined operationally by *"the amount of input* (e.g., number of trials, pairings, bits of information, etc.) *which must occur before that output* (responses, acts, repertoire, etc.), *which is construed as evidence of acquisition, reliably occurs"* (Seligman, 1970, p. 408, italics in original). An organism that takes only a few trials to form an association between a CS and a US is said to be prepared to form that association. One that takes many trials is said to be *contraprepared.* Seligman's timely paper was intended to summarize and integrate the new findings and show how troublesome they were for older, more traditional views.

There was and is, however, an important lack of specificity and some obvious circularity in this doctrine of preparedness. The lack of specificity is in

94

the failure to consider parametric factors when discussing the ability of animals to form associations. The circularity is in the general view that you can tell how prepared an animal is by how quickly it learns. For Seligman, the pigeon is prepared to peck a lighted key (CS) that is paired with food (US) because it will peck the key even though there is no operant contingency between peck and food. But it can take 20 or 100 pairings of keylight with food to establish autoshaping depending on the intertrial interval (Terrace, Gibbon, Farrell, & Baldock, 1975). So by Seligman's criterion for preparedness (number of trials to establish the response), the pigeon is prepared at one intertrial interval to form an association between keylight and grain, but is contraprepared (or unprepared) at another. Seligman also suggests the possibility of a direct relationship between preparedness and resistance of associations to extinction. Again parametric and other considerations would suggest caution. First of all, it could just as readily be argued that the better-prepared animal should extinguish more *quickly*. Certainly it would be more biologically sensible to give up unadaptive behavior as quickly as possible and move on to something else. This becomes a matter of opinion as to what is adaptive. But however this argument goes, we do know that here again parametric considerations are involved. The relationship between trials-to-extinction and number of reinforced trials, at least in man and many other mammals, is curvilinear; there is an overlearning-extinction effect after continuous reinforcement—fast extinction after a small number of acquisition trials, slower extinction after an intermediate number, and faster extinction again after a large number of trials. After partial reinforcement training, the picture is entirely different; the relationship between number of acquisition trials and trials to extinction continues to increase almost monotonically. It is this kind of parametric complexity, along with the paradoxical effects that result *even within a single species,* that must be accounted for by any adequate treatment of learning; a simple preparedness notion, while intuitively appealing, doesn't begin to do the job. Statements such as "pigeons are prepared to associate key lights with grain," or "preparedness retards (or facilitates) extinction" are unsatisfactory because they fail to take into account even some of the more fundamental parameters and paradoxes of learning.

A Modernization of Hull's Position

For Hull, in this 1945 paper, the solution to the problem of species and individual preparedness to learn was in the " *'empirical constants' which are essential constituents of the equations expressing the primary and secondary laws of behavior"*

95

(pp. 56–57). He pointed out that none of the 20 or so "constants" he had identified had yet been determined and that an account of species differences in these terms would be very difficult. He alludes to "a very promising technique [which] is being developed" (p. 60), an obvious reference to the quantification work he, Felsinger, Gladstone, and Yamaguchi published in 1947 and 1948 (see next section), as offering "renewed hope." After almost 40 years, the search for some kind of general principle of species differences in learning appears to be going on in ways very different from Hull's—but the principle appears to be just as elusive.

Michael Domjan and Sara Shettleworth, two of the original proponents of a "constraints" position, have recently commented on that entire enterprise from the perspective of the mid-1980s. They appear to concur in the view that the "general lawfulness" position has not been weakened by the "constraints" episode.

After an extensive review and analysis of ten years of experimental work on biological constraints and its implications for general process theory, Domjan (1983) arrives at the conclusion that such investigations do not force a retreat from the search for general principles of learning. "Studies of constraints on learning," he writes, "have provided numerous new insights into the mechanisms of classical and instrumental conditioning [and have, at the same time] significantly contributed to our knowledge of elementary general mechanisms of learning."

To our ears, Shettleworth's summary is written in a decidedly more Hullian key. She writes:

> In fact, however, most recent research on "constraints on learning" shows that conditioned flavor aversion and other examples of "constrained" learning display the same properties as other forms of associative learning, once some degree of specificity in what stimuli can enter into associations is taken into account. . . . Similarly, the interval between events over which associations can be formed can be regarded as a variable that depends on the particular events and species involved. Rather than weakening it, the investigation of "constraints on learning" has broadened and enriched the study of general mechanisms of associative learning. (Shettleworth, 1984, p. 174).

Quantification of Intervening Variables

17. A proposed quantification of habit strength. (1947)

18. Characteristics of dispersions based on the pooled momentary reaction potentials ($S^{\dot{E}}R$) of a group. (1948)

These were the second and fourth of five papers on quantification, four published in the space of a single year, June 1947 to June 1948, under the same multiple authorship in permuted order, and a fifth published in 1950. The other three appeared in the *Journal of Experimental Psychology* (Felsinger, Gladstone, Yamaguchi, & Hull, 1947; Gladstone, Yamaguchi, Hull, & Felsinger, 1947; Wilcoxon, Hays, & Hull, 1950). Hull obviously felt strongly the importance of this work and conveyed this feeling in a letter to Spence dated February 16, 1948, and earlier in two Research Memoranda dated 1943 and one dated 1945 (see Koch, 1954, p. 110), and in Idea Books entries (May 24, 1945; September 2, 1947). At the time of writing, three of the four papers in this series were already in print. The letter to Spence reads in part as follows:

> I have read over your chapter manuscript [for Stone's *Comparative Psychology*, third edition (1951)] and find it grand. . . . There is only one thing that might possibly be added to the statement of our system. This is that recently, by the use of a Thurstone statistical technique, an empirical equation has been secured which joins the beginning (antecedent) part of the system with the end (consequent) part of the system. The equation in question is #9 of the article by Gladstone, Yamaguchi, Hull, and Felsinger, shown on pages 517–518. Since you already have a heavy loading of our material, something else could be dropped out if this is added. In a way this equation integrates the chain on page 383 of P.B. which you suggested and which you persuaded me to publish. [11]
>
> . . . I think you have it right in your chapter when you say that Tolman's stuff if quantified would look about like ours. But he never has quantified anything in the way of theory. And what do you think of his optimism that in twenty years general agreement will be reached? For quite a while I have felt that the time is ripe for a great advance and general convergence of opinion on behavior theory. Who knows? *You* may even live to see it.

11. Hull is referring here to a diagram in the final chapter of the *Principles* summarizing the major constructs of the theory. "Chain" refers to a form of the diagram which moves from independent to dependent variables through successively higher-order constructs.

Section 3. Commentaries on Papers

In an interesting—and tangential for present purposes—final paragraph in this letter, Hull, as did Tolman (1942) in his monograph, *Drives Toward War*, and as he had done earlier in a New York Academy of Sciences paper (Hull, 1945), expresses his faith in a science of behavior and his revulsion against wars:

> There is even reason to think that if the superstition which a good solid behaviorism would destroy were eliminated much of the fighting in the world, e.g., Jerusalem and India, would disappear and a great deal of war would cease.

Papers 17 and 18 deal with the application of Thurstone's (1927) scaling techniques to the quantification of the two major intervening variables, habit, strength and momentary effective reaction potential ($S\dot{E}R$). The first paper in the series (Felsinger et al., 1947) is not like the other three in that it does not apply the scaling methodology, but is a painstaking empirical study which deals with the form of the function relating reaction latency to number of reinforcements when trials are separated by 24 hours. The purpose of the long intertrial interval was to provide learning data of great purity that would reflect the growth of habit, and therefore excitatory potential, while inhibitory factors were minimized (by trial spacing) and drive factors were held constant. The latencies were taken in a bar-press learning situation from each of 59 rats on every trial in the course of response acquisition and on a large number of trials after the asymptote of response latency had been reached. Hull apparently regarded this study as yielding the first more or less exact form of the quantitative molar law of behavior, $S^HR = f(N)$. The other papers in this series are methodological and theoretical and are based on the data from the first one. The third paper (Gladstone et al., 1947), while published in the *Journal of Experimental Psychology*, is not an experimental article but is an attempt to relate the quantification of reaction potential (Paper 17) to a number of other constructs such as the absolute zero of reaction potential, the maximum (M') reaction potential "attainable under ordinary [experimental] conditions," the reaction threshold (S^LR), and primary hunger motivation defined by hours of deprivation (h).

Hull saw these studies as yielding derived scales of excitatory potential and habit, not different in principle from the scaling of temperature (see Gladstone et al., 1947, p.513). He was obviously sensitive to the criticism of his use in the *Principles* of such terms as wat, hab, mote, and pav (after Watson, habit, motivation, and Pavlov), and he believed that the quantification work gave these terms more substance and respectability (see Felsinger et al., 1947, p. 214). In a review of the *Principles*, Skinner (1944) wrote: "The mathematics [in the equations at the end of several of the chapters] is also occasionally rather wishful, as, for example, when detailed instructions are given for 'calculating habit strength,' although no techniques have been discovered for making the necessary measurements." One of Hull's major preoccupations from 1943 until his death was in finding a way to make these "measurements."

Whereas it was the belief of Clark Hull that the work on quantification of the intervening variables was a major intellectual achievement that would in twenty-years' time be the most important surviving part of his work (Idea Books, May 24, 1945; September 2, 1947), this prediction of his was not confirmed by passing time and events. For one thing, Hull's followers did not take up the work in great numbers. As far as we are aware, none of Hull's collaborators pursued the work. Kenneth Spence, who of the Hullians was surely closest to Hull in his wish to make learning theory quantitative, chose almost to ignore the quantification studies themselves. His paper, entitled "Mathematical Formulations of Learning Theory" (published in Spence, 1960), in a symposium of the American Statistical Association held in Chicago in 1950, when these papers should have been fresh in his mind, makes no mention of the quantification work. Nor does his Kentucky Symposium article mention it, although in this article he writes, "I have for a number of years been interested in extending the quantitative aspects of this type of theory [of Hull's] to more complex learning phenomena . . ." (Spence, 1954, p. 8). The Silliman lectures book (Spence, 1956) refers to one of the five articles, but only in connection with the disagreement with Hull on the form of the distribution defining oscillatory inhibition. It is the case, however, that Spence employs the elements of Thurstone's metric to outline a procedure in which differences between the hypothetical excitatory potentials of two competing responses can be determined (Spence, 1956, pp.203–5 and pp.237–42).[12]

As we see it, the closest Spence came to acknowledging the actual articles on quantification is a doctoral dissertation at Iowa by Cletus Burke which he supervised. (Burke then went to Indiana where he teamed with Estes and helped to develop Statistical Learning Theory). Burke's dissertation[13] showed that the distribution of behavioral oscillation (or oscillatory inhibition, as Spence pre-

12. Grice (1963, p. 363) points out that Spence's theory of choice behavior reveals "the remarkable similarity between the Hull-Spence approach and TSD [theory of signal detectability]." In a personal communication (January 6, 1983), Professor Grice points out the very interesting fact that in his first paper in this series Hull published a figure "that is the mathematical equivalent of an ROC" (Hull et al., 1947, p. 251, Fig. 3).

13. Perhaps the best early brief explications of the logic of Hull's quantification procedure are contained in a publication derived from Burke's dissertation (Burke, 1949) and in a paper by Burros (1951) that provides a variant of Thurstone's scaling technique, which the author takes to be simpler and to provide approximately equivalent scale values as Hull's for reaction potential. For further explication and a critique of Hull's post-1943 preoccupation with quantification as it relates to postulate construction, the reader is referred to Koch (1954).

99

ferred) was normal and not leptokurtic as Hull and others had found. The leptokurtosis, Burke demonstrated, was an artifact of using a distribution of pooled subjects. As we have seen, the argument over the shape of this distribution was an important one between Hull and Spence: a leptokurtic distribution, Spence felt, would represent a serious impediment to quantitative theorizing.

Of Spence's students, besides Burke, the only references of which we are aware to Hull's quantification procedure is in the work of Logan and Grice. In his book, *Incentive* (1960), Logan compares speeds scaled as excitatory strengths in the manner of Hull et al. with "raw" speeds (reciprocals of times) for three alley segments from his basic runway procedure. His evaluation is: "On balance, scaled speeds offer promise of providing a simpler, more consistent picture of performance in the alley than do the raw speeds reported here" (p. 131). He concludes that further research would be needed to determine whether this is in fact the case. We are not aware of any further work on this problem.

Grice's work (e.g., 1968, 1977) is probably the most extensive subsequent use of the quantitative approach. Working with data from eyelid conditioning and reaction-time experiments, Grice employs little if any of the structure of Hull's theorizing, but uses the concept of excitatory strength, the reaction threshold (criterion), and Thurstone's metric. Hull never reached the stage in which he could write equations describing a set of data in which more than one variable was manipulated. In Grice's work equations are written describing data derived from manipulation of number of conditioning trials, response latency, stimulus intensity, stimulus similarity, individual differences, and motivational and other variables influencing the criterion or threshold. Grice's view [14] is that Hull's progress was probably impeded by two factors: his finding of leptokurtic distributions of behavioral oscillation (momentary effective reaction potential), and the impossibility of applying the quantification procedure to a theory as general as he (Hull) wanted to have.

The mathematical learning theorists (e.g., Bush & Mosteller, 1951, 1955; Estes, 1950; Estes & Burke, 1953), whose work followed on the heels of the quantification studies, made no references to it, even though Bush and Mosteller characterized their version as a "Hullian model." An anthology on mathematical learning theory (Bush & Estes, 1959) contains no reference to the work of the "four horsemen," as Hull (Idea Books entry, September 2, 1947) called his group. Neither did two general texts in mathematical psychology (Atkinson, Bower, & Crothers, 1965; Coombs, Dawes, & Tversky, 1970) make any textual reference to this work, although the Atkinson et al. book includes in its

---

14. Personal communication, January 6, 1983.

Section 3. Quantification

bibliography three of the papers. This latter is the only, albeit tacit, acknowledgment that the quantification papers were in any way relevant or related to the work in mathematical learning theory. In the light of our earlier comment (Footnote 12) about the similarity of TSD and ROC to Hull-Spence quantitative theory, it is interesting to note that in both of these books, there are more page references to theory of signal detectability than to any other entry in the subject indexes.

Whereas on first consideration one might think that evidence of such relatedness should have been seen, further reflection suggests otherwise. The fact is that the mathematical models, which were so prominent in the 1960s and 1970s, were attempts to provide mathematical characterizations of the learning curve, and the kind of activity they represent had a history that antedated the quantification work, perhaps the most prominent attempts before the Estes/Bush-Mosteller era being at the hands of Thurstone (1919, 1930), Gulliksen (1934), and Hull himself in the *Principles*. The quantification studies of Hull and his three collaborators were addressed to the intervening variables ($S^H R$, $S^E R$) in Hull's theory with the purpose of showing that a mensurational system could be developed to give them quantitative meaning. These studies were indeed different in intent from the various (mostly descriptive) mathematical (probabilistic, stochastic) treatments of the various growth functions that represent learning. The mathematical descriptions of learning curves that were derived, starting in 1950, from a variety of laboratory situations did not deal in the kinds of hypothetical states and processes that are postulated in Hull's theory. The closest to this kind of theoretical statement at that time was Estes' (e.g., 1955, 1958) use of a stimulus-sampling model to account, in nonincremental terms, for the apparently incremental nature of learning, for spontaneous recovery, and for the role of drive conceptualized as stimulus variation. In recent years, the equations of the Rescorla-Wagner model (1972) seem a blend of the two influences, the associative-strength factor (V) being somewhat akin to Hull's $S^H R$, or perhaps $S^E R$—there are no nonassociative factors in the Rescorla-Wagner model as there were not in its immediate precursors in mathematical learning theory— whereas their equations follow the linear-operator form. A recent extension by Daly and Daly (1982) of the Rescorla-Wagner model, which includes additional assumptions from Amsel's (1967) Frustration Theory, and is designed to explain a large number of reward-schedule effects, is of the same linear-operator form. But like their precursors, the Rescorla-Wagner and Daly models do not address quantification, even though they deal in hypothetical associative strengths. Their predictions, however, are entirely ordinal.

Hull was careful to state that his equations and his quantifications, e.g.,

101

$S^H R = f(N)$, were "for albino rats in the present simple learning situation (Gladstone et al., 1947, p. 525). The implication was that the same techniques of quantification applied to other strains or species in other situations and under other motivations would yield habit and excitatory growth functions reflecting these differences. Hull, as we have seen, had earlier (Paper 14) addressed himself in a preliminary way to the problem of innate individual and species differences and had taken the position that across mammals, at least, individual and species differences would be conceptualized as empirical constants in the equations of learning theory. His correspondence and his notebook entries make it clear that he saw the work on quantification as a step toward the solution to the problem of individual differences, a solution to which Grice came closer some two decades later.

The First Revision of the Principles

20. Behavior postulates and corollaries—1949. (1950)

This paper is Hull's first formal revision of the postulates of the *Principles*. It was followed in the next year by a little book, *Essentials of Behavior* (1950), which was an expanded, in the sense of annotated, version of these revised postulates. There had been several experimental developments just before and after publication of the *Principles* that required amendments of the 1943 postulates, and Hull showed he was prepared to be flexible and to be led by these new data. The major changes had to do with stimulus intensity as an energizer (V) and the definition of habit strength. We will restrict this commentary to the latter, as stimulus-intensity dynamism has been treated previously. The problem in the definition of habit strength was the general equation: $S^HR = f(N,w,t)$, habit strength is a function of number of reinforcements, and amount and delay of reinforcement.

The problem of $S^HR = f(N)$ was still not addressed in the 1949 postulates. Its history is somewhat as follows: a direct, monotonic relationship between habit strength and number of reinforcements (N) was difficult to hold in the face of the work of Humphreys on partial reinforcement, work Hull knew about but obviously did not take seriously before the *Principles* was published. In a letter to Spence from Hull dated December 8, 1939, there is a reference to a manuscript that was to be the first in a series of experiments by Humphreys (1939a) and the problems it created. (Subsequent experiments [Humphreys, 1939b, 1940, 1943] confirmed that this was a serious problem for the theory, and by 1949 Hull should have seen that this was a problem in the definition of S^HR, but instead, as we shall see, he tried to argue the problem away.)

> Humphrey's [sic] letter [arrived] with its very interesting data and I am, if anything, more puzzled than ever [about certain aspects of the data]. . . . [H]ow does one account for more conditioning or even as much under 50% reinforcement as 100% reinforcement by our present concepts? Does one assume that inhibition of conditioning is very great and that 50% training tends to greater disinhibition of it? I strongly suspect that such results would not be found in infrahuman subjects and I would therefore be inclined to lay it to the effects of different voluntary sets produced in the subject. However, these are problems which I have given little or no thought to and these notions are probably terrifically naive.

SECTION 3. COMMENTARIES ON PAPERS

Humphreys had shown that acquisition of a conditioned eyeblink response was almost as good under 50 percent as under 100 percent reinforcement and that extinction was retarded following the smaller percentage relative to the larger. In the *Principles,* Hull had taken the position that resistance to extinction was a measure of habit strength. He based this mainly on the Perin-Williams data (Perin, 1942; Williams, 1938), but he had held this view for some years previously, as a letter to Spence dated February 5, 1937, shows:

> Using rats in our experimental set-up, we train two habits, one based on the horizontal bar and the other based on the vertical bar, employing the Skinner apparatus. Suppose the horizontal bar is a strong habit based on 80 reinforcements, and the vertical bar (to be pressed sideways) is a weak habit based on 20 reinforcements. The two habits are set up independently on successive days. On the third day, both bars are put in simultaneously, and the wiring is fixed so that when the strong habit is operative no food is forthcoming, but when the vertical bar is operated the food comes down as usual. In this way the strong habit is systematically extinguished, but the weak habit is systematically built up and finally the animal will give consistent reactions to the vertical bar but not to the horizontal bar. Now suppose we wish either at the end of the process or at any arbitrary point throughout the process to find out how strong either one of the tendencies is at that time. All it is necessary to do is to remove the bar not involved in that particular process and leave the animal alone with the bar which is involved in that process, merely changing the wiring of the food apparatus so that this particular bar no longer gives any food. The number of times the animal operates the bar before complete extinction indicates in an objective way something of the actual strength of the particular habit at the point immediately preceding the beginning of this extinction.

Humphreys' experiments showed that either this was not the case, or that 50 percent reinforcement yielded greater H than did 100 percent, a highly unpalatable proposition for Hull. Humphreys interpreted his findings in terms of a difference in expectancy, and Hull regarded this as a major challenge to S-R theory. There followed attempts at Iowa and at Yale to salvage the S-R position by showing that the acquisition results could be due to uncontrolled secondary reinforcement on nonreinforced trials of the 50 percent schedule (Denny, 1946), and that the extinction finding could be explained by the fact that, in massed acquisition trials but not in spaced, the response becomes conditioned to cues characteristic of extinction (V.F. Sheffield, 1949). This latter explanation, referred to in the literature at the time and since as the Hull-Sheffield hypothesis of the partial reinforcement extinction effect, was called into question by later experiments (Weinstock, 1954, 1958; Wilson, Weiss & Amsel, 1955). Of course, this latter work was not available to Hull in 1949.

104

SECTION 3. REVISION OF *PRINCIPLES*

What Hull did change in the 1949 Postulates was $S^H R = f(w,t)$. In the *Principles,* habit strength was taken to be a function of magnitude (w) and time of delay (t) of reinforcement. In 1949 magnitude (K) and delay (J) of reinforcement are taken to affect excitatory potential ($S^E R$) and not habit strength. In this Hull was strongly influenced by the data of Crespi (1942)—Zeaman's (1949) data were a later confirmation—on shifts in reward magnitude during instrumental training producing "elation" and "depression" effects (what we now call successive positive and negative contrast). These shifts produced relatively abrupt changes in direction of response strength, making it unlikely they could be due to habit factors.

Apparently, Hull was unaware of Crespi's (1942) paper which appeared as the *Principles* was being completed. The circumstances under which Hull encountered Crespi's work are described in the following comments to Spence in a letter dated October 13, 1944. The passage we quote is interesting historically and because it is an acknowledgment by Hull at this early date that an expectancylike construct would be required in future versions of his system:

> One other matter in regard to your interest in motivation. A day or two ago I received a set of galley proof sheets from Langfeld [editor of the *Psychological Review*], from an article which I gather will be in the next issue of the *Review*. This material has been written up by a chap named Crespi [a theoretical article (Crespi, 1944)]. This fellow bases his article to a large extent on my treatment of habit strength as a function of the amount of reinforcement, and he took a number of rather dirty cracks at me apparently because I had not been very critical of the studies of Grindley and Gantt. Apparently the chap was motivated to write this article in order to call attention to the fairly good experimental study which he published in the *American Journal of Psychology,* October, 1942. I should judge that his article came out about two months before I sent the manuscript of my book to the publishers. Actually, I am sorry to say that I had never seen it or even heard of it until this proof came in. I am afraid this chap's experimental work means that I shall need to expand my theoretical system to take formal notice of what Tolman and some others have been calling *expectancy*. Crespi has some experimental work which shows that immediate experimental extinction effects definitely depend upon the amount of reward that the organism has been receiving previous to the extinction process. This, anthropomorphically, is almost self-evident. Crespi himself regards his experiment as essentially motivational.

The significance of Crespi's data for theories of learning and extinction in the 1940s and through the 1970s is reviewed elsewhere (Mackintosh, 1974; Rashotte, 1979b,c).

A letter from Spence to Hull dated February 10, 1948, makes it very plain that, even before the publication of the *Principles,* Spence had differed with Hull

SECTION 3. COMMENTARIES ON PAPERS

on whether the limit of habit was a function of magnitude of reinforcement. By the time of this "I-told-you-so" letter, Hull had come around to Spence's position, terming the magnitude factor K (for Kenneth, it is said). In our excerpt from this letter, Spence provides r_G-s_G as the mechanism for K, and mildly scolds his mentor for leaving this factor out of the *Principles*.

> And now to the role of size of reward and its influence on behavior: You may recall at the time of Crespi's article we had some correspondence (see my letter of October 17, 1944, to you) in which I recalled an earlier letter to you (January 31, 1941) in which I differed with your interpretation that the limit of habit strength varies with size of reward. I have always held to the view that habit growth is independent of size of reward and that the influence of the latter is a motivational one. . . . I have recently elaborated this conception considerably in my lecture notes and think I have the thing pretty well worked out. The germ of it was given in that Athens [Ohio] Symposium, and it is mentioned by [Howard] Kendler in the 1946 *J. Exper.* article mentioned above. Essentially the whole thing is based on your old notion of fractional anticipatory goal reaction and its motivational properties. Without going into detail, I may indicate how this conception leads to two somewhat different formulations of classical conditioning and instrumental conditioning or all other forms of learning involving instrumental acts. According to your P.B.
>
> *Classical conditioning*
> $$S^E R = f(S^H R, D)$$
> Here habit $S^H R$ is determined by magnitude of reward, number of reinforcements, etc.
>
> *Instrumental conditioning* is different as follows:
> $$S^E R = f(S^H R, r_G\text{-}s_G, D)$$
> Here there is the added component of the classical conditional (fractional goal) resonse which is always present in instrumental learning. In your earlier theoretical articles you always had this $r_G - s_G$ factor but you left it out of the P.B. In my opinion it should have been included in the treatment of simple instrumental learning.
>
> Quite frankly, I am not sure whether r_G-s_G contributes to $S^E R$ as an H or a D; that is why I have kept it separate. I think it can be shown both to provide an additional H component and also to increase the value of D.
>
> Returning now to equation (3) of your letter, you will see that you no longer assume that H is a function of the size of reward (w) but give it [w] an independent status in determining E. This, it is interesting to note, is the same conclusion which I reached. I believe, in other words, that the mechanism underlying your factor K is that described above.

On the matter of the contribution of r_G-s_G to H or D, Spence's later writings (e.g., 1956) included both although they tended to stress the latter, whereas

106

Section 3. Revision of *Principles*

Hull's early papers dealt exclusively with the associative contribution of r_G-s_G as a "pure-stimulus act." As Spence's letter indicates, the fractional anticipatory goal reaction in Hull's early papers did not have "motivational properties." Spence's 1948 letter was quickly followed by a chapter in the third edition of Stone's *Comparative Psychology* (Spence, 1951) in which there was the specific assumption that r_G-s_G contributed to excitatory potential *both* through associative and non-associative mechanisms, that is to say through H and through K.

As we have indicated (p. 41), it is puzzling that in his article, "Reinforcement, Expectancy, and Learning," Bolles (1972) offers a critique of so-called "classical incentive motivation theory" in which he asserts that in the Hull-Spence theory of incentive motivation "its effect on instrumental behavior is [only] nondirectional." While it is true that Spence stressed the K factor in his later work (the r_G-s_G designation does not appear in Bolles' article on expectancy), he certainly referred to *both* the associative and nonassociative (motivational) properties of r_G-s_G in his theorizing, as we have already seen (Spence, 1951, pp. 272–73; 1956, p. 50). And most of Amsel's work since the 1950s has stressed these directional properties in both positive and negative incentive systems (see, for example, Amsel, 1958, 1967, 1972), as has Logan's (1960), and Mowrer's (1960). To repeat, Hull's papers on the fractional anticipatory goal response published in the *Psychological Review* dealt *exclusively* with the *directional* properties of "goal attraction" and "purpose" through the mechanism of the "pure-stimulus act," r_G-s_G.

ı

Clark L. Hull's
Psychological Review Papers

Offprinted from PSYCHOLOGICAL REVIEW, Vol. 36, No. 6, Nov., 1929

A FUNCTIONAL INTERPRETATION OF THE CONDITIONED REFLEX

BY CLARK L. HULL

Yale University

INTRODUCTION

PAPER

1

The experimental evidence now available shows quite clearly that the conditioned reflex is a two-phase phenomenon. One phase is obviously primary and the other is definitely secondary. Viewed physiologically, the primary phase is positive or excitatory in its nature; the secondary phase is negative or inhibitory. Functionally regarded, the primary phase appears to be a tentative trial, or first-approximation aspect of an adaptative process, while the secondary phase is the selective, corrective, or precision-insuring aspect. These two phases of the conditioned reflex, operating jointly, thus stand revealed as an automatic trial-and-error mechanism which mediates, blindly but beautifully, the adjustment of the organism to a complex environment.

The primary or excitatory phase of the conditioned reflex is the one which is best known and which has been employed most extensively as an explanatory principle. The knowledge of certain aspects of it, indeed, is as old as associationism itself. A much more comprehensive view of the process has recently been exploited to considerable advantage by H. L. Hollingworth under the name of *redintegration*. As applied to the conditioned reflex, this term represents the fact that all elements of a stimulus complex playing upon the sensorium of an organism at or near the time that a response is evoked, tend themselves independently and indiscriminately to acquire the capacity to evoke substantially the same response. For our present purposes the indiscriminateness of the tendency is particularly to be noted.

But the redintegrative aspect is only one of at least four which are discernible in the primary phase of the conditioned

498

reflex. A second significant tendency is an almost total lack of responsiveness to the patterning of the stimulus complex. A third is a remarkable lack of specificity of the conditioned reactions as regards the conditioned stimuli which may evoke them; the reflexologists call this *irradiation*. A fourth characteristic of great significance is the curious tendency, where the conditioned stimulus precedes the unconditioned one in the conditioning process, for the reaction to be attracted forward toward the former. Under certain circumstances the reaction (after a number of reenforcements) may begin a considerable interval before the delivery of the unconditioned stimulus. In the case of certain defense reactions this may even result in the organism not receiving the nocuous unconditioned stimulus at all.

The secondary or inhibitory phase of the conditioned reflex appears to be less widely appreciated. For the most part this phase is not open to ordinary observation, only becoming manifest as the result of ingenious experimental procedures. Corresponding to the four aspects of the excitatory phase, each to each, we find here four parallel inhibitory aspects. They are: (1) inhibition from experimental extinction, (2) conditioned inhibition, (3) differential inhibition, and (4) inhibition of delay. In this connection it is to be noted that a given inhibitory tendency can only be developed on the basis of a corresponding excitatory tendency which must previously have been established.

PAPER

1

We may now proceed to the consideration of the biological function performed by the several phases of the conditioned reflex process.

Redintegration and Experimental Extinction

Of what biological utility is the redintegrative tendency? It clearly results in the multiplication of the stimulus complexes which are capable of evoking particular reactions. With certain limitations, these conditioned stimulus complexes become equivalent to, *i.e.*, substitutable for, the corresponding native or unconditioned stimuli. But just how does this substitution tendency result in augmenting the

survival chances of the organism? It is quite clear, for
example, that for any and every stimulus complex to have the
capacity to evoke any and every response would not be good
biological economy. Such an arrangement could lead to
nothing but a wild and unadaptive chaos of behavior. No
doubt many psychologists and biologists with a vitalistic
leaning will urge that, if the process be really blind and automatic as assumed, we should expect exactly such a chaos.
The problem deserves serious consideration.

The solution of the problem is seen perhaps most readily
in the conditioning of defense reactions. The unconditioned
stimuli for such reactions are ordinarily genuine injuries.
With such unconditioned stimuli the organism will rarely or
never make an unnecessary defense reaction for the reason
that a defense will always be needed. Such certainty could
hardly be attained with any other type of stimulus. This is
a characteristic example of biological conservatism. The
trouble with this particular type of arrangement is that, in
order for the defense reaction to take place, the organism
must always receive an injury. This is bad biological
economy. Clearly a corrective accessory mechanism is
needed. This exists in the substitution-of-stimulus tendency
characteristic of redintegration.

Now the nature of nocuous stimuli practically limits them
to such as involve actual contact with the organism before
being effective. But if, as will usually be the case, the
nocuous stimulus is of such a nature as also to stimulate a
distance receptor like the eye, this latter stimulus is likely to
get conditioned to the defense reaction. Here we have a
means whereby effective defense behavior may be evoked
without always being preceded by an injury. The retinal
image of the threatening object when at a moderate distance
will be sufficiently like that which is received when it is close
enough to deliver the injurious stimulus, to evoke the defense
reaction (withdrawal, flight) early enough for the organism
to escape the injury altogether. Indeed it may very well be
that the frequency among primitive conditioned reflexes of
the substitution of distance receptors for contact receptors
is due to this combination of circumstances.

Granting the tremendous biological advantage of occasionally being able to substitute certain stimulus complexes for certain others we still are pursued by the threat of a behavior chaos. There remains, in short, the difficulty presented by the indiscriminateness of the redintegrative tendency. Quite irrelevant stimulus elements will almost certainly find their way into every stimulus complex. By the principle of redintegration alone these irrelevant ones must get conditioned exactly as do the relevant. Why does not this produce the blind chaos of behavior previously suggested?

The answer is found in the corrective principle of experimental extinction. Stimulus elements which are not biologically relevant will not accompany a given unconditioned stimulus with any regularity, whereas the truly significant elements must do so. The latter, of course, will develop ordinary conditioned reflexes. The former, also, will tend to do so during their first accidental reinforcements or occasional short unbroken sequences of reinforcements. In so far as this accidental reinforcement takes place there may be realized a genuine unadaptiveness of behavior. Presumably this mechanism is responsible for a certain amount of human and other animal error.

PAPER
1

Fortunately complete functional conditioning usually does not take place until after repeated combined stimulations. Except for very unusual runs of chance coincidences of stimuli, the irrelevant stimulus would appear one or more times *unaccompanied* by the unconditioned stimulus before the accidentally initiated redintegrative tendency should have risen above the functioning threshold. Such failures of reinforcement at once produce a tendency to experimental extinction. In this connection it must be remembered that experimental extinction is not a mere passive failure to strengthen an excitatory tendency according to the so-called 'law of use.' Instead it is a very potent tendency to repress existent excitatory tendencies, particularly the one from which it has taken its origin.[1] Since chance alone will ordinarily present the irrelevant stimulus without reinforcement much

[1] See I. P. Pavlov's Conditioned reflexes, pp. 54*ff* (Oxford University Press, 1927).

more frequently than with it, the resulting inhibitory tendency will very soon become much more potent than the positive redintegrative tendency. Even if by some chance the false conditioned tendency should have gotten above the reaction threshold, the combination of circumstances just referred to would very soon convert it into a permanently inhibited and impotent state.

PATTERNED STIMULI AND CONDITIONED INHIBITION

After observing the utter indiscriminateness of the primary phase of the conditioned reflex as to the components of the stimulus complex which it tends to endow with action-evoking powers, we should not be greatly surprised to find a similar obtuseness as regards sensitivity to the particular combination or patterning of such complexes. Extensive experiments show, as a matter of fact, that the primary conditioning tendency leaves the components of the conditioned stimulus in an essentially unorganized state as regards the evocation of response. It is true that, if only a part of the original stimulus complex be presented, the intensity and promptness of the response will be reduced. This, however, is an addition-subtraction type of reaction rather than a sensitivity to organization or pattern. Barring accidental variability in the potency of the several components of the conditioned stimulus, this reduction in the magnitude of the response closely parallels the reduction in the number of the conditioned stimulus elements. With the same reservation, it may be said that one combination of stimulus elements from an original conditioned stimulus complex, will evoke the same response (both qualitative and quantitative) as any other combination having the same number of elements. Similarly, if two distinct stimuli which have been independently conditioned to a given response be presented together, the intensity of the resulting response is likely to approach closely the arithmetical sum of the responses to the two stimuli if presented separately. It is accordingly clear that, except for characteristic differences in potency, the individual components of a primarily conditioned stimulus

PAPER

1

complex are completely interchangeable and appear to have little or no functional individuality. Under such circumstances there is naturally no differential sensitivity to any particular combination or pattern of stimulus components.

Now it is evident to ordinary observation that the simple addition-subtraction relationship obtaining among the components of a conditioned stimulus in the primary phase of the conditioning process, is a fairly adequate first approximation for many life situations. Indeed, if the vertebrate organism were to be dependent upon but a *single* stimulus mechanism, it is doubtful whether any other conceivable one would be more conducive to successful environmental adjustment and survival. In the long run, where fewer signs of danger appear, the less danger there is likely to be. Similarly, where two signs of danger appear, both of which independently are tolerably reliable, the organism is pragmatically justified by the law of chance alone in making unusually prompt and vigorous defense reactions. The same may be assumed to hold for positive reactions such as those involved in food getting.

Even so, innumerable life situations arise where the simple addition or subtraction of the potencies of the several components of a stimulus complex is not adequate. In many situations a particular combination or pattern of stimulus components (either simultaneous or temporally extended) is the very essence of the stimulus. To change a single minute component of certain stimuli will completely change the nature of the appropriate response. A telegram is an example of such a patterned stimulus complex. If a single letter in it be changed, the reaction of the receiver may be made either one of joy or of despair.

Numerous experimental examples of differential sensitivity to the patterning of stimuli are found in the conditioned reflex literature. We reproduce from Pavlov one involving a temporal pattern:

The following is an experiment by Dr. Ivanov Smolensky. The positive conditioned alimentary stimulus was made up of a hissing sound (H), a high tone (hT), a low tone (lT), and the sound of a buzzer (B), applied in that order, namely H–hT–lT–B. The inhibitory stimulus was made up with the order of the two middle components reversed, namely H–lT–hT–B.

Time	Conditioned Stimulus	Secretion of Saliva in Drops During 30 Seconds	Remarks
3:10 P.M.	H–hT–lT–B	4	Reinforced
3:17 P.M.	H–lT–hT–B	0	Not reinforced
3:27 P.M.	H–hT–lT–B	3	Reinforced
3:32 P.M.	H–hT–lT–B	4	"
3:38 P.M.	H–lT–hT–B	0	Not reinforced
3:46 P.M.	H–hT–lT–B	2	Reinforced

The formation of these inhibitory reflexes usually required a great deal of time; although a relative differentiation could sometimes be observed quite early, absolute differentiation was obtained in extreme cases only after more than one hundred repetitions without reinforcement.[2]

PAPER

1

How is this obvious inadequacy of the primary phase of the conditioned reflex met? As in the case of the primary redintegrative tendency, a corrective appears in the corresponding inhibitory phase, *i.e.*, in experimental extinction. This was implied in the example just cited.

A special case of this is known in the literature as *conditioned inhibition*. This is of particular interest because it reveals in some detail one of the simplest mechanisms by which sensitivity to the patterning of a stimulus is mediated. Again we choose an example from Pavlov.[3]

A positive conditioned stimulus is firmly established in a dog by means of the usual repetitions with reinforcement. A new stimulus is now occasionally added, and whenever the combination is applied, it is never accompanied by the unconditioned stimulus. In this way the combination is gradually rendered ineffective, so that the conditioned stimulus when applied in combination with the additional stimulus loses its positive effect, although when applied singly and with constant reinforcement it retains its full powers.

[2] I. P. Pavlov, Conditioned reflexes, pp. 146–147.
[3] Idem., *op. cit.*, p. 68.

Irradiation and Differential Inhibition

One of the most clearly marked of the primary tendencies of the conditioning process is that of spontaneous generalization. When a conditioned reflex has been set up in the usual manner, it is found that many other stimuli of a somewhat similar nature will also evoke the response. This is particularly common where a pseudo-conditioned stimulus operates through the same sensory analyzer as the true conditioned stimulus. Under certain circumstances this vicarious spreading of the conditioned tendency may extend even into entirely different sense fields such as from the skin to the senses of the eye and the ear. This primitive tendency to generalization is known among the reflexologists as *irradiation*.

It is evident upon only a little reflection that irradiation is a tendency of enormous importance. Indeed it is hard to conceive how any organism requiring very complex learned adjustments could survive without it. It is a commonplace observation in the animal world that stimuli varying within a rather wide range may require substantially the same reaction. Take, for example, a simple command. Physical analysis of sound shows that the particular stimulus complex constituting a vowel sound such as ä is largely different as spoken by a man and a woman, and even as spoken by the same person at different pitches or different persons of the same sex at the same pitch. Similar variability is found among all sorts of other stimuli which, for most purposes, are considered the same. Indeed it is doubtful whether, in a strict sense, a given stimulus is ever exactly repeated. It follows that if the conditioning process were to be based upon a principle of strictly exact repetitions of the conditioned stimulus, even within the differentiating limits of the analyzer, rarely or never would a sufficient number of such identical repetitions accumulate to raise the conditioning tendency above the functioning threshold. But even if by some miracle of chance a conditioned reflex should get set up under such conditions, of what biological

PAPER
1

value would it be? Without the principle of irradiation, it could never function except on the rare chance that the organism should encounter the particular shade of the stimulus upon which the conditioned reflex tendency was originally based. All of the innumerable other shades of variability of the stimulus biologically requiring the reaction could be of no adaptive value to the organism. To be so, each possible shade of the stimulus would need to be separately conditioned. But since the number of such differences would be indefinitely great, the organism might well consume the better part of its life in perfecting the conditioning process of a single response. It is very clear that irradiation is an indispensable principle of learned adjustment.

There is, however, a decided disadvantage in the unlimited tendency to irradiation. If irradiation were extended to its logical limit, it would ultimately bring about a state in which any stimulus whatever would tend to evoke, with little or no distinction, every conditioned response possessed by the organism. This would indeed produce an unadaptive behavior chaos. But, just as we have observed in the two preceding aspects of the primary phase of the conditioning process, an inhibitory tendency enters to save the biological situation. In this third case the corrective tendency is known as *differential inhibition.*

Let us suppose that a conditioned alimentary reflex has been set up to a bell of a certain pitch. Our knowledge of the irradiation tendency makes it quite safe to assume that another bell of a pitch and quality measurably different from the first will also evoke the response. We will assume that the second bell is not a biologically relevant stimulus. In this case it will not, when presented, receive reinforcement. This in turn (assuming an adequately discriminative analyzer mechanism) will gradually develop an inhibition for the pseudo-conditioned stimulus. Meanwhile the true bell will be steadily reinforced which will preserve the biologically valuable conditioned tendency intact. Thus the two tendencies, working jointly, bring about a most excellent adaptation which neither alone could conceivably effect.

PAPER 1

118

THE ANTICIPATORY TENDENCY AND INHIBITION OF DELAY

Pavlov describes an experiment[4] in which a dog was given a tactile stimulus continuously for one minute, after which there was a pause of one minute, whereupon some dilute acid was introduced into the dog's mouth. Such an introduction of acid is always followed after a brief interval by a flow of saliva—an unconditioned reflex. Pavlov seems not to have interested himself in the phenomenon here emphasized, so that the detailed timing of the process is not given in his report. It is plain, however, that at the beginning of the experiment the flow of saliva could not have taken place until some seconds *after the termination* of the one-minute pause. After the procedure described above had been repeated a number of times, a significant change takes place. The saliva begins to appear during the one-minute pause *i.e.*, *preceding* the introduction of the acid. The first time there was only half of a drop, presumably appearing just at the close of the period. Ten minutes later, ten drops appear during the pause. Since each drop requires some time for secretion, the first of these drops must have preceded the acid by a considerable part of the one-minute pause. A later repetition yielded fourteen drops during the pause, the first drop of which presumably preceded the introduction of the acid by a still longer interval. This experiment illustrates very nicely a most interesting and significant aspect of the excitatory phase of the conditioned reflex. It is the tendency of the reaction to creep forward in time toward the conditioned stimulus in such a way as to lessen the interval originally separating the two and to make the reaction antedate the presentation of the unconditioned stimulus.

We can now ask what may be the survival value of this anticipatory characteristic of the conditioned reflex. The writer ventures a fairly confident prediction that this primitive mechanism will be found intimately connected with the 'short circuiting' so essential a part of the more complex forms of learning. By *short circuiting* is here meant the tendency of a significant or critical reaction in a learning

PAPER

1

[4] I. P. Pavlov, Conditioned reflexes, p. 40.

behavior sequence, to move forward in the series in such a way as to antedate (and thus eliminate) useless and irrelevant behavior segments formerly preceding it. But quite apart from this possibility, the shortening of the time interval between the conditioned stimulus and its response has a most obvious and immediate biological significance. As usual this is most easily seen in the case of defense reactions, particularly those involving withdrawal and flight. If the conditioned defense reaction were to preserve unchanged its temporal distance from the conditioned stimulus, the organism would (assuming the conditioned stimulus to be related in a constant temporal manner to the unconditioned stimulus) encounter the injurious stimulus on every occasion. It would thus in no wise profit by the conditioning of the defense reaction, say, to a distance receptor. This would obviously be very bad biological economy. Clearly, for a defense reaction to be wholly successful, it should result in a complete escape from injury. The only way this can be effected is to have the flight reaction antedate the possibility of the impact of the nocuous stimulus. This the basic anticipatory tendency of the conditioned reflex brings about.

But not all reactions are defensive in this sense. Certain behavior acts such as the various delayed reactions, require for their success in mediating biological adjustment that the period of latency or delay, instead of being reduced to a minimum, shall be separate from the stimulus by a quite definite and fairly prolonged period. This *inhibition of delay*, as it is called, has been studied experimentally by the reflexologists. By special techniques they have been able in dogs to condition periods of delay up to thirty minutes, with considerable precision. These experiments yield convincing evidence that the delay results from an inhibition which represses what would otherwise be an overt tendency for the reaction to follow the conditioned stimulus at once. The following report taken from Pavlov describes one of the more illuminating of these experiments: [5]

[5] *Op. cit.*, p. 41.

The animal can be given food regularly every thirtieth minute, but with the addition, say, of the sound of a metronome a few seconds before the food. The animal is thus stimulated at regular intervals of thirty minutes by a combination of two stimuli, one of which is the time factor and the other the beats of the metronome. Further, if the sound is now applied, not at the thirtieth minute after the preceding feeding, but, say, at the fifth or eighth minute, it entirely fails to produce any alimentary conditioned reflex. If it is applied slightly later, it produces some effect; applied at the twelfth minute the effect is greater; at the twenty-fifth minute greater still. At the thirtieth minute the reaction is of course complete. If the sound is never combined with food except when applied at the full interval, in time it ceases to have any effect even at the twenty-ninth minute and will only produce a reaction at the thirtieth minute—but then a full reaction.

Once more, then, we observe the primary excitatory phase and the secondary inhibitory phase of the conditioned reflex combining in a kind of trial-and-error process to bring about a type of biological adaptation which neither tendency could possibly produce alone.[6] The tentative or trial process is mediated by the excitatory phase; the selective or corrective process is effected by the inhibitory phase—at bottom, experimental extinction brought about automatically by failure of reinforcement.

PAPER
1

The Dilemma of the Conditioned Defense Reaction

In connection with that aspect of the conditioned reflex last considered, a curious and rather sharp distinction appears between positive reactions such as those involved in the taking of food, and defense reactions such as involve withdrawal or flight. In the case of an alimentary reaction, a successful response would ordinarily be followed each time by the consumption of food. This means, of course, that the conditioned tendency is continuously reinforced, which will keep it up to full strength. In this respect the case of the defense reaction is quite otherwise. As pointed out above,

---

[6] While undoubtedly related, this process is not to be confused with the trial-and-error of ordinary learning such as of the maze. The author hopes in a later paper to elaborate this distinction.

for a defense reaction to be wholly successful, it should take place so early that the organism will completely escape injury, *i.e.*, the impact of the nocuous (unconditioned) stimulus. But in case the unconditioned stimulus fails to impinge upon the organism, there will be no reinforcement of the conditioned tendency which means (one would expect) that experimental extinction will set in at once. This will rapidly render the conditioned reflex impotent which, in turn, will expose the organism to the original injury. This will initiate a second cycle substantially like the first which will be followed by another and another indefinitely, a series of successful escapes always alternating with a series of injuries. From a biological point of view, the picture emerging from the above theoretical considerations is decidedly not an attractive one.

PAPER

1

The sharpness of the conflict here, invites speculation as to how the problem is met by nature. One possibility which suggests itself is that the greater potency of the defense reaction tendencies may make them less subject to the weakening tendencies of experimental extinction. Another possibility is that the tendency to experimental extinction may be more or less in abeyance where defense reactions are concerned. But as soon as the principle of experimental extinction becomes inoperative, the organism is exposed to the dangers resulting from accidentally conditioned irrelevant stimuli (p. 501). There is thus presented a kind of biological dilemma apparently not at all the product of misplaced ingenuity on the part of the theorist. If experimental extinction operates fully the organism seems doomed to suffer the injury of the nocuous stimulus periodically in order to renew the strength of its conditioned defense reactions. If, on the other hand, experimental extinction does not operate, the organism seems doomed to dissipate much of its energy reacting defensively to irrelevant stimuli.

It is suggested on the basis of mere casual observation that what might be called a kind of organic compromise may be operating in this curious situation. It may be that experimental extinction becomes progressively in abeyance as the gravity of the injury increases. Thus slight injuries would suffer considerably from experimental extinction and would consequently require more frequent nocuous reinforcement. Reactions to grave injuries would be affected relatively little by experimental extinction but for this reason would be very prone to become attached to irrelevant stimuli. This last, indeed, may account for the prevalence of phobias which appear, at least superficially, to be more or less accidental conditionings of irrelevant stimuli to strong emotional reactions. On the other hand very mild punishment is very likely to require frequent repetition. The problem presents a fascinating field for experimental investigation.

[MS. received April 20, 1929]

Offprinted from PSYCHOLOGICAL REVIEW, Vol. 37, No. 3, May, 1930

SIMPLE TRIAL–AND–ERROR LEARNING: A STUDY IN PSYCHOLOGICAL THEORY

BY CLARK L. HULL

Institute of Human Relations, Yale University

I

Science proceeds by a double movement. For the most part, scientific discoveries are accomplished by means of observation and experiment. Occasionally, however, it happens that a discovery is made by means of a more or less complex logical process or 'gedanken experiment.' Einstein's mathematical deduction and prediction of what may be observed in the behavior of light when it passes near the sun is perhaps as good an example of this as any.

Frequently, after the existence and characteristics of natural phenomena have been discovered empirically, it is seen that these things might very well have been deduced from facts and principles already known. When the deduction is thus performed, as a kind of afterthought, the process is more properly termed explanation. Actual prediction is more dramatic than explanation, but the two processes are logically very similar. A true deductive explanation possesses a quality of logical necessity closely akin to prediction regardless of when the empirical observation takes place. It is of the mass of such interlocking deductive explanations that scientific systems are made. In general, that science is most perfectly systematized which can show the greatest proportion of its phenomena as logically deducible from recognized principles and other known phenomena. Moreover it seems reasonable that rival systems within a science may also be evaluated on the basis of this same criterion.

It is evident that much of what passes for explanation fails of this true deductive quality. It avails little merely to

PAPER

2

241

subsume a known phenomenon under some more or less general principle. It is true enough to say of any actual event that it is a case of conservation of energy, or of cause and effect. But such bare general principles of themselves alone can hardly enable one to deduce the existence and characteristics of natural phenomena. In a similar manner, the typical undergraduate behaviorist's glib explanation of the more complex forms of habit phenomena by saying of each that it is a case of stimulus and response, utterly fails of the true deductive quality. The same may be said of the fairly common, but equally futile, invocation of complexes, equilibrium, *Gestalten*, closures, *Einsicht* and the like for a similar purpose.

PAPER

2

For an explanation to form the substance of a true system, the deduction must eventuate in some kind of genuine novelty as compared with what is contained in the original premises. This element of novelty is what was referred to above as a predictive quality in real explanation. The deductive process is a true generative activity. The known principles give rise to new knowledge as the result of a causal sequence in a high-class redintegrative organism. According to one plausible hypothesis, principles are symbolic habits which, as a result of their functional interaction within the organism possessing them, give rise to new and distinct habits. These latter constitute the new knowledge. Thus the new knowledge, while derived from the original principles, is not the principles, but something newly come into existence. By the accumulation of these bits of deductive explanation, scientific systems become enlarged very much as have systems of mathematics.

Perhaps no theorists have been more naïve in their attempts at system construction than those who seek in the principles of stimulus-response the main explanation of those forms of behavior usually called mental. It may even be that, thus far, none have failed much worse in evolving the solid substance of genuine explanation. Even so, the author has considerable confidence in the possibilities of this point of view. As a concrete example in miniature of what is believed to be a desirable direction for this movement toward systematization to take, there is given the following account of a *simple* type of trial-and-error learning. This may be taken as a relatively uninvolved example of what has been spoken of above as a deductive explanation.

II

There appear to be a number of fairly distinct types of trial-and-error learning. The particular principles necessary to employ in their explanation, as well as the mode of combining the principles, differ somewhat according to the type of learning to be explained. Of the true trial-and-error learning, we have the relatively complex type exemplified by maze learning, where the *obvious* reinforcement of the conditioning process (or the lack of reinforcement) for the most part comes only at the end of a series or particular combination of trial acts. A strict deductive explanation of this type of learning presents special difficulties and very probably will turn out to involve some principles not needed for the explanation of the less complex types. A second and relatively simple type of trial-and-error learning is seen where each act or trial is definitely and immediately reinforced positively, if successful, or is followed by punishment (negative reinforcement) if unsuccessful. A still different, and perhaps simpler, type is where each trial act is reinforced, if successful, but is followed by no special stimulus (is merely unreinforced) if unsuccessful. It is this last type of learning *only* which we shall consider in the following paragraphs.

Numerous phenomena characteristic of this third type of learning call for explanation. These problems can perhaps best be formulated as a series of questions:

1. Why does the organism persist in its trials or attempts even after repeated failure?

2. Why, in case success does not result from its first attempts, does the organism vary its reactions, often over a very wide range?

3. What principle or mechanism limits the range of the variation of the reactions which an organism will make to any problem situation?

4. Why do organisms of the same general type sometimes differ so widely from each other in their reactions to the same (external) problem situation?

5. What principle determines the order of appearance of the several trial acts of a trial-and-error sequence?

6. Why, in the series of trial acts preceding the first success, does the organism often stupidly commit the same erroneous reaction repeatedly?

7. What constitutes success itself?

8. Why should the trial sequence come to an end as soon as success has been attained? Why should it not continue exactly as before?

9. Why, even after the successful reaction cycle has been performed one or more times, do reactions, repeatedly found to be unsuccessful, quite illogically continue sometimes to be made?

10. Why, in general, do these erroneous reactions become less and less frequent with each successful solution, and why do they at length cease altogether?

11. Why, for a particular organism, are certain trial-and-error problems so much more readily solved than are others? Why, for certain organisms, is the same problem so much more difficult of solution than for other organisms, presumably of equally good natural endowment?

12. Why, on the whole, are the trial reactions in 'blind' trial-and-error learning so much more likely to prove successful than would be a mere random sampling from the entire repertory of the organism's possible movements? Why is the organism so much more likely to try a successful act early in the trial-and-error sequence than pure random sampling might be expected to bring about?

III

Let it be assumed, at the outset, that there exist a number of unconditioned stimuli, S_x, S_y, and S_z; and that these stimuli evoke in a certain organism the responses R_x, R_y, and R_z, respectively. It is assumed, further, that these responses involve the same 'final common path' so that no two of them can take place simultaneously. Let S_1 represent a very mild neutral stimulus evoking at the outset no observable response whatever.

Now if S_1 should accompany S_x in the same stimulus complex a number of times there will be set up the conditioned reaction tendency

$$S_1 \longrightarrow R_x.$$

In a similar manner, if S_1 accompanies S_y in another stimulus complex a number of times there will be set up the conditioned reaction tendency

$$S_1 \longrightarrow R_y.$$

Similarly, there may also be set up the conditioned reaction tendency

$$S_1 \longrightarrow R_z.$$

Thus S_1 may come to possess a number of distinct and mutually incompatible excitatory tendencies or 'bonds.' Presumably each of these tendencies to action will have a strength or potency different from that of the others. For the sake of definiteness and simplicity of the logical consequences, we may let the strength of these excitatory tendencies stand, at this stage, in the ratio respectively of 3, 2, and 1. Lastly let it be assumed that reaction R_z is the one and only response which is biologically successful, *i.e.*, the one which is followed by reinforcement and which terminates the stimulus S_1.

Under the conditions as assumed, what might logically be expected to result in case the organism should be stimulated by S_1, either alone or in conjunction with certain other approximately neutral stimuli? It is obvious at once that there will arise a kind of competition or rivalry among the three mutually incompatible excitatory tendencies. This competition may conveniently be represented thus:

PAPER

2

Since the excitatory tendency flowing from S_1 to R_x is strongest, this reaction will be the first trial act. By hypothesis this reaction will not be reinforced. According to the principle of experimental extinction this failure of reinforcement will weaken the tendency of S_1 to evoke R_x, leaving it, let us say, with a value of 2.1.[1] But since this excitatory tendency, even after its weakening, is stronger than either of the other two, it will still be dominant. By hypothesis, S_1 continues without interruption. Accordingly, after the brief refractory phase following the R_x response, this same reaction will be repeated as the second trial act. A second experimental extinction at once reduces the tendency to R_x to a strength of 1.2. This leaves the tendency to R_y dominant at the beginning of the third trial. S_1 continues to act. Accordingly R_y is evoked as the third trial. Here, for the first time, we note the phenomenon of variability in the trial acts.

But since R_y will not be reinforced, this excitatory tendency also will suffer extinction, reducing it to 1.1. Meanwhile, R_x has spontaneously recovered to a strength of 1.5. By hypothesis, S_1 still persists. As a result, R_x is evoked as the fourth trial of the series. Failure of reinforcement at once reduces it to the value of .6. During this time R_y has recovered to 1.4, which gives it a position of dominance. S_1 accordingly evokes this reaction for a second time, as the fifth trial act of the trial-and-error series. Failure of reinforcement reduces its excitatory potentiality to .5. Meanwhile, R_x has recovered to a strength of .9, but this is not enough to equal that of R_z, which now for the first time becomes dominant. S_1 accordingly evokes R_z as the sixth trial of the series. By hypothesis this reaction is a success and is followed by reinforcement. Since this act also terminates S_1, R_z is the last trial of the first trial-and-error sequence or behavior cycle.

[1] See Table I. for a systematic and detailed summary of the characteristic incidents of this hypothetical learning episode. No special significance should be attached to the quantitative values employed. Presumably the several types of loss and gain in strength of excitatory processes in all cases should become progressively less as the maximum effect is approached, instead of being constant as shown. The simpler constant values have been chosen with a view to simplifying the exposition. For the same reason forgetting tendencies have been neglected as well as complications involved in the acquisition of the three conditioned reactions.

TABLE I

Table showing the progressive changes that would take place in a simple case of trial-and-error learning if the influence of experimental extinction each time should be to diminish an unreinforced excitatory tendency .9 points,[2] the influence of spontaneous recovery should be to restore the loss from experimental extinction .3 points for each interval between successive trials (say one hour) and for the interval between problem cycles (say 24 hours) to restore two-thirds of the maximum diminution resulting from the experimental extinction of the preceding cycle.[3] Each successful reaction reinforces its excitatory tendency by .3 points,[4] this reinforcement being assumed to take place immediately.

Trial No.	Behavior Cycle I.		Behavior Cycle II.		Behavior Cycle III.		Behavior Cycle IV.	
	Status of Excitatory Tendencies Preceding Reaction	Resulting Reaction	Status of Excitatory Tendencies Preceding Reaction	Resulting Reaction	Status of Excitatory Tendencies Preceding Reaction	Resulting Reaction	Status of Excitatory Tendencies Preceding Reaction	Resulting Reaction
1	$x = 3.0$ $y = 2.0$ $z = 1.0$	R_x	$x = 2.2$ $y = 1.5$ $z = 1.3$	R_x	$x = 1.7$ $y = 1.2$ $z = 1.6$	R_x	$x = 1.4$ $y = 1.2$ $z = 1.9$	R_z
2	$x = 2.1$ $y = 2.0$ $z = 1.0$	R_x	$x = 1.3$ $y = 1.5$ $z = 1.3$	R_y	$x = .8$ $y = 1.2$ $z = 1.6$	R_x		
3	$x = 1.2$ $y = 2.0$ $z = 1.0$	R_y	$x = 1.6$ $y = .6$ $z = 1.3$	R_x				
4	$x = 1.5$ $y = 1.1$ $z = 1.0$	R_x	$x = .7$ $y = .9$ $z = 1.3$	R_z				
5	$x = .6$ $y = 1.4$ $z = 1.1$	R_y						
6	$x = .9$ $y = .5$ $z = 1.0$	R_z						

PAPER

2

The second time the organism encounters the stimulus S_1 (the beginning of the second behavior cycle) the values of all the excitatory tendencies have increased over those existent at the conclusion of the previous behavior cycle. The tendency to R_x is dominant, and this reaction follows at once. The trial is unsuccessful, extinction follows, and stimulus S_1

[2] I. P. Pavlov, Conditioned reflexes, pp. 48 ff.

[3] Idem, op. cit., p. 58.

[4] Idem, op. cit., p. 40.

131

persists. Thereupon R_y becomes dominant, and therefore becomes the second trial act. This also is an error. Meanwhile, R_x once more has recovered to a state of dominance, and it accordingly becomes the third trial. R_x is weakened again by failure of reinforcement, which leaves dominant the correct reaction R_z. This reaction brings the second problem cycle to a successful conclusion and R_z is reinforced a second time.

The third time the stimulus S_1 is encountered it finds the three excitatory tendencies in still a different combination of strengths. R_x is dominant and becomes the first trial, an error. Its consequent weakening leaves R_z dominant. S_1 accordingly evokes R_z as the second trial. This success, as before, is followed by reinforcement.

On the fourth occasion that the organism encounters the stimulus S_1, for the first time it finds R_z dominant at the outset. Accordingly the first trial act is a success. At this point the process of trial-and-error learning may be considered as functionally complete.

IV

We may now summarize the results of our deduction by answering the questions formulated above.

1. The organism persists in its attempts because the stimulus which evokes the attempts itself persists.

2. The organism varies its reaction, when one reaction fails, because the consequent weakening of the primarily dominant excitatory tendency leaves dominant a second and distinct excitatory tendency conditioned to the same stimulus situation.

3. The range or variety of reactions which may be evoked by a given problem situation is limited to the reactions which have become conditioned during the life of the organism to one or another stimulus component of that situation.

4. Organisms superficially quite similar in general constitution may differ very widely in the nature of their trial attempts at problem solution, because their previous life history has resulted in both qualitative and quantitative

differences in their stock of excitatory tendencies evocable by the several stimulus components of the problem situation.

5. The principle which determines which of the possible trial acts shall be evoked first, second, third, etc., in the trial-and-error series is: That trial act is evoked at any given stage of the trial-and-error process which at that time is dominant, *i.e.*, strongest.

6. The reason that the organism frequently, and apparently quite stupidly, tries an unsuccessful act over and over during the first problem cycle, despite failure of reinforcement, is quite simply that the several processes which are continually varying the strengths of the different excitatory tendencies may on more than one occasion leave any particular excitatory tendency dominant. This may even result in the same erroneous act taking place two or more times in immediate succession, as in trials 1 and 2 of Behavior cycle I. (See Table I.)

PAPER

2

7. Not enough is yet known concerning the psychology of learning to give a completely general definition of success in objective biological terms. In the case of hunger, success consists in the eating of food. Ordinarily the successful act results in a cessation of the persisting stimulus S_1. In the case of hunger, S_1 is generally considered to be the cramping of the walls of the upper digestive tract.

8. The trials cease after success has been attained simply because success terminates the stimulus (S_1) which evokes the trials.

9. Erroneous acts continue to be made even after the correct solution has been 'discovered' one or more times by successful trials because the reinforcement, by success, of a weak excitatory tendency is not always great enough to make it equal in strength to excitatory tendencies which were originally more potent and which have had time to recover greatly from the effects of experimental extinction suffered just previous to the successful reaction.

10. The erroneous reactions become less and less frequent as the trial-and-error process continues, because the basic superiority in the strength of the excitatory tendencies leading

to erroneous responses becomes less and less dominant. This in turn is owing (*a*) to the action of experimental extinction which continually weakens such erroneous reactions as chance to become functionally dominant, and (*b*) to the action of reinforcement which strengthens the excitatory tendency which, when dominant, evokes successful responses. Ultimately this process must lead to a state in which the successful excitatory tendency will be dominant at the very outset of a behavior cycle.

If this first case of success on the initial trial of a behavior cycle should chance to take place under circumstances such that the spontaneous recovery from extinction by the unsuccessful tendencies had not had time to take place (as might have happened if Cycle II. had begun very soon after the conclusion of Cycle I.), then we should expect to find errors made repeatedly after one or several perfect initial performances had occurred.

11. One problem is more readily solved than another for a given organism because in its particular stock of reaction tendencies the one tending to the successful reaction chances to be relatively stronger than in the other problem situation. In case the excitatory tendency evoking the successful reaction chances to be dominant at the outset, the correct reaction will be made at the first trial and no errors whatever will occur. On the other hand, the same problem may be more difficult for one organism than another, both of which can ultimately master it, because the previous history of the two organisms has so conditioned them that the successful tendency is relatively more dominant in one than in the other. Such relative similarity in the difficulty of problems for different specimens of a given type of organism as actually exists presumably depends upon the relative similarity in the stimulating situations encountered in their lives. This is usually considerable.

12. From the foregoing, it is obvious that trial-and-error learning, while 'blind' in the sense that it is not assumed that there is available for its guidance and control any disembodied soul or spirit, is *not* blind in the sense that it does not operate according to recognized principles. In the first place, the

trials are not made from the total repertory of the organism, but from only those movements which have by previous stimulation become conditioned to one or another stimulus component of the problem situation. This fact at once automatically limits enormously the number of trial reactions from which selection must be made, and thus largely accounts for such efficiency as it displays. In the second place, of those acts which may be evoked by the stimulus situation, it seems reasonable to expect that in the long run the stronger excitatory tendencies will be more likely to evoke successful reactions than the weaker, and the weaker ones than those reactions within the repertoire of the organism, which have not become conditioned at all to any component of the problem stimulus complex.[5] Since the trial acts are evoked in the order of their strength, this factor will also greatly favor an early success over a mere random sampling from the possible reactions of the organism. It is true that such a system would not always succeed early, and might fail completely of the solution of a problem. Unfortunately this also agrees with the facts of life. Problems are often solved only after much delay, and not infrequently they are not solved at all.

PAPER

2

V

From the point of view of the longevity of hypotheses, it is extremely dangerous for them to become thoroughly definite and specific. The very definiteness of an hypothesis makes it possible to determine with relative ease whether its implications agree with the known phenomena which it proposes to explain. In case of failure to conform, the unambiguous nature of the comparison is peculiarly fatal. Worse yet, an unambiguous hypothesis is likely to permit the deductive forecast of what should be observed under various experimental conditions which may as yet be untried. A single well-planned experiment may at any moment yield results quite different from the deductive forecast, and thus topple

---

[5] Space is inadequate to elaborate this point. It is touched on briefly, however, in 'A functional interpretation of the conditioned reflex,' this JOURNAL, 1929, 36, p. 498.

the entire hypothetical structure. This, of course, is all quite as it should be. The healthy development of a science demands that the implications of its hypotheses be deduced as promptly and unambiguously as possible. This will make it possible for them, if verified by experiment, to be incorporated into the structure or system of the science; or, if found to disagree with experimental findings, the hypotheses may be recast or simply discarded as errors in the long trial-and-error process of system construction. At the least, such hypotheses may be credited with the virtue of having stimulated experimental research. But if an hypothesis be so vague and indefinite, or so lacking in relevancy to the phenomena which it seeks to explain that the results neither of previous experiments nor those of experiments subsequently to be performed may be deduced from it, it will be difficult indeed to prove it false. And if, in addition, the hypothesis should appeal in some subtle fashion to the predilections of a culture in which it gains currency, it should enjoy a long and honored existence. Unfortunately, because of its very sterility and barrenness in the above deductive sense, such an hypothesis should have no status whatever in science. It savors more of metaphysics, religion, or theology.

PAPER

2

Substantially the only significant criticism of the stimulus-response, or mechanistic movement in psychology, has been made by members of the Wertheimer branch of the *Gestalt* school, notably by W. Köhler and K. Koffka, particularly the latter. This painstaking criticism of theoretical stimulus-response constructs has been a distinct service to science. Better still, they have put forward a quite different set of principles to explain the same phenomena, which are proposed as alternative, because assumed to be superior, concepts. The issue has thus been joined in a manner quite frank and deliberate. Best of all the contest, instead of taking place in a field of pure speculation where a decision can rarely be reached, is to be conducted in the laboratory where the decision must ultimately be submitted to the impartial arbitration of the facts. That hypothesis, or set of hypotheses, which can show the highest achievement in the things which are recognized by scientists as the functions or virtues of hypotheses must in the end be judged the superior.

As a beginning in this direction there may be considered the above theoretical construct concerning one extremely limited type of trial-and-error learning. Here the question at once arises: Are the concepts or principles, by which the *Gestalt* psychologists would explain the kind of behavior under consideration, of such a nature that answers to the above questions can also be deduced from them? The present writer is frank to confess that such concepts as closure, *Pragnanz, Einsicht* and the like appear to him either too vague or too general to permit any significant deductions whatever to be drawn. He is quite free to admit, however, that this may be due merely to his failure to grasp the true significance and virtue of these concepts. The real test is whether the *Gestalt* psychologists themselves can do so. It is entirely possible, of course, that they may repudiate in whole or in part the very existence of conditions implied in the questions propounded. In that event it would seem fair to expect an exhibition of the deductive explanation of parallel phenomena as they conceive them to exist.

PAPER
2

VI

It is admitted on all hands that one of the very best tests of an hypothesis or explanatory system is to deduce correctly the result of experimental observations not yet made, particularly when the latter are made by observers disinterested in the outcome. This is a severe test, but it is a fair one, and no system should shrink from it. A number of such possibilities lie sufficiently near to the range of the very simple conditions assumed above for first-approximation forecasts of the outcome of certain experimental procedures to be ventured. Space is lacking for the presentation of but one of these. We shall make our own deduction from the same set of principles already employed. A friendly invitation is extended to the *Gestalt* psychologists, and to such other schools as put forward distinctive theories of learning, to exhibit in similar detail a similar deduction from their own principles. If no such deductive forecast can be derived, there will be an indication of immaturity, possibly of inadequacy. If a deduction is evolved in which recognized stimulus-response principles are employed, the indication will be that the psychology in question is not so distinct as might otherwise have been supposed. If a rigorous deduction from genuinely distinct principles should appear, but one in which the same outcome is arrived at as by the stimulus-response principles here employed, an extremely interesting situation of parallelism would be presented, which might very well be mutually illuminating to all parties to the discussion. Finally, if any two deductions should arrive at quite distinct forecasts as to the outcome of the experimental procedures, the laboratory may be evoked as the final court of appeal.   Indeed, the laboratory must pass the final verdict even if there were no difference of opinion whatever.

PAPER

2

Forecast: In cases of relatively simple trial-and-error learning by mammalian organisms below the anthropoids where, as above, but a single act is required for success; where the several trial acts are relatively distinct and uniform; and where the first one-fourth of the behavior cycles required for complete learning have been both fairly protracted and in fairly close succession: it is predicted that there will be a tendency for the proportion of erroneous acts (R_x and R_y) to successful acts (R_z) to be greater at the first trial act of new cycles when the new cycle begins a relatively long time after the conclusion of the preceding one than when it begins relatively soon after.

Deduction: From Table I it is quite obvious that if Behavior cycle II. should begin at once after the conclusion of Cycle I., R_z will be dominant since the status of the excitatory tendencies will be:

$$x = .9$$
$$y = .5$$
$$z = 1.3$$

But if, instead, an hour intervenes, the relative strength of the tendencies will be:

$$x = 1.2$$
$$y = .8$$
$$z = 1.3$$

At this point R_z and R_x are about equally likely to take place. Or if, as a third alternative, still more time elapses between the close of Cycle I. and the beginning of the next cycle, R_x and R_y will both become progressively more dominant over R_z until at length we shall have the condition obtaining at the first trial act of Cycle II. as shown in Table I.

It must be especially emphasized that the type of learning here considered is not only very simple, but very special in its simplicity. Its nature is perhaps best indicated in the early parts of sections II. and III. It naturally will require some ingenuity fully to satisfy these conditions in an experiment. In particular it may be difficult to set up an experimental situation where all the components of the stimulus complex, except a single dynamic core (S_1), will remain practically neutral throughout the reaction sequence.[6] However, ingenious experimentalists will be able to approach those conditions closely enough to make possible significant comparisons of results.

PAPER
2

VII

In conclusion it may be observed that the behavior deduced above, particularly the persistence of effort at solution by means of varied response, is one of the most commonly remarked differences between behavior, usually called psychic or mental, and that of ordinary automatic machines. Indeed it is common, by way of contrast, to call such behavior 'intelligent' and 'purposive.' It is the belief of the present author that these latter terms represent extremely important aspects of mammalian behavior, but that instead of being

---

[6] In this connection it may be asked why the implications of such a simplified situation should be studied. The answer is found in the history of mathematical procedures. It is often possible to understand the implications of simple situations when, at the outset, the understanding of more complex situations would be impossible. The previous solution of simple situations should make the later solution of progressively more complex situations possible. There is reason to hope that this shall prove to be the case in the present instance.

ultimate entities, all may be derived from certain combinations of more basic principles. It is believed, for example, that the account sketched above in section III. deduces a type of behavior which, if observed in an animal, would be called purposive by most psychologists though it does not show the type of purpose involving plan.[7]

Moreover, if the type of explanation put forward above be really a sound deduction, it should be a matter of no great difficulty to construct parallel inanimate mechanisms, even from inorganic materials, which will genuinely manifest the qualities of intelligence, insight, and purpose, and which, in so far, will be truly psychic. Such a mechanism would represent a radically new order of automaticity, one not yet dreamed of by the ordinary designer of automatic machinery. That such mechanisms have not been constructed before is doubtless due to the paralyzing influence of metaphysical idealism. The appearance of such 'psychic' mechanisms in the not very remote future may be anticipated with considerable confidence. Dr. H. D. Baernstein, in collaboration with the present author, has already succeeded in constructing an electro-chemical mechanism which shows the more important of the phenomena of the simple conditioned reflex.[8] There has also been constructed a model which manifests the phenomenon of simple rote learning. It is not inconceivable that 'psychic' machines may ultimately play an appreciable rôle in the life of industrialized communities. On the side of psychology it is possible that these mechanisms may dissolve the age-old problem of the opposition of mind to matter by practically demonstrating the characteristic mechanisms by means of which matter manifests the forms of behavior called psychic.

[MS. received November 13, 1929]

[7] It is a plausible hypothesis that the type of purpose involving plan and fore-sight (or fore-knowledge) requires, in addition to a persisting dynamic core in the stimulus complex, as in the case elaborated above, a flexible symbolic habit system. The implications of such an accessory habit system for trial-and-error learning, as well as further implications of the persisting-stimulus principle, are reserved for later examination.

[8] C. L. Hull and H. D. Baernstein, A mechanical parallel to the conditioned reflex, *Science*, 1929, **70**, pp. 14–15.

PAPER
2

Offprinted from PSYCHOLOGICAL REVIEW, Vol. 37, No. 6, November, 1930

KNOWLEDGE AND PURPOSE AS HABIT MECHANISMS

BY CLARK L. HULL

Institute of Human Relations, Yale University

It is only with the greatest difficulty that scientists are able to maintain a thoroughly naturalistic attitude toward the more complex forms of human behavior. Our intellectual atmosphere is still permeated in a thousand subtle ways with the belief in disembodied behavior functions or spirits. The situation is aggravated by the fact that the details of the more complex action patterns are so concealed as to be almost impossible of observation. Even so, the outlook is hopeful. The work of many ingenious investigators is bringing to light important details of the hidden processes, and enough evidence has already accumulated to enable us in a number of cases to discern with tolerable clearness the broad naturalistic outlines of their operation.

PAPER

3

I

One of the oldest problems with which thoughtful persons have occupied themselves concerns the nature and origin of knowledge. How can one physical object become acquainted with the ways of another physical object and of the world in general? In approaching this problem from the point of view of habit, it is important to recognize that knowledge is mediated by several fairly distinct habit mechanisms. In the present study but one of these will be elaborated.

Let us assume a relatively isolated inorganic world sequence taking place as shown in Fig. 1. Here S_1, S_2, etc.,

THE WORLD: $S_1 \longrightarrow S_2 \longrightarrow S_3 \longrightarrow S_4 \longrightarrow S_5 \longrightarrow \cdots$

FIG. 1

represent typical phases of a sequential flux, the time intervals between successive S's being uniform and no more than a few

511

seconds each.   Let us suppose, further, that in the neighborhood of this world sequence is a sensitive redintegrative
organism. The latter is provided with distance receptors and
is so conditioned at the outset as to respond characteristically
to the several phases of the world sequence. Each S accordingly becomes a stimulus complex impinging simultaneously
on numerous end organs. As a result, each phase of the
world sequence now becomes a cause, not only of the succeeding phase in its own proper series, but also of a functionally
parallel event (reaction) within the neighboring organism.
The organismic responses of the series thus formed have no
direct causal relationship among themselves.[1] R_1 in itself
has no power of causing (evoking) R_2. The causal relationship essential in the placing of R_2 after R_1 is that of the
physical world obtaining in the S-sequence; R_2 follows R_1
because S_2 follows S_1. The situation is represented diagrammatically in Fig. 2.

PAPER

3

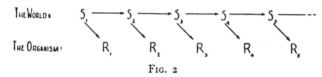

FIG. 2

Now a high-grade organism possesses internal receptors
which are stimulated by its own movements. Accordingly
each response (R) produces at once a characteristic stimulus
complex and stimuli thus originated make up to a large
extent the internal component of the organism's stimuli
complexes.   Let these internal stimulus components be represented by s's. If we assume, in the interest of simplicity of
exposition, that the time intervals between the phases of the
world flux selected for representation are exactly equal to
those consumed by the $S \rightarrow R \rightarrow s$ sequences, the situation

---

[1] This neglects the original dynamic influence of the ever-present internal component of the organismic stimulus complex into which each phase of the world sequence
enters to evoke the corresponding organismic reaction. The excitatory potency of
this internal component is here supposed to be minimal. Its influence is neglected in
the interest of simplicity of exposition. Its undeniable presence clearly introduces an
element of subjectivity into reactions which appear superficially to be evoked purely
by the external world.

will be as shown in Fig. 3, S_2 coinciding in time with s_1, S_3 with s_2 and so on.

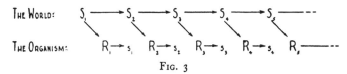

FIG. 3

Now, by the principle of redintegration, all the components of a stimulus complex impinging upon the sensorium at or near the time that a response is evoked, tend themselves independently to acquire the capacity to evoke substantially the same response. We will let a dotted rectangle indicate that what is enclosed within it constitutes a redintegrative stimulus complex; and a dotted arrow, a newly acquired excitatory tendency. After one or more repetitions of the world sequence, the situation will be as shown in Fig. 4.

PAPER

3

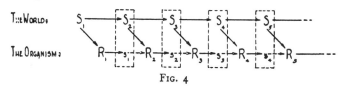

FIG. 4

As a result of the joint operation of the several factors summarized in Fig. 4, the organismic reactions (R's) which at the outset were joined only by virtue of the energies operating in the outer world sequence of S's, are now possessed of a genuine dynamic relationship lying within the organism itself. To make this clear, let it be assumed that the world sequence begins in the presence of the organism, but is at once interrupted. The resulting situation is shown diagrammatically in Fig. 5. The newly acquired excitatory tend-

THE WORLD: S_1 ——— --

THE ORGANISM: $R_1 \rightarrow s_1 \cdots \rightarrow R_2 \rightarrow s_2 \cdots \rightarrow R_3 \rightarrow s_3 \cdots \rightarrow R_4 \rightarrow s_4 \cdots \rightarrow R_5$ ——— --

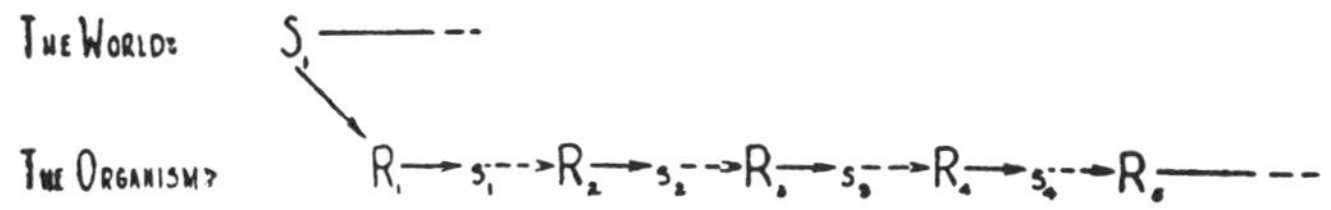

FIG. 5

encies, unless interrupted by some more potent influence, should continue the organismic sequence of responses very much as when they were first called forth as the result of the stimulation by the world sequence.

In summary it may be said that through the operation of a variety of principles and circumstances, the world in a very important sense has stamped the pattern of its action upon a physical object. The imprint has been made in such a way that a functional parallel of this action segment of the physical world has become a part of the organism. Henceforth the organism will carry about continuously a kind of replica of this world segment. In this very intimate and biologically significant sense the organism may be said to know the world. No spiritual or supernatural forces need be assumed to understand the acquisition of this knowledge. The process is entirely a naturalistic one throughout.

II

Once the organism has acquired within its body this subjective parallel to the ways of the physical world, certain other activity patterns or habit mechanisms at once become operative. One of the more important of these is the power of foresight or fore-knowledge. A great deal of mystery has surrounded this problem. Foresight may be defined for our present purpose as *the reaction to an event which may be impending, but which has not as yet taken place.* The difficulty seems largely to have been concerned with the problem of how an organism can react to an event not yet in existence. The reasoning runs: An event not yet in existence cannot be a stimulus; and how can an organism react to a stimulus which does not exist? In terms of our diagram, how can R_5, which is a reaction to the stimulating event S_5, take place before S_5 itself has occurred?

An important circumstance connected with foresight is the fact that the tempo of the acquired subjective parallel to the outer world sequence is not limited to that of the latter. Indeed, there is evidence indicating a tendency for a primary conditioned reaction to run off at a higher speed than that of the master world sequence which it parallels.[2] Thus it comes

[2] C. L. Hull, A functional interpretation of the conditioned reflex, PSYCHOL. REV., 1929, 36, p. 507 *ff*. A quite distinct mechanism serving much the same function as that here emphasized has its basis in the peculiar advantage afforded by distance

about that, even when both series begin at the same instant, the end-reaction of the subjective series may actually antedate the stimulus in the world sequence which exclusively evoked it previous to the conditioning shown in Fig. 4. It is evident that this possibility of the heightened tempo on the part of the organismic act sequence is intimately connected with the possession by the organism of knowledge of events before they actually take place.

The biological advantage of antecedent knowledge of impending events is great. This is particularly clear in the case of defense reactions. These latter fall into two main types— flight and attack. Let us suppose that in the example elaborated above, S_5 is a seriously nocuous stimulus and R_5 is a successful flight reaction. Foresight will result from the reeling off of the R-series faster than the S-series so that s_4 will evoke R_5 before S_5 has occurred. In this event S_5, when it does occur, will not impinge on the organism for the reason that the latter will have withdrawn from the zone of danger as the result of the act R_5. In case R_5 is an act of attack rather than flight it must, to be successful, bring the organismic series into contact with the world sequence in such a manner as to interrupt the latter before S_5 is reached. In this case also, the organism clearly escapes the injury. Thus the supposed impossibility of an organismic reaction to a situation before it exists as a stimulus is accomplished quite naturally through the medium of an internal substitute stimulus.

PAPER

3

III

A reflective consideration of the habit mechanisms involved in anticipatory defense reactions reveals a phenomenon of the greatest significance. This is the existence of acts whose sole function is to serve as stimuli for other acts. We shall accordingly call them *pure stimulus acts*. Under normal conditions practically all acts become stimuli, but ordinarily

receptors. The stimulus of a distant object through a distance receptor is often sufficiently like that when the object is near and nocuous to evoke a successful defense reaction before the source of danger can get near enough to produce injury. This has been discussed in detail by Howard C. Warren, *J. Phil., Psychol. & Scient. Meth.,* 1916, **13**, p. 35 *ff*.

the stimulus function is an incidental one.   The consideration of the approach of an organism to food may clarify the concept.   Each step taken in approaching the food serves in part as the stimulus for the next step, but its main function is to bring the body nearer the food.   Such acts are, therefore, primarily instrumental.   By way of contrast may be considered the anticipatory defense sequence presented above. R_5, the actual defense reaction, obviously has instrumental value in high degree. R_4, on the other hand, has no instrumental value.   This does not mean that it has no significance. Without R_4 there would be no s_4, and without s_4 there would be no R_5 *i.e.* no defense.   In short, R_4 is a pure stimulus act. In the same way R_3 and R_2 serve no instrumental function but, nevertheless, are indispensible as stimulus acts in bringing about the successful defense response.

PAPER
3

A simple experiment which can be performed by anyone in a few moments may still further clarify the concept of the pure stimulus act.   Ask almost any psychologically naïve person how he buttons his coat with one hand—which finger, if any, he puts through the buttonhole, what the last act of the sequence is—and so on.   The average person can tell little about it at first.   If wearing a coat, he will usually perform the act forthwith.   If warned against this, the hand may quite generally be observed to steal close to the position at which the buttoning is usually performed and to go through the buttoning behavior sequence *by itself*.   After this the nature of the final buttoning act may be stated with some assurance.   Clearly, the earlier acts of this pseudo-buttoning sequence are pure stimulus acts since they serve no function whatever, except as stimuli to evoke succeeding movements and ultimately, the critical final movement which is sought.

It is evident upon a little reflection that the advent of the pure stimulus act into biological economy marks a great advance.   It makes available at once a new and enlarged range of behavior possibilities.   The organism is no longer a passive reactor to stimuli from without, but becomes relatively free and dynamic.   There is a transcendence of the limitations of habit as ordinarily understood, in that the organism can

react to the not-here as well as the not-now. In the terminology of the *Gestalt* psychologists, the appearance of the pure
stimulus act among habit phenomena marks a great increase
in the organism's 'degrees of freedom.' The pure stimulus
act thus emerges as an organic, physiological—strictly internal and individual—symbolism.[3] Quite commonplace instrumental acts, by a natural reduction process, appear
transformed into a kind of *thought*—rudimentary it is true,
but of the most profound biological significance.

Thus the transformation of mere action into thought,
which has seemed to some as conceivable only through a kind
of miracle, appears to be a wholly naturalistic process and
one of no great subtlety. Indeed, its obviousness is such as
to challenge the attempt at synthetic verification from inorganic materials. It is altogether probable that a 'psychic'
machine, with ample provision in its design for the evolution
of pure stimulus acts, could attain a degree of freedom,
spontaneity, and power to dominate its environment, inconceivable alike to individuals unfamiliar with the possibilities
of automatic mechanisms and to the professional designers of
the ordinary rigid-type machines.

PAPER
3

IV

Pure stimulus-act sequences present certain unique opportunities for biological economy not possessed by ordinary
instrumental-act sequences. In the first place, there is the
ever present need of reducing the energy expenditure to a
minimum while accomplishing the ordinary biological functions in a normal manner. It is clear that pure stimulus-act
sequences, since they no longer have any instrumental function, may be reduced in magnitude to almost any degree
consistent with the delivery of a stimulus adequate to evoke

[3] This peculiarly individual form of symbolism is not to be confused with the
purely stimulus acts of social communication. Neither is it to be confused with what
appears to be a derivative of the latter by a reduction process, the subvocal speech
emphasized by Watson. The special stimulus-response mechanisms by which the
evolution of these latter forms of symbolism take place, together with their peculiar
potentialities for mediating biological adjustment and survival, are so complex as to
preclude consideration here.

the final instrumental or goal act.[4] Observation seems to indicate that this economy is operative on a very wide scale. It may even be observed in the buttoning experiment previously cited. The hand while going through the buttoning sequence by itself will ordinarily make movements of much smaller amplitude than when performing the instrumental act sequence with a real button.

A significant observation made by Thorndike in the early days of animal experimentation illustrates the same tendency, though in a very different setting. He placed cats in a confining box from which they sought to escape. Some he would release only when they licked themselves, others only when they scratched themselves. After an unusually long training period the cats finally learned to perform the required acts and thus to escape fairly promptly. In this connection, Thorndike remarks:

PAPER
3

"There is in all these cases a noticeable tendency, of the cause of which I am ignorant, to diminish the act until it becomes a mere vestige of a lick or a scratch. After the cat gets so it performs the act soon after it is put in, it begins to do it less and less vigorously. The licking degenerates into a mere quick turn of the head with one or two motions up and down with tongue extended. Instead of a hearty scratch the cat waves its paw up and down rapidly for an instant." [5]

The ordinary scratch of a cat is an instrumental act. It must have a certain duration and intensity to serve its function. In the present instance the scratch served only as a visual stimulus to Dr. Thorndike. As such, a small movement was presumably quite as effective as a large one.

In the second place there is, particularly in the case of primitive defense acts, the need to economize time so as to increase the promptness of the defense reaction. This de-

[4] Movements greatly reduced in magnitude tend to become vestigial. This suggests a possible explanation of the extreme subjectivity of imagery. Just how far the weakening of pure stimulus acts may go and still serve their stimulus function is a question which may yield to experimental approach. That they should diminish to an actual zero, with nothing but a neural vestige remaining to perform the stimulus function, is conceivable though hardly probable. It is believed that the present hypothesis is general enough to fit either alternative.

[5] E. L. Thorndike, Animal intelligence, MacMillan, 1911, p. 48.

sideratum appears to be accomplished by the same means as the first—the reduction in the magnitude of the acts. A movement of small amplitude should be more quickly performed than one of large amplitude.

But the maximum of economy, both as to energy and as to time, demands not only that the units of the stimulus-act sequence shall be small in amplitude, but that they shall also be as *few* as possible. If a single stimulus-act is sufficient to furnish the necessary stimulus for the defense reaction, the existence of all the other stimulus acts in the series is a sheer waste, both of time and energy. This means that biological efficiency demand on two separate counts the dropping out of large sections of purely stimulus-act sequences.

V

The importance of the serial-segment elimination tendency in pure stimulus-act and other complex learning sequences raises very insistently the question as to what stimulus-response mechanisms may bring it about. Observation suggests that one condition favorable for 'short circuiting' is that the process shall be strongly 'purposive.' *In the present study the purpose mechanism shall be understood as a persisting core of sameness in the stimulus complexes throughout the successive phases of the reaction sequence.* We will symbolize this persisting stimulus by S_p. This may be thought of concretely as a continuous strong red light, or a continuous gripping of a dynamometer, or the continuous knitting of the brows, or (more typically) the continuously recurring crampings of the digestive tract as in hunger.

When the principle of the persisting stimulus is joined to the set of principles represented as operating in Fig. 5, a number of novel consequences at once appear. The situation is represented in Fig. 6. An examination of this diagram shows that S_p has a unique advantage over all the other components in the several stimulus complexes. Thus, S_1, S_2, etc. and s_1, s_2, etc. can get conditioned, except for remote associative tendencies,[6] only to the response in each case

PAPER

3

[6] These are here neglected in order to simplify the exposition. Ultimately they must, of course, be taken fully into account.

which immediately follows, *i.e.* to but a single response each. But S_p, since it is present in all the stimulus complexes of the series, *gets conditioned to all the reactions* taking place in it.

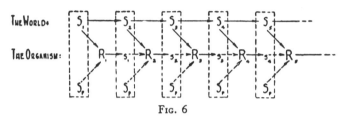

Fɪɢ. 6

This multiplicity of excitatory tendencies resulting from the situation shown in Fig. 6, is represented diagrammatically in Fig. 7.

Tʜᴇ Oʀɢᴀɴɪsᴍ:

Fɪɢ. 7

VI

It is evident that in a situation such as is presented in Fig. 7, a competition of the several excitatory tendencies will follow. Since this competition must be between the several parts of the series, it will be called *intraserial competition.* We may safely assume that the several excitatory tendencies radiating from S_p will have varying strengths. There also enter into this competition, of course, the stimulus elements which may be present in the stimulus complex from other sources at any particular moment. We will simplify the stimulus situation somewhat by assuming that the world sequence is interrupted at once after its first phase, S_1. What, then, will be the state of this intraserial competition at the second stimulus complex of the diagram?

If we assume that s_1 has an excitatory tendency toward R_2 of 2 units, that S_p also has an excitatory tendency toward

R_2 of 2 units, toward R_3 of 3 units, towards R_4 of 4 units and towards R_5 of 5 units, the competition among the several segments of the series will be that shown in Fig. 8. From

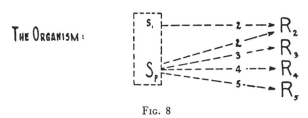

Fɪɢ. 8

this diagram it may be seen that the immediately following reaction (R_2) in the original action sequence has the advantage of a double excitatory tendency, whereas the more distant reactions such as R_3, R_4, and R_5, have but a single excitatory tendency each, that arising only from S_p. But if at any time one of the single (S_p) excitatory tendencies should chance to be stronger than the combination of the two tendencies leading to the immediately following act of the original sequence, the elimination of a segment of the pure stimulus-act sequence will take place.

PAPER 3

In order to understand how the purposive mechanism, through intraserial competition, may bring about serial segment elimination, let us observe the sequel to the following hypothetical situation. It may very well prove to be the case that S_p gets conditioned more strongly as the final or critical response in a behavior cycle is approached.[7] Accordingly a rough approximation to such a system of excitatory tendencies has been assigned to the bonds presented in Fig. 8. We may summarize the several competing excitatory tendencies radiating from the second stimulus complex as follows:

[7] It would not appear to be an over difficult task to test this hypothesis experimentally. If it should prove true it would have extensive theoretical implications and would clear up a number of questions in the theory of learning. However, almost any other hypothesis which provides considerable variation in the strength of the excitatory tendencies radiating from S_p will produce substantially similar results. It may be added that an irregular distribution of intensities of excitatory tendencies from S_p offers special opportunities for backward serial segment elimination as contrasted with the more usual forward variety here emphasized.

$$R_2 = 4,$$
$$R_3 = 3,$$
$$R_4 = 4,$$
$$R_5 = 5.$$

This shows that the reaction following the second stimulus complex must be, not R_2 as in the original act sequence, but R_5. But if R_5 follows immediately after R_1, the behavior segment shown in Fig. 9 drops completely out of the series. This is inevitable because no stimulus now remains in the series adequate to evoke it.

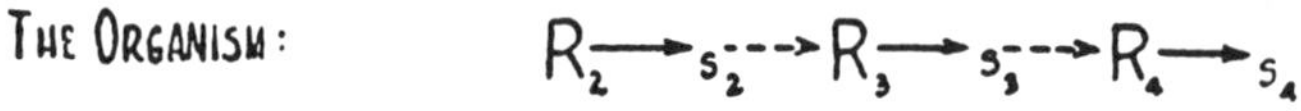

THE ORGANISM:

$$R_2 \longrightarrow s_2 \dashrightarrow R_3 \longrightarrow s_3 \dashrightarrow R_4 \longrightarrow s_4$$

Fig. 9

PAPER
3

One of the most baffling theoretical problems related to experimental psychology has been that of explaining how errors or unnecessary acts in behavior sequences get eliminated. Nevertheless, few psychological phenomena are more common. One is asked the product of 49 × 67. He writes the numbers down on paper, certain multiplication-table and addition-table habits of childhood are evoked in an orderly succession, and at length there is written down by successive stages the number, 3283. If, not too long afterwards, the individual is again asked the product of 49 × 67, he may respond by saying 3283 at once. In thus passing directly from the question to the answer, the behavior sequence of pure stimulus acts which constituted the detailed multiplication of 49 × 67 has completely dropped out of the sequence.

The difficulty of accounting for this phenomenon has been due to a considerable extent to the fact that the serial segment elimination must take place in the face of the so-called law of use or frequency. According to this principle (alone) practice or repetition might be expected blindly to fix the undesirable behavior segment in its place more firmly than ever. Perhaps such inadequacies as these have contributed much to bringing the simple chain reaction theory into its deserved ill repute as a universal explanatory principle. As a matter of plain fact, the principle of redintegration from which may be derived the simple chaining of reactions, implies with equal cogency the evolution of a stimulus-response mechanism which appears to be capable on occasion of completely transcending the chaining tendency.[8] According to this principle any stimulus such as an organic craving which persists as a relatively constant component throughout the otherwise largely changing stimulus complexes of a behavior sequence, must become conditioned to every act of the series. The implications of this for complex adaptive behavior are far reaching. It is our present concern only to point out that the persisting stimulus, through the sheaf of excitatory tendencies emanating from it to every act of the series, provides a unique dynamic relationship between each part of the series and every other part. This, as we have seen above, gives rise to a significant competition among the several potential action tendencies within the series. While final decision must be reserved until the facts are determined by experiment, the probability seems to be that this intraserial competition may easily become sufficiently potent to over-ride the simple chain-reaction tendency and produce a leap in the behavior sequence from the beginning of a series at once to the final or goal reaction, thus eliminating the intervening unnecessary action segment.

PAPER

3

VII

The results of the present inquiry may be briefly summarized.

Sequences in the outer world evoke parallel reaction sequences in sensitive organisms. By the principle of redintegration the organismic sequences acquire a tendency to run off by themselves, independently of the original world sequences. The organism has thus acquired an intimate functional copy of the world sequence, which is a kind of knowledge.

In case the two sequences begin at the same time but the organismic or behavior sequence runs off at a faster rate, the knowledge becomes fore-knowledge or foresight. This has great significance in terms of biological survival.

[8] See E. L. Thorndike, The original nature of man, New York, 1913, 186–187.

The possibility of more or less extended functional habit sequences being executed by the organism with an instrumental act only at the end, gives rise to the concept of the pure stimulus act. Such behavior sequences have great biological survival significance because they enable the organism to react both to the not-here and the not-now. Incidentally it accounts for a great deal of the spontaneity manifested by organisms.

The concept of the pure stimulus act appears to be the organic basis of symbolism but is believed to be a more fundamental one than that of symbolism as ordinarily conceived.

Pure stimulus-act sequences offer possibilities of biological economy, both of energy and of speed, through the reduction in the amplitude of the acts in the sequence. Further analysis reveals the fact that both energy and time would be economized with no incidental sacrifice if the acts between the beginning of an action cycle and its goal act should drop out of the sequence. Observation seems to show that the dropping out of such intervening pure stimulus acts occurs very extensively.

PAPER 3

The problem arises as to how this dropping out of undesirable behavior segments may come about, since it appears to be a violation of the 'law of use.' A plausible explanation is found in the peculiar potentialities of stimuli which persist relatively unchanged throughout a behavior sequence. A persisting stimulus component is regarded as one of the characteristic mechanisms of purposive behavior. We should expect such a stimulus to get conditioned to every act of the sequence, presumably most strongly to the goal act and those acts immediately preceding the goal act. The resulting multiplicity of excitatory tendencies emanating from the persisting stimulus is found to generate an important phenomenon—the competition among the several potential segments of the behavior series. This intraserial competition, if sufficiently strong, could easily over-ride the simple chaining of contiguous acts produced by the 'law of use' and enable the final act of the original series to be evoked at once after the first act of the series, thus producing what is rather inappropriately called 'short-circuiting.' Thus may a persistent problem in the theory of mammalian adaptive behavior be on its way to solution.

The general plausibility of the foregoing theoretical deductions as well as the probable biological significance of several of the deduced mechanisms, suggests strongly the desirability of an intensive program of experimental research designed to test their actuality. In that way the true function of theoretical analysis may be realized.

[MS. received June 5, 1930]

GOAL ATTRACTION AND DIRECTING IDEAS CONCEIVED AS HABIT PHENOMENA

BY CLARK L. HULL

Yale University

I

When an animal long without food is first placed in a maze or other problem situation it will usually, after a momentary pause, move about vigorously but more or less at random. These seeking movements are understood without great difficulty as the result of the combination of (*A*) the changing sensory stimulation emanating from the environment as the animal moves from place to place; (*B*) the changing proprioceptive stimulation resulting from the immediately preceding movements of the animal itself; and (*C*) a sensibly *non*-changing dynamic internal core of stimulation emanating from the continually recurring hunger cramps of the digestive tract. The changing stimulus components account to a considerable extent for the variability characteristic of the trial-and-error seeking behavior, the particular acts taking place at each instant being determined by the nature of the habituation tendencies set up in the previous history of the organism. The unchanging stimulus component, on the other hand, gives the various action segments of the behavior flux its characteristic unity by tending largely to limit the behavior to acts which in the past have been associated with the securing of food and which are therefore more likely than pure chance to result in securing it again. And when, at length, the food is found and eaten and the digestive crampings have ceased, the food-seeking behavior naturally comes to an end because its stimulus motivation has ended. Such, in brief, is the account of trial-and-error behavior conceived as motivated primarily by physiological drive.

But this is by no means the whole story. While probably

487

accurate enough so far as it goes, the above account presents but the first part of the learning process. Experimenters report that once the animal has found food at the end of the maze a few times, his behavior undergoes a striking qualitative change. The new behavior is often characterized as appearing to be more 'purposeful' than at the beginning; he acts, as Gengerelli remarks, as if he were 'going somewhere.' Beneath this rather vague characterization there may be discerned certain fairly concrete and definite behavior tendencies, the most notable of which involve anticipatory movements. When an animal is approaching his goal (the food box) he is apt progressively to speed up his pace. Another significant observation is that when an animal is approaching a familiar 90° turn in a maze, he quite generally begins his turning movements some time before he reaches the corner. Perhaps most significant of all is the phenomenon observed not only in all sorts of vertebrates but in young children and naive adults as well, that as a food goal is neared the organism tends to make mouth movements of a masticatory nature. It is probably not without significance that such movements are particularly prominent in cases where the sequence of acts leading to the goal is, for some reason, interrupted.

To casual observation such acts as the premature or anticipatory movements just cited are likely to appear as interesting symptoms of an obscure psychic tendency but in themselves to be of no functional value whatever to the organism. If this were the case they would, of course, be positively detrimental, since they would involve a wasteful expenditure of energy. In direct contrast to this view, it is the purpose of the present paper to elaborate the hypothesis that anticipatory goal reactions, as distinct from organic drives, play an indispensable rôle in the evolution of certain of the more complex forms of mammalian adaptive behavior and that the understanding of this rôle will render explicable on a purely naturalistic and physical basis the profoundly significant influence of rewards, goals, and guiding ideas upon behavior sequences.

II

Let it be assumed that a relatively isolated inorganic world flux takes place in time. Characteristic phases of the world sequence, separated from each other by but a few seconds each, are represented by S_1, S_2, S_3, etc., as they appear in Fig. 1. In the neighborhood of this world sequence is a

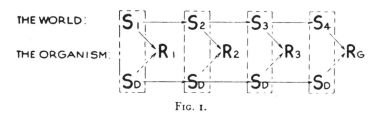

FIG. 1.

sensitive redintegrative organism provided with distance receptors and so constituted as to respond characteristically to the several phases of the world flux with a parallel behavior flux. Phases of the response flux corresponding to the world-stimulus flux are represented in Fig. 1 by R_1, R_2, etc., the final or goal reaction being indicated by R_G. Let it be assumed, further, that within the organism there is a source, such as hunger, which produces the continually recurring stimulation represented in Fig. 1 by S_D. Now, according to the principle of redintegration, all the components of a stimulus complex which may be impinging on the sensorium at or near the time that a response is evoked tend themselves independently to acquire the capacity to evoke substantially the same response. The stimulus complexes in Fig. 1 which fall under this principle are each enclosed within a dotted rectangle. It may be seen from an examination of the diagram that S_D, owing to the fact that it persists throughout the entire behavior sequence, will acquire a tendency to the evocation of R_1, R_2, R_3, and R_G, *i.e.*, to the evocation at any moment of *every* part of the reaction sequence. These newly acquired excitatory tendencies are indicated in the diagram by dotted arrows.

To amplify this part of the picture, there must be added the fact that each act, as R_1, gives rise to a proprioceptive stimulus, s_1. These proprioceptive stimuli are added to the

PAPER
4

159

diagram in Fig. 2. Through the operation of redintegration, they likewise tend to acquire the capacity to evoke the reactions immediately following them. This second group of

THE WORLD:

THE ORGANISM:

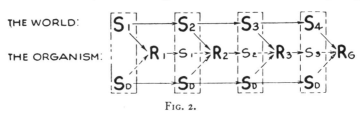

Fig. 2.

newly acquired excitatory tendencies is also represented by dotted arrows.

III

It has been shown elsewhere [1] that under certain conditions, notably when the behavior sequence is made up of symbolic or pure-stimulus acts, the multiple excitatory tendency of the persisting stimulus, S_D, may evoke the final or goal reaction of the series almost or quite at the outset of the movement, thus dropping out the useless and actually wasteful intervening acts formerly leading to the goal. But in cases where the intervening acts are mainly instrumental in nature, as is obviously the case with the locomotor activities involved in maze running, it is physically impossible to drop out any of the acts involved in traversing the *true* pathway and at the same time reach the goal.[2] With the maze remaining con-

[1] C. L. Hull, Knowledge and purpose as habit mechanisms, PSYCHOL. REV., 1930, **37**, 511–525.
    It should be noted that the mechanism of short circuiting behavior sequences there described is not adequate, as it stands, to explain the dropping of blind-alley entrances in maze learning. Space is here lacking for the elaboration of the particular mechanism involved in that specialized form of behavior sequence. Contrary to what seems to have been assumed by some, maze learning, instead of being a relatively simple process, is in reality one of great complexity. See C. L. Hull, The goal gradient hypothesis and maze learning, This journal, (In press).
    [2] Perhaps this difference in short circuiting of pure-stimulus acts as contrasted with instrumental acts is their most revealing distinction. Pure-stimulus acts are defined as acts whose sole function is to evoke other acts through the proprioceptive stimuli which they give rise to. They thus conform in a physical sense to the concept of symbolism though the entire process may be confined to a single organism in contrast to communicational symbolism which involves the acts of one organism serving as stimuli to another. The pure stimulus acts considered in the present paper are entirely of the first or individual type.

stant, the space between the starting point and the goal must, somehow, be gotten over if the food is to be obtained. Consequently, if the anticipatory invasion by the goal reaction of the instrumental behavior sequence normally leading to the goal should result in the interruption of the sequence, the actual goal will never be reached and the episode will be biologically abortive. Such an interruption will inevitably take place either when (*A*) the invading goal reaction is of such a nature that it cannot be performed by the organism at the same time as the antecedent instrumental acts leading up to it, or (*B*) when the execution of the goal reaction results in the removal of the source of the physiological drive stimulus (S_D).

In view of the ever-present potentiality of a strong drive stimulus for producing anticipatory invasions of behavior sequences by goal reactions, it should not occasion surprise if these invasions should occasionally take place even in genuinely instrumental sequences. Those common wish-fulfilling delusions so characteristic of certain forms of dementia precox are probably cases where the miscarriage of this mechanism has led to its natural maladaptive issue. Indeed, all wish fulfillments appear to be of this nature, which doubtless explains their bad repute among psychopathologists. The sexual orgasm which takes place during the ordinary erotic dream is evidently of the same nature. Extreme *ejaculatio precox* in anticipation of the sex relationship is a still clearer example of the abortive results of the goal reaction being displaced forward in time, producing the typical biologically disastrous result of preventing the completion of a reproductive cycle.

That this abortive anticipatory invasion of the antecedent instrumental sequence by the goal reaction does not take place with as great frequency as does the biologically valuable short-circuiting of pure-stimulus-act sequences raises an important theoretical question. A plausible explanation of this difference is found in the nature of the stimuli complexes operative in the two cases. Except for remote excitatory tendencies, which are here neglected in the interest of simplicity of exposition, the typical stimulus complex of the in-

PAPER
4

strumental sequence leading to a goal is shown in Fig. 2. Consider, for example, the stimulus complex immediately preceding R_2. It consists of the external stimulus S_2, the proprioceptive stimulus, s_1, arising from the preceding activity, and the persisting or drive stimulus, S_D. The typical symbolic series, on the other hand, being ordinarily an internal process, characteristically lacks in its stimulus complex the external factor, S_1, at least as a dynamic and coercive component. The significance of this stimulus difference becomes apparent when it is observed that the S_2- and s_1-components operate in the direction of a simple and stable chain-reaction tendency whereas the S_D, in addition to a chaining tendency, may have at the same time a very strong tendency to evoke other reactions, and especially the goal reaction. The relative potentialities of the two stimulus systems may be seen very readily by an inspection of Fig. 3, where arbitrary nu-

PAPER
4

THE WORLD:

THE ORGANISM:

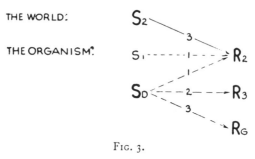

Fig. 3.

merical values have been assigned to the several excitatory tendencies. The simple summation of the potentialities of the several excitatory tendencies of the instrumental stimulus complex, $S_2\ s_1\ S_D$, yields the following values:

$$R_2 = 5$$
$$R_3 = 2$$
$$R_G = 3$$

Here R_2 is definitely prepotent and the original sequence will not be interrupted. Clearly the chaining tendency is greatly stabilized by the presence of S_2. A similar casting up of the action potentialities when S_2 is neutral or functionally absent (as in symbolic sequences) shows the following:

$$R_2 = 2$$
$$R_3 = 2$$
$$R_G = 3$$

In this case, R_G becomes prepotent. Here the chaining tendency is very obviously threatened with disruption as the result of R_G following immediately after R_1 with the consequent dropping out of R_2 and R_3.

From the foregoing it is evident that in genuinely instrumental sequences the goal reaction is not likely to be displaced backward in the behavior sequence if it is of such a nature as seriously to compete with the latter for control of the final common path. The powerful influence of the external component of the stimulus complex (S_2) ought normally to prevent this. But in case the goal reaction does not, either as a whole or in part, compete with the instrumental sequence, there seems to be no reason why the former should not undergo such displacement. In that case, the anticipatory goal reaction would not disrupt the instrumental sequence, but the two would take place concurrently. Presumably, however, goal reactions spread rather widely and ordinarily involve a large part of the organism. A wide involvement of the organism in the goal act would naturally tend strongly to interfere with any other complex concurrent activities with which it might be associated. Thus the appearance of complete goal reactions simultaneously with what previously were their antecedents should be rare.

There remains the more likely alternative that a split-off portion of the goal reaction which chances not to be in conflict with the antecedent instrumental series may be so displaced. Unfortunately, little is known experimentally of the dynamics of this fascinating possibility. Observation, however, supporting theoretical expectation, seems to indicate that anticipatory goal reactions appearing in the midst of normally antecedent instrumental act sequences are generally incomplete, fractional, imperfect, and feeble. Fortunately, with pure-stimulus acts, weakness within limits is of no disadvantage.[3]

Moreover, anticipatory goal reactions appear to manifest themselves with special frequency, vigor and completeness on occasions when, for any reason, the smooth flow of the instrumental sequence has been interrupted. This, again, is in harmony with theoretical expectation, since at such times there would presumably be less competition for the final common path. As an illustration of this there may be mentioned a recent observation made in a Boston restaurant. A man and woman were leisurely eating their dinner. Sitting bolt upright at the table on a third chair was a handsome bull terrier. Throughout the meal the dog watched his master and mistress consuming the tempting morsels without himself making the slightest overt instrumental act leading to the obvious goal. Moreover, all overt anticipatory goal reactions (such as masticatory movements) appeared also to have been inhibited, quite in accordance with the best New England traditions. After a time, however, an implicit fractional component of the anticipatory goal reaction manifested itself; a long, thick thread of saliva was observed hanging from each corner of the dog's mouth. The carefully studied salivation of Pavlov's dogs evidently also represents anticipatory goal or terminal reactions. The less inhibited Russian dogs executed gross mouth movements such as vigorous licking of the lips as well.[4]

Despite the superficial appearance of a lack of physiological conflict between two such processes as locomotion and the goal activity of mastication, general observation leads rather strongly to the expectation that there would be considerable interference even in such cases. Carefully controlled experiments will probably show, for example, that salivation is more active when the normally antecedent instrumental acts are temporarily interrupted than when they are proceeding in full vigor. If this principle can be established experimentally it will have special theoretical significance.

[3] C. L. Hull, Knowledge and purpose as habit mechanisms, PSYCHOL. REV., 1930, **37**, p. 515.
[4] I. P. Pavlov, Conditioned reflexes, p. 22.

IV

Having the phenomenon of the anticipatory goal reaction clearly before us, we may proceed to the consideration of some of its functional potentialities. Let us assume that in the dynamic situation represented in the diagram of Fig. 3, one portion of the goal reaction is not in conflict (competition) with its antecedent reactions, whereas the remainder is so. For convenience we may designate this non-conflicting component as r_G and the conflicting component as R'_G. It is assumed that as learning proceeds, S_D gets conditioned to the several phases of the reaction sequence and with an intensity roughly proportional to the proximity of each to the goal, the goal reaction itself possessing the most strongly conditioned excitatory tendency of all.[5] It is assumed, further, that this tendency, at least occasionally, will be sufficiently strong to evoke a weak r_G-reaction even at the outset of the series. This movement of the fractional goal reaction to the beginning of the behavior sequence together with its subsequent persistence throughout the cycle is indicated diagrammatically in Fig. 4. The persistence of r_G is due to the parallel persistence of S_D which continuously evokes it.

PAPER
4

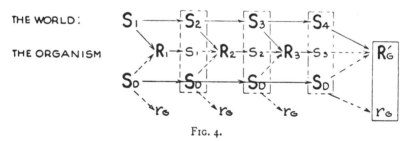

FIG. 4.

Like all other movements, r_G causes characteristic proprioceptive stimulations to arise from the muscles involved. This complex of stimulation flowing from r_G may be represented conveniently by s_G (Fig. 5). It is obvious that since r_G persists throughout the behavior sequence, s_G must also do so.

[5] C. L. Hull, Knowledge and purpose as habit mechanisms, PSYCHOL. REV., 1930, **37**, p. 521. This as yet hypothetical drive stimulus excitatory gradient will be taken up in some detail in a forthcoming paper. A rather numerous and varied assortment of experimental observations substantiates the hypothesis.

It thus comes about that our dynamic situation is possessed of two persisting stimuli, S_D and s_G. Some of the potentialities of the drive stimulus (S_D), have been elaborated elsewhere.[6] The second persisting stimulus (s_G), by way of con-

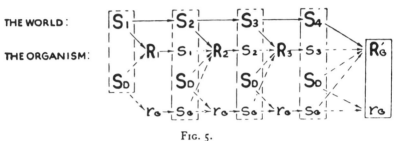

THE WORLD:

THE ORGANISM:

FIG. 5.

trast, will be called the *goal stimulus*.

It is at once apparent from an examination of Fig. 5 that, just as in the case of the drive stimulus, the principle of

redintegration ought to set up excitatory tendencies from s_G to every reaction of the behavior sequence including, apparently, tendencies to both components of the goal reaction, the one to r_G being circular. The multiple excitatory tendencies in question are represented diagrammatically in Fig. 6.

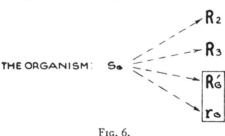

THE ORGANISM:

FIG. 6.

Despite the very significant similarity of the goal stimulus to the drive stimulus there are equally significant differences which need carefully to be noted. In the first place, the two stimuli differ radically in their source, or origin. The drive stimulus, in the typical case of hunger already before us, evidently has its origin in the physico-chemical processes involved

[6] C. L. Hull, Knowledge and purpose as habit mechanisms, PSYCHOL. REV., 1930, **37**, p. 519. In that article the drive stimulus, here represented by S_D, was represented by S_p. The present notation is believed to be the more appropriate.

in nutrition. The goal stimulus, on the other hand, is dependent, in the main at least, upon the existence of the drive stimulus and the conditioning of it to the goal reaction. The drive stimulus thus has an essentially non-redintegrative origin, whereas the goal stimulus is preeminently a redintegrative phenomenon. The drive stimulus is not likely to be greatly disturbed by either the presence or absence of the goal stimulus, but anything which terminates the drive stimulus will automatically bring the goal stimulus to an end.[7]

A second significant difference between the drive stimulus and the goal stimulus arises from the fact that from a single drive stimulus there may evolve many tolerably distinct goals. A rat, for example, will, when hungry, eat many different kinds of food. The eating of each kind of food may become a different goal with the goal reaction in each case presumably in some sense distinct. Moreover, the same kind of food may constitute the goal in many different mazes. It is evident that this possibility of a multiplicity of goal stimuli for each drive stimulus has important dynamic potentialities, especially in view of the small number of drives as contrasted with the immense variety of mammalian goals.

PAPER
4

V

With the contrasted concepts of the drive stimulus and the goal stimulus well before us, we may now turn to the consideration of the rôles played by them in certain typical situations which are known rather well on the basis of specific experiment. The first situation to be studied is the well known one where an animal which has learned a maze with a reward of food consistently given, for a number of trials receives no reward of any kind. Under such circumstances the maze habit progressively disintegrates. Our interest is concerned with the mode of this disintegration. There is, of course, nothing surprising in the fact that a food reaction should suffer experimental extinction upon consistent failure of rein-

[7] This neglects the possibility that once S_D has brought r_G into the antecedent reaction sequence, stimuli there resident may acquire a tendency to evoke r_G themselves and thus bring into existence s_G independently of S_D. An example of such a possibility would be the excitatory tendency represented by $s_1 \rightarrow r_G$.

forcement. Nothing is more common in the conditioned reflex literature.[8] But this, as it stands, would seemingly account for nothing but the inhibition of the act immediately preceding the failure of the customary reward. The particular question which primarily interests us here is: Why does the habit sequence disintegrate as a whole? Why should an event (failure to receive food) taking place at the conclusion of a long series of reactions produce a disintegration of those habit segments most remote from the active origin of disintegration, quite as promptly and completely as of the segment (goal reaction) immediately adjacent? In terms of our diagrams (Figs. 4 and 5) why should an event taking place at S_4 produce a disintegration of habit organization at S_1?

PAPER
4

The first hypothesis which appears to offer anything in the way of explaining this extensive disintegration is that the drive stimulus might acquire generalized inhibitory properties. Specifically, once the drive stimulus (S_D) has suffered experimental extinction as regards its goal reaction, this inhibition might conceivably spread to every other reaction into which S_D enters as a stimulus. But since S_D is present throughout the series the tendency to inhibition would thus spread from the termination of the sequence at once throughout its whole length and might, therefore, produce the generalized disintegration known to exist.[9]

As yet our knowledge of secondary inhibitory tendencies is too meager for us to express an opinion with any confidence as to whether a spread of inhibition would be brought about by the mechanism sketched above, and, if so, whether the tendency would be strong enough to produce the disintegration just referred to. The following consideration makes it seem doubtful: If the inhibitory tendency to reactions emanating from S_D were strong enough to over-ride the chaining excita-

[8] It is here tacitly assumed as a useful working hypothesis that principles found to be operative in conditioned reflexes are also operating in maze learning. This paper may be regarded as essentially an exploration of what might be expected in a complex learning situation in case this were true. Once the implications have been drawn, the way will be open for the setting up of critical experiments which may clarify the present unfortunate uncertainty concerning the relationship between the two phenomena.

[9] I. P. Pavlov, Conditioned reflexes, pp. 48, ff.

tory tendencies holding the behavior segments together in the series in which the frustration took place, it should also be strong enough to produce a similar disintegrative tendency in every other sequence which this drive (S_D) enters as a stimulus. This means that if the organism were consistently disappointed in finding food in one accustomed place until it would no longer seek it in that location there would also result a similar paralysis of all attempts to seek food in any place at all, at least until the inhibitory tendency should have subsided. And in that event the organism would be about as likely to seek food in the place previously proven disappointing as in some alternative place which has consistently yielded food. Since these deductions are obviously contrary to fact, at least in this extreme form, [10] we must seek some further or supplementary mechanism for the explanation of habit disintegration which results from withdrawal of reward.

A second mechanism which appears with somewhat greater probability as mediating the generalized disintegration of maze habit organization at the failure of the reward is the *goal stimulus*. We have already pointed out in connection with the discussion of the rôle of the drive stimulus that the goal reaction (r_G) would naturally be the one to be eliminated at once as the result of failure of reinforcement by food. But when r_G is eliminated, there is automatically eliminated s_G also, together with the influence of its multiple excitatory tendencies (Fig. 5). And, since s_G is a stimulus component of all the reactions of the sequence, they will all be correspondingly weakened by its absence, thus accounting for the spread of the effects of the failure of reward so effectively throughout the entire series.

The extent to which this weakening takes place will de-

PAPER
4

[10] The *a priori* probability that the inhibition resulting from failure of reward in one situation should inhibit to a certain extent other tendencies to action from the same drive stimulus, at least for a time, is sufficient to warrant the setting up of a carefully controlled experiment to determine whether or not it exists. If, for example, a rat has learned two distinct mazes to a known and equal degree and then the habit of running maze No. 1 is disintegrated by failure of reward, the rat should show a perceptible tendency to disintegration of the second maze habit when comparison is made with a suitable control. A fundamental principle of considerable importance may thus merge.

pend to a considerable degree upon whether the stimuli
throughout the action sequence are in the state of mere
unorganized complexes or whether they are organized more
or less perfectly into stimulus patterns. In the former case
any stimulus component, by dropping out of the complex, will
withdraw from its joint excitatory tendency no more than
what it would exert if acting alone. But in case the stimuli
have become organized into patterns the dropping out of any
customary component may result in the profound weakening
of the joint excitatory tendency and even its complete aboli-
tion.[11]

Our main objective, however, is to emphasize a radical and
significant difference between the habit mechanisms of drive
stimulus and goal reaction stimulus respectively. We have
already seen that a strictly generalized inhibitory tendency
from S_D alone, if such exists, would spread alike to all reaction
sequences which are mediated by this drive and would not
permit of the differentiation of a successful series from an
unsuccessful one. This would present an impossible biological
dilemma. The goal stimulus supplies the key to the situation. Since r_G is peculiar to the one sequence of which it is the
terminal action, the effect of its inhibition will weaken its
own series alone. This will leave all other series, even when
motivated by the same drive, essentially intact except possibly
for weak inhibitory radiation effects. Thus an animal disappointed in finding food at one place, will no longer seek it there
but will, nevertheless, proceed to seek it elsewhere. The
disintegration of maze habits under the influence of withdrawal of reward thus serves nicely to illustrate both the
inadequacy of the drive stimulus as a sole explanatory concept
and the distinct explanatory possibilities of the goal-stimulus
concept.

PAPER
4

VI

The concept of anticipatory or premature goal reactions
appearing in fragmentary form concurrently with acts origi-

[11] Presumably habits range everywhere between these two extremes of degree of
patterning and any given stimulus may be in a constant state of flux in this respect.
The experimental determination of the factors governing this fundamental tendency
offers a rich field for systematic exploration.

nally antedating them presents a very striking similarity to what has long been known as ideo-motor action. Some concrete cases of what is meant by this latter term may assist in the grasping of this point. A familiar example of ideo-motor action is found in the pressure of the inexperienced billiard player against the edge of the table while observing the movement of a ball which he has just activated, particularly when the ball threatens not quite to reach the mark at which he has aimed. A somewhat similar example is seen in the common tendency of people when watching a football game to lean and even push in the direction that they wish the play to move.

To most psychologists in the past, ideo-motor action has been regarded as no more than an interesting curiosity—a kind of abortive activity having no functional value in itself but serving, perhaps in large part by virtue of its very maladaptive nature, to indicate strikingly the existence of a tendency which might be really adaptive under other circumstances.[12] From the point of view of instrumental behavior the maladaptive nature of most ideo-motor acts is evident. Nothing could well be conceived as more stupid and less calculated to influence the course of a billiard ball than a gentle pressure on the side of the billiard table. Few things could be imagined which would be more futile as regards the outcome of a football play than the sympathetic movements on the part of the spectators. In this, ideo-motor action presents an exact parallel to implicit anticipatory goal reactions such as the licking of the lips and the salivation of the dogs of the conditioned reflex experiments. Indeed if we consider that the pressure delivered to the side of the billiard table really would function on the ball if the hand had traversed the distance from the edge of the table to the position of

PAPER
4

[12] This seems to have been true even of William James, despite the fact that he regarded ideo-motor action as intimately related to will. "Wherever movement follows *unhesitatingly and immediately* the notion of it in the mind, we have ideo-motor action. . . We think the act and it is done. . . Dr. Carpenter, who first used, I believe, the name of ideo-motor action, placed it, if I mistake not, among the curiosities of our mental life. The truth is that it is no curiosity but simply a normal process stripped of disguise." (William James, Principles of psychology, 1908, Vol. II., p. 522.)

the ball, and that the movements of the spectator of a football game really would affect the outcome of the play if he had traversed the distance separating him from the players, these movements appear quite literally as anticipatory goal reactions. As instrumental acts they are, and must always be, abortive, maladaptive, wasteful and stupid.

It by no means follows from the foregoing, however, that ideo-motor action is really maladaptive. On the contrary the view is here put forward that ideo-motor reactions and anticipatory goal reactions in general are really guiding and directing pure-stimulus acts and as such perform the enormously important functions ordinarily attributed to ideas. Considered merely as acts they are negligible; as pure-stimulus acts and sources of stimuli to control other action, they at once take on the very greatest importance. While indubitably physical they occupy at the same time the very citadel of the mental. The classical view was that a non-physical idea of an act preceded the act and somehow commanded the energy to evoke it, such act in consequence being called ideo-motor. In contrast to that view, the hypothesis here put forward is (1) that ideo-motor acts are in reality anticipatory goal reactions and, as such, are called into existence by ordinary physical stimulation; and (2) that these anticipatory goal reactions are pure-stimulus acts and, as such, guide and direct the more explicit and instrumental activities of the organism. In short, ideo-motor acts, instead of being *evoked* by ideas, *are* ideas. Thus the position of the classical psychology in this field is completely inverted.

Healthy individuals, uncontaminated by psychological and metaphysical theory, generally have quite simply and naturally held that ideas were dynamic—that somehow they exert a physical control over instrumental activity. The prevailing metaphysics, with its roots far back in the unscientific past, has insisted that ideas are not physical. The combination of the two points of view produced the logical absurdity of hypothesizing a physical interaction where one of the two entities involved was non-physical. Among other difficulties, such an interaction found itself in direct conflict with the principle of the conservation of energy. The present hypothesis, according to which the idea [13] is physical and at the same time an action and a stimulus, completely dissolves this logical absurdity, opens the door for an objective study of ideas, and offers a legitimate and unambiguous status for them in science.

But granting, for the sake of argument, that a non-physical idea could somehow evoke physical movements, there still remains the fundamental question of how, in detail, such an idea could evoke the particular actions which would be necessary to lead to a particular goal even in the relatively simple situations considered above. Schools of psychology dominated by metaphysical idealism have been peculiarly insistent upon the obligation of physical psychological theories to explain the guidance or control of action by ideas. The fact that the mentalists themselves have not been able to do this seems hardly to have been noticed, either by themselves or anyone else. Possibly in a system already filled with the incredible an additional incredibility attracts little notice. The fact remains that there exists no magic which absolves *any* system which purports to give a thoroughgoing account of human nature from the obligation of showing how purposive ideas [14] are able automatically to guide and direct action to the realization of a goal or reward. The problem is admittedly a difficult one. However, considerations already put forward in this paper furnish some grounds for optimism concerning its final solution on a strictly physical basis. At any rate the challenge is accepted.

PAPER
4

[13] It is not to be understood that the anticipatory goal reaction is the only physical basis for what have in the past been called ideas. There certainly are some others and probably a good many others, particularly with human subjects. What was lumped together by the classical psychologists as a single thing is turning out to include a number of fairly distinct things. Thus the old terminology becomes inadequate for modern needs.

[14] In a previous paper purpose was tentatively identified with the drive stimulus (S_D). Upon more mature consideration the writer is inclined to revise this judgment in favor of the goal stimulus (s_G), largely on the ground that the latter stimulus both represents the goal and provides the more intimate mechanism of its attainment, even though the goal stimulus is ultimately dependent for its existence upon the drive.

VII

We may now briefly summarize the results of our discussion:

The drive stimulus accounts very well for the random seeking reactions of a hungry organism, but alone it is not sufficient to produce the integration of complex behavior sequences such as is involved in maze learning. There must always be a reward of some kind. Once the reward has been given, however, the behavior undergoes a marked change most definitely characterized by evidences of actions anticipatory of the goal, which actions tend to appear as accompaniments to the sequence ordinarily leading to the full overt goal reaction.

It is shown how these fractional anticipatory goal reactions could be drawn to the beginning of the behavior sequence and maintained throughout it by the action of the drive stimulus (S_D). The kinaesthetic stimulus resulting from this persistent anticipatory action should furnish a second stimulus (s_G) which would persist very much like S_D. These two persisting stimuli alike should have the capacity of forming multiple excitatory tendencies to the evocation of every reaction within the sequence. They should differ, however, in that the anticipatory goal reaction stimulus would be dependent for its existence upon the integrity of the drive stimulus. A second difference is that a single drive stimulus may generate many distinct goal stimuli.

The general *a priori* probability of the existence of the goal stimulus finds confirmation in the fact that it affords a plausible explanation of a class of experimentally observed facts hitherto inexplicable. It enables us to understand, for example, why withholding the usual reward at the end of an accustomed maze run will cause a disintegration of that particular habit sequence while leaving the organism free to pursue alternative sequences based on the same drive. It offers an explanation of why, during a maze learning process, the substitution of one reward for another presumably of about the same attractiveness should produce a transitory slump in the learning scores. It throws light on why an animal evidently motivated by the anticipation of one kind of

PAPER
4

food will leave untouched a different but otherwise acceptable type of food which has been surreptitiously substituted. There is reason to believe that as the experimental literature on the motivating influence of rewards increases the goal stimulus mechanism will find enlarged application.

Moreover, there is strong reason for believing that the fractional anticipatory goal reaction is the actual basis of what has long been known as ideo-motor action. This latter phenomenon emerges from the analysis as a dynamic mechanism, a pure-stimulus act, rather than an end product as was formerly supposed. This means that ideo-motor acts are not caused by ideas. On the contrary, they are themselves ideas. It has long been recognized that one of the prime functions of ideas is to guide and control instrumental acts in cases where the situation to which the acts really function is absent and, as a consequence, is unable to stimulate the organism directly. The capacity of anticipatory goal reactions as stimuli to control and direct other activity renders intelligible on a purely physical basis the dynamic guiding power of ideas. This, in turn, makes still more plausible the hypothesis that anticipatory goal reactions are the physical substance of purposive ideas.

PAPER
4

For the sake of definiteness and additional clarity the hypotheses elaborated above may be assembled in brief dogmatic form: Pure-stimulus acts are the physical substance of ideas. Ideas, however, are of many varieties. Among them are goal or guiding ideas. The physical mechanism constituting these particular ideas is the anticipatory goal reaction. This appears to be substantially the same as ideo-motor action. The anticipatory goal reaction seems also to constitute the physical basis of the somewhat ill-defined but important concept of purpose, desire, or wish, rather than the drive stimulus as has sometimes been supposed, notably by Kampf. This interpretation of purpose explains its dynamic nature and at the same time removes the paradox arising under the classical psychology where the future appeared to be operating causally in a backward direction upon the present. This hypothesis also renders intelligible the 'realization of an anticipation' by an organism. It is found in situations where a fractional anticipatory goal reaction as a stimulus has motivated a behavior sequence which culminates in a full overt enactment of a goal-behavior complex of which it is a physical component.

[MS. received March 25, 1931]

Offprinted from PSYCHOLOGICAL REVIEW, Vol. 39, No. 1, Jan., 1932

THE GOAL GRADIENT HYPOTHESIS AND MAZE LEARNING

BY CLARK L. HULL

Yale University

One of the most persistently baffling problems which confronts modern psychologists is the finding of an adequate explanation of the phenomena of maze learning. The writers in this field a generation ago seem to have regarded it as a relatively simple process. This view is rapidly losing ground. It is now quite generally agreed by those familiar with the experimental literature on the subject that the process is in reality an exceedingly complex one, that it differs in important respects from the numerous other forms of trial-and-error learning, and that no mere chain-reaction hypothesis alone is adequate to account for the various known facts. The revolt against the over-simple view continues, nevertheless, to motivate a great deal of experimental work. This has, for the most part, been conducted with animals, usually rats. Upon the whole, this work has been admirably conceived and the results have a significance far beyond the negative one of disproving the efficacy of the law of frequency as a sole explanatory principle. It is noteworthy, however, that writers in this field have been conspicuously more successful in disproving the explanatory potency of hypotheses of the early Watsonian type than in devising more adequate formulæ. Meanwhile the steady accumulation of well authenticated maze-learning phenomena, all demanding explanation by any thoroughgoing explanatory hypothesis, is making the task constantly more insistent and at the same time more complex and difficult. These problems present two major aspects, each dependent upon a fairly distinct mechanism. It is believed that the *modus operandi* of the two mechanisms is sufficiently distinct to make separate treatment desirable.

The mechanism which in the present paper will be mainly depended upon as an explanatory and integrating principle is

PAPER
5

25

that the goal reaction gets conditioned the most strongly to the stimuli preceding it, and the other reactions of the behavior sequence get conditioned to their stimuli progressively weaker as they are more remote (in time or space) from the goal reaction.   This principle is clearly that of a gradient, and the gradient is evidently somehow related to the goal.[1]   We shall accordingly call it the *goal gradient hypothesis.*

I

One of the simplest and at the same time most illuminating experiments in maze learning is one which presents the animal with two alternative paths from the starting point to the food box.   At first the rat will take one or the other path, more or less at random.   In case one of these paths is distinctly longer than the other, however, the animal will gradually come to choose the shorter path.[2]

PAPER 5In order to consider the theoretical aspects of the situation, let it be supposed that a hungry albino rat has been released at (S) in the maze shown in Fig. 1.   He has found his way to

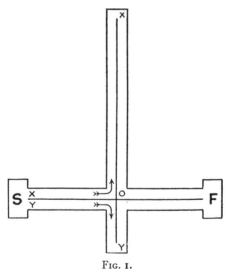

Fig. 1.

[1] This principle has been used to advantage by Washburn in the development of the theory of learning presented in the third edition of The animal mind (1926).   See especially p. 329 ff.

[2] J. E. DeCamp, Relative distance as a factor in the white rat's selection of a path, *Psychobiology*, 1920, 2, p. 245.

the food (F) an equal number of times by the long path (X) and the short path (Y). For convenience we shall divide these paths up into sections of equal length, the X-path totaling six units in length, and the Y-path, three.

The stimulus-response dynamics of this situation at a fairly advanced stage of practice is conceived to be as represented in Fig. 2 for paths X and Y separately. The upper

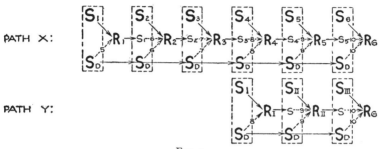

PATH X:

PATH Y:

FIG. 2.

PAPER
5

series of S's in each sequence represents the external stimulation. The R's represent the responses by the organism. The s's represent proprioceptive stimulations resulting from these movements and the S_D's represent the persisting or drive stimulus. The dotted rectangles represent redintegrative stimulus complexes. It will particularly be noted that the respective sequences, in addition to possessing a common drive stimulus, are also alike in possessing a common beginning and a common ending; the former, however, being a *stimulus* and the latter a *reaction*.

The dotted arrows extending from the s's and the S_D's indicate excitatory tendencies acquired through the process of association or conditioning. At this point enters the principle of the goal gradient according to which these acquired tendencies leading to the goal reaction are strongest, and are progressively weaker to reactions more and more remote from the goal. In this connection a very simple gradient has been assumed—that the excitatory tendency to the R_G at some advanced stage of training is ten units, and that at each step removed from the goal the strength of the excitatory tendency is diminished by one unit. These values have been placed

3

on the lines representing the excitatory tendencies in Fig. 2. Presumably this gradient is operating on all the acquired excitatory tendencies. In the interest of simplicity of exposition, however, only those values emanating from the drive stimulus will be discussed in the following pages.

From an inspection of this figure it is easy to see that the choice of the shorter of the two paths must follow. The stimulus leading to the alternative responses at the outset being the same, the issue as to which path will be chosen must depend upon the relative strengths of the divergent excitatory tendencies, the one to the first act of the X path (R_1), and the other to the first act of the Y path (R_I). The strength of the tendency to the former is 5 units, whereas that to the latter is 8 units. Evidently R_I must take place rather than R_1. The principle of the goal gradient thus clearly generates the preferential choice of the shorter of two alternate paths to a goal. In this important sense the former may be said to explain the latter.

PAPER

5

II

In the preceding discussion of the choice of the shorter path, as well as in two previously published studies involving rather distinct aspects of adaptive behavior, the concept of the goal gradient has been utilized in its simplest possible form, *i.e.*, as a uniform slope. This type of gradient is shown diagrammatically in Fig. 3. Because of its simplicity it is

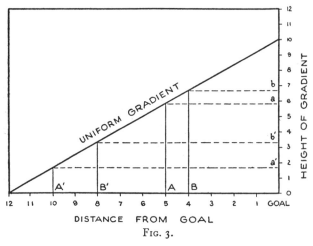

FIG. 3.

admirably adapted to the needs of exposition. Moreover, where only very elementary results were to be deduced from the principle, such as the short-circuiting of pure-stimulus act sequences,[3] the evolution of goal attraction motor mechanisms [4] and the choice of the shorter of alternative paths in the maze, an excitation gradient sloping generally upward in the direction of the goal was all that the situation required. But with the attempt to utilize the principle for the explanation of the finer and more exact details of adaptive behavior there comes the necessity of inquiring rather specifically into the mathematical characteristics of this slope. The method to be followed will be to determine which of various conceivable slopes is required to generate the phenomena revealed by one of the best, and, from the present point of view, one of the most exacting of recent maze investigations.[5] Having determined the nature of the gradient in this manner, various behavioral phenomena of maze learning will be deduced from it, some of them known from experiments already performed, some of them not as yet submitted to experiment. In the former case the hypothesis will appear in the rôle of an explanatory principle in the most significant meaning of the term. In the latter it will serve as the basis for prediction.

Yoshioka's excellent experiment furnishes evidence peculiarly adapted to give us at least a first approximation to the curve of the goal gradient. He ran rats on two mazes of the alternate-pathway type represented by Fig. 1. One maze was exactly twice as large as the other as regards the length of the pathways, the standard path in the smaller measuring 211 inches in length, whereas the corresponding path of the larger maze measured 422 inches. The second alley of each maze was so constructed that it could be shortened at will. The problem was to determine the ease of discrimination by the rats of various absolute and relative amounts of difference

[3] C. L. Hull, Knowledge and purpose as habit mechanisms, PSYCHOL. REV., 1930, 37, 511–525.

[4] C. L. Hull, Goal attraction and directing ideas conceived as habit phenomena, PSYCHOL. REV., 1931, 38, 487–506.

[5] J. G. Yoshioka, Weber's law in the discrimination of maze distance by the white rat, *Univ. of Calif. Publications in Psychol.*, 1929, 4, 155–184.

between the alternate pathways. Groups of 20 rats were run on each of five different settings of each of the two mazes, nearly 200 animals in all being used. The *relative* length of the long alternative to the short one at each of the five settings was the same for both mazes, the ratios being: 1.07, 1.14, 1.23, 1.33, and 1.44. The *absolute* differences between alternate paths were, of course, twice as great in the large as the small maze. Within the range explored by Yoshioka the results show a very definite tendency for the discrimination of equal ratios to be equally difficult, regardless of the absolute amount of difference between the lengths of the paths being compared. Thus the small maze, with a difference between alternative pathways of 65 inches, gives almost exactly the same mean discrimination score as the long maze with a difference between its paths of 130 inches.

PAPER
5

The implication of these results as to the shape of the goal gradient may be best appreciated by first considering what results might be expected from an experiment of the Yoshioka type, with various assumed gradients. A preliminary analysis of the shapes a goal gradient might conceivably take reveals three typical ones. The first is the uniform slope represented by the straight line and already discussed. The second is a curve of negative acceleration, the increase in the excitatory tendencies being more rapid at the beginning of the sequence and growing less and less as the goal is approached. The third is a curve of positive acceleration in which the increase in the excitatory tendency is relatively slight at the outset of the behavior sequence, but grows progressively greater as the goal is approached.

The situation as regards the uniform gradient is represented in Fig. 3. Let us suppose that the standard path in the small maze is 5 units long, and in the large one it is 10 units long. Suppose, further, that the alternative path in the long maze is 8 units long, and in the short one it is 4 units long. The difference in length between the alternative paths of the large maze is two units, and between those of the small one it is one unit. Turning to Fig. 3 it will be seen at once that the difference between the stimulus gradients (projected by means of

TABLE I

	Small maze	Large maze
Standard path...................	5 units long	10 units long
Comparison path.................	4 units long	8 units long
Difference in excitation gradient.....	1 unit	2 units

the broken lines upon the scale at the right) in the first case is twice as great as in the second. Since it is assumed that the degree of the preference for the shorter path is based upon the absolute difference in the excitatory gradient between the two alternatives, a straight-line goal gradient would produce a much more ready discrimination in the long maze than in the short one. This, we have seen, is contrary to Yoshioka's results. These demand equal discrimination in our supposi-tional situation, since the differences in distance are propor-tional (1/5) in both cases. Clearly the evidence does not point to a goal gradient of uniform slope.

We may inquire, secondly, what might be expected if the gradient were one of negative acceleration, such as that shown in Fig. 4. As before, we measure off on the base line values of

PAPER
5

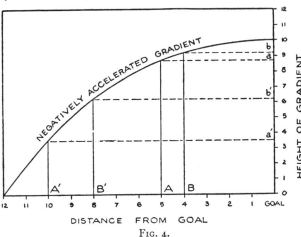

DISTANCE FROM GOAL

FIG. 4.

5 and 4 units for the short maze, and of 10 and 8 units for the long maze, and then erect a perpendicular from each point so as to locate the excitatory tendency to the choice of each at the entrance to the respective pairs of paths. We then project these gradient values by means of broken lines upon

the scale at the right.   Inspection of the figure shows that the gradient difference in favor of discrimination of the long pair is about three times as great as for the short pair.   This is in even more violent disagreement with Yoshioka's results than the corresponding implications from assuming the uniform gradient of Fig. 3.

By a process of elimination we thus arrive at the tentative conclusion that the goal gradient must have a positive acceleration.   There remains, however, the question of determining the exact nature of this type of acceleration.   Mathematicians have devised and studied a great variety of plane curves and curved figures, certain portions of which satisfy equally well the rather inexact requirement of manifesting positive acceleration.   There are, for example, the circle, the elipse, the

TABLE 2

PAPER
5

This table shows the strength of the excitatory tendency of the drive stimulus to evoke reactions habitually taking place at different unit distances from the goal reaction, on the hypothesis that the goal reaction has a strength of ten points and that the strength of the excitatory tendency to the remaining reactions diminishes progressively with remoteness from the goal according to the logarithmic principle.

Units distant from goal	Strength of excitatory tendency	Units distant from goal	Strength of excitatory tendency
1	10.000	26	1.903
2	8.277	27	1.809
3	7.270	28	1.718
4	6.554	29	1.631
5	6.000	30	1.547
6	5.547	31	1.465
7	5.164	32	1.386
8	4.831	33	1.310
9	4.539	34	1.236
10	4.277	35	1.164
11	4.040	36	1.094
12	3.824	37	1.026
13	3.625	38	.959
14	3.441	39	.895
15	3.270	40	.832
16	3.109	41	.771
17	2.958	42	.711
18	2.816	43	.652
19	2.682	44	.595
20	2.554	45	.539
21	2.433	46	.484
22	2.317	47	.431
23	2.207	48	.379
24	2.101	49	.327
25	2.000	50	.277

parabola, the hyperbola, the cardoid, the logarithmic curve, the cissoid, the witch, the conchoid, the lemniscata, the sine curve, the cycloid, and the various spirals, to mention but a few. It remains to select that curve which will, so long as the relative difference between the longer and the shorter of alternate paths to a goal remains constant, and regardless of their absolute difference, yield the same excitatory difference.

These conditions are, as a matter of fact, satisfied by the logarithmic curve, quite as the tradition associated with Weber's law prepares us to expect. A series of values based on the logarithmic principle and adapted to the present situation are given in Table 2. These values have been plotted accurately, and appear in Fig. 5. Just as with the two previous gradients considered, the 5- and the 10-unit

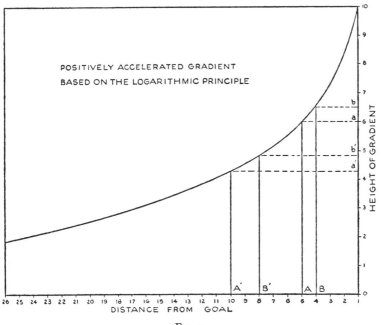

PAPER

5

FIG. 5.

discrimination problem has been projected upon this logarithmic curve. Inspection. of the diagram shows that the difference in excitatory tendency at the beginning of each pair of paths is sensibly the same. Reference to Table 2 yields numerical values to the same end. These are summarized in Table 3. Yoshioka's experiment thus indicates that the goal

TABLE 3.

	Small maze	Large maze
Long path excitatory strength	6.554	4.831
Short path excitatory strength	6.00	4.277
Gradient difference	.554	.554

gradient of excitation in maze learning of the rat is one of positive acceleration and that it conforms very closely to the logarithmic law.

A corollary deducible immediately from Table 2 is that *the smaller the relative difference between two alternative mazes, the more difficult will be the discrimination.* Thus, in the case of the 10-unit maze just considered, a difference of one unit or one-tenth yields a gradient difference of .262 point, whereas a coarser one of two units, or one-fifth, yields the larger excitation difference of .554 point. The general *a priori* probability of such an issue as deduced from the above table is fully substantiated by Yoshioka's experimental results. He found that with a constant standard alley of 211 inches, a difference of 65 inches yielded a discrimination value of 18.85, one of 52 inches yielded a discrimination value of 17.65, 39 inches yielded 14.74, 26 inches yielded 11.89, and 13 inches yielded 10.80. Upon this basis we venture the fundamental generalization that *the larger the gradient difference between two alternative tendencies, the more perfect the preferential differentiation; whereas the smaller the gradient difference, the less perfect will be the differentiation.*

PAPER
5

III

We may now proceed to the consideration of the problem of the elimination of blind alleys from the final path in maze learning. In general the operation of the goal gradient mechanism presents the elimination of blind alleys as a special case of the preference for the shorter path. At any point in the maze, as point *B* in Fig. 6, the animal has the choice of (1) proceeding directly to the food at *F*, or (2) going down the blind to *B'*, back to *B*, and then down to *F*. Clearly the direct path is the shorter. Other things equal, it follows at once from the theorem developed in the preceding section that in the competition between the two paths, the one including the blind alley must be eliminated.

The conclusion thus arrived at on general principles may be demonstrated quantitatively. In the maze of Fig. 6, the blinds and the intervals between blinds are assumed all to be of equal traversing length. The distance between blinds will

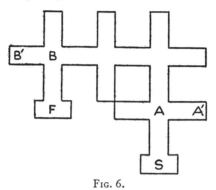

Fig. 6.

PAPER

5

accordingly be taken as the unit of space traversed. Thus it is one unit from *B* directly to *F*. If, however, the animal goes from *B* to *B'*, then back to *B*, and finally to *F*, the distance traversed will be approximately three units. Referring to Table 2 we find that the goal gradient or excitatory tendency to acts leading directly to *F* has a value of 10.00 points, whereas the excitatory tendency leading to acts which are the beginning of a different behavior sequence and one three units distant from the goal is 7.270 points. In this conflict of excitatory tendencies, the one leading to the direct path is obviously prepotent with an excitatory margin of 2.730 points. Thus will the blind alley be eliminated.

In a similar manner it may be shown that in so far as this particular mechanism is operative a long blind alley will be eliminated more readily than a short one. Suppose for example, that blind *B'* were two units in length instead, of the one unit as shown in Fig. 6. To traverse this 2-unit blind on the way to the goal would add four units to the one unit of the true path, making five in all. The gradient

value for one unit is 10.000; that for five units is 6.000. There
is accordingly available for the elimination of the 2-unit blind
4 gradient points, as against the 2.730 points for a 1-unit
blind. The greater gradient difference should produce a
more ready elimination of the long blind.

The above deductions, while not necessarily demanding
that the animal shall have as many cases of going directly to
the food as of reaching it by way of the blind at B', may
possibly demand that the number of occasions of entering the
blind shall not exceed the number of direct runs by an amount
more than equivalent to the 2.730 points of natural goal
gradient advantage of the direct path. In this connection it
may be pointed out that there appears to be some mechanism
within the rat's organism which makes for spontaneous variability of response, and which thus tends to insure the rather
full exploration of all possibilities until definite conditioned
excitatory tendencies get set up which are strong enough to
over-ride the spontaneous tendency to variability. Fortunately the bulk of this spontaneous variability of reaction
precedes the setting up of the excitatory tendencies, at which
time it should produce a fairly equal distribution of practice.
This should enable the goal gradient principle to play an important rôle in bringing about the elimination of the blind
alleys.

There is good evidence that if by special experimental
means the animal were induced to go into the wrong alley a
quite disproportionate number of times, the blind would still
be eliminated.[6] It is believed that at this point a second
principle of considerable importance enters, which may be
called provisionally the principle of habit families, or preferential hierarchies. This principle is a kind of second order
phenomenon, being itself dependent upon the goal gradient
and the resultant preference for the shorter path. A number
of hitherto puzzling maze phenomena appear to be explained
by it. This is the second of the two major aspects of maze
learning mentioned in the introduction to the present paper.
Space is here lacking for further elaboration of the principle.

[6] J. A. Gengerelli, Preliminary experiments on the causal factors in animal learning,
J. Comp. Psychol., 1928, **8**, 1–23.

IV

We may now inquire the significance of the goal gradient hypothesis as regards the order of elimination of blinds in maze learning. The implication for the rat is very clear. In so far as this principle is operating it should produce an elimination of blinds first at the goal and then progressively backward towards the beginning of the maze. Consider, for example, the relative margin of excitatory strength furnished by the goal gradient for the elimination of blind alley A' at the beginning of the maze (Fig. 6) as compared with blind alley B' near the goal and already considered. Point A is 4 units distant from F by the direct path, whereas it is 6 units distant by way of A'. Referring to Table 2 we find that the excitatory tendency to movements in a sequence 4 units distant from the goal is 6.554 points, whereas that 6 units distant is 5.547 points, a gradient difference available for blind elimination of 1.007 points. We have already seen in the last section that the gradient advantage available for elimination of blind B' was 2.730, or over twice as much. Clearly other things equal, B' at the goal should be eliminated more readily than A' at the beginning of the maze. By means of Table 2, anyone interested may easily verify this principle with other values. The goal gradient hypothesis clearly operates in the direction of the backward elimination of blinds in maze learning.

By a simple extension of the above reasoning, there may also be deduced from the principle of the goal gradient the well-known fact that long mazes in general require more repetitions to learn than do short ones. Thus in Table 2 the difference in gradient made by entering a blind at the beginning of a maze is 2.730 points, at ten units from the goal it is .453, at twenty units from the goal it is .237 point, at fifty units from the goal it shrinks to .098 point. It is likely that for any given organism there is a gradient threshold below which the gradient difference corresponding to a blind alley may not fall if the blind is to be eliminated. This amounts to a deduction from the principle of the goal gradient that a maze may be too long to be learned at all.

PAPER

5

A further extension of the above reasoning is that the steeper the goal gradient the more rapid the process of elimination, whereas the flatter the gradient the slower the elimination of errors. At the outset of the learning process the entire gradient is of course uniformly flat. The basic part of the learning process would seem to be the rise of the excitatory gradient. It should be possible to deduce the curve of the rise of this function with continued practice from the joint consideration of the nature of the mathematical characteristics of the goal gradient and the rate of elimination of blinds at the different stages of practice. Once the characteristics of the curve of acquisition of the goal gradient has been determined, numerous new relations may be deduced which will open the way for still further experimental testing of the hypothesis, with resulting additions to our knowledge of the learning process.

V

PAPER

5

Just as in Section II we had occasion to inquire the implication of the three type gradients upon alternate maze-path discrimination, so now we may ask a similar question regarding the implication of the two types not yet considered as to the order of blind alley elimination. The answer is quite clear and unambiguous. A glance at the uniform gradient of Fig. 3 shows by simple inspection that for constant differences in the length of the maze path there will be equal amounts of excitation difference at all points of the maze. This means that blind alleys at one point will be eliminated, so far as the goal gradient is concerned, exactly as easily as at any other point. The curve of negative acceleration, however, presents a somewhat more interesting situation. An inspection of Fig. 4 shows at a glance that by this principle the nearer to the beginning of a maze, the greater the difference in goal gradient for a given distance traversed and, hence, the more readily will blind alleys be eliminated. In a word, *a negatively accelerated goal gradient should produce elimination of errors in a forward order.*

Two major combinations of the positively and negatively accelerated gradients are conceivable. One case would be where the gradient begins as a positively accelerated curve but at some point in the sequence passes over into a negatively accelerated gradient. Such a combination gradient would produce the curious result of most rapid learning at some place in the midst of the maze and the slowest learning at the two ends. No such learning as this seems to have been reported.

The opposite combination would be a gradient beginning with a negative acceleration but reversing in the midst of the maze and finishing as positive acceleration. Such a gradient is shown in Fig. 7. This combination gives progressive elimin-

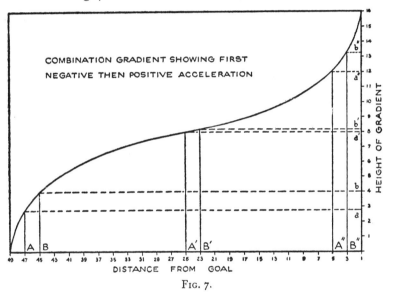

PAPER
5

Fig. 7.

ation from both ends toward the interior with the slowest elimination at the point of inflection between the two types of acceleration. Thus the gradient difference for the elimination of blinds at *AB* and *A″B″* is greater than at *A′B′*. This second acceleration combination is of special interest because it would generate what is believed by some to be the typical order of blind alley elimination of humans as contrasted with lower forms. If this should turn out to be true the interesting possibility would emerge that the basic type of gradient would be a combination one with the higher forms having the

inflection far up towards the goal, whereas lower forms
would find their inflection progressively nearer the beginning,
the rat in this respect possibly representing a limiting case.
This combination gradient presents numerous intriguing
implications as to learning phenomena, which can not be
entered into at this time.

VI

There remains to be considered one of the most interesting
of all the implications of the goal gradient hypothesis—the
rate of locomotion through the different portions of the maze.
Since in the ordinary maze the rate of locomotion is complicated by conflicts between two competing gradient tendencies
which result in such irrelevancies as blind alley elimination in
a characteristic order, such mazes are hardly suitable for
testing the principle under consideration. The simplest case
is where the animal is running from one end to the other of a
long straight alley with food at the termination of the run.
Under such conditions, since according to the goal gradient
hypothesis the excitatory tendencies are progressively stronger
as the goal is approached and since response is more vigorous
and rapid with increased stimulation, it is reasonable to suppose that the animal would show a progressively more rapid
rate of locomotion from the start to the finish of the run.   In
other words, if there is a well-marked stimulus gradient from
the beginning of the maze to the goal, there should be a speed-
of-locomotion gradient in some sense paralleling it throughout.
This matter is of sufficient theoretical significance to be well
worth an attempt at verification. A straight alley forty or
fifty feet long with provision for the automatic recording of
the moment at which the animal passes each of a half dozen
points located at uniform distances through its length, should
suffice as a basic apparatus.

A second test of the goal gradient hypothesis from the
angle of the speed of locomotion is found in the relative rate
at which animals move in the early portions of alternative-
pathway mazes such as that shown in Fig. 1.   Place easily
visible doors at the entrance to paths X and Y.   In the experiment let one door be closed and the other open.   Determine

PAPER
5

the length of time required by the animal to pass from S to the entrance of alleys X and Y respectively.   Since, according to the goal gradient hypothesis, the strength of excitation to action is less on the longer path, we should expect a perceptibly slower pace from S to the entrace of X than from S to the entrance of Y.   In a similar manner the time required for the animal to traverse the length of the first straight section of paths X and Y respectively could be determined experimentally.   Here again, the goal gradient hypothesis demands that the speed of locomotion in the first section of path X should be slower than in the parallel section of path Y.

By way of contrast, a similar determination could be made for the final parallel sections of the two paths.   Here, since each is the same distance from the goal, the gradient should be the same for both paths.   The hypothesis accordingly demands that the speed on both paths should be approximately the same, except as it might be influenced by possible warming- up, fatigue, and similar effects.

Finally there may be considered the influence on the speed of locomotion produced by the conflict of the excitatory tendencies where a blind alley is in process of being eliminated in favor of the direct path.   In this connection we may recall the values involved in the competition which resulted in the elimination of blind alley A' of the maze represented in Fig. 6. We saw that at point A there came to be an excitatory tendency of 5.547 points strength to movements in the direction of A', whereas the excitatory tendency to going straight ahead on the direct path amounts to 6.554 points.   Clearly if these two tendencies were equal and no other factor of importance were involved, they would neutralize each other and there would be no action, i.e., the animal would pause at A, the point of choice.

In a more advanced stage of the evolution of the goal gradient (learning), where the gradient difference between the alternative tendencies has risen above the response threshold, it is reasonable to expect that the speed of locomotion at point A will be perceptibly reduced.   If the two competing tendencies are positive quantities and fairly equal in size, the

CLARK L. HULL

difference between them available for motivation must be smaller than either. And since speed and amplitude of response is a function of the strength of the stimulus, there should be at first a tendency to slow down in the speed of locomotion as the animal passes the entrance of a blind alley previously eliminated.

VII

We may now survey the results of our inquiry. From the hypothesis that there exists an excitatory gradient extending with positive acceleration approximately according to the logarithmic law in an upward direction from the beginning of a maze to the reward box, there may be deduced the following principles of behavior:

1. That the animal will tend to choose the shorter of two alternative paths to a goal.

2. That the greater the difference between the length of the paths (the standard path remaining constant), the more readily will the shorter path be chosen.

3. That the readiness of choosing the shorter path will not be affected by the absolute difference between the alternates, provided the paths to be discriminated maintain a constant ratio to each other. (Weber's law.)

4. That animals will come to choose the direct path to a goal rather than enter blind alleys.

5. That long blinds will be more readily eliminated than short ones.

6. That the order of elimination of blind alleys will tend to be in the backward direction.

7. That long mazes will be learned with greater difficulty than short ones.

8. That animals in traversing a maze will move at a progressively more rapid pace as the goal is approached.

9. That of two alternative paths to a common goal the animal will traverse the early section of the shorter path at a faster rate than that of the parallel section of the longer one.

10. That the final parallel sections of two alternate paths each of different length leading to a common goal will be traversed at approximately equal speed.

11. That animals after having eliminated a blind will tend to pause at its entrance while pursuing the shorter path.

To this list there may be added from previously published studies the deductions:

12. That under certain circumstances segments of pure-stimulus-act sequences will drop out, producing what is known as 'short-circuiting.'

13. That fragments of goal reactions will tend to intrude into instrumental act sequences, producing the phenomenon of ideo-motor action and directive or guiding ideas.

The fact that it has been possible to deduce ten or so important behavior phenomena from a single hypothesis can scarcely be due to chance. It is hardly accidental that a single principle should be able to explain in the above deductive sense, and thus to integrate, such diverse phenomena as the choice of the shorter path, Weber's law, the elimination of blind alleys, the order of their elimination, the rate of locomotion through the different portions of a maze, the short-circuiting of symbolic-act sequences, and the origin of ideo-motor action. It encourages the belief that the science of mammalian behavior may be entering an era of systematic development more nearly comparable with that of the older, more exact, and more fully systematized sciences.

[MS. received June 15, 1931]

PAPER
5

Offprinted from PSYCHOLOGICAL REVIEW, Vol. 41, No. 1, Jan., 1934

THE CONCEPT OF THE HABIT–FAMILY HIER-
ARCHY AND MAZE LEARNING:[1]
PART I

BY CLARK L. HULL

Yale University

I. The Principles of Divergent and of Convergent Associative Tendencies

Our conception of habit is necessarily expanded with the increase in our comprehension of its phenomena. Instead of presenting a single unvarying and indistinguishable sameness, as is too often assumed, habits, even to our present meager knowledge, present a remarkably varied series of patterns. In this multiplicity it is possible, from the point of view of the present paper, to distinguish two major types. One type is characterized by a fan-like series of divergent excitatory tendencies radiating from a single stimulus, each leading to a distinct reaction. This type will be called the *divergent* mechanism. The other is characterized by the convergence of a number of excitatory tendencies from separate

PAPER

6

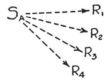

FIG. 1. The divergent excitatory mechanism. Ordinarily the different tendencies will be of widely varied strength.

stimuli, all upon a single response. The second type will consequently be called the *convergent* mechanism. The divergent mechanism is represented diagrammatically in Fig. 1,

[1] The substance of the major portion of the material contained in this paper has been used as a bound manuscript in certain of the writer's classes since June, 1931. During that time the author has received many valuable criticisms and suggestions from his students. Those of Dr. Kenneth W. Spence and of Mr. Neal E. Miller have been particularly valuable.

33

the convergent mechanism, in Fig. 2 (**13**).   In these diagrams and those to follow, the S's represent stimuli and the R's represent responses.   Arrows with broken lines indicate acquired tendencies to action; arrows with solid lines indicate unlearned tendencies to action.

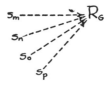

FIG. 2.   The convergent excitatory mechanism.

As might readily be anticipated from the sharpness of the contrast between these two stimulus-response mechanisms, the functions performed by each in mediating adaptive behavior are characteristically distinct.   Compound habit mechanisms have not been sufficiently studied from the present point of view to warrant any ultimate or comprehensive statement regarding the functional dynamics of either of the types. It is clear, however, that the first or divergent mechanism, in case the several radiating excitatory tendencies within it are antagonistic (incompatible with one another in the sense that they cannot be executed by the organism simultaneously) will give rise to a competition among themselves.   This identifies the mechanism at once as the basic one responsible for the variability of response in trial-and-error learning (**13**). When originating in the drive stimulus (S_D), this mechanism also appears to bring about the intra-serial competition which is responsible for the serial segment elimination or 'short-circuiting' characteristic of pure-stimulus or symbolic act sequences (**14**).   Much the same mechanism seems also to be responsible for anticipatory intrusions (**22, 23**), particularly of the fractional component of the anticipatory goal reaction which has been supposed to bring about the phenomenon of ideomotor action and its tremendously important functional correlate, guiding or directive ideas (**15**).   No doubt other and equally important functions performed by this mechanism are yet to be discovered.

The second or convergent type of compound excitatory tendency clearly presents as a primary characteristic a response equivalence of the various stimuli involved; S_m, S_n, S_o, etc., are all functionally equivalent in that all alike evoke R_G. The functional dynamics of this mechanism have been studied even less than have those of the divergent mechanism, but it is believed that they have far-reaching implications for the explanation of the more subtle forms of mammalian adjustment. In particular there is reason to believe that functional equivalence of stimuli plays an important rôle in bringing it about that habits established under certain stimulus conditions will function with little or no delay in new situations having nothing whatever as *objective* stimuli in common with the conditions under which the habit was originally formed.

This capacity to react appropriately to wholly new stimulus situations is of enormous biological importance because it not only saves the organism the labor of learning by trial and error to react to each new situation as it arises, but, in cases of danger where prompt and appropriate defense reactions are needed, it may make the difference between continued life and sudden death. In many such cases practice of the ordinary trial-and-error variety would be maladaptive because even one error might be fatal. This particular mechanism has an added theoretical interest because certain writers (**19**, **170**) [2] seem to have supposed that the types of behavior mediated by it are quite impossible of explanation by any principle of association or habit action.

PAPER
6

II. ASSOCIATIVE CONVERGENCE A MECHANISM OF AUTOMATIC HABIT TRANSFER

The power of the convergent mechanism to mediate transfer of reaction from one situation to a second which, *objectively* considered, may be totally different, is not difficult to show. Suppose that after the formation of the excitatory tendencies shown in Fig. 2, the combination $S_m \rightarrow R_G$ has been extended by conditioning or otherwise into a sequence

[2] Throughout this paper, numbers in bold-face type refer to items in the list of references; the associated numbers refer to pages of publications cited.

(Fig. 3) which eventuates in the terminal defense reaction R_x. Now suppose, after this has taken place, that the organism is stimulated by S_p. The sequence which would be expected to follow on the principle of ordinary habit activity is shown diagrammatically in Fig. 4. By Fig. 2, S_p must give rise to

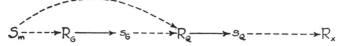

FIG. 3.   A chain reaction formed by extending one of the convergent excitatory tendencies shown in Fig. 2.

R_G and this, in turn, to s_G. But since s_G has been conditioned to R_Q, the chain of reactions leading to R_Q will be initiated much as in Fig. 3, with the result that S_p, even though never associated with it, will bring about the terminal reaction R_x. There will be the difference, however, that R_Q will not have the support of the remote excitatory tendency from S_m (**14**, 519) which it had in the original sequence (Fig. 3).[3]

PAPER
6

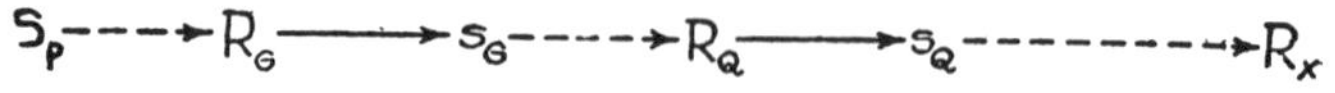

$$S_P\text{---}\!\!\!\rightarrow R_G \longrightarrow s_G\text{----}\!\!\!\rightarrow R_Q \longrightarrow s_Q\text{-------}\!\!\!\rightarrow R_x$$

FIG. 4.   Diagram illustrating the possibility of a transfer of reaction originating from one stimulus (S_m) to another (S_p) which is assumed, objectively, to be totally different.

Thus we observe the superficially impossible is really quite easily conceivable without the assumption of any principles beyond the commonplace ones of conditioning or habituation. From a common-sense point of view, the explanation of the paradox lies in the fact that while, objectively considered, S_m and S_p are entirely distinct, they have, possibly by chance association, acquired identical excitatory potentialities in the body of a particular organism. This identity of excitatory capacity brings about substantially the same outcome as if they possessed an objective identity (**12**).[4]

[3] In case the sequence of Fig. 3 were highly patterned (**15**, p. 500, note), e.g., by a large amount of over-training, the reaction shown in Fig. 4 would probably become exceedingly weak and might not take place at all, because the remote bond $S_m \rightarrow R_Q$ would be lacking in the stimulus combination shown in Fig. 4.

[4] As a result of this difference in the basic mechanism involved, it is to be expected that transfer on the basis of objective identity in the stimulus situation should be largely common to the members of a given species, whereas transfer based on acquired

The habituation transfer mechanism presented above abstractly may be clarified and emphasized by means of an experimental example. Such a case on the conditioned-reaction level seems to be furnished by a recent investigation reported by Shipley (**28**). Eleven human subjects were first stimulated by a faint flash of light, followed by the tap of a padded hammer against the lower eyelid. This has been shown by experiment normally to give rise to a conditioned tendency for the flash to evoke the wink. Next the subject was stimulated repeatedly by an induction shock on the fingers of one hand which, in addition to the sharp retraction of the hand from the electrodes delivering the shock, normally also gives rise to a wink. Here, then, we have two stimuli independently able to evoke the same reaction, which constitutes the convergent mechanism. This is shown diagram-

FIG. 5. Shipley's convergent conditioning situation. Here as elsewhere in the present study, the solid line represents what is presumably an unlearned tendency, and the broken line, an acquired tendency.

PAPER

6

matically in Fig. 5, exactly paralleling the relationship shown in Fig. 2.

After the training with the shocks, the flash was given alone and, in a small percentage of the subjects, this now evoked a finger retraction despite the fact that the *flash had never previously been associated either with the shock or the finger retraction*. A control experiment involving the same number of shocks similarly timed, etc., gave no finger retractions, which would seem to make it reasonably certain that the results in the case cited above were not due to mere irradiation.

The observed results of Shipley's experiment may easily be deduced from the principles of ordinary conditioning, just as was the case of transfer abstractly considered above. Since

identical excitatory potentialities should be very unevenly distributed within a population. Such generality as the latter would show, would be based on the similarity of environmental circumstances. In some cases even this might produce considerable uniformity in transfer capacity.

the shock evokes both the wink and the retraction, the proprioceptive stimuli from each should become conditioned to the other reaction either by a simultaneous, or at least by a backward (**31**), process, as shown in Fig. 6. Accordingly, when later the organism is stimulated by the flash, this gives

FIG. 6. Diagram showing how mutual conditioned reactions may be set up among the several part-reactions to a single stimulus.

rise to the retraction by means of the stimulus-response sequence shown in Fig. 7. Naturally the tendency would be very weak, in part because of the specific weakness of simultaneous or backward conditioned tendencies (**38**), and doubt-

$$\text{FLASH} \dashrightarrow \text{WINK} \longrightarrow P_w \dashrightarrow \text{RETRACT}$$

PAPER
6

FIG. 7. Diagram showing the hypothetical manner in which the flash was able to evoke the finger retraction with which it had never been associated (Shipley's 'Group *C*').

less also in part because the transfer involved the breaking up of a stimulus pattern.

III. Associative Divergence and Convergence the Basis of the Habit-Family Hierarchy

With this introduction to the mechanisms of divergent and convergent excitatory tendencies, we may now turn to our main concern, which is a higher synthesis obtained by combining the two into a single functional unit. The synthesis in question is represented diagrammatically in Fig. 8. It will be observed that this figure begins with the divergent mechanism of Fig. 1, and ends with the convergent mechanism of Fig. 2. Extending between the two and connecting the S_A with the R_G are a number of distinct behavior sequences which are supposed to differ greatly from one another both as to the qualitative nature of their activity and as to length of sequence, the first sequence (initiated by s_1) being shortest, the second and third progressively longer, and the fourth longest of all.

It is to be expected that the adaptive potentialities of the mechanism obtained by combining the two dynamic tendencies discussed above should differ in certain respects from those manifested by either alone.   Whereas the one mechanism by itself mediates alternative reactions, and the other brings about transfer through equivalence of reaction potentiality, there emerges from the combination (Fig. 8) the sig-

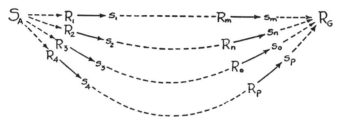

Fɪɢ. 8.   The habit family hierarchy which consists of combining the divergent and the convergent excitatory mechanisms shown in Figs. 1 and 2.   The length of the sequences represents inversely the excitatory strength of each at point S_A.   It is probable that this mechanism is related to Tolman's 'means-end-field' (33, 177).

PAPER

6

nificant novel phenomenon of the *habit family*.   A family of habits may be defined in general as a group of two or more habit sequences, all of which may be initiated by a particular stimulus and terminated by a particular reaction.[5]   Despite the 'emergent' nature of the habit-family mechanism, it nevertheless retains clear functional evidences of its origin. The individual habit sequences of a particular family are still alternative in that but a single member can be active at once. At the same time they are equivalent in that all are alike in bringing about substantially the same final reaction or adjustment to the problem situation presented by S_A.

Perhaps the simplest and most obvious examples of habit families are found in alternative locomotor sequences through space.   If, while following a footpath we encounter a pool of water, the problem may be solved by detouring in either the right-hand or the left-hand direction.   The respective behavior sequences are alternative in that we cannot go in both

[5] The term 'families' is here used in much the same sense that geometers use the term to designate a series of curves, such as parabolas, which originate at the same point but thereafter follow different courses, all being generated by a single formula but each having a different value for one of the parameters.

directions at the same time. They are equivalent in that each without distinction brings us again upon our path.

The alternative-pathway maze, represented conventionally in Fig. 9, gives rise to what, from the point of view of simplicity, is a limiting case of the habit-family hierarchy. As in the diagram, it is usual for such mazes to have one path somewhat shorter than the other. On the basis of trustworthy experiment (2), it is known that the shorter of the two paths, presumably in conformity with the principle of the goal

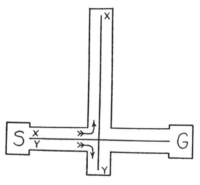

Fig. 9. Example of a simple habit family hierarchy which has been investigated experimentally. Path Y is the preferred member of the hierarchy.

gradient (16), will come to be preferred by animals which have become familiar with both. The fact that both of the action sequences begin with the same stimulus (S) and terminate in the same reaction (G) constitutes them a habit family; the fact that one sequence is preferred above the other constitutes them a hierarchy. By increasing the number of pathways and keeping the pathways all of a different length, there obviously may be generated in an animal fairly large habit-family hierarchies.

It should be especially noted, however, that the principle of habit-family hierarchy is not limited to the field of spatial orientation here emphasized. It is operative in all situations wherever there is more than one distinct action sequence which will lead to the attainment of a particular goal or subgoal. It is believed, for example, that the habit-family hierarchy constitutes the dominant physical mechanism which mediates such tests of truth and error as organisms employ—that it provides the basis for a purely physical theory of knowledge.[6]

IV. The Habit-Family Hierarchy and the Automatic Transfer of Practice Effects

The deductive explanations of maze phenomena which will be attempted in the following pages rest, for the most part, upon the following two related hypotheses:

1. *That in the albino rat, habit-family hierarchies based primarily on locomotion are set up very early in life, presumably as the result of locomotion in free space, with the result that the animal at the beginning of a maze experiment is already in possession of a vast repertoire of equivalent but fairly distinct locomotor habits, any one of which, in free space, would mediate a transition of his body from the starting point to the goal.*

2. *That when one member of a habit-family hierarchy has attained a goal in an objectively novel situation, the learning thus acquired is transferred without specific practice to the remaining members of the hierarchy.*

PAPER
6

A crucial experimental test of the incidental assumption in the first hypothesis (that locomotor habit-family hierarchies are acquired by early running in free space) is difficult. Some general indications as to its validity might be obtained, however, by determining whether *very* young rats, *e.g.*, animals under ten or (possibly) twenty days of age, would manifest less strongly the phenomena to be expected on the assumption of the truth of the hypothesis than would older animals. Another test, though again not a crucial one, might be made by determining whether rats raised in total darkness, suspended in a hammock through which their legs would protrude so as to touch a miniature treadmill, say (thus allowing free movement and a certain amount of exercise but no genuine transit in space), would show as strong evidences of the existence of a habit-family hierarchy as would animals of the same age reared under ordinary conditions. The hypothesis leads to the expectation that they would not. By similar reasoning, animals reared in

[6] This matter is reserved for elaboration in a subsequent paper.

very small cages would show less evidences of orientation than animals raised in a cage as large as an ordinary room.

The validity of the second hypothesis must be judged in the main by the extent to which the deductions based primarily upon it agree with the facts of mammalian behavior as the latter shall finally come to be known. It is exactly this type of evidence which supports such belief as we have in molecules, atoms, and electrons.

It may be stated at once, however, that this hypothesis is definitely not put forward as an ultimate principle. On the contrary, it is confidently expected that in case it turns out to be sound, it will be found to be deducible from certain still more general principles.[7] As an illustration of the general course which this deduction (or perhaps more properly, *reduction*) is likely to take, the following sketch is offered. The principles are fairly simple and the most of them are reasonably well authenticated.

From the nature of the habit family, it follows that in it all behavior sequences terminate at the same point, or in the same final act. This will often be consummatory in nature. Now there is considerable evidence that terminal reactions have a strong tendency to come forward in their entirety, as shown by abortive intrusions into behavioral sequences, which sequences were originally antecedent. Not only this, but there is evidence (**29**; **30**) that reactions some distance from the goal also tend to come forward in the behavioral sequence, though these latter reactions appear to possess less strength in this respect than do goal reactions or reactions closely antecedent to the goal reactions. There is reason to believe, however, that in case the goal reactions or pre-goal reactions as a whole are in physiological conflict with the sequence properly leading to them, some *portion* of the goal reaction which chances not to be in such conflict will be temporarily detached from the goal aggregate and will move forward in the sequence independently and rather freely (**15**).

As yet this subject has been little investigated experimentally, so that the extent and variety of such fractional

[7] This statement also holds for the principle of the goal gradient (**16**).

anticipatory reactions is very imperfectly known. Fortunately, salivation, a well-known type of anticipatory reaction, has been extensively studied. It is of significance for the understanding of the probable mechanism mediating transfer in the habit-family hierarchy that the amount and quality of anticipatory salivation is known to vary widely according to the adjustment situation (25, 184). Much less is known experimentally about fractional anticipatory sex behavior, though clearly this species of behavior manifests not only complex secretional activities but extensive and profound circulatory changes as well. Tumescence may be mentioned as a characteristic fractional anticipatory sex reaction. In addition to these rather gross and obvious forms of fractional anticipatory behavior, it is probable that rich variety exists, of which we as yet know little or nothing. It is conceivable, for example, that the mere visual stimulation by a light pattern may evoke hidden but characteristic reactions in the organism which could play the anticipatory rôle. At all events, it is not purely gratuitous to assume that both goal reactions and pre-goal reactions may possess characteristic fractional components which will be drawn forward to the beginning of all action sequences originally leading to them, and which, after each family has attained a moderate degree of integration, will be present everywhere throughout all members of a given family.[8]

PAPER

6

It thus seems probable that the fractional anticipatory goal reaction (r_G, Fig. 10) is the major mechanism which brings about the integration of the habit-family hierarchy. It is this mechanism which appears to be mainly responsible for the important and characteristic phenomenon of the transfer of practice effects from a less preferred member of a habit hierarchy to a more favored one. There is also reason to believe that under certain circumstances the fractional anticipatory goal reaction will be powerfully supported in this action by the drive stimulus (S_D, Figs. 10 and 11) in

[8] A somewhat detailed discussion of one mechanism by which goal and near-goal reactions may be displaced forward in a behavior sequence may be found in reference 14. A second mechanism has been proposed by Lepley (21).

PAPER

6

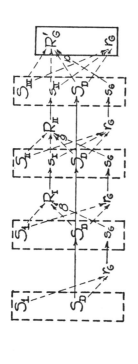

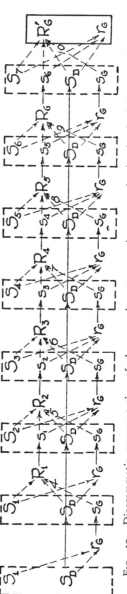

Fig. 10. Diagrammatic representation of the more important excitatory tendencies involved in two behavior sequences belonging to a habit-family hierarchy. Numbers corresponding to a conventional rectilinear goal gradient are inserted on the various lines representing excitatory tendencies from s_G to the several R's. It is to be noted that s_G leads to R_I with a strength of 8 units and to R_1 with a strength of only 4 units. The repetition of S_1 at the outset indicates a hesitation of the animal until S_1 has had time to arouse r_G.

case the latter is the same in the new situation as in the old. Even in cases where the drive may be superficially distinct, there is some reason to believe that there may be an inner core of identity which, if present, would doubtless aid considerably in mediating a transfer. While the inadequacy of our knowledge about these matters is such that we must be very tentative at present as to the precise details of the processes involved, it may be worth while to give an account of how the vicarious transfer under consideration might conceivably take place.

Let us suppose that the reaction sequences represented in Fig. 10 correspond to the first and last members respectively of the habit-family hierarchy shown in Fig. 8, as in their original setting. The S's represent external stimuli; the R's, the gross reactions; the r_G's represent fractional anticipatory goal reactions; S_D, the persisting drive stimulus, *e.g.*, hunger; and the s's represent proprioceptive stimuli from preceding reactions. The final or goal reaction is represented as consisting of two components, R'_G and r_G. The latter is assumed usually to be relatively insignificant in absolute magnitude but, because of its supposed ability to move forward rather freely in the behavior sequence, to be of the greatest significance as the physical substance of goal or directive ideas. Solid arrows indicate what are presumed to be unlearned sequences, and broken lines terminating in arrows indicate tendencies to action which have been acquired by association or conditioning.

PAPER
6

Suppose that the organism possessing the combination of excitatory tendencies shown in Fig. 10 should find itself in a somewhat novel situation presenting an initial external stimulus S_1', and a different drive (S_D') as well.[9] Suppose, further, that by trial-and-success the organism finds its way to the goal over the route involving the action sequence

[9] The deduction would be considerably easier if the original drive (S_D) were assumed in the new situation, but the outcome would be less general than to assume a distinct drive. It may easily be deduced from these and related considerations that, other things being equal, transfer should be distinctly more effective where the same drive (*e.g.* hunger) is involved in both the old and the new situations. This deduction may easily be checked by experiment.

R_1, R_2, R_3, R_4, R_5, R_6, R_7, R_G. Now, if this action sequence is repeated a few times, r_G will become conditioned to S_D' and so will be brought forward to the beginning of the series (15). By virtue of this fact, r_G *will be brought into the presence of S_1' and will therefore become conditioned to it* (Fig. 11). Accordingly, whenever the animal finds himself in the presence of S_1', particularly if there is a pause before the beginning of locomotion, S_1' as a stimulus will evoke r_G, which will bring with it the proprioceptive stimulus s_G. But s_G, by virtue of previous

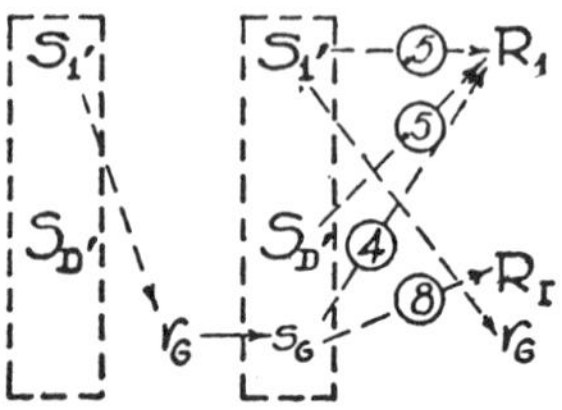

PAPER
6
Fig. 11. Diagrammatic representation of the competition between the excitatory tendencies leading to R_1 and R_I upon the transfer of the habit system shown in Fig. 10 to a new situation permitting the same behavior adjustments but having different external stimuli and also a different drive (S_D'). S_1' indicates the initial external stimulus complex characteristic of the new situation. It is also assumed that the goal was attained the first few times exclusively by the longer path, *i.e.*, the one beginning with act R_1, and that during these repetitions incipient excitatory tendencies were set up leading to R_1 from S_1' and S_D'.

conditioning (Fig. 10), possesses excitatory tendencies both to R_1 and to R_I. Since, assuming a simple goal gradient, R_1 has at this point a strength of 4 units (Fig. 10) and R_I a strength of 8 units, this competition of excitatory tendencies will eventuate in reaction R_I, *which has never before taken place in this (objective) situation.* We accordingly have here a mechanism adequate to produce the transfer of practice effects which we have been seeking.[10]

Perhaps as good an experimental example of the concrete working out of this principle as any is found in a minor detail of a study by Johnson (18, 37). In this portion of Johnson's experiment, two dogs, blind from the first few days of life,

[10] It will be noted that the mechanism here indicated as mediating the transfer of habituation, while differing in important respects from that presumably responsible for the transfer in Shipley's conditioned reflex experiment, resembles it in that the element upon which the transfer was based is an *act*.

together with one normally seeing dog, were trained to open the door of a box containing food, by lifting a latch. The door of the box during the training period was always situated at the northwest corner of the box. After all three dogs had completed the learning in the original position, the box was turned 90° to the right. When the dogs had adjusted themselves to this position, the box was again turned to the right 90°. Thus the door was opened by the dogs successively at the N.W. corner, the N.E. corner, and the S.E. corner. One of Johnson's diagrams seems to indicate that the dogs always approached the box from the south. It was observed that when the door of the box was in the third or S.E. position the two blind dogs, even after 44 and 47 successive trials, always approached it by the roundabout way of the northwest and the northeast corners. This was the course by which the successive turnings of the box had originally led them. The seeing dog, on the other hand, took the direct route to the S.E. corner after the seventh trial.

PAPER
6

The present hypothesis would explain these observations by supposing that in the free locomotion of the seeing dog there had been developed an effective hierarchy of locomotor habits in which the shorter path possessed a distinct preference. It required seven repetitions by the non-preferred member of the hierarchy to condition the anticipatory terminal reactions to the stimuli present at the point of choice. When this had taken place, however, the s_G at once evoked the dominant sequence of taking the shorter path to the S.E. corner, i.e., practice effects acquired in a previous situation were first transferred to a non-preferred member of a simple hierarchy by means of practice and then automatically transferred to a preferred member of the hierarchy without any additional practice whatever in the latter act. It seems reasonable to suppose that the blind dogs, because of their sensory limitation, had not been able during their previous lives to build up such effective locomotor habit hierarchies as the seeing dog was able to do, which would account for their failure of transfer at this point in the experiment. However, these animals on still another turn of the

box to the right, which naturally brought about a still greater
difference between the two paths to the door, succeeded
rather tardily in making the transfer, which indicates that
they possessed the habit-hierarchy mechanism at least to a
limited degree.

V. THE HABIT-FAMILY HIERARCHY AND THE PRINCIPLES OF FRUSTRATION AND DISINHIBITION

It must now be noted that the situation as represented in
the preceding section will normally present certain significant
complications not there discussed.   In the process of conditioning S_1' to r_G, additional conditioned excitatory tendencies,
which may be represented by $S_1' \rightarrow R_1$, would naturally arise.
Now such excitatory tendencies must be in direct competition
with R_I, and so are opposed to the transfer under consideration.   If, however, the conditions of the experiment are such
as to leave these excitatory tendencies fairly weak, e.g., as
shown in Fig. 11, the strengths of the respective excitatory
tendencies might sum up as follows:

$$R_1 = 4 + .5 + .5 = 5,$$
$$R_I = 8.$$

Under these conditions the excitatory tendency to R_I would
still be clearly dominant and the transfer would take place,
though somewhat less promptly and with somewhat less
certainty than without this complication.

If, on the other hand, a considerable amount of training
should be given to the non-preferred member of the habit-
family hierarchy under conditions such as that shown in
Fig. 12, in which the preferred path is an integral part of the
non-preferred path, as was the case in the experiments by
Higginson, Gengerelli, and Valentine (36), a rather different
situation arises.   It is understood that during the main part
of the training the door at E is always closed when the animals
pass it on the way to D, but it is open when they return so
that they can enter and go to the food at F.   Under such
conditions the excitatory tendencies emanating from S_1' and
S_D' (see Fig. 11) may become fairly strong.   Moreover, once

PAPER

6

the long path has been traversed a number of times, transfer should take place to the preferred member of the hierarchy, at which time the animals will begin attempting to take the short path to *F* even though the door at *E* is closed. But under these circumstances we should expect to have a dominant excitatory tendency undergoing frustration, *i.e.*, being prevented from functioning. Under such conditions,

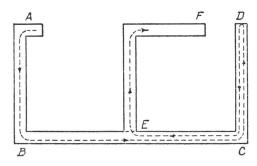

FIG. 12. Diagram of Valentine's maze (36). The broken line represents the required path of the rat during the early trials. The door at *E* was closed when the rat passed from *B* in the direction of *C*, but when he returned from *D* it was always open. *F* represents the point at which food was given.

PAPER
6

there is reason to believe that an 'internal' inhibition will develop which is substantially like the experimental extinction observed in conditioned reactions.[11] We shall let the inhibitory tendency be represented by $a - 1$ and the two positive excitatory tendencies, one from S_1' and the other from S_D', each by $a + 1$. With a moderate amount of training, then, the following situation might result:

$$R_1 = 4 + 1 + 1 = 6,$$
$$R_I = 8 - 1 = 7.$$

Even here the animal would still usually take the short path if the door were open on his way down from *B*. This actually took place in the experiments by Higginson (8) and Gengerelli (6).

But suppose that the training to go into the blind *D* (Fig. 12) were very great. Then one might expect the positive

[11] See Part II for an elaboration of this point.

tendencies to R_1 to be greater and the inhibitions of the tendency to go to R_l to be more profound, in which case the excitatory tendencies might sum up as follows:

$$R_1 = 4 + 1 + 1 + .5 + .5 = 7,$$
$$R_l = 8 - 4 = 4.$$

In such an event the animal would be expected to continue to follow the longer path unless the advantage possessed by it should be upset in some way. As a matter of fact, Valentine's animals did continue to take the longer path with fair regularity for a long time, though finally all came to take the shorter path.

But how are we to explain the fact that Valentine's animals all finally learned to take the shorter route? It might be supposed, for example, that once an animal has practiced the longer, naturally less preferred, path until the excitatory tendency to it has become dominant, he would PAPER
6 always continue to follow it and would never thereafter eliminate the blind alley, succeeding practice serving to fixate the blind still more firmly rather than to eliminate it. This paradox, like so many that have arisen in the theory of learning, comes from assuming that only one principle, or at most a very few principles, are operating in the learning process at one time.

It happens that in this particular case, a principle from the conditioned reflex literature offers a ready explanation. It is well known (**25**, **44**) that when an extra (disturbing) stimulus (or its after-effect) impinges on an excitatory tendency, the latter will be weakened; and when such a disturbing stimulus impinges on a situation where a previous excitatory tendency has suffered extinction, the inhibition becomes temporarily disinhibited, which enables at least a considerable portion of the excitatory tendency previously active to become active again (**25**, 49 *ff.*). We have already presented reasons for believing that there should arise such an inhibition of the tendency to go into alley F when coming down from B.

Let us suppose that we have one of Valentine's animals which is taking consistently the long path, *i.e.*, that the rat goes from A to B, past the open door at E to C, then to D, back by C, through E and up to F. Suppose, now, that just before point E is reached (on the way to C) a loud buzzer is sounded. The excitatory tendency to C will be weakened according to the principle of *external inhibition*, whereas the inhibited tendency to go into F will suffer *disinhibition*, the latter reanimating the excitatory tendency to go directly to F. The respective tendencies which were originally as appear on p. 49 would be transformed somewhat as follows: [12]

$$R_1 = 4 + 1 + 1 + .5 + .5 = 7 - 2 = 5,$$
$$R_I = 8 - 4 = 4 + 2 = 6.$$

The excitatory tendency of R_1 which stood at 7 is weakened by two points through external inhibition, leaving 5, whereas the strength of R_I, previously weakened by experimental extinction from 8 to 4, recovers two points through disinhibition so that it now stands at 6. The tendency to R_I consequently becomes dominant. Therefore, after a disturbing stimulus, the animal might be expected to drop the blind into which he has been trained to go,[13] *i.e.*, to take the turn to the left even though previously he has always entered this alley by making a turn to the right.

A second deduction which is of considerable potentiality as an experimental test of the above hypothesis depends upon the well-known fact (**25, 65**; **32**) that external inhibitions and disinhibitions are notoriously transitory. This means that

[12] It is not yet clear from the experimental work on conditioned reflexes whether a disinhibiting stimulus affects only the inhibitory component or whether its effect is also upon the excitatory component as well. It seems reasonable to assume that the latter is the case. The net gain in strength of reaction in such a case would be due to the well-known fact (**25**, 66) that inhibitory tendencies suffer much greater external inhibition from stimuli of moderate strength than do excitatory tendencies. Thus the net gain in the strength of R_I of two points (from 4 to 6) might result from a combined reduction of the basic excitatory tendency of 8 to 7 through external inhibition and a gain in effective excitatory strength through a reduction by disinhibition of the four units of inhibition to 1. Thus the application of the results of conditioned reflex experiments to more complex situations give a unique significance to certain phases of conditioned reactions hitherto disregarded.

[13] Perhaps one of the most important biological functions performed by external inhibition (and disinhibition) is to prolong trial-and-error and prevent permanent fixation of maladaptive habit tendencies of which the long path in Valentine's experiment is an example.

under ordinary conditions a shortly succeeding test carried out like the above but without the buzzer should be about as likely to result in the entry of alley D as were those trials made previous to the trial with the buzzer, except for the positive conditioning influence of taking on this one occasion the shorter path from A to F.

The application of these principles to Valentine's experiment is obvious. Even under the most favorable experimental conditions, slight disturbing stimuli are constantly impinging on the experimental animal; they may come from the environment, or they may originate within the animal's own body. An obvious source of external inhibition would be the open door which the animal is not accustomed to see when on his way from B, especially if a strong light should be shining through it. Other sources of disturbance might be slight sounds, odors, the bites of parasites, etc. These disturbing stimuli should produce the combination of external inhibition and disinhibition exactly as described above, and thus bring about occasional choices of the shorter path.

Since external inhibition in its various forms is inherently transitory, such short-path choices are likely to be followed by runs on the long path, particularly if the interval between trials were as much as five minutes. Thus there might be expected to take place an irregular alternation between choices of short and long paths. Since it is probable that the experimenter would not be able to sense the majority of the stimuli disturbing the animal, particularly those of internal origin, these alternations would appear to ordinary observation to take place in an entirely fortuitous manner.

THE CONCEPT OF THE HABIT–FAMILY HIER-
ARCHY AND MAZE LEARNING: PART II

BY CLARK L. HULL

Yale University

VI. Automatic Habit Transfer when the Principle of Frequency must be Overridden

We must now consider the question of how the tendency to take the long path, which is clearly dominant with many of the animals in Valentine's experiment at the beginning of the 'critical runs,' *i.e.*, that portion of the practice in which the door at E was open throughout each trial, finally gives place to a dominance of the tendency to take the short path. We have shown in the preceding section how occasional choices of the shorter path might be expected to take place through the influence of chance sensory disturbances. But in many cases, at least, the external inhibitions at E would be of relatively infrequent occurrence and the proportion of long-path to short-path choices would still greatly favor the choice of the longer path. Suppose, for example, that we assume only one short choice out of six. A naïve interpretation of the principle of frequency would demand that such a ratio not only would not increase the proportion of short-path choices but that the short-path choices should steadily decrease until they would entirely disappear. Such an interpretation of the principle of frequency implicitly assumes that frequency is the only principle operative. It is to be doubted whether anyone has ever utilized this principle under such an assumption. At all events, there is reason in this particular case to believe that at least two other factors are also operating simultaneously and in such a way as to oppose and over-ride it.[14]

[14] To over-ride a principle or factor by opposing to it one or more factors which possess in the aggregate a greater strength should not be considered as a disproof of the existence and significance of the first principle. Thus, for a balloon or an airplane or a thrown object to rise from the earth in opposition to gravity is in no sense a proof of the non-existence of gravity or that gravity need not be taken into consideration, as many an aviator has found to his sorrow.

134

The first opposing factor to be adduced in this connection is the empirical principle discovered in conditioned reaction experiments that the restoration of an experimentally extinguished tendency to action is much more rapid than was its original acquisition. Thus Hilgard and Marquis (9) report that the restoration of an experimentally extinguished lid reaction recovered in the case of three dogs in approximately one-fifth, one-fourth, and two-fifths respectively of the numbers of reinforcements originally required to produce the same increase in strength of the tendency. If we may take the middle of these three values as a first rough approximation and apply it tentatively to Valentine's rats, this principle alone would allow the animals to take the long path three times out of four and still have a substantial margin of practice effects in favor of the shorter path.

A second principle which presumably contributes to the same end is that of the goal gradient (16). Let us assume in the interest of simplicity of exposition that increase in strength of excitatory tendency per repetition within a moderate range is constant under given experimental conditions. Now, from the choice point E in Valentine's maze, the long path is nearly four times as great as the short one. Turning to the table of hypothetical goal gradient values (16, 32) and giving the short and the long paths distance values of 10 and 38 respectively, it is easy to see that one repetition of the short path will strengthen the tendency to repeat that act on a subsequent occasion much more at point E than one repetition of the long path will strengthen the latter tendency at the same point. Under these assumptions the short path would increase in strength per trial in the proportion of 4.28 whereas the long path would increase in strength per trial in the proportion of only .96. Thus, by this principle alone the short path would ultimately become dominant, even though it were chosen only a fourth as often as the longer one.[15] This pro-

PAPER

7

[15] Suppose that a given degree of perfection would be attained in ten repetitions. By 16, p. 32, each trial would increase the strength of the tendency to take the short path by .428 unit, whereas it would increase the strength of the tendency to take the long path by .096 unit. It follows that two runs on the short path would strengthen that tendency by .856, whereas eight runs on the long path would increase the strength of that tendency by only 8 × .096, or .768 unit. This would leave a net advantage of .088 to the tendency to take the short path.

portion would vary with the absolute size of the maze, but the general principle ought to hold if the goal gradient hypothesis is sound.

We do not yet know enough about the two processes just considered to be able to say whether they would combine in an additive or a multiplicative manner, but it is evident that they would summate in some way. The nature of the relationship would seem to favor a multiplicative mode of combination. If that were true, the above numerical assumptions would lead to the expectation that an ultimate giving up of the blind alley in Valentine's experiment during the 'critical' runs would still take place even if disinhibition should occur on the average in only one trial out of ten or twelve. By similar reasoning, the more frequently disinhibition takes place at point E, in this stage of the learning process, the more rapidly the blind will be eliminated. On the other hand it is conceivable that distractions might be so far eliminated that occasional animals would never make the correction at all. From this general angle may possibly be explained the stubborn cases of 'fixation' which have puzzled many experimenters; it may be that certain animals, by constitution or the accidents of life, are relatively immune to disinhibition.

PAPER
7

VII. The Predilection of Animals for Entering Goalward-Pointing Blinds

We come now to the consideration of the behavior of the rat in an ordinary single-path maze such as that shown in Fig. 13. Experimentalists frequently report two characteristic phases in the process of a hungry rat learning a maze. The first is a slow, hesitant groping until the food is found. Soon after, the behavior of the rat changes markedly: he goes about his searching in a business-like way, as if he were 'going somewhere' (6). The same thing is often expressed by saying that the rat has become oriented. It will be recalled that according to the hypothesis here being presented, orientation itself consists in the anticipatory goal reaction (r_G) becoming conditioned to the external stimulus complex S_1' (Figs. 10 and 11). But we have already seen that when this takes place the practice effect of traversing the path by which the food (*F*) was reached is at once transferred to all other members of the particular habit family, especially to those which are shorter and therefore occupy a superior position in the hierarchy. It follows, provided the animal

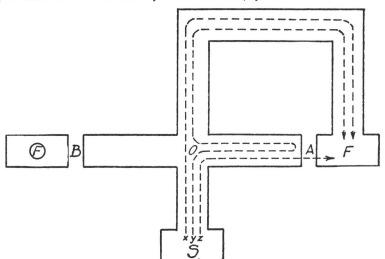

PAPER

7

FIG. 13. Conventional maze to represent the predilection of animals for entering blind alleys which point in the direction of the place where food is obtained. The *F* in the circle at the left of *B* represents food inaccessible to the animal but placed in such a position as to give the same olfactory cues at the choice point *O* as that which is ultimately eaten. The broken lines indicate three conventional paths; path *Z* represents the path of the preferred member of the habit-family hierarchy which the animal would take if the blind end of alley *A* did not prevent. It is to be noted that this maze would not be suitable to test experimentally the existence of the tendency to enter goal-pointing blinds because it would also evoke the tendency to make an anticipatory right turn (**22, 30**).

cannot see the end of the alley in question, that every blind is the beginning of a path to the goal. It is obvious that blinds like *A*, Fig. 13, pointing in the direction of the goal, are the beginnings of paths which, if completed, would be among the shorter ones of the animal's habit family and hence are to be preferred to the longer, more roundabout path, *X*. It accordingly follows at once that *animals will show a marked predilection for blinds pointing in the direction of the goal, as contrasted with alleys pointing in the opposite direction.*[16]

[16] Both Dashiell (**1**) and Tolman and Honzik (**33**, 119 *ff.*) have reported this significant phenomenon on the basis of experiment.

As a corollary of the foregoing, it follows directly that for blind alleys pointing in the direction of the food box there will be a period in the learning of the maze, *i.e.*, through the acquisition of orientation, during which these errors will progressively increase. Thus we arrive, by a purely deductive procedure, at the paradox that *for certain specific portions of the maze an increase in training will make the score worse rather than better.* This deduction may easily be checked by appropriate experiment.

This brings us to the second phase of the maze learning process, the elimination of the blind alleys. It is evident from the preceding discussion that this must be to a considerable extent the elimination of the blinds pointing toward the goal, a form of maladaptive behavior inherently characteristic of the habit-family mechanism. It is to the consideration of the details of this process that we must now apply ourselves.

VIII. The Elimination of Goalward-Pointing Blinds

There is reason to believe that the maladaptive aspect of the habit hierarchy system just referred to, the predilection for entering blinds pointing in the direction of the food box, is corrected by at least two tendencies. Each of these is fairly distinct, and both presumably operate simultaneously. The first and more basic mechanism is that of the direct effects of the goal gradient (16) which would make path X (Fig. 13) preferable to path Y because the former is shorter. This principle, however, cannot alone account for the final preference of path X, unless there is assumed to be a moderate number of spontaneous choices of the shorter of the two paths during the early practice trials.[17] But the habit-family

---

[17] On the principle of the goal gradient alone, assuming the latter to operate according to the logarithmic law, and, in the interest of simplicity of exposition, assuming an approximately straight curve of learning, it would be possible for the choice finally to settle on path X, even though there should be distinctly more trials on Y than on X. Path X from point O is about 27 units long, and path Y, about 41. By Table 2 of (16), path X should have, at point O, an excitatory strength in the proportion of 1.81, whereas path Y would have a strength in the proportion of .77. Since .77 is contained in 1.81 twice with .27 left over, it follows that path X would finally come to preponderate over Y even if the former had initially only half as many choices as the latter.

principle, as applied to paths X and Y, would, by virtue of the principle of transfer, shift the dominance of reaction from Y to Z, once orientation had taken place on the basis of runs in Y, *even though not a single run had ever been made by path Z.* Thus, the situation is complicated by the necessary implication that, as already noted in the preceding section, the habit-family principle also produces the strong maladaptive tendency to attempt to take path Z, quite apart from any specific practice whatever on this particular path. We must now consider what phenomena should be expected under these circumstances to result from repeated trials.

In order to understand the outcome of this complex situation, it will be necessary to put forward a supplementary hypothesis already referred to and employed in another connection (p. 49, Part I). This may be called the *frustration hypothesis.* The term frustration is here used to indicate any situation in which an acquired excitatory tendency, and particularly an excitatory tendency located posterior to a chain of such excitatory tendencies making up an appreciable segment of a behavior cycle, is for any reason prevented from evoking its accustomed reaction. The hypothesis is that *under such circumstances internal inhibitions will be developed which will manifest substantially the same characteristics as result from the experimental extinction of conditioned reactions.* Among the phenomena to be expected on this hypothesis are the gradual cessation of attempts to perform the act which has been frustrated, spontaneous recovery of the tendency with the passage of time, and disinhibition (**25**, 66).

PAPER

7

It will be necessary also to recall in this connection the famous study of Ebbinghaus (**4**; **7**). In that investigation he obtained experimental evidence indicating that in series of nonsense syllables learned by rote, there were set up by the learning process excitatory tendencies not only connecting each syllable with the next but also remote excitatory tendencies between syllables as far apart as seven intervals in the series (**4**, 106). It is the existence of these remote excitatory tendencies that is of special significance in the present connection.

With these principles especially in mind, let us proceed to the consideration of what might logically be expected to take place in the behavior of the rat upon repeated entries into blind alley *A* of Fig. 13. Suppose that the stimulus and behavior flux of potential path *Z*, from choice point *O* to the goal *F*, be represented by the arbitrary action phases shown in Fig. 14, with the barrier (the end of the blind) falling just

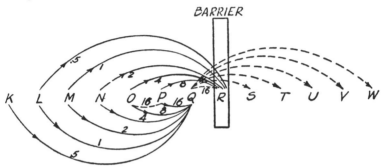

PAPER

7

FIG. 14. Diagrammatic representation of some of the immediate and remote excitatory tendencies involved in a typical behavior sequence where an animal in a maze enters a blind alley pointing in the direction of the food box. The letters *K*, *L*, *M*, *N*, etc., represent both stimuli and reactions at closely spaced intervals in the behavior flux. For purposes of simplifying the exposition, the goal gradient as such is ignored. The gradient of the remote excitatory tendencies of Ebbinghaus is represented conventionally by giving each value one-half the strength of that preceding it. Each point is understood as having six excitatory tendencies emanating from it when considered as a stimulus, and six excitatory tendencies converging upon it when considered as a reaction. Only a few of these could be represented without unduly complicating the figure.

before reaction *R*. Now, according to the Ebbinghaus hypothesis, there should be an immediate excitatory tendency with a strength of 16 units, say, from *Q* to *R*; a remote excitatory tendency of less strength, say one-half as great (8 units), from *P* to *R*; a second remote excitatory tendency, one-fourth as great (4 units), from *O* to *R*, and so on. The excitatory tendencies of this series will yield a total aggregate excitatory tendency of approximately 32 units. It is important to note that because of the habit-family principle there will be at all times, in addition to the tendency of path *Z* to lead into alley *A*, a relatively weaker excitatory tendency to go *out* of alley *A* by path *Y*. Let us assume that this latter and opposing tendency has a strength of 14 units.

But the barrier, by preventing act R from taking place, according to the frustration hypothesis, will produce an inhibition at all points from L to Q, presumably of a strength at each point in proportion to the strength of the original excitatory tendency from each point to R (**25**, 100). Now it is known that when one excitatory tendency suffers extinction, the resulting internal inhibition has a tendency to irradiate, as secondary inhibition, to closely related excitatory tendencies (**25**, 61, 171). Thus it would be reasonable to suppose that the frustration of the 8-unit remote excitatory tendency from P to R, together with probable additional inhibitions resulting from the frustration of the excitatory tendency from P to S, P to T, P to U, etc., will spread in such a way as to inhibit to a considerable extent the immediate excitatory tendency from P to Q, and to a progressively lesser extent to the excitatory tendency from O to P, from N to O, from M to N, and so on. Thus there would result from the frustration at R *an inhibitory gradient extending backward from R as a focus* at which point it presumably will be nearly equal to the inhibitory tendency upon which it is based. This means that there must be a parallel but reversed excitatory gradient extending backward from R, at which point the effective limiting excitatory value would be zero.

PAPER 7

Now, by hypothesis, the moment that inhibition has weakened the excitatory tendency to go forward at any point below the assumed level of 14 units, the animal will turn and take path Y out of the blind to the food box F. It is clear that this turning must take place first at point R, since that is the initial focus of frustration at which the inhibition is maximal. Upon repetitions of frustration at successive trials, the inhibition (and so the secondary inhibition) will grow more profound, the gradient at the same time extending farther backward beyond M, L, etc. As a result, the critical excitatory level of 14 units on path X will move backward toward L progressively and as this takes place the point at which turning occurs will also move backward. But when the turning point begins to move backward, *e.g.*, when the turning takes place at Q, this itself will create a

225

new set of immediate and remote frustrations substantially like those which resulted when the barrier prevented act *R* from taking place. This new set of inhibitions will cause the animal to turn and follow path *Y* at a still earlier point; the earlier turning will produce another new crop of frustrations, which will result in a still earlier turning, and so on. *Thus the animal may be expected, in general, to penetrate the blind alley shorter and shorter distances on successive trials until finally he will not enter it at all*, but will proceed directly to the food by way of path *X* (**3**; **17**).[18]

It should be noted that this explanation of the elimination of a blind alley is distinctly related to the important hypothesis put forward by Holmes around 1910 (**11**, 164 *ff.*). Holmes' principles, however, are inadequate to explain the elimination of a blind alley from a maze because they do not show how the end of an alley can lead to an 'incongruous' act (**10**). The checking of locomotion or the necessity of turning about at the end of a blind alley only becomes 'incongruous' on the assumption that there is a definite excitatory tendency to go directly through the space occupied by the end of the blind. This is not provided by Holmes' hypothesis. There is no reason to believe, for example, that a rat would develop any inhibition from going into a blind alley during random exploration, for the reason that in such a case there would exist to be frustrated no excitatory tendencies to go anywhere in particular. The principle of the habit-family hierarchy furnishes a clear basis for a definite frustration, and the results from conditioned reflex experiments furnish a principle by which this frustration could be converted into an inhibition without which repetition could hardly produce the elimination. It also affords a deduction of the *mode* of elimination, *i.e.*, the progressively shortened entrances, a matter of considerable corroborative significance.

PAPER

7

[18] Several writers, perhaps the earliest of whom is Peterson (**26**), have noted the progressively shortening penetrations of animals into blinds. Perhaps the most convincing study illustrating this tendency is that by Robinson and Wever (**27**), a truly beautiful experiment. Though the conditions of this latter investigation differ in certain respects from those assumed in the above deduction, it is believed that the explanation here offered holds substantially for them also.

IX. EIGHT COROLLARIES INVOLVING BLIND ALLEY ELIMINATION

A number of corollaries flow from the deduction presented in the preceding section:

The first concerns the relative ease of eliminating long vs. short blinds. It has been shown elsewhere (**16**) that the mechanism of the goal gradient alone would lead to the more ready elimination of long than of short blinds. Since, other things equal, alleys not pointing toward the food box are believed to be eliminated largely by the goal gradient mechanism, it follows that with such alleys hungry animals will eliminate long alleys more readily than short ones.

In the case of alleys pointing in the direction of the goal, however, the principles put forward above lead to a different expectation. Since the elimination is a progressive or stepwise process, it would seem that the deeper the alley, the more steps of a given length it would require to complete the elimination. Consequently long alleys pointing in the direction of the food box should be eliminated less readily than short ones.

PAPER
7

The third corollary concerns the behavior of the animal between S and O, Fig. 13, when he is about to discontinue entering A. Because of the progressive backward movement of the inhibitory gradient, the forward excitatory tendency of path Z should show a perceptible degree of weakening, presumably in the form of reduced speed, for some distance preceding the arrival at the point at which the turning takes place. It would seem logical to expect that as the critical turning point reaches the entrance to the blind (O) this antecedent segment of inhibition should have spread downward on path Z towards S. Since inhibitions are known to persist to a certain extent, this should manifest itself by a reduction in the speed of locomotion as the animal approaches O, even on occasions when he has ceased to show any other tendency whatever to enter alley A.

A fourth corollary is dependent on the additional assumption that the dominant principle of the elimination of alleys pointing away from the goal depends upon a rather different principle, *i.e.*, upon the competition at point O (**16**, **34**) between the excitatory tendencies to take paths of the X and Y type. If the Y path should triumph on any given occasion, it is difficult to see what, save some scant and rapidly fading inhibitions resulting from the conflict, could prevent the animal from running the whole length of the alley at each entrance, or at least to a point from which the blind end would be visible (**17**). But since alleys pointing away from the food box are the beginnings of possible, even though non-preferred, paths to the goal, there probably would be some tendency to inhibitory phenomena here also, though it should be weaker than in alleys pointing toward the food box. Accordingly it is believed that if an average were made of the depth of penetration into the two types of alleys on those occasions where a clear tendency to enter appeared, the alleys pointing away from the goal would display the greater mean depth of penetration.

A fifth corollary is that, since the failure to enter alley A is essentially an inhibitory phenomenon, some disturbance like the weak sounding of a buzzer taking place when the animal is on his way between S and O should produce a dis-inhibition; in which case the animal might be expected again to enter alley A. If a much stronger disturbance should take place it ought also to produce external inhibition of the movements constituting path X, in which case the animal would be likely to cease locomotion altogether. Moreover, upon resumption of locomotion the animal might be expected to go sometimes into alley B, though there would still probably be somewhat of a predilection for entering alley A.

But since the results of both of these types of disturbance are distinctly transitory (**25**), it may be anticipated with some confidence that after a few minutes of quiet following entrances into the blinds the animal's behavior should show little or no tendency to deviations from its former errorless performance.

The fact of spontaneous recovery from experimental extinction demonstrates that inhibitory tendencies disintegrate more rapidly with the elapse of time than do the excitatory tendencies upon which they are based. It seems likely that the principle of the more rapid disintegration of inhibitory tendencies may be rather general, regardless of their origin (**25**, 66). If we are warranted in making this assumption, it follows that the frustrational inhibitions by which goalward-pointing alleys are eliminated would accumulate more slowly if a few hours should intervene between repetitions than if they are *immediately* consecutive, *i.e.*, other things equal, goalward-pointing alleys will be eliminated less easily by distributed than by massed practice. This principle would be much less active in alleys pointing away from the goal because their elimination is less dependent on inhibition. It follows that with distributed practice there should be relatively a greater difference between the ease of eliminating the two types of alleys than with massed practice, particularly where the alleys appear near the posterior end of the maze.[19]

It is stated (**5**, 365) that caffeine tends to facilitate the acquisition of excitatory tendencies, but to retard the development of inhibitions. In this connection it will be remembered that alleys pointing away from the goal are believed to be eliminated largely on the basis of competing excitatory tendencies, whereas the major factor in the elimination of blinds pointing toward the goal is believed to be inhibitory in nature. If we make the rather dubious assumption that the action of caffeine on the nervous system is as simple as just stated, the above considerations lead to a further corollary: rats learning a maze under the influence of caffeine will eliminate alleys pointing away from the goal more readily

PAPER

7

---

[19] It is easy to deduce from Lepley's hypothesis (**21**) that rote series of nonsense syllables will be more easily learned by distributed practice. Presumably the same principles apply to mazes, particularly if most of the alleys point away from the goal. This would explain the well-known economy in maze learning by distributed practice. The action of the Lepley principle and the present one are thus in opposite directions, with the evidence favoring the dominance of the former. Even so, the above hypothesis seems to demand that there should be relatively less advantage from distributed practice on mazes made up largely of goalward-pointing blinds than on mazes made up largely of blinds pointing away from the goal. At the very least the predominant direction of the blinds becomes a matter of significance in maze studies involving distributed vs. massed practice.

than when in the normal condition, but will eliminate alleys pointing toward the goal with greater difficulty than when in the normal condition. Related implications may also be drawn from the alleged action of bromides (**5**, 365).

X. The Concept of Habit-Family Hierarchies based on Subordinate Goals

The above deductions from the concept of the habit-family hierarchy are drawn, for the most part, from the relatively simple situation in which the goal reaction (r_G) or some closely related reaction is the dominant factor. There is evidence, however (30; 22; 23), that distinctly subordinate goal reactions also tend to come forward in behavior sequences in a manner substantially similar to goal reactions themselves, though doubtless less strongly. A large number of experimental phenomena may be deduced, and thus explained, on this assumption by methods analogous to those employed above. Space here is sufficient only to list two or three major type situations.

The first is dependent upon positive transfer on the basis of an r_G from a subordinate goal reaction. Here belong Maier's ingenious experiments which indicate that even in the rat the more remote end of a segment of a pathway leading to the goal is able to attract to itself, though weakly, a second segment appropriate in combination to make it possible for the animal to reach the food box (24). The second type is represented concretely by a nice experiment reported by Tolman and Honzik (35; 34). In this study, evidence was obtained which indicates that when an animal encounters a barrier in the segment of a path common to the terminal portion of two alternative paths leading to food, there results an inhibition not only of a previously existent tendency to enter the path traversed on the occasion of the frustration, but of the tendency to enter the other path as well. This phenomenon is explained on the basis of negative transfer, *i.e.*, the transfer to one path of an inhibition acquired in association with the other.

But once the principle of transfer on the basis of subordinate habit families based upon the anticipatory nature of subgoals is recognized as a general proposition, each subordinate goal with its habit family may be conceived as possessing numerous goals of a still lower order, each with a lower-order habit-family hierarchy, and so on. In this way the principle of transfer obviously may be extended downward almost indefinitely to even the most minute details of behavior adjustment. On this hypothesis the rich variability, the almost fluid flexibility of behavior characteristic of mammals even in well-practiced action sequences, is a phenomenon not only wholly to be expected from the present point of view, but definitely demanded by it.

XI. Summary

We may now summarize our conclusions in brief dogmatic form.

The convergent excitatory mechanism is capable of mediating the transfer of reactions from one stimulus situation to another where the two stimulus situations externally may contain no common element whatever. When the divergent and the convergent mechanisms are combined, there emerges a new mechanism which may be called a habit-family hierarchy. The hypothesis is put forward that when an organism for any reason succeeds in solving a problem by a sequence of acts which is substantially that of one member of a habit family, the other members of the family, particularly those occupying a more favored position in the hierarchy, will automatically become active in the new situation without any specific practice whatever. This transfer may be thought of as being mediated mainly through the anticipatory reaction (r_G) which is common to all members of the habit-family hierarchy and which therefore as a stimulus is conditioned to evoke the initial reactions of each member. It seems likely that this mechanism of transfer may prove to have an extremely wide application as an explanatory principle in many subtle and otherwise inexplicable forms of behavior at present usually designated indiscriminately as intelligence. The habit-family hierarchy is accordingly put forward as one of

PAPER

7

the basic mechanism of insight; presumably there are numerous other such mechanisms. Thus we seem to be on our way to an objective and discriminating definition of this immensely important but badly understood phenomenon.

In making the application of the principle to the particular problems of maze learning in the rat, it is assumed that a great number of habit families of the locomotor variety have been established by the locomotion of the animal in free space during its early life. From these principles a number of deductions may be made, though in some cases the certainty of the deductions is limited by uncertainty as to the facts concerning conditioned reflexes upon which they are based. The more important of these deductions are as follow:

1. Animals which through lack of practice or otherwise have not had a normal opportunity to set up initial habit-family hierarchies, should show little or no signs of transfer.

2. Other things equal, immediate transfer in the maze to a shorter path should be distinctly more effective where the drive stimulus in the old and the new situations is the same than where it is different.

3. In case an animal is specifically trained to go into a blind alley, he will, if the training has not been too extensive, eliminate the blind at the first opportunity to take the direct path.

4. If the training to take the blind has been very extensive, the animal will normally continue to take the blind if undisturbed, even after the door which would permit him to take the direct path is opened.

5. If, under these conditions, the animal is disturbed shortly before the choice point is reached, he will be likely to omit the blind and take the direct path.

6. Shortly after such a choice, provided the disturbing stimulus has ceased, the animal will be likely to revert to his accustomed use of the blind, though in general the tendency to take it will not be so strong as it was previously.

7. If such disturbing stimuli should repeatedly produce the choice of the shorter path, even though interspersed with a considerably larger number of choices involving entrances into

the blind, the animal will come ultimately to choose the shorter path on most occasions.

8. The more frequently, relatively, choices are made as a result of disturbing stimulations, the more quickly will the animals acquire a fixed habit of choosing the direct path.

9. Animals in learning a maze will tend to show a predilection for blinds pointing in the direction of the food box, as contrasted with blinds originating near the same point and leading in the opposite direction.

10. Of two blind alleys pointing in the direction of the food box, other things equal, the one closer to it by direct line will be more favored by the animals and will be more difficult of elimination from the path.

11. Blinds pointing in the direction of the food box will show at first an increase in the percentage of entrances per trial, after which there will follow a gradual decrease. Blinds pointing away from the goal, other things equal, will show in general a progressive decrease in per cent of entrances from the beginning of practice.

PAPER
7

12. On successive complete entrances to a blind pointing in the direction of the goal, the animal will proceed at a progressively slower pace especially as he approaches the blind end, whether the latter is visible or not.

13. The process of eliminating blinds pointing in the direction of the goal will be characterized by the animal turning around and coming out before reaching the end, and even before being able to see the blind end.

14. The depth of such partial entrances will tend to become less and less with continued practice, until finally the blind will not be entered at all.

15. The mean depth of all penetrations after the first partial entrance has taken place will average less for alleys pointing in the direction of the goal than for those pointing in the opposite direction.

16. Short blind alleys pointing away from the goal will be less readily eliminated by hungry animals than will long blinds.

17. Short blind alleys pointing in the direction of the goal

will be more readily eliminated by hungry animals than will long blinds.

18. After the animal has consistently eliminated a blind alley and has made repeated perfect runs, a slight disturbance just before he reaches the opening to such a blind will be likely to cause an entrance into the alley. A slightly stronger stimulus should cause an entrance also into alleys extending in the opposite direction. Such tendencies to enter blinds, however, should be of relatively short duration.

19. With distributed practice there should be a relatively greater difference between the ease of eliminating goalward and nongoalward-pointing blinds than there would be under immediately consecutive massed practice.

20. Alleys pointing in the direction of the food box should be eliminated with greater difficulty when the animal is under the influence of caffeine, whereas alleys pointing away should be eliminated with greater ease.

Several of the above deductions are known on the basis of experiment to be true, though many of them have never been subjected to experiment. The latter may, therefore, present an opportunity to test the truth of the basic hypothesis from which they logically flow. Hypotheses (in psychology too often called theories) are not matters of faith to be defended with religious zeal. On the contrary they are to be subjected to the most rigorous experimental tests possible at the earliest feasible opportunity. Those hypotheses which clearly fail by this test must be ruthlessly discarded. And, by the same token, no hypothesis which fails to yield such deductions (as distinguished from the intuitions of its originator or protagonists) has any status in science.

REFERENCES

1. DASHIELL, J. F., Direction orientation in maze running by the white rat, *Comp. Psychol. Monog.*, 1930, **7**, No. 32.
2. DE CAMP, J. E., Relative distance as a factor in the white rat's selection of a path, *Psychobiol.*, 1930, **2**, 245–253.
3. DENNIS, W., A study of learning in the white rat, *J. Genet. Psychol.*, 1930, **37**, 294–308.
4. EBBINGHAUS, H., Memory (Trans. by Ruger), New York: Teachers Coll., Columbia Univ., 1913 (original date, 1885).

5. EVANS, C. L., Recent advances in physiology, 4th ed., Philadelphia: P. Blakiston's Son and Co., 1930.
6. GENGERELLI, J. A., Preliminary experiments on the causal factors in animal learning, *J. Comp. Psychol.*, 1928, **8**, 435–457.
7. HALL, M. E., Remote associative tendencies in serial learning, *J. Exper. Psychol.*, 1928, **11**, 65–76.
8. HIGGINSON, G. D., Visual discrimination in the white rat, *J. Exper. Psychol.*, 1926, **9**, 337–347.
9. HILGARD, E. R., AND MARQUIS, D. G., Acquisition, extinction, and retention of conditioned lid responses in dogs (to appear).
10. HOBHOUSE, L. T., Mind in evolution, London: Macmillan and Co. Ltd., 1926.
11. HOLMES, S. J., The evolution of animal intelligence, New York: Henry Holt and Co., 1911.
12. HULL, C. L., Quantitative aspects of the evolution of concepts, *Psychol. Monog.*, 1920, **28**, No. 123.
13. ——, Simple trial-and-error learning: a study in psychological theory, PSYCHOL. REV., 1930, **37**, 241–256.
14. ——, Knowledge and purpose as habit mechanisms, PSYCHOL. REV., 1930, **37**, 511–525.
15. ——, Goal attraction and directing ideas conceived as habit phenomena, PSYCHOL. REV., 1931, **38**, 487–506.
16. ——, The goal gradient hypothesis and maze learning, PSYCHOL. REV., 1932, **39**, 25–43.
17. ——, Differential habituation to internal stimuli in the albino rat, *J. Comp. Psychol.*, 1933, **16**, 255–273.
18. JOHNSON, H. M., Audition and habit formation in the dog, *Behav. Monog.*, 1913–15, **2**, No. 8.
19. KOFFKA, K., The growth of the mind (Trans. by Ogden), New York: Harcourt, Brace and Co. Inc.; London: Kegan, Paul, Trench, Trubner and Co. Ltd., 1925.
20. LASHLEY, K. S., The effects of strychnine and caffeine upon the rate of learning, *Psychobiol.*, 1917, **1**, 141–170.
21. LEPLEY, W. M., A theory of serial learning and forgetting based upon conditioned reflex principles, PSYCHOL. REV., 1932, **39**, 279–288.
22. LUMLEY, F. H., An investigation of the responses made in learning a multiple choice maze, *Psychol. Monog.*, 1931, **42**, No. 189.
23. ——, Anticipation as a factor in serial and maze learning, *J. Exper. Psychol.*, 1932, **15**, 331–342.
24. MAIER, N. R. F., Reasoning in white rats, *Comp. Psychol. Monog.*, 1929, **6**, No. 29.
25. PAVLOV, I. P., Conditioned reflexes, an investigation of the physiological activity of the cerebral cortex (Trans. by Anrep), London: Oxford Univ. Press, 1927.
26. PETERSON, J., The effect of length of blind alleys on maze learning: an experiment on twenty-four white rats, *Behav. Monog.*, 1916–19, **3**, No. 15.
27. ROBINSON, E. W., AND WEVER, E. G., Visual distance perception in the rat, *Univ. Calif. Publ. Psychol.*, 1930, **4**, 233–239.
28. SHIPLEY, W. C., An apparent transfer of conditioning, *J. General Psychol.*, 1933, **8**, 382–391.
29. SPENCE, K. W., The order of eliminating blinds in maze learning by the rat, *J. Comp. Psychol.*, 1932, **14**, 9–27.

PAPER 7

30. Spragg, S. D. S., Anticipation as a factor in maze errors, *J. Comp. Psychol.*, 1933, 15, 313–329.
31. Switzer, S. A., Backward conditioning of the lid reflex, *J. Exper. Psychol.*, 1930, 13, 76–97.
32. ——, Disinhibition of the conditioned galvanic skin response, *J. General Psychol.*, 1933, 9, 77–100.
33. Tolman, E. C., Purposive behavior in animals and men, New York and London: The Century Co., 1932.
34. ——, Sign-Gestalt or conditioned reflex? Psychol. Rev., 1933, 40, 246–255.
35. Tolman, E. C., and Honzik, C. H., 'Insight' in rats, *Univ. Calif. Publ. Psychol.*, 1930, 4, 215–232.
36. Valentine, H. M., Visual perception in the white rat, *J. Comp. Psychol.*, 1928, 8, 369–375.
37. Wheeler, H. W., and Perkins, F. T., Principles of mental development, New York: Thomas Y. Crowell Co., 1932.
38. Wolfle, H. M., Conditioning as a function of the interval between the conditioned and the original stimulus, *J. General Psychol.*, 1932, 7, 80–103.

[MS. received July 26, 1933]

Offprinted from Psychological Review, Vol. 42, No. 3, May, 1935
Printed in U. S. A.

THE MECHANISM OF THE ASSEMBLY OF BE-HAVIOR SEGMENTS IN NOVEL COMBINATIONS SUITABLE FOR PROBLEM SOLUTION [1]

BY CLARK L. HULL

Institute of Human Relations, Yale University

I. The General Problem of Adaptive Novelty in Mammalian Behavior

Many persons have been puzzled by the paradox of the presumptive fertility and originality of the processes of reasoning on the one hand, as contrasted with the remarkable sterility of the syllogism on the other. It has been urged that if one already knows a major premise such as,

All men are mortal,

and that if an organism passing by the name of Socrates manifests traits generally characteristic of a man, it requires no particular originality or perspicacity to conclude that Socrates will himself prove ultimately to be mortal also. Fertility, originality, invention, insight, the spontaneous use of implements or tools—these things, clearly, do not lie in the syllogism. The fact that it has been found possible to construct a relatively simple mechanism of sliding disk segments of sheet metal which will solve automatically, *i.e.*, exhibit the conclusions logically flowing from, all of the known syllogisms and which will automatically detect all of the formal fallacies,[2]

PAPER
8

---

[1] The writer is indebted to the members of his seminar for a number of valuable criticisms and suggestions, notably, to Dr. T. L. McCulloch, Mr. S. D. S. Spragg, and Dr. J. B. Wolfe. Dr. N. R. F. Maier also read a preliminary draft of the manuscript.

[2] Such a mechanism has been designed and constructed by the author, but a description has not yet been published.

219

emphasizes the crudely mechanical characteristics of the syllogism.[3] The solution of the paradox is, of course, that the genuinely creative and novelty-producing portions of the reasoning processes take place in advance of the emergence of the substance or materials of the syllogism; *i.e.*, the solution consists in the *assembly*, from the considerable store of such materials presumably possessed by the more versatile and adaptive organisms, of the particular set of premises which are relevant to the problem situation in question. An understanding of the dynamics of the presumably numerous forms of intelligence,[4] insight, thought, and reasoning must therefore be sought not in the mechanism and use of the syllogism as such, but in this period *antecedent* to the explicit emergence of the material which may be susceptible later of being arranged in the form of a syllogism.[5] It accordingly becomes our task to discover the principles by which, on the occasion of need,

PAPER

8

[3] So far as the writer is able to see, there is no *a priori* impossibility of constructing a mechanism which will display genuine thinking capacity. Indeed, it is expected with some confidence that such mechanisms will ultimately be constructed. But when, and if, this takes place the thinking mechanism will surely be of a far more subtle and complex character than a mere logic machine consisting of sliding disks (1, 2, 11, 12).

[4] By a curious hemianopsia, workers in intelligence testing have confined their activities almost exclusively to the field of tests, and their methods have been largely limited to the computation and manipulation of correlation coefficients. The test-correlation approach is admirably adapted for immediate practical application; but, even when supplemented by the more powerful methods of Spearman (24), Kelley (9), Hotelling (3), and Thurstone (28), it is difficult to see how such a method can possibly yield deductions (and thus, explanations) concerning such fundamental phenomena as those propounded by Maier's analysis. Present indications are that the task of developing a systematic scientific theory of intelligence in this sense will be performed mainly by students of animal behavior, a group almost entirely distinct from that professionally engaged in intelligence testing. It may be that it would not be economical for many individuals to attempt to pursue both, though a more intimate linking of the two fields would seem to be desirable for the robust development even of intelligence testing, as is illustrated by the work of E. L. Thorndike (27). Lippmann, in his attack on psychologists engaged in intelligence testing (13), was probably wrong when he urged that they could not measure a thing of whose nature they had little comprehension. Nevertheless it would seem that improvements in the validity of such measurements might be facilitated by a serious effort to understand the numerous mechanisms which presumably lie behind the various manifestations of intelligence.

[5] As a matter of fact, John Stuart Mill long ago pointed out that the syllogism is primarily a device for testing the accuracy of reasoning processes which have already taken place (20, Book II).

there emerge the habit segments or premises in the particular combination necessary for problem solution.

Something of the theoretical urgency of this problem is brought home to us when we consider the blind chaos which would result if, in problem situations, premises or habit segments should appear by pairs as if drawn by chance from a huge urn from the supply possessed by the organism. The probability that a particular pair of numbers would be drawn from a supply of 100 on any particular occasion is something like 1 in 10,000. Chance is evidently an element in intelligent behavior but, clearly, the dice of chance must be loaded in some way or problems would never get solved. In short, any adequate theory of higher adaptive behavior must show how the dice are loaded, *i.e.*, how the characteristics of the problem situation are able to evoke the particular combination of acts which alone will serve to extricate the organism from its difficulty.

PAPER

8

II. THE SPECIFIC PROBLEM OF THE ADAPTIVE ASSEMBLY OF HABIT SEGMENTS IN NOVEL COMBINATIONS

As a rule it is more economical and generally effective to attack difficult problems by investigating at the outset their simpler aspects and manifestations rather than their more complex ones. In accordance with this principle, we shall begin our analysis of the dynamics of novelty in mammalian behavior by the consideration of a concrete form of intelligent or insightful behavior to which attention has been directed by Norman Maier. In this connection he has remarked significantly, ". . . the combination of two patterns in the solution of a problem is at the bottom of theories of reasoning that make reasoning more than 'trial-and-error' . . ." (**17**). As a result of ingenious experimental procedures, Dr. Maier believes that he has demonstrated the existence of such capacity in the albino rat.

In order to make the substance of Maier's fundamental bit of analysis explicit, let us consider a somewhat modified and conventionalized version of his experimental arrangement

(**17**). This may be understood with the aid of Fig. 1. Sections R, U, X, and H represent enclosed boxes each of distinct shape. Distinctive cutaneous stimuli are provided for the animals' feet by the character of the floor of each box, on the assumption that a characteristic stimulus will lead to a distinct

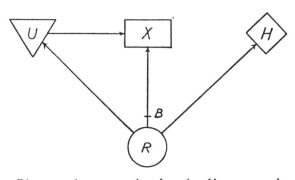

PAPER
8

FIG. 1. Diagrammatic representation of a series of locomotor paths representing a somewhat conventionalized form of Maier's 'reasoning' experiment with rats (**17**). The pathways are enclosed, as are the areas R, X, U, and H. The floor of X would be of soft, flossy silk, say; that of U, of cold metal with rough, sharp points; that of H, of polished warm metal; and that of R, of several layers of thin rubber dam. When training on one path is taking place, all others are closed.

reaction while in each box, and so favor the arousal of partially distinct anticipatory reactions (**5**). For the same reason, additional special devices calculated to induce markedly characteristic and distinct postures in the animals whenever traversing the respective boxes, should probably be provided (**21**). The animal will be trained first to go from R to X, and from U to X as distinct habits, and will receive food. Next he will be trained to go from R to U and from R to H as distinct habits for the reward of water, say. Following this there should probably be given a few more forced runs on UX and RX with food reward, after which the animals should be given an opportunity to choose between RU and RH a number of times to determine objectively the relative strength of the tendency of each individual to enter the respective alleys. Then, with all the four paths open but with a barrier in RX at point B (Fig. 1), the rat will be placed at R, very hungry but with the thirst drive thoroughly satiated. Insight in the sense here used will be shown by the animals' tending, in general, to choose path *RU* (and then *UX*) rather than path *RH* a significantly greater proportion of the trials than was the case on the control choices.

Let us now, for convenience and definiteness in exposition, represent schematically our conception of the essentials of the organization of the several habit segments generated by the foregoing procedure. We shall begin with that leading from *R* to *X*, Fig. 1. We shall suppose that a mammalian organism in an external stimulus situation, S_R, and with an internal stimulus situation (drive), S_D, possesses at the end of some training the habit sequence,

(Sequence I)
$$S_R \searrow \atop S_D \nearrow R_P \to R_Q \to R_X$$

PAPER
8

Here S_R represents the visual, auditory, and other external stimuli coming to the organism from box *R*, and S_D represents proprioceptive stimuli such as result from hunger cramps of the digestive tract, say. R_X represents the final or consummatory reaction which abolishes S_D and thus naturally terminates the cycle. In this sense R_X may be said to be the solution of the problem jointly presented by S_R and S_D. R_P and R_Q represent the locomotor and other activity involved in traversing path $R \to X$.

Let us suppose, also, that in a different external stimulus situation, S_U, but one possessing the same drive as that of Sequence I, *i.e.*, S_D, there has been formed a second behavior sequence which terminates in the same solution or goal reaction as Sequence I:

(Sequence II)
$$S_U \searrow \atop S_D \nearrow R_U \to R_V \to R_W \to R_X$$

This corresponds to the habit segment leading from *U* to *X*, Fig. 1. Here S_U represents the visual, olfactory, and other external stimuli coming to the organism from box *U* (Fig. 1). R_U, R_V, and R_W represent the activity of traversing the path from box U to box X, and R_X represents the final or consummatory response as in Sequence I.

In addition there are postulated two further sequences, both originating at S_R:

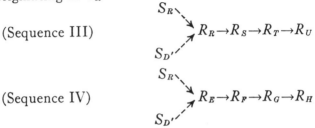

(Sequence III)

(Sequence IV)

Sequence III represents the path from R to U, and Sequence IV represents the path from R to H (Fig. 1). It is to be noted, however, that Sequence III and Sequence IV are each supposed to have a drive (*e.g.*, thirst) which is different from that of Sequences I and II. We accordingly represent the drive of Sequences III and IV by $S_{D'}$. R_U and R_H represent that portion of the final or consummatory segments of the respective sequences which are characteristic and distinctive of each.

PAPER

8

Now, suppose that Sequence I should be prevented from taking place by the barrier placed between S_R and R_P as indicated in Fig. 2 and point B, Fig. 1. How can the solution (reaction R_X) to the problem thus precipitated be brought about? In external stimulus situation S_R the organism now has but two choices, Sequence III or Sequence IV. If Sequence IV is taken, this act leads only to R_H, which for the drive, S_D, is a mere blind alley and a failure, since it does not eliminate S_D. But if Sequence III is taken, this leads to Sequence II which, in turn, leads to R_X, the solution, thus:

$$S_R$$
$$\searrow$$
$$R_R \to R_S \to R_T \to R_U \to R_V \to R_W \to R_X$$

In any realistic consideration of this problem it is important to note that there is always a possibility that the organism will find its way from S_R to S_U by mere chance (trial-and-

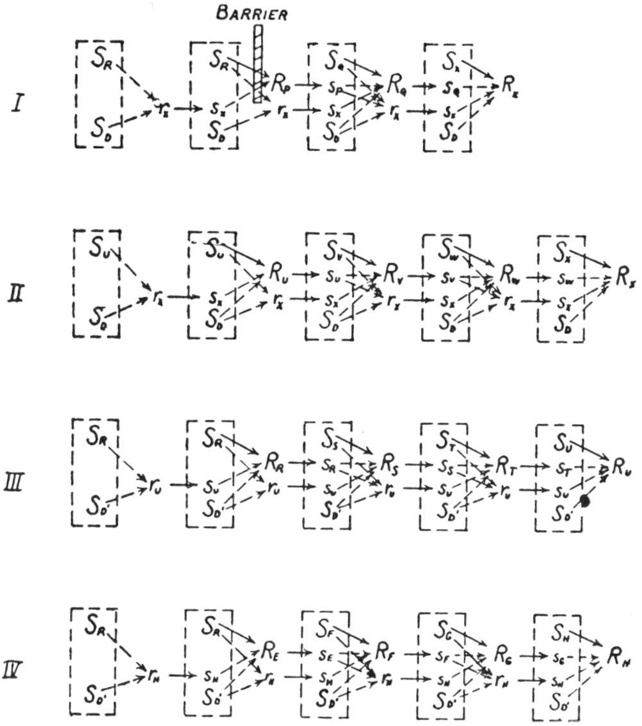

FIG. 2. Diagrammatic representation of the major immediate excitatory tendencies in action sequences I, II, III, and IV, which correspond to Paths $R \rightarrow X$, $U \rightarrow X$, $R \rightarrow U$, and $R \rightarrow H$, respectively, of Fig. 1. Remote excitatory tendencies are not represented. The barrier is assumed to have been placed before R_P after Sequence I had become fairly well practiced and was working smoothly.

PAPER
8

error), in which case Sequence II would presumably follow at once and the problem would be solved for the organism but no insight would be involved. Since the trial-and-error type of behavior is almost certain to be present to a greater or less degree in situations such as the one here supposed, it is necessary to have in the experimental set-up some unambiguous opportunity for trial-and-error to operate relatively uncomplicated by other factors in order to have a basis for comparison and possible contrast with a situation in which insight may be an appreciable additional element. It is to be noted that such an opportunity for the manifestation of pure trial-and-error behavior is provided for by the path from R to H of

Fig. 1 (and Sequence IV in Fig. 2). Thus if upon the whole, after the frustration of Sequence I, Sequence IV is chosen as frequently by the organism as Sequence III, no insight is indicated. If, however, Sequence III is chosen a significantly greater proportion of the trials, this excess constitutes an indication of intelligence or insight and demands genuine explanation by any systematic theory of mammalian behavior.

Whatever may be the final conclusion regarding the abilities of albino rats in this respect, there can be little doubt that man and, presumably, some of the higher mammals show such a capacity.[6] Therefore we must face the question of why the organism should choose Sequence III, which will ultimately lead to success, rather than Sequence IV, which will not. How is the possession by the organism of the latent or implicit habit sequence (II) able to influence in any way the choice between III and IV in favor of III? If we can succeed in answering this question we shall probably not only have isolated one important and basic mechanism of intelligence and insight, but may possibly have made a step forward in the understanding of the more elaborate forms of reasoning proper where verbal symbolic reactions are primarily involved.

PAPER

8

III. Maier's *Gestalt* Interpretation

Before proceeding to the consideration of our own interpretation of this fascinating problem, it will be well to glance briefly at that offered by Maier himself. He states that when he attempted to account for the animals' alleged preference for the path from R to U over that from R to H, by means of associative principles, he encountered difficulties. He argues, first, that since S_R has associations leading both to Sequences III and IV ($R \to U$ and $R \to H$, Fig. 1), it should be expected that the animals would choose the one as readily as the other. But insightful behavior demands that some preference should be shown to III over IV. Thus he concludes that association cannot account for the phenomenon (17, p. 92).

[6] Recently Wolfe and Spragg (29) have reported results which, taken in conjunction with certain characteristics of Maier's technique, lead them to question whether the albino rat can combine habit segments, as supposed by Maier.

He accordingly turns from association to *Gestalt* concepts as offering more promising possibilities. His remarks concerning a substantially similar situation appear also to be applicable to the one before us:

The concept of patterns or *Gestalten* thus seems to be a necessary assumption to explain these complex types of behavior. The fact that a rat can choose the . . . means to an end without previously having reached this end by any of these means, seems to make a pattern concept almost a necessity. A temporal chain is not sufficient; it must be an immediate whole.

A little examination of the nature of our problem seems to show, however, that the concept of *Gestalten* leads to the same sterile issue as the naïve associative view which Maier quite properly rejected. It is to be observed that Maier does not claim to have demonstrated exactly how patterns lead in the above situation to correct rather than incorrect choices. One might say, of course, that under the stress created by the frustration of I, Sequences III and II become fused into a *Gestalt* or unity in the sense that together they somehow solve the problem, whereas Sequences IV and II do not so fuse. But such an interpretation of *Gestalten* as an explanatory principle would naïvely beg the question, since the deduction of this fusion from more basic principles is the essence of the problem before us. Such a utilization of the concept of *Gestalten* would be a mere tautological gesture; it would merely re-assert the fact of problem solution in a new terminology without in any sense deducing the outcome from any principles whatever. It is true that the history of science reveals many cases of such naïve procedures, though, so far as the writer is aware, no one has ever put forward this particular argument.

PAPER 8

But if ordinary association and *Gestalt* principles have both failed, what other possibility remains? The writer is inclined to the view that the principles of association between stimuli and responses, particularly as revealed in modern conditioned-reaction experiments,[7] offer a possibility of explana-

---

[7] In order to correct a frequent misunderstanding, due presumably to the wide dissemination of the views of J. B. Watson, the writer wishes to make it quite clear

tion in a manner which Maier's analysis failed to take into consideration. We shall now proceed to an examination of this possibility.

IV. A Suggested Stimulus-Response Explanation of the Adaptive Assembly of Habit Segments

A somewhat detailed stimulus-response analysis of action Sequences I, II, III, and IV, as sketched above, is given in Fig. 2. The S's at the top of each diagram represent typical stimuli as received from the external receptors. S_D and $S_{D'}$ represent persisting internal stimuli such as hunger, thirst, sex, etc., and the s's represent proprioceptive stimulations. Broken arrows indicate acquired or learned tendencies, whereas solid lines indicate what are presumed to be innate or unacquired tendencies.

In this connection it is to be noted that an anticipatory goal

reaction appears in the first segment of each of these sequences (5). For example, in the first sequence there appears r_x, which is supposed to be a relatively inconspicuous component of the goal reaction R_x, brought forward to the beginning of the series presumably through its association with S_D or through the action of trace reactions while in their early stages (or both), and which, once there, becomes associated with S_R. In the same way we find r_x at the beginning of Sequence II (having originally been a component of R_x),[8] r_U at

that neither here nor in any previous publications has he assumed that the more complex forms of behavior are synthesized from reflexes which play the rôle of building blocks. This may or may not be true. His working hypothesis is, rather, that the *principles of action* discovered in conditioned reaction experiments are also operative in the higher behavioral processes. The compound adjective in the expression, 'conditioned-reflex principles,' accordingly refers to the locus of *discovery* of the principles rather than to their locus of *operation*.

[8] That terminal or goal and near-goal reactions do come forward in behavior sequences is amply substantiated by a number of investigations, among which may be mentioned those by Lumley (14, 15, 16), Mitchell (22), Spragg (25), and Miller (21). In some of the investigations just mentioned, the anticipatory (or antedating) reactions actually come forward in their entirety and supplant reactions properly belonging in the positions in question. Spragg's study also shows anticipatory tendencies not only for goal reactions, but for sub-goal reactions as well. Moreover, it suggests that sub-goal reactions tend to come forward with less vigor than goal reactions, quite as the goal gradient hypothesis would lead us to expect.

the beginning of Sequence III (having originally been a component of R_U), and r_H at the beginning of Sequence IV (having originally been a component of R_H). It is assumed, further, that similar components of all reactions in any given series tend to come forward and become associated with the external stimulus component in the same manner, though because of the difficulty of representing them in detail only the anticipatory goal reactions are shown in Fig. 2. A complete set of anticipatory reactions, emanating from both goal and sub-goal reactions, are, however, shown in the first segment of Fig. 3.

Fig. 3 is designed to show the dynamics of the situation at point S_R after the barrier comes in to frustrate and extinguish Sequence I. This is regarded as the crucial point of the theoretical problem. A study of Fig. 3, in conjunction with Fig. 2 from which it was derived, shows that the ordinary principles of the association of stimuli and responses, when applied in a thorough-going fashion, actually lead in a logical and straightforward manner to the expectation that an organism capable of functional anticipatory reactions (*e.g.*, r_U) would be more likely to react with the sequence

PAPER
8

$$R_R \rightarrow R_S \rightarrow R_T \rightarrow R_U \rightarrow R_V \rightarrow R_W \rightarrow R_X$$

and consequently with a successful solution, than by the reaction

$$R_E \rightarrow R_F \rightarrow R_G \rightarrow R_H$$

which is not a solution.

At bottom the decisive factor in this competition (Fig. 3) is the presence of s_U, with its excitatory tendency to evoke R_R rather than R_E. But s_U, in turn, was necessarily dependent upon the presence of r_U, an anticipatory or antedating reaction. The details of the dominance of r_U over the other anticipatory reactions, and of R_R over R_E, are explained in the legend of Fig. 3, which must be traced through in detail if the reader is to understand the deduction. It may be noted that r_U is a pure-stimulus or symbolic act (4), since the only function that it performs is to release by its action the propriocep-

PAPER
8

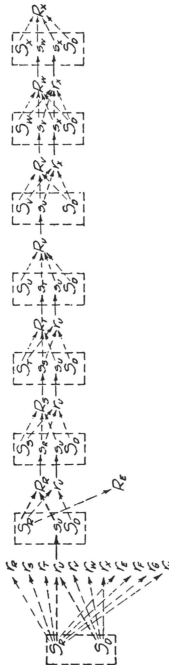

Fig. 3. Diagrammatic representation of the dynamics of the situation at the problem point S_R after the frustration and extinction of the excitatory tendencies originally emanating from it to the sequence $R_P \to R_Q \to R_X$. Note that all of the excitatory tendencies here represented are taken from Fig. 2. Thus the excitatory tendencies from S_R to r_R, r_S, r_T, and r_U come from Sequence III, those from S_R to r_E, r_F, r_G, and r_H come from Sequence IV, and those from S_D to r_U, r_V, r_W, and r_X come from Sequence II. Referring, now, to the above figure, it may be seen that of the several anticipatory reactions just mentioned, r_U, only, has more than one excitatory tendency. The one from S_R comes from the beginning of Sequence III, whereas the one originating in S_D comes from the first reaction of Sequence II ($S_D \to R_U$). All the other r's are accordingly assumed to play minor rôles and are dismissed from further consideration.

At the next segment there appears another critical situation, the actual competition between R_R and R_B. It may be seen from the diagram that R_R has two excitatory tendencies, both originally functioning at the beginning of Sequence III, whereas R_B, its competitor, has only one excitatory tendency, that originating from the beginning of Sequence IV. Because of the advantage of the bond emanating from s_U to R_R, the latter reaction must have the advantage over R_B. Thus the presence of s_U raises the reaction from the status of trial-and-error into the realm of insight or intelligence without the intervention of any special psychic agent.

tive stimulus s_U, which ultimately leads to an intelligent rather than to a stupid reaction.[9]

Here, then, we appear to have laid bare before us the mechanism of *one* type of intelligence or insight. It turns out, in fact, to be associative in nature, though distinctly not in the simple and direct fashion conceived by Maier. Thus there has apparently evolved on a purely physical basis a type of reaction which has sometimes been supposed possible only by a kind of miraculous intervention of some non-physical (psychic) agent called mind or consciousness. To state the same thing in other words, we appear to have before us here a deduction of insight in terms such that it might conceivably be constructed by a clever engineer as a non-living—even an inorganic—mechanism.

V. Seven Corollaries

A study of Figs. 3 and 4 leads to the statement of a number of corollaries.

PAPER 8

(1) One of these takes its origin from the remoteness and general tenuity or feebleness of the mechanism leading to the resolution of the competition in favor, first, of r_U and, second, of R_R, upon which this supposed act of intelligence depends (Fig. 3). Because of the obviously unstable nature of this mechanism, it might naturally be expected that it would be easily upset, that even weak antagonistic trial-and-error impulses would frequently over-ride it, and that, as a consequence, only too often it would fail completely. Thus if the excitatory tendency from S_R to R_E chanced to be much stronger than that from S_R to R_R, the 'intelligence' mechanism of s_U to R_R would be over-ridden. The relative rarity of genuinely 'intelligent' action of the kind here under consideration, even among humans with the advantage of their pre-

[9] It seems probable that when the animal meets the barrier (Sequence I, Fig. 1), R_P will be extinguished but r_X may largely escape extinction, and perseverate (see pp. 238 ff.) to the point where the choice is made between the two other paths. In that event s_X would appear in the first stimulus complex (and perhaps later ones) of Fig. 3. This would give r_U, as well as r_V and r_W (Sequence II, Fig. 1), an additional excitatory tendency at the outset. In the interest of simplicity of presentation this is left out of Fig. 3, since the deduction does not require it.

sumably additional verbal-symbolic powers, constitutes substantial general corroboration of this deduction.

(2) The excitatory tendencies behind the sequence $R_R \rightarrow R_S \rightarrow R_T \rightarrow R_U$ (Fig. 4) lack the strong support of the $S_{D'}$ which it has in III of Fig. 2. From this consideration follows the corollary that this particular segment of the completed act of insight should be made more slowly and haltingly, that it should be more easily over-ridden by contrary tendencies and more subject to disruption by external inhibitions, etc., than would the final section, $R_U \rightarrow R_V \rightarrow R_W \rightarrow R_X$, which has its accustomed support of S_D (Sequence II, Fig. 2).

(3) As a further corollary it may be pointed out that the particular weakness just mentioned should be especially marked at the outset of the sequence; *i.e.*, at act R_R, since this act lacks its accustomed stimulus $S_{D'}$ and also the proprioceptive stimulus from a preceding act in the series such as is found elsewhere throughout all sequences which are really integrated. This, however, is also true of the first act of all series (Fig. 2).

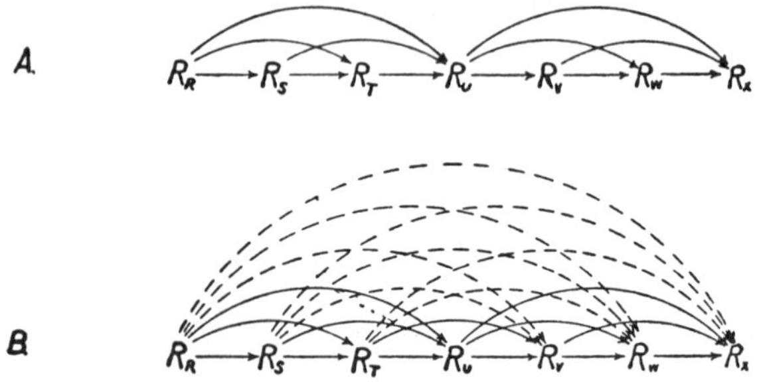

FIG. 4. Diagrammatic representation of both immediate and remote excitatory tendencies when (A) Sequences III and II of Fig. 1 first function as a (frail) unity, and when (B) they have functioned together with reward frequently enough to produce a thoroughly integrated whole with a full set of remote excitatory tendencies. The broken lines in the lower diagram represent the additional remote excitatory tendencies which constitute the basis of the more complete integration of the two habit segments supposed to come with contiguous association.

As a matter of observed fact, long series, at least, do commonly show at their beginning exactly the sluggishness which a mechanism of this kind would produce (8).

(4) As a fourth corollary, it should be pointed out that on

the average there ought to be a slight tendency to a relatively lower speed of locomotion especially in the neighborhood of R_U at the first execution of a complete intelligent act. The reason for this expectation is that since each of the two segments has been practiced as a unit, there should be remote excitatory tendencies extending throughout each series which should support the action of each segment. But, since the two segments have not been practiced in immediate succession, we should not expect such facilitating tendencies to extend across the junction from one to the other. The situation is shown in section A of Fig. 4. The relative lack of remote excitatory tendencies in the neighborhood of R_U should diminish the vigor of reaction at this point below what it would be in a well-integrated sequence, which, among other things, should diminish the speed of locomotion. It is to be expected, however, that this tendency may be difficult to detect unless comparison is made with a good control because the sequence beginning with R_U (Corollary 2) presumably will have a faster rate than the one immediately preceding it.

PAPER
8

(5) After a small amount of rewarded practice, however, the act would cease to be specifically intelligent in the sense of depending upon the r_U-mechanism elaborated above, and the remote bonds would be formed as in B, of Fig. 4. At this latter stage there would, obviously, be no tendency to retardation in the neighborhood of R_U. Moreover, the fractional goal reaction of R_X (*i.e.*, r_X) would become associated with the reactions of the sequence $R_R \rightarrow R_U$ as well as $R_U \rightarrow R_X$, so that what were two segments before would become in a functional sense a single segment, though doubtless in certain situations (**8**, 406 *ff.*) the components would retain a capacity to unite separately in new combinations.

(6) It is clear that the combination of two habit segments is a special case because the posterior segment has its posterior end securely anchored at the goal reaction (R_X), and the anterior segment has its anterior end securely anchored to the external stimulus of the problem situation (S_R). The more general case is that in which the solutional sequence is made up from three or more segments; in the case of a spontaneous

assembly of such habit segments, the middle segment would be attached directly neither to the goal reaction nor to the external stimulus component of the problem situation. A careful examination of the presumptive behavior of the type of anticipatory mechanism such as r_U and r_R (Fig. 2) leads to the belief that such an event might possibly occur. The linkage in this case would, however, appear to be far more tenuous even than that represented in Fig. 3 and emphasized in Corollary 1 above. It is accordingly believed that such a type of spontaneous habit synthesis will be very rare indeed, even in organisms especially gifted in the functioning of anticipatory goal and sub-goal reactions.

(7) It is evident, however, that chains of three or more segments may easily be formed on separate occasions by the action of the intelligence mechanism elaborated in Section IV above, supplemented by the consolidating or integrating principle of association by contiguity which would begin operating immediately upon the initial act of insight. Thus segments 'one' and 'two' might be joined on one occasion by insight; later, segments 'two' and 'three' might be similarly joined. Now, the two newly compounded segments overlap with respect to segment 'two'; this overlapping reduces the three original segments to the functional status of two, thus permitting the insight mechanism to operate substantially as elaborated in Section IV.

VI. THE PROBLEM OF THE INITIAL SPONTANEOUS USE OF IMPLEMENTS

Special interest attaches to the results of the preceding analysis because it rather looks as if the associative mechanisms there elaborated are also responsible for the spontaneous utilization of objects as implements or tools. An instance often cited as an example of such action is that described by Köhler, on the part of his chimpanzee, Sultan (**10,** 132 *ff.*). In this case the ape had learned to drag in through the bars of his cage a bit of fruit placed a certain distance outside. On a particular trial, however, Köhler put in the cage two bamboo sticks, neither of which was long enough to reach the food.

The animal first tried to obtain the fruit with one of the short sticks. After repeated failure he began playing with the two sticks. This (apparently) random manipulation finally resulted in the insertion of the end of the smaller stick into the hollow end of the larger. Soon after this took place, the animal reached through the bars with the combination stick and obtained the fruit. This union of action segments constituted the solution of the problem. Unfortunately it is not entirely clear whether the animal had ever before joined two objects in a somewhat similar manner, and there is no control in the plan of the experiment to show that the solution was not a mere accident. To be a clear case of insight in the sense of the term here employed, the joining of the sticks should have been performed a number of times in the recent past in random play, but should never have been used in the securing of food.

An experimental arrangement which promises less ambiguous evidence of insight in the field of implement or tool using might be set up on the analogy of the Maier experiment, somewhat as follows:

PAPER 8

Sequence I. An ape is trained to press upward, by means of a stick three feet long, against a toggle electric switch placed on the wall out of his reach; after which an electrically operated automatic machine close at hand will give him a grape.

Sequence II. A similar switch is placed three feet higher on the wall of another room, and the ape is trained to operate this with a six-foot stick which must be chosen from among two three-foot ones also available. After the pushing of the switch, a machine similar to that of Sequence I will give the animal a grape.

Sequence III. The animal is trained to put two sticks, each three feet long, together in such a way that one fits into a socket in the end of the other, making a stick six feet long. This training should be in still a different room. The reward in this case must be different from that of Sequences I and II, possibly the release from the room to return to the animal's living quarters.

Sequence IV. In a fourth room, the ape learns to place two sticks (other than those used in Sequence III) together so as to make a T, the reward in this case to be the same as that of Sequence III. One of the above sticks must have a socket in its middle instead of at its end, in order to permit the construction of the T.

The Problem. This would be set by placing the animal in the room with the high switch, as usual, but with two short sticks instead of the long one. This situation corresponds to the barrier placed in Path R → X, in the rat experiment discussed above. The stick to be inserted into a socket would be like that in Sequences III and IV, but the other stick would have sockets both at one end and in the middle. *Insight would be shown by the animal tending to put the sticks together end to end rather than in the form of the T.*

A great variety of problems bearing on the nature of the presumably numerous mechanisms mediating intelligent behavior may be set up on this general pattern. In addition to the use of children at various ages, rich returns probably await the systematic utilization of such experimental approaches with the various intellectual levels of young adults in homes for the feebleminded. It is conceivable that, in addition to filling out the picture of intelligence as delineated by investigations concerned mainly with intelligence testing, a matter of pure science and of the greatest importance, the leads so obtained might yield valuable hints for increasing the validity of the tests in actual practice.

PAPER
8

VII. A Second Case of Supposed 'Reasoning' in Rats, by way of Contrast

It may be well at this point to consider a second case of 'reasoning' in rats which Maier has bracketed with that discussed above on the grounds that in both, the animals are able to solve a problem by 'combining two experiences' (**19**). A diagram of the 'Y' maze employed in this second experiment is shown in Fig. 5. After being allowed to explore the maze for some hours, the rats were given from three to six days of 'preliminary tests,' the results of which are not reported. These may be regarded as practice or training in the act later to be tested. In this practice the animal was placed on one of the table tops, at X for example, where he found some food which he ate in part. The animal was then placed at Y and permitted to take his choice between going to Z or X. In case of the latter choice at point Q, the remainder of the food would be found and eaten. This would

involve turning to the right.   At other times, with the food
tasted at X as before, the animal was placed at Z and allowed
to take his choice of going to X or Y at point Q, which required a *left* turn to reach the food.   In a similar manner all
the combinations in both directions, a total of six, would be
practiced.

Then the routine or recorded tests were begun.   So far
as one can determine from the published report, these were

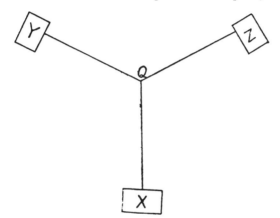

PAPER

8

Fig. 5.   Diagram of a rat maze used by Maier.   *X*, *Y*, and *Z* are small table
tops.   These are connected by pathways which intersect at *Q*.   In the present theoretical analysis, the alleys are assumed to be closed, though Maier actually used open
pathways.

substantially the same as the training tests just considered.
The problem was to determine whether, after such preliminary training, the animals would choose at point Q the
correct one of the two possible paths more frequently than
chance; *i.e.*, more than 50 per cent of the trials.   Under these
conditions, Maier reports in one typical experiment involving
18 trials on each of 19 normal animals (**19**), that 80.7 per cent
of the choices were correct, *i.e.*, were such as to lead directly
back to the food just tasted.   How is this excess of some 30
per cent above chance to be accounted for?

It is probable that a number of different mechanisms are
jointly operative in this situation.   It is believed, however,
that the following one, if not dominant, is a major component

and quite sufficient alone to account for all the phenomena so far reported.[10]   At bottom the explanatory hypothesis here to be presented is that the animal, having eaten food on a given table, *e.g.*, Table X (Fig. 5), has his body thrown into a characteristic posture which is to a certain extent distinct from that resulting from eating on any other table, and that this distinct action tendency (r_x) may persist to progressively diminishing degrees for a certain length of time.   When, now, the animal is taken from Table X, at which he has just eaten, and placed on Table Y, this reaction (r_x) may be assumed to persist throughout the action sequence involved in traversing alley YQ, so that at critical choice point Q there will be present as a decisive component in the combination of stimuli preceding a rewarded right turn the proprioceptive stimulus element s_x.   The same would be true of the action sequences leading to the other two tables.

Additional stimuli in the combination evoking the reaction at Q will be the perseverative effects of the sequence of acts, from Y to Q.   We will pool all these under the expression S_Y. Lastly, we shall let the visual and other stimuli of Q, as viewed from alley Y, be represented by S_{YQ}.   As a result we have at the critical choice point Q the following stimulus combination always preceding a rewarded right turn:

$$(\mathrm{I}) \qquad \boxed{\begin{array}{c} S_{YQ} \\ S_Y \\ s_x \end{array}} \rightarrow \text{Right turn (to alley } QX)$$

[10] The principles put forward in Section IV above lead to the expectation that animals would tend to go to a table on which they had just tasted food even if they had received no specific training with the tasting technique but had merely been trained to go from one table to another with a food reward.   The detailed deduction is too complicated to be given here.   Its substance is that this training would bring forward in the behavior sequence the fractional goal reaction, *e.g.*, r_x; thus s_x would be present in the stimulus complex at Q much as in formula I (p. 28).   When, later, the animal is given the tasting test for the first time, the perseverating s_x so aroused would summate with the s_x produced by the anticipatory mechanism.   But increase in the strength of a conditioned stimulus increases the strength of the reaction tendency (**23**, 384).   The s_x so enhanced would therefore be prepotent in evoking a choice of alley QX over any other action tendency due to the stimulus arising from an anticipatory reaction alone.

In a similar manner we have preceding the rewarded choice from Y to Z:

(II) $\begin{array}{|c|} \hline S_{YQ} \\ S_Y \\ s_Z \\ \hline \end{array}$ $\rightarrow$ Left turn (to alley QZ)

Likewise the two rewarded choices, when the animal starts at X, will be preceded and (later) controlled by the stimulus combinations or patterns:

(III) $\begin{array}{|c|} \hline S_{XQ} \\ S_X \\ s_Y \\ \hline \end{array}$ $\rightarrow$ Left turn (to alley QY)

(IV) $\begin{array}{|c|} \hline S_{XQ} \\ S_X \\ s_Z \\ \hline \end{array}$ $\rightarrow$ Right turn (to alley QZ)

PAPER
8

Lastly, the two rewarded choices at Q when the animal starts at Z will be preceded and (later) controlled by the stimulus combinations or patterns:

(V) $\begin{array}{|c|} \hline S_{ZQ} \\ S_Z \\ s_X \\ \hline \end{array}$ $\rightarrow$ Left turn (to alley QX)

(VI) $\begin{array}{|c|} \hline S_{ZQ} \\ S_Z \\ s_Y \\ \hline \end{array}$ $\rightarrow$ Right turn (to alley QY)

By a study of these stimulus formulæ it will be seen that there is a different pattern or combination of stimuli in each of the six cases. In particular, it is to be noted that the otherwise puzzling question of why, for example, the organism should turn *right* at Q when going to X from Y and to the *left* when going to the same table from Z is answered by the distinctiveness of stimulus *combinations* shown in formulæ I and V respectively. Thus is explained the excess of 30 per cent of correct choices beyond chance as reported by Maier and cited above.

Several corollaries flow from the above deduction. In the first place, the situation in formula I, say, because two of the components (S_{YQ} and S_Y) are also found in stimulus formula II which is conditioned to a left turn, still presents a picture of competition of two excitatory tendencies. It follows from this that accidental factors causing variation in the relative strength of these excitatory tendencies would frequently produce choices of the 'incorrect' path in spite of the generally dominant tendency. Secondly, since perseverations are usually short-lived and progressively diminish in strength through the passage of time, we would expect a diminution in the per cent of 'correct' choices with an increase in the time between the preliminary feeding and the test. Further, this diminution should increase *progressively* with the increase in the intervening time interval. It is also to be expected that during this period any 'extra' stimulation (**23**, **46**) evoking more or less violent reaction in the organism would tend to break up this perseverative activity. This would weaken or abolish the special increment to the strength of s_X resulting from the perseveration of the effects of eating at X, which, in turn, would diminish the strength of the tendency to make correct choices. Moreover, this weakening, other things equal, should be progressively greater the more intense the disturbing reaction.

A final corollary concerns Maier's experimental distinction between the kind of behavior which we have attributed above to the operation of a perseverating fractional goal reaction, on the one hand, and what he calls 'L' or learning, on the other. Maier produced this latter type of action by giving on a day preceding the test eight consecutive rewarded runs (with preliminary feeding, as usual) from Y to X, say. This increased amount of practice, particularly by reason of its relative recency, would be expected to strengthen the tendency of stimulus formula I (pp. 238 f.) to evoke a right turn at Q. Assuming that this compound stimulus has not wholly crystallized into a pattern and that the individual elements possess a considerable degree of individual excitatory potentiality, it follows that S_{YQ} and S_Y, even when separated from the customary s_x, would have a considerably enhanced tendency to evoke a right turn as the result of this special training. Then, on the day of the test, even if the trial should be made without any preliminary feeding on either tables X or Z, we should have the situation represented by the following formula:

(VII)

$$\boxed{\begin{array}{l} S_{YQ} \\ S_Y \end{array}} \longrightarrow \text{Right turn (to alley QX)} \\ \longrightarrow \text{Left turn (to alley QZ)}$$

The extra shaft (dotted line) on the upper arrow indicates the enhanced strength of the tendency to turn right due to the recent practice; Maier calls this 'L' or learning.

If, however, the animal has been fed at X just before the trial, this adds to the stimulus complex the element s_x which contributes another considerable element favorable to the right turn. The stimulus formula for this situation will be:

(VIII)

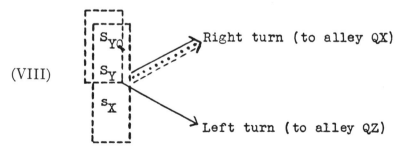

The third shaft (broken line) added to the upper arrow represents the increment to the strength of the right-turning tendency produced by adding s_x to the stimulus complex. This is the element which Maier calls 'R.' Accordingly, under these conditions we should expect an increase in the per cent of correct choices over conditions shown in formula VII. Formula VIII represents what Maier calls 'R + L.'

But if, instead, the animal is first allowed to taste on table Z, the stimulus formula will be:

(IX)

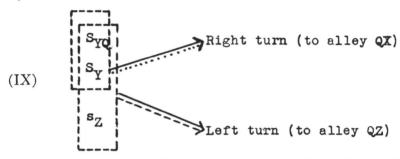

Here the dotted line ('L') leads to a right-turning action, and the broken line ('R') leads to a left-turning movement. Accordingly we should expect the two special tendencies to be opposed, i.e., the situation is what Maier has called 'R − L.' Clearly, then, stimulus formula IX should give a smaller percentage of reactions of the kind associated with the perseverating reaction than should stimulus formula VIII.

Once experimental values are available for 'R + L' and 'R − L,' there may be computed from them approximations to the values of 'R' and 'L' separately.[11] By means of this combination of techniques, Maier reports that, on the average, gross brain lesions were followed by a marked diminution in the 'R'-factor, but by no detectable change in the 'L'-factor.

PAPER
8

[11] One set of Maier's results is reported to yield, in round numbers:

$$R + L = 89 \text{ per cent} \tag{1}$$
$$R − L = 70 \text{ " " } \tag{2}$$

Adding (1) and (2), we have

$$2R = 159 \quad \text{per cent}$$
$$R = 79.5 \text{ " " } \tag{3}$$

Substituting (3) in (1), and solving for L, we have

$$L = 9.5 \text{ per cent}$$

Under these conditions 'R,' or the perseverational factor, turns out to be about eight times as potent as this amount of special training on 'L.' It seems likely that this general approach to such complex problems is capable of much wider use than is the case at present.

In this way, assuming that the experiment substantially survives repetition, Maier appears to have proved effectively both the reality and the distinctiveness of the two mechanisms or principles of action quite as is to be expected on the basis of the preceding analysis. But to have shown that the two processes, '*R*' and '*L*', are genuinely distinct is by no means to have shown that '*R*' in the *Y*-maze situation just considered is the same in its essential structure as what Maier calls reasoning in the situation described in Section II above, much less that it is a case of reasoning in any generally recognized sense. The results from the experiment discussed in Sections II to IV have the appearance of a spontaneous combination of two habit segments originally of independent acquisition. The *Y*-maze experiment shows, on the other hand, no indications of combined habit segments. It appears, rather, to be essentially a case of the perseveration of a goal reaction as a pure-stimulus act from one stimulus situation to a closely following one, the proprioceptive stimulus from this perseverating goal reaction becoming the critical element in differential stimulus compounds or patterns. Indeed, if the hypothesis of a perseverative goal reaction should prove to be sound, it seems doubtful whether it would be legitimate in this second case to designate (1) the preliminary eating, and (2) the conditions of the subsequent choice at *Q*, even as separate 'experiences'; such a continuity would seem to make them one.

PAPER

8

VIII. Summary

Taking as a point of departure an analysis of intelligent behavior published by Norman Maier, the view is put forward that a basic mechanism mediating one great class of such behavior is that of the spontaneous assembly of habit segments never previously associated with each other. Behavior of this kind is deduced from stimulus-response principles. If this deduction should turn out to be sound, it would amount to a proof that at least one form of insightful behavior is not an ultimate, unanalyzable entity but is, instead, a special, though somewhat complicated, case of association between stimuli and reactions. Indeed, the principles of action which appear by this deduction are of such a nature that they might conceivably be incorporated into an inorganic machine which would automatically solve such problems. This is not to deny either the reality or the importance of such forms of behavior. On the contrary, it leads to the view, mainly on the grounds of the novel character and distinctiveness of the mechanism mediating it, that an adequate understanding of such behavior is of special importance, both theoretical and practical. The above analysis does lead, however, to the denial of the necessity of postulating any peculiarly experiential, psychic, or configurational factors in order to explain the existence of this particular form of intelligent action.

Whether the forms of behavior involving the spontaneous assembly of habit segments shall be called 'reason' as Maier and Shepard are inclined to do, is not primarily a question of science, but, rather, one of taste and convenience. The present writer inclines to reserve the term 'reason' for application to those problem situations in which the solution is mediated through the action of symbolic verbal reactions. There seems even less justification for applying the term 'reasoning' to the behavior of animals on the Y-maze under the tasting technique which we have explained on the basis of perseveration.

PAPER
8

REFERENCES

1. BAERNSTEIN, H. D., AND HULL, C. L., A mechanical model of the conditioned reflex, *J. General Psychol.*, 1931, **5**, 99-106.
2. BENNETT, G. K., AND WARD, L. B., A model of the synthesis of conditioned reflexes, *Amer. J. Psychol.*, 1933, **45**, 339-342.
3. HOTELLING, H., Analysis of a complex of statistical variables into principle components, *J. Educ. Psychol.*, 1933, **24**, 417-441; 498-520.
4. HULL, C. L., Knowledge and purpose as habit mechanisms, PSYCHOL. REV., 1930, **37**, 511-525.
5. ———, Goal attraction and directing ideas conceived as habit phenomena, PSYCHOL. REV., 1931, **38**, 487-506.
6. ———, The goal gradient hypothesis and maze learning, PSYCHOL. REV., 1932, **39**, 25-43.
7. ———, The concept of the habit-family hierarchy and maze learning, PSYCHOL. REV., 1934, **41**, Part I (Jan.), 33-52; Part II (March), 134-152.
8. ———, The rat's speed-of-locomotion gradient in the approach to food, *J. Comp. Psychol.*, 1934, **17**, 393-422.

9. KELLEY, T. L., Crossroads in the mind of man, Stanford Univ. Press, 1928.

10. KÖHLER, W., The mentality of apes, Harcourt Brace and Co., 1925.

11. KRIM, N. B., Electrical circuits illustrating mammalian behavior and their possible engineering value, Thesis presented for the degree of Bachelor of Science, Mass. Institute of Technology, 1934; copy deposited in the Yale Library.

12. KRUEGER, R. G., AND HULL, C. L., An electro-chemical parallel to the conditioned reflex, *J. General Psychol.*, 1931, 5, 262–269.

13. LIPPMANN, W., A future for the tests, *The New Republic*, 1922, 33, 9–11.

14. LUMLEY, F. H., An investigation of the responses made in learning a multiple choice maze, *Psychol. Monog.*, 1931, 42, No. 189.

15. ——, Anticipation of correct responses as a source of error in the learning of serial responses, *J. Exper. Psychol.*, 1932, 15, 195–205.

16. ——, Anticipation as a factor in serial and maze learning, *J. Exper. Psychol.*, 1932, 15, 331–342.

17. MAIER, N. R. F., Reasoning in white rats, *Comp. Psychol. Monog.*, 1929, July, No. 29.

18. ——, Reasoning and learning, PSYCHOL. REV., 1931, 38, 332–346.

19. ——, The effect of cortical destruction on reasoning and learning in white rats, *J. Comp. Neurol.*, 1932, 54, 45–75.

20. MILL, J. S., A system of logic (8th edition), Harpers, 1887.

21. MILLER, N. E., A reply to 'Sign-Gestalt or Conditioned Reflex?' PSYCHOL. REV., 1935, 42, 280–292.

22. MITCHELL, M. B., Anticipatory place-skipping tendencies in the memorization of numbers, *Amer. J. Psychol.*, 1934, 46, 80–91.

23. PAVLOV, I. P., Conditioned reflexes: an investigation of the physiological activity of the cerebral cortex (trans. and ed. by G. V. Anrep), London: Oxford Univ. Press, 1927.

24. SPEARMAN, C., Abilities of man, N. Y.: The Macmillan Co., 1927.

25. SPRAGG, S. D. S., Anticipation as a factor in maze errors, *J. Comp. Psychol.*, 1933, 15, 313–329.

26. ——, Anticipatory responses in the maze, *J. Comp. Psychol.*, 1934, 18, 51–73.

27. THORNDIKE, E. L., Animal intelligence, N. Y.: The Macmillan Co., 1911.

28. THURSTONE, L. L., The theory of multiple factors, 1932, Edwards Bros., Ann Arbor, Mich.

29. WOLFE, J. B., AND SPRAGG, S. D. S., Some experimental tests of 'reasoning' in white rats, *J. Comp. Psychol.*, 1934, 18, 455–469.

PAPER
8

[MS. received November 9, 1934]

Offprinted from PSYCHOLOGICAL REVIEW, Vol. 42, No. 6, November, 1935
Printed in U. S. A.

THE CONFLICTING PSYCHOLOGIES OF LEARNING
—A WAY OUT [1]

BY CLARK L. HULL

Yale University

INTRODUCTION

One of the most striking things about the present state of the theory of learning and of psychological theory in general is the wide disagreement among individual psychologists. Perhaps the most impressive single manifestation of the extent of this disagreement is contained in 'Psychologies of 1925' (**14**) and 'Psychologies of 1930' (**15**). In these works we find earnestly defending themselves against a world of enemies, a hormic psychology, an act psychology, a functional psychology, a structural psychology, a Gestalt psychology, a reflexology psychology, a behavioristic psychology, a response psychology, a dynamic psychology, a factor psychology, a psychoanalytical psychology, and a psychology of dialectical materialism—at least a dozen.

No one need be unduly disturbed by the mere fact of conflict as such; that in itself contains an element of optimism, since it indicates an immense amount of interest and genuine activity which are entirely favorable for the advancement of any science. What disturbs many psychologists who are solicitous for the advancement of the science of psychology is

[1] The substance of this paper was read as a portion of the symposium on 'Psychological theories of learning,' at the Pittsburgh meeting of the A. A. A. S., December 28, 1934.

The writer is indebted to Dr. Robert T. Ross for the material appearing in notes 7 and 8. Dr. Ross has also read and criticized the entire manuscript. Professor Max Wertheimer and Dr. George Katona also read and criticized an early form of the manuscript.

491

that of which these disagreements are symptomatic. To put the matter in an extreme form: if all of these twelve psychologies should be in specific disagreement on a given point, then at least eleven of them must be wrong, and in such a welter of error the twelfth may very well be wrong also; at all events, it is difficult under such circumstances to see how all can be right about everything.

The obvious implication of this general situation has recently called out a timely little book by Grace Adams (1) entitled, 'Psychology: science or superstition?' In this work she points out what we all know only too well—that among psychologists there is not only a bewilderingly large diversity of opinion, but that we are divided into sects, too many of which show emotional and other signs of religious fervor. This emotionalism and this inability to progress materially toward agreement obviously do not square with the ideals of

objectivity and certainty which we associate with scientific investigation; they are, on the other hand, more than a little characteristic of metaphysical and theological controversy. Such a situation leads to the suspicion that we have not yet cast off the unfortunate influences of our early associations with metaphysicians. Somehow we have permitted ourselves to fall into essentially unscientific practices. Surely all psychologists truly interested in the welfare of psychology as a science, whatever their theoretical bias may be, should cooperate actively to correct this.

But before we can mend a condition we must discover the basis of the difficulty. A clue to this is furnished by the reassuring fact that persisting disagreements among us do not concern to any considerable extent the results of experiment, but are confined almost entirely to matters of theory. It is the thesis of this paper that such a paradoxical disparity between scientific experiment and scientific theory not only ought not to exist but that it need not and actually will not exist if the theory is truly scientific. It will be convenient in approaching this problem first to secure a little perspective by recalling the essential characteristics of some typical scientific procedures.

Four Typical Scientific Procedures

There are many approaches to the discovery of truth; for our present purposes these may be grouped roughly under four heads.

The simplest method of discovery is random observation —the trusting to chance that some valuable datum may turn up in the course of miscellaneous search and experiment. It is hardly conceivable that there ever will come a time in science when an experimenter will not need to be on the alert for the appearance of significant but unexpected phenomena. A classical example of the occasionally immense significance of such accidentally encountered observations is the discovery of the X-ray.

A second method of very wide and successful application in the search for truth is that sometimes known as systematic exploration. This seems to be the method advocated by Francis Bacon in his 'Novum Organum' (2). In modern times the discovery of salversan, by Ehrlich, illustrates in a general way this indispensable type of research procedure.

PAPER 9

A third method widely employed in scientific investigations is that of the experimental testing of isolated hypotheses. Such isolated hypotheses often come as intuitions or hunches from we know not where; they occasionally appear in the form of prevailing traditions which are as yet inadequately tested by experiment. An example of the latter is the widespread belief that tobacco smoking interferes with the learning and thought processes (9).

A fourth procedure in the discovery of truth, and the one which particularly concerns us here, is found in experiments which are directed by systematic and integrated theory rather than by isolated and vagrant hypotheses. Such systematic theoretical developments are exemplified by relativity theory, chiefly in the hands of Einstein (7, 299), and by quantum theory (20), in the hands of a large number of individuals including Bohr, Rutherford, Heisenberg, Schrodinger, Dirac, and others. Perhaps the best-known investigation motivated by relativity theory is the astronomical observation whereby it was demonstrated that the image of a star whose light rays had passed close to the sun showed a certain amount of displacement from its true position, conforming both as to direction and amount with deductions made from the theory (7, 370). Possibly one of the most striking recent experiments based on quantum theory is the well-known discovery and isolation of 'heavy' water, at Columbia University a few months ago, by Professor Urey.

Our special concern here is to point out that this fourth type of investigation, in addition to yielding facts of intrinsic importance, has the great virtue of indicating the truth or falsity of the theoretical system from which the phenomena were originally deduced. If the theories of a science really agree with the experimental evidence, and if there is general agreement as to this evidence, there *should* be a corresponding agreement regarding theory. An examination of the nature of scientific theoretical systems and their relationship to the fourth type of scientific procedure just considered should aid us in coping with the paradox presented by the present unfortunate state of psychological theory.[2]

Four Essentials of Sound Scientific Theory

It is agreed on all hands that Isaac Newton's 'Principia' is a classic among systematic theories in science. It starts with eight explicitly stated definitions and three postulates (laws of motion) (16, pp. 1–13), and from these deduces by a rigorous process of reasoning the complex structure of the system. Many persons who may not be overly familiar with the technical details of classical mathematical physics will be able to understand the essentials of such a system from our knowledge of ordinary Euclidian geometry, which as a systematic structure is substantially similar. In the geometries we have our definitions, our postulates (axioms), and, following these, the remarkable sequence of interrelated and inter-

[2] This emphasis on the fourth type of experimental approach is not to be understood as an advocacy of it as an exclusive method in psychology; neither is it being urged that theoretical considerations are paramount. Many approaches are necessary to produce a well-rounded science. Some temperaments will prefer one approach, some another, thus leading to a useful division of labor.

locking theorems which flow so beautifully by deduction from the basic assumptions. In a truly scientific system, however, a considerable number of the theorems must constitute specific hypotheses capable of concrete confirmation or refutation. This was eminently true of Newton's system. For a very long time the Newtonian physics stood this test, though finally certain important deductions from his postulates failed of confirmation, and it fell. Had Newton's system not been firmly anchored to observable fact, its overthrow would not have been possible and we would presumably be having at the present time emotionally warring camps of Newtonians and Einsteinians. Fortunately, we are spared this spectacle.

To summarize in a formal and systematic manner, it may be said that for a candidate to be considered as a sound scientific theory it must satisfy four basic criteria.[3]

I. The definitions and postulates of a scientific system should be stated in a clear and unambiguous manner, they should be consistent with one another, and they should be of such a nature that they permit rigorous deductions.

PAPER 9

II. The labor of deducing the potential implications of the postulates of the system should be performed with meticulous care and exhibited, preferably step by step and in full detail. It is these deductions which constitute the substance of a system.

III. The significant theorems of a truly scientific system must take the form of specific statements of the outcome of concrete experiments or observations. The experiments in question may be those which have already been performed, but of particular significance are those which have not previously been carried out or even planned. It is among these latter, especially, that crucial tests of a theoretical system will be found.[4]

[3] As the reader examines these items it might be illuminating for him to consider the particular theoretical system which is his special aversion, and judge whether or not it passes each successive criterion. After having thus fortified himself, he might proceed cautiously to a similar examination of the system which he favors.

[4] For this reason it is especially desirable for the advancement of science that the proponents of theoretical systems publish the deductions of the outcome of as yet untried experiments. The failure of subsequent experimental verification of such de-

IV. The theorems so deduced which concern phenomena not already known must be submitted to carefully controlled experiments. The outcome of these critical experiments, as well as of all previous ones, must agree with the corresponding theorems making up the system.

Let us consider briefly some of the more important reasons why a sound scientific system should possess these four characteristics. Consider the first: If the postulates of an alleged system are not stated clearly they can hardly be known to the scientific public which may wish to evaluate the system. Moreover, if the postulates have never been explicitly written out by the sponsor of the system, the chances are high that they are not clear even to him. And, obviously, if the definitions and postulates of a system are not clear to the sponsor of the system, neither he nor anyone else can make specific and definite deductions from them.

PAPER

9

Second, deductions must be performed with rigor because only in this way can their implications become known. Obviously, until the implications of the postulates are known they cannot possibly be submitted to experimental test; and unless the deductions are rigorous the experimental test will be futile because it will have no real bearing on the soundness of the postulates. Indeed, without rigorous deductions a would-be system is nothing more than a vague and nebulous point of view.

Third, the deductions must be related specifically to the concrete data of the science in question, since otherwise they cannot be submitted to the absolutely indispensable experimental test. It is here that scientific theory differs (or *should* differ) sharply from metaphysical speculations such as concern ethics and theology. Metaphysics does not permit this continuous check on the validity of the deductions, which largely accounts for the interminable wrangles characteristic of that literature. This criterion accordingly becomes in-

ductions should not be regarded as in any way discrediting the author. Instead, it should be considered merely a normal incident in the evolution of science. Fortunately, in such situations it is the hypothesis which is on trial, not the proponent's reputation as a seer.

valuable in distinguishing psychological metaphysics from scientific psychological theory. By this criterion much of what at present passes as theory in our literature must be regarded as metaphysical, *i.e.*, as essentially unscientific.

Fourth, the labor of setting up the critical experiments designed to verify or refute the theorems thus rigorously deduced from the postulates must be performed thoroughly and impartially because, once more, we shall otherwise lack the indispensable objective test of the truth of the system.

It scarcely needs to be added that there is nothing either radical or new in the above criteria of sound scientific theory; on the contrary, the program is conservative and respectable to an eminent degree. Indeed, it has been accepted in science for at least two hundred years. Our purpose is mainly to urge that we really put into practice what we, with the other sciences, have known for a very long time. This we evidently have not done; otherwise we would not be confronted with the glaring paradox of the wildest confusion in the matter of theory coupled with substantial agreement in the field of experiment.

PAPER
9

Is Rigorous Theory in Psychology Possible?

No doubt many will feel that such standards of scientific theory may be suitable for theoretical physics, but that they are quite impossible in psychology, at least for the present. To take such a view is equivalent to holding that we can have no genuinely scientific theory in psychology. This is indeed conceivable, but if so we ought not to pretend to have theories at all. If scientific theories are really impossible in psychology, the quicker we recognize it, the better. There are signs, however, that the beginnings of a genuinely scientific theory of mammalian behavior are already on their way. Extremely promising examples of such achievements in intimately related fields have been published by Crozier (3) and by Hecht (8). The recent work of Gulliksen (6), in which he presents a genuinely rational equation for the learning curve, as distinguished from an empirically fitted formula, offers promise of a larger development in the field of mammalian learning.

It is probably not accidental that all three of the above studies are essentially mathematical. At present, on the other hand, the superficial appearance of the concepts regarding learning which are current among our theorists does not suggest ready mathematical treatment. And while this condition is probably more apparent than real, it serves to raise the important question as to whether rigorous logical deductions can be made on the basis of such quasi-mathematical concepts as have so far emerged from behavior experiments.

There is reason to believe that a genuinely scientific system may be constructed from such materials, and that the difficulty of making such theoretical constructs is not nearly so great as their rarity might lead one to expect. Obviously, the best evidence for such a belief is actual performance. Accordingly, the following section (pp. 501 *ff.*) of this paper is given over to the presentation of a suggested miniature scientific system based on typical quasi-mathematical concepts. This has been developed by means of a form of reasoning analogous to that employed in ordinary geometrical proofs. In it an effort has been made to conform to the criteria laid down above as necessary for a sound theoretical development. It is hoped that it will aid in making clear in some concrete detail the theoretical methodology here being advocated. Let us, accordingly, proceed to the critical examination of this miniature theoretical system in the light of our four formal criteria of what scientific theory should be.

At the beginning (pp. 501 *ff.*) there will be found a series of eleven definitions: of rote series, of the learning of rote series, of excitatory tendency, of inhibitory tendency, of spanning, of actual and of effective strength of excitatory tendencies, of remote excitatory tendency, of trace conditioned reaction, and so on.

Next there appears (p. 503) a series of explicitly stated postulates: that the remote excitatory tendencies of Ebbinghaus exist; that remote excitatory tendencies of Ebbinghaus possess the same behavior characteristics as do the trace conditioned reflexes of Pavlov (Lepley's hypothesis); that the period of delay of trace conditioned reflexes possesses an inhibition of delay; that inhibitions are additive; that caffeine retards the accumulation of inhibition; that inhibitions diminish more rapidly with the lapse of time than do related excitatory tendencies, and so on. So much for the first criterion.

There follows (pp. 504 *ff.*) a series of eleven theorems derived by a formal process of reasoning from the preceding postulates and definitions. For the most part each step of the reasoning is explicitly stated and the logical source of each is conscientiously given. In this connection it is to be observed that the deduction or proof of each theorem is a complex multiple-link logical construct involving the joint action of numerous principles or postulates, as contrasted with simple syllogistic reasoning where but two premises are employed. Moreover, it is to be noted that the system is an integrated one not only in that all the theorems are derived from the same postulates, but also in that the later theorems are dependent on the earlier ones in the form of a logical hierarchy, very much as in systems of geometry. In the derivation of these eleven theorems an attempt has thus been made to conform to the second criterion of a satisfactory scientific system.

Let us now proceed to the examination of this theorem hierarchy from the point of view of the third and fourth criteria.

The first four theorems, while logically necessary for the derivation of the later ones, do not themselves permit any direct experimental test. It is believed, however, that all of the others are sufficiently concrete and specific to permit definite experimental confirmation or refutation. Consider, for example, Theorem V. In plain language, this states that *the central portion of a rote series is more difficult to memorize than are the two ends.* This is, of course, a fact long known to experimentalists (**21**).[5] Theorem VI, which states that

[5] It is to be noted, however, that while the general picture of series difficulty as shown by experiment agrees with the theorem, there is disagreement in detail. The theorem demands that the maximum difficulty appear in the exact center of the series, whereas it actually appears a little posterior to the center. This, of course, reflects an inadequacy in the theory and calls for a revision of postulates. This systematic reconstruction has already gone far enough to correct the difficulty here considered. This

*the difficulty of learning syllables increases most rapidly at the
ends of the series but the rate of increase is less and less as the
point of maximum difficulty is approached,* has also long been a
laboratory commonplace (21). Theorem VII states that
*the reaction times of the syllables of a rote series will be shortest
at the ends and progressively longer as the middle is approached;*
this is a case of a deduction actually made in advance of
experiment. Recently, however, the deduction has had
experimental confirmation (24).

Now, let us look at Theorem VIII. This theorem means
that *syllables in the middles of partially learned series are known
better a short time after the termination of practice than they
are immediately at the conclusion of practice.* It is particularly
to be noted that this theorem flies directly in the face of the
old and time-honored principle of forgetting; *i.e.,* it demands
that performance shall *improve* instead of deteriorate with the
passage of time. When this deduction was first performed
our logic seemed to be carrying us into a topsy-turvy world,
but our postulates presented us with no alternative; scientific
theory is concerned with inflexible logic rather than with
predictions based on intuitions or wishes. A year or two
after the deduction was made, Ward submitted it to critical
experimental test and found the theoretical expectation
fully and completely substantiated (24).

And so we could go on through Theorems IX and X. It
will suffice to say that Theorem IX has recently been experimentally verified by Ward (24) after the deduction was made,
and that Theorem X states a striking law of economy of
learning long known to the literature (18, 375 *ff.*).

Finally we come to Theorem XI. Stripped of technical
verbiage, this theorem means that *the peak of difficulty in the
middle of a rote series when learned by massed practice under the
influence of caffeine will be lower than when learned by massed
practice in the normal condition.* Two or three years after this
deduction had been made, the author set up an experiment

may serve as an example of the successive-approximation procedure characteristic of
theoretical development in science.   The revised construct will be given in connection
with a full statement of the system to be contained in a contemplated publication.

PAPER
9

especially to test it. When the experiment was completed and the data tabulated, it was found that the deduction was *not* verified—the peak of difficulty in the middle of the series was a little higher under caffeine than in the control series, where the subjects learned the material in a normal condition (**10**). Here, then, is a case where a definite deduction has been flatly controverted by fact.

Clearly, where a theory is opposed by a fact, the fact has the right of way. In a situation of this kind something is obviously wrong, presumably with one or more of the postulates involved in the deduction. In this particular case suspicion naturally rests most heavily on Postulate VI. At all events, Theorem XI serves to round out and give a further note of realism to this miniature scientific theoretical system. It is a noteworthy event, in the present status of psychological theory, to have a deduction sufficiently anchored by logic to the postulates of the system that a collision with a stubborn experimental fact shall be able to force a revision of the system. It is reasonably safe to assume that the rarity of such collisions at present is not due to the infallibility of current theoretical constructs. Until our systems become sufficiently clear and definite for this kind of event to be of fairly frequent occurrence, we may well suspect that what passes as theory among us is not really making contact with our experimental facts.

A Miniature Scientific Theoretical System by Way of Illustration

Definitions

I. A rote series is a number of nonsense syllables presented visually one at a time for constant periods (*e.g.*, three seconds) with only a fraction of a second between exposures. The subject learns to speak each syllable while its predecessor is still in view, the overt immediate stimulus for each overt reaction being the visual stimulus arising from the preceding syllable.

II. A rote series is said to be learned when the subject can correctly anticipate each successive syllable throughout a single repetition.

III. An 'excitatory tendency,' as emanating from a stimulus, is a tendency for a reaction to take place more certainly and, in case it does occur, to do so more vigorously other things equal, soon after the organism has received said stimulus than at other times.

IV. An 'inhibitory tendency' is one which has the capacity to weaken the action potentiality of a concurrent excitatory tendency.

V. A syllable reaction tendency is said to be spanned by a remote excitatory tendency and by the parallel inhibition of delay (Postulate III) when said syllable reaction tendency falls between the stimulus syllable and the response syllable associated with the remote excitatory tendency and the parallel inhibition of delay in question.

VI. The 'actual' strength of an excitatory tendency is that strength it would display for action if uncomplicated by concurrent inhibitory tendencies.

VII. The 'effective' strength of an excitatory tendency is that strength it displays in action under whatever conditions of inhibition may exist at the time.

VIII. A remote excitatory tendency is an excitatory influence, initiated by a syllable as a stimulus, exerted upon any other syllable as a reaction with the exception of the syllable immediately following the stimulus syllable.

IX. A trace conditioned reaction is an S → R relationship (acquired in isolation by a special conditioning technique) which has the characteristic that an appreciable interval (e.g., sixteen seconds) may elapse between the presentation of the overt stimulus and the taking place of the overt response.[6]

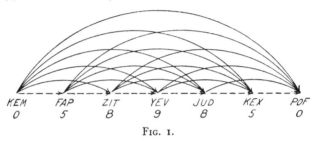

KEM	FAP	ZIT	YEV	JUD	KEX	POF
0	5	8	9	8	5	0

Fig. i.

Diagrammatic representation of both the immediate and the remote forward excitatory tendencies assumed to be operative in rote series. The straight broken arrows represent immediate excitatory tendencies and the curved solid arrows represent remote excitatory tendencies. The number of remote excitatory tendencies spanning a given syllable, such as ZIT, is given by the formula $(n - 1)(N - n)$ where N is the total number of syllables in the series and n is the ordinal number of the syllable whose span value is under consideration. Thus, in the above example, $N = 7$ and the n for ZIT $= 3$. Accordingly, $n - 1 = 2$ and $N - n = 4$. Consequently, ZIT should have 2×4 or 8 remote excitatory tendencies spanning it. The truth of this computation may be verified by counting the number of curved lines immediately above the syllable in question. The number of remote excitatory tendencies spanning the several syllables is given beneath each.

[6] What is spoken of as the 'overt' stimulus of a trace conditioned reaction is not regarded as the 'actual' stimulus. The 'overt' stimulus is supposed to set in motion some kind of slowly changing internal sequence more or less characteristic of each such stimulus. It is the stimulus value of the phase of this sequence immediately preceding the reinforcing stimulus which is regarded as the 'actual' stimulus of the trace conditioned reaction. It thus comes about that the stimulus of POF (Fig. 1) is compounded of 6 elements from as many different sources, whereas that of FAP arises from a single source. But, so far as is now known, the ease of conditioning is not influenced by the complexity of the stimulus, so that the 'actual' strength of the excitatory tendencies to the arousal of POF and FAP should be alike so far as this factor is concerned. This means, necessarily, that the *immediate* excitatory tendency from KEX to POF must be appreciably weaker than that from KEM to FAP or even from ZIT to YEV. This last deduction is obviously capable of experimental test.

X. 'Massed practice' is a method of learning in which the series is run through from beginning to end almost continuously, *i.e.*, with a pause only of from ten to twenty seconds between successive repetitions.

XI. 'Distributed practice' is a method of learning in which an appreciable interval of time (*e.g.*, one hour or more) is interposed between successive repetitions; otherwise it is the same as 'massed practice.'

Postulates

I. Rote series possess functionally potent remote excitatory tendencies extending forward from each syllable of the series as an overt stimulus to every syllable placed later in the series as an overt response except the response syllable immediately following the stimulus syllable. (Ebbinghaus, **4**, 106.)

II. The remote excitatory tendencies of Ebbinghaus possess the same characterstics as the trace conditioned reflexes of Pavlov. (Lepley's hypothesis, **12**; **13**.)

III. The period of delay of trace conditioned reflexes possesses a power to inhibit (temporarily) to a certain extent the functional strength of excitatory tendencies, the reactions of which would otherwise tend to take place during such period. (Pavlov, **17**, 173.)

IV. The inhibition of delay of each succeeding degree of remoteness (distance between overt stimulus and overt response) decreases progressively, each additional increment in remoteness diminishing the inhibition, on the average, by a constant amount. (Assumed by rough analogy to corresponding excitatory tendencies, **4**, 106.)

V. Inhibitions of delay operative at the same time summate arithmetically. (Assumed from analogy to excitatory tendencies, **22**, 36 *ff*.)

VI. Inhibitions of delay accumulate to a lesser degree when the subject is under the influence of caffeine than do associated excitatory tendencies. (Evans, **5**, 365.)

VII. When learning is performed by massed practice, the ratio of the actual strength of excitatory tendency to the inhibition of delay is, on the average, constant throughout the learning process, and such as usually to leave a positive effective strength of excitatory tendency. (Assumed as a first approximation.)

VIII. Inhibitory tendencies in the early stages of weakening through the lapse of time diminish more rapidly than do associated excitatory tendencies. (Pavlov, **17**, 99 and 58 *ff*.)

IX. A constant minimal strength of excitatory tendency is necessary to make recall possible even when no concurrent inhibition is present. (Assumed.)

X. The total aggregate actual excitatory tendency exerted on a syllable as a reaction tendency is, on the average, a constant for all syllables in a given list at a given time. (Assumed.)

XI. A constant minimal 'effective' strength is required of any given excitatory tendency for it to pass the threshold of overt reaction. (Assumed.)

XII. Under the conditions of rote learning, each repetition of a rote series adds, on the average, a constant positive increment to the actual strength of each excitatory tendency of the series. (Pillsbury, **18**, 370.)

XIII. The greater the functional or 'effective' strength of the excitatory tendency evoking a reaction, the less, on the average, will be the time elapsing between the stimulus and the reaction. (Simley, **23**.)

XIV. The 'actual' strength of excitatory tendencies accumulated through repetitions is not influenced by the previous presence of superposed inhibitions of delay. (Assumed.)

PAPER
9

Theorems

I

If the number of syllables in a rote series is N, and the ordinal number of a particular syllable counting from the beginning is n, the syllable as a reaction tendency will be spanned by $(n - 1)(N - n)$ remote excitatory tendencies.

1. It is evident (Postulate I and Fig. 1) that a given syllable in a rote series (Definition I) is spanned (Definition V) by remote excitatory tendencies (Definition VIII) all of which originate in the syllables anterior to itself and which terminate in syllables posterior to itself; *i.e.*, each syllable anterior to a given syllable has a remote excitatory tendency extending to each syllable posterior to said syllable n.

2. Since there are $(n - 1)$ syllables anterior to a given syllable and $(N - n)$ syllables posterior to it, it follows from (1) and Postulate I that there must be $(n - 1)$ $(N - n)$ remote excitatory tendencies spanning any given syllable as a reaction.

II

Within any rote series, the mean degree of remoteness of remote excitatory tendencies spanning a given syllable is the same for all syllables, viz., $\dfrac{N + 1}{2}$.

1. In continuous series the terms of which increase by constant steps, the mean of the series as a whole will be given by the mean of the values appearing at the respective ends of the series.

2. By Postulate I (and Fig. 1), the remote excitatory tendencies spanning a given syllable and originating in a particular syllable, satisfy the conditions of (1).

3. Take any syllable, n, of a rote series. It is evident (Fig. 1 and Postulate I) that those remote excitatory tendencies originating in syllable 1 and which span syllable n must have as their greatest length the distance in intervals from the last syllable of the series to the first syllable of the series, *i.e.*, $N - 1$ intervals, and for their shortest value the distance in intervals from syllable 1 to syllable $n + 1$, *i.e.*, $n + 1 - 1$, or simply n intervals.

4. From (1), (2), and (3) it follows that the remote excitatory tendencies of the set emanating from syllable 1 have as their mean that of $N - 1$ and n, or $\dfrac{N + n - 1}{2}$.

5. It is evident also (Postulate I and Fig. 1), that the excitatory tendencies of the set emanating from the second syllable must all be one step less in distance than those emanating from syllable 1, *i.e.*, that their mean value must be $\dfrac{N + n - 1}{2} - 1$; that the mean of those emanating from syllable 3 must be $\dfrac{N + n - 1}{2} - 2$, and so on, the amount subtracted from the fraction in the case of the mean of the last set being one less than the total number of sets.

6. But by (2) of Theorem I, the number of such sets is $n - 1$. It follows from (5) that the value subtracted from the fraction which appears in the formula representing the mean of the last set must be $(n - 1) - 1$, or $n - 2$.

7. From (4), (5), and (6), the final mean of the series must be $\dfrac{N + n - 1}{2}$ $- (n - 2)$. But by (5) and (6) the means of the several series constitute a continuous series exhibiting constant step intervals. Therefore, by (1), the mean of these means must be given by the mean of the first and last means of the series.

PAPER
9

8. By (5), (6), and (7), the mean extent of the series of means must be

$$\frac{\dfrac{N + n - 1}{2} + \dfrac{N + n - 1}{2} - (n - 2)}{2}$$

which becomes

$$\frac{N + n - 1 + N + n - 1 - 2n + 4}{4}.$$

The n's disappear, leaving

$$\frac{2N + 2}{4} \quad \text{or} \quad \frac{N + 1}{2}.$$

9. But since by assumption n was *any* syllable, it follows from (7) that the mean length of remote excitatory tendencies spanning any syllable is like that of all the others, viz., $\dfrac{N + 1}{2}$.

III

The total inhibition of delay operative at any given syllable position is measured by the number of remote excitatory tendencies spanning that syllable position.

1. By Postulates II and III and Definition IX, the intervals of delay of remote excitatory tendencies are the loci of inhibitions of delay.

2. By Postulate IV, the magnitude of these inhibitions of delay is a decreasing linear function of the degree of remoteness of the excitatory tendency in question.

3. It follows from (1) and (2) and Theorem II that the mean magnitude of inhibition (Definition IV) effective at any given syllable position in the series must be like that of all other syllable positions.

4. But if the mean inhibition of delay at all syllable positions is the same, it follows that the total inhibition at any given syllable position must be strictly proportional to the number of remote excitatory tendencies spanning that syllable position.

5. From (4) and Postulate V the theorem follows.

IV

The number of repetitions required for mastery of any particular syllable of a rote series is $T + R_I$, where T is a constant representing the number of repetitions required to produce learning when no inhibition is present, and R_I is a linear function of the number of spannings, i.e. of $(n - 1) (N - n)$.

1. By Postulates IX and XII and Definition II, a finite basic number of repetitions, T, will be required to produce the strength of excitatory tendency (Definition III) necessary to evoke reaction when there is no inhibition present.

2. By Postulate X and Definition VI, T must be a constant throughout any given rote series.

3. By Postulates XI and XII and Definitions IV and VII, there must be added to the threshold constant, T, certain repetitions to overcome any inhibitions present.

4. By Postulates V and XII, the number of repetitions at a given syllable will be a direct linear function of the aggregate inhibition at that syllable.

5. By (4) and Theorem III, the number of repetitions required to override the inhibition at any point within a given series must be a linear function of the value $(n - 1) (N - n)$.

6. From (2) and (5) it follows that the number of repetitions required for mastery of a rote series at any given point must be the sum of those required to pass the thres-

PAPER
9

279

hold of recall, T, plus those required to overcome the adverse influence of inhibition, $(n - 1) (N - n)$, *i.e.*, it must be $T + R_I$ where the latter is a linear function of $(n - 1) (N - n)$.

V

The number of repetitions required for mastery of the individual syllables of a rote series is greater in the central region of the series than at either end, the position of maximum difficulty falling at point $\frac{N + 1}{2}$.

1. Since, by Theorem IV, T in the expression $T + R_I$ is a constant, it follows that the variability in the number of repetitions required for the mastery of the several portions of a rote series will be a direct linear function of $(n - 1) (N - n)$ only, since R_I is a linear function of $(n - 1) (N - n)$.

2. If, now, we substitute in this formula the successive ordinal values at the beginning of any rote series, taking the length of the series at any convenient value such as $N = 9$, we have,

Syllable number (n),	1	2	3	4	5	6	7	8	9
Units of repetition to learn,	0	7	12	15	16	15	12	7	0

3. It may be seen by an inspection of the series of values in (2) that the number of repetitions required for mastery increases continuously from the ends toward the middle of the series, the maximum falling at point 5, which may be expressed by $\frac{N + 1}{2}$. Thus we have a concrete demonstration of the truth of the theorem for a particular series.[7]

VI

The rate of increase in the number of repetitions required for mastery in a rote series progressively diminishes as the point of maximal difficulty is approached from either end,

1. Taking any convenient length of series such as one of eight syllables ($N = 8$),

---

[7] A deduction of the essential portion of this theorem is yielded by the calculus:

$$R_I = a + m(n - 1)(N - n)$$

Expanding we have,

$$R_I = a - m[+ n^2 + n(N + 1) - N]$$

Differentiating with respect to n,

$$\frac{dR_I}{dn} = m[-2n + (N + 1)]$$

at the maximum,

$$\frac{dR_I}{dn} = 0$$

whence

$$- 2n + (N + 1) = 0$$

and solving for n we have,

$$n = \frac{N + 1}{2}$$

therefore, the position of maximum difficulty falls at the point $\frac{N + 1}{2}$.

we have by Theorem IV the formula $T + R_I$, remembering that T is constant and R_I is a linear function of $(n - 1)(N - n)$.

Syllable number (n),	1	2	3	4	5	6	7	8
Units of repetition to learn,	0	6	10	12	12	10	6	0

2. Here it may be seen that the units of repetition required for mastery increase by 6 points from syllable 1 to syllable 2, by 4 points from syllable 2 to syllable 3, and by 2 points from syllable 3 to syllable 4; *i.e.*, the rate of increase in difficulty progressively diminishes as the middle is approached.

3. A corresponding inspection reveals the same type of progression from the posterior end of the series as po.$_{int}$ $\frac{N + 1}{2}$ is approached.

4. (1), (2), and (3) constitute a concrete demonstration of the truth of the theorem for a particular series.[8]

VII

The reaction times of the syllables of a rote series learned by massed practice will be shortest at the end positions and progressively longer the farther the syllable from the ends of the series.

1. By Theorem V, syllables require an increasing number of repetitions to learn as the point of maximal difficulty of the series is approached from either end.

2. From (1) and Postulates XI and XII and Definition VII, it follows that the syllables near the ends of the series will rise above the threshold of recall progressively earlier than the syllables farther from the ends.

PAPER

9

---

[8] A deduction of the essential portion of this theorem is yielded by the calculus (see note to Theorem V):
It follows from

$$\frac{dR_I}{dn} = m[- 2n + (N + 1)] \text{ (where } m \text{ is positive)}$$

that

$$\frac{d^2R_I}{dn^2} = - 2m$$

whence, if

$$n < \frac{N + 1}{2}$$

$\left.\begin{array}{l} \dfrac{dR_I}{dn} \quad \text{is positive} \\[2mm] \dfrac{d^2R_I}{dn^2} \quad \text{is negative} \end{array}\right]$ whence, the curve increases toward the right with decreasing slope

if

$$n > \frac{N + 1}{2}$$

$\left.\begin{array}{l} \dfrac{dR_I}{dn} \quad \text{is negative} \\[2mm] \dfrac{d^2R_I}{dn^2} \quad \text{si negative} \end{array}\right]$ whence, the curve decreases toward the right with increasing (negative) slope.

3. From (2), Definition I, and Postulate XII, it follows that the syllables near the ends of the series will be overlearned more than those at the middle, *i.e.*, they will have progressively stronger effective excitatory tendencies (Definition VII) as their distance from the middle of the series increases.

4. By (3) and Postulate XIII the theorem follows.

VIII

In rote series learned to a variable but incomplete degree by massed practice, the number of successful reactions in the middle portion of the series will be greater after a certain period of no practice than at once after the conclusion of learning.

1. By Theorems I and III and Postulate VII, it follows that throughout the learning of rote series where the learning is performed by massed practice there will be variable but finite amounts of inhibition operative on the excitatory tendencies of syllables in the interior of series, *i.e.*, upon all but the two end syllables.

2. By Definition IV, this will depress the effective reactive capacity of such excitatory tendencies (Definition VII) below their actual values.

3. But, by Postulate VIII, inhibitions at first diminish more rapidly during the passage of time than do the associated excitatory tendencies.

4. By (3), during a given interval of no practice the inhibitory tendency will decrease by a finite amount.

5. It follows from (2) and (3) and Postulate XIV that in the early stages of a period of no practice following the learning of a rote series, the effective excitatory strengths of the interior syllables as reaction tendencies will be greater by finite amounts than at the conclusion of learning.

6. From (5) it follows that all syllables as reaction tendencies whose excitatory strengths are above the reaction threshold at the conclusion of incomplete learning will remain above after the period of no practice.

7. Since the degree of learning before interruption varies from one series to another (as here assumed), it follows that of those reaction tendencies which are below the threshold of recall some will differ from the threshold by an amount less than the finite amount indicated in (4).

8. From (3) and (7) it follows that certain syllables which are below the threshold of recall at the conclusion of incomplete learning will be above it at the conclusion of an optimal interval early in the period of no practice.

9. The group of effective reaction tendencies above the threshold at the conclusion of learning (6) added to the group which pass the threshold after an optimal interval of no practice (8) will make a sum larger than the former alone, from which the theorem follows.

IX

In just barely learned rote series the reaction time of syllables in the interior of the series will be shorter after an optimal period of no practice than for the corresponding individual syllables at the conclusion of learning by massed practice.

1. By reasoning analogous to that of (1), (2), (3), and (4) of the proof for Theorem VIII, it follows that the effective excitatory strength of just-learned syllables in the middle of rote series will be greater at some point early in the period of no practice than at the conclusion of learning by massed practice (Definition X).

2. By (1) and Postulate XIII, this increased excitatory strength will be accompanied by shortened reaction time, from which the theorem follows.

X

Rote series will be learned with fewer repetitions by distributed practice than by massed practice.

1. By Theorems II, III, and IV, the most difficult syllables to memorize of a rote series are loaded with inhibitions of delay.

2. By Definition XI, the method of distributed practice involves appreciable periods of time between repetitions. By Postulate VIII these time intervals, if not too long, will dissipate the inhibition more rapidly than the associated excitatory tendency. It follows that for a given amount of training the method of distributed practice will yield relatively less accumulated inhibition than by massed practice.

3. From (2) it follows (Postulates XI and XII) that the method of distributed repetitions will bring the most difficult syllable above the threshold of recall with fewer repetitions than will be the case by the method of massed repetitions.

4. But, by Definitions I and III, the number of repetitions required to learn rote series is that required to learn the most difficult single syllable.

5. By (3) and (4), the theorem follows.

XI

The value obtained by dividing the number of repetitions required to bring syllables above the threshold at the ends of rote series, by the number required in the middle of the same series, will be larger when the learning is done under the influence of caffeine than when done in the normal condition, the learning in both cases to be performed by massed practice.

1. By Theorem V, the middles of rote series learned by massed practice require more repetitions for learning than do the ends.

2. From (1) it follows that the number of repetitions per syllable for learning at the ends divided by the number at the middle R_E/R_M will yield a value less than 1.

3. Now, by Postulate VI, inhibitions accumulate to a lesser degree, other things equal, when the learning is performed under the influence of caffeine. It follows from this and Theorems II and III that less inhibition will accumulate in the middle of the series in question when learning is performed under the influence of caffeine.

4. By (3), Definition IV, and Postulate XII, it follows that the middle syllables will be learned with less repetitions under caffeine than in the normal condition, *i.e.*, that R_M will be smaller than normal. Since caffeine has no such influence on syllables not inhibited, R_E will remain the same.

5. But to reduce R_M in the division R_E/R_M will increase the resulting values.

6. From (5) the theorem follows.

PAPER
9

SOME PROBLEMS CONNECTED WITH THE EVALUATION OF PSYCHOLOGICAL THEORY

The recognized principles of science, then, provide us with a method which seems capable of bringing some kind of order out of the present chaos in theoretical psychology. Moreover, the program appears to be one to which all theorists, however diverse their postulates provided they are not essentially metaphysical or mystical, may subscribe. Indeed, it seems to be so firmly rooted in the traditions and essential logic of science that all would-be theoretical work will ultimately come to be judged by the scientific public according to this standard, regardless of the views of the theorists themselves. This brings us to the consideration of certain concrete problems which arise when an attempt is made to evaluate the claims of competing theoretical systems.

In the first place, it should be obvious that all mere systems of classification must be rejected. A dictionary may be systematic, but it can hardly be rated as a theoretical system even when the terms are largely of new coinage. Merely to call a bit of learning behavior a case of 'closure' or 'insight' on the one hand, or a case of 'conditioning' or 'trial-and-error' on the other, will not serve. Such systems cannot pass even the first criterion.[9]

Next we must consider the nature of the concepts and postulates which are admissible as the basis for psychological theory. Some psychologists appear to have assumed that only principles incapable of direct observational verification [10] should be admitted as postulates, whereas others may conceivably have assumed that only principles capable of direct observational verification should be admitted. In a similar manner, one group of theorists may insist that the postulates from which psychological systems evolve must be concerned with *parts*, while another group may insist that they must concern *wholes*. One group of theorists may insist that the postulates must come solely from conditioned reflex experiments, whereas to another group such postulates might not be at all acceptable.

[9] It appears to be at this point that most current attempts in the field of psychological theory break down. Their concepts appear not to be of such a nature that significant theorems may be drawn from them by a rigorous logic. A theoretical system without proven theorems is a paradox, to say the least.

[10] The postulates of a system may be susceptible of two types of verification—one indirect and the other direct. Indirect verification occurs when a deduction from a combination of postulates is observationally confirmed. The failure of such a verification throws doubt on the soundness of all of the postulates involved. This particular doubt is removed when appropriate change is made in one or more of these postulates so that deductions from them conform not only to the new observations but to all those phenomena previously deduced and verified. All postulates are susceptible of indirect verification, but some postulates permit direct verification and some do not. Postulates regarding the positions and movements of electrons, for example, permit indirect verincation but not direct observation.

From the present point of view this argument is quite footless. Actually, all such groups beg the main question. The question at issue is: Can more theorems which will be confirmed in the laboratory be deduced from postulates which are principles of dynamics, or more from postulates which are principles of mechanics, or more from a combination of both types of postulates; can more sound theorems be deduced from postulated parts, or more from postulated wholes, or more from a combination of the two? These are matters which should properly await the outcome of trial; it is conceivable that numerous distinct sets of postulates may prove more or less successful.

The history of scientific practice so far shows that, in the main, the credentials of scientific postulates have consisted in what the postulates can *do*, rather than in some metaphysical quibble about where they came from. If a set of postulates is really bad it will sooner or later get its user into trouble with experimental results. On the other hand, no matter how bad it looks at first, if a set of postulates consistently yields valid deductions of laboratory results, it *must* be good.[11] In a word, a complete *laissez-faire* policy should obtain in regard to postulates. Let the psychological theorist begin with neurological postulates, or stimulus-response postulates, or structural postulates, or functional postulates, or factor postulates, or organismic postulates, or Gestalt postulates, or sign-Gestalt postulates, or hormonic postulates, or mechanistic postulates, or dynamic postulates, or postulates concerned with the nature of consciousness, or the postulates of dialectical materialism, and no questions should be asked about his beginning save those of consistency and the principle of parsimony.

PAPER
9

Third, we must be extremely careful to insure the rigor of our deductions. Perhaps the most common fallacy in current would-be theories is the *non sequitur*—the supposed conclusion simply does not follow from the postulates.

[11] Consider the Riemannian geometry, which insists that the sum of the angles of a triangle is greater than two right angles (**19**, 58). This is repugnant to common sense, yet Einstein used the Riemannian geometry as the basis for making the greatest single advance in scientific theory since the time of Newton.

In particular we must be on our guard against what might be called the 'anthropomorphic fallacy.' By this is meant a deduction the critical point of which turns out to be an implicit statement which, if made explicit, would be something like, "If I were a rat and were in that situation I would do so and so." Such elements in a deduction make it a travesty because the very problem at issue is whether a system is able to deduce from its postulates alone what a normal man (or rat) would do under particular conditions. It is this fallacy which justifies the inveterate aversion of scientists for anthropomorphism. It is true that as a practical guide to the expectation of what a rat, or an ape, or a child, or another man will actually do in an as yet untried situation such an approach is, of course, of value and should be used. But predictions arrived at in such a way are of no value as scientific theory because a truly scientific theory seeks to deduce what

anthropomorphism reaches by intuition or by naïve assumption. Prophecies as to the outcome of untried experiments based merely on such anthropomorphic intuitions should be credited to the intuitional genius of the prophet rather than to the theoretical system to which the prophet may adhere. Predictions, however successful, can have no evidential value as to the credibility of the prophet's system until he is willing and able to exhibit the logic by which his predictions flow from the postulates of that system, and until this logic is really rigorous, until it consists of something more than the feeble *non-sequiturs* too often presented in our literature as scientific explanations.

Summary and Conclusions

Scientific theory in its best sense consists of the strict logical deduction from definite postulates of what should be observed under specified conditions.[12] If the deductions are lacking or are logically invalid, there is no theory; if the deductions involve conditions of observation which are impossible of attainment, the theory is metaphysical rather than scientific; and if the deduced phenomenon is not observed

[12] Truth, for the purposes of the present paper, is to be understood as a theoretical deduction which has been verified by observation.

when the conditions are fulfilled, the theory is false. Classifications of the phenomena of a science may have distinct expository and pedagogical convenience, but convenience cannot be said to be true or false. Points of view in science may possess the virtue of fertility by suggesting new directions of investigations, but neither can fertility be said to be true or false. On the other hand, truly scientific theory, from its very nature, must permit the observational determination of its truth or falsity.

It is believed that upon the above conceptions of scientific theory may be based a robust hope of bringing order out of our present theoretical chaos. It is conceivable, of course, that more than one scientific system may be able to deduce the major phenomena of learning. However, the history of scientific theory has shown that successful duplicate explanations of the same natural phenomena have usually turned out to be at bottom the same. Accordingly, we may expect that when we have put our scientific house in order there will be little more disagreement in the field of theory than in the field of experiment, and presumably such disagreements as appear will prove to be but temporary.

PAPER
9

Assuming both the possibility and the desirability of such an outcome, the question arises as to how it can most promptly be achieved. First, it is believed that the thing most urgently needed at the present moment is a clear statement of postulates with accompanying definitions of terms. Second, these postulates should be followed by the step-by-step deduction of the theorems making up the body of the system. No doubt the meticulous presentation of the logic behind the theorems of a system may at first strike certain readers as pedantic. Moreover, it is an unfortunate fact that for persons untrained in a particular system, the more rigorous the logic the more difficult it becomes to comprehend. It is encouraging, however, to note that difficulty of comprehension by the tyro has not prevented the development of mathematical theory in the older sciences, and with them rigor of deduction has not usually been regarded as pedantry. A number of indications point to a considerable development of this kind of theoretical work in psychology within the immediate future.

As this development proceeds, we may anticipate that those systems or points of view which are unable to satisfy the postulational requirements of truly scientific theory will come to be known for what they are, and will lose adherents. The proponents of other points of view may be expected gradually to clarify their basic postulates and from these to evolve systems of rigorously proved theorems. Of this latter group of systems, presumably, it will be found impossible to apply the experimental check to the theorems of some because the systems in question either do not specify clearly the conditions under which phenomena should occur or else they are not clear as to exactly what phenomena are to be expected. Some systems, on the other hand, will doubtless succeed in making genuine contact with experimental facts. Of these, some will probably present such a high proportion of experimental non-confirmations that the confirmations actually observed may be attributable to mere chance.

Finally, let us hope, there will survive a limited number of systems which show a degree of successes appreciably in excess of what chance would produce. Occasionally, in such cases, a failure of a theorem to agree with experimental observation may be accounted for plausibly on the basis of a known and recognized factor operating in such a way as to over-ride the action represented by the theorem. Unless this can be done, however, the postulates of the system must be revised until they yield theorems agreeing with both the new and the old facts, after which there will be made new deductions which will be checked against new experiments, and so on in recurring cycles. Thus theoretical truth is not absolute, but relative.

It seems likely that as the process of theoretical development goes on the surviving systems will show two fairly distinct types of relationship. First, there will be systems which attempt explanations on different levels such as the perceptual level, the stimulus-response level, the neuro-anatomical level, and the neuro-physiological level. It is conceivable that each might develop a perfect system on its own level. In that case each lower level should be able to deduce the relevant basic postulates of the system above it in the hierarchy of systems. Here, of course, would be supplementation rather than conflict.

Second, there may be some systems which attempt explanation at the same level. However diverse such systems may appear at the beginning, they may be expected gradually to display an essential identity as they go through successive revisions, the differences at length consisting in nothing but the terms employed. Those systems which concern different but related aspects of learning, by the process of expansion, will finally come to overlap. This overlapping will convert them into approximately the same status as the groups just mentioned, and a gradually approached outcome of substantial agreement may similarly be anticipated. Thus systems may expand by a process of integration.

Finally, sound scientific theory has usually led not only to prediction but to control; abstract principles in the long run have led to concrete application. With powerful deductive instruments at our disposal we should be able to predict the outcome of learning not only under untried laboratory conditions, but under as yet untried conditions of practical education. We should be able not only to predict what rats will do in a maze under as yet untried circumstances, but what a man will do under the complex conditions of everyday life. In short, the attainment of a genuinely scientific theory of mammalian behavior offers the promise of development in the understanding and control of human conduct in its immensely varied aspects which will be comparable to the control already achieved over inanimate nature, and of which the modern world is in such dire need.

PAPER
9

REFERENCES

1. ADAMS, G., Psychology: science or superstition?, New York; Covici Friede, 1931.
2. BACON, F., Advancement of learning and novum organum, Revised edition, Colonial Press, 1900.
3. CROZIER, W. J., Chemoreception, from A handbook of general experimental psychology, edited by Carl Murchison, Worcester: Clark University Press, 1934.

4. EBBINGHAUS, H., Memory (trans. by H. A. Ruger and C. E. Bussenius), N. Y.: Teachers College, Columbia University, 1913.
5. EVANS, C. L., Recent advances in physiology, Phila.: P. Blakiston's Son and Co., 1926.
6. GULLIKSEN, H. A., A rational equation of the learning curve based on Thorndike's law, *J. General Psychol.*, 1934, **11**, 395–434.
7. HAAS, A., Introduction to theoretical physics, Vol. II (trans. from the 3rd and 4th editions by T. Verschoyle), London: Constable and Co., 1925.
8. HECHT, S., Vision: II. The nature of the photoreceptor process, from A handbook of general experimental psychology, edited by Carl Murchison, Worcester: Clark University Press, 1934.
9. HULL, C. L., The influence of tobacco smoking on mental and motor efficiency, *Psychol. Monog.*, 1924, **33**, No. 150.
10. ——, The influence of caffeine and other factors on the phenomena of rote learning, *J. General Psychol.*, 1935, **13**, 249–274.
11. KREUGER, W. C. F., Effect of overlearning on retention, *J. Exper. Psychol.*, 1929, **12**, 71–78.
12. LEPLEY, W. M., A theory of serial learning and forgetting based upon conditioned reflex principles, PSYCHOL. REV., 1932, **39**, 279–288.
13. ——, Serial reactions considered as conditioned reactions, *Psychol. Monog.*, 1934. No. 205.
14. MURCHISON, C., (Editor), Psychologies of 1925, Worcester: Clark University Press, 1925.
15. ——, Psychologies of 1930, Worcester: Clark University Press, 1930.
16. NEWTON, ISAAC, Mathematical principles (Trans. by F. Cajori), Univ. of California Press, 1934.
17. PAVLOV, I. P., Conditioned reflexes (trans. by G. V. Anrep), Oxford University Press, 1927.
18. PILLSBURY, W. B., The fundamentals of psychology, N. Y.: Macmillan, 1927.
19. POINCARÉ, H., The foundations of science (trans. by G. B. Halsted), The Science Press, 1929.
20. REICHE, F., The quantum theory (trans. by H. S. Hatfield and H. L. Brose), N. Y.: E. P. Dutton and Co., 1930.
21. ROBINSON, E. S., AND BROWN, M. A., Effect of serial position on memorization, *Amer. J. Psychol.*, 1926, **37**, 538–552.
22. SHERRINGTON, C. S., The integrative action of the nervous system, New Haven: Yale University Press, 1906.
23. SIMLEY, O. H., The relation of subliminal to supraliminal learning, *Arch. Psychol.*, 1933, No. 146.
24. WARD, L. B., Retention over short intervals of time, Thesis presented for the degree of Doctor of Philosophy, Yale University, 1934 (on file in the Yale University Library).

PAPER 9

[MS. received April 12, 1935]

Reprinted from PSYCHOLOGICAL REVIEW, Vol. 44, No. 1, January, 1937
Printed in U. S. A.

MIND, MECHANISM, AND ADAPTIVE BEHAVIOR [1]

BY CLARK L. HULL

Institute of Human Relations, Yale University

INTRODUCTION

Since the time of Charles Darwin it has become clear not only that living organisms have gradually evolved through immense periods of time, but that man is evolution's crowning achievement. It is equally clear that man's preëminence lies in his capacity for adaptive behavior. Because of the seemingly unique and remarkable nature of adaptive behavior, it has long been customary to attribute it to the action of a special agent or substance called 'mind.' Thus 'mind' as a hypothetical entity directing and controlling adaptive behavior attains biological status possessing survival value and, consequently, a 'place in nature.' But what is this mysterious thing called mind? By what principles does it operate? Are these principles many or are they few? Are they those of the ordinary physical world or are they of the nature of spiritual essences—of an entirely different order, the non-physical?

It will, perhaps, be most economical to begin our examination of this important problem by passing briefly in review some typical phenomena of adaptive behavior which have led to the assumption of a special psychic entity. Among these may be mentioned the following: When obstacles are encountered, organisms often persist in making the same incorrect attempt over and over again; they vary their re-

PAPER
10

[1] Presidential Address delivered before the American Psychological Association, Hanover, New Hampshire, September 4, 1936.

The author is indebted to Professor Max Wertheimer for a critical reading of this paper.

I

actions spontaneously; they display anticipatory reactions antedating the biological emergencies to which the reactions are adaptive; they present the phenomena of disappointment and discouragement; they strive to attain states of affairs which are biologically advantageous; they transfer to new problem situations adaptive behavior acquired in situations which, objectively considered, are totally different. The behavior of organisms is purposive in that they strive for goals or values, and in so doing manifest intelligence or insight and a high degree of individual freedom from current coercion of the environment. Whatever may be the final conclusion as to the ultimate nature of these phenomena, their biological significance in terms of survival must be immense. The task of understanding and controlling them is surely worthy of the best coöperative efforts of the biological and social sciences.

PAPER
10

The Controversy Regarding Adaptive Behavior Is Theoretical, Not Factual

Historically, two main views have been held as to the ultimate nature of adaptive behavior. The most widely accepted of these, at the present time, is also the most ancient; its roots lie far back in primitive animism. According to this view, the principles governing adaptive behavior are essentially non-physical, mental, or psychic. The second view, despite its austerity, has received a certain amount of favor among men of science. It assumes that adaptive behavior operates ultimately according to the principles of the physical world. In our consideration of these contrasting views, it will be convenient to begin with the latter.

The physical or mechanistic view of the nature of adaptive behavior can best be stated by quoting the beautiful presentation of the raindrop analogy written by the late Albert P. Weiss:

> We may best visualize the relationship between the responses that make up the so-called purposive behavior category by the raindrop analogy. We may start with the assumption that every drop of rain in some way or other gets to the

ocean. . . . . Anthropomorphizing this condition we may say that it is the *purpose* of every drop of rain to get to the ocean. Of course, this only means that virtually every drop *does* get there eventually. . . . Falling from the cloud it may strike the leaf of a tree, and drop from one leaf to another until it reaches the ground. From here it may pass under or on the surface of the soil to a rill, then to a brook, river, and finally to the sea. Each stage, each fall from one leaf to the next, may be designated as a *means* toward the final end, the sea, . . . Human behavior is merely a complication of the same factors.[2]

The nub of Weiss's statement lies in his concluding remark that adaptive behavior is merely a 'complication' of the same factors as those which are involved in the behavior of a drop of water finding its way from an inland cloud to the sea. Obviously, Weiss did not mean to say that the several forms of seeking and striving behavior characteristic of the higher organisms are brought about by the various compoundings of such processes as evaporation, condensation, splashing, and flowing. The context of the quotation shows that he meant that ultimately the complex forms of purposive behavior would be found to derive from the same *source* as those from which the raindrop phenomena are derived; *i.e.*, from the basic entities of theoretical physics, such as electrons and protons. He discusses these latter concepts explicitly and at length.

PAPER
10

Passing to the more orthodox view, that adaptive behavior is essentially non-physical, or psychic, the words of A. S. Eddington may be taken as a point of departure. In his book, 'The nature of the physical world,'[3] Eddington remarks:

> Conceivably we might reach a human machine interacting by reflexes with its environment; but we cannot reach rational man morally responsible. [P. 343.] . . . In a world of æther and electrons we might perhaps encounter *nonsense;* we could not encounter *damned nonsense.*

[2] Albert P. Weiss, A theoretical basis of human behavior, Columbus, Ohio: R. G. Adams and Company, 1925, pp. 346–347.
[3] New York: The Macmillan Company, 1929, p. 345.

The significance of Eddington's statement centers around the word *reach*. From the present point of view, he seems to be saying that we cannot reach the highest forms of adaptive behavior, such as complex problem solution (rational behavior) and certain complex forms of social behavior involving the implicit verbal coercion of the behavior of the individual (moral behavior) if we start out merely with æther and electrons; we must begin with something non-physical, or psychic—presumably consciousness.

Thus the issue is joined. We are presented with the paradox of Eddington, the physicist, apparently insisting that the higher forms of behavior are at bottom non-physical, whereas Weiss, the psychologist, insists that they are fundamentally non-phychological!

PAPER

10

But what, exactly, is the issue? Is it, for example, a difference as to an ordinary matter of observed fact? Do Eddington and those who share his view claim to have made certain observations which are in conflict with a corresponding set of observations supposed to have been made by Weiss and those with a mechanistic leaning? The dispute involves nothing of this nature. It is clear that the controversy is definitely a theoretical one. Eddington seems to be implying that we *can not* reach a sound theory of rational, purposive and moral behavior if we set out with nothing but æther and electrons. Weiss is saying, by implication, that a sound theory of such behavior *can* be reached by setting out with nothing but electrons and protons.

The Methodology of Scientific Theory Differentiated from That of Philosophical Speculation

Having located definitely in the field of theory the contrasted views represented in a general way by Weiss and Eddington, we face at once the critical question of whether the problem lies within the range of the operation of scientific methodology. If it does, what is that methodology? How is it to be applied to the question before us in a way which will avoid the interminable wrangles and philosophical futilities so long associated with the mind-body problem? It will be necessary to go into the matter of methodology rather thoroughly, in part because of its central importance for our present problem, but in part also because of the widespread misconceptions regarding it due to our early associations with philosophy. With the question of methodology clarified we shall return to Weiss and Eddington in the hope of demonstrating its concrete application.

The essential characteristics of a sound scientific theoretical system, as contrasted with ordinary philosophical speculation, may be briefly summarized under three heads:

1. A satisfactory scientific theory should begin with a set of explicitly stated postulates accompanied by specific or 'operational' definitions of the critical terms employed.

2. From these postulates there should be deduced by the most rigorous logic possible under the circumstances, a series of interlocking theorems covering the major concrete phenomena of the field in question.

PAPER
10

3. The statements in the theorems should agree in detail with the observationally known facts of the discipline under consideration. If the theorems agree with the observed facts, the system is probably true; if they disagree, the system is false. If it is impossible to tell whether the theorems of a system agree with the facts or not, the system is neither true nor false; scientifically considered, it is meaningless.

Since concrete example is more illuminating and more convincing than abstract statement, there is reproduced below a small scientific theoretical system in which an attempt has been made to conform to the above principles. There may be found (p. 15 ff.) a number of definitions, which are followed (p. 16 ff.) by six postulates. The system concludes with a series of thirteen theorems (p. 17 ff.), each derived from the postulates by a process of reasoning analogous to that ordinarily employed in geometry.

At first sight the formal characteristics of scientific theory look very much like those of philosophical speculation and even of ordinary argumentation, from which philosophical speculation can scarcely be distinguished. At their best, both scientific theory and philosophical speculation set out from explicit postulates; both have definitions of critical terms; both have interlocking theorems derived by meticulous logic. Consider, for example, Spinoza's 'Ethic,' a philosophical work of the better sort. This has all of the above characteristics in almost exactly the same form as the miniature scientific system which is presented below. Where, then, lie the great difference and superiority of the scientific procedure?

The answer, while extending into many complex details, rests upon a single fundamental principle. The difference is that *in philosophical speculation there is no possibility of comparing a theorem with the results of direct observation.* An obvious example of this impossibility is seen in Spinoza's famous pantheistic theorem, Proposition XIV, from Part One of his 'Ethic':

Besides God no substance can be, nor can be conceived.

It is difficult to imagine subjecting such a theorem as that to an observational test.

Consider, by way of contrast, a really scientific procedure, one carried out by Galileo at about the same time that Spinoza was writing. The Copernican hypothesis concerning the nature of the solar system was then in violent dispute. From this hypothesis, together with a few familiar principles concerning the behavior of light, it follows logically as a theorem that the planet Venus, like the moon, should show the crescent and all the other stages between the full and dark phases. Presumably led by this deduction, Galileo, with a telescope of his own construction, made the necessary observations on Venus and found the phases exactly as demanded by the theorem. Here we have the indispensable observational check demanded by science but lacking in philosophy.

But why, it will be asked, is it so imperative to have an observational check on the theorems of a system if the system is to merit serious consideration by scientists? To answer this question adequately it will be necessary to consider in a little detail the characteristics of postulates, the procedure in selecting them, and the methodology of their substantiation.

It is important to note at the outset that in scientific theory postulates tend to be of two kinds. First, there are postulates which are mere matters of fact; *i.e.*, they are matters of relatively simple and direct observation. Second, there are postulates which by their nature cannot conceivably be matters of direct observation. The classical investigation of Galileo just considered contains examples of both types. The principles of light and shadow upon which lunar and planetary phases depend are obviously matters of ordinary, everyday, direct terrestrial observation, and so represent postulates of the first type. On the other hand, the Copernican hypothesis as to the relative movements of the several components of the solar system is not susceptible to direct observation, and so represents postulates of the second type.

In scientific theory, owing to the continuous checking of theorems arrived at deductively against the results of direct observation, both types of postulates are constantly receiving *indirect* verification or refutation. Thus postulates capable of the direct approach are susceptible of two independent kinds of test, the direct and the indirect. But the continuous indirect test is of special importance for the postulates incapable of the direct approach. Were it not for this they would be subject to no observational verification at all, and scientific theory would in this respect have no more safeguard against erroneous basic assumptions than has philosphical speculation. Thus Galileo's brilliant observations of the phases of Venus not only gave the scientific world some new facts but, of far greater importance, they substantiated in a convincing, though indirect, manner the fundamental Copernican hypothesis.[4]

PAPER
10

[4] Many persons have been puzzled by the paradox that in science a deduction frequently sets out with postulates which are by no means securely established, whereas in ordinary argumentation there is the greatest insistence upon the certainty of the premises upon which the argument is based. The explanation of this paradox lies largely in the difference of objective in the two cases. Argument ordinarily seeks to convince by a deductive procedure of something which under the circumstances is not directly observable; otherwise there would be no point in performing the deduction. It is clear that if the person to whom the argument is directed does not agree with the premises he will not agree with the conclusion and the whole procedure will

Whenever a theorem fails to check with the relevant facts, the postulates which gave rise to it must be ruthlessly revised until agreement is reached. If agreement cannot be attained, the system must be abandoned. In this constant revision there is a definite tendency to choose and formulate the postulates in a way which will make them yield the deductions desired. Such a procedure involves an obvious element of circularity. This is particularly the case where the system is small and where the postulates are purely symbolic constructs or inventions and therefore not subject to direct investigation. Even so, the choice of postulates to fit the facts is methodologically legitimate and, upon the whole, desirable. One important reason for this is that a postulate or hypothesis so arrived at may lead to a *direct*, experimental confirmation in case it is capable of the direct approach.[5] In such an event, of course, all circularity disappears.

PAPER
10
But if the system is truly scientific in nature, the circularity just considered is only a temporary phase even when one or more of the postulates are insusceptible to direct investigation. It is precisely in this connection that scientific method shows its incomparable superiority over philosophical speculation. A sound set of postulates should lead to the deduction of theorems representing phenomena never previously investigated quite as logically as of theorems representing phenomena already known when the postulates were formulated. When a theorem representing novel phenomena receives direct observational confirmation there is no possi-

be futile. In science, on the other hand, the situation may be almost completely reversed; the conclusion (or theorem) may be known observationally at the outset, but the premises (or postulates) may at first be little more than conjectures and the logical process quite circular. For the methodology of resolving this circularity, see p. 8 ff.

[5] From the experimental point of view the process of developing systematic theory thus leads in two directions. On one hand it leads to the investigation of theorems derived from postulates of the system, and on the other to the direct investigation of postulates which appear to be required as assumptions for the deductive explanation of facts already known. Since phenomena of the latter type are fundamental in a strict sense, their investigation is of the highest significance. A background of systematic theory thus often directly suggests fundamental investigations which might be indefinitely delayed under the usual procedure of random, and even of systematic, exploration.

bility of circularity; as a consequence the probability that the postulates directly involved are sound is very definitely increased.[6] Thus the fact that Venus shows lunar phases could not have been known to Copernicus when he formulated his epoch-making hypothesis, because the telescope had not yet been invented. Accordingly their discovery by Galileo constituted strong positive evidence of the essential soundness of the Copernican hypothesis regarded as a postulate. This classical example of the observational but indirect confirmation of the soundness of postulates will serve as a fitting conclusion for our general consideration of theoretical methodology.

The Recognized Scientific Methodology Has Not Been Applied to the Behavior Controversy

We turn now to the question of whether the recognized scientific methodology is really applicable to a resolution of the controversy concerning the basic nature of adaptive behavior. At first glance the prospect is reassuring. It becomes quite clear, for example, what Weiss and Eddington should have done to substantiate their claims. They should have exhibited, as strict logical deductions from explicitly stated postulates, a series of theorems corresponding in detail to the concrete manifestations of the higher forms of human behavior. Then, and only then, they might proceed to the examination of the postulates of such system. To substantiate his position Weiss would have to show that these postulates concern essentially the behavior of electrons, protons, etc.; and Eddington to support his assertions would need

PAPER
10

[6] A single unequivocal disagreement between a theorem and observed fact is sufficient to assure the incorrectness of at least one of the postulates involved. But even if the postulates of a system generate a very long series of theorems which are subsequently confirmed without exception, each new confirmation merely adds to the *probability* of the truth of such postulates as are incapable of direct observational test. Apparently this indirect evidence never reaches the crisp certainty of a deductive conclusion in which the postulates are directly established, except in the highly improbable situation where all the possible deductions involving a given postulate have been tested with positive results. According to the theory of chance, the larger the sample from this possible total which has been tried and found without exception to be positive, the greater the probability that a new deduction based on the same set of postulates will be confirmed when tested.

to show that the postulates of a successful system are primarily phenomena of consciousness.[7] The formal application of the methodology is thus quite clear and specific.

But here we meet an amazing paradox. In spite of the calm assurance of Weiss as to the truth of his statement that purposive behavior is at bottom physical, we find that he neither presents nor cites such a system. Indeed, he seems to be quite oblivious of such a necessity. Turning to Eddington, we find exactly the same paradoxical situation. Notwithstanding his positive, even emphatic, implications that moral behavior must be conscious or psychic in its ultimate nature, we find him neither presenting nor citing a theoretical system of any kind, much less one derived from psychic or conscious postulates. This paradox is particularly astonishing in the case of Eddington because he has been active in the field of physical theory and should, therefore, be sophisticated

regarding the essential methodology involved in scientific theory in general. Surely the same logic which demands strict deduction from explicitly stated postulates in physical theory demands it for the theory of adaptive and moral behavior. And surely if we demand it of a mechanistic theory of the more recondite forms of human behavior, as Eddington seems emphatically to do, there is no hocus-pocus whereby a psychic view of such behavior may be maintained without the same substantial foundation.

A Demonstration of the Application of Theoretical Methodology to Adaptive Behavior

But if neither Weiss nor Eddington, nor any other writer in this field, has been able to bring forward the indispensable systematic theory as a prerequisite of the logical right to express a valid conclusion concerning the ultimate nature of higher adaptive behavior, may this not mean that the attainment of such a system is impossible, and that, consequently,

[7] It is here assumed as highly probable that if the two approaches are strictly in conflict, only one would be successful. In the course of the development of scientific theoretical systems, however, it is to be expected that during the early stages several different systems may present appreciable evidences of success. See The conflicting psychologies of learning—A way out, Psychol. Rev., 42, 1936; especially pp. 514–515.

the problem still remains in the realm of philosophical speculation? There is reason to believe that this is not the case. The ground for optimism lies in part in the small theoretical system which is presented below (p. 15).

By way of introduction to the system we may begin with the consideration of Theorem I (p. 17). In brief, this theorem purports to show that Pavlov's conditioned reactions and the stimulus-response 'bonds' resulting from Thorndike's so-called 'law of effect' are in reality special cases of the operation of a single set of principles. The major principle involved is given in Postulate 2. Briefly, this postulate states the assumption of the present system concerning the conditions under which stimuli and reactions become associated. The difference in the two types of reaction thus turns out to depend merely upon the accidental factor of the temporal relationships of the stimuli to the reactions in the learning situation, coupled with the implication that R_G, which in part serves to mark a reinforcing state of affairs, is also susceptible of being associated with a new stimulus.[8] The automatic, stimulus-response approach thus exemplified is characteristic of the remainder of the system.

PAPER
10

A consideration of Theorem II will serve still further as an orientation to the system before us. We find this theorem stating that both *correct* and *incorrect* reaction tendencies may be set up by the conditioning or associative process just referred to. Our chief interest in this theorem, as an introduction to the system, concerns the question of whether the terms 'correct' and 'incorrect' can have any meaning when they refer to reaction tendencies which are the result of a purely automatic process of association such as that presented by Postulate 2. It is believed that they have a very definite meaning. Definitions 7 and 8 state in effect that correctness or incorrectness is determined by whether the reaction tendency under given conditions is, or is not, subject to experimental extinction. Such purely objective or behavioral

---

[8] In effect this deduction purports to show that the Pavlovian conditioned reflex is a special case under Thorndike's 'law of effect,' though Thorndike might not recognize his favorite principle as formulated in Postulate 2. For a fuller but less formal discussion of this point see *Psychol. Bull.*, 1935, **32**, 817–822.

definitions of numerous terms commonly thought of as applying exclusively to experience, as distinguished from action, are
characteristic of the entire system.

With this general orientation we may proceed to the theorems more specifically concerned with adaptive behavior.
The proof of the first of these, Theorem III, shows that under
certain circumstances organisms will repeatedly and successively make the same incorrect reaction. At first sight this
may seem like a most commonplace outcome. However,
when considered in the light of the definition of correctness
given above it is evident that this theorem differs radically
from what might be deduced concerning the behavior of a
raindrop or a pebble moving in a gravitational field.[9]

Theorem IV states that after making one or more incorrect
reactions an organism will spontaneously vary the response
even though the environmental situation remains unchanged.
PAPER 10 This theorem is noteworthy because it represents the classical
case of a form of spontaneity widely assumed, as far back as
the Middle Ages, to be inconceivable without presupposing
consciousness.

Theorem V states that when an organism originally has
both correct and incorrect excitatory tendencies evoked by a
single stimulus situation, the correct tendency will at length
be automatically selected in preference to stronger incorrect
ones.[10] This theorem, also, has been widely regarded as
impossible of derivation without the presupposition of consciousness. Otherwise (so it has been argued) how can the
organism know which reaction to choose?

[9] It may be suggested that if water should fall into a hollow cavity on its way
to the sea, it might at first oscillate back and forth vigorously and then gradually
subside, each oscillation corresponding to an unsuccessful attempt and the gradual
cessation, to experimental extinction. In all such cases the discussion as to whether
the observed parallelism in behavior represents an essential similarity or a mere superficial analogy requires that both phenomena possess a thorough theoretical basis.
*If the two phenomena are deducible from the same postulates and by identical processes of
reasoning, they may be regarded as essentially the same, otherwise not.* But if one or
both lacks a theoretical basis such a comparison cannot be made and decision can
ordinarily not be reached. Much futile argument could be avoided if this principle
were generally recognized.

[10] See Simple trial-and-error learning: A study in psychological theory, PSYCHOL.
REV., 1930, 37, 241–256; especially pp. 243–250.

Theorem VI represents the deduction that in certain situations the organism will give up seeking, *i.e.*, cease making attempts, and thus fail to perform the correct reaction even when it possesses in its repertoire a perfectly correct excitatory tendency. The substance of this proof lies in the expectation that the extinction resulting from repeated false reactions will cause indirectly a critical weakening of a non-dominant but correct reaction tendency. This theorem is of unusual importance because it represents the deduction of a phenomenon not as yet subjected to experiment. As such it should have special significance as a test of the soundness of the postulates.

With Theorems VII and VIII we turn to the problem of anticipatory or preparatory reactions. The proof of Theorem VII derives, from the principles of the stimulus trace and conditioning (Postulates 1 and 2), the phenomenon of the antedating reaction. The substance of this theorem is that after acquisition, learned reactions tend to appear in advance of the point in the original sequence at which they occurred during the conditioning process.[11] Pursuing this line of reasoning, Theorem VIII shows that in the case of situations demanding flight, such antedating reactions become truly anticipatory or preparatory in the sense of being biologically adaptive to situations which are impending but not yet actual. Thus we arrive at behavioral foresight, a phenomenon evidently of very considerable survival significance in animal life and one frequently regarded as eminently psychic, and inconceivable without consciousness.[12]

Passing over Theorem IX, which lays some necessary groundwork, we come to Theorem X. Here we find a deduction of the existence of the fractional anticipatory goal reaction. Of far greater significance from our present point of view, the deduction purports to show that through the action of mere association the fractional anticipatory reaction tends automatically to bring about on later occasions the

PAPER
10

[11] See A functional interpretation of the conditioned reflex, PSYCHOL. REV., 1929, **36**, 498–511; especially pp. 507–508.

[12] See Knowledge and purpose as habit mechanisms, PSYCHOL. REV., 1930, **37**, 511–525; especially pp. 514–516.

state of affairs which acted as its reinforcing agent when it was originally set up. For this and other reasons it is believed that the anticipatory goal reaction is the physical basis of expectation, of intent, of purpose, and of guiding ideas.[13]

Theorem XI represents a deduction of the phenomenon of behavioral disappointment [14] as manifested, for example, by Tinklepaugh's monkeys. When these animals had solved a problem with the expectation of one kind of food they would tend to refuse a different kind of food, otherwise acceptable, which had been surreptitiously substituted.[15]

Theorem XII purports to be the deduction of the principle that organisms will strive actively to attain situations or states of affairs which previously have proved to be reinforcing. The automaticity deduced in the proof of Theorem X has here reached a still higher level. This is the capacity to surmount obstacles. But with the ability to attain ends in spite of obstacles comes automatically a genuine freedom (Definition 18), of great biological value but in no way incompatible with determinism.[16]

Theorem XIII is also derived with the aid of the fractional anticipatory goal reaction. This theorem represents the phenomenon of the adaptive but automatic transfer of learned reactions to situations having, as regards *external* characteristics, nothing whatever in common with the situations in which the habits were originally acquired. This, once more, is a form of adaptive behavior of the greatest survival significance to the organism, and one supposed in certain quarters to be impossible of derivation from associative principles.

PAPER
10

[13] See Goal attraction and directing ideas conceived as habit phenomena, PSYCHOL. REV., 1931, 38, 487–506.

[14] It is to be observed from a comparison of Definitions 9 and 16 that *Disappointment* necessarily presupposes a specific expectation or intent (r_G), whereas *Discouragement* does not.

[15] O. L. Tinklepaugh, An experimental study of representative factors in monkeys, *J. Comp. Psychol.*, 1928, 8, 197–236. See especially p. 224 ff.

[16] An additional element of interest in this theorem is the fact that the fundamental phenomenon of motivation seems to have been derived from the ordinary principle of association (Postulate 2). If this deduction should prove to be sound, it will have reduced the two basic categories of motivation and learning to one, the latter being primary.

This is believed to be a low but genuine form of insight and a fairly high order of the 'psychic.'

This concludes the list of formally derived theorems. They have been selected from a series of fifty or so which are concerned with the same subject. None of these theorems 'reaches' Eddington's 'rational man morally responsible.' They accordingly are not offered as a basis for deciding the ultimate nature of such behavior. They *are* offered as a concrete and relevant illustration of the first and most essential step in the methodology which must be followed by Eddington, or anyone else who would determine the basic nature of the higher forms of behavior. Incidentally they are offered as specific evidence that such problems, long regarded as the peculiar domain of philosophy, are now susceptible of attack by a strictly orthodox scientific methodology.

ADAPTIVE BEHAVIOR—A SCIENTIFIC THEORETICAL SYSTEM IN MINIATURE [17]

PAPER 10

Definitions

1. A *reinforcing state of affairs* (Postulate 3) is one which acts to give to the stimulus-trace component (Postulate 1) of preceding or following temporal coincidences consisting of a stimulus trace and a reaction, the capacity to evoke the reaction in question (Postulate 2).

2. *Experimental extinction* is the weakening of a conditioned excitatory tendency resulting from frustration or the failure of reinforcement (Postulate 4).

3. *Frustration* is said to occur when the situation is such that the reaction customarily evoked by a stimulus complex cannot take place (Postulate 4).

4. *Seeking* is that behavior of organisms in trial-and-error situations which, upon frustration, is characterized by varied alternative acts all operative under the influence of a common drive (S_D).

5. An *attempt* is a segment of behavior the termination of which is marked by either reinforcement or extinction.

6. A *simple trial-and-error situation* is one which presents to an organism a stimulus complex which tends to give rise to multiple reaction tendencies which are mutually incompatible, one or more of them being susceptible to reinforcement and one or more of them not being so susceptible.

7. A *correct* or 'right' reaction is a behavior sequence which results in reinforcement.

8. An *incorrect* or 'wrong' reaction is a behavior sequence which results in experimental extinction.

---

[17] The author is greatly indebted to Dr. E. H. Rodnick and Mr. D. G. Ellson for detailed criticisms and suggestions during the original preparation of the system which follows. Thanks are also due Professor K. F. Muenzinger, Dr. R. T. Ross, and Dr. R. K. White for criticisms given since the presentation at Hanover.

9. *Discouragement* is the diminution in the power of one excitatory tendency to evoke its normal reaction, this diminution resulting from one or more unsuccessful attempts involving a second reaction.

10. A behavior sequence is said to be *directed* to the attainment of a particular state of affairs when there appears throughout the sequence a characteristic component (r_G) of the action (R_G) closely associated with the state of affairs in question and this component action (r_G) as a stimulus tends to evoke an action sequence leading to the total reaction (R_G) of which the component constitutes a part.

11. Striving is that behavior of organisms which, upon frustration, displays varied alternative action sequences, all *directed* by an intent (r_G) to the attainment of the same reinforcing state of affairs.

12. A *goal* is the reinforcing state of affairs towards the attainment of which a behavior sequence of an organism may be directed by its intent (r_G).

13. An organism is said to *anticipate* a state of affairs when there is active throughout the behavior sequence leading to the state of affairs a fractional component (r_G) of the action associated with the state of affairs in question.

14. *Success* is the culmination of striving which is characterized by the occurrence of the full reaction (R_G) of which the fractional anticipatory component (r_G) is a part.

15. *Failure* is the culmination of striving which is characterized by the lack of the enactment of the full reaction (R_G) of which the fractional component (r_G) is a part.

PAPER
10

16. *Disappointment* is the diminution in the power of one reinforcing situation to evoke appropriate consummatory reaction, this diminution (Postulate 4) resulting from the failure of a second reaction sequence directed (by an intent, or r_G) to a different reinforcing situation from that to which the first was directed, both being based on the same drive (S_D).

17. A *habit-family hierarchy* consists of a number of habitual behavior sequences having in common the initial stimulus situation and the final reinforcing state of affairs.

18. *Individual freedom* of behavior, so far as it exists, consists in the absence of external restraint.

Postulates

1. The adequate stimulation of a sense organ initiates within the organism a neural reverberation which persists for some time after the stimulus has ceased to act, the absolute amount of the reverberation diminishing progressively to zero but at a progressively slower rate. (Stimulus trace.)

2. When a reaction and a given segment of a stimulus-trace (Postulate 1) repeatedly occur simultaneously and this coincidence occurs during the action of a drive (S_D) and temporally close to a reinforcing state of affairs (Definition 1), this and stronger segments of the stimulus trace tend progressively to acquire the capacity to evoke the reaction, the strength of the association thus acquired manifesting a negatively accelerated diminution with distance of the associates from the reinforcing state of affairs. (Positive association.)

3. A characteristic stimulus-reaction combination ($S_G — — \rightarrow R_G$) always marks reinforcing states of affairs (Definition 1). The particular stimulus-response combination marking the reinforcing state of affairs in the case of specific drives is determined empirically, *i.e.*, by observation and experiment. (Mark of reinforcing state of affairs.)

4. When a stimulus evokes a conditioned (associative) reaction (Postulate 2) and this event does not occur within the range of the reinforcing state of affairs (Defi-

nition 1 and Postulate 3), or when an excitatory tendency in a behavior sequence encounters a situation which makes the execution of the act impossible (Definition 3), the excitatory tendency in question undergoes a diminution in strength with a limit below the reaction threshold (Definition 2), this diminution extending in considerable part to other excitatory tendencies which may be operative at the same time or for some time thereafter. (Negative association or experimental extinction.)

5. The strength of any given increment of either positive or negative association (Postulates 2 and 3) diminishes with the passage of time, and the portion remaining shows a progressively greater resistance to disintegration with the increase in time since its acquisition, a certain proportion of each increment being permanent. (Negative retention or forgetting.)

6. Each reaction of an organism gives rise to a more or less characteristic internal stimulus. (Internal stimulation.)

Key to Diagrams

S = an adequate stimulus together with the resulting trace (Postulate 1).
S_D = the stimulus associated with a drive, such as hunger.
S_G = the stimulus associated with the goal or reinforcing state of affairs.
s = an internal stimulus resulting from a reaction.
R = a reaction.
R_G = the reaction associated with the goal or reinforcing state of affairs.
r_G = a fractional component of the goal reaction.
$—\,—\!\rightarrow$ = excitatory tendency from stimulus to reaction.

$\rightsquigarrow$ = causal connection of a non-stimulus-reaction nature.

$\cdots$ = a continuation or persistence of a process, as of a drive (S_D).
Distance from left to right represents the passage of time.

PAPER
10

Theorems

I

The Pavlovian conditioned reaction and the Thorndikian associative reaction are special cases of the operation of the same principles of learning.

1. Suppose that in the neighborhood of a sensitive organism stimuli S_C and S_G occur in close succession, that these stimuli in conjunction with the drive (S_D) evoke reactions R_C and R_G respectively, that S_m coincides in time with S_C while S_n coincides in time with S_G, and that (Postulate 1) the stimulus trace of S_m extends to R_C, and the stimulus trace of S_n extends to R_G.

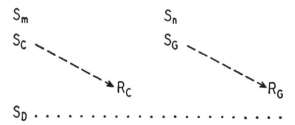

2. From (1) and Postulate 1, it follows that one phase of the stimulus trace of S_m will coincide with R_C and one phase of the stimulus trace of S_n will coincide with R_G.

3. Now, by Postulate 3, the combination $S_G - - - \rightarrow R_G$ marks a reinforcing state of affairs.

4. From (1), (2), (3), and Postulate 2 it follows, among other things, that the trace of S_n will become conditioned to R_G, and the trace of S_m will be conditioned to R_C, yielding the following excitatory tendencies:

$$S_m - - - \rightarrow R_C$$
$$S_n - - - \rightarrow R_G$$

5. But by (3) and (4) the reaction of the newly acquired excitatory tendency $S_n - - - \rightarrow R_G$ is that intimately associated with the reinforcing state of affairs, which identifies it as a conditioned reaction of the Pavlovian type.

6. On the other hand, by (3) and (4) the reaction of the excitatory tendency $S_m - - - \rightarrow R_C$ is a reaction distinct from that of the reinforcing state of affairs, which identifies it as an associative reaction of the Thorndikian type.

7. By (5) and (6) both the Pavlovian and the Thorndikian types of reaction have been derived from (1), (2), (3), and (4) jointly, and these in turn from the same principles of learning (Postulates 1, 2, and 3).

8. From (7) the theorem follows.

Q. E. D.

II

Both correct (right) and incorrect (wrong) reactions may be set up by the conditioning (associative) process.

1. Let it be supposed that an organism capable of acquiring associative reactions (Postulate 2) is, a number of times, stimulated simultaneously by S_A, S_B, S_C, and S_D; that S_C evokes reaction R_C; that the stimulus trace (Postulate 1) of S_A and S_B extend as far as R_C; that the object represented by S_B, in conjunction with act R_C, produces (causes) in the external world the event yielding the stimulus S_G; and finally that S_G evokes R_G.

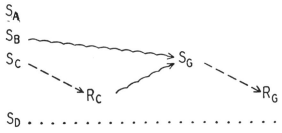

2. By Postulate 3, $S_G - - - \rightarrow R_G$ marks a reinforcing state of affairs.

3. From (1), (2), and Postulates 1 and 2, it follows that among other associative tendencies the following must be set up:

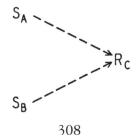

308

4. Now suppose that at a later time, S_B *alone* should evoke R_C. It follows from (1) that S_B, in conjunction with R_C, will cause to occur the event in the external world which will yield the stimulus S_G which, in turn, will evoke R_G.

5. But, once more, by Postulate 3, $S_G \text{—} \text{—} \rightarrow R_G$ marks a reinforcing state of affairs from which it follows that under the special new conditions of (4) the reaction tendency $S_B \text{—} \text{—} \rightarrow R_C$ will still be reinforced.

6. From (5) and Definition 7 it follows that $S_B \text{—} \text{—} \rightarrow R_C$ must be a correct or 'right' reaction.

7. Let us suppose, on the other hand, that S_A *alone* should evoke R_C. It follows from (1) that the external event giving rise to S_G will not occur (S_B being absent), and the excitatory tendency $S_A \text{—} \text{—} \rightarrow R_C$ will not be reinforced and, by Postulate 4, will suffer experimental extinction.

8. From (7) and Definition 8 it follows that $S_A \text{—} \text{—} \rightarrow R_C$ will be an incorrect or 'wrong' reaction.

9. From (6) and (8) the theorem follows.

Q. E. D.

III

Simple trial-and-error situations may arise in which the organism will make repeated incorrect reactions.

1. Let it be supposed that we have the simultaneous stimulus situation $S_T S_B S_D$ with the component S_B (step 3, Theorem II) evoking R_C; that S_B and R_C when operating jointly cause S_G, S_G evoking R_G, whereas S_T evokes R_V with an excitatory tendency exceeding that of S_B to R_C by an amount greater than the weakening effect (Postulate 4) of several unreinforced attempts (Definition 5); that R_V is not followed by its usual reinforcing sequence ($S'_G \text{—} \text{—} \rightarrow R'_G$); and that the external stimulus situation after each attempt becomes exactly the same as before. PAPER 10

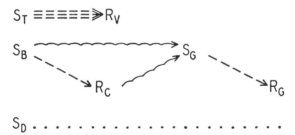

2. From (1) it follows that reaction R_V will take place at once after the organism encounters the compound stimulus $S_T S_B S_D$.

3. Now, by (1) the situation is such that R_V cannot be followed by its accustomed reinforcing sequence, so that this behavior sequence must be interrupted.

4. From (3) and Postulate 4, the excitatory tendency from S_T to R_V will be weakened by experimental extinction.

5. By (4) and Definition 8, R_V is an incorrect reaction.

6. By (1) and (2) the stimulus situation after the first R_V reaction must be the same as at the beginning, and the excitatory tendency to R_V must still be considerably in excess of that to R_C, from which it follows that R_V will occur a second time, and so on.

309

7. But, by (2), we have a first reaction (R_V), which, by (5) is incorrect and by (6) we have a repetition of this incorrect reaction, from which the theorem follows.

Q. E. D.

IV

Organisms in simple trial-and-error situations may manifest spontaneous variability of reaction, the objective situation remaining constant.

1. Suppose the situation in (1) of Theorem III with the additional assumption that excitatory tendency $S_B \text{---} \rightarrow R_C$ shall be strong enough to resist all generalized inhibitory effects (Postulate 4) sufficiently to escape becoming subliminal.

2. By (1) and Theorem III, it follows that reaction R_V will take place repeatedly.

3. By (1) and (2), reaction $S_T \text{---} \rightarrow R_V$ will not be followed by reinforcement (neither $S'_G \text{---} \rightarrow R'_G$ nor $S_G \text{---} \rightarrow R_G$), which failure (Postulate 4) will progressively weaken the tendency to R_V.

4. From (1) and (3) it follows that the reaction tendency to R_V must finally become weaker than that to R_C, at which point the stimulus complex $S_T S_B S_D$ will evoke reaction R_C.

5. But the shift from reaction R_V (2) to R_C (4) constitutes a variability of reaction.

6. Meanwhile, by (1) the objective situation has not changed.

7. From (5) and (6) the theorem follows.

Q. E. D.

V

Organisms in simple trial-and-error situations beginning with erroneous reactions may, after a sufficiently large number of attempts, come to give an indefinitely long series of successive correct reactions.

1. Let us assume the situation in step (1) of the deduction of Theorem IV.

2. By (1) and steps (2), (3), and (4) of Theorem IV, reaction tendency R_V will be progressively weakened by extinction until it is below the level of R_C, when the latter will take place.

3. Moreover, by (1), R_C in conjunction with S_B causes S_G; and S_G evokes R_G which, by Postulate 3, marks a reinforcing state of affairs.

4. It follows from (2), (3), and Postulate 2 that the excitatory tendency $S_B \text{---} \rightarrow R_C$ will be reinforced, and therefore strengthened.

5. But a certain amount of time must elapse while reaction R_C is taking place; by Postulate 5, this time must permit a certain amount of spontaneous recovery from experimental extinction on the part of R_V.

6. Now, the rate of the spontaneous recovery of R_V (5) may be either (*A*) more rapid than the gain in strength of R_C through the latter's reinforcement, or (*B*) it may be less rapid, or (*C*) the two processes may take place at the same rate. If it is less rapid, or if the two processes take place at the same rate, R_C will maintain its dominance, thus giving an indefinitely long series of correct reactions (Definition 7); from which the theorem follows.

7. But suppose, on the other hand, that the rate of the spontaneous recovery of R_V from its experimental extinction is faster than the gain in strength of R_C through its reinforcement (6). It follows that on this alternative R_V must again become dominant.

8. From (7) it follows by reasoning analogous to that in (2) that R_V will occur repeatedly until depressed by further experimental extinction below the strength of R_C when the latter will again occur, to be further reinforced, and so on.

310

9. Now it follows from (4) and (8) together with Postulate 5, that after each complete cycle of reversal of R_V and R_C, the former will retain a certain amount of its weakening which will not yield to spontaneous recovery and the latter will retain a certain amount of the strengthening which will not yield to forgetting.

10. It follows from (9) that if the cyclical alternation were to go on indefinitely, the tendency to R_V must be weakened to zero and that to R_C must be strengthened to its maximum.

11. It is evident from (10) that at some point in the progressive shift in the basic strengths of R_V and R_C the two movements must cross, at which point R_C will be permanently dominant over R_V irrespective of spontaneous recovery or forgetting, and there will then follow an indefinitely long series of successive correct reactions.

12. From (6) and (11) the theorem follows.

Q. E. D.

VI

In simple trial-and-error learning situations, failure of final correct reaction will, under certain conditions, result from discontinued effort.

1. Suppose the situation in (1) of Theorem III except that the excitatory tendency $S_B \text{ ---} \rightarrow R_C$ is at the outset only a little above the reaction threshold.

2. From (1) and Theorem III, false reaction R_V will be made repeatedly.

3. By (1) and (2), reaction tendency $S_T \text{ ---} \rightarrow R_V$ will not be followed by reinforcement, which failure (by Postulate 4) will, if not interrupted, gradually weaken $S_T \text{ ---} \rightarrow R_V$ to zero.

4. By (3) and Postulate 4, the weakening of $S_T \text{ ---} \rightarrow R_V$ will extend in considerable part to $S_B \text{ ---} \rightarrow R_C$.

5. Now, by (1) the super-threshold margin of strength of $S_B \text{ ---} \rightarrow R_C$ may be smaller than any assigned finite value, from which it follows that it may be smaller than the depressing effects (4) arising from the extinction of $S_T \text{ ---} \rightarrow R_V$.

6. It follows from (5) that before $S_T \text{ ---} \rightarrow R_V$ may be extinguished beneath the level of $S_B \text{ ---} \rightarrow R_C$ the latter will also have been depressed below the reaction threshold so that when $S_T \text{ ---} \rightarrow R_V$ reaches zero and ceases action, the potentially correct reaction tendency, $S_B \text{ ---} \rightarrow R_C$, will also be unable to function even though without any competition whatever.

7. But the depression of both the tendency to R_V and R_C as shown in (6) will bring about a cessation of attempts (Definition 5), the latter of which (1) would have been a correct reaction (Definition 7).

8. From (3), (4), and (7) the theorem follows.

Q. E. D.

Corollary 1.

Organisms capable of acquiring competing excitatory tendencies will manifest discouragement.

This follows directly from Theorem VI and Definition 9.

VII

Reactions conditioned to a late segment of a stimulus trace will subsequently occur as antedating reactions.

1. Suppose that stimulus S_B precedes stimulus S_C by several times the latency of conditioned reactions; that S_C evokes reaction R_C; that the stimulus trace of S_B extends as far as R_C; that the physical event responsible for S_C, jointly with reaction

PAPER
10

R_C, causes S_G; that S_G evokes R_G; and that S_D begins at S_C and persists throughout the remainder of the process.

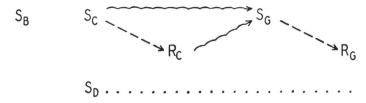

2. From (1) and Postulate 1, a segment of the stimulus trace initiated by S_B will coincide with R_C.

3. By (1) and Postulate 3, $S_G \text{---} \rightarrow R_G$ marks a reinforcing state of affairs and follows the coincidence of R_C with the trace of S_B.

4. By (2), (3), and Postulate 2, reaction R_C will become conditioned to a late coinciding segment of the trace of stimulus S_B, *i.e.*, that portion which coincides temporally with R_C.

5. Now, by Postulate 1, stimulus trace S_B at the point of the onset of the stimulus is substantially the same as at the segment conditioned to R_C, except that it is stronger.

PAPER

10

6. From (5) and Postulate 2 it follows that once R_C has been conditioned to a late segment of the trace of stimulus S_B with a supraliminal strength, the reaction will be evoked by any portion of the same trace which is as strong as, or stronger than, the segment conditioned.

7. But since, by (1), the initial portion of the stimulus trace of S_B will occur several times the latency of such a reaction in advance of the original point of the occurrence of R_C, it follows from (5) and (6) that after conditioning, R_C will be evoked in advance of the point of its original occurrence.

8. From (7) the theorem follows.

Q. E. D.

VIII

Organisms capable of acquiring trace conditioned reactions will be able to execute successful defense reactions.

1. Let it be supposed that an organism capable of acquiring trace conditioned reactions is stimulated by S_B, that the external world event responsible for S_B initiates a causal sequence several times the length of a conditioned reaction latency, which sequence terminates in S_G and S_D, the two latter jointly constituting an injury and evoking R_G, a flight reaction, which terminates their impact on the organism; and that the stimulus trace of S_B reaches well beyond the point at which R_G occurs.

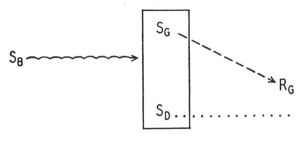

2. From (1) and Postulates 1 and 2 it follows that R_G will be conditioned to the trace of S_B.

3. From (1), (2), and Theorem VII it follows that if S_B occurs on a later occasion, reaction R_G will occur in advance of situation $S_G S_D$, which, if it impinges on the organism, will be injurious.

4. But, by (1), R_G is a flight reaction. It follows from (3) that the organism will not be present when the situation otherwise giving rise to $S_G S_D$ occurs and so will escape the injury, thus:

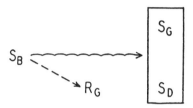

5. From (1) and (4) the theorem follows.

Q. E. D.

IX

PAPER

10

In stable behavior sequences terminating in reinforcement, each reaction, in general, becomes conditioned (A) to the proprioceptive stimulus arising from the action immediately preceding it, and (B) to the drive stimulus (S_D), each with an intensity diminishing according to a negatively accelerated rate with distance from the reinforcing state of affairs.

1. Let it be supposed that there impinges on an organism a uniform sequence of external stimuli S_1, S_2, S_3, etc.; that these stimuli evoke in the organism reactions R_1, R_2, R_3, etc.; that these reactions produce (Postulate 6) proprioceptive stimuli s_1, s_2, s_3, etc.; that R_3 by an external causal sequence produces a state of affairs which includes S_G; that S_G evokes R_G; that the combination S_G — — → R_G marks (Postulate 3) a reinforcing state of affairs; and that throughout the sequence there occurs the persisting drive stimulus S_D.

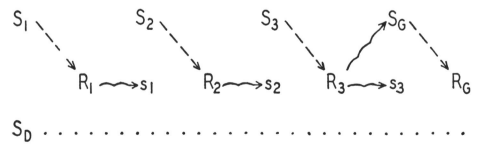

2. By Postulates 1 and 2 the situation supposed in (1) will give rise to an association between each proprioceptive stimulus and the reaction immediately following thus:

313

$$s_1 \ -\!-\!\to R_2$$

$$s_2 \ -\!-\!\to R_3$$

$$s_3 \ -\!-\!\to R_G$$

3. Also, since by (1) S_D occurs at every point throughout the series, it follows from (1) and Postulate 2 that S_D will be conditioned to every reaction in the series, thus:

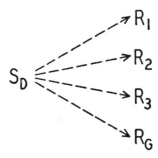

4. By (2) and Postulate 2,

$$s_3 -\!-\!\to R_G \ > \ s_2 -\!-\!\to R_3 \ > \ s_1 -\!-\!\to R_2$$

and

$$(s_3 -\!-\!\to R_G) - (s_2 -\!-\!\to R_3) \ > \ (s_2 -\!-\!\to R_3) - (s_1 -\!-\!\to R_2)$$

5. Also by (3) and Postulate 2,

$$S_D -\!-\!\to R_G > S_D -\!-\!\to R_3 > S_D -\!-\!\to R_2 > S_D -\!-\!\to R_1$$

and

$$(S_D -\!-\!\to R_G) - (S_D -\!-\!\to R_3) \ > \ (S_D -\!-\!\to R_3) - (S_D -\!-\!\to R_2) \ > \ (S_D -\!-\!\to R_2) - (S_D -\!-\!\to R_1)$$

6. But the expressions in (4) and (5) represent negatively accelerated excitatory gradients diminishing with distance from the reinforcing state of affairs.

7. From (2), (3), and (6) the theorem follows.

Q. E. D.

X

A fractional anticipatory goal reaction as a stimulus will tend to bring about the reinforcing state of affairs with which the total goal reaction, of which it is a constituent part, is associated.

1. Suppose the situation in (1) of Theorem IX with the additional assumption that the goal reaction (R_G) is composed of two components, a major one which cannot take place without the aid of the object represented by S_G and which is incompatible with the several acts of the sequence preceding it, and a minor one (r_G) which is not mechanically dependent on S_G and which may take place simultaneously with the antecedent reactions of the series.

2. Now, by Theorem IX, S_D is conditioned to R_G and, since by (1) r_G is a constituent part of R_G, S_D is also conditioned to r_G.

3. Since, by (1), S_D occurs throughout the series, it follows that it will evoke r_G at all points in the behavior sequence R_1, R_2, R_3, etc.

4. From (3) and Postulates 1 and 6 it follows that the trace of the internal stimulus produced by r_G, *i.e.*, s_G, will tend to occur in conjunction with all the reactions of the sequence R_1, R_2, R_3, etc.

5. Now, each time the situation represented in (4) occurs it is followed (1) by the reinforcing state of affairs marked by $S_G - - \rightarrow R_G$, from which it follows by Postulate 2 that s_G will ultimately become associated with all of the reactions of the sequence, thus:

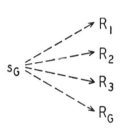

PAPER
10

very much as in the case of S_D (Theorem IX).

6. From (5) it follows that s_G will tend, on subsequent occasions, to bring about reactions R_1, R_2, R_3. By (1), R_3 causes S_G, and S_G evokes R_G.

7. But by (1), r_G is a constituent part of R_G which, with its S_G, marks (*i.e.*, is associated with) the reinforcing state of affairs.

8. But if (6 and 7) r_G, through the action of s_G, brings about the inevitable mark of its reinforcing state of affairs ($S_G - - \rightarrow R_G$), it must at the same time bring about the reinforcing state of affairs itself.

9. From (7) and (8) the theorem follows.

Q. E. D.

XI

Organisms capable of acquiring functionally potent anticipatory reactions intimately associated with the reinforcing state of affairs, will manifest a weakened tendency to the consummatory reaction if, at the completion of the action sequence, the state of affairs then presented does not permit the occurrence of the complete reaction of which the anticipatory reaction is a constituent part.

1. Suppose that an organism which has been in a situation such as (1) in Theorem IX later finds itself in the same situation with the exception that the terminal conditions, instead of permitting reaction $S_G - - \rightarrow R_G$, permit a different reaction, $S'_G - - \rightarrow R'_G$, which is appropriate to the same drive (S_D) and is in the repertoire of the organism in question but has a strength only slightly above the reaction threshold.

2. By step (1) of the proof of Theorem IX, together with Theorem IX itself, the customary stimulus complex giving rise to the terminal reaction must be:

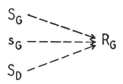

3. Now, by (1) and Theorem IX, the s_G of (2) represents r_G, and r_G (Definition 13) is both a reaction anticipatory of, and a fractional component of, R_G.

4. On the other hand, by (1), (2), and Theorem IX, the excitatory tendencies under the changed conditions of the present theorem will be:

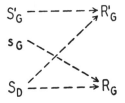

5. From (1) and (4) it follows that the excitatory tendencies leading to R_G must be frustrated (Definition 3) which (by Postulate 4) will set up experimental extinction at the point in question.

6. From (5) and Postulate 4 it follows that as a result of the extinction of the tendencies to R_G there will occur simultaneously a weakening of the tendency to reaction R'_G.

7. But by (1) the tendencies to R'_G may be as small as desired and therefore smaller than the generalized extinction of (6), from which it follows that under these circumstances the excitatory tendencies to R'_G will pass below the reaction threshold.

8. From (3) and (7) the theorem follows.

Q. E. D.

Corollary 1.

Organisms will display disappointment.

This follows directly from Theorem XI and Definition 16.

XII

Organisms capable of acquiring anticipatory goal reactions will strive to bring about situations which are reinforcing.

1. Let it be assumed that an organism has acquired a habit-family hierarchy (Definition 17) of two distinct action sequences of the type described in (1) of Theorem X, both originating in the external stimulus situation S_1, terminating in the reinforcing situation $S_G —— → R_G$ and associated with the drive S_D; that the initial acts of one of the sequences are R_I, R_{II}, etc., and those of the other are R_1, R_2, etc.; that the excitatory tendency initiating the sequence beginning with R_1 is dominant over that beginning with R_I, but that the tendency to R_I is far enough above the reaction threshold to survive the weakening effect which would result (Postulate 4) from the frustration of the tendency to R_1.

2. Now suppose that an obstacle is interposed which effectually prevents the completion of R_1 and the remainder of that sequence (1). It follows from Postulate 4 that this excitatory tendency will suffer extinction, with no limit above zero.

3. From (1) and (2) it follows that the sequence beginning with R_I and terminating with R_G will be executed after the frustration of the excitatory tendency leading to R_1.

4. Now, from (1) it follows by reasoning strictly analogous to steps (2), (3), (4), (5), and (6) of the deduction of Theorem X, that s_G will acquire during the acquisition of the habit family the tendency to evoke (A) reaction sequence R_1 and all those acts following it in the sequence leading to R_G, and (B) reaction sequence R_I together with all those leading from it to R_G.

5. From (2), (3), (4), and Definition 10 it follows that under these circumstances the introduction of a barrier will cause the organism to shift from one behavior sequence *directed* to a reinforcing state of affairs to another *directed to the same* reinforcing state of affairs.

6. But by (5) and Definition 11, when the interposition of an obstacle leads an organism to choose an alternative action sequence *directed* to the same reinforcing state of affairs as that interrupted by the obstacle, the behavior in question is striving.

7. From (6) the theorem follows.

Q. E. D.

Corollary 1.

Organisms will strive for goals.

This follows directly from Theorem XII and Definitions 11 and 12.

PAPER
10

XIII

When an organism has attained a reinforcing state of affairs in a situation which, objectively considered, is totally novel, but by means of a member of a previously established habit-family hierarchy, there may follow without specific practice a tendency to a transfer to the new situation of the behavior tendencies represented by one or another of the remaining members of the habit-family hierarchy in question.

1. Let it be assumed that an organism has acquired a habit-family hierarchy (Definition 17) of two distinct action sequences of the type described in (1) of Theorem X, both originating in the external stimulus situation S_1, terminating in the reinforcing situation $S_G — — → R_G$ and associated with the drive stimulus S_D; that the initial act of one of the sequences is R_I and that of the other is R_1.

2. From (1) it follows by reasoning strictly analogous to steps (2), (3), (4), (5), and (6) of the deduction of Theorem X, that s_G will acquire during the acquisition of the habit family the tendency to evoke (A) reaction sequence R_1 and all those acts following it in the sequence leading to R_G, and (B) reaction sequence R_I together with all those leading from it to R_G.

3. Now, suppose that this same organism in a novel external situation S'_1 and acting under the same drive stimulus S_D reaches, a few times, by the process of trial and error the reinforcing state of affairs marked by $S_G — — → R_G$, by an action sequence the same as that beginning with R_1 of one of the members of the habit-family hierarchy of (1).

4. From (3) it follows by reasoning similar to steps (2) and (3) of the deduction leading to Theorem X, that r_G will be present throughout the behavior sequence beginning with S'_1.

5. It follows from (4) that there will be a coincidence of r_G and the stimulus trace of S'_1.

6. Since by (3) the coincidence of the stimulus trace of S'_1 and r_G (5) is followed by $S_G \text{---} \rightarrow R_G$, it follows by Postulates 1 and 2 that there will be set up the excitatory tendency $S'_1 \text{---} \rightarrow r_G$.

7. From (6), (2), and Postulate 6 it follows that S'_1 will tend to initiate the behavior sequence (omitting internal stimuli after R_1):

$$S'_1 \text{--} \rightarrow r_G \longleftrightarrow s_G \text{--} \rightarrow R_1 \text{--} \rightarrow R_2 \text{--} \rightarrow R_3 \rightsquigarrow s_G \text{--} \rightarrow R_G$$

and also

$$S'_1 \text{--} \rightarrow r_G \rightsquigarrow s_G \text{--} \rightarrow R_I \text{--} \rightarrow R_{II} \text{--} \rightarrow R_{III} \rightsquigarrow s_G \text{--} \rightarrow R_G$$

or, combining the two sequences,

$$S'_1 \text{--} \rightarrow r_G \rightsquigarrow s_G \Big\langle {\nearrow R_1 \text{--} \rightarrow R_2 \text{--} \rightarrow R_3 \searrow \atop \searrow R_I \text{--} \rightarrow R_{II} \text{--} \rightarrow R_{III} \nearrow} \Big\rangle s_G \text{--} \rightarrow R_G$$

PAPER
10

8. Now, suppose that at this point an obstacle is interposed such that R_1 cannot take place, and that $s_G \text{---} \rightarrow R_I$ is far enough above the reaction threshold to resist the weakening effect of the frustration of the excitatory tendency to R_1. With the competition of R_1 thus removed from the excitatory tendency to R_I, s_G will initiate R_I (7); this will lead to R_{II}, this to R_{III}, etc., and finally to $S_G \text{---} \rightarrow R_G$.

9. But the shift from the sequence beginning with R_1 to that beginning with R_I as in (8) is a transfer without specific practice from an old to a new situation because R_I, R_{II}, etc., have never taken place in the external stimulus situation beginning with S'_1.

10. From (9) the theorem follows.

Q. E. D.

The Nature of Adaptive Behavior as Indicated by the Postulates of the Present System

We come now to the second step in our exposition of the procedure which should have been carried out by Eddington and Weiss before they presumed to state the ultimate nature of the more complex forms of adaptive and moral behavior. In this step we turn, mainly for purposes of illustration, to the direct examination of the postulates which gave rise to the system, to see whether they are, in fact, physical or psychic. Let us pass them in review. Postulate 1 states that the physiological effects of a stimulus persist for a certain time even after the stimulus has ceased. Postulate 2 indicates the conditions under which stimuli and reactions become associated or conditioned. Postulate 3 gives the marks of reinforcing situations. Postulate 4 states the conditions under which associations are unlearned. Postulate 5 gives the conditions under which positive and negative learning are lost. Postulate 6 states the well-known fact of internal stimulation.

At first glance most persons would probably say that these postulates represent the behavior of what has always been regarded as physical. Moreover, the postulates appear to be phenomena of physical structures which most theoretical physicists believe will ultimately be derived, *i.e.*, deduced, by them from electrons, protons, deutrons, etc. According to this view the theoretical physicists will ultimately deduce as theorems from electrons, protons, etc., the six postulates which we have employed as the basis for the deduction of adaptive behavior. If this deduction were accomplished we should have an unbroken logical chain extending from the primitive electron all the way up to complex purposive behavior. Further developments may conceivably extend the system to include the highest rational and moral behavior. Such is the natural goal of science. This is the picture which a complete scientific monism would present. Unfortunately, theoretical physics is very far from this achievement, and judgment regarding its ultimate accomplishment must be indefinitely suspended. At most such a view, attractive as it is, can be regarded only as a working hypothesis.[18]

PAPER
10

[18] There is conceivable, however, a kind of experimental shortcut to the determination of the ultimate nature of adaptive behavior. Suppose it were possible to construct from inorganic materials, such as the theoretical physicists have already succeeded in deriving from electrons and protons, a mechanism which would display exactly the principles of behavior presented in the six postulates just examined. On the assumption that the logic of the above deductions is sound, it follows inevitably that such a 'psychic' machine, if subjected to appropriate environmental influences, must manifest the complex adaptive phenomena presented by the theorems. And if, upon trial, this *a priori* expectation should be verified by the machine's behavior, it would be possible to say with assurance and a clear conscience that such adaptive behavior may be 'reached' by purely physical means. A beginning in the direction of such constructions has already been made. See R. G. Krueger and C. L. Hull, An electro-chemical parallel to the conditioned reflex, *J. Gen. Psychol.*, 1931, 5, 262–269; G. K. Bennett and L. B. Ward, Synthesis of conditioned reflex, *Amer. J. Psychol.*, 1933, 45, 339; D. G. Ellson, A mechanical synthesis of trial-and-error learning, *J. Gen. Psychol.*, 1935, 13, 212–218.

But What of Consciousness?

But what of consciousness, of awareness, of experience—those phenomena of which the philosophers and theologians have made so much and upon the priority of which they are so insistent? An inspection of the postulates of the miniature system of adaptive behavior presented above certainly shows no trace of any such phenomena. It is clear, therefore, that so far as that considerable array of complex behavior is concerned, consciousness or experience has no logical priority. In the field of scientific theory no other form of priority is of primary significance.

What, then, shall we say about consciousness? Is its existence denied? By no means. But to recognize the existence of a phenomenon is not the same thing as insisting upon its basic, *i.e.*, logical, priority. Instead of furnishing a means for the solution of problems, consciousness appears to be itself a problem needing solution. In the miniature theoretical system, no mention of consciousness or experience was made for the simple reason that no theorem has been found as yet whose deduction would be facilitated in any way by including such a postulate. Moreover, we have been quite unable to find any other scientific system of behavior which either has found consciousness a necessary pre-supposition or, having assumed it, has been able to deduce from it a system of adaptive behavior or moral action.[19] There is, however, no reason at all for not using consciousness or experience as a postulate in a scientific theoretical system if it clearly satisfies the deductive criteria already laid down.

PAPER
10

[19] It is rather hoped and expected that this statement will be challenged. In the interest of the clarification of an important problem, it is desirable that the challenge be accompanied by a formal exhibition of the structure of the system supposed to manifest the critical characteristics. As illustrated above, a theoretical system is a considerable sequence of interlocking theorems, all derived from the same set of postulates. Too often what pass as systems in psychology are merely informal points of view containing occasional propositions which, even if logically derived, would be nothing more than isolated theorems. Some authors are prone to the illusion that such propositions could be deduced with rigor in a few moments if they cared to take the trouble. Others assert that the logic has all been worked by them 'in their heads,' but that they did not bother to write it out; the reader is expected to accept this on faith. Fortunately, in science it is not customary to base conclusions on faith.

If such a system should be worked out in a clear and un-ambiguous manner the incorporation of consciousness into the body of behavior theory should be automatic and immediate. The task of those who would have consciousness a central factor in adaptive behavior and in moral action is accordingly quite clear. They should apply themselves to the long and grinding labor of the logical derivation of a truly scientific system. Until such a system has been attained on a consider-able scale, the advancement of science will be favored by their limiting their claims to statements of their hopes and wishes as such. Meanwhile, one cannot help recalling that for several centuries practically all psychological and philosophi-cal theorists have set out precisely with the assumption of the priority of consciousness or experience. Considering the practically complete failure of all this effort to yield even a small scientific system of adaptive or moral behavior in which consciousness finds a position of logical priority as a postulate, one may, perhaps, be pardoned for entertaining a certain amount of pessimism regarding such an eventuality.

PAPER
10

In view of the general lack of the kind of evidence which would be necessary to show the logical priority of conscious-ness, it may naturally be asked why there is such insistence upon its central significance. While there are many con-tributing factors, it can scarcely be doubted that an important element in the situation is found in the perseverative influences of medieval theology. During the Middle Ages, and for centuries thereafter, social or moral control was supposed to be effected largely through promises of rewards or punish-ments after death. Therefore something had to survive death to reap these rewards. Consciousness as a non-physical entity was considered incorruptible and thus immune to the disintegration of the flesh. Consequently it offered a logical possibility of something surviving physical death upon which scores might be evened among the shadows beyond the river Styx. But to be convincing, it was necessary for the thing rewarded or punished to be an essentially causal element in the determination of moral conduct or behavior. Thus it was imperative not only that consciousness be non-physical, but also that it be the basic factor in determining action. Such a view is incompatible with the belief that the more complex forms of human behavior could be derived without any reference whatever to consciousness. Tradition is strong, especially when fostered by powerful institutions. Accordingly, the frequent insistence on the logical priority of consciousness is not surprising, even when coming from persons who have no clear notion as to the origin of their feelings in the matter.

Thus it can hardly be doubted that psychology in its basic principles is to a considerable degree in the thrall of the Middle Ages, and that, in particular, our prevailing systematic outlook in the matter of consciousness is largely medieval. The situation depicted in a remarkable panel of the fresco by Orozco in the Dartmouth Library gives a powerful artistic representation of this. There, lifeless skeletons in academic garb assist solemnly at the gruesome travail of a reclining skeleton in the act of reproducing itself. What a picture of academic sterility! Fortunately the means of our salvation is clear and obvious. As ever, it lies in the application of scientific procedures. The methodology is old and tried; it goes back even to the time of Galileo. The present paper is, in reality, an exposition of the specific application of this technique in a systematic manner to the problems of complex adaptive behavior. Galileo practiced this methodology at the imminent risk of imprisonment, torture, and death. For us to apply the methodology, it is necessary only to throw off the shackles of a lifeless tradition.

Reprinted from Psychological Review, Vol. 45, No. 4, July, 1938
Printed in U. S. A.

THE GOAL–GRADIENT HYPOTHESIS APPLIED TO SOME 'FIELD–FORCE' PROBLEMS IN THE BEHAVIOR OF YOUNG CHILDREN [1]

BY CLARK L. HULL

Yale University

The hypothesis of the goal-excitatory gradient (8),[2] as well as that of the habit-family hierarchy (9),[3] was originally expounded in connection with a consideration of the behavior of albino rats in the ordinary enclosed maze. In such mazes the possible pathways of approach to the goal as well as the range of vision are greatly limited. Indeed, in former papers the sense of vision as a distance receptor was almost entirely neglected. The present paper, on the other hand, is concerned with some of the implications of the two hypotheses and a number of closely related principles when behavior, chiefly locomotor, is taking place in situations such that the field of vision is practically unobstructed. And, while certain limita-

PAPER

11

[1] The substance of this article has been in occasional use in the form of a bound manuscript as a seminar reference since the spring of 1934. In this way a number of valuable criticisms have been received; the author is especially indebted to Dr. Neal E. Miller and to Dr. Carl I. Hovland. Mr. Donald T. Perkins has contributed the mathematical portions of notes 6, 12, 16, and 19.

[2] A certain amount of misunderstanding concerning the goal-gradient hypothesis has arisen from confusing one of the implications of the hypothesis under particular conditions (20, 153) with the hypothesis itself. The hypothesis, as originally stated (8, 26) is, "that the goal reaction gets conditioned the most strongly to the stimuli preceding it, and the other reactions of the behavior sequence get conditioned to their stimuli progressively weaker as they are more remote (in time or space) from the goal reaction." The 'goal' is the point of reinforcement. Because of the somewhat anthropomorphic connotation of the term 'goal' it would, perhaps, be better if this principle could be known as the 'gradient of reinforcement,' as suggested by Miller and Miles (16).

[3] A habit-family hierarchy consists of a number of habitual alternative behavior sequences having in common the initial stimulus situation and the final reinforcing state of affairs (11, 16).

271

tions will be placed on the opportunities for locomotion in the situations to be considered, freedom in this respect will be comparatively unrestricted. Lastly, the phenomenon to be studied will be mainly the naïve striving behavior of organisms such as young children who are only slightly sophisticated regarding obstacles at distances greater than the arm's length.[4] A number of the problems to be examined have already been subjected to a Gestalt analysis by Lewin (**13**, **14**).

I

PAPER

11

We shall begin by considering the influence of the subject's being able to see clearly, though usually at some distance, the lure or goal (G) from the starting point of his sequence of locomotion (S), together with numerous discriminable aspects of the intervening space. It is clear that the visual stimulation changes constantly, particularly as to the size of the image on the retina, as the subject approaches the lure, *i.e.*, the point of reinforcement. According to the goal excitatory gradient hypothesis, the several phases of the flux of this stimulus complex will become conditioned to the accompanying movements leading to the point of reinforcement with a strength increasing with proximity to the goal. Thus, after a certain amount of training the organism should advance more vigorously the closer it is to the goal (**10**).[5]

[4] Striving is that behavior of organisms which, upon frustration, displays varied alternative action sequences, all directed by an intent (fractional anticipatory goal reaction or r_G) to the attainment of the same reinforcing state of affairs (**11**, **16**). The naïveté here assumed involves as a minimum the absence of effective speech symbolism. Accordingly the present analysis should apply both to young children and to feeble-minded, of whatever chronological age, who have a mental age under about two years (**17**).

[5] This is on the assumption that the stronger the excitatory tendency, the stronger and more rapid will be the reaction dependent upon it. The experimental results reported by Bruce (**3**), and one or two other studies which have been communicated privately, seem to indicate that the relationship between the speed-of-locomotion gradient and the hypothesis of the goal gradient may not be so simple as appeared in the author's study just cited and in an independent confirming experiment by Miller and Miles (**16**). Evidently further experimental work will be needed to clarify this relationship. On the other hand, a recent experiment involving compound trial-and-error, reported by Muenzinger, Dove, and Bernstone (**18**), presents reassuring evidence of the substantial truth of the basic goal-excitatory-gradient hypothesis (see note 2 above). Incidentally, these writers show that when conditions permit, a similar

Yoshioka's experiment involving the power of rats to discriminate short from long paths indicates that this increase in excitatory tendency follows rather closely the logarithmic principle (22).[6]

A convenient presentation of such a logarithmic function is shown in Table 1. By means of this table it will be easy to see in a clear and precise manner the quantitative [7] implications of the goal-gradient hypothesis as bearing on the locomotor excitatory tendencies of a considerable variety of situations. Let us take as our first example one in which the visual stimulus of the lure (G) is placed at two distances from the subject, the second distance being three times as great as the first (Fig. 1). Suppose that the first starting point (S) is 5 units distant from the goal, and that the second is 15 units distant.[8] By Table 1, the excitatory potentiality of

---

gradient of excitation also *follows* the point of reinforcement quite in harmony with the well-established conditioning or learning experiments of Thorndike (21; 2).

[6] This may be demonstrated as follows. Yoshioka's experiment showed that the length-discrimination threshold in rats for pairs of distinct paths to the same reward point was inversely proportional to the distance. If we assume that the *difference* between the excitatory tendencies (E) leading to the initial acts of the alternative pathways is the same for the various length-discrimination thresholds, then the decrease in excitatory strength per unit increase in distance (D) from the goal is inversely proportional to the distance, *i.e.*,

$$\frac{dE}{dD} = -\frac{b}{D},$$

where b is a positive constant. Hence, integrating, we have:

$$E = a - b \log D,$$

where a is a constant (and must be positive, since E is positive). This is the equation upon which Table 1 is constructed. It is to be noted, however, that this is but a tentative, and probably not a very accurate, representation of the exact nature of the relationship. Two considerations argue against its finality. (1) At $D = 0$, E becomes infinite, and (2) with very large values of D, E becomes negative instead of becoming asymptotic to zero. A plausible alternative equation is:

$$E = ae^{-hD}$$

In this connection see Guilford (6).

[7] This quantitative approach with the attendant possibilities of utilizing the potentialities of a metricized mathematics for the purpose of exploring the implications of its postulates is somewhat in contrast to the topological approach emphasized by Lewin with its seeming limitation to the qualitative (14).

[8] It is to be emphasized that the principles of alternative reaction sequences here considered are intended to apply to all sorts of behavior and are definitely not restricted

PAPER
11

TABLE 1

This table shows the hypothetical strength of the conditioning of stimuli received at different distances from the goal to reactions occurring simultaneously. This is on the assumption that the excitatory tendency one unit from the goal acquires a strength of ten units and that the strength of the excitatory tendency acquired at each of the remaining distances diminishes with their remoteness according to the equation

$$E = a - b \log D,$$

where a has a value of 10, b has a value of 4, and the logarithms are taken with a base of 5.

Units Distant from Goal (D)	Strength of Excitatory Tendency (E)	Units Distant from Goal (D)	Strength of Excitatory Tendency (E)
1	10.000	26	1.903
2	8.277	27	1.809
3	7.270	28	1.718
4	6.554	29	1.631
5	6.000	30	1.547
6	5.547	31	1.465
7	5.164	32	1.386
8	4.831	33	1.310
9	4.539	34	1.236
10	4.277	35	1.164
11	4.040	36	1.094
12	3.824	37	1.026
13	3.625	38	.959
14	3.441	39	.895
15	3.270	40	.832
16	3.109	41	.771
17	2.958	42	.711
18	2.816	43	.652
19	2.682	44	.595
20	2.554	45	.539
21	2.433	46	.484
22	2.317	47	.431
23	2.207	48	.379
24	2.101	49	.327
25	2.000	50	.277

PAPER
11

the visual image encountered at 5 units distant has a value of 6.00 points, whereas its strength at 15 units is only 3.27 points, a difference of 2.73. This fundamental relationship may be represented graphically as in Fig. 2.

It follows from the preceding that if an experimental situation should be so arranged that two distinct alternative paths of these respective lengths *both* lead from S to G, path

to locomotion in space. When non-spatial sequences are involved, the distance from the goal should be thought of as time (8) or, possibly, energy consumption. Spatial examples have certain advantages for exposition because of the ease of diagrammatic representation, but it is believed that they actually present greater theoretical difficulties than do non-spatial sequences.

A would be chosen in preference to path *B* because the stimulus at the point of choice would have an excitatory tendency leading to the acts constituting *A* nearly twice as great as to those constituting *B*. A situation of this kind is, of course, the limiting case of a habit-family hierarchy: the fact that two paths begin and end at the same points makes them a family; the fact that one is preferred above the other constitutes them a hierarchy (**9**).

By a simple extension of the above reasoning, certain corollaries may be derived. It may be shown, for example, that the difference in excitatory tendency leading to the locomotor action of traversing pairs of paths differing in length by a constant amount grows less and less as the paths

PATH A:

PATH B:

PAPER

11

FIG. 1. Two paths to the same goal; *S*, starting point of one path and *S'*, of the other. Path *A* is represented as being 5 units in length and path *B* as 15 units in length. The dynamics of the two situations are represented in Fig. 2. It is to be observed that if Path *S'* → *G'* were suitably curved and shifted about in a manner such that point *S'* would coincide with point *S*, and point *G'* would coincide with point *G*, the combination of paths thus resulting would constitute a habit-family hierarchy (see text, pp. 274–275).

jointly become longer and longer. Suppose, for example, that the shorter path in the above example increases from 5 to 20 units in length and the longer one from 15 to 30. The difference in excitatory strength produced by the difference of 10 units in length would (Table 1) shrink from 2.73 points to 1.00 point. When the shorter path is further increased to 40 units in length, a second path 10 units longer makes a difference in excitatory tendency of only .56 of a point, and so on. Conversely, by shortening both paths a constant difference in their lengths will give rise to greater and greater differences in their excitatory potentialities. This principle has important implications which will be taken up below. So far as the author is aware, these corollaries have not been subjected to experimental test; they offer a ready means of further testing the hypothesis.

II

At this point we may conveniently consider the bearing of the present system of hypotheses on the interesting problem of the allegedly deleterious influence of increasing the excita-

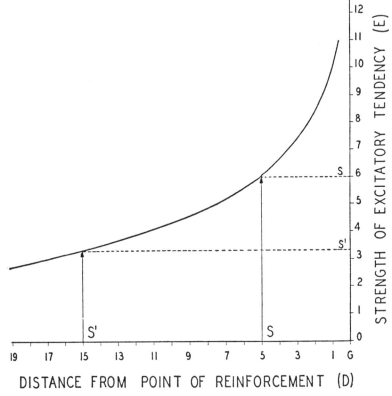

FIG. 2. Diagrammatic representation of the hypothetical dynamics of the two paths to goal *G* shown in Fig. 1. The curve represents the excitatory potentialities of the visual stimulus of the goal complex at all distances from 1 to 19 units according to the equation,

$$E = a - b \log D.$$

The strengths at 5 and 15 units distant have been projected upon the scale at the right. It is evident to inspection that *S* has nearly twice as great excitatory potentiality as has *S'*.

tory strength of the lure upon the solution of certain types of problems (**12**). Let us assume once more that a naïve organism has two distinct habit sequences corresponding to paths *A* and *B* of Fig. 1, each leading to the same goal or point of reinforcement. In this case, however, there is supposed to be an effective physical barrier at the beginning

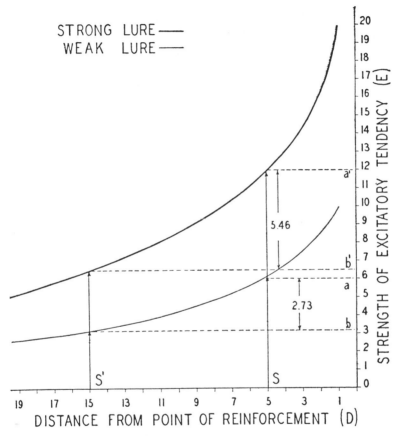

STRONG LURE ——
WEAK LURE ——

PAPER
11

FIG. 3. Diagrammatic representation of the dynamics of doubling the strength of the lure at 1 unit from *G*, Fig. 1. The two curves represent the hypothetical strength of excitatory tendency of the optical image of the respective lures for all distances between 1 and 19 units of remoteness from *G*. The equation for the weak lure (lower curve) is

$$E_w = 10 - 4 \log_5 D,$$

whereas that for the strong lure (upper curve) is

$$E_s = 20 - 8 \log_5 D.$$

The excitatory potentialities (*E*) at *S* and *S'* are projected upon the scale at the right. It is evident to inspection that the difference between *S* and *S'* is greatly increased by adding to the strength of the lure.

of the shorter path (A) so that solution of the problem consists in traversing the longer path (B). Let us assume, further, that in one situation the excitatory potentialities of the goal one unit distant have been doubled, say, by increasing the quantity of the reward. Presumably the remainder of the gradient would rise proportionately.[9] On this assumption the resulting situation may be represented with precision by plotting the values of Table 1 on two different ordinate scales, one twice as great as the other. Graphs produced in this manner are presented in Fig. 3. An inspection of this figure shows that the difference between the excitatory tendency to take the respective paths under the weak lure is only 2.73 units (6 − 3.27), whereas this difference rises to 5.46 units (12 − 6.54) in the presence of the strong lure.

Here it becomes necessary to introduce a second hypothesis, which is that a strong excitatory tendency diminishes the same number of units in excitatory strength from a given amount of frustration [10] as does a weak excitatory tendency.[11] Applying this principle to the supposititious case before us, it follows that it would take as long (or as many futile at-

PAPER

11

[9] It would seem that this assumption could be tested experimentally without great difficulty. Perhaps the technique of Muenzinger, Dove, and Bernstone (18) might here be employed to advantage.

[10] The frustration hypothesis is to the effect that whenever an excitatory tendency is prevented, for any reason, from evoking its accustomed reaction, a state ensues substantially like the experimental extinction or internal inhibition long known to be characteristic of conditioned reactions (19). This hypothesis has been elaborated to a certain extent in (9, p. 139). A special case of wide occurrence not yet elaborated is where an organism is learning by simple trial-and-error to choose consistently one of a pair of alternative reactions such as the two turns of a single T maze. According to the frustration hypothesis, whichever alternative is chosen, the excitatory tendencies otherwise leading to the other must be frustrated and so generate a certain amount of inhibition. This would be true even though the alternative chosen should be correct and receive reinforcement. According to this hypothesis, a constant number of reinforcements to one of two alternative reactions, with the stimulus otherwise evoking the other reaction present, should add less to the extinctive resistance of the reinforced reaction than they would if the stimulus normally evoking the weaker alternative were absent. This deduction suggests an experimental test of the hypothesis.

[11] No really satisfactory evidence on this point is available. The present situation makes the experimental determination of this relationship especially urgent. Actually, the following deductions would still hold even if the absolute diminution in excitatory tendency should be faster in initially strong than in initially weak excitatory tendencies, provided that the relative *rate* in the former were slower.

tempts on the part of the organism) for the presence of the barrier to path A to diminish by 4 units an excitatory tendency initially with a strength of 12 units (strong lure) as one initially with a strength of only 6 units (weak lure). In the former case the problem would not have been solved in this length of time, since the obstructed path would still have a strength of 8 units (12 — 4) which would be well above the strength of the long but unobstructed path (6.54). In the case of the weak lure, on the other hand, the obstructed path would have, after the same period (or amount) of frustration, a strength of only 2 units (6 — 4). Since this is well below the strength of the long path (3.27) the latter would presumably have been chosen some time before the end of the period in question, solving the problem of the organism. Thus the paradox of an increased lure interfering with, rather than facilitating, the solution of certain problems apparently finds an explanation.[12]

PAPER

11

[12] The preceding demonstration holds, of course, only for the particular supposititious values employed. The general theorem may be derived by ordinary mathematical procedures, as follows:

Let the initial excitatory tendency in the case of the weak lure be:

$$E_w = a - b \log D$$

and in the case of the strong lure be:

$$E_s = K(a - b \log D) \text{ where } K > 1.$$

Then, after a certain number (n) of frustrations, these excitatory tendencies will have reduced to:

$$E_w(n) = a - b \log D - f(n),$$
$$E_s(n) = K(a - b \log D) - f(n),$$

where $f(n)$ is an increasing function of n.

Now let path A, of length D_1, be obstructed; and let path B, of length $D_2(D_2 > D_1)$, be unobstructed. Then, the number (n_w) of frustrations required to make the excitatory tendency along A less than that along B is:

$$n_w = [f^{-1}\left(b \log \frac{D_2}{D_1}\right) + 1],$$

where f^{-1} is the inverse function of f, and the brackets mean 'largest integer not greater than.'

Likewise, the corresponding number (n_s) of frustrations required in the case of the strong lure is:

$$n_s = [f^{-1}\left(Kb \log \frac{D_2}{D_1}\right) + 1],$$

but

$$K > 1,$$

In this same general category probably will be found to fall phenomena resulting from increasing the craving of the organism. If the lure is food, general observation as well as experimental results (10) indicates that increased hunger (food privation) heightens the excitatory gradient very much as does increasing the quantity of the lure. By the same reasoning as that of the immediately preceding paragraph, increasing hunger with a constant food lure should impede the solution of this type of problem very much as would increasing the lure with constant craving or drive.

Another situation closely paralleling the influence of increasing the excitatory value of the lure while leaving the lure itself objectively unchanged ought, according to the present set of hypotheses, to result from progressively shortening both paths at the same time keeping the absolute difference between them the same. A special case of this kind studied by Lewin (13, 14) is presented by the two situations shown in Fig. 4. Suppose that direct path A is approximately 5 units long. Then indirect path B will be about 29 units long. By Table 1 (leaving out of consideration for the moment the directional factor), the excitatory tendency at point S to take these respective paths should be 6.00 units and 1.63 units respectively; this leaves a difference of 4.37 points of excitatory potentiality to be extinguished by the barrier in path A before path B can become active. In the case of the right-hand figure, direct path A' has a length of 12 units and indirect path B' has a length of approximately 35

PAPER 11

hence

$$Kb \log \frac{D_2}{D_1} > b \log \frac{D_2}{D_1},$$

hence

$$f^{-1}\left(Kb \log \frac{D_2}{D_1}\right) + 1 > f^{-1}\left(b \log \frac{D_2}{D_1}\right) + 1,$$

hence

$$n_s \geq n_w,$$

i.e., the number of frustrations on the shorter path necessary to produce the successful (long-path) reaction will be greater with the strong than with the weak lure provided the difference between the lengths of the two paths is great enough to be equivalent to at least a single attempt. The outcome of the two remaining cases in this section may be derived in an analogous manner, but space in which to do this is not available in the present paper.

units. By Table I, the excitatory tendency at choice point S to take paths A' and B' to G' should be 3.82 units and 1.16 units respectively, with a difference of only 2.66 units to be worn down by the barrier frustration before path B' can become active. Assuming, again, something like a constant rate of extinction from the frustration produced by the barriers to the direct paths, goal G' should be easier of attainment than goal G, in some inverse function of the proportion of 4.37 to 2.66.

To sum up, then, we arrive at the tentative conclusion that three different changes in a problem situation are substantially equivalent in their supposed paradoxical ten-

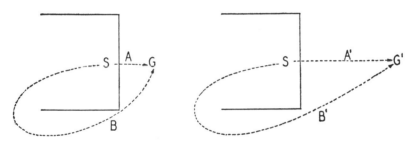

PAPER
11

FIG. 4. The figures represent an organism located at S and observing a lure G and G' respectively. There are two potential paths to G, A and B, and two to G', A' and B'. The problem is which goal will be more easily attained, and why. The present system of hypotheses favor G', providing no other lures complicate the situation by leading the organism around the barrier.

dency to impede the solution of problems involving alternative paths to a goal where the shorter, or preferred, path has a barrier: increasing the strength of the lure, increasing the strength of the drive or craving, and decreasing the remoteness of the lure. The last two of the three cases are capable of general demonstration by the ordinary mathematical procedures analogous to those applied to the first (see note 12). This analysis serves to raise not only the experimental question as to the postulates involved, such as the shape of the goal excitatory gradient and the rate of weakening of excitatory tendency under frustration, but, quite as insistently, the question of the reality in detail of the three supposed paradoxical tendencies themselves. It is highly doubtful whether either set of phenomena is as simple as the above treatment would imply.

III

Consider once more the situation represented in Figs. 1, 2, 3 and 4, on the former assumption that the short path A has a barrier near its beginning. In the preceding sections we have proceeded on the tacit assumption that the only thing necessary before path B will be chosen is that the strength of the tendency to take path A shall be weakened from s (Fig. 2) to a value somewhat below s'.[13] It now becomes necessary to point out in the competitional situations considered, the operation of a factor—temporarily ignored—which is variously called the irradiation of inhibition or the generalization of extinction (frustration). From the present point of view this principle is that every extinguished reaction has a tendency to inhibit (weaken) all other reaction tendencies, the stimuli of which impinge on the organism closely following the extinction process.[14] It follows from this principle that when A is being extinguished from s to s', B has been undergoing a secondary extinction which will depress its excitatory potentiality appreciably below s', say to s''. As a result the extinction of A must go on below s' to s''. But by this time path B will have suffered further secondary weakening.

This raises the question as to how far the extinction of A must go before it will actually reach a level beneath that of B. So far as the present writer is aware, this problem has not

PAPER
11

[13] It is believed that the perseveration principle will insure that the effect of trials on A will actually persist somewhat beyond the point at which the strength of A has become equal to that of B, which would bring it about that B would have an appreciably higher excitatory potentiality than A when the first trial on the former would take place. Otherwise spontaneous recovery of A would instantly recall the subject to that reaction again, and the organism would vibrate frantically from one to the other like too sensitive thermostats which sometimes oscillate continuously between turning the heat on and off.

[14] That this principle is operative in the free and dynamic behavior of rats in the simple trial-and-error situation has been abundantly demonstrated in unpublished work of R. E. P. Youtz (23) and of D. G. Ellson (4). Mitrano (17) has shown it to be operative with feeble-minded children. In the situations so far investigated the generalized weakening effect seems to be around 50 per cent.

yet been investigated experimentally, though it should be a relatively straightforward matter on the conditioned-reflex level. In advance of the possession of actual knowledge of this relationship, however, it is easy to tell roughly what should result under various suppositions. It is clear, for example, that, other things equal, the shorter the distance between s and s', the less inhibition there will be to irradiate and the shorter the distance below s' at which reaction B will take place. Secondly, the smaller the proportion of inhibition which irradiates, the shorter will be the distance below s' at which B will take place.

There remains to be considered the special case of the possibility that A could be extinguished to a functional zero, yet reaction B never take place at all. It seems inevitable that this would occur under certain conditions: Suppose that 50 per cent of the inhibition of A irradiates to B and that at the outset A stands at 6.00 and B at 2.00. When A has reached zero, B would have suffered 3 units of inhibition; this would place it at $-$ 1.00, *i.e.*, one unit below zero (19). In this case striving for this particular goal (reinforcing state of affairs) would cease altogether, at least for a time. If the time available for solution is limited it follows that the organism may completely fail to solve its problem.

PAPER
11

IV

At this point we must return to the consideration of a principle which was latent in the situation considered in Section II above, especially as represented in Fig. 4. This is the influence (in the case of very naïve subjects) of the angle which any path except the one leading directly to the goal makes with the latter. The consideration of this problem may be facilitated by referring to the diagram shown as Fig. 5. The question is: What bearing does the size of the angles of paths B, C, D, E, and F with path A at point S have on the relative strengths of excitatory tendency of the paths in question?

The hypothesis here tentatively put forward is that in the random locomotion, and even hand movements, of the organism (7) [15] throughout its previous existence, a movement terminating at G but initiated in the direction of path B at point S will, *on the average*, require the traversing of a distance something like that of path B.   The same is assumed of the initial angles of paths C, D, E, and F.   As a result, the principle of the goal excitatory gradient demands that the greater the angle of the path at point S, the weaker will be

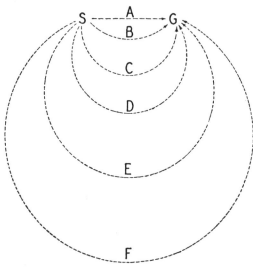

PAPER
11

FIG. 5.   Diagrammatic representation of what are conceived to be approximations to typical *mean* pathways by which the organism has passed by means of random locomotion in its previous history from one point (S) to another point (G).   It will be noted that the angle which each path makes with path A at point S is a direct function of the length of the path—the larger the angle, the longer the path.   It is understood that a substantially similar family of potential circular paths lies on the other side of direct path A.

the tendency to take the particular path.   Thus path F as represented in Fig. 5 is about eight times as long as path A. Assuming path A to be 5 units in length, and path F to be 40, the respective excitatory tendencies will be, according to Table 1, in the proportion of 6.00 to .83; *i.e.*, the strength of the tendency to start for G in the initial direction of path A

[15] Halverson's analysis of hand and arm movements in the act of prehension among young children (7, 175) shows that the pathway of the arm and hand in reaching for a small cube at 28 weeks is a decidedly circuitous one but, with increasing age (52 weeks) its course becomes practically a straight line.

would be over seven times as great as the tendency to set out in the initial direction of path *F*. This hierarchy of excitatory tendencies based on the initial angles of locomotion toward a goal thus appears to be a special case of the habit-family hierarchy (**9**).

It follows at once from these considerations that in certain situations the difference between the excitatory tendencies of a naïve organism to take the initial steps of two paths may

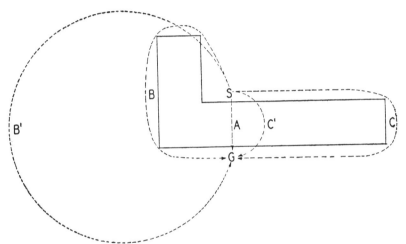

PAPER
11

F*ɪɢ*. 6. Diagrammatic representation of an experimental situation designed to show the influence of the angle of the initial portion of a path upon the strength of its tendency. *S* is the organism, *G* is the lure. The right-angled figure in bold outline represents a barrier. Path *B* is actually shorter than path *C*, yet it is assumed that the naïve organism will choose *C* rather than *B* because at the outset *C* is the beginning of paths which, on the average, in the past have been approximately of the length of path *C'*, and path *B* at the outset is the same as paths which in the past have averaged in length something like that of *B'*.

be considerably greater than the difference between the actual lengths of the two paths would warrant. This may be illustrated by the situation represented in Fig. 6. Let us suppose that the organism at *S* has the choice of paths *B* and *C* around the barrier to *G*. Path *C* is 26 units long, whereas path *B* is only 22 units long. Nevertheless, a naïve organism might be expected to choose path *C* because the initial angle of path *C* has presumably in its past history represented, on the average, a path something like *C'*, of only 8 units, whereas the

initial angle of path B has, on the average, represented a path
something like that of B', which has a length of 42 units.   By
Table 1, the angles therefore represent naïve excitatory
tendencies in the proportion of 4.8 to .7 in favor of path C,
i.e., from the point of view of the initial angle of the pathway
the excitatory tendency to take path C should be something
like seven times as great as that to take path B, even though
path B is actually the shorter of the two.

It is to be expected, of course, that the principle of the
goal gradient operating directly (*e.g.*, under conditions such
that the organism would be forced to take the two paths of
Fig. 6, say, in alternation each being followed by reinforcement) would ultimately lead to the giving up of path C and
to the preferential choice of path B, because the beginning of
path B is actually much nearer the point of reinforcement
than is that of path C.   Such training accordingly leads to a
form of sophistication distinct from the individual use of
speech as pure-symbolic acts.   Thus we arrive at a kind of
operational definition of the term 'sophistication' as here
employed.[16]

V

With admirable perspicacity, Lewin has called attention
to a very important series of problems involving conflicting
tendencies to action, *i.e.*, situations which involve simultaneous impulses both to approach and to retreat.   Such conflicts
of excitatory tendency he has aptly termed *tensions* (**13**).
One supposititious case illustrating this point is that of a child

[16] It is possible to state the angle-hierarchy hypothesis (Fig. 5) in exact mathematical terms.   On this hypothesis the distance (D) as a function of the angle made by the
tangent of the arc at point S with the straight line joining S and G (the distance SG
being taken as the unit of measurement) is given by the equation,

$$D = \frac{A}{\sin A}.$$

Since the excitatory tendency (E) at the beginning of a pathway on the goal-gradient
hypothesis is a function of D, E may be expressed in terms of the same variables by the
equation,

$$E = a + b \log \sin A - b \log A.$$

This, of course, can be regarded as no more than a very rough first approximation to the
actual relationship.   It is hoped, however, that it may serve as an entering wedge to an
investigation of the whole problem.   It may at least claim the virtue of being sufficiently definite to be susceptible of experimental verification.

on the shore looking at a toy swan floating in the water. The swan as a stimulus object tends to evoke in the child movements of approach, whereas the water as a stimulus object tends to evoke movements of flight. In this connection Lewin remarks (13, p. 607), "It is important that here, as frequently in such cases, the *strength* of the field forces which correspond to the negative valence diminishes much more rapidly with increasing spatial *distance* than do the field forces corresponding to the positive valence. From the direction and strength of the field forces at the various points of the field it can be deduced that the child must move to the point P where *equilibrium* occurs. (At all other points there exists a resultant which finally leads to P.)" [17]

A still more striking and dramatic form of this general problem is found where the positive and negative stimulus objects are both small and occupy substantially the same point in space. It is assumed, further, that the negative gradient at one unit distant from the object, say, has a greater excitatory potentiality than the positive excitatory gradient at the same distance but, owing to its steeper slope, the negative gradient soon diminishes to a strength of excitation below that of the positive gradient, thereafter remaining permanently in an inferior position. As pointed out above, there is evidence indicating that the positive excitatory gradient possesses a roughly logarithmic shape. Corresponding study of negative excitatory tendencies has not yet been made. Analogy, however, suggests that negative excitatory tendencies may show at least a negative acceleration.[18]

PAPER
11

[17] It is to be regretted that Lewin did not work out in detail the deduction which he mentions as a possibility. The above quotation suggests that had this been done his assumptions would turn out to be substantially the same as the relevant assumptions of the present study (see summary) and the form would not be very different from that represented by note 19, below. It is believed that if such practices could become general the genuine disagreements among the psychologies would prove to be much less than now appears from the divergence of their vocabularies.

[18] Here evidently lies a virgin field for investigations both theoretical and experimental. Will, for example, a negative gradient lead to the elimination of blinds in a maze? If so, will the order be backward or forward or in some more complex mode? Ordinary observation suggests the probability that suitable measurements would readily reveal a marked speed-of-locomotion gradient (10); *i.e.*, that the organism would proceed more slowly the more remote it is from the point of retreat.

A situation based on these assumptions is represented diagrammatically in Fig. 7. The positive gradient *JJ'*

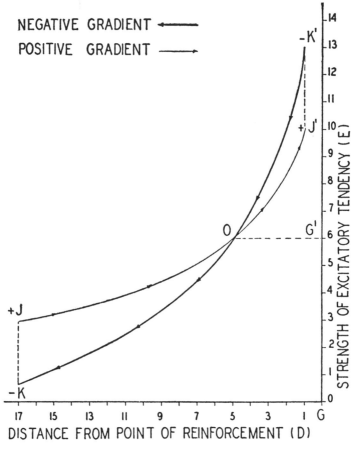

FIG. 7. Diagrammatic representation of the functional relationships of two gradients of different sign and different slope. The positive gradient is represented by the equation,

$$E_+ = 10 - 4 \log D,$$

and the negative gradient is drawn according to the equation,

$$E_- = 13 - 7 \log D.$$

The two gradients intersect at $D = 5$ with a common E value of 6 (see note 18).

represents the excitatory potentialities of *G* as a stimulus to distance receptors leading to locomotor reactions of approach, whereas the negative gradient KK' represents the excitatory potentialities of G at the various distances to evoke movements of retreat or flight. It may be seen in the figure that at a distance of 17 units the positive gradient dominates; accordingly the organism should move forward with a force corresponding to the difference in excitatory tendency between J and K. However, as locomotion continues it should diminish in speed progressively until point O is reached, at which forward locomotion should cease altogether except for momentum effects. If, on the other hand, the organism should find itself at a distance of one unit from G, locomotion would take place in an opposite direction. The rate of locomotion in this case, as in the one just considered, would presumably correspond to the difference in excitatory tendency existing between K' and J'. This should diminish progressively as point O is approached, at which it should cease just as when the movement was in a forward direction.[19]

[19] The general case takes the following form:

Let the gradient of the positive excitatory tendency (E_+) be represented by the equation,

$$E_+ = a - b \log_f D,$$

and the equation representing the negative excitatory tendency (E_-) be

$$E_- = c - d \log_f D,$$

where

$$c > a$$

and

$$d > b.$$

The point at which the difference between the two gradients will be zero will be where they intersect, i.e., where

$$E_+ - E_- = 0,$$

i.e.,

$$E_+ = E_-.$$

Then,

$$a - b \log_f D = c - d \log_f D,$$

i.e.,

$$a - c = (b - d) \log_f D,$$

hence

$$\log_f D = \frac{a - c}{b - d},$$

therefore

$$D = f^{\frac{a - c}{b - d}},$$

where f is the base of the system of logarithms employed. This is the equation expressing the point at which tensional equilibrium should occur, i.e., the distance from the

As a corollary from the above deduction it is evident that, assuming radial symmetry of the positive and negative gradients about point G, distance OG must be constant in all directions. It follows from this that the locus of tensional equilibrium about point G must be a circle (Fig. 8). Assuming the presence in the situation of stimuli leading to action in the direction of numerous minor goals located according to

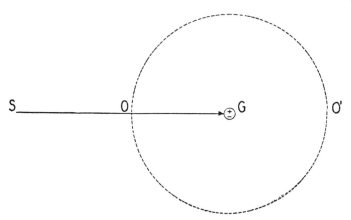

FIG. 8. Diagrammatic representation of the locus of the point of equilibrium when the critical stimulus giving rise to two gradients of opposite sign such as those represented in Fig. 7, emanates from a single point G. So long as the gradients remain constant, distance OG must remain constant, which necessarily makes the locus of equilibrium circular, as shown by the fine dotted line.

chance, it is to be expected that there will occur irregular oscillations not only toward and away from point G, but laterally as well. In the former case it is to be expected that such oscillatory tendencies will be opposed by the summation gradient tending to the locus O, whereas those tangent to this locus will meet with no such opposition. It follows that

object precipitating the ambivalent situation at which the organism will come to rest. Thus in the gradients represented in Fig. 7,

$$a = 10, b = 4, c = 13, d = 7,$$

and the base of the log system is 5.

Substituting these values in the above equation, we have

$$D = 5^{\frac{10 - 13}{4}} - 7 = 5^{\frac{-3}{-3}} = 5,$$

i.e., the gradients intersect at a distance of 5 units from the goal, as appears in Fig. 7.

the lateral movements will display a greater amplitude than those perpendicular to locus O. Accordingly the naïve organism if given time enough may be expected to make completely circular movements about point G, though these will be complicated by approaches, retreats, and much retracting.

As a second corollary it should be pointed out that even without the presence of distracting stimuli the organism at point O (Fig. 8) probably will not remain absolutely passive, *i.e.*, in a state indistinguishable from mere idleness characteristic of no effective stimulation whatever. On the contrary, it is reasonable to expect that, since there is a great deal more stimulation of a dynamic sort present in conflict situations than in a case where inaction is due to the lack of effective stimulation, the muscles of the organism should show a conspicuous excess of tonicity in the former case as contrasted with the latter. Muscular tonicity may accordingly offer a convenient supplementary means for gauging the extent of this type of conflict.

PAPER 11

The deductions of the preceding paragraph tacitly assume a constancy of both the positive and the negative gradients while the organism remains suspended, as it were, between the antagonistic difference gradients to action which the situation evokes within him. There is strong reason to doubt such a constancy. In addition to the very general empirical principle that in organisms tendencies to action are always in a state of flux, there is in this case the specific expectation that, assuming an objectively constant G as a stimulus object, both gradients should diminish in height, presumably throughout their whole effective length. This follows from the frustration hypothesis already considered (p. 278).[20]

A test of the above hypothesis which immediately suggests itself could be arranged as follows: Place two objects, one with

[20] There is abundant evidence to support this hypothesis where the frustration is produced by an external barrier of some sort. But the writer is unaware of any evidence bearing directly on situations like the one here under consideration in which the same object gives rise to what is, in some sense, an internal conflict of two gradients of opposite sign. Deductions based on this more inclusive interpretation of the frustrational hypothesis must accordingly be regarded with more than usual caution until definite evidence on the point is available.

a negative value and the other with a positive value, one above the other so as to produce the conflicting gradients shown in Fig. 7. Determine the initial potentialities of each object separately at the outset by measuring the speed-of-locomotion of given organisms in a positive or negative direction at representative distances from G. Then place both objects together and let the organism remain at point O (Figs. 7 and 8) in the state of tensional equilibrium for about as long as this will persist. At once repeat, with separate subgroups, the test of the excitatory potentiality of each object singly, as at the beginning of the experiment. The frustration hypothesis demands that in this latter case the rate of locomotion toward the positive object and that away from the negative object shall both be diminished.

Two corollaries flow from this deduction. The first, based on the principle of spontaneous recovery (**19**), is that after a lapse of time (possibly within the range of one or two hours) the speed of locomotion in both cases should have increased to a very considerable extent, though the recovery should not be perfect. A second corollary, again based on principles derived from conditioned-reflex experiments, is that an organism placed in the state of tensional equilibrium a second time will show both a more rapid inhibition of the respective excitatory tendencies than it did on the first occasion and also a slower and more imperfect spontaneous recovery.

PAPER
11

One of the most obvious questions which arise from the consideration of conflict situation when the latter is viewed in the light of the frustration hypothesis, is the effect of the continuation of the state of tensional equilibrium upon the distance (OG) from the goal objects (G), which the organism at first maintains. It is obvious, of course, that if both gradients should decline simultaneously and at a certain relative rate the distance OG would remain constant. When we consider the number of other possibilities of variation, however, the chance that this particular set of changes should take place is exceedingly improbable. It accordingly seems almost certain that the distance OG will undergo a progressive change in length with the duration of the conflict or tension.

Whether, upon the whole, the change will be to diminish or to increase distance OG can only be predicted when we know more concerning the resistance of positive and negative, steep and gentle, gradients. It is evident that here is a rich and almost virgin field for investigation, both with animals and with young children. One apparently relevant principle we have, however, thanks to the work on conditioned reactions. Other things equal, that gradient which is the oldest should resist frustration the best. This factor should tend to lengthen or shorten distance OG according to whether the older gradient is the negative or positive one respectively.

In this connection there should also be considered the matter of progressive changes in the drive. As already pointed out above, an increase in a drive such as hunger presumably increases both the height and the slope of the positive gradient. This increase should obviously diminish the distance OG and reduce the radius of the circular locus of tensional equilibrium.

Finally, the significance of this whole psychology of conflicting excitatory gradients as a challenge to experimental psychology should be emphasized. Its importance for psychopathology, particularly the conflicts of the positive sexual gradient and the specific negative gradient based on social tabus and prudential considerations, has been emphasized in the clinical field by the psychiatrists for many years (5). Coitus interruptus and what, in current slang, is called 'petting,' are cases in point. The bad repute of these practices in mental hygiene emphasizes the possible significance of conflicting gradients in either time or space. In this connection it is to be noted that the mutual checking of two impulses as represented in Fig. 7 might be expected to produce something like twice as great an amount of internal inhibition as would be the case where one tendency was completely over-ridden by the other because in the one case two excitatory tendencies are frustrated, whereas in the other, only

PAPER
11

one is thwarted. It would not be surprising if this mechanism should be found to play an important role in the so-called psychogenic disorders.

Summary

The preceding analysis of certain problems in the behavior dynamics of naïve organisms has proceeded mainly on the following assumptions:

1. That simultaneously occurring stimuli and reactions (both of approach and flight) tend to be associated more strongly the closer they are to a reinforcing state of affairs, the diminution in excitatory tendency with remoteness from the point of reinforcement proceeding with a negative acceleration.

2. That situations may arise where stimuli originating in substantially the same point in space will give rise in a given organism to incompatible excitatory tendencies, notably the opposing tendencies to acts of approach and of flight.

3. That the flight gradient may, at least under certain circumstances, be both steeper and higher near the stimulus object.

4. That an organism in which positive and negative excitatory tendencies are active behaves at any given instant according to the algebraic sum of such tendencies.

5. That the positive gradient of excitation grows both higher and steeper with the increase in the drive, e.g., food privation.

6. That, other things equal, this gradient of excitation grows higher and steeper with the increase in the amount of reward.

7. That a strong functional excitatory tendency is weakened after a given amount of frustration by a smaller proportion of its original strength than is a weak functional excitatory tendency.

8. That spontaneous recovery from extinction effects will occur but this will not be complete.

9. That a second extinction will occur more rapidly than the first and its spontaneous recovery will be less complete.

PAPER 11

10. That in the history of organisms it is a fact that upon the whole the larger the angle the beginning of a pathway makes with the straight line leading to the object, the longer the path to the object.

11. That the prevention by any circumstance of the reaction normally evokable by any stimulus or stimulus component results, other things equal, in weakening (extinguishing) the particular excitatory potentiality of such stimulus or stimulus component.

12. That the older an excitatory tendency, the more resistant to the extinction from frustration.

13. That a considerable weakening of a given excitatory tendency appears at once following the extinction of another excitatory tendency.

From these assumptions in the main the following conclusions have been drawn concerning the behavior of naïve organisms, unmentioned factors being assumed as equal:

PAPER
11

1. In a problem situation such as shown in Fig. 4, a naïve organism will have more difficulty in solving the problem where the lure is large than where it is small.

2. There will be more difficulty where the lure is close to the barrier than where it is farther away.

3. There will be more difficulty where the drive is strong than where it is weak.

4. The functional excitatory tendency of weak alternatives in a habit-family hierarchy may be depressed to 'below zero' by generalized extinction effects from the frustration of a stronger member of the hierarchy.

5. This depression below zero is the more likely to occur, the greater the percentage of the extinction effects in the strong tendency which are generalized to the weak tendency.

6. The depression below zero is more likely to occur the weaker the absolute strength of the weak tendency.

7. The depression below zero is more likely to occur the greater the difference between the competing excitatory tendencies.

8. For a naïve organism, the larger the angle which the beginning of a pathway to a point makes with the straight line

to the point, the weaker the excitatory tendency to execute the acts which constitute taking the divergent path.

9. Naïve organisms through the misleading action of the angular hierarchy will, under certain circumstances, choose the longer of two paths.

10. With sophistication of the organism consisting of actually traversing both of such paths as considered in (9), the tendency to take the longer path will gradually give place to a degree of preference to be expected on the basis of the uncomplicated goal excitatory gradient hypothesis.

11. Under the conditions of assumptions 2 and 3, there will be a distance (D) from the ambivalent stimulus object at which the two opposed excitatory tendencies of a tensional situation will be equal.

12. Under the conditions of (11), the organism will tend to move toward this point of equal excitatory tendency.

PAPER
11

13. Under the conditions of (11), assuming an unchanging stimulus object and the presence of minor lures of appreciable potentiality distributed in a chance manner throughout the neighborhood, the organism will tend to take a roughly circular course around the ambivalent stimulus object.

14. These circular movements will be very irregular in rate and extent, and be characterized by much retracing.

15. There will be some irregular oscillation toward and away from the ambivalent stimulus.

16. The movements of (15) will, upon the whole, be less in extent than will those of (14).

17. Where cases of tensional equilibrium persist for an appreciable period, both excitatory tendencies arising from an ambivalent stimulus object will be weakened progressively.

18. With the passage of time there will be a progressive recovery from this weakening.

19. Recovery from this frustrational weakening will never be complete.

20. A second period of tensional equilibrium will produce an extinctive weakening more rapid than the first.

21. The second recovery will be less rapid than the first.

22. The second recovery will be less complete than the first.

23. As the state of tensional equilibrium continues there will usually occur a progressive shift in the distance the organism maintains from the stimulus object.

24. This shift will tend to be in the direction of the older of the two opposed excitatory tendencies.

25. The secondary frustration effects will be greater in cases of tensional equilibrium than in cases where one tendency is strong enough to over-ride the other.

Of the forty or so propositions assembled above from the preceding theoretical analysis, scarcely one is yet established on a secure quantitative experimental basis. Perhaps the chief outcome of the analysis is the sharp realization of our profound ignorance concerning the essential principles operative in such relatively simple dynamical situations. However, admissions of ignorance, while momentarily depressing, are likely to be wholesome. Each recognized item of basic ignorance constitutes a challenge to a critical experimental determination. Thus a resolute attempt at theoretical integration naturally leads the way to a systematically coördinated program of investigation. In the present case, such an integrated program of research appears to fall into three portions or phases.

PAPER
11

The first phase consists of the direct experimental determination of the principles or laws, now almost entirely in the state of hypothesis or guesswork, which are suggested by the first of the above lists of propositions. These determinations should be quantitative in nature and so designed as to yield functional curves of basic relationships. Equations fitted to such data become the postulates of the system.

The second phase is logical and mathematical. It consists of deriving by means of mathematics, and perhaps of symbolic logic, the behavioral implications of the postulates yielded by the first movement when acting in the greatest possible variety of conditions. The substance of note 12 gives an indication of the general nature of this theoretical portion of the program.

The third phase consists of the systematic experimental verification of the behavioral expectations resulting from the mathematical activities of the second movement. Whenever this systematic verifying procedure reveals disagreements, work on the first movement is resumed in an effort to rectify presumptive defects in the postulate determinations. Following such new postulate determinations, new implications are drawn, new verification experiments are set up, and so on in continuously recurring cycles until disagreements fail to manifest themselves, if such a time ever comes.

Such a self-conscious scientific procedure may with some propriety be called 'logical empiricism.' It begins with an empirical determination of its postulates and ends with an empirical check on the validity of its theorems; between the two lies the integrating symbolic structure of logic and mathematics.

PAPER
11

REFERENCES

1. ANDERSON, A., Runway time and the goal gradient, *J. Exper. Psychol.*, 1933, **16**, 423–428.
2. BRANDT, H., The spread of the influence of reward to bonds remote in sequence and time, *Arch. Psychol.*, 1935, **180**, pp. 40, 41.
3. BRUCE, R. H., An experimental investigation of the thirst drive in rats, with especial reference to the goal gradient hypothesis, *J. Gen. Psychol.*, 1937, **17**, 49–62.
4. ELLSON, D. G., Quantitative studies of the interaction of simple habits; I. Recovery from specific and generalized effects of extinction (to be published).
5. FREUD, S., Selected papers on hysteria and other psychoneuroses. (Trans. by A. A. Brice), pp. 141–142, Journal of Nervous and Mental Disease Publishing Company, 1909.
6. GUILFORD, J. P., A generalized psychophysical law, PSYCHOL. REV., 1932, **39**, 73–85.
7. HALVERSON, H. M., An experimental study of prehension in infants by means of systematic cinema records, *Genet. Psychol. Monog.*, 1931, **10**, 107–286.
8. HULL, C. L., The goal gradient hypothesis and maze learning, PSYCHOL. REV., 1932, **39**, 25–43.
9. ——, The concept of the habit-family hierarchy and maze learning, PSYCHOL. REV., 1934, **41**, Part I, 33–52; Part II, 134–152.
10. ——, The rat's speed-of-locomotion gradient in the approach to food, *J. Comp. Psychol.*, 1934, **17**, 393–422.
11. ——, Mind, mechanism, and adaptive behavior, PSYCHOL. REV., 1937, **44**, 1–32.
12. KÖHLER, W., The mentality of apes, New York: Harcourt, Brace and Co., 1925.
13. LEWIN, K., Environmental forces, in 'A Handbook of Child Psychology' (edited by C. Murchison, 2nd edition revised), Worcester: Clark Univ. Press, 1933, Chapter 14, pp. 590–625.

14. ——, A dynamic theory of personality (Trans. by D. K. Adams and K. E. Zener), New York: McGraw-Hill Book Co., 1935, pp. ix + 286.
15. ——, Principles of topological psychology (Trans. by F. and G. M. Heider), New York: McGraw-Hill Book Company, 1936, pp. xv + 231.
16. MILLER, N. E. AND W. R. MILES, Effect of caffeine on the running speed of hungry, satiated, and frustrated rats, *J. Comp. Psychol.*, 1935, **20**, 397–412.
17. MITRANO, A. J., A preliminary investigation of human motivation by conditioned reaction methods, Ph.D. thesis, 1937, Yale University Library.
18. MUENZINGER, K. F., DOVE, C. C. AND BERNSTONE, A. H., Serial learning: II. The bi-directional goal gradient in the endless maze, *J. Genet. Psychol.*, 1937, **50**, 229–241.
19. PAVLOV, I. P., Conditioned reflexes (Trans. by G. V. Anrep), Oxford: Oxford Univ. Press, 1927.
20. SNYGG, D., Mazes in which rats take the longer path to food, *J. Psychol.*, 1936, **1**, 153–166.
21. THORNDIKE, E. L., An experimental study of rewards, Contributions to Education (see pp. 54–55), No. 580, New York: Bureau of Publications, Columbia University, 1933.
22. YOSHIOKA, J. G., Weber's law in the discrimination of maze distance by the white rat, *Univ. Calif. Publications in Psychol.*, 1929, **4**, 155–184.
23. YOUTZ, R. E. P., The trial and error reaction as a type of conditioned response, Ph.D. thesis, 1937, Yale University Library.

PAPER

[MS. received November 8, 1937]

11

Reprinted from Psychological Review, Vol. 46, No. 1, January, 1939
Printed in U. S. A.

THE PROBLEM OF STIMULUS EQUIVALENCE IN BEHAVIOR THEORY [1]

BY CLARK L. HULL

*Institute of Human Relations,
Yale University*

INTRODUCTION

In his presidential address (**18**, 14), Tolman remarked incidentally that the writer's theory of adaptive behavior contains no explanation of stimulus equivalence.[2] At about the same time, Adams complained (**1**, 10) in a particular context that the writer has given no definition of the term *stimulus*. In a certain important sense both criticisms involve the same question. Moreover, they represent what has been implicit for a long time in the attacks of *Gestalt Theorie* on behaviorism. These considerations emphasize the fact that the problem of stimulus equivalence is a fundamental one. This is true not only for behaviorism but for any psychology purporting to deal in a thorough-going manner with adaptive behavior. It accordingly deserves the most serious consideration by all schools of psychology.

PAPER
12

The problem of stimulus equivalence is essentially this: How can we account for the fact that a stimulus will sometimes evoke a reaction to which it has never been conditioned, *i.e.*, with which it has never been associated? For example, it is evident that a given physical object as sensed by the eye, say, probably never presents the same physical pattern of light energy to the retina on any two occasions. On the other hand, we have the equally well recognized fact that within

[1] The author is indebted to Dr. Donald T. Perkins for the mathematical derivation of equation 7, p. 20 ff.

[2] In the same connection Tolman expresses the belief that there is in the writer's system a corresponding lack of an explanation of response equivalence. It is impossible to agree with Tolman on this point; a serious attempt has been made really to account for numerous phenomena involving response equivalence by means of the mechanism called the *habit-family hierarchy* (**8**).

9

limits mammalian organisms will react to such an object or situation in substantially the same way, or at least in such a way as to attain the same goal or reinforcing state of affairs (response equivalence) on the different occasions of its presentation. Thus a rat's eyes probably never receive exactly the same combination of physically stimulated points on any two occasions as he approaches the choice point in a simple T-maze, yet the hungry animal will, after a time, learn consistently to turn into the alley which leads to the food.

At the outset it is important to note that there are at least three forms of the phenomenon of stimulus equivalence, according as it is dependent upon one or another of three fairly distinct principles or mechanisms. The first and most obvious mechanism responsible for evoking the same or equivalent reactions is the *partial physical identity* of the stimulus complexes involved. This principle is so obvious and has been so fully elaborated by behavioristic writers that it will not be discussed here (17, p. 32; 7). The second principle of stimulus equivalence we shall call *primary generalization* (Definition 8). This is the empirically determined behavioral phenomenon first described by Pavlov as irradiation (12, 3, 5). The third principle mediating stimulus equivalence we shall call *secondary generalization* (Definition 9). This term has been chosen because in this case stimulus equivalence is conceived to come about indirectly through the previous widespread conditioning of the stimulus continuum to some other reaction.

In order to proceed effectively to a more detailed consideration of the problem of stimulus equivalence, it is expedient to give an elucidation [3] of a number of terms, some of which have already been employed and all of which will be utilized in a more or less technical manner:

[3] It is recognized that as soon as possible precise definitions should be formulated of most of the critical concepts of the system by means of a limited number of undefined terms, the meanings of which can be no more than elucidated. The technique of symbolic logic promises to be of invaluable aid in this task, as is emphasized by the success attained by J. H. Woodger in the field of biology (20). Thanks to the generous collaboration of Professor Woodger, the task of thus laying the formal foundations of the present system has already begun.

1. *Stimulus equivalence:* the equivalence of various stimuli for evoking the (qualitatively) same reaction. Quantitative equivalence is not intended.

2. *Response equivalence:* the equivalence of various action sequences which are alike in that they all serve to attain the same goal, *i.e.,* to bring about the same reinforcing state of affairs. This is believed to be mediated by the habit-family hierarchy (8).

3. *Stimulus object:* the physical origin or critical source of a pattern of energy capable of affecting a sense organ. An example would be a half-inch white die with the usual black spots (Fig. 1).

4. *Potential stimuli:* The infinite number of physically distinct patterns or combinations of physical energy emanating from a stimulus object and capable of affecting a sense organ. An example of such a family of potential stimuli is the infinite number of physically distinct light patterns emanating from an ordinary white die (S_2 S_3, S_4, etc., Fig. 1) corresponding to the infinite number of possible angles. Other examples are the infinite gradations of sizes of retinal image, of intensities of light, shadow, etc.

5. *Stimulus continuum* or *stimulus dimension:* an unbroken ordered sequence of potential stimuli. For example, a stimulus continuum would be the sequence of physical light patterns falling at a given point in space from the white die instanced above (Fig. 1) if it were turned about an axis, *e.g.,* one at right angles to a line extending

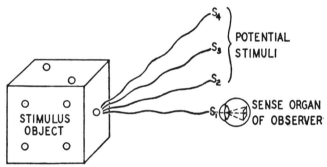

FIG. 1. Diagrammatic representation of a stimulus object, a sheaf of potential stimuli, an actual stimulus (S_1), and the sense organ of the observer upon which the actual stimulus impinges.

from the point to the center of the die. Another stimulus continuum of a far less complicated nature would be the range of simple sound waves from 16 to 30,000 vibrations per second. This latter type of continuum has been called *stimulus dimension* by Boring (4) and Spence (15).

6. *Stimulus* or *actual stimulus:* one of the infinite number of potential stimuli emanating from an object or combination of objects which actually makes an impact upon the sensorium of an organism. An example would be one of the infinite number of possible light-wave patterns emanating from the white die instanced above (Fig. 1), as transformed by the refracting media of the eye, which makes a junction with the system of visual end organs and finally gives rise to a stimulus trace.

7. *Stimulus trace:* an unspecified physiological reverberation within the organism presumed to occur during the impact of the stimulus and to persist for some time after its termination, diminishing to zero with a negative acceleration and capable at any point in its course of becoming conditioned to (associated with) a reaction (9).

8. *Primary* or *physiological generalization* (irradiation): the fact that when a reaction has been conditioned to the trace of a stimulus, the traces of other stimuli from the same stimulus continuum and adjacent to the first will evoke the reaction with an intensity which decreases as the difference between the stimuli increases, the rate of the decrease in the irradiation gradient showing a negative acceleration when the distance from the stimulus conditioned is expressed in units of discrimination thresholds (j.n.d.'s).

9. *Secondary generalization:* the presumptive situation where primary generalization to one or more reactions has been set up to this stimulus continuum and where, if another reaction is then conditioned to a single point on this continuum, all points, however distant, will have a finite excitatory potentiality toward the evocation of this reaction. A somewhat detailed deduction of this phenomenon from lower-level principles is presented in a later section of the present study (pp. 27–28).

10. *Reaction threshold:* the amount of excitatory potential which is required before an overt reaction may be evoked by a stimulus. An illustration of this phenomenon appears in the fact that in most learning situations one or more reinforcing repetitions are necessary before a conditioned stimulus will actually evoke the reaction being conditioned to it (14).

CHARACTERISTICS OF PRIMARY OR PHYSIOLOGICAL GENERALIZATION

If the notion of existence be added to the ten concepts elucidated in the preceding section, most of them are at once transformed into natural-science postulates. This is especially obvious in the case of (8), which concerns primary or physiological generalization (irradiation). This principle deserves special elaboration because of its importance in the understanding of stimulus equivalence.

Historically, the principle of physiological generalization has been taken in the main directly from conditioned-reaction investigations and is primarily an empirical finding concerning a relation existing between stimulus continua and reactions originally conditioned to a single point on such a continuum or dimension. Beyond implying that the explanation (theoretical deduction) of this principle, when and if an explanation is achieved, will be physiological, no physiological hypothesis, Pavlovian or otherwise, is intended. In the present systematization it has the status of a behavioral postulate or primitive assumption, with no assumptions as to its origin.

Relevant experimental studies in this field are that of Anrep, working in Pavlov's laboratory (2); that of Bass and Hull (3); and that of Hovland (5). These investigations, while differing much in the organisms and the experimental conditions employed, and more than one would like in the details of the findings, nevertheless are completely consistent in showing two essential characteristics:

1. If a reaction (R_x) is well conditioned to one point on a stimulus continuum, other points adjacent to the point conditioned will evoke the reaction without further reinforcement.

2. There is a gradient in the intensity or amplitude of these generalized reactions; the more the stimulus evoking the reaction differs from the stimulus originally conditioned to the reaction, the weaker the reaction evoked.

However, a number of important points concerning this type of generalization are not adequately covered as yet by empirical investigation. Some of these will be discussed in the following pages.

PAPER

12

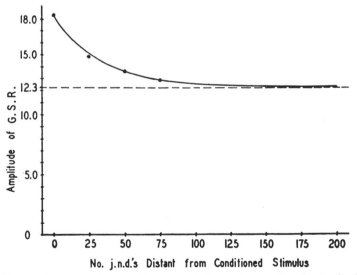

FIG. 2. The curve is a graphic representation of the equation (see text) which has been fitted to the four values of Hovland's physiological generalization gradient of excitatory potential, the latter being represented by the solid circles.   Note that if D (the number of j.n.d's) should be increased without limit, the amplitude of the galvanic-skin reaction, according to this equation, could never fall below 12.3. This means that in a situation of this kind all points in the stimulus continuum have already attained a stimulus equivalence through the physiological generalization gradient alone.

Hovland's experimental results (5) on the gradient of generalization of excitatory potential over the continuum of frequency of simple sound waves, uncomplicated by intensity, as manifested by the amplitude of the galvanic-skin reaction, will serve conveniently as a concrete point of departure in discussing primary generalization. His experimental findings are shown by the solid circles in Fig. 2. An equation fitting these values well enough for the present purpose is:

$$\text{Amp.} = 12.3 + \frac{6}{10^{.0135D}},$$

where *Amp.* is the mean amplitude of the galvanic-skin reaction as recorded by Hovland's apparatus and D is the number of discrimination thresholds, or j.n.d.'s on the stimulus continuum separating the stimulus actually conditioned from that evoking the reaction. For example, suppose that the sensorium of an organism should receive the impact of a stimulus at a point in a stimulus continuum differing by 25 j.n.d.'s from that originally conditioned to the reaction R_x. Substituting 25 in place of D in the equation, we have:

$$\text{Amp.} = 12.3 + \frac{6}{10^{.0135\times25}}$$

$$= 12.3 + \frac{6}{10^{.3375}}.$$

The value of 10 to the .3375 power is given directly by an ordinary table of logarithms as 2.175. Accordingly we have:

$$\text{Amp.} = 12.3 + \frac{6}{2.175}$$

$$= 12.3 + 2.75$$

$$= 15.05.$$

The curve in Fig. 2 is a line drawn through a series of points determined from the equation by a series of such substitutions.

The curved line in Fig. 2 may be seen at a glance to conform to the two characteristics of generalization mentioned above as well established by experiment. In addition it presents the gradient as one of negative acceleration. This is here provisionally adopted as the basis for the present explorational analysis.[4] Finally, it is evident from an inspection of the equation that such a gradient will never fall below a rather large value, in the present case 12.3. This means that under the conditions of Hovland's experiment the conditioning of a single point at once makes all other points within the particular stimulus continuum qualitatively equivalent in their capacity to evoke the reaction conditioned (R_x), at least to some degree.

That this is true for all continua and for all reactions is to be doubted for the following reasons: it is known (1) that the galvanic-skin reaction is evokable by practically all stimuli even at moderate intensities previous to any overt conditioning whatsoever, and (2) that merely shocking a subject without association of the shock with any point on the conditioned stimulus continuum will greatly heighten such generalization tendency. On this assumption the value of 12.3 drops out of the equation, as probably an artifact, leaving it as

PAPER

12

$$\text{Amp.} = \frac{6}{10^{.0135D}}, \tag{1}$$

in which 6 represents the amount of excitatory potential susceptible to diminution through the generalization process, and D is the difference in j.n.d.'s between the point on the stimulus continuum at which reinforcement occurred and the point at which the test stimulus was applied.

Since the excitatory potential at the point conditioned is dependent upon the number of reinforcements received, it is

[4] Spence (15) has recently suggested that the generalization function follows, throughout the greater part of its course, a negatively accelerated diminution as here postulated, but postulates a brief initial section possessing a positive acceleration. A number of experimental findings seem in an indirect manner to support the hypothesis. According to this view, the failure of Hovland's experiment to show any indications of this preliminary period of positively accelerated diminution might be due to the fact that the experiment did not explore the interval between 0 and 25 j.n.d.'s from the point conditioned. For this reason, among others, the assumption regarding the exact mathematical characteristics of the generalization function represented by equation (1) must be regarded as especially tentative until more adequate evidence is available.

evident that a thoroughgoing working hypothesis of any concrete generalization situation requires a statement of the excitatory potential at the point conditioned (E_c) as a function of the number of repetitions (R). As a first approximation to this relationship we shall assume throughout the present paper the relationship to be [5]

$$E_c = A - \frac{A}{e^{hR}},\qquad(2)$$

where h is a constant dependent in the main upon the relative magnitude of the units selected for E and R, and A is the physiological limit of the organism for acquiring excitatory potential.   Thus if $A = 100$, $e = 10$, $h = .04$, and $R = 25$, the equation becomes

$$E_c = 100 - \frac{100}{10^{.04\times25}}.\qquad(3)$$

PAPER

12

Solving this equation we find that

$$E_c = 90.$$

With the value of the excitatory potential at the point conditioned at our disposal we may now rewrite equation (1) as follows:

$$E_D = \frac{E_c}{e^{kD}},\qquad(4)$$

[5] It is important to note that while equation (2) purports to be a curve of learning, it must not be confused with any of the numerous curves of learning plotted directly from empirical data.   On the contrary, it represents a preliminary attempt to state in quantitative terms the basic excitatory potentiality which is postulated to lie behind the various observable manifestations of learning.   Among these are: the decrease in reaction (with continued repetition); the increase in the amplitude or vigor of reaction; the increase in the resistance to extinction; the decrease in the number of errors made; the increase in the number of items recalled; and so on.   It is to be noted, further, that equation (2) represents a negatively accelerated learning function.   In view of our great ignorance regarding these matters, this equation is put forward very tentatively, largely with a view to calling attention in a concrete and specific manner to the various problems involved.   Actually, a number of known facts are consistent with the assumption that the rise of excitatory potential as a function of repetitions, at least during the early stages of learning, may be represented by a straight line.   Hull and Perkins (11) have found, for example, excitatory potential (E) to be a very clear linear function of the oscillation or distractibility threshold of rats during compound trial-and-error learning.

where D is the number of j.n.d.'s separating the point on the stimulus continuum conditioned from the point at which the generalization tendency is tested, E_D is the generalized excitatory potential at the point tested, and k is a constant depending in the main upon the units chosen in which to measure E and D. If, now, we take $e = 10$ and $k = .01$ we have as a concrete working equation,

$$E_D = \frac{E_c}{10^{.01D}},\qquad (5)$$

which will serve for illustrative purposes. A double-winged generalization gradient plotted from values computed from equations (2) and (4) appears as the upper curve in Fig. 3.

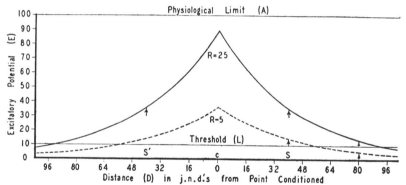

PAPER

12

FIG. 3. Diagrammatic representation of two generalization gradients, the upper one based on an original conditioning of 25 reinforcements, and the lower based on 5 reinforcements. The height of each at the point conditioned ($D = 0$) is based on equation (3), whereas that on the respective wings of generalization is based on equation (5). The threshold (L) is assumed to be 10 and the physiological limit (A) is assumed to be 100. The unit of measurement of excitatory potential is assumed to be 1/100 of the distance from zero to the physiological limit.

To the generalization gradient of equation (5) thus arrived at we have only to add the concept of the reaction threshold (see Definition 11). It is accordingly assumed for purposes of concrete illustration that 10 units of excitatory potential (E) are required to overcome the inertia of the reactive mechanism before overt reaction can occur, i.e., that

$$L = 10,\qquad (6)$$

where L is the reaction threshold. This hypothetical threshold is represented in Figs. 3, 4, 5, 6, and 7 in relation to various generalization gradients presently to be discussed.

Some Elementary Theorems Based on Primary Generalization

It is more common than one might wish for a writer to rename a well-known phenomenon and thereupon to be credited with having somehow explained it.[6] Accordingly we must inquire whether the present attempt at a solution of the problem of stimulus equivalence is of this fallacious nature. Fortunately there is available a straightforward objective technique for determining whether the renaming fallacy has been committed: A theoretically significant explanatory concept can be cast into the form of a postulate from which, in conjunction with other postulates of the system with which it is associated, an appreciable number of verifiable characteristics of the phenomenon in question may be deduced. On the other hand, a mere renaming of the phenomenon is theoretically sterile in that it mediates the deduction of no verifiable theorems. Indeed, the renaming maneuver is apt to give an illusion of accomplishment and thus actually to retard efforts to secure genuine explanations.

PAPER
12

We proceed now to apply this test to our use of the concept of primary or physiological generalization for the explanation of the phenomena of stimulus equivalence:

1. *In a given stimulus dimension the primary generalization gradient may extend in two, and only two, directions.*

This proposition may be illustrated as follows: Let it be assumed that we have given a single stimulus dimension such as the number of sound vibrations per second, other things such as intensity remaining constant. Let it be assumed, further, that some point (c) a considerable number of j.n.d.'s removed from either extreme has been conditioned, in a particular organism, to the reaction R_X by 25 reinforcements. We have already seen (p. 16) that by equation (3) this number of reinforcements yields an E_c of 90. Suppose that, later, the sensorium of this organism receives the impact of S, a point on the same stimulus dimension 40 j.n.d.'s removed from c in the direction of a more rapid vibration. Substituting 90 in place of E_c, and 40 in place of D in

---

[6] Perhaps as good an example of this type of confusion as any is that associated with the *Gestalt* concept known as *Einsicht*. In this connection see Spence's criticism (16, 214).

equation (5), we obtain for the excitatory potential to the evocation of R_X at S a value of 35.7 (Fig. 3). Suppose, next, the test is made at point S', 40 j.n.d.'s distant from c but in the direction of *fewer* vibrations per second. Since the value of D is the same as before, substitution in equation (5) yields the same value for E_D, *i.e.*, 35.7. Thus we see the stimulus gradient extending symmetrically in two directions.

2. *Many stimulus objects possess generalization gradients extending in an infinite number of directions.*

Suppose we have the stimulus object represented in Fig. 1, and the subject is conditioned to S_1 as there shown. Now it is evident that this die may be rotated about an infinite number of axes, each of which will present to the subject's eye a different continuum of physically distinct stimulus combinations each with its own series of j.n.d.'s and so on, and consequently each with its own gradient of generalization.

3. *The farther removed, in j.n.d.'s of the stimulus continuum concerned, a test stimulus is from the point conditioned, the smaller will be its excitatory potential.*

Now, let us assume that the organism conditioned as in (1) later receives the impact of S'' (Fig. 3, the S'' not shown), a point on the same continuum as S, but 80 j.n.d.'s removed from c, the point previously conditioned to R_X. Substituting 80 in equation (5), we obtain a value for E_D in this case of 14.2 (Fig. 3). It will be recalled from (1) that S, a point 40 j.n.d.'s removed from c, gave an E_D value of 35.7. The value of 14.2 is very much smaller than this. Thus the principle finds illustration.

4. *The excitatory potential of a point on a generalization gradient midway between the point conditioned and some other point will have a value intermediate between the two, and this value will differ from the value at the point conditioned by more than it differs from the value at the more remote test point.*

PAPER

12

By further comparing the E_D-values in (3) and Fig. 3, it is evident that 35.7 falls between 90 and 14.2. Moreover,

$$90 - 35.7 > 35.7 - 14.2$$
$$54.3 > 21.5.$$

Thus the principle is illustrated.

5. *The farther removed, in terms of the j.n.d.'s of a stimulus continuum, a test stimulus is from the point conditioned, the weaker will be the reaction evoked.*

There are good experimental grounds (6) for assuming that *the smaller the excitatory potential, the smaller the extent (amplitude) of the associated reaction.* From this and (3) the proposition follows.

6. *The farther removed, in terms of the j.n.d.'s of a stimulus continuum, a test stimulus is from the point conditioned, the longer the latency of the action evoked.*

There are good experimental grounds (14) for assuming that *the weaker the excitatory potential, the longer the reaction time.* From this and (3) the proposition follows.

7. *The farther removed, in terms of the j.n.d.'s of a stimulus continuum, a test stimulus is from a point conditioned, the fewer the unreinforced reactions which will be required to produce experimental extinction.*

There are good experimental grounds (19) for assuming that *the weaker the excitatory potential, the fewer the unreinforced reactions required for experimental extinction.* From this and (3) the proposition follows.

8. *The farther removed, in terms of the j.n.d.'s of a stimulus continuum, a test stimulus is from the point conditioned, the shorter the time required for experimental extinction to a given criterion.*

There are good experimental grounds (19) for assuming that *the weaker the excitatory potential, the shorter the time required for experimental extinction.* From this and (3) the proposition follows.

9. *The fewer the number of reinforcements, the less extended is the supraliminal generalization gradient.*

Let the situation of (1) be assumed, with the exception that the number of reinforcing repetitions is 5 instead of 25. Substituting the 5 in place of R in equation (3), we arrive at 36.9 as the value of E_c. Substituting this value in equation (5), first with the value $D_1 = 40$ and next with the value $D_2 = 80$, we arrive at the two excitatory potentialities 14.6 and 5.8 respectively (Fig. 3). But 5.8 is less than 10, the value of L (equation 6). This means that with only 5 reinforcements a functional generalization gradient does not extend as far as 80 j.n.d.'s from the point conditioned, whereas by (3) with 25 reinforcements the functional gradient extends well beyond this point (Fig. 3). Thus the proposition finds illustration.

10. *The fewer the number of reinforcements, other things equal,*

(a) *the weaker the generalized reaction;*
(b) *the longer the generalized reaction latency;*
(c) *the fewer the number of unreinforced reactions required to extinguish the generalized reaction;*
(d) *the shorter the time required to produce extinction of the generalized reaction.*

From reasoning analogous to that following proposition (9), together with principles put forward in connection with propositions (5), (6), (7), and (8), may be derived the preceding propositions, assuming as constant both the number of reinforcements and the number of j.n.d.'s difference between the point tested and that conditioned.[7]

11. *The excitatory potential at a given point within the range of the generalization gradients originating at two distinct points on the same stimulus continuum is equal to the sum of the two generalized excitatory potentials taken separately, less the quotient obtained by dividing the product of the two potentials by the physiological limit of such potentials, i.e.,*

$$E_T = E_{T_c} + E_{T_{c'}} - \frac{E_{T_c}E_{T_{c'}}}{A} . \qquad (7)$$

In equation (7), T is the point on the stimulus continuum tested, c and c' are the points originally conditioned, and A is the physiological limit.[8]

Let it be supposed that the same reaction (R_x) is conditioned to two distinct points on a stimulus continuum (Fig. 4) separated by a number of j.n.d.'s less than the sum of the near wings of the super-threshold generalization ranges of the two excitatory tendencies. Let it also be assumed that *overlapping generalization gradients combine in the same manner to produce a joint excitatory potential as would two sets of repetitions each sufficient to produce one of the generalized excitatory potentials in question.*

We have given by equation (2) above,

$$E_c = E_{(R)} = A(1 - e^{-hR}),$$

letting $E_{(R)}$ be the excitatory potential produced at the point conditioned by R rein-

PAPER

12

---

[7] It is to be observed that sets of corollaries parallel to these four follow from propositions 12, 13, 14, 16, 17, 19, 23, 27, and 28.

[8] It is believed that the derivation of the other propositions of the present series is sufficiently obvious to make rigorous proof of them undesirable in this place. Partly as an illustration of what is presumably possible in all cases, and partly because the derivation of the present proposition is more complicated than that of the others, it is here given in some detail.

forcements. We wish to show, first, that

$$E_{(R_1+R_2)} = E_R + E_{R^2} - \frac{1}{A} E_{R_1} \times E_R .$$ (8)

To prove this we observe that,

$$
\begin{aligned}
E_{(R_1+R_2)} + \frac{1}{A} E_{(R_1)} \times E_{(R_2)} &= A(1 - e^{-h(R_1+R_2)}) \\
&\quad + A(1 - e^{-hR_1})(1 - e^{-hR_2}) \\
&= A(2 - e^{-hR_1} - e^{-hR_2}) \\
&= E_{(R_1)} + E_{(R_2)},
\end{aligned}
$$

from which equation (8) follows.

Now in the case of the generalization gradient tested at point T at a distance D from the point of conditioning, we have by equation (4),

$$E_{T_c} = E_c(D) = E_c e^{-kD}.$$

Substituting in this equation the value of E_c from equation (2) we have

$$E_{T_o} = E(R, D) = A e^{-kD}(1 - e^{-hR}).$$

Let $\bar{R}$ be the number of repetitions which it *would* take to create E_{T_o} by a direct learning process. Then,

$$E(\bar{R}) = E(R, D).$$

Solving for $\bar{R}$, we have

$$\bar{R} = -\frac{1}{h} \log \left[1 - e^{-kD}(1 - e^{-hR}) \right].$$

PAPER

12

To simplify the notation we shall write this as

$$\bar{R} = f(R, D).$$

Now by previous assumption, the total amount of excitatory potential due to the combination at point T of two generalizations from learning at two points c and c' at distances D and D' from T, after R and R' repetitions respectively, will be

$$E(\bar{R} + \bar{R}') = E[f(R, D) + f(R', D')].$$

Now, by (8),

$$E(\bar{R} + \bar{R}') = E(\bar{R}) + E(\bar{R}') - \frac{1}{A} E(\bar{R}) \cdot E(\bar{R}').$$

Hence,

$$
\begin{aligned}
E[f(R, D) + f(R', D')] &= E[f(R, D)] + E[f(R', D')] \\
&\quad - \frac{1}{A} E[f(R, D)] \cdot E[f(R', D')],
\end{aligned}
$$

i.e.,

$$E_T = E_{T_c} + E_{T_{c'}} - \frac{E_{T_c} E_{T_{c'}}}{A} .$$

Q.E.D.

12. *When two points separated by less than half the superthreshold generalization range of either are equally conditioned to the same reaction* (R_X), *the conditioning of the second will increase the excitatory potential effective at the point first conditioned.*

Now let the situation of (11) be assumed, the two overlapping gradients being 48 j.n.d.'s apart with 10 reinforcements given to each. By equation (3), 10 reinforcements give an E_c of 60.2. The two overlapping gradients are shown in Fig. 4. The generalization gradient of the second at the point S_c, by equation 3, is 19.9. Substituting the values of 60.2 and 19.9 in equation (7) we arrive at a joint value of 68.1 at point S_c. But this is larger by 7.9 than the value originally conditioned.

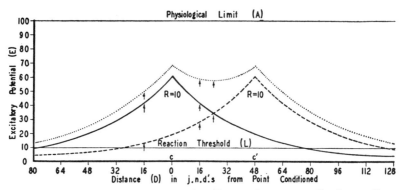

FIG. 4. Diagrammatic representation of two primary generalization gradients set up 48 j.n.d.'s apart, each alike with 10 reinforcements. The dotted line above represents the functional summation of the two overlapping gradients according to equation (7).

PAPER

12

13. *When two points separated by less than half the superthreshold generalization range of either are equally conditioned to the same reaction (R_X) the conditioning of the second will increase the excitatory potential effective at points on the far generalization wing of the first.*

Assuming the same situation as in (12), computation shows (Fig. 4) that 16 j.n.d.'s beyond S_c the first gradient has a value of 41.5 and the second one has a value of 13.8. By equation (7) this gives a joint excitatory potential of 49.7, which is larger than 41.5.

14. *When two points separated by less than half the superthreshold range of either are equally conditioned to the same reaction (R_X), the conditioning of the second will increase the excitatory potential effective at points on the near wing of the first by an amount greater than at an equal distance on the far wing.*

Assuming the same situation as in (12), computation shows (Fig. 4) that at a distance of 16 j.n.d.'s from the first toward the second, the first has an excitatory potential of 41.6 and the second has an excitatory potential of 28.7. By equation (7) this gives a joint excitatory potential of 58.4. But $58.4 - 41.6 = 16.8$ and $49.7 - 41.6 = 8.1$, and $16.8 > 8.1$.

15. *When two points separated by less than half the superthreshold generalization range of either are equally conditioned to the same reaction (R_X), the slope of the summation gradient is less than that of the major of the two components but is in the direction of the latter.*

From (12) and (14) we have (Fig. 4), as the difference between the excitatory potential of the major generalization gradient at the point conditioned and at a point 16 j.n.d.'s distant,

$$60.2 - 41.6 = 18.6.$$

The difference between the joint values of the two gradients at the same points is

$$68.1 - 58.4 = 9.7,$$

but

$$9.7 < 18.6.$$

16. *When two points separated by less than half the superthreshold generalization range of either are equally conditioned to the same reaction (R_X) the functional summation values show a minimum at the point of intersection of the near wings of the two gradients.*

The near generalization gradients of the two conditioned parts of Figure 4 intersect 24 j.n.d.'s from each point of origin with an excitatory potential of 34.6 each. This yields a joint excitatory potential of 57.4, which is the lowest point between the two points conditioned.

17. *When two points separated by less than half the mean superthreshold generalization range of either are conditioned to an unequal degree, the joint values from the combining of the near wings of each at a given point of overlapping will show a minimal value at a point nearer the point of weaker reinforcement.*

Suppose one point is conditioned to a stimulus continuum to the extent of 10 repetitions and a second point 48 j.n.d.'s distant is conditioned to the same stimulus continuum to the extent of 5 reinforcements. The primary and summation gradients of this combination are shown in Fig. 5. An inspection of this figure shows that in

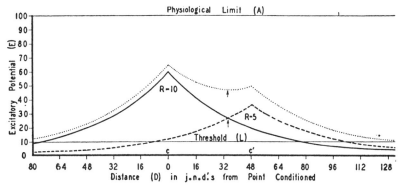

Fig. 5. Diagrammatic representation of the overlapping primary generalization gradients set up 48 j.n.d.'s apart, the left-hand one with 10 reinforcements and the right-hand one with 5 reinforcements. The dotted line above represents the functional summation of these two unequal overlapping primary generalization gradients according to equation (7).

this situation there is also a minimum, but it falls at a point nearer the point of origin of the weaker excitatory potential.

18. *When two points separated by less than half the mean superthreshold generalization range of either are conditioned to an unequal degree, the joint values from the combining of the near wings of each at a given point of overlapping show a steeper slope at the point more strongly conditioned than at the point less strongly conditioned.*

Illustration of this principle appears in the upper curve of Fig. 5.

19. *When a supraliminal generalized excitatory potential overlaps a sublimina generalized excitatory potential, the joint excitatory potential of the two is stronger than the stronger excitatory potential alone.*

Suppose that two points 192 j.n.d.'s apart are conditioned to the same reaction (R_X) each to the extent of 10 reinforcements. The near gradient of one at 48 j.n.d.'s difference from the point conditioned falls on the same stimulus as does the near gradient of the other at 144 j.n.d.'s difference from the point conditioned (Fig. 6). By equation (5) these values yield excitatory potentials of 19.9 and 4.7 respectively, the 4.7 being subliminal since it is well below the threshold value of 10 (equation 6). Combining these by equation (7) we obtain a joint value of 23.7, a gain over 19.9 of 3.8 units (Fig. 6).

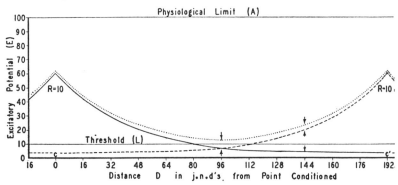

PAPER

12

Fɪɢ. 6. Diagrammatic representation of two primary generalization gradients set up 192 j.n.d.'s apart, each alike with 10 reinforcements. The dotted line represents the functional summation of the overlapping gradients according to equation (7).

20. *If sufficiently close to the reaction threshold two subliminal overlapping generalization gradients will combine to produce an excitatory potential strong enough to produce overt reaction.*

Suppose the situation presented in (19). The gradients intersect at 96 j.n.d.'s from each point of reinforcement where the excitatory potential of each, by equation (5), is 6.6. This is below the reaction threshold (Fig. 6). The joint excitatory potential, by equation (7), is 12.8, which is well above the reaction threshold.

21. *The conditioning of the same reaction (R_X) at a finite number of points properly placed throughout any stimulus continuum will serve completely to generalize the reaction throughout that stimulus continuum.*

Suppose the situation assumed in (19). An inspection of the resulting excitatory potentials (Fig. 6) shows that the sum of the ranges of the two near superthreshold generalization ranges taken separately is approximately 160 j.n.d.'s, whereas the superthreshold combined generalization inner range is evidently something in excess of 192 j.n.d.'s. Moreover, the combination of the excitatory potential of the inner wing of one with the outer wing of the other (Fig. 6) will evidently also extend slightly the outer ranges of the joint gradient over either single gradient alone. From the preceding it is clear that a finite number of conditioned points so distributed over any stimulus continuum will render it wholly generalized to the reaction so conditioned.

22. *When a generalized excitatory potential is extinguished at a given point until it yields a zero reaction, there is still an appreciable amount of latent excitatory potential (E) at that point and an amount of inhibitory potential (I) is generated at that point equal to the difference between the original excitatory potential and the magnitude of the reaction threshold (L).*

Let it be supposed that a point on a stimulus continuum is conditioned to a re-action (R_x) by 25 reinforcements, as in (1). Substitution in equations (3) and (5) shows that under these circumstances the point conditioned will have an excitatory potential of 90, and a point 32 j.n.d.'s removed from the point of reinforcement will have an excitatory potential of 43.1 units. Now suppose that the stimulus at this latter point is presented repeatedly to the subject without reinforcement until no reaction occurs, when presentations will be discontinued. By Definition 10, this will have brought the excitatory potential to the threshold, which by equation (6) is 10.

There is much reason to postulate that situations of this kind generate an inhibitory potential (I) which generalizes in the same way that the excitatory potential does, *i.e.*, according to equation (5). Now, assuming (Fig. 7) that the inhibitory potential is

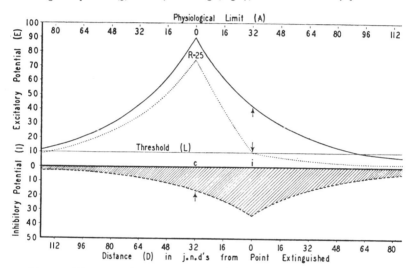

PAPER

12

FIG. 7. Diagrammatic representation of a primary positive generalization gradient based on 25 reinforcements and an inhibitory generalization gradient produced by the experimental extinction to the reaction threshold of the generalized excitatory gradient at a point 32 j.n.d.'s from its point of reinforcement. The dotted line between shows the functional summation (effective excitatory potential, or $\bar{E}$) of the positive and negative excitatory potentials according to equation (9).

measured in the same units as the excitatory potential, it follows that the inhibitory potential generated must be the same as the amount of excitatory potential lost, *i.e.*, it will be:

$$43.1 - 10.0 = 33.1.$$

23. *When a generalized excitatory potential is extinguished to the point of zero re-action, the excitatory potential at the point originally conditioned also suffers an appreciable amount of diminution.*

Let us assume the situation of (22). Substituting 33.1 in equation (5) together with a D of 32, we find that the generalized inhibitory potential at a point 32 j.n.d.'s distant in either direction from the point of extinction has an inhibitory value of 15.8. It follows that one of these directions will coincide with the point of original rein-forcement.

It is assumed that in situations of this kind the actual effective excitatory potential is given by the equation:

$$\bar{E}_T = E_T - I_T, \tag{9}$$

where $\bar{E}_T$ is the effective excitatory potential at the point tested. Substituting appropriately in equation (9) we have (Fig. 7)

$$\bar{E}_c = 90.0 - 15.8 = 74.2.$$

24. *When a generalized excitatory potential has been extinguished to a point of zero reaction the resulting gradient of effective excitatory potential between the point of conditioning and the point of extinction is steepened.*

By means of computations similar to those outlined in (22) and (23), Fig. 7 has been constructed. By inspecting the curve of effective excitatory potential ($\bar{E}$) lying between the point of conditioning and the point of extinction, it will be seen that the slope is steeper than the slope of the corresponding section of the gradient of excitatory potential.

25. *When a generalized excitatory potential has been extinguished on one wing until it yields a zero reaction, the resulting gradient of effective excitatory potential on that same wing beyond the point of extinction lies entirely below the threshold, and the gradient of diminution in this region is less steep than was the original excitatory gradient.*

If we inspect the curve of effective excitatory potential ($\bar{E}$) in Fig. 7 at the right of the extinction point, illustration of this proposition will be observed.

26. *When a generalized excitatory potential has been extinguished at a point on one wing until it yields a zero reaction, the superthreshold range of this wing of generalization in terms of j.n.d.'s is greatly reduced, depending on how close the point of extinction is to the point of original reinforcement.*

This proposition is a corollary dependent upon proposition (25). In the situation represented by Fig. 7, the generalization range on the wing extinguished is reduced by approximately 60 j.n.d.'s.

27. *When a generalized excitatory potential has been extinguished at a point on one wing until it yields a zero reaction, the gradient of effective excitatory potential of the other wing is lower throughout than was the original excitatory gradient, but the lowering is less at all points than at corresponding points on the wing subjected to extinction.*

The left-hand portion of Fig. 7 illustrates this proposition.

28. *When a generalized excitatory potential has been extinguished on one wing until it yields a zero reaction, the superthreshold portion of the gradient of effective excitatory potential on the other wing is diminished but not to so great an extent as on the wing where the extinction occurred.*

This is a corollary from (27). (See Fig. 7.)

29. *When a generalized excitatory potential has been extinguished on one wing until it yields a zero reaction, the resulting gradient of effective excitatory potential on the other wing is less steep at all points than was the original gradient of generalized excitation.*

The left-hand portion of Fig. 7 illustrates this proposition.

Numerous other propositions could be derived with the aid of the principles associated with the concept of primary generalization. It is believed, however, that the twenty-nine propositions already presented are ample to show that the introduction of this concept to explain one type of stimulus equivalence is not an empty renaming of the phenomenon in question.

SECONDARY GENERALIZATION

It will be recalled (p. 10) that cases of stimulus equivalence were separated into at least three types, depending upon the presumptive principle or mechanism mediating the equivalence. The fact of partial physical identity of the stimulus was dismissed as not requiring elaboration. The second principle of primary or physiological generalization was discussed in detail in the preceding section. It will be our task in the present section to consider stimulus equivalence as mediated by the third mechanism, that of *secondary generalization*.

The principle of secondary generalization, unlike that of primary or physiological generalization, is not a postulate but is, instead, a theorem derived from other postulates of the system. For that reason a rough outline of the logical procedure whereby it is derived will be given:

PAPER

12

1. Let us assume the existence of a stimulus continuum several times wider than the range of any generalization gradient.

2. It is further assumed that at very many places throughout the stimulus continuum of (1) R_x (*e.g.* the blinking of the eyelid) has been conditioned.

3. From (2) and proposition (21) of the preceding section, it follows that all points throughout this stimulus continuum, whether specifically conditioned to it or not, will evoke R_x to a high and fairly uniform degree; *i.e.*, any two points on the stimulus continuum such as S_a and S_n would evoke R_x to a high and approximately equal degree regardless of the number of j.n.d.'s separating them, thus:

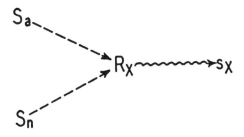

where s_x is a proprioceptive stimulus arising from reaction R_x.

4. Now, let us suppose that a given point, S_a, of this continuum is later conditioned rather strongly to the reaction R_y (*e.g.* a hand movement).

371

5. From (3) and (4) the process of conditioning would be as follows:

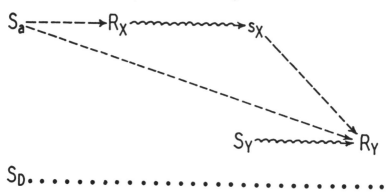

6. Suppose, now, the organism is stimulated by S_n, a number of primary supraliminal generalization spans removed from S_a.

7. From (3), (5), and (6) we have

$$S_n \dashrightarrow R_X \rightsquigarrow s_X \dashrightarrow R_Y$$

8. Generalizing (7) we may accordingly say that,

Even though S_n has never been conditioned to R_Y, and even though S_n is beyond the primary generalization range of S_a, nevertheless S_n is able to evoke R_y, i.e., S_a and S_n are equivalent in their capacity to evoke the same reaction.

Fairly convincing experimental evidence that indirect generalization or equivalence of stimuli really occurs has been reported by Shipley (**13**). A somewhat detailed analysis of one of Shipley's experimental findings has already been published by the present author (**8**), and need not be repeated here.

Numerous corollaries flow from the preceding theorem. A sampling of them are:

1. *All points beyond the superthreshold generalization range of the point conditioned to the second reaction will evoke it, but with a weaker intensity than at the point conditioned.*

2. *All points beyond the superthreshold generalization range of the point conditioned to the second reaction will evoke it with approximately an equal intensity, so far as generalization is concerned.*

3. *All points within the superthreshold generalization range of the point conditioned to the second reaction will evoke it to a stronger degree, the closer their proximity to the point conditioned.*

SUMMARY

In the preceding pages we have attempted to show in a number of ways how physical stimuli, as distinguished from stimulus objects, possess equivalence in the sense of being able to evoke qualitatively the same, or equivalent, reactions. *Quantitatively*, reactions from equivalent stimuli are usually weaker when evoked by the stimulus not specifically conditioned (associated).

Three fairly distinct principles or mechanisms have been isolated as mediating stimulus equivalence: (1) the partial physical identity of the stimulus compounds; (2) primary or physiological generalization (Pavlov's 'irradiation'); and (3) secondary or indirect generalization through the arousal of a reaction previously conditioned to the same stimulus continuum. These three forms of stimulus equivalence are conceived to combine their action in various degrees in different situations. Many cases which may appear through our present ignorance to be of the second form may in the end prove physiologically to be of the first. Moreover, the third is dependent upon the second; it is a theorem and not an original postulate. While there probably are other mechanisms mediating stimulus equivalence, it is believed that the three listed above account for most of the behavior properly classed as due to stimulus equivalence.

Incidentally the analysis has enabled us to give what we hope will prove to be a clear and unambiguous elucidation of the term *stimulus*. It is in terms of physical energies such as light waves, sound waves, heat waves, and the like, exactly as these are conceived in the physical sciences. In this way an unambiguous contact of psychology with the physical sciences is established, and its traditional isolation is abolished, at least at this point. At the same time, the traditional confusion of the stimulus with the stimulus object has been definitely clarified. Thus on this count, it is hoped, we have put the behavioristic house in order.

PAPER
12

But what of Tolman and the psychologists of various other *Gestalt* groups? How do *they* meet the problem of stimulus equivalence? Surely organisms for them must somehow react to the physical world and, if so, the distinction between the actual stimulus and the stimulus object must exist also. Meanwhile we remind ourselves that merely renaming the thing will not suffice as an explanation however impressive the process of re-christening. Neither will the mere introduction of a non-physical perceptual process between the physical world and the physical reaction solve the problem; consciousness as such no longer possesses this kind of magic in the scientific world. Despite the monotony of the refrain we must repeat again and again that nothing will serve as scientific explanation except logical deductions from known postulates.

REFERENCES

1. ADAMS, D. K.   Note on method. PSYCHOL. REV., 1937, **44**, 212–218.
2. ANREP, G. V.   The irradiation of conditioned reflexes. *Proc. Royal Soc. London*, 1923, **94**, Series B, 404–425.
3. BASS, M. J. & HULL, C. L.   The irradiation of a tactile conditioned reflex in man. *J. comp. Psychol.*, 1934, **17**, 47–66.
4. BORING, E. G.   The physical dimensions of consciousness. New York: The Century Co., 1933, pp. ix + 251.
5. HOVLAND, C. I.   The generalization of conditioned responses: I. The sensory generalization of conditioned responses with varying frequencies of tone. *J. gen. Psychol.*, 1937, **17**, 125–148.
6. ——.   The generalization of conditioned responses: IV. The effects of varying amounts of reinforcement upon the degree of generalization of conditioned responses. *J. exper. Psychol.*, 1937, **21**, 261–276.
7. HULL, C. L.   Quantitative aspects of the evolution of concepts. *Psychol. Monogr.*, 1920, **28**, No. 123, pp. 85.
8. ——.   The concept of the habit-family hierarchy and maze learning. PSYCHOL. REV., 1934, **41**; Part I, 33–52; Part II, 134–152.
9. ——.   Mind, mechanism, and adaptive behavior. PSYCHOL. REV., 1937, **44**, 1–32.
10. ——.   A comment on Dr. Adams' note on method. PSYCHOL. REV., 1937, **44**, 219–221.
11. —— & PERKINS, D. T.   Analysis of compound trial-and-error behavior in the rat. (In prep.)
12. PAVLOV, I. P.   Conditioned reflexes: an investigation of the physiological activity of the cerebral cortex. (Trans. and ed. by G. V. Anrep.) London: Oxford Univ. Press, 1927, pp. xv + 430.
13. SHIPLEY, W. C.   An apparent transfer of conditioning. *J. gen. Psychol.*, 1933, **8**, 382–391.
14. SIMLEY, O. A.   The relation of subliminal to supraliminal learning. *Arch. Psychol.*, 1933, No. 146.
15. SPENCE, K. W.   The differential response in animals to stimuli varying within a single dimension. PSYCHOL. REV., 1937, **44**, 430–444.
16. ——.   Gradual versus sudden solution of discrimination problems by chimpanzees. *J. comp. Psychol.*, 1938, **25**, 213–224.
17. THORNDIKE, E. L.   Educational psychology, Vol. II, The psychology of learning. Teachers College, Columbia Univ., 1913, pp. xi + 452.
18. TOLMAN, E. C.   The determiners of behavior at a choice point. PSYCHOL. REV., 1938, **45**, 1–41.
19. WILLIAMS, S. B.   Resistance to extinction as a function of the number of reinforcements. *J. exper. Psychol.* (in press).
20. WOODGER, J. H.   The axiomatic method in biology. Cambridge Univ. Press, 1937, pp. x + 174.

[MS. received September 15, 1938]

PAPER 12

THE PROBLEM OF INTERVENING VARIABLES IN MOLAR BEHAVIOR THEORY [1]

BY CLARK L. HULL

Yale University

I. Introduction

There is a striking and significant similarity between the physicalism doctrine of the logical positivists (Vienna Circle) and the approach characteristic of the American behaviorism originating in the work of J. B. Watson (13). Intimately related to both of the above movements are the pragmatism of Peirce, James, and Dewey on the one hand, and the operationism of Bridgman (4), Boring (1), and Stevens (11), on the other. These several methodological movements, together with the pioneering experimental work of Pavlov and the other Russian reflexologists, are, I believe, uniting to produce in America a behavioral discipline which will be a full-blown natural science; this means it may be expected to possess not only the basic empirical component of natural science, but a genuinely scientific theoretical component as well. It is with the latter that the present paper is primarily concerned.

PAPER
13

II. Probability Versus Natural Law in the Behavior Sciences

Now, scientific theory is concerned with natural laws. These are conceived as being uniform. Do such isolable uniformities exist in the field of behavior? Of the present panel, Lewin and I believe they do; Brunswik, on the other hand, is convinced that no such uniformities exist, that the best we may hope for is to find correlations among phenomena which will always lack appreciably of being 1.00, possibly ranging mostly

[1] Thanks to the kindness of Brunswik, I have had his revised manuscript before me while preparing the revision of the present paper. Owing to the delay in the revision of my paper, it is doubtful whether either Brunswik or Lewin was able to utilize in any way the copies which were sent them immediately on its completion.

273

between .40 and .60. Since this disagreement concerns whether something can or cannot be done, it should ultimately be capable of unambiguous decision. If a set of such laws are actually isolated, the question will receive an affirmative answer, but if after a very prolonged effort directed specifically to this task, no such laws are discovered, there will gradually arise an increasingly formidable presumption that the answer to the question is negative.

But since the verdict from trial is very laborious and time-consuming, it is desirable to make as shrewd an estimate of the outcome as possible from evidence now available, because if the quest appears hopeless, all of us may as well give it up, as Brunswik seems already to have done. In this connection Brunswik points to the indisputable fact that under the complex conditions of life, the behavior of organisms is variable. This variability, except possibly in the matter of degree, is not peculiar to the field of behavior. It is easily accounted for without assuming any lack of uniformity in the supposed laws involved: The outcome of a dynamic situation depends upon (1) a set of antecedent conditions and (2) one or more rules or laws according to which, given a certain period of time, these conditions evolve into different conditions or events. It is evident that such a situation implies some degree of uncertainty of dynamic outcome, because we always lack absolutely exact knowledge concerning *conditions*. It does *not* necessarily imply that within the causal segment under consideration stable and uniform sequences may not occur which can be formulated into absolutely uniform rules of molar action. Accordingly, the uncertainty or probabilism of the situation may lie entirely in the conditions and not at all in the rules or laws.

This uncertainty may be illustrated by the following example. In the case of falling bodies, the *law* is represented by the form of the equation,

$$s = \tfrac{1}{2}gt^2,$$

and the *conditions* of its operation are represented by the empirical values of s, g, and t, which must be substituted in the equation if the law is to be verified. In this case the equation is universally believed to be exact, *i.e.*, it is believed that if the measurement of s on the one hand and of g and t on the other were exact, the equation would hold absolutely when applied to objects falling in a vacuum at the earth's geographical pole; in that case the correlation between the right- and the left-hand sides of the equation would be 1.00. But as a rule, errors of measurement are appreciable, which is to say that it is impossible to know the exact conditions in any given case of a falling body. Therefore, the actual correlation of the values on the respective sides of even the most fully authenticated equations of physics is bound to be something less than 1.00. That this lack of perfect correlation is due to the difficulty of measurement of the conditions rather than to the capriciousness of the alleged law is suggested by the fact that as measurements are improved, repeated, and pooled, the verification of the formula becomes increasingly exact, *i.e.*, the correlation becomes progressively higher. It seems reasonable to suppose that the same situation may exist in the field of behavior.

A second and more serious *a priori* argument against the probable success of the attempt to isolate true natural science laws in the behavior sciences is that any theory of behavior is at present, and must be for some time to come, a molar theory.[2] This is because neuroanatomy and physiology have not yet developed to a point such that they yield principles which may be employed as postulates in a system of behavior theory; consequently, both for empirical and theoretical purposes, behavior must be broken up into relatively coarse causal segments, the interior conditions of which cannot be subjected to observation and measurement. It follows from considerations put forward above that even if the action of the ultimate molecular units of the causal segment were absolutely lawful, the molar outcome of the joint action of the numerous internal elements composing a molar causal segment would vary, because the conditions, being unknown, would presumably vary from one molar situation to another. It would follow that

PAPER
13

[2] Molar behavior theory is here opposed to the molecular. The latter would presumably deal with the action of the ultimate nerve cell, the protoplasmic molecules making up the neuron or perhaps the atoms constituting the molecule, or even the electrons, protons, neutrons, etc., constituting the atom. Thus the term *molar* as here used corresponds approximately to the term *macroscopic*, or *coarse-grained*.

molar laws cannot be expected to be absolutely exact. This statement must, I think, be granted.

It would seem, however, that the smaller the molar segment employed, the less will be the uncertainty regarding the conditions and so the smaller will be the role of probabilism in molar dynamic outcomes. By the sagacious pooling of the data obtainable from experimental situations when controlled as well as possible, the net results of the chance variability of the molecular conditions will be largely equalized, and from these there may emerge quantitative laws characteristic of a stable central tendency of the conditions in question.[3] The laws of thermodynamics in gases rest upon exactly this basis; where moderately large samples of gas are involved these laws have a precision which represents a probability of substantially 1.00, something far beyond anything usefully measured by a Pearsonian coefficient of correlation. I conclude, then, that it is not unreasonable to hope for the isolation of both primary and secondary behavioral laws which will hold within a narrow margin of error for averages secured from carefully controlled empirical conditions.[4]

PAPER
13

III. Symbolic Constructs Are Widely Used in Behavior Theory

As Brunswik points out, a second indirect effect of the present molar status of the behavior sciences is the resort to

[3] Under the rubric of the oscillation (O) of habit strength below its standard or maximal strength (**8**, p. 76; **7**), there is incorporated in my own theoretical systematization an explicit recognition of a particular phase of this presumptive variability of conditions. This oscillation is tentatively attributed to the random spontaneous firing of the individual nerve cells (**7**).

[4] I do not at all mean to imply by the above that Brunswik's program of empirical correlational determinations is not without great scientific value. On the contrary, I believe that it is an extremely valuable mode of approach. I do mean, however, that I should expect to derive from molar behavior laws exactly the type of correlations which he finds between the relative potency of the several visual cues in the determination of the verbal responses of his subjects in judging third dimensional distance. Indeed, I am of the opinion that adequate molar laws are even now available which would make this possible; however, such a deduction has not yet been made in rigorous detail, and of course achievements of this kind cannot be claimed with certainty in advance of performance. If Brunswik is prepared publicly to challenge the possibility of such a derivation, I am prepared to attempt it and publish in this journal the outcome, whatever it turns out to be. My program thus does not oppose that of Brunswik, but merely attempts to supplement it.

symbolic constructs or intervening variables.   This is a wide-spread and wholly respectable practice, not only in the behavior sciences but in the physical sciences as well.   Actually the physical sciences are molar in much the same sense as are the social sciences, and they are similarly forced to piece out by hypothetical entities the region not directly observable.   In addition to molecules, atoms and the various hypothetical subatomic entities such as electrons, protons, etc., are for the most part not only unobserved but presumably unobservable.

In this connection it may be of interest to observe that the use of theoretical constructs or intervening variables is practically universal among writers who have seriously attempted the theoretical systematization of behavior.   As the first example, let us take a statement by a leading logical positivist, Rudolph Carnap: "At ten o'clock Mr. A was angry" (6, p. 89). Carnap argues that for this statement to have scientific significance, the state of anger must be publicly observable, either directly or indirectly; in this connection he mentions the characteristic behavior which is ordinarily taken as indicating the condition called anger.   This behavior, being observable, clearly permits an *indirect* observation of a condition within the body of Mr. A through the conversion, translation, or transformation of the statement about the behavior into a statement about the anger.   Thus it becomes apparent that anger, typical of the psychic element in the classical psychology, lies between (1) the antecedent conditions of frustration and what not which precipitated the state, and (2) the observable consequences of the state; *i.e.*, anger is an *unobserved intervening variable*.   This dynamic situation is repre-

PAPER

13

CARNAP

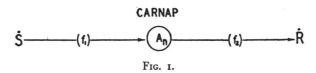

Fig. 1.

sented conveniently by the diagram of Figure 1, where $\dot{S}$ represents the antecedent conditions which precipitated the anger, $\dot{R}$ represents the observable response, A represents the anger,

f_1 and f_2 represent quantitative functional relationships between $\dot{S}$ and A and between A and $\dot{R}$ respectively. A circle is drawn around A to indicate that it is a symbolic construct, something not directly observable and measurable.

Passing to the more comprehensive statements of Brunswik (2), who is both a logical positivist and a psychologist, we have the situation represented by the diagram of Figure 2, where

BRUNSWIK

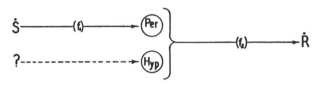

FIG. 2.

$\dot{S}$, $\dot{R}$, f_1, and f_2 mean the same as in Figure 1, Per represents *perception*, and Hyp, *hypothesis*. Here we find not one intervening variable or construct, but two of them operating jointly. Circles are drawn around Per and Hyp to indicate that they are regarded as symbolic constructs.

A third systematic approach is that of Tolman (12). I have attempted to represent this from the present point of view by the diagram shown in Figure 3, where $\dot{S}$, $\dot{R}$, f_1, f_2, and

TOLMAN

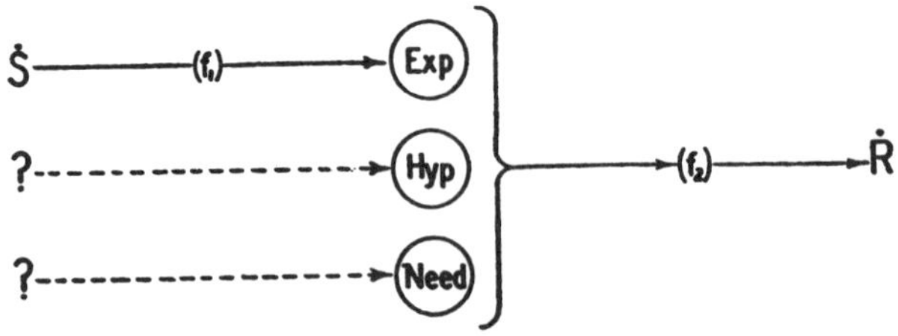

FIG. 3.

Hyp mean the same as above, Exp represents *expectation*, and *Need* is unabbreviated. The circles, as above, indicate the symbolic constructs.

A fourth example of the use of symbolic constructs is found in a study by Buxton (5).[5]   It may be represented as shown in Figure 4, where $\dot{S}, f_1, f_2, f_3$, Per, Need, and $\dot{R}$ mean the same as above, Cog represents *cognition*, and Force, *psychological force*.

BUXTON

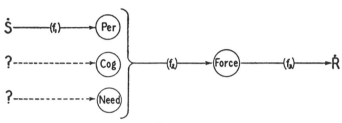

Fɪɢ. 4.

It may be noticed that the Buxton diagram has *two* links in its chain of symbolic constructs, rather than the single link represented in the preceding diagrams.

Finally I may mention my own use of symbolic constructs (7). A considerably abbreviated representation of this is shown in Figure 5,[6] where S, R, G, and N represent the stimulus energy, the response, the nature of the reinforcement, and the number of reinforcements of the original reinforcement or learning situation respectively; $\dot{S}$ represents the evocation or stimulus energy; $\dot{s}$, the afferent neural impulse initiated by the receptor discharge; Need, the number of hours of food privation, for example; D, the state of organic drive resulting from the privation; $\dot{s}E\dot{R}$, excitatory or reaction potential;[7] $\dot{R}$, the

PAPER

13

[5] At this point I would have preferred to give a representation of Lewin's (10) use of symbolic constructs, but I felt even more uncertain in attempting this than in the case of the representations which were attempted.   There seems no doubt, however, that Lewin does employ symbolic constructs both explicitly and on a considerable scale.   Perhaps the diagram of Buxton's usage may be considered a rough approximation to that of Lewin, as Buxton in his theorizing seems to have followed Lewin to a considerable degree.

[6] I am indebted to Kenneth W. Spence for the general methodology of representing intervening variables here employed.   In this connection see especially page 318 of Spence's Chapter 11, Theoretical interpretations of learning, in *Comparative Psychology* (revised edition), edited by F. A. Moss, New York, Prentice-Hall, Inc., 1942; also see page 11 of Bergmann, G., and Spence, K. W., Operationism and theory in psychology, Psᴄʜᴏʟ. Rᴇᴠ., 1941, 46, 1–14.

[7] It is probable that the construct *reaction potential* ($\dot{s}E\dot{R}$) corresponds rather closely to Buxton's construct called *Force*, and to Lewin's *vector* concept.

reaction itself; $_SP_R$, the probability of reaction evocation; $_St_R$, the latency of reaction evocation; $_SA_R$, the amplitude of reaction evocation; and $_Sn_R$, the number of unreinforced reaction evocations to extinguish the reaction potential to a subthreshold value. As in the preceding figures, circles are drawn around the symbolic constructs.

HULL

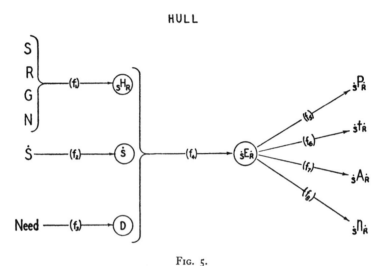

PAPER

13

FIG. 5.

It is quite clear from the above examples that the use of symbolic constructs by behavior theorists is both explicit and general.

IV. REQUIREMENTS FOR THE SATISFACTORY USE OF SYMBOLIC CONSTRUCTS

It would appear that Brunswik also has considerable pessimism concerning the utility of symbolic constructs in behavior theory, even though he himself in his visual constancy studies seems at certain moments at least to introduce perception as a variable intervening between the physical stimulation of his subjects and their verbal responses. While I would not go so far as to exclude the use of symbolic constructs, I do believe that their use is attended by serious risks which can be avoided only by taking certain definite precautions.

It is quite clear that in the case of all the above diagrams, symbolic constructs can have nothing more than a rather dubious expository utility unless they are anchored to observable and measurable conditions or events on both the antecedent and consequent sides. It follows that some means must be found of determining the value of the intervening variable from the measurement of the antecedent conditions and, knowing this, some means must be found of determining what amount of the consequent observable conditions or event corresponds to the value of the construct.

Specifically, my own system, as represented by the diagram shown in Figure 5, requires that the habit strength (sH_R), afferent impulse $(\dot{s})$, and drive intensity (D) must each be calculable from their antecedent conditions, that the nature and magnitude of the reaction potential (sE_R) must be calculable from the values of sH_R, $\dot{s}$, and D taken jointly, and that the nature and magnitude of the several reaction functions $(sP_R, st_R, sA_R,$ and $sn_R)$ must each be calculable from sE_R. This is necessary because if the values of the constructs are indeterminate, the theory of the relationship between the antecedent and the consequent conditions cannot be verified empirically, and an unverifiable theory has no place in science.

PAPER 13

In every case of the proper use of a symbolic construct the calculation must, of course, be performed by means of equations representing the functional relationship in question. In the evolution of my own system considerable effort has been devoted to the derivation of such equations, and numerous tentative ones have been worked out. For example, on the antecedent side (assuming S, R, and G to be practically simultaneous),

$$sH_R = w - w(10^{-hN}) \tag{1}$$

where w is an increasing function of the nature and amount of the reinforcing agent (G), and h is an empirical constant of the order .03 (7). Next,

$$sE_R = f(D) \times f(sH_R) \tag{2}$$

where $f(D)$ and $f(sH_R)$ are rather complex increasing functions of drive intensity and habit strength respectively (7).

As an example of the final link in this chain of functional relationships we have,[8]

$$\dot{S}n_{\dot{R}} = .66_{\dot{S}}E_{\dot{R}} - 4 \tag{3}$$

It is evident that this equational mode of anchoring symbolic constructs to objectively observable and measurable antecedent and consequent conditions or phenomena is necessary, because otherwise their values would be indeterminate and the theory of which they constitute an essential part would be impossible of empirical verification. If left permanently in that state the theory would be reduced to something appreciably worse than nonsense. This seems to be what Brunswik charitably calls the "encapsulation" of symbolic constructs.

V. POSSIBILITY OF DETERMINING UNAMBIGUOUSLY THE FUNCTIONAL RELATIONSHIPS OF BEHAVIORAL UNOBSERVABLES TO OTHER BEHAVIORAL VALUES

PAPER
13

It is quite clear that the determination of the functional relationship of an unobservable to anything else cannot be carried out merely by the direct fitting of equations to empirical data, because there can be no empirical data on the side of the relationship represented by the construct. This means that the determination must be somewhat indirect and in part trial-and-error. Such procedures are common in the more mature sciences. Suppose, for example, that a person unacquainted with the law of falling bodies,

$$s = \tfrac{1}{2}gt^2,$$

were given the task of determining it directly by empirical methods. He would first let weights fall repeatedly in a

[8] Tentative equations have now been derived for all of the relationships represented in Figure 5, and the most of the empirical constants involved have been roughly determined. In addition, a number of other functional relationships not represented in the diagram have been worked out in the same tentative manner. It is accordingly possible, given the objective measurable antecedent conditions, S, R, G, H, $\dot{S}$, and D, to calculate the value of the consequent or terminal events, $\dot{S}P_{\dot{R}}$, $\dot{S}t_{\dot{R}}$, $\dot{S}A_{\dot{R}}$, or $\dot{S}n_{\dot{R}}$. These are all given in considerable detail in a book now in press (7). However, an immense amount of research must be performed before the relationships in question can be regarded as satisfactorily determined.

vacuum from various heights, and average the falling time associated with the different distances. These means, with the corresponding distances, would make up two parallel columns of numbers. Then he would begin to try out various simple equational forms, to find one in which the substitution of the t-value would yield the corresponding value in the s-column. He would discover by trial that an exact agreement in any given case could be obtained if the value of t were multiplied by some number called a constant, but this coefficient would need to be different for every pair of values and so could not constitute a true solution to the problem. Similarly, it would be found that if one of these coefficients were kept really constant, s could be derived by multiplying the coefficient by various powers of t. But in that case a different exponent would be required for each pair of empirical s and t values, most of the exponents being fractional. Finally, in the search for simplicity, integral exponents might be tried, among which would be 2. This procedure, of course, would require approximately the *same* coefficient for all pairs of values, the coefficient being what appears in the formula as $g/2$. This finding would constitute a solution.[9]

A criticism of such a procedure might be that it is circular, since the value of the number, $g/2$, follows from the assumption that the t should be squared. The reply to this, of course, is that by the procedure outlined neither the $g/2$ nor the t^2 is assumed at first, but that that particular combination of values, *i.e.*, that particular coefficient and that particular exponent in combination, will yield the empirical value of s, and that *no other possible combination will do so*.

In an exactly analogous manner, if a single symbolic construct stands between two observable and measurable conditions ($\dot{S}$ and $\dot{R}$), and it is found by trial that two particular equations, *and those only*, mediate in conjunction with the

---

[9] As a matter of fact, once it is postulated that the equation has the general form of

$$s = at^x$$

the values of both a and x can be calculated by means of simultaneous equations from only two pairs of s and t empirical values. Such calculations, of course, will not reveal the exact values of either s or t, but only rather close approximations, because s and t are themselves only approximations.

symbolic construct the precise calculation of $\dot{R}$ from $\dot{S}$, it is submitted that the determination of neither equation may be considered viciously circular. At all events, that is the general method which has been employed in the derivation of the equations given above. The presence of more than one construct (horizontally or vertically, as represented in Figures 1 to 5) considerably complicates the task of working out the equations, but does not change the essential logic.

VI. The Scientific Status of Symbolic Constructs When Unambiguously Determined

At this point in the discussion it is easy to imagine a rock-ribbed positivist like my friend Woodrow (14) saying, "If you have a secure equational linkage extending from the antecedent observable conditions through to the consequent observable conditions, why, even though to do so might not be positively pernicious, use several equations where one would do?" It is quite true that in my own equations (1) can be substituted in (2), and (2), thus amplified, can be substituted in (3); in which case we would have a single equation relating the antecedent conditions directly to the consequent ones, though it would be exceedingly complex. Indeed, if the situation were as simple as this question implies, there would hardly be any point in the derivation of multiple equations where one would fit the entire situation equally well. It does not seem to me that any single equation would really fit the situation equally well.

In reaching a decision concerning this question, two considerations should be kept in mind. One is that if the antecedent and consequent values have been determined with great precision, only one particular equation will *exactly* satisfy them and that equation would, it is assumed, be no other than the one resulting from the telescoping of the three equations as above suggested. In other words, for the multiple equations to be justified, the single equation giving the best attainable fit to the empirical data would be found in fact to contain within itself in some form or other the mathematical equivalents of the various equations linking the observable and the hypothetical unobservable elements of the situation.

PAPER 13

A second and more decisive consideration involved in reaching a decision in this matter is that the occasion of the action of $\dot{S}$, $\dot{R}$, G, and N may be very remote temporally from that of the action of S and the Need. While it is perfectly possible to put into a single equation the values of events which occur at very different times, it is hard to believe that an event such as a stimulation in a remote learning situation can be causally active long after it has ceased to act on the receptors. I fully agree with Lewin that all the factors alleged to be causally influential in the determination of any other event must be in existence at the time of such causal action. I believe that it is some such consideration as this which has led to the universal common-sense use of the concept of habit; in my system ${}_S H_{\dot{R}}$ is merely a quantitative representation of the perseverative after-effects of the no-longer-existent compound events represented by $\dot{S}$, $\dot{R}$, G, and N. It follows that the value of ${}_S H_{\dot{R}}$ will need to be calculated separately before the influence of $\dot{S}$, $\dot{R}$, G, and N can be combined with that of the reaction-evocation situation represented by S and the Need. It is an obvious convenience to be able to concentrate the influence of four quantitative variables, such as $\dot{S}$, $\dot{R}$, G, and N, into a single numerical value or index. Since this index is not $\dot{S}$ or $\dot{R}$ or G or N, but something distinct from each, convenient symbolic manipulation demands a distinct symbolic representation, i.e., ${}_S H_{\dot{R}}$. Semantic exigencies also require the use of a name or term; the universally used word *habit* has been adapted to this use by quantitative redefinition.

PAPER
13

In an analogous manner it is hoped that the factors which determine primary drive (such as the number of hours of food or water privation, the intensity of an electric shock, or the number of degrees of temperature below or above the optimum) may each also be convertible into a standard index of motivation (D), presumably by means of a different equation for each type of need. If wholly successful, such a treatment of primary motivation would yield a standard D or drive value in each case which could be *substituted without distinction in the same single equation (2) yielding* ${}_S E_R$ in such a way as to mediate within the limits of errors of measurement the observable behavioral phenomena, $_sP_R$, $_st_R$, etc. If a program like that just outlined should turn out to be successful, it would practically require the use of multiple equations and so of the special signs which we have called symbolic constructs.

It is possible, of course, that animals are so constituted that a program such as has been implicitly outlined in the present paper can never be successfully carried through. Whatever may be our several *a priori* prejudices in the matter of the probable outcome of such a program, I think we should be able to agree upon two propositions relating to it. One is that if such equations could be found, they would greatly facilitate the theoretical integration of the behavior sciences as well as their practical application to the needs of man. The second proposition is that the only wholly convincing way of demonstrating this possibility is for some person or, preferably, some group of persons, actually to derive the equations in question and show that they do indeed mediate rather precisely the derivation of consequent behavior from the measured complex antecedent conditions as outlined above. Naturally such work will be done by those who hope for its achievement and believe in its possibility; those who do not share these hopes and beliefs will engage in other ventures. In the end, if the equations are derived successfully they will be available for all to use, and both groups should rejoice in the contemplation of the advantages ultimately to accrue. On the other hand, if the quest proves unsuccessful, those engaged in it will have had the thrill of high adventure and the satisfaction of having made a worthy effort.

Supplementary Note

Professor Lewin's manuscript did not become available to me until after the preceding portion of the present contribution to the symposium had been sent in. I have accordingly availed myself of the editor's permission to comment briefly in this note.

I am in complete agreement with Lewin when he remarks, "In other words, field theory can hardly be called a theory in the usual sense" (though possibly my understanding is not exactly what he intends). I believe the statement quoted above to be literally true when taken in conjunction with the methodology favored by Lewin.

I do not believe it to be true of field theory in general, nor in particular of the view of it put forward in a passage from Hilgard and Marquis, a portion of which is quoted by Lewin.[10]

The main reason why I believe the methodology favored by Lewin cannot yield a satisfactory natural-science theory of behavior, field or otherwise, is that his field when secured is primarily subjective and his preferred method of securing it is primarily introspective. As I read him, experimental extinction occurs because 'the individual catches on,' conditioned reactions are evoked in part because of a concurrent 'expectation,' and so on. Moreover, when attributed to inarticulate organisms, subjective entities such as 'expectancy,' 'catching on,' 'life space,' 'subjective probability,' and the like would seem to degenerate to sheer anthropomorphism; the investigator in effect projects himself into the rat, the cat, the dog, the monkey, the ape, or the young child, and says, "If I were in that situation I would perceive, cognize, feel, think, or hypothesize so and so."

The main trouble with the subjective and anthropomorphic methodology which Lewin seems to say he favors is that the entities which it yields are not really measurable, whereas the satisfactory verifiability of natural-science theory requires rather precise quantification; in so far as a theory or hypothesis is incapable of verification, it falls short of the scientific ideal. For example, the trouble with such a concept as expectancy, as employed by Hilgard and Lewin, is that when we attempt to verify the hypothesis in which it appears we cannot tell how much expectancy to expect; neither do we know the magnitude of the reaction which the expectancy is expected to mediate. This lack of determinate quantitative relationship to objectively observable and measurable states and events is, I

PAPER
13

[10] The entire passage is as follows:

"As I see it, the moment one expresses in any very general manner the various potentialities of behavior as dependent upon the simultaneous status of one or more variables, he has the substance of what is currently called field theory. My habit-family hypothesis is presumably a field principle in this sense. It is probable that my equation expressing the goal gradient hypothesis (gradient of reinforcement) and even the one expressing the generalization gradient (gradient of irradiation of Pavlov) might also qualify as bits of field theory. On the other hand, some might object to this usage on the ground that equations of this nature are not peculiar to gravitational or electromagnetic fields but are almost universal in natural science theory. Moreover the variables and the constants, together with their inter-relationships, which have so far appeared in equations expressing behavior theories, seem to differ radically from those which appear in the equations of physical field theories. The notable lack of such equations in current Gestalt field formulations, while paradoxical, is probably symptomatic. For such reasons I prefer to be rather sparing in my use of the expression 'field theory'; if one has the substance, the use of the term is scientifically unimportant however valuable it may be for purposes of propaganda. But if one means by field theory what I have indicated, I am all for it and I see no inherent disagreement on this point between stimulus-response theory and Gestalt theory."

believe, what Brunswik means by 'encapsulation.' If so, I quite agree with his objections to it.

It seems inevitable that as the behavior sciences evolve, the relationships where multiple causes are involved will be expressed more and more precisely in the form of equations; if someone wishes to liken this tendency to the phase in the evolution of gravitational and electromagnetic science, I have no objection. The main thing is that the task be accomplished, that the joint causal relationships be determined with a high degree of precision. It is hardly to be doubted that the behavior sciences are rapidly moving in this direction. On the other hand, in every culture there are to be found individuals who prefer their portraits to be artistically out of focus. Similarly, there will always be found scientists who prefer their theories to be vague, who fear that exact formulation will freeze them or constitute a kind of harness restricting the freedom of the workers. But two swallows do not make a spring. I cannot agree that American psychology is moving in the direction of more introspection, subjectivity, anthropomorphism, or vagueness.

It may be, of course, that I have totally misunderstood Lewin's meaning. I would like to believe that he has not been advocating the things to which I have taken exception above, because, if generally accepted, they would have an unfortunate effect on the development of the behavior sciences.

PAPER
13

Remarks to Mr. Hull's Supplementary Note by Kurt Lewin

Professor Hull states, "It may be, of course, that I have totally misunderstood Lewin's meaning. I would like to believe that he has not been advocating the things to which I have taken exception above." Happily, I feel sure he did misunderstand me. I have never expressed the opinion "that American psychology is moving in the direction of more introspection, subjectivity, anthropomorphism, or vagueness," and I would not agree to such a statement about psychology—American or otherwise.

Mr. Hull may not have realized that my little sketch, which describes a typical reconditioning set-up in common language, was not meant to be more than a 'description.' As Mr. Hull knows, if I present 'theories' they are usually expressed in mathematical terms of geometrical regions, vectors, and equations. In other words, in regard to theory we both feel compelled and justified to use a straight scientific terminology. But I have been so frequently accused of using too highbrow or too physicalistic a language that outside the level of 'explanatory theory,' I try to keep to the common language— even if speaking of conditioning situations. I, too, have been slightly bothered by certain terminologies; for instance, why use the term 'goal response' instead of the perfectly good common term 'consumption' if one actually does not mean all types of reactions to a goal, but just consummatory actions? There is a danger that the use of a terminology might put up the appearance of a theory when there is but an uncommon descriptive term inserted for a common term. It might be quite healthy for widening the range of the theories which should be considered as possible explanations for certain phenomena if one realized that these phenomena can be described in various ways.

Hull says: "For example, the trouble with such a concept as expectancy, as employed by Hilgard and Lewin, is that when we attempt to verify the hypothesis in which it appears we cannot tell how much expectancy to expect; neither do we know the magnitude of the reaction which the expectancy is expected to mediate"; but looking over the literature on the Level of Aspiration, Hull would quickly see that reliable quantitative data about 'expectancy' can be obtained, that the conditions for changing expectancy and the 'magnitude of reaction' can be studied, at least in human beings. I hope he will be pleased to see that it is even possible to make rather specific theoretical predictions about expectancy and to prove them experimentally (5).[11]   Certainly it is a legitimate question to ask at what age level or what phylogenetic level one can adequately speak of 'expectation,' how behavior differs in case of certain expectation or non-expectation, etc.   There may be differences of opinion among animal psychologists as to whether or not today a satisfactory operational definition can be given for this term in regard to animals. These, however, are technical problems and no question of principle is involved.

PAPER

13

I suppose Mr. Hull is not likely to be persuaded that the term 'expectation' is at least as well defined operationally—and, in my mind, better defined conceptually—as many terms in psychology of perception or conditioning which he accepts.   Neither am I likely to be persuaded that some of the alleged 'stimuli' referred to in conditioning are not altogether too vague, unrealistic, and inadequate, in spite of their emphasized front of 'objectivity.'   My main criticism against some of these concepts or theories has been their lack of analytical clarity (12), and I was pleased to notice recent changes in this direction.   These criticisms of specific points, however, did not make me feel justified to accuse anyone of 'advocating' vague, subjective and unanalytical thinking.   Mr. Hull knows as well as I do that in actual research we all have to give operational definitions, that no one yet has been able to eliminate from the operational definitions in psychology what so wittingly is called 'language reaction,' that we all have to be ready to prove the relia-

[11] References in Dr. Lewin's 'Remarks' are to be found in the bibliography of his original article, pp. 309–310.

bility of our observational instruments, and that all our data must be ready to face the same scrutinizing criteria for their significance. Why, then, bring up the problem of "advocating vagueness, introspection, subjectivity, anthropomorphism"? Frankly, I have been bored for a decade by the dispute about these fetishes of a theological controversy which in actual research has died long ago. I hope that this point of satiation will be reached by all of us soon because that would help considerably in straightening out the real issues.

These issues behind Mr. Hull's note seem to be two:

1. Are we ready to apply in an unemotional, unbiased and fair manner the same test of 'scientific objectivity'—on which we all pretty well agree—to such terms as 'expectation,' 'hope,' and even to such cultural or sociological terms as 'generosity,' 'fairness,' or 'friendship' that we apply to terms like 'nonsense syllables,' 'goal,' or 'goal response'?

2. Some aspects of the classical theory of association and conditioned reflex have correctly been characterized as 'psychology without organism.' I suppose that we all agree in principle that psychology cannot leave out the organism. But some of us seem to be too timid to believe that a real science of the organism is possible. They prefer the most peculiar round-about routes to a recognition of the simple principle that all psychological concepts, including 'physical stimuli,' have finally to be expressed in terms which relate to the organism in its particular state. These psychologists seem to suffer from a too generalized concept of subjectivity and to be haunted by the fear that someone will call them subjective in the sense of unscientific if they think in terms of the specific situation of the particular organism. I had felt that in Mr. Hull's and my original articles we had overcome some unnecessary misunderstandings in this matter.

Finally, a word about Hull's remark on the poor way in which such field theorists, as I, are handling field theory. I suppose that Mr. Hull will understand that even the cry "Let's take field theory away from the field theorists" would be sweet music for the latter. I am even optimistic enough to believe that, in time, Hull and I will agree as to the main characteristics of field theory, in particular that this is a method of analyzing causal relations and constructing theories and concepts rather than a 'theory' in the usual sense of the term. In the meantime what counts is that after a decade of refutation, psychology is turning more and more toward field theory.

REFERENCES

1. BORING, E. G. *The physical dimensions of consciousness.* New York: The Century Co., 1933.
2. BRUNSWIK, E. Psychology as a science of objective relations. *Philos. Sci.,* 1937, 4, 227–260.

3. ———. Organismic achievement and environmental probability. PSYCHOL. REV., 1943, 50,
4. BRIDGMAN, P. W. *The logic of modern physics.* New York: Macmillan Co., 1938.
5. BUXTON, C. E. Latent learning and the goal gradient hypothesis. *Contr. psychol. Theor.*, 1940, 2, No. 2.
6. CARNAP, R. *Philosophy and logical syntax.* London: Kegan Paul, Trench, Trubner and Co., Ltd., 1935.
7. HULL, C. L. *Principles of behavior.* D. Appleton-Century Co. (in press).
8. ———, HOVLAND, C. I., ROSS, R. T., HALL, M., PERKINS, D. T., & FITCH, F. B. *Mathematico-deductive theory of rote learning.* New Haven: Yale Univ. Press, 1940.
9. LEWIN, K. The conceptual representation and the measurement of psychological forces. *Contr. psychol. theor.*, 1938, 1, No. 4.
10. ———. Defining the 'field at a given time.' PSYCHOL. REV., 1943, 50, 292–310.
11. STEVENS, S. S. The operational basis of psychology. *Amer. J. Psychol.*, 1935, 47, 323–330.
12. TOLMAN, E. C. *Purposive behavior in animals and men.* New York: The Century Co., 1932.
13. WATSON, J. B. *Psychology from the standpoint of a behaviorist* (2nd ed.). Philadelphia: J. B. Lippincott Co., 1924.
14. WOODROW, H. The problem of general quantitative laws in psychology. *Psychol. Bull.*, 1942, 39, 1–27.

Reprinted from PSYCHOLOGICAL REVIEW, Vol. 52, No. 2, March, 1945
Printed in U. S. A.

THE PLACE OF INNATE INDIVIDUAL AND SPECIES DIFFERENCES IN A NATURAL–SCIENCE THEORY OF BEHAVIOR

BY CLARK L. HULL

Institute of Human Relations, Yale University

INTRODUCTION

The natural-science approach to behavior theory presents two major tasks. The first is to make a satisfactory working analysis of the various behavior processes; this consists in deriving, *i.e.*, deducing, from the primary laws of the system the characteristic observable phenomena of the behavior process in question as displayed by the modal or average organism under given conditions. This is the task which engages the efforts of the traditional academic theorist (4, 6). It leads to attempts to deduce, and thereby explain, such processes as simple discrimination learning, simple trial-and-error learning, complex discrimination learning, compound (chain) trial-and-error learning, the acquisition of skill, rote learning, generalizing abstraction, the evolution of concepts, primary motivation, secondary motivation, the assembly of behavior segments in problem solution, abstract (verbal) reasoning (3, pp. 220, 244), fallacies, rationalizations, delusions—in short, to an analysis of all sorts and varieties of adaptive and maladaptive behavior.

The second major task of a natural-science approach to behavior theory concerns the problem of innate behavioral differences under identical conditions between different species and between the individuals within a given species. It involves such questions as these: Given two rats with similar antecedent life histories, why can one learn a particular maze more quickly than the other? Why is it that an occasional rat can master the double alternation temporal maze problem, whereas most rats, apparently, will never master it regardless of the amount of training devoted to the task (7, 8)? Why is it that dogs can master certain tasks impossible to rats, that apes can master certain tasks impossible to dogs, and that men can master very many tasks impossible to apes? Why does one of two human individuals with comparable previous environmental influences progress satisfactorily in school while the other is a dismal failure? Why does one individual under given circumstances develop a weak, yielding personality, a second develop an aggressive, overbearing personality, and a third develop a furtive, secretive personality? Such questions could be multiplied almost indefinitely.

Both types of task cry loudly and insistently for completion. But most neglected of all is the relationship between the two approaches. We are accordingly here devoting ourselves briefly to the consideration of this relationship, with special reference to its bearing on

PAPER
14

55

the theory of individual and species differences in behavior potentiality.

One obvious, even commonplace, cause of individual differences in behavior is a difference in the previous histories of the organism involved. Differences in individual histories inevitably result in different sets of habits in each organism and so in different behavior under exactly similar external stimulating conditions. This environmental source of individual behavioral differences is of immense importance and there is no intention here of minimizing it. There is much reason to believe, however, that even if organisms could be subjected to identical environmental conditions from the moment of conception, great differences would still be displayed in the behavior of different species as a whole and in the behavior of the individual organisms of each species. Such differences must presumably be regarded as dependent upon, *i.e.*, derived from, differences in the innate or original nature and constitution of the individual organism. We shall accordingly call them *innate* differences.

THE THEORETICAL DILEMMA PRESENTED BY INNATE INDIVIDUAL DIFFERENCES AND ITS FORMAL SOLUTION

At this point in our analysis a critical dilemma emerges. The natural-science theory of behavior being developed by the present author and his associates assumes that all behavior of the individuals of a given species and that of all species of mammals, including man, occurs according to the same set of primary laws. These laws typically take the form of equations. Prediction of the behavior theoretically to be expected under particular conditions is made by substituting quantitative values representing the situation in question in the equations which are statements of the laws. *But if the laws (equations) are*

the same for all organisms, the equal values corresponding to identical reaction-instigating conditions when substituted in these equations would necessarily produce identical predictions of behavioral outcome for all organisms. This, of course, amounts to a denial of innate individual and species differences.

The paradox just proposed probably arises in the main from the ambiguity of the notion of identical natural laws. This ambiguity may be clarified by a citation from elementary physics. The law which expresses the distance (*s*) that a body will fall from rest within a certain time (*t*) is given by the equation,

$$s = \tfrac{1}{2}gt^2.$$

The *form* of the equation represents the law. But nearly all such equations contain one or more of what are known as *empirical constants*, values which must be determined by empirical investigation before the equation can be used in actual prediction. The *g* in the above equation is such a constant. Now, it has long been known that *g* varies appreciably from one point on the earth to another. For example, *g* at Hammerfest is 32.2364 feet, whereas at Madras it is 32.0992 feet and at New York it is 32.1594 feet. But this variation in the value of *g* does not change the *general form* of the equation, and so is not regarded as constituting a violation of the generality of the law.

This example of a natural law containing a variable empirical constant paves the way for the statement of the hypothesis which is believed to offer a solution to the paradox presented by the assumption of strict natural primary behavioral laws and the assumption of important innate individual and species differences in behavior potentiality. The hypothesis may be stated very simply: *Innate individual and species differences find expression in the 'empirical con-*

stants' which are essential constituents of the equations expressing the primary and secondary laws of behavior. This is the central point of the present paper.

A FORMAL ILLUSTRATION OF THE WORKING OF THE HYPOTHESIS

An example worked out in detail may make clear the meaning of the hypothesis just presented. Though empirical validation is not yet available, there is some *a priori* reason to believe that a close approximation to the discrimination threshold or difference limen (DL) of any individual organism (or the mean discrimination threshold for the individuals of a given species) when based upon a large number of distributed trials at the limit of training in simple separate-stimulus-presentation discrimination, is given by the equation (6),

$$DL = \frac{\log \dfrac{M_E}{M_E - 3\sigma_0}}{h + i} \quad (1)$$

where,

DL is the difference limen as obtained by the method of separate stimulus presentation in j.n.d. units, the latter as determined on a standard group of organisms under conditions of *joint* stimulus presentation (the method ordinarily employed),[1]

[1] In simple *separate*-stimulus-presentation discrimination, the times of the delivery of the stimuli to be discriminated are spaced far enough apart (*e.g.,* twenty-four hours) for the perseverative stimulus trace of the first of the pair to be dissipated before the delivery of the second of the pair. In simple *joint*-stimulus-presentation discrimination, the procedure commonly employed in discrimination experiments, the second stimulus is presented soon enough after the presentation of the first for the stimulus perseveration of the first still to be active in the nervous system when the second occurs. This latter circumstance presents the possibility of an afferent neural interaction effect between the two impulses (4), which presumably favors discrimination. For this reason, the difference limen (DL) as

M_E is the magnitude of the excitatory potential of the organism at the point of reinforcement in wats (4, p. 239),

σ_0 is the standard deviation of the behavioral oscillation function (4, p. 319),

h is the exponent appearing in the equation which represents the generalization of positive habit strength (4, p. 199),

and

i is the exponent appearing in the equation which represents the generalization of extinctive inhibition (4, pp. 264, 283).

In order to show how this equation illustrates the present hypothesis, let it be assumed that we have a standard situation in which $M_E = 70$ wats, $h = .01$, $i = .01$, and $\sigma_0 = 6$ wats. Substituting these values in equation 1, we have

PAPER 14

$$DL = \frac{\log \dfrac{70}{70 - 3 \times 6}}{.01 + .01}$$

$$= \frac{\log \dfrac{70}{70 - 18}}{.02}$$

$$= \frac{\log 1.346}{.02}$$

$$= \frac{.12905}{.02}$$

$$= 6.45.$$

determined by separate stimulus presentation will be different from, and presumably considerably greater than, the j.n.d. as determined by joint stimulus presentation. Accordingly in equation 1 the DL (of separate-stimulus-presentation discrimination) is expressed in terms of the (presumptive) j.n.d. of joint-stimulus-presentation discrimination. This is the reason why in the illustrative computations which follow, the DL (of separate-stimulus-presentation discrimination) is represented as several times (*e.g.,* 6.45) the size of the j.n.d. as determined by joint-stimulus-presentation discrimination.

This value (6.45) will be taken as the basis of comparison with a succession of other situations in which one empirical constant will be varied at a time.

Suppose, first, that M_E be increased from 70 wats to 90 wats. We then have

$$DL^{\cdot} = \frac{\log \dfrac{90}{90 - 3 \times 6}}{.01 + .01}$$

$$= \frac{\log \dfrac{90}{90 - 18}}{.02}$$

$$= \frac{\log 1.25}{.02}$$

$$= \frac{.09691}{.02}$$

$$= 4.84.$$

Thus, increasing M_E from 70 to 90 improves the discrimination by decreasing the discrimination threshold from 6.45 units to 4.84 units. Generalizing on the preceding considerations, we arrive at our first exemplary corollary concerning individual (or species) differences:

I. *Other things equal, in simple separate-stimulus-presentation discrimination by distributed trials, that organism (or species) which has the larger reaction potential will have the finer (smaller) discrimination threshold.*

Suppose, next, that either h or i be increased from .01 to .02. We then have

$$DL = \frac{\log \dfrac{70}{70 - 3 \times 6}}{.01 + .02}$$

$$= \frac{\log \dfrac{70}{70 - 18}}{.03}$$

$$= \frac{\log 1.346}{.03}$$

$$= \frac{.12905}{.03}$$

$$= 4.30.$$

Thus, increasing either h or i from .01 to .02 (thereby steepening one or the other gradient of generalization) decreases the reaction threshold from 6.45 to 4.30. Generalizing on the preceding considerations we arrive at our second exemplary corollary concerning individual (or species) differences:

II. *Other things equal, in simple separate-stimulus-presentation discrimination by distributed trials, that organism (or species) which has the steeper excitatory and/or inhibitory generalization gradient will have the finer (smaller) discrimination threshold.*

Finally, let us suppose that the value of σ_0 be increased from 6 to 7 wats. We then have

$$DL = \frac{\log \dfrac{70}{70 - 3 \times 7}}{.01 + .01}$$

$$= \frac{\log \dfrac{70}{70 - 21}}{.02}$$

$$= \frac{\log 1.429}{.02}$$

$$= \frac{.15503}{.02}$$

$$= 7.75.$$

Thus the increase in σ_0 from 6 to 7 units *increases* the discrimination threshold from 6.45 to 7.75. Generalizing on these considerations we arrive at our third exemplary corollary concerning individual (or species) differences:

III. *Other things equal, in simple separate-stimulus-presentation discrimination by distributed trials, that organism (or species) which has the larger standard deviation of oscillatory variability (σ_0) will have the coarser (larger) discrimination threshold.*[2]

[2] While the present paper was in press, a review of *Principles of Behavior* (4) appeared (*J. genet. Psychol.*, 1944, **65**, 3–52), in which it was pointed out that the book contained no

PAPER
14

POSSIBLE BEARING OF THE PRESENT
HYPOTHESIS ON FUTURE RESEARCH

From the three preceding examples we are able to see not only how in general the variation in empirical constants can account for individual differences in an adaptive capacity wholly within the framework of a strict natural-science theory, but specifically how variations in three empirical constants may influence adaptive capacity in simple separate-phase discrimination. Differences in M_E, h, i, and σ_0 accordingly play the role of *primary* individual differences, whereas the resulting differences in the $D\,L$ become *secondary* individual differences. This means that if independent determinations could be made of M_E, h, i, and σ_0 for a given organism (or species) its discrimination threshold at a particular point on a given stimulus continuum could be calculated directly from equation 1.

At this point we encounter a second paradox. This is that from the analysis of animal behavior in the main (6) there emerges quite unexpectedly the indication for a new approach to the prediction of individual differences in human aptitudes (2, p. 21 ff.). It is only necessary to consider the $D\,L$ as the criterion score of an aptitude, and M_E, h, i, and σ_0 as test scores, to see the relationship to aptitude prediction, though there are significant differences. Equation 1 as an aptitude-prediction formula is radically different from the multiple-regression equation traditionally employed in aptitude prediction (2, p. 457 ff.), and M_E, h, i, and σ_0 purport at least to be

"capacity laws," *i.e.*, no "principles that relate differences of learning capacity to differences of species, age, and IQ." Actually the principles put forward above embrace not only learning, but the whole field of behavior. It may be added that the present paper has been taken with only minor changes from the manuscript of a book now in preparation (6) which is to be the second volume in the series on behavior theory.

innate tendencies. Thus M_E, h, i, and σ_0 are closely analogous to the group factors in Spearman's approach to aptitudes, though the present methodology of identifying the 'factors' is also radically different (10) from that employed either by Spearman or by any factor analysis based on correlation. Even so, one factor in our exemplary analysis (σ_0) corresponds closely to one which Spearman has stressed. Symptomatic of the correspondence is the fact that Spearman has called this factor, 'oscillation' (10, p. 319 ff.).

It is important to note that the present type of analysis may also be applied to differences which take place in the behavior of organisms as the result of drug action and various pathological conditions. Familiar examples of drug action are those of caffeine on the one hand and the bromides on the other. These were investigated to some extent by Pavlov and his pupils (9, pp. 127, 300), but not from the point of view of changes in the empirical behavior constants as here conceived; the latter seems not to have been attempted as yet by anyone.

Another extremely intriguing research possibility would be to ascertain what behavior constants are changed, and in what manner, when individuals pass into mild or violent manic states with the characteristic distractibility, 'flight of ideas,' and so forth. A possible molar cause of the marked lack of adaptive continuity in the behavior of such individuals may be found to lie in a considerably shortened duration in the perseverative stimulus trace (4, p. 42). Another possible molar cause may be that the magnitude of the strictly internal component of the oscillation function (4, pp. 304 ff.) is greatly increased. The research opportunities offered by these theoretico-empirical approaches to psychopathology are believed to be typical of many to be found in this enor-

PAPER
14

mously important field. It is not inconceivable that such researches might have considerable practical value by suggesting causal factors and therapeutic procedures.

It is to be regretted that no factual evidence in support either of the central hypothesis of the present paper as to the nature of individual or species differences, or of the soundness of equation 1 can be given at this time. Judging by the author's experience to date, the task of empirically validating quantitative secondary molar behavioral laws (represented by equation 1 above) is very difficult, and the validation of equations representing the primary behavioral laws (and the incidental determination of the values of the empirical constants appearing in these equations) is excessively so. Despite the fact that a program of empirical research directed to this latter end has been in progress in the author's laboratory for more than a year, it must be confessed that not a single empirical constant of the twenty or so contained in his systematic approach to behavior (4; 5, pp. 176–177) has been satisfactorily determined. However, a very promising technique is being developed and we now have renewed hope.

SUMMARY

A strict quantitative natural-science approach to the theory of behavior presents a serious dilemma as to the place in it occupied by individual and species differences. This dilemma is easily resolved on a purely formal level by assuming that the *forms* of the equations representing the behavioral laws of both individuals and species are identical, and that the differences between individuals and species will be found in the empirical constants which are essential components of such equations. The validity of this hypothesis would seem to be susceptible to an empirical determination but as yet the necessary experimental work has not been performed. If the hypothesis should turn out to be true, it is conceivable that it would open up an entirely new approach to the scientific study of the nature of aptitudes and liabilities. If this should occur it would mark a genuine junction between pure and applied psychology, which of late have seemed to be drifting farther and farther apart (1). It might even lead to a situation such that clinical psychologists, aptitude psychologists, psychiatrists, penologists, sociologists, and cultural anthropologists will study attentively the theory of animal behavior as an essential background, at least where research and creative scholarship are contemplated. This would be in accordance with the practice of engineers who now receive training in the basic disciplines of mathematics, physics, and chemistry throughout the most of their academic training.

REFERENCES

1. BABCOCK, H. The bottleneck in psychology as illustrated by the Terman vocabulary. PSYCHOL. REV., 1943, 50, 244–254.
2. HULL, C. L. *Aptitude testing*. Yonkers-on-Hudson, New York: World Book Co., 1928.
3. ——. The mechanism of the assembly of behavior segments in novel combinations suitable for problem solution. PSYCHOL. REV., 1935, 42, 219–245.
4. ——. *Principles of behavior*. New York: D. Appleton-Century Co., 1943.
5. ——. *Psychological memoranda, 1940–1944*. Bound sets of mimeographed sheets on file in the libraries of the University of Iowa, University of North Carolina, and Yale University.
6. ——. *Elementary theory of individual behavior* (in prep.).
7. HUNTER, W. S. The behavior of raccoons in a double alternation temporal maze. *J. genetic Psychol.*, 1928, 35, 374–388.
8. ——, & NAGGE, J. W. The white rat and the double alternation temporal maze. *J. genetic Psychol.*, 1931, 39, 303–319.
9. PAVLOV, I. P. *Conditioned reflexes* (trans. by G. V. Anrep). London: Oxford Univ. Press, 1927.
10. SPEARMAN, C. *The abilities of man*. New York: The Macmillan Co., 1927.

Reprinted from Psychological Review, Vol. 53, No. 3, May, 1945
Printed in U. S. A.

THE DISCRIMINATION OF STIMULUS CONFIGURATIONS AND THE HYPOTHESIS OF AFFERENT NEURAL INTERACTION [1]

BY CLARK L. HULL

*Institute of Human Relations,
Yale University*

I. INTRODUCTION

Long ago William James called attention to the fact that a lion behind the bars of a cage presents a very different behavior situation from that of a lion in front of the bars. Ordinary observation abundantly confirms the generalization that organisms react to stimulus combinations, as such, as well as to the separate stimulus elements making up the compound (**9, 10**). A red light in a drugstore window causes no retardation in the locomotion of a pedestrian, but a red light above a street intersection causes him to halt; neither the red light alone nor the street intersection alone would, as a stimulus aggregate, halt locomotion, but the combination or configuration of both does so. When a person is riding in an automobile and approaches a red light at a street intersection, his behavior is different if he is behind the steering wheel than it would be if he were merely a passenger. In the former case the foot is removed from the throttle and may press down on the brake, but in the latter case, especially if the passenger is in the rear seat, usually no foot movements at all occur unless an accident is threatened.

The examples just given are all cases of differential response to identical elements in *simultaneous* stimulus configurations.

A second and closely related behavioral situation involves *temporal* stimulus configurations. If, after suitable instructions, I spell out the letters N–O, the literate subject reacts promptly by pronouncing the word 'No'; but if I spell out the letters O–N, the subject unhesitatingly pronounces the word 'On.' The same letters (stimulus aggregates) are employed in both cases but their temporal order is different, *i.e.*, they constitute distinct temporal configurations. A situation possessing greater dramatic potentialities is that in which someone apologizes after stepping on our toes as contrasted with apologizing first and *then* stepping on our toes. The apology in the first case would be a courtesy, in the second it would be an affront. An experimental example of a temporal stimulus configuration is found in a sequence of musical notes making up a melody such as, 'Home, Sweet Home.' Humphrey has shown that subjects trained to respond to an isolated tone which appears repeatedly in this melody, but *not* to respond to certain other isolated tones which also appear in it, usually responded to none of the tones when they were presented in the temporal sequence of the melody itself (**4**, pp. 198, 237).

These examples could be extended almost indefinitely. The ubiquity of stimulus configurations in adaptive situations really comes home to us

[1] Portion of a paper read before the staff of the Institute of Human Relations, January 18, 1943 (**2**, pp. 99–103), somewhat revised, and supplemented with portions of a paper read before the same group on December 1, 1941 (**2**, pp. 86–98), and a seminar memorandum bearing the date of December 27, 1943 (**2**, p. 179). The writer is indebted to J. F. Brown, W. O. Orbison, J. P. Seward, and K. W. Spence for criticizing a preliminary draft of the manuscript.

PAPER
15

133

when we attempt to think of a natural example (or to devise an artificial one) where the combination or configuration of the stimuli as such plays no role whatever. This aspect of behavior dynamics has been and still is greatly neglected, perhaps especially by psychologists trained in the British tradition. The *Gestalt* psychologists are unquestionably correct in stressing its importance.

II. AN EXPERIMENTAL EXAMPLE OF STIMULUS-CONFIGURATIONAL DISCRIMINATION

The essential nature of learning to discriminate between stimulus configurations is perhaps most sharply and unequivocally brought out in the controlled experimental procedures originally devised by the workers in Pavlov's laboratory (**7**, p. 141 ff.). These experiments are especially illuminating because they represent quantitative results from the limiting case of stimulus configurational discrimination, namely, that between the configuration and its essential components taken separately. Recently the Russian experimental procedures were adapted by Woodbury to the motor response of dogs (**11**). As our illustrative example we shall take Woodbury's experiment employing the dog Dick, in which the stimulus configuration as a whole was positive, and the stimulus components were negative.[2]

The dog stood on a laboratory table within a wooden stock or pen. Just in front of his head was a light wooden bar. Early in the experiment, whenever the animal nosed this bar upward

[2] Woodbury reports experiments on five dogs: one trained to discriminate between the component stimulus aggregates S_H and S_L, one trained positively to the simultaneous stimulus configuration, one trained negatively to the simultaneous stimulus configuration, one trained positively to the temporal stimulus configuration, and one trained negatively to the temporal stimulus configuration.

an electromagnetic mechanism would release a cylinder of appetizing dog food, which dropped into the food dish. Later, a thin wooden shutter was lowered between the dog and the bar, and an auditory configuration consisting of a high-pitched buzzer (S_H) and a low-pitched buzzer (S_L) was introduced. On the positive trials the two buzzers would be sounded simultaneously; then the shutter would be lifted and the bar exposed, the dog would nose the bar upward, the food would rattle down the chute into the food dish, and the dog would eat it greedily. On other occasions one or the other buzzer would be sounded alone, after which the shutter would be raised exactly as with the full configuration. In this latter case, however, if the dog nosed the bar the apparatus would give no food. Out of each 100 trials, 50 were positive with the configuration followed by reinforcement, and 50 were negative with one or the other of the stimulus components, 25 of each, followed by no reinforcement. The three types of stimuli were delivered according to a carefully planned randomization. This alternate reinforcement of the reaction to one stimulus arrangement and non-reinforcement of the reaction to a contrasted stimulus arrangement is called *differential reinforcement*.

Woodbury's results show that this type of learning is rather difficult for dogs. After some 1300 trials, however, the animal had approximately perfected the discrimination. The figure shows the course of the positive learning for the compound or configuration, and of the negative learning for each of the components.

III. A CONVENTIONAL BUT FALSE ANALYSIS OF CONFIGURATIONAL-DISCRIMINATION LEARNING

We may now turn to the intriguing question of how the learning repre-

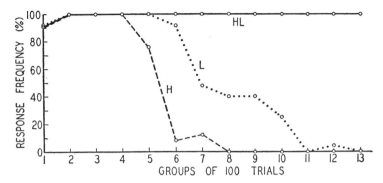

Graph showing the course of the learning by Woodbury's dog Dick of an auditory configurational discrimination, in which the compound made up of the high- and the low-pitched buzzers presented simultaneously (*HL*) was positive, and the separate components (*H* and *L*) were negative. (Adapted from Woodbury, **11.**)

sented in the figure is to be explained. According to what principles does it take place, *i.e.*, from what principles, if any, may it be deduced? It has frequently been supposed that this type of learning cannot be explained by means of behavioristic, non-mentalistic principles. Indeed, up to quite recently this view has been practically undisputed. Unfortunately the logic behind this conclusion has been so clouded with metaphysical and other vague and irrelevant considerations that the exact grounds for it have not been entirely evident. In order to make them quite explicit we shall begin our exposition of the theory of the discrimination learning of stimulus configurations with a quantitative theoretical analysis which takes this mistaken approach and, naturally, eventuates in this erroneous conclusion:

1. Let it be assumed that through learning, the stimulus compound in the experiment just described, S_H and S_L, has been conditioned to reaction, R, to the extent of 80 units, *i.e.*,

$$\left.\begin{array}{c} S_H \\ S_L \end{array}\right\} \,-\,-\,-\rightarrow R = 80 \text{ units of reaction potential,}$$

where S_H is the stimulus produced by the high-pitched buzzer and S_L is the stimulus produced by the low-pitched buzzer, and where the combination, $\left.\begin{array}{c} S_H \\ S_L \end{array}\right\}$ or $\left\{\begin{array}{c} S_H \\ S_L \end{array}\right.$, represents the simultaneous presentation of S_H and S_L.

2. This means that,

$$\left[\begin{array}{l} S_H \,-\,-\,-\rightarrow R = 40 \text{ units of reaction} \\ \qquad\qquad\qquad\qquad\text{potential} \\ S_L \,-\,-\,-\rightarrow R = 40 \text{ units of reaction} \\ \qquad\qquad\qquad\qquad\text{potential.} \end{array}\right.$$

$$\overline{\quad\quad}$$

Total = 80 units of reaction potential.

3. Next, by unreinforced reaction evocation,

$$S_H \,-\,-\,-\rightarrow R$$

taken by itself is gradually reduced by experimental extinction to a strength of zero, and, in a similar manner,

$$S_L \,-\,-\,-\rightarrow R$$

is also reduced to a strength of zero.

4. It follows from (3) that when S_H and S_L are subsequently presented together, their combined strength for the evocation of R will be zero, *i.e.*,

PAPER

15

$$\begin{cases} S_H - - - \to R = 0 \text{ units of reaction} \\ \qquad\qquad\qquad \text{potential} \\ S_L - - - \to R = 0 \text{ units of reaction} \\ \qquad\qquad\qquad \text{potential} \end{cases}$$

$$\text{Total} = 0 \text{ units of reaction potential.}$$

5. But a habit of zero strength cannot mediate action (1, p. 344).

6. It accordingly follows from (4) and (5) that when the components of a configuration have no power to evoke a reaction, the stimulus configuration resulting from their combination will also have no power to evoke the reaction.

7. But this conclusion is patently false because, as shown in the figure, the dog really did learn to perform the discrimination. Therefore something must be seriously wrong with one or more of the assumptions upon which the analysis is based.

And so it has frequently been concluded that a non-mentalistic, objective, or so-called 'mechanistic' or 'atomistic' psychology is necessarily inadequate for the explanation of configurational-discrimination learning and of the differential reaction to stimulus configurations in general.[3]

IV. A More Adequate Analysis of Configurational-Discrimination Learning

It is true that the analysis of configurational learning just given is quite inadequate and that this fact does reveal a serious inadequacy in the assumptions upon which the deduction was based. It does not follow from

[3] The author has not been able to understand exactly what the terms *mechanistic* and *atomistic* mean when applied to behavior theory. However, the ultimate question is not whether the principles of a system are mechanistic, atomistic, field-force, phenomenalistic, or holistic. It is solely: Do the principles mediate a quantitative deduction of the relevant phenomena?

this, however, that all non-mentalistic approaches are similarly ineffective. We proceed now to present an analysis which, while by no means offered as the last word on the subject, is believed to mark a definite advance over the preceding one.

1. At the outset it is to be noted that associative connections are not conceived as being set up directly between stimuli (S) and responses (R); the connections between stimuli and responses are believed to be indirect, the intervening links being afferent and efferent neural impulses, s and r, just as in the conventional accounts of neurophysiology. The relationship is conceived to be as represented by the following diagram:

$$S \longrightarrow s - - - \to r \longrightarrow R$$

in which the arrow with the broken shaft represents the acquired associative connection or habit, and the other arrows represent non-learned neurophysiological connections.

2. The next assumption which we need to take note of is that of *afferent neural interaction* (1, p. 42 ff.). This hypothesis is to the effect that all afferent neural impulses (s) which are active within the nervous system at any given time change one another more or less into a state represented by the symbol $\breve{s}$.[4] For example, in the Woodbury experiment, S_H and S_L when presented separately would yield the afferent impulses s_H and s_L respectively, but when presented simultaneously as a stimulus configuration they would result in $\breve{s}_H$ and $\breve{s}_L$. Now, $\breve{s}_H$ and s_H are assumed to resemble each

[4] It is highly probable, as Köhler suggests (5, p. 132) that this interaction occurs in the gray matter of the nervous system, the most of which is found in the brain. The term *afferent* in the expression, 'afferent neural interaction,' refers to the neural impulses mainly involved, rather than to the point at which the interaction presumably occurs.

other in that both fall on the same generalization continuum, but to differ in that a reaction conditioned to one will be evoked by the other with a greater or less diminution according to the amount of afferent neural interaction that has occurred. Thus the functional consequences of afferent neural interaction are thought of in the molar conceptual framework of stimulus generalization.[5]

3. From the foregoing it follows that the quantitative reaction evocation situation assumed by the false analysis given above becomes transformed into:

$$\begin{cases} S_H \longrightarrow \check{s}_H ---\!\!\rightarrow r \longrightarrow R = 40 \text{ units of reaction potential} \\ S_L \longrightarrow \check{s}_L ---\!\!\rightarrow r \longrightarrow R = 40 \text{ units of reaction potential} \end{cases}$$

$$\text{Total} = 80 \text{ units of reaction potential.}$$

4. But, by (2), in the separate presentations of S_H and S_L during the extinction process there results:

$S_H \longrightarrow s_H$, instead of $\check{s}_H$ which by (3) was conditioned to $r \longrightarrow R$,

and

$S_L \longrightarrow s_L$, instead of $\check{s}_L$ which by (3) was conditioned to $r \longrightarrow R$.

5. Since $\check{s}_H$ and s_H are on the same stimulus continuum (step 2), s_H will, by the principle of stimulus generalization (1, pp. 183 ff.), tend to evoke R, but less strongly than would $\check{s}_H$ which was originally conditioned to it. Let us say that in the shift from $\check{s}_H$ to s_H

[5] It is well known, for example, that a reaction conditioned to one tonal frequency (S_1) such as 1000 vibrations per second, will be evoked by tones at other frequencies (S_2) such as 1200, 1500, or 1800, though in general the strength of the tendency to such evocations decreases progressively as the difference (d) between the frequencies of S_1 and S_2 increases; specifically, this generalization gradient is believed to be a negative growth function of d when the latter is measured in j.n.d.'s (1, pp. 183 ff.).

there will be a loss of 50 per cent in reaction evocation potential. On this assumption, then, we have

$s_H ---\!\!\rightarrow r \longrightarrow R = 50$ per cent of 40 units, or 20 units,

and

$s_L ---\!\!\rightarrow r \longrightarrow R = 50$ per cent of 40 units, or 20 units.

6. Now, s_H and s_L are the afferent impulses which evoke the reactions extinguished during the process of differential reinforcement. This means that only 20 units of habit strength will need to be converted into inhibition by the extinction process associated with S_H and S_L respectively. It also means that when this inhibition is generated it will be conditioned to s_H and s_L (1, pp. 281 ff.) and not to $\check{s}_H$ and $\check{s}_L$, i.e.,

$s_H ---\!\!\rightarrow I = 20$ units of inhibitory potential

and

$s_L ---\!\!\rightarrow I = 20$ units of inhibitory potential.

7. But when the complete stimulus configuration, $\begin{Bmatrix} S_H \\ S_L \end{Bmatrix}$, is again presented following the extinction process, the afferent impulses active in the joint reaction evocation will be $\check{s}_H$ and $\check{s}_L$, and not s_H and s_L which were involved in the extinction process.

8. Now, inhibition generalizes with loss very much as does positive habit strength, and, so far as is now known, with the same steepness of gradient (1, p. 275). We accordingly assume that the inhibition generalizes from s_H

PAPER

15

and s_L back to $\check{s}_H$ and $\check{s}_L$ respectively, also with a loss of 50 per cent. Thus 50 per cent of the 20 units of inhibition attached to s_H, or 10 units, will generalize back to $\check{s}_H$, and similarly 10 units of inhibition will generalize from s_L to $\check{s}_L$.

9. As a result, the 40 units of habit strength originally attached to $\check{s}_H$ by the conditioning process, will be diminished to the extent of the 10 units of inhibition generalized to it from s_H. Exactly the same reasoning will apply to $\check{s}_L$ and s_L. From this it follows that we have as the reaction potentiality of the configuration at the conclusion of the extinction process of the separate components,

$$\begin{cases} S_H \longrightarrow \check{s}_H \dashrightarrow r \longrightarrow R = 40 - 10 = 30 \text{ units of reaction potential} \\ S_L \longrightarrow s_L \dashrightarrow r \longrightarrow R = 40 - 10 = 30 \text{ units of reaction potential} \end{cases}$$

$$\text{Total} = 60 \text{ units of reaction potential}$$

PAPER
15

10. Accordingly we find that by the present analysis the process of differential reinforcement ends with 60 units of effective reaction potential, instead of zero units as by the false analysis given above. This, of course, is ample to yield prompt, vigorous, and regular reaction to the stimulus configuration, and yet no reaction whatever will be evoked by either isolated stimulus component.[6] Thus it

[6] The reader should take note of the fact that the example of stimulus configuration discrimination learning just worked out has, in the interest of expository clarity, been somewhat over-simplified. In particular, the above computations have neglected the influence of certain complex considerations such as the physiological summation (+) of excitatory and inhibitory habit tendencies (1, p. 223), and the presumptive existence of subthreshold reaction potentials (1, p. 322 ff.). It is believed, however, that these factors are not of sufficient magnitude to alter materially the theoretical outcome under the assumed conditions. If a more meticulous derivation is desired it may be found elsewhere (1, p. 349 ff.).

is possible quite easily to derive in a quantitative manner the differential response of organisms to stimulus configurations, without resort to either mentalistic or phenomenalistic hypotheses.

V. QUANTITATIVE ASPECTS OF AFFERENT NEURAL INTERACTION

It is to be noted that the novelty in the above derivation does not lie in any of the principles employed, but rather in their choice and the manner of their combination. Even so one of the principles, that of afferent neural interaction, has been very little employed as yet in theoretical studies[7] so that some elaboration of the matter here may not be out of place, particularly on the quantitative side.

In Pavlov's classical statement of this principle he remarks (7, p. 70):

When the additional stimulus or its fresh trace left in the hemispheres coincides with the action of the positive stimulus, there must result some sort of special physiological fusion of the effect of the stimuli into one compound excitation *partly differing from and partly resembling* the positive one. [Italics ours.]

In the italicized portion of this quotation, Pavlov clearly raises the question

[7] Köhler, more than anyone else, has employed the principle, or one closely resembling it (5, p. 132; 6, p. 55). Tolman also has used an interaction principle according to which "stimuli S_1, S_1S_2, and S_2 $\cdots$ interacting among themselves" tend "as a whole to evoke the unified sign-Gestalt" (8, pp. 137–138). These words, coupled with their context, seem to suggest an interaction among the stimuli as distinguished from the afferent neural impulses released by the stimuli, though Tolman's usage of the term 'stimulus' may include both.

of the *amount* of afferent neural interaction. So far as the present writer's knowledge goes, this is the only specific reference yet made by any writer to the quantitative aspects of this principle.

Now, as science develops its theory tends inevitably to become quantitative. This means that before the principle of afferent neural interaction can be of much value in the behavior sciences, we shall need to know the major molar laws of its occurrence, *i.e.*, it must be possible to determine how much interaction results in the various configurational conditions under which it is assumed to arise. We shall, for example, need to know the quantitative law of the amount of afferent interaction that takes place between neural impulses within the same receptor field; between those from different receptor fields; between the neural impulses arising from different intensities of stimulation; between those from stimuli which arise at different distances from each other on the same generalization continuum; between old and young perseverative stimulus traces; and so on. So far as the present writer is aware, no quantitative experimental work bearing directly on these problems has yet been reported in the reflexological, the behavioristic, or the *Gestalt* literature. Indeed, no method of measuring the amount of interaction and no unit for this measurement appear yet to have been proposed. As a tentative contribution to this end, the following suggestions are offered:

It has already been pointed out (footnote 5) that the afferent neural interaction hypothesis has a molar setting of stimulus generalization. Let it be supposed, then, that the molar law of stimulus generalization has been determined with quantitative precision, and that it turns out to be

$$s'E_R = sE_R \times 10^{-jd} \qquad (1)$$

where

sE_R is the potentiality of S (the stimulus originally conditioned) to evoke R,

$s'E_R$ is the potentiality of some other stimulus, S' (which lies on the same stimulus continuum as S), to evoke R,

j is an empirical constant depending upon the steepness of slope of the generalization gradient (here assumed to have the value of .0135), and

d is the difference between S and S' in j.n.d. units.

On these assumptions, we may rewrite equation 1 as

$$\varepsilon'E_R = \varepsilon E_R \times 10^{-jd} \qquad (2)$$

where

ε represents the afferent neural impulses as originally conditioned to R, and
ε' represents these afferent neural impulses as changed through the introduction of a new stimulus element into the configuration, which would precipitate Pavlovian external inhibition (1, p. 217 ff.).

It is evident from the foregoing that just as d in equation 1 is a measure of the difference between S and S', so in equation 2, d becomes a measure of the difference between ε and ε', *i.e.*, of the amount of afferent neural interaction generated in a Pavlovian external-inhibition situation. It accordingly becomes desirable to express d as a function of the other elements in equation 2. Thus we have, by easy stages:

$$\varepsilon'E_R = \frac{\varepsilon E_R}{10^{jd}}$$

$$10^{jd} = \frac{\varepsilon E_R}{\varepsilon'E_R}$$

$$jd = \log \frac{\varepsilon E_R}{\varepsilon'E_R}$$

$$d = \frac{\log \dfrac{\varepsilon E_R}{\varepsilon'E_R}}{j} . \qquad (3)$$

PAPER
15

Next, let it be supposed that an external inhibition experiment [8] is set up from which the values of $_iE_R$ and $_{i'}E_R$ are determined, and that these values are found to be 50 wats and 40 wats respectively. We are now in position to calculate the value of d by substituting appropriately in equation 3:

$$d = \frac{\log \frac{50}{40}}{.0135}$$

$$= \frac{\log 1.25}{.0135}$$

$$= \frac{.09691}{.0135}$$

$$= 7.1785.$$

PAPER
15

Accordingly in the suppositious case before us, the afferent interaction effect of introducing the new stimulus element into the stimulus configuration originally conditioned to R amounts to a little more than 7 j.n.d. units on the original S-generalization continuum. *Thus we appear to have both a unit and a methodology for the measurement of afferent neural interaction.*

If, upon experimental trial, the methodology sketched above should prove to be substantially sound, the way would presumably be open for the empirical determination of the numerous molar laws relating the amount of afferent neural interaction to the various factors within the stimulus configuration which produce it. For example, let it be supposed that we have six large groups of subjects and that each group is conditioned to one

[8] This is an experiment in which a reaction is first conditioned to a stimulus (S) and then S is presented to the organism in conjunction with S' which supposedly is a neutral stimulus. Pavlov reports that the presence of S' usually weakens the power of S to evoke the reaction earlier conditioned to it.

of a series of sound intensities in a constant known amount ($_sE_R$); following this the groups are divided into six equal subgroups and each subgroup is subjected to external inhibition by one of six lights of different known intensities. From the results so secured the residual reaction potential ($_{s'}E_R$) can be determined. Ideally, the series of six tones and the series of six lights should be spaced at equal j.n.d. intervals on the respective continua. With these values available the amount of afferent neural interaction (d) may be calculated in each case by the use of equation 3.

This experiment would yield a six-by six-way table of d-values as a joint function of the intensities of the six sound stimuli originally conditioned (S_1) and of the intensities of the six interfering light stimuli (S_2). Now, columns proportional to these d-values, if mounted on such a table, would determine a surface. An equation fitted to this surface, *i.e.*,

$$d = f(S_1, S_2), \qquad (4)$$

will evidently be a first approximation to the molar law of the amount of afferent neural interaction as a function of the intensity of sound stimuli conditioned to the reaction and of light stimuli introduced into the original conditioned-stimulus configurations. By analogous procedures, numerous other molar laws governing the amount of afferent neural interaction produced in stimulus configurations may presumably be determined experimentally.[9]

[9] While the present article was in press, two reviews of the author's recently published book (1) severely criticized the afferent neural interaction hypothesis. One reviewer remarks, "But in the principle of afferent neural interaction we have no way of estimating, for example, the degree of similarity between the compound afferent impulse and its component impulses, when taken separately. Any such

VI. SUMMARY

That mammalian organisms respond to individual stimuli or stimulus aggregates, in part, according to the other stimuli which are acting at the same time or which have acted shortly before, is a matter of ordinary observation. Quantitative experiment has confirmed the soundness of these observations. Results secured by means of such investigations probably cannot be deduced either from the unsupplemented principles of the early behaviorism or from the unsupplemented principles of *Gestalt Theorie*. However, it has been found possible to derive configurational discrimination rather easily from a set of Pavlovian principles, even though Pavlov himself did not do this. The critical Pavlovian principle employed in this derivation which is not found among either the Watsonian or the Thorndikian principles is afferent neural interaction.

estimate must perforce be ad hoc, . . ." (*Psychol. Bull.*, 1944, **41**, pp. 642–643). In somewhat similar vein, the other reviewer says, ". . . it is desirable that the principle of afferent interaction should be operationally meaningful. . . . What is the difference produced in 'each' afferent neural impulse? How much are afferent impulses modified, and what factors produce much or little effect? . . . it would be hard to find in psychology a principle that is more nearly meaningless than this one of Hull's." (*J. genet. Psychol.*, 1944, **65**, pp. 25–26). While by no means as dissatisfied with the original formulation of the afferent neural interaction hypothesis as the reviewers quoted above, the author felt keenly the need of a unit of measurement and a mode of calculating the amount of the effect in question. This led to a derivation of equation 3 and the related unit of measurement as early as December 27, 1943 (2, p. 179). These are believed to yield an acceptable operational definition and, together with the associated program of experimental research as sketched in section V above, may be expected to yield adequate methods of quantitative determination.

But before this promising principle can be of much scientific use the quantitative molar laws according to which it occurs under various stimulus configurational conditions must be determined experimentally. The attainment of these results, in turn, requires both a methodology and a unit of measurement. One basis for such a methodology is believed to lie in the Pavlovian experimental procedure designed to produce external inhibition; the amount of afferent neural interaction which results from this experimental procedure may presumably be calculated by means of an equation derived from the empirical formula for stimulus generalization. The unit of measurement is found in the j.n.d. of the stimulus aggregate which undergoes the afferent neural interaction.

This proposal is, of course, entirely programmatic as yet and a large amount of experimental work must be performed before it can be accomplished. It is believed, however, that the potential importance of the matter is sufficient to warrant a very considerable expenditure of time and effort. Moreover, this potentiality does not lie merely in the field of theory; there is considerable reason to believe that an adequate understanding of some of the more important practical educative processes of our schools involves stimulus configurations (3), and these cannot be understood until we know more about the quantitative laws of afferent neural interaction.

PAPER
15

REFERENCES

1. HULL, C. L. *Principles of behavior.* New York: D. Appleton-Century Co., Inc., 1943.
2. ——. *Psychological memoranda, 1940–1944.* Bound mimeographed material on file in the libraries of the University of Iowa, University of North Carolina, and Yale University.

3. ——. *Elementary theory of individual behavior* (in prep.).
4. HUMPHREY, G. *The nature of learning.* New York: Harcourt, Brace and Co., 1933.
5. KÖHLER, W. *Gestalt psychology.* New York: Liveright Pub. Co., 1929.
6. ——. *Dynamics in psychology.* New York: Liveright Pub. Co., 1940.
7. PAVLOV, I. P. *Conditioned reflexes* (trans. by G. V. Anrep). London: Oxford Univ. Press, 1927.
8. TOLMAN, E. C. *Purposive behavior in ani-*

mals and men. New York: D. Appleton-Century Co., Inc., 1933.
9. WARDEN, C. J., & ROWLEY, J. B. The discrimination of absolute versus relative brightness in the ring dove, Turtur risorius. *J. comp. Psychol.*, 1929, 9, 317–337.
10. WOLFLE, D. L. Absolute brightness discrimination in the white rat. *J. comp. Psychol.*, 1937, 24, 59–71.
11. WOODBURY, C. B. The learning of stimulus patterns by dogs. *J. comp. Psychol.*, 1943, 35, 29–40.

THE PROBLEM OF PRIMARY STIMULUS GENERALIZATION

BY CLARK L. HULL

Institute of Human Relations,
Yale University

The genuineness of primary stimulus generalization has recently been seriously challenged (12) as not being in agreement with experimental facts. It accordingly becomes necessary in the interest of the advancement of science to reëxamine the available evidence with care, and to secure such additional evidence as is possible.

PRELIMINARY HISTORY OF THE PROBLEM

PAPER
16

Pavlov, presumably some time previous to 1910 (15, p. 114), made the empirical discovery that salivary reactions in dogs conditioned to a particular stimulus were evokable by other stimuli but to a diminished degree, the magnitude of the response constituting a falling gradient the height of which at any given point is a decreasing function of the difference between the stimuli in question. In this connection Pavlov states (15, pp. 112–113):

"The successful development of analysis of external agencies by means of conditioned reflexes is always preceded by what we call a 'period of generalization' (which may possibly be regarded as some form of synthesizing activity).

For instance, if a tone of 1000 d.v. is established as a conditioned stimulus, many other tones spontaneously acquire similar properties, such properties diminishing proportionally to the intervals of these tones from the one of 1000 d.v. Similarly, if a tactile stimulation of a definite circumscribed area of skin is made into a conditioned stimulus, tactile stimulation of other skin areas will also elicit some conditioned reaction, the effect diminishing with increasing distance of these areas from the

one for which the conditioned reflex was originally established. The same is observed with stimulation of other receptor organs. The spontaneous development of accessory reflexes, or, as we have termed it, *generalization of stimuli,* . . . ." [Italics ours.]

Subsequently, in discussing the matter of how to secure stimulus discrimination, Pavlov remarked (15, p. 117):

"Formerly we were inclined to think that this effect could be obtained by two different methods: the first method consisted in repeating the definite conditioned stimulus a great number of times always accompanied by reinforcement, and the second method consisted in contrasting the single definite conditioned stimulus, which was always accompanied by reinforcement, with different neighbouring stimuli which were never reinforced. At present, however, we are more inclined to regard this second method as more probably the only efficacious one, since it was observed that no absolute differentiation was ever obtained by the use of the first method, even though the stimulus was repeated with reinforcement over a thousand times. On the other hand, it was found that contrast by even a single unreinforced application of an allied stimulus, or by a number of single unreinforced applications of different members of a series of allied stimuli at infrequent intervals of days or weeks, led to a rapid development of differentiation."

Several years later (1917–18) Anrep, one of Pavlov's pupils and the translator of his major work, made systematic measurements of this 'generalization of stimulation,' as Pavlov calls it, in the field of cutaneous stimuli, determining the generalization gradients for positive learning in terms of the short trace conditioned salivary secretions of dogs (1). The interval separating the two stimulations involved in each reinforcement was four or five seconds. Anrep found the response gradient to be a decreasing function of the distance of the points stimulated from the point originally conditioned on two animals. His graphs representing two sets of typical measurements of this gradient on a single dog are reproduced as Fig. 1.

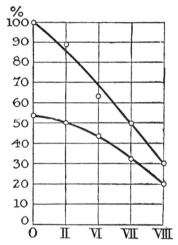

FIG. 1. Two graphic representations of the gradient of cutaneous stimulus generalization of a conditioned salivary reaction in a single dog. The upper curve represents the original gradient, the lower one, the same gradient at a later stage of experimentation after the dog had developed an appreciable amount of 'spontaneous inhibition.' The abscissa values (Roman numerals) represent roughly equal increments in distance from the point on the left thigh originally conditioned, as it extended forward on the right side of the animal to the chest and thence down the front leg. (After Anrep, 1, p. 412.)

Some ten years after the publication of Anrep's study, Loucks (13) published an elaborate criticism of certain experimental work emanating from Pavlov's laboratory. This criticism was directed in the main against an hypothe-

sis of Pavlov's which is that the results of stimulation progress through the brain in a sluggish wave and that this progression is manifested as a parallel temporal phenomenon in the responsiveness of organisms to cutaneous stimulation. The alleged wave-like phenomenon in question we shall, for the sake of clearness in the present exposition, call *irradiation*. This, be it noted, is quite a different notion from the phenomenon represented in Fig. 1. Despite the fact that Anrep seems clearly to refer to the phenomenon represented by Fig. 1 as irradiation (1, p. 407), we shall here call it *generalization*,[1] as Pavlov himself does in the quotation cited above.

Because of the relative freedom of the Anrep data from the usual variability characteristic of mammalian behavior, Loucks refused to accept them as having definite scientific value. In this connection he says (13, p. 43):

"From first hand experience with experiments of this type, from a study of the

PAPER

16

[1] Perhaps the clearest difference between the two concepts is that irradiation is conceived as a progressive spread of the effect of stimulation extending over a few minutes only, whereas stimulus generalization is a relatively permanent potentiality of reaction evocation which seems to exist regardless of any recent stimulation whatever. In the terms here specified it may be said that Pavlov believed that stimulus generalization was functionally dependent on, and so, closely related to, irradiation. This supposed causal relationship naturally augmented the tendency to confuse the two concepts. Bass and Hull unintentionally contributed to this confusion by using the term 'irradiation' in the title of their article (2). This was done with a view to making obvious the relevancy of their work to Pavlovian phenomena. They hoped to protect themselves from misunderstanding by inserting a footnote (2, p. 47) categorically denying subscription to any neurological theory whatever, Pavlovian or otherwise, in their use of the terms, 'spread,' 'irradiation,' and 'generalization.' That they were not wholly successful may be seen by consulting Loucks (14, p. 329 ff.).

protocols of other Russian investigators . . . the writer is forced to question the completeness of the data [of Anrep] as standing for the raw measurements, uninfluenced by any selective factor. . . . the writer feels it must be regarded with suspended judgment. . . . If it were not for the fact that this work, taken at its face value, appears of more significance than almost any other in this field, . . . it would not be necessary to raise these questions."

While not particularly sharing Loucks' skepticism as to the scientific significance of Anrep's published results but nevertheless being somewhat disturbed that such a presumably sound and important principle should be called in question even indirectly, Bass and Hull (2) set out to test experimentally the genuineness of the stimulus generalization gradient. They employed in all two groups of eight human subjects, using the conditioned galvanic skin reaction originally evoked by an electric shock. One group of subjects was used for determining the generalization gradient of positive excitation, and one for determining the gradient of extinction effects (inhibition). The Bass-Hull study clearly confirmed the falling gradient of cutaneous stimulus generalization as reported by Anrep. They also reported a closely analogous gradient of the stimulus generalization of extinction effects. Bass and Hull's graph representing their cutaneous stimulus generalization gradient of conditioned response is reproduced as Fig. 2. Despite the use of different types of subjects and very different reactions, the resemblance between Figs. 1 and 2 is striking.

In 1937 Hovland carried out a number of meticulous studies with human subjects on the generalization of positive reaction tendencies to auditory vibration frequency (7, p. 128 ff.), auditory vibration intensity (8), and cutaneous vibration intensity (9). Hov-

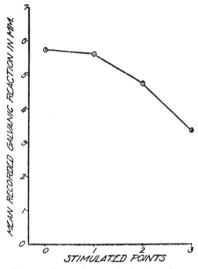

FIG. 2. Composite graph showing the cutaneous stimulus generalization gradient of the conditioned galvanic skin reaction in man based on eight subjects. (From Bass and Hull, 2, p. 60.)

land's work has the great advantage over previous investigations in employing more subjects and in the precise determination of the numerical magnitude of the differences separating the several stimuli involved, which permitted the fitting of equations to his empirical results. His graph of the stimulus generalization of the galvanic skin reaction to excitation by auditory vibration frequency before the use of any additional reinforcement of the conditioned stimulus is reproduced as Fig. 3. It is notable that there is a clear and unambiguous falling gradient having its maximum at the point of reinforcement, i.e., the magnitude of the galvanic response is a decreasing monotonic function of the degree of separation of the stimuli from the stimulus originally conditioned. This, of course, is true of the graphs published by Anrep and by Bass and Hull. There is, however, a distinct difference in the nature of the curvature of the first two functions (Figs. 1 and 2) and that of Hovland.

Hovland reports experimental evidence (7) that responses evoked by wide stimulus generalization are distinctly more susceptible to experimental extinction than are those evoked by stimuli differing less from the conditioned stimulus, and that the conditioned stimulus is least of all influenced by extinction. The results of a second study in this field, by Hovland, show the generalization gradient on the first, second, and third unreinforced tests of a generalization to tonal intensity. There was found a practically horizontal gradient on the first trial with a fairly conventional gradient of increasing steepness on the second and third trials. A graphic representation is presented as Fig. 4. Hovland also reports

a meticulous experiment (7) which yielded a primary stimulus generalization gradient of extinction effects closely resembling that reported by Bass and Hull.

The next experimental study which we notice in the recent history of stimulus generalization was reported in 1942, by Brown (5). In this experiment two groups of albino rats totaling 36 animals were trained to traverse a 60-inch straight runway under a hunger motivation to go to food at the end, where an illuminated ground-glass screen was placed. Half of the animals were trained to go to a screen of .02 apparent foot-candles, and half to a screen of 5000 apparent foot-candles. After 18 reinforced trials of this sort, each group was tested at intervals of 10 minutes with the screen set at .02, at 5.0, and at 5000 foot-candles. The test con-

PAPER

16

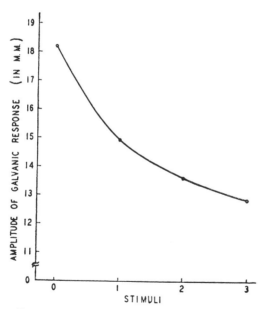

FIG. 3. Composite graph showing the auditory stimulus generalization on the vibration frequency dimension of the conditioned galvanic skin reaction in man. This graph is based on data from 20 subjects. (From Hovland, 7, p. 136.)

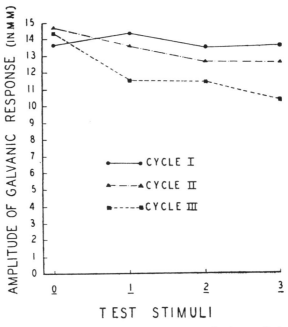

FIG. 4. Graphic representation of the generalization gradients of conditioned galvanic skin responses to tonal stimulus intensity. Note the practically horizontal nature of the results of Test I. (Reproduced from Hovland, **8**, p. 286.)

sisted in the animal being placed in a light harness of rubber bands which was connected by a cord to a recording spring dynamometer. The length of the cord was such that the pulling occurred half way from the starting point to the screen or reward point. At each test two scores were obtained, (1) the time required by the rat to traverse the distance from the starting end of the runway to the middle where the pulling occurred, and (2) the maximum pull exerted during 5 seconds devoted to this activity. At the end of the pulling test the animals were in all cases picked up without feeding. Thus the 'conditioned' stimulus was subjected to nonreward exactly as much as were the stimuli which had not been reinforced. Three such tests were given each rat.

The composite results of the 36 animals show clearly marked stimulus generalization gradients in both strength of pull and reaction latency. It may be noted also that the light-trained (5000 apparent foot-candles) animals showed a steeper gradient of generalization than did the dark-trained (.02 apparent foot-candles) animals, which means that intensity *per se* has an effect on the magnitude of response. This observation is in agreement with Hovland's findings in the generalization of sound intensities (8) with human subjects, though Brown's results in this respect are not so extreme as are those of Hovland. Brown's graph showing stimulus generalization as indicated by reaction latency is reproduced as Fig. 5.

A significant detail, which also is in

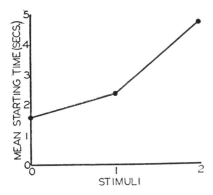

FIG. 5. Composite curve representing the light stimulus generalization gradient as shown by reaction latency by 36 albino rats. Since reaction latency is inversely related to, *i.e.*, is a decreasing monotonic function of, reaction potential, it follows that a generalization gradient plotted as this one is must have its low extreme at the point of reinforcement. (After Brown, 5, p. 216.)

agreement with the Hovland findings noted above, is that the generalized reaction tendencies were markedly more susceptible to experimental extinction than were those evoked by the conditioned stimulus, and the farther away a stimulus was from the conditioned stimulus, the greater the tendency to extinction. Actually the first trial showed a practically horizontal gradient, just as Hovland's did. This means that almost all of the gradient shown in Fig. 5 is due to the differential extinction effects. A graph showing these results is reproduced as Fig. 6, which should be compared with Fig. 4.

The next study to be considered in this survey of the empirical evidence bearing on the problem of stimulus generalization was reported by Wickens. This differs from the other studies included in this summary, because it involves response generalization as well as stimulus generalization. It is included here in the main because its outcome has been supposed, though not by

Wickens himself, to be inconsistent with the results of other experiments in this field. Wickens states (21, p. 226):

"The present experiment was designed to test for the possibility of stimulus generalization of the generalized conditioned response. Three groups of subjects were conditioned to tonal stimuli. Shock served as the unconditioned stimulus, and finger extension was the conditioned response. The Ss's hands were then turned over and the tone alone was sounded. For one group the same tone was used, for another the test tone differed by one octave from the training tone, and for the third group a two-octave difference was employed."

The outcome of the experiment in so far as it concerns us here is represented graphically in Fig. 7. In regard to this Wickens states (21, p. 226):

"The data show some tendency for the same tone to be more effective in eliciting the transferred conditioned response than were the generalized tones, if direct comparison of the means is made. Treatment of the data by an analysis of variance, however, produces an F-ratio of less than one. Thus, there is no statistical evidence that any one of these stimuli are more effective than any of the others. This re-

PAPER
16

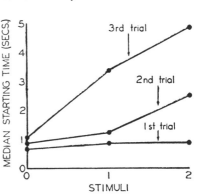

FIG. 6. Graphic representation of the stimulus generalization gradients based on reaction latency as produced by different numbers of unreinforced reaction evocations. Figure 5 is the composite of these three gradients. (Reproduced from Brown, 5, p. 218.)

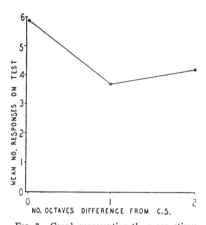

Fig. 7. Graph representing the mean stimulus generalization tendencies of what is in the main a generalized conditioned hand response as a function of the auditory octave. Note that both generalized responses are lower than those to the conditioned response, but that the value at two octaves is higher than at one octave. (Plotted from data published by Wickens, 21, p. 225.)

PAPER
16

sult is probably to be expected on several counts. Humphreys has shown that losses in the magnitude of the response during stimulus generalization are not great if the test tone bears an octave relationship to the training tone. Secondly, it will be recalled that the tonal stimulus was brief in duration, and had a sudden onset. This would result in a large number of similar component frequencies during the onset of each of the tones."

A Revolutionary Re-interpretation of the Phenomena of Stimulus Generalization

The above may probably be taken as a fair summary of the consensus of opinion in this field (6, p. 176 ff.) up to a few months ago when Lashley and Wade (12) published their paper on the subject. While apparently the facts as reported by the various investigators are not disputed (with the possible exception of Anrep's results), a radically different interpretation is given to them. Insofar as it is closely related to the

investigations summarized above, Lashley and Wade's central position seems to be substantially that (12, p. 74):

"There is no 'irradiation' or spread of effects of training during primary conditioning."

In an amplification of the above statement made in a private communication, Lashley states that the quotation just cited constitutes a "categorical denial that a stimulus generalization gradient is generated by training with a single stimulus." As an example of his position in this matter he states in the same communication that, "in conditioning a white stimulus on a uniform unvarying ground," he "would be confident that no gradient would develop." Thus the central issue emerges as a concrete and specific one of experimental fact.

There are, however, a number of collateral but subordinate issues which tend to bear on the central problem and which therefore need to be considered:

1. Alternative explanations are given to certain experimental results hitherto regarded as evidence indicating the genuineness of primary stimulus generalization:

(A) it is held that neither the salivary nor the galvanic skin reaction yields dependable evidence for the generalization of training effects because (12, p. 84):

"These indicators [salivary and skin secretions] are cumulative, build up gradually, so that increase in reaction time with difficulty of discrimination results in a graduated intensity of response."

(B) It is held that only lower animals make suitable subjects for experiments on primary stimulus generalization. Likewise, the position is taken that adult human subjects are objectionable for such purposes because for such subjects "the stimulus series represented familiar relational sequences, that initial tests directed attention to the dimensions investigated." Finally, it is held that (12, p. 75),

"To demonstrate irradiation in primary conditioning the subject must be inexperienced with respect to the stimulus dimension used, in order to rule out any tendency to identify a single stimulus as belonging in a familiar graded series or to use habits of relational thinking."

(C) Apparently Anrep's stimulus generalization results with dogs are dismissed from consideration because of the Loucks criticism of the irradiation experiments reported from Pavlov's laboratory.

(D) Lashley and Wade seem to take the position (1) that generalization can occur only on the basis of a stimulus dimension and (2) that a stimulus dimension is only brought into existence by a comparison of at least two stimuli possessing the same dimension. They say, for example (12, p. 74),

"The 'dimensions' of a stimulus series are determined by comparison of two or more stimuli and do not exist for the organism until established by differential training."

This point is clarified somewhat in a private communication which states that when generalization gradients occur "it is the result of comparison which is an essential feature of discrimination and the formation of differential reactions." The context seems to indicate that one necessary condition for comparison to take place is the reception of the stimuli to be compared either simultaneously or in close succession, *i.e.*, the reception of the two stimuli within a few seconds of each other.

2. It is held that experimental results on gradients of stimulus generalization have not been consistent. In this connection the work of Wickens (21) and that of Razran (16) are cited as being inconsistent, apparently, with the results of Bass and Hull and of Hovland.

3. It is held that evidence definitely contradictory to the gradient of primary stimulus generalization has arisen from certain hitherto unpublished experiments from Lashley's laboratory. These experiments involve (1) a process of simultaneously presented visual stimuli (one figured and the other plain black) in which discrimination was produced by differential reinforcement after which (2) the original figured stimulus was paired simultaneously with a new figured stimulus in the same dimension and discrimination learning was finally effected between these stimuli by differential reinforcement. In contrast to what we above called 'Pavlovian differential reinforcement,' we shall call this simultaneous presentation of the stimuli to be discriminated, 'Lashleyan differential reinforcement.'

4. As an incident to Lashley and Wade's discussion of primary stimulus generalization they remark in connection with their own experimental results (12, p. 79):
"We have not attempted to reduce these 'habit strengths' to the equations of the neo-Pavlovian system. The spurious character of its quantitative and mathematical treatment of learning is illustrated by the definition of its units of measurement, the hab and wat. . . ."

This serves to raise the far more important question of whether any quantitative and mathematical treatment of learning or behavior phenomena is either desirable or possible. Lashley and Wade do not specifically commit themselves on these points, but the general context suggests deep pessimism if not actual opposition.

SOME COMMENTS ON LASHLEY AND
WADE'S CRITICISM OF PRIMARY
STIMULUS GENERALIZATION
EXPERIMENTS

We may now comment on the various attempts made by Lashley and Wade to

PAPER
16

explain away the experimental facts hitherto regarded as evidence of the reality of a gradient of stimulus generalization. We shall take them up in the order in which they have been presented above, and under the same numbers.

1. (A) Unfortunately, Lashley and Wade do not make clear the logic behind their objection to the use of the salivary and the galvanic skin reaction as an indication of the existence of gradients of stimulus generalization. Here, as frequently throughout their paper, they content themselves with a brief, dogmatic statement. A process of gradual accumulation of a secretion, even if significantly existent in the experiments, could only produce a constant error in such a way as to cause a spurious appearance of a stimulus generalization gradient in case the stimuli were delivered in the experiments in question, *both* (1) within a few moments of each other and (2) in an order progressing along the stimulus dimension from a remote point toward the point of reinforcement. In the Pavlovian experiments the test trials were usually given at relatively long intervals and apparently in a random fashion (15, pp. 55, 57, 63, etc.). Accordingly, failure to conform to the first of the above conditions would rule out the objection to the salivary experiment. In regard to the galvanic skin reaction experiments, elaborate precautions were taken to eliminate any such constant errors by systematically varying the order of stimulation (2, pp. 56, 62; 7, pp. 134, 135). This failure to conform to the second of the above conditions rules out the objection to the galvanic skin reaction experiments. We must accordingly conclude that Lashley and Wade's hypothesis that the generalization gradients based upon the salivary and galvanic skin reactions are mere artifacts or constant errors owing to some hypo-

PAPER
16

thetical cumulative characteristics of these reactions, is without foundation.[2]

(B) It must be confessed that we ourselves have in general a considerable amount of sympathy with the preference for lower animal subjects as contrasted with humans, especially with adult humans where behavior is likely to be influenced by stimuli arising from subvocal speech. However, Lashley's objections on this score have only the status of a mere possibility and this possibility is rather remote owing to the relatively non-voluntary character of galvanic skin reaction. To this difficulty must be added the important empirical consideration that at the first trial in some of Hovland's experiments (Fig. 4) and probably in all of them (though the critical evidence is not reported), the gradient at the first test trial was horizontal, *i.e.*, there was no evident slope at all, exactly as with Brown's rats. If the gradient eventually found were due to the indirect effect of previously formed habits, *e.g.*, of speech, it should have appeared in fully developed form at the very first trial because the speech habits were presumably as fully formed at that time as at the time of the subsequent trials. Actually the gradient occurred only as the result of a number of unreinforced separate-presentation reaction evocations. Therefore Lashley and Wade's objection to the acceptance of data from human subjects, plausible as it

[2] Lashley, in a second communication which he transmitted to the writer of the present article after a perusal of the manuscript sent him upon its completion, makes the following statement which is designed to clarify the position taken in the Lashley-Wade article on this point and, specifically, that portion of it quoted above under 1 (A), p. 126. He says, "My argument concerning the relation of salivary secretion and galvanic response to reaction time was not directed against the existence of a sensory gradient but against the use of these quantitative data as evidence for strength of association."

sounds at first hearing, proves on closer examination not to be in harmony with the relevant facts.

(C) Suppose, now, for the sake of getting on with the argument, we should throw out of present consideration all of the experiments involving galvanic skin reactions and human subjects. There would still remain numerous positive experiments employing dogs and rats. But when we consider the dog experiments we encounter Lashley and Wade's reference to Loucks' criticism of results from Pavlov's laboratory. In this connection it must be recalled that Loucks' criticisms are directly concerned only with irradiation, which is quite distinct from stimulus generalization; stimulus generalization as an empirical phenomenon stands on its own feet wholly irrespective of the genuineness of irradiation. There of course remains the possibility of attributing Anrep's quantitative results to slightly attenuated fraud or nature faking. But even though that hypothesis should be adopted there would still remain the definite statement by Pavlov (quoted above, p. 120) which clearly indicates a stimulus generalization gradient. There would also remain the difficult question of explaining how Anrep could have fabricated in advance a measured gradient which agrees so closely with the gradient found by Bass and Hull, even though the abscissa points of the Anrep gradient are somewhat arbitrarily spaced.[3]

(D) We come now to what appears to be the final criticism of the stimulus generalization experiments. This is that they may in some way be owing to Lashley's type of differential training made on the basis of direct (simultaneous) comparison of the contrasted stimuli. Now, *in not a single one of the experiments cited above were the stimuli involved in the gradients contrasted in Lashley's sense by being presented either simultaneously or within a few seconds of each other.* Therefore, differential reinforcement in Lashley's sense was not involved in any of the experiments used as evidence of this phenomenon. It is true that Pavlov (in Anrep's translation) frequently uses the expressions 'contrast' and 'differential reinforcement' to designate a systematic reinforcement of the conditioned stimulus and systematic non-reinforcement of evocations of the response by other (generalized) stimuli, but *the stimuli were never presented simultaneously* (15, p. 55; 7, p. 135; 2, p. 52 ff.). The results from Pavlov's laboratory, and those from the Bass-Hull study as shown in Fig. 2, are in part owing to the *Pavlovian* type of differential reinforcement, not that of Lashley. Lashley's simultaneous-presentation contrast hypothesis as to the origin of these gradients must accordingly be dismissed as not being in harmony with the relevant facts.

It remains to be added that the gradients of Hovland (Fig. 3) and of Brown (Fig. 5) did not even involve the Pavlovian type of differential reinforcement; no reinforcement whatever was given between the beginning of the tests and their termination.[4]

PAPER
16

[3] In the second communication referred to in footnote 2 above, Lashley explains that his objective in citing the Loucks criticism of the Russian experiments on irradiation was not to question the scientific authenticity of Anrep's published data on stimulus generalization. In this connection Lashley makes the following categorical statement: "I do not question that Pavlov and Anrep got a graded series of responses."

[4] In Lashley's second communication, referred to in footnote 2 above, he points out more specifically his meaning of the terms 'comparison' and 'stimuli' in the present connection (12, p. 74). He says, "The statement quoted [under 1 (D) above, p. 127] does not imply simultaneity or close succession of stimuli. Training with one stimulus leaves a trace, which I think of as nervous patterning

2. We now come to the supposedly inconsistent results of Razran and Wickens. The reference given by Lashley and Wade to Razran has been gone over with great care, but the present writer has been quite unable to find anything which would cast doubt on the reality of the falling gradient of stimulus generalization. Hovland's generalization results are cited by Razran, along with the results from the Russian laboratories, apparently with approval. The article is essentially a contribution to a controversy concerned with responses to explicit *patterns* of stimulation, a matter which is not here under consideration.

The Wickens experiment has already been described. We have seen that the stimulus-generalization means in both cases are less than the non-generalized means, which so far is in conformity with other experiments in the field. Nevertheless, when the rather exacting criteria of the analysis of variance are applied to the data the outcome is not such as to permit the conclusion that a typical gradient is proved. But to say that something is not proved is by no means the same thing as to say that it is disproved or that it constitutes any grounds whatever for rejecting the results of some other experiment. As a matter of fact, computations based on Wickens' published results show that the critical ratio based on the standard deviations involved of the difference between points 0 and 1 is 1.70, and that between points 0 and 2 is 1.41. The first gives as a probability that a difference as great as the one observed and in the same direction would occur by

and which is rearoused in later trials. The 'comparison' may be between this trace and later stimuli (between a memory image and a stimulus, if I must be anthropomorphic to be understood)." It may be noted that a statement of the expanded meaning of 'stimulus' to include the concept of 'trace' was not contained in the Lashley-Wade article.

chance alone only about 4.5 times in 100 in the first pair, and about 12 times in the second pair. In a private communication Wickens states,

". . . it is worth noting that the percentage of subjects responding in the groups 0, 1, and 2 is 87, 69, and 62 per cent. Plotted, these data give a gradient similar to that obtained by Hovland. When Chi square is calculated, however, none of these differences reach the 10 per cent level. In summary I would like to state that I do not believe the data of my experiment to be at variance with Hovland's type of gradient. In some respects the data are quite harmonious with his findings, although they do not go so far as to offer any *conclusive* statistical support of his gradient."

Thus the general probabilities in this case, so far as they go, are quite in line with the results of the other experiments in the field of primary stimulus generalization.

3. We come now to the experiments from Lashley's own laboratory. Lashley and Wade report that they carried out numerous experiments, all of which were incompatible with the assumption of stimulus generalization. They say (12, p. 78):

"On the contrary, training with one stimulus fails to produce a significantly greater strength of association with that stimulus than with others on the same stimulus dimension. Under conditions which rule out pre-existing habits of relational thinking, no evidence for any graduated spread of effects of training is obtained."

The most impressive mass of data cited by Lashley and Wade are the ten sets of relatively homogeneous rat experiments. Unfortunately the numerical results of all but two of these experiments are not available for statistical analysis. A private communication states that they were accidentally destroyed. But certain significant things are stated about these results.

(A) Lashley and Wade's experiments yield results which are *opposite* to what is held to be the implication of stimulus generalization by a falling gradient or even a horizontal gradient.

(B) All ten experiments agree in this reverse outcome. In this connection Lashley and Wade remark (12, p. 76):

"In every case a differential reaction was established more quickly when the training involved extinction of the initial reaction to a single stimulus than when that reaction was reinforced. The differences are statistically unreliable but are consistent in all 10 experiments."

Now from a statistical point of view it is quite true that the single toss of a coin does not decide anything any more than does a single statistically unreliable experiment. However, in case a coin is tossed ten times in succession with the same result in each case, it is truly remarkable; the probability that this would occur by pure chance is $(1/2)^{10}$, which is but one chance in 1,024. Taking this report at face value, then, it indicates that a generalization gradient of high statistical reliability was really operating in the experiment but that its slope was in the opposite direction from that implied by the stimulus generalization experiments. Thus Lashley and Wade's experiments have a considerably more revolutionary implication than they have claimed. Moreover, these results flatly contradict Lashley and Wade's own conclusion (quoted above) that no graduated spread of the effects of training is obtained. There purports, on the contrary, to be a genuine spread of the effects of the preliminary training, but in the opposite direction.

This naturally raises the question of whether this generalization with the low end of the slope of reaction potential at the point of reinforcement is contained in Lashley's own theory of behavior. If not, then the outcome of his experi-ment presents an acute explanatory problem to him quite as much as to those who credit the experiments on primary stimulus generalization. So far as the present writer can discover, Lashley and Wade's assumption is that the central figure involved in the first discrimination phase of their experiments, *i.e.*, a concrete representation of the critical stimulus dimension, has received no learning whatever because not previously contrasted with anything in the same dimension. We find, however, that taken at face value their rat experiments indicate that the conditioned stimulus somehow did acquire a *negative* value—some potentiality which interfered with the generation of an approach reaction on the part of the animals. The brief description of the experiments and the fragmentary data available concerning them make it difficult to hazard a guess as to what could have produced an apparent effect which is opposed to the views of both parties to the issue, and points to a type of stimulus generalization never held by anyone, so far as the present writer is aware.

But the situation as a whole is not so confused and hopeless as the Lashley-Wade experiment might suggest. It happens that there have recently become available some experimental results involving simultaneous discrimination in rats which apply directly to the present issue. Spence (18) reports that he trained 20 albino rats for four days to take a single black (or white) runway to food on a special apparatus (17). After a total of 40 trials of this training the animals were divided into four groups and trained by differential reinforcement to choose either the shade of alley which they were previously habituated to choose, or the opposite shade. The mean outcome of the experiment in terms of number of errors is as follows:

PAPER

16

1. Trained on White	1. Trained on Black	1. Trained on White	1. Trained on Black
2. Trained on W + vs. B − (++)	2. Trained on B + vs. W − (++)	2. Trained on B + vs. W − (+−)	2. Trained on W + vs. B − (+−)
.4	7.2	31.4	12.6

It may be noticed, as we have had occasion to point out in certain other experiments on black and white discrimination, that the animals show a special tendency to learn to go to white, the physically more intense of the two opposed stimuli employed. Thus the combination of the first and fourth values given above, where white was the positive stimulus, gives a mean of 6.5 errors, whereas the combination of the second and third values, where black was the positive stimulus, yields a mean of 19.3 errors. However, since this factor is presumably equalized in the two ++ groups as well as in the two +− groups, the two of each are averaged to secure the results of training transfer due to primary stimulus generalization with the effects of stimulus intensity equalized. In the notation employed by Lashley these means are:

$$++ = 3.8 \text{ errors}$$
$$+− = 22.0 \text{ errors}$$

Thus the animals which in the discrimination experiment were trained to choose the brightness to which they had been trained in the preliminary nondiscriminatory learning, learned the discrimination with considerably fewer errors than did the animals which had to reverse the habit formed during the preliminary single shade training, the difference being 18.2 errors. A test of this difference by the 't' statistic gives a value of 4.09, which is beyond the .001 level of significance.

4. It is difficult to believe that any behavior scientist would actively oppose the placing of the behavior sciences on a secure quantitative, mathematical basis. On the other hand, it is axiomatic that until reaction potentiality and habit strength as such are measured in appropriate units a true basis for a mathematical systematization does not exist. In this connection reaction potential as such is to be contrasted with various phenomena taken as indicating its presence, *i.e.*, as having a monotonic functional relation to it. A number of such indicators are: (1) the number of reinforcements, (2) the amount of conditioned secretion, (3) the degrees of arc moved by a galvanometer, (4) the number of non-reinforced responses evoked, (5) the number of grams lifted in a conditioned muscular contraction, (6) the number of centimeters moved in a conditioned muscular contraction, (7) the number of seconds involved in the reaction latency, (8) the number of errors occurring per trial in a learning situation, and (9) the per cent probability of response occurrence following a given kind of stimulation. Under favorable conditions all nine of the above measurable phenomena are recognized as indicators of reaction potential or habit strength, but we have as yet no equations for converting any of them into reaction potential or *vice versa*. The situation is analogous to that in the history of heat measurement previous to Joule's classical experiments which demonstrated the mechanical equivalent of heat. But the history of thermometry and calorimetry should warn us that the adequate quantification of the behavior sciences will be neither swift nor easy (3; 4).

In 1943 a largely programmatic sketch of what the behavior sciences might be like if so quantified and mathematically systematized was published (11, p. 327). Since that time, work toward realizing this program has gone forward continuously in the writer's laboratory. It may merely be said here that, utilizing substantially the logic implicit in the classical work in psychophysics as elaborated by Thurstone (20), we appear to have made numerous approximate quantitative determinations of reaction potential ($_s E_R$) as such. The unit of measurement used so far (as might be anticipated from the relationship of psychophysical determinations and scaling) is the standard deviation of the probability function or, what in the present system is the same thing, the σ of the oscillation function ($_s O_R$) (11, p. 304 ff.). Several papers devoted to the empirical aspects of this subject are at the present time in preparation, one by Sprow (19) being in press. It may be added that a tentative equation has even now been derived for converting the reaction latencies, into reaction potential ($_s E_R$). Space is here lacking for a detailed explanation of the methodology employed to do this, except to say that it is analogous to the somewhat abbreviated one used by Sprow.[5] The equation in question is

$$_s E_R = 2.85\ _s t_R^{-.483} - .60.$$

[5] In connection with the discussion of the mathematical treatment of learning, Lashley in the second communication mentioned in our footnote 2 amplifies the statement of Lashley and Wade quoted above (p. 131) as follows: "I certainly do not oppose the placing of behavior sciences on a secure quantitative mathematical basis. But the making of consistent mathematical constructs and determination of their fit to observable phenomena are different matters. *The implication of my . . . footnote is that the values or constants necessary for your equations are indeterminable.*" (Italics added.) We have in the italicized sentence quoted just above a confident and unequivocal, though characteristically unsupported, statement that the scientific goal in question is a human impossibility. Lashley thus deliberately puts himself on record. The next few years should begin to show whether his intuition on this point is correct.

SUMMARY AND CONCLUSIONS

We may now sum up the conclusions at which we arrived in the preceding pages.

1. Early in the conditioning process primary generalization is complete, or nearly so, within the stimulus field originally conditioned, *i.e.*, the gradient of generalization shows little or no slope downward from the point conditioned (Pavlov, Hovland, Brown).

2. With continued reinforcement of the conditioned stimulus, a downward sloping gradient of primary stimulus generalization of reaction strength gradually and spontaneously develops (Pavlov).

3. This generalization gradient of reaction strength is a monotonic decreasing function of the magnitude of the differences between the conditioned stimulus and the unconditioned stimuli (Pavlov, Anrep, Bass and Hull, Hovland, Brown, Wickens).

4. Primary stimulus generalized conditioned reaction tendencies are much more susceptible to experimental extinction than are reactions actually conditioned to the response; and the wider the generalization, the greater the susceptibility. Equal numbers of unreinforced reaction evocations by all the stimuli involved (including the originally reinforced stimulus) accordingly result in a marked steepening of the generalization gradient (Hovland, Brown).

5. Another very effective method of steepening the primary stimulus generalization gradient in the case of the single-presentation or Pavlovian type of discrimination is differential reinforcement or contrast, *i.e.*, systematic reinforcement of the conditioned stimulus while systematically extinguishing one or more generalization stimuli (Pavlov, Hovland).

6. Stimulus intensity as such has a marked tendency to evoke reactions in the stimulus generalization situation

PAPER
16

(Hovland, Brown). This principle deserves a more explicit place in a comprehensive theoretical formalization than it has yet received.

7. The stimulus generalization gradient manifests itself with rats even in the complex differential reinforcement with simultaneously presented stimuli as employed by Lashley and Wade, and apparently directly contrary to their reported findings (Spence).

8. Differential reinforcement with simultaneous stimulus contrast critically involving the dimension in question is not necessary as a pre-condition of primary stimulus generalization (Pavlov, Anrep, Bass and Hull, Hovland, Brown, Wickens).

9. Lashley and Wade's statement of their belief in the absurdity of attempting to reduce the habit strength and reaction potential resulting from learning to mathematical treatment in the form of quantitative equations, ironically comes at the moment (June, 1946) when this seems actually to be taking place.

In conclusion the author wishes to thank Dr. Lashley for an advance copy of the Lashley-Wade manuscript, and for his kind invitation to write a reply to it. This courtesy greatly facilitated the relatively early preparation of the present study.

PAPER 16

REFERENCES

1. ANREP, G. V. The irradiation of conditioned reflexes. Proc. Royal Soc. London, 1923, 94B, 404–425.
2. BASS, M. J., & HULL, C. L. The irradiation of a tactile conditioned reflex in man. J. comp. Psychol., 1934, 17, 47–65.
3. BOYER, C. B. History of the measurement of heat. I. Thermometry and calorimetry. Scientific Monthly, 1943, 57, 442–452.
4. ——. History of the measurement of heat. II. The conservation of energy. Scientific Monthly, 1943, 57, 546–554.
5. BROWN, J. S. The generalization of approach responses as a function of stimulus intensity and strength of motivation. J. comp. Psychol., 1942, 33, 209–226.
6. HILGARD, E. R., & MARQUIS, D. G. Conditioning and learning. New York: Appleton-Century Co., Inc., 1940.
7. HOVLAND, C. I. The generalization of conditioned responses: I. The sensory generalization of conditioned responses with varying frequencies of tone. J. gen. Psychol., 1937, 17, 125–148.
8. ——. The generalization of conditioned responses: II. The sensory generalization of conditioned responses with varying intensities of tone. J. genet. Psychol., 1937, 51, 279–291.
9. ——. The generalization of conditioned responses: III. Extinction, spontaneous recovery, and disinhibition of conditioned and of generalized responses. J. exp. Psychol., 1937, 21, 47–62.
10. HULL, C. L. The problem of stimulus equivalence in behavior theory. PSYCHOL. REV., 1939, 46, 9–30.
11. ——. Principles of behavior. New York: D. Appleton-Century Co., Inc., 1943.
12. LASHLEY, K. S., & WADE, M. The Pavlovian theory of generalization. PSYCHOL. REV., 1946, 53, 72–87.
13. LOUCKS, R. B. An appraisal of Pavlov's systematization of behavior from the experimental standpoint. J. comp. Psychol., 1933, 15, 1–45.
14. ——. Reflexology and the psychobiological approach. PSYCHOL. REV., 1937, 44, 320–338.
15. PAVLOV, I. P. Conditioned reflexes (trans. by G. V. Anrep). London: Oxford Univ. Press, 1927.
16. RAZRAN, G. H. S. Transposition of relational responses and generalization of conditioned responses. PSYCHOL. REV., 1938, 45, 532–538.
17. SPENCE, K. W. An experimental test of the continuity and non-continuity theories of discrimination learning. J. exp. Psychol., 1945, 35, 253–266.
18. ——. An experimental investigation of Lashley's interpretation of primary stimulus generalization (in manuscript).
19. SPROW, A. J. Reactivity homogeneous compound trial-and-error learning with distributed trials and terminal reinforcement. J. exp. Psychol. (in press).
20. THURSTONE, L. L. Stimulus dispersions in the method of constant stimuli. J. exp. Psychol., 1932, 15, 284–297.
21. WICKENS, D. D. Studies of response generalization in conditioning. I. Stimulus generalization during response generalization. J. exp. Psychol., 1943, 33, 221–227.

Reprinted from Psychological Review, Vol. 54, No. 5, September, 1947
Printed in U. S. A.

A PROPOSED QUANTIFICATION OF HABIT STRENGTH [1]

BY CLARK L. HULL, JOHN M. FELSINGER, ARTHUR I. GLADSTONE
AND HARRY G. YAMAGUCHI

Institute of Human Relations,
Yale University

INTRODUCTION

The central factor of a science of behavior naturally is behavior itself. It inevitably follows that the central problem of a systematic natural-science approach to behavior is that of determining from given antecedent events and conditions what behavior will follow. Such a determination amounts to a prediction, *i.e.*, a statement of the behavioral potentiality (sE_R) which lies in the relevant antecedent events and states. Now, the critical immediately preceding event in the case of reaction evocation appears to be stimulation (S), and the critical immediately preceding states involved are (1) the strength of the habit (sH_R) and (2) the primary motivation or drive (D), *e.g.*, hunger.[2] There is some reason to believe that the potentiality of the evocation of a reaction in a simple, *i.e.*, a non-competitional, situation will turn out one

day to be multiplicative in nature. More specifically, it is believed that when these three functions are suitably quantified it will be found that

$$sE_R = sH_R \times D. \qquad (1)$$

On this assumption, if the stimulation and the drive at the several trials are kept constant as they ordinarily are during experimental learning processes, the responses obtained at the successive trials will be substantially a function of habit strength alone, quite as is ordinarily assumed. Actually, of course, the habit strength will throughout such a series be multiplied by a constant value of drive which, strictly speaking, makes it a case of reaction potential.[3] The purpose of the present paper is primarily to propose a methodology for quantifying a sequence of habit strengths (reaction potentials with motivation constant) which results from a simple learning situation of this kind.

One major difficulty in the way of satisfactorily quantifying reaction potential is that its objective manifestations take so many different forms. These manifestations, while measurable, are usually measured in different units and rarely or never, even when measured in the same units, yield results which are comparable. Moreover, in some cases, *e.g.*, muscular

PAPER
17

---

[1] This is the second study in the series by the present authors. The experimental work, as described in the previous study (7), was performed by Mr. Felsinger, the statistical analysis was carried out by Mr. Yamaguchi and Mr. Gladstone, and Mr. Hull supervised the investigation and prepared the manuscript in frequent consultation with the other three authors. The senior author takes entire responsibility for the methodology and the interpretations here given. The authors are indebted to Professors Irvin L. Child, Mark A. May, and Kenneth W. Spence for a critical reading of a preliminary draft of the manuscript. Dr. H. O. Gulliksen also contributed a valuable suggestion.

[2] Secondary motivation is here neglected, partly in the interest of expository simplification but mainly because of uncertainty as to its exact status.

[3] On the other hand, if the sH_R of equation 1 is kept constant and the D is varied, the resulting series of reaction potentials will be substantially a function of primary motivation alone, *i.e.*, the product of a variable D multiplied by a constant value of sH_R.

237

contraction, several different aspects of the response, such as latency, amplitude, and force, can be employed as indicators of what at bottom is presumably the same thing. A number of phenomena recognized as associated quantitatively with reaction potential are listed in Table 1. All these presumably possess a monotonic relationship to reaction potential, and all are evidently increasing functions of it except reaction latency and number of errors which obviously have a decreasing or inverse functional relationship. But $_sE_R$ itself clearly is not necessarily a certain number of degrees of arc, a certain number of grams, millimeters, cubic centimeters, seconds, or errors.

Moreover, all quantifications of reaction potential, however empirically manifested, should be expressible on the same scale and in terms of the

TABLE 1

A tabular summary of various objectively observable and quantifiable manifestations of reaction potential ($_sE_R$), the aspect of the manifestation quantified, the unit ordinarily employed in this quantification, and typical references to experimental work.

PAPER
17

Phenomenon	Aspect of phenomenon quantified	Customary unit	Typical references
1. Conditioned secretion	Saliva	Drops or cubic centimeters	24; 1
2. Galvanic skin reaction	Electric potential	Degrees of arc moved by galvanometer	2; 18
3. Striated muscular contraction	Intensity of contraction	Grams	8
4. Striated muscular contraction	Amplitude of resulting movement	Centimeters	22; 17
5. Striated muscular contraction	Reaction latency	Seconds	12; 9; 28; 30
6. Change in size of optic pupil	Length of cross-section	Millimeters	19
7. Breathing amplitude	Chest expansion as recorded by pneumograph	Millimeters	10; 21
8. Pulse rhythm	Variability in amplitude of pulse beats as graphically recorded	Oscillometer units	29
9. Occurrence of erroneous response	Ratio of errors to total relevant trials	Probability of erroneous reaction ($\bar{p}$)	14; 31
10. The mere occurrence of the response, whatever it is	Ratio of response occurrence to total suitable stimulations	Probability of a given response occurrence (p)	6; 37; 27
11. Experimental extinction	Unreinforced reaction evocations	Number of extinctive responses (n)	36; 25
12. Vocal squeak	Latency and intensity	Seconds and amplitude of graphic record	5; 16

same unit. This principle at once renders questionable for quantification the cubic centimeter because this is peculiar to salivary secretion and does not directly apply, for example, to the galvanic skin reaction. It renders questionable for this purpose intensity of muscular contraction because this will not directly apply to salivary secretion. It rules out in the same sense the number of degrees of arc moved by a galvanometer, because most manifestations of sE_R are not primarily electrical in nature. It rules out the intensity and the amplitude of muscular contraction because many reactional manifestations are not of a muscular nature and so cannot be measured in grams or centimeters. It rules out number of erroneous reactions because some processes, such as the salivary secretion and the galvanic skin reaction, are not associated with competing reactions capable of displacing them as is ordinarily the case with reactions called errors.

A second major difficulty in the way of the proposed quantification is that habit strength, drive, and reaction potential are never available as such to direct observation of the scientist (20, p. 21). In a word they are logical constructs much as are the atoms and molecules of physics and chemistry. It is instructive to note in this connection that in spite of the fact that individual atoms are never observed, much less placed in a balance and weighed, their masses have been determined with great accuracy by indirect means. It is true, of course, that the fact that atomic phenomena have been quantified successfully by indirect means does not imply that the quantification of habit phenomena will be achieved, much less that any particular methodology of such quantification will be successful. The facts of atomic quantification do negate, on the other hand, the major pre-

mise prevalent in certain psychological circles (38) that indirect methods of the quantification of theoretical constructs is absurd because *a priori* impossible. True, the process of atom quantification has consumed much time, together with great labor and profound thought. On the other hand, the quantification of reaction potential as such has hardly yet been proposed, much less seriously attempted. Until the problem is attacked in a vigorous and protracted manner it cannot be said whether it will be more or less difficult than have been parallel tasks in the physical sciences. Meanwhile we submit that the quantification of atoms, even of uranium or plutonium, is of no greater ultimate significance for the welfare of man than is that of behavior potentiality.

The Principles Upon Which the Proposed Quantification is Based

In order to facilitate the reader's comprehension of the statement of methodology which follows, it has been thought desirable to state the major principles upon which the methodology is based and which serve as a kind of background for it, together with a general outline of their operation in the present situation.

1. It is assumed with confidence that with distributed trials and minimum work load, habit strength (sH_R) increases up to a maximal asymptote as the reinforcements (N) increase.[4]

2. It has been shown experimentally (7) that reaction latency (st_R) decreases to a minimal asymptote as the reinforcements (N) increase.

3. From (1) and (2) it follows that habit strength (or reaction potential, D constant) has an inverse mono-

PAPER
17

---

[4] This is believed to hold where reaction latency is not specifically trained to be slow, as in delayed conditioned reactions (20, p. 337).

tonic functional relationship to reaction latency.

4. It follows from (3), other things equal, that if reaction latency B is found to be less than reaction latency A, then the momentary reaction potential ($_s\dot{E}_R$) corresponding to B must be greater than that corresponding to A.

5. It is a universal empirical observation that reaction latency where the related reaction potential ($_sE_R$) is presumably constant, e.g., at the $_sl_R$ asymptote, varies from instant to instant, and so from trial to trial.

6. It follows from (3), (4), and (5) that the momentary reaction potential ($_s\dot{E}_R$) must vary from instant to instant (20, p. 319).

7. Further, it is specifically assumed that the spontaneous variability in the momentary reaction potential ($_s\dot{E}_R$) approximates the normal form of distribution (20, p. 304 ff.), $_sE_R$ remaining constant.[5]

8. It is a statistical commonplace that the differences between two sets of uncorrelated values which are themselves distributed normally will be normally distributed (13, pp. 218, 219).

9. It is self-evident that if a considerable number of reaction latencies, all secured after a given organism has reached its latency asymptote, are available and these are drawn at random and compared, it will be found that except for occasional cases of equality about half of the latencies chosen first will be shorter than those chosen second, and about half will be longer.

10. It follows from (6), (7), and (8) that the two halves of the distribution of reaction-latency differences of (9) correspond to the two symmetrical wings of a normal or Gaussian distribution of reaction-potential differences.

[5] Certain indirect evidence bearing on the soundness of this assumption will be presented later in the present paper (p. 250 ff.).

11. It is also a statistical commonplace (13, pp. 218, 219) that if a random comparison of two normal uncorrelated distributions A and B occurs and significantly more than 50 per cent of the B's are found to be greater than the A's, the mean of the B's must be greater than the mean of the A's.

12. By (10), (11), and related statistical principles, it follows that if the latencies of two groups of $_sl_R$'s, A and B, are compared and more than 50 per cent of the B's are shorter than the A's, this not only implies that the $_sE_R$ of the B's must be greater than is that of the A's, but that this difference has a determinate magnitude. The logic behind the quantification of the difference in reaction potential is illustrated in Fig. 1. For example, suppose that the A's are reaction latencies from a habit with two reinforcements and the B's are from a habit of three reinforcements, and that 40 of the comparisons out of a total of 59 show the B's to be shorter, i.e., $\frac{40}{59}$ or 67.8 per cent of the B momentary reaction potentials ($_s\dot{E}_R$) to be greater than the A's. By consulting a suitable table of the normal probability integral it will be found that the 17.8 per cent that 67.8 per cent exceeds 50 per cent corresponds to .462 of the standard deviation (σ) of the normal distribution of the differences here involved. In a word, the reaction potential of B exceeds that of A by $.462\sigma_{\text{diff}}$. By this quantification of the *difference* between two reaction potentials, a major step toward the quantification of the reaction potentials themselves is attained.

13. In case a situation should chance to arise in which there is an analogous quantification of the difference between habit strength A and the absolute zero of habit strength (Z), i.e., just no habit strength at all, the difference between this zero and the value of A would be the habit strength of A;

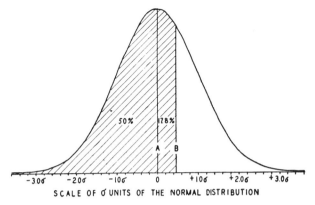

FIG. 1. Diagrammatic representation of the determination of the implied behavioral differences between a habit of two reinforcements (*A*) and one of three reinforcements (*B*). The normal distribution represented above is that of the differences between the parallel items of two independent, non-correlated distributions. The σ units should really be marked σ_diff. to indicate that they refer to a set of differences.

the sum of *A* and the difference between *A* and *B* would be the habit strength of *B*; and so on for all the other habits in the series. Thus would be finally attained, in an indirect manner it is true, the quantification of a series of habit strengths which it is the objective of the present paper to describe.

14. The close analogy of the procedure so far described to that employed in the methodology of judgmental paired comparisons as employed in traditional psychophysics must have struck the reader. Among the similarities are: the momentary variability in the judgmental response when everything else is constant; the assumption of the Gaussian nature of the variability of these judgmental responses; the per cent excess of one type of judgment over the other; the general method of calculating the difference represented by a given per cent of judgmental difference; and the unit of quantification, the σ of the dispersion of the relevant differences (**13**, p. 219). Nevertheless, the present data do *not* arise from judgments in any ordinary sense. In psychophysics

the judgments ordinarily are based on a comparison of stimulations which are systematically varied, the judgmental response being evoked on the basis of an identical internal condition of relevant habit strength possessed by the judges. In the present situation, on the other hand, the stimulation is in all cases identical while the relevant habit strength which mediates the reaction is the critical difference.

15. Moreover, in psychophysical judgments the two things compared are ordinarily present as stimuli simultaneously or in close succession, whereas the present states under comparison cannot possibly exist simultaneously because only one strength of a given habit can be possessed at a time. This is because when a habit strength is increased the previous strength of that habit no longer exists as such. By the present methodology, the reaction latency is permanently recorded at the time each habit strength exists (even though changed immediately thereafter by reinforcement or non-reinforcement) and the numerical comparison of these records, which may represent states as much as 80

days distant from each other, may be made (by the investigator) at any time whatever after the second event has occurred.

16. Owing also to the fact that only one strength of a given habit can be possessed by a given organism at a given time, there arises a limitation not encountered in ordinary psychophysical experiments. Only one reaction latency can be secured from the reaction potential based on a given habit strength because a response evocation must be either reinforced or not reinforced. If a response evocation is reinforced, it will strengthen the reaction potential; if it is not reinforced, it will weaken it. Therefore the reaction potential can never again be assumed with certainty to be the same as it was. Consequently only one significant comparison can ever be secured from any two habit strengths of a given organism. It thus comes about that in order to secure adequate numbers of comparisons of what correspond to the same habit strength, many different organisms are placed in a comparable learning sequence so that all acquire corresponding habits, it being assumed that the increments in habit strength at the successive reinforcements are in some sense comparable, though hardly equal because of individual differences in learning capacity. For this reason the latencies of a given organism are here only compared with each other, never with those of other organisms.

17. It thus follows that habit strength difference quantifications secured by the present methodology are those between the central tendency of the many habit strengths of the group of organisms as a whole at two different numbers of reinforcements, in terms of the standard deviations of the pooled reaction potential variabilities of the same group of organisms as a whole. In some respects this is analogous to Thorndike's method of pooling the judgments of a large number of persons concerning the quality of concrete samples of handwriting (32) where the unit in which the resulting differences were quantified was a function of the pooled variability differences of the group of judges who chanced to be employed. As Thurstone (33) has pointed out, this pooling of the variability of numerous somewhat different organisms introduces an additional uncertainty regarding the normality of the distribution of the differences, the σ of which is here used as the preliminary measuring unit of the quantification of reaction potential. Sooner or later, of course, the characteristics of this pooling of many variability distributions must be objectively determined if possible (11). Provisionally it is assumed to approximate closely enough to normality to permit useful employment of the usual tables of the probability integral.

THE DETAILED QUANTIFICATIONAL
PROCEDURE

A detailed account of the subjects and experimental procedure which yielded the data of the study now being reported was given in the first article of the present series (7). It will be necessary here only to say that 59 male albino rats were employed as subjects and that they were trained to move a brass tube to the left a minimum of one-sixteenth of an inch. This tubular manipulandum projected five-eighths of an inch into the animal's chamber and required a lateral pressure of seven and a half grams. The motivation throughout was 22 hours of food privation. A single operation of the manipulandum, always immediately reinforced by a small cylinder of food, was given each animal every day, including week-ends, throughout the training. The aspect of the reaction directly measured was the time from the lifting of the shutter giving the animal access to the manipulandum until the completion of the animal's reaction. As a sample of the data with which we start, we give in Table 2 the first nine latencies of the first ten of the 59 animals.

There were available for our quantification the experimental data from more than 60 trials of our 59 animals. Such a number of quantifications by the present methodology would involve a prohibitive amount of labor. For this reason a judicious sampling[6] of 25 trials distributed over the entire range of 60 was chosen as the basis for our major investigation (11). But the tables associated with the simultaneous quantification of even 25 variables are very bulky and hardly possible of publication in an ordinary journal. Since, however, the present methodology had not hitherto been applied to the present type of problem, it was felt that a detailed example would ma-

[6] The trials actually chosen are presented on the abscissa of Fig. 2. Every second trial was chosen early in the series where change is more rapid, and thereafter every third trial was chosen.

terially facilitate the exposition. Accordingly the quantification of the first nine only of the 60 trials was worked out for illustrative purposes, and will be presented here. The outcome of the quantification of the 25 trials will be presented in analytical detail elsewhere (11).

The first step in the methodology of paired comparisons is to compare each of the items under consideration with every other. Such a set of comparisons for our example, that for subject No. 2, is shown in detail in Table 3. In each comparison there is involved the latency of primary reference, the numbered rows of Table 3, and the latency of secondary reference, the numbered columns. The numbers of the rows and columns represent the number of the superthreshold trials during the learning process. In case the latency of primary reference has a shorter duration (which implies a greater reaction potential) than its secondary-reference comparison, a value of unity is placed in the cell marked by the intersection of row and column, e.g., row 2 and column 1. In case the reverse comparison is made, a zero is placed in the cell of opposite combination, e.g., row 1 and column 2. Thus where row and column differ in num-

PAPER

17

TABLE 2

A sample of the original data employed in the present study, the first nine latencies (in seconds) of each of the first ten subjects

Rat No.	Trial numbers								
	1	2	3	4	5	6	7	8	9
1	3.50	4.01	10.03	8.21	25.00	1.00	2.57	2.54	.80
2	27.50	15.41	7.61	18.00	1.43	25.00	6.50	5.82	3.86
3	13.00	9.00	13.50	8.80	20.00	17.00	41.00	10.05	2.00
4	13.00	11.50	5.00	2.00	1.00	1.00	.80	2.00	1.50
5	6.00	4.00	2.80	6.00	8.56	2.27	1.01	1.23	2.07
6	2.50	3.00	1.50	148.00	16.50	25.00	33.50	40.00	22.80
7	5.50	10.05	21.00	9.00	16.00	270.00	4.21	2.56	2.07
8	31.50	39.50	210.00	112.00	258.00	36.00	53.00	62.50	
9	6.20	3.77	8.31	7.26	4.43	16.50	1.81	2.36	1.21
10	49.00	33.00	6.71	27.36	44.00	5.50	3.70	1.51	2.36

TABLE 3

Table of the paired comparisons of the nine reaction latencies of a typical subject, No. 2. Note that each pair of latencies yields two comparison scores because each is used once as the primary reference and once as the secondary reference. The sum of the entries of the columns and the rows of the same number must equal the number of items compared (nine), which makes possible a convenient check of the accuracy of each tabulation.

Ordinal number of latency trials of primary reference	Reaction latencies compared	Ordinal number of latency trials of secondary reference									Check column summating the total of row and column having the same number
		1	2	3	4	5	6	7	8	9	
1	27.50	.5	0	0	0	0	0	0	0	0	0.5+ 8.5 = 9.0
2	15.41	1	.5	0	1	0	1	0	0	0	3.5+ 5.5 = 9.0
3	7.61	1	1	.5	1	0	1	0	0	0	4.5+ 4.5 = 9.0
4	18.00	1	0	0	.5	0	1	0	0	0	2.5+ 6.5 = 9.0
5	1.43	1	1	1	1	.5	1	1	1	1	8.5+ 0.5 = 9.0
6	25.00	1	0	0	0	0	.5	0	0	0	1.5+ 7.5 = 9.0
7	6.50	1	1	1	1	0	1	.5	0	0	5.5+ 3.5 = 9.0
8	5.82	1	1	1	1	0	1	1	.5	0	6.5+ 2.5 = 9.0
9	3.86	1	1	1	1	0	1	1	1	.5	7.5+ 1.5 = 9.0
Σ		8.5	5.5	4.5	6.5	.5	7.5	3.5	2.5	1.5	40.5+40.5=81.0

ber, the comparison score appears twice in the table. In case the two latencies under comparison are the same, a value of .5 is placed in each of the two cells.[7] If a row and column have the same number, only one entry is made, that of .5; hence the diagonal row of .5 values dividing the table into halves. This is in conformity with a psychophysical convention (13, p. 226) and represents the fact that the comparison of a value with itself yields a zero difference.

[7] When a value of .5 appears in a table of the type of Table 3, i.e., where the two latencies compared are equal, we have in the present situation what corresponds to an "equal" judgment in ordinary psychophysics. This situation accordingly has substantially the logical status of the "equal" judgments which involve a special relationship to the magnitudes judged (13, p. 195). The assignment of a .5 to such cases in effect divides them equally between the two situations being compared. While this probably produced an error in the results, it was slight owing to the small number of such "tied" comparisons. The increased accuracy to be obtained in giving separate treatment to these data was not believed to warrant the added labor in a preliminary determination such as the present one.

The second step in the procedure is to go through all the paired comparison tables, such as Table 3, of the 59 individual animals and find the total of the scores falling in each of the 81 cells. Each one of these totals is then divided by the total number of subjects, here 59. This yields the equivalent per cent of the latencies of each of the pairs compared in which the latency of primary reference is the shorter and therefore the reaction potential the greater. These means are shown in Table 4, corresponding cell for cell to Table 3.

Our third step is to convert the empirical probability values of Table 4 into quantificational separations or differences in units of the standard deviation of the difference variability of the group as a whole, as described above (p. 242). For example, in the first data column of Table 4, it appears in row 2 that 57.6 per cent of the second superthreshold trials of the 59 animals proved to have shorter reaction latencies than the first superthreshold trials. Looking up the cor-

TABLE 4

Means of the several reaction-latency comparison scores of the first nine reactions of the 59 subjects. The values of the cells in this table are the averages of the corresponding cells of the type of Table 3, for the entire group of 59 animals.

Ordinal number of latency trial of primary reference	Ordinal number of latency trials of secondary reference								
	1	2	3	4	5	6	7	8	9
1	.500	.424	.390	.280	.322	.322	.170	.119	.102
2	.576	.500	.322	.288	.322	.305	.170	.153	.119
3	.610	.678	.500	.263	.305	.339	.195	.186	.195
4	.720	.712	.737	.500	.407	.458	.305	.314	.136
5	.678	.678	.695	.593	.500	.517	.348	.356	.305
6	.678	.695	.661	.542	.483	.500	.390	.305	.195
7	.831	.831	.805	.695	.653	.610	.500	.426	.373
8	.881	.848	.814	.686	.644	.695	.576	.500	.331
9	.898	.881	.805	.864	.695	.805	.627	.670	.500

responding σ values in an appropriate table of the probability integral, e.g., Guilford (**13**, p. 537 ff.), we find that this corresponds to .192 $\sigma_{diff.}$ as shown in the same position in Table 5. Similarly, the third set of 59 super-threshold latencies shows 61.0 per cent shorter than the first set, as presented in row 3, column 1 of Table 4, which

by the same table corresponds to .280 $\sigma_{diff.}$ as given by the next entry in Table 5; and so on for all the other comparisons with the first super-threshold reaction latency. The 67.8 per cent value and the .462 $\sigma_{diff.}$ value used for illustrative purposes in Fig. 1 appear at the intersection of row 3 and column 2 in Tables 4 and 5 respec-

PAPER 17

TABLE 5

Quantificational separations of the nine variables of the group of 59 organisms as a whole in all combinations in terms of the standard deviations of response variability of the variables involved, as found by looking up in a table of the normal probability integral the values corresponding to those of Table 4.

Ordinal number of latency trials of primary reference	Ordinal number of latency trials of secondary reference								
	1	2	3	4	5	6	7	8	9
1	.000	−.192	−.280	−.584	−.462	−.462	−.956	−1.182	−1.272
2	.192	.000	−.462	−.559	−.462	−.510	−.956	−1.026	−1.182
3	.280	.462	.000	−.635	−.510	−.415	−.860	− .891	− .860
4	.584	.559	.635	.000	−.236	−.106	−.510	− .486	−1.100
5	.462	.462	.510	.236	.000	.042	−.392	− .369	− .510
6	.462	.510	.415	.106	−.042	.000	−.280	− .510	− .860
7	.956	.956	.860	.510	.392	.280	.000	− .192	− .324
8	1.182	1.026	.891	.486	.369	.510	.192	.000	− .439
9	1.272	1.182	.860	1.100	.510	.860	.324	.439	.000
Means	.5989	.5517	.3810	.0733	.0490	.0221	−.3820	− .4686	− .7274
Means squared	.3587	.3044	.1452	.0054	.0024	.0005	.1495	.2196	.5291

PAPER

17

tively. In a similar manner were obtained from the proportion or probability values of Table 4 all the other quantitative behavioral differences shown in Table 5.

At this point we introduce into our quantificational methodology a unique procedure devised by Thurstone (33, 34)—the so-called Case III of his paired-comparisons methodology. This yields an estimate of the dispersion of each of the individual variables involved (σ_k) and mediates an important rectification of the scale-difference values as secured from the table of the probability integral. The procedure of securing the σ_k's consists of several stages, the results of which are summarized in Table 6. It begins with the calculation of the standard deviation of each column of Table 5. To do this each item in each column of Table 5 is squared and the squares are added and divided by the number of items; this gives the mean of the X^2's, i.e., $\frac{\Sigma X^2}{N}$. Then the squares of the means of the columns of Table 5 are transferred and placed in the formula

$$V_k = \sqrt{\frac{\Sigma X^2}{N} - M^2} \qquad (1)$$

in Guilford's notation. For example, by this formula the standard deviation of column 1, Table 5, becomes

$$V_k = \sqrt{\frac{4.8122}{9} - .3587}$$

$$= \sqrt{.5347 - .3587,}$$

$$V_k = .4195.$$

These V_k values for the present data are given as the first row of Table 6.

The next stage of the process is to find the reciprocal of each V_k value, e.g.,

$$\frac{1}{.4195} = 2.384.$$

These appear as the second row of values in Table 6. All the nine $\frac{1}{V_k}$ values are then added, which comes to 20.211, as shown in the Σ column at the right. With the $\Sigma \frac{1}{V_k}$ values available the value, a, may be calculated by the formula

$$a = \frac{2n}{\Sigma \dfrac{1}{V_k}}. \qquad (2)$$

Substituting in our example,

$$a = \frac{2 \times 9}{20.211};$$

$$\therefore \quad a = .8906.$$

We now have the values necessary for finding the σ_k's which are our immediate objectives. These are given by the formula

$$\sigma_k = a \frac{1}{V_k} - 1. \qquad (3)$$

Substituting, we have as σ_k of variable 1

$$\sigma_k = \frac{.8906}{.4195} - 1$$

$$= 2.123 - 1;$$

$$\therefore \quad \sigma_k = 1.123.$$

The values of the σ_k's as so calculated appear in the third line of Table 6.

Now, the ultimate object of calculating the σ_k's as above is to enable us to rectify certain distortions in the scale-difference values as they come from the probability table as shown in Table 5. This arises from the facts (1) that these latter values are in terms of σ_{diff}, and (2) that these σ_{diff}'s as units of quantification are tacitly assumed to be equal. Actually they are not equal, as is shown by implication in the third line of Table 6. To understand this we need to recall

TABLE 6

Stages in the calculation of the σ_k's which are the estimates of the dispersions of the several individual variables. It will be noticed that the smaller the V_k, the greater the σ_k.

Symbolic representation of the several computational stages	Ordinal number of the several variables									
	1	2	3	4	5	6	7	8	9	Σ
V_k	.4195	.4295	.4823	.5559	.3760	.4387	.4580	.4864	.4084	
$\dfrac{1}{V_k}$	2.384	2.328	2.073	1.799	2.660	2.279	2.183	2.056	2.449	20.211
σ_k	1.123	1.073	.846	.602	1.369	1.030	.944	.831	1.181	8.999
σ_k^2	1.261	1.151	.716	.362	1.874	1.061	.891	.691	1.395	9.402

a fundamental equation used by Thurstone (**33**, p. 280),

$$S_2 - S_1 = X_{21} \cdot \sqrt{\sigma_2{}^2 + \sigma_1{}^2} \quad (4)$$

in which

$S_2 - S_1$ represents the difference between any pair of quantified reaction potentials used as variables;

X_{21} = the sigma value of the difference between 1 and 2 as derived from Table 4 and appearing in Table 5 as described above;

σ_2 = the dispersion of variable No. 2;

σ_1 = the dispersion of variable No. 1.

The σ_k's are given in Table 6, e.g., 1.123 and 1.073. Substituting in equation (4), we have

$$S_2 - S_1 = .192\sqrt{1.261 + 1.151}$$
$$= .192 \times 1.553$$
$$= .298.$$

Carrying out similar statistical maneuvers for all of the other combinations we have the values of Table 7,

PAPER 17

TABLE 7

Quantificational separations of the nine variables of the group of 59 subjects as a whole as derived from Tables 5 and 6, with the aid of Formula 4.

Ordinal number of latency trials of primary reference	Ordinal number of latency trials of secondary reference								
	1	2	3	4	5	6	7	8	9
1	.000	−.298	−.394	−.744	−.818	−.704	−1.402	−1.651	− 2.073
2	.298	.000	−.631	−.688	−.803	−.758	−1.366	−1.392	− 1.886
3	.394	.631	.000	−.659	−.821	−.553	−1.090	−1.057	− 1.250
4	.744	.688	.659	.000	−.353	−.126	− .571	− .499	− 1.459
5	.818	.803	.821	.353	.000	.072	− .652	− .591	− .922
6	.704	.758	.553	.126	−.072	.000	− .391	− .675	− 1.348
7	1.402	1.366	1.090	.571	.652	.391	.000	− .242	− .490
8	1.651	1.392	1.057	.499	.591	.675	.242	.000	− .634
9	2.073	1.886	1.250	1.459	.922	1.348	.490	.634	.000
Σ	8.084	7.226	4.405	.917	−.702	.345	−4.740	−5.473	−10.062

the first item in row 2 being the .298 calculated above.

It may next be noticed that in Table 7 we have eight distinct measures of the scale difference between the members of each successive pair of reaction potentials. If we let S with a subscript corresponding to the number of the superthreshold trial (including the first) represent the nine reaction potentials here under consideration, it is evident (assuming a normal distribution and a very large sample of data) that the value of $(S_3 - S_1)$ less the value of $(S_3 - S_2)$ must represent the value of $(S_2 - S_1)$, and so on. Stated formally and systematically,

$$(S_3-S_1)-(S_3-S_2)=S_2-S_1=d_{12}$$
$$(S_4-S_1)-(S_4-S_2)=S_2-S_1=d_{12}$$
$$(S_5-S_1)-(S_5-S_2)=S_2-S_1=d_{12}$$
$$\cdots \cdots \cdots \cdots \cdots$$
$$(S_9-S_1)-(S_9-S_2)=S_2-S_1=d_{12}.$$

These seven values together with that secured directly by subtracting S_1 from S_2 give in all eight values for d_{12}, or one less than the total number of the variables involved. Actually, since $(S_3 - S_1) \cdots (S_9 - S_1)$ constitutes column 1 of Table 7 and $(S_3 - S_2) \cdots (S_9 - S_2)$ constitutes column 2, this series of mathematical expressions amounts to a mere subtraction of the entries of column 2 of Table 7 from the corresponding values of column 1. These differences are recorded appropriately in column 1 of Table 8. In a similar manner the subtraction of column 3 from column 2 yields the eight values of d_{23}, the subtraction of column 4 from column 3 yields the eight values of d_{34}, and so on.

Now, the mean of each column of scale-difference values will in general yield a more reliable measure of the quantificational differences in question than will any single difference value. The eight versions of the quantitative difference between each of the successive variables are accordingly averaged and appear as the next-to-last line of Table 8. These represent the culmination of our

TABLE 8

Eight different evaluations of each of the eight quantificational differences between the reaction potentials separating each successive pair of trials, together with their means and cumulations.

Ordinal number of trials	The eight types of differences involved							
	d_{12}	d_{23}	d_{34}	d_{45}	d_{56}	d_{67}	d_{78}	d_{89}
1		.096	.350	.074	−.114	.698	.249	.422
2	.298		.057	.115	−.045	.608	.026	.494
3	−.237	.631		.162	−.268	.537	−.033	.193
4	.056	.029	.659		−.227	.445	−.072	.960
5	.015	−.018	.468	.353		.724	−.061	.331
6	−.054	.205	.427	.198	−.072		.284	.673
7	.036	.276	.519	−.081	.261	.391		.248
8	.259	.335	.558	−.092	−.084	.433	.242	
9	.187	.636	−.209	.537	−.426	.858	−.144	.634
Σ of sE_R differences	.560	2.190	2.829	1.266	−.975	4.694	.491	3.955
M of sE_R differences	.0700	.2738	.3536	.1583	−.1219	.5868	.0614	.4944
Cumulative sE_R values	.0700	.3438	.6974	.8557	.7338	1.3206	1.3820	1.8764

quantifications of reactional-potential differences.

There remains, however, the task of finding the relative magnitude of the several reaction potentials from the lowest available reference point, which is arbitrarily taken as zero. This naturally is the reaction potential of the first trial during the learning process showing a conditioned reaction, *i.e.*, a minimum superthreshold reaction potential. This means that reaction No. 1 has a value of zero; No. 2 has a reaction potential represented by the difference between 1 and 2, *i.e.*, d_{12}, which is .07; the reaction potential of No. 3 is at that distance above zero which is the sum of $d_{12} + d_{23}$; and so on for the other values up to trial No. 9, which has a value of 1.8764. These values, consisting of the cumulation of successive differences, are shown in the last line of Table 8.

Thus reaction-potential differences as generated by a simple learning process have been quantified and, in some sense, measured (**4, 3, 15, 23, 26**). The quantificational unit employed is the joint standard deviation of the oscillatory tendencies of the 59 organisms employed as subjects on the trials quantified. By the same token the present description of the operations involved in this quantification constitutes a detailed operational definition of reaction potential ($_sE_R$) itself.

The Variation in σ_k as Learning Progresses

The central concept under examination in the present section is Thurstone's 'confusion range' (**33**, p. 285), which is said by him to 'fluctuate' (**33**, p. 274). This fluctuation of judgmental reactions is evidently related

PAPER
17

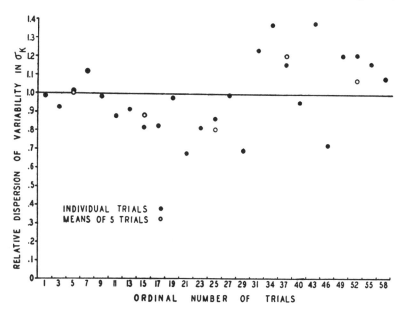

Fig. 2. A graphic representation of the relative dispersion estimates (σ_k) of the variables used as the basis for measuring the respective reaction potentials at 25 of the 60 learning trials selected for the purpose of quantification.

functionally to what the senior author of the present article has called the 'oscillation' ($_sO_R$) of reaction potential (**20**, p. 304). The question of primary interest now before us is whether, except for the influence of sampling, the dispersion range of the individual variable (σ_k) varies systematically as the learning process progresses. Fortunately, as we have seen, Thurstone has provided us with a procedure for estimating the relative dispersion of the several elements entering into paired comparisons with every other in a quantificational situation such as the present. This is an approximation based on the assumption that the actual differences in dispersion are not very great; e.g., that (**33**, p. 286) the dispersion of one of the compared elements (No. 2) will not be more than about twice that of another (No. 1) as a maximum difference.

PAPER

17

The calculated estimates of the σ_k magnitudes as worked out in our example given above are presented on p. 247. From an inspection of these it is clear that there is a good deal of variation in the estimated dispersions. It is evident, of course, that considerable variability in this function would occur in the present empirical situation owing to the relatively small number of comparisons (59) in each quantification. An inspection of these σ_k values shows that the largest value (1.369) is slightly more than twice that of the smallest one (.602).

The above group of σ_k's, coming as they do from a set of genuine but exemplary data, are presented essentially to illustrate the methodology. Our main evidence in regard to the degree of dispersion of the present quantification data concerns the selection of the 25 learning trials mentioned earlier (p. 243). In order to facilitate the reader's comprehension of this rather complex set of 25 σ_k's, they are presented graphically in Fig. 2. There it may be seen that just as in our sample of nine, the variability from trial to trial is considerable. The largest value (1.381) is also slightly more than twice that of the smallest (.678).

An inspection of Fig. 2 shows in general a tendency of the σ_k's to fall to a minimum near $N = 25$, after which they rise. To reduce the confusing effect of random variability apparently due largely to sampling limitations, the σ_k's were averaged by successive 5's. The results are represented in Figure 2 by hollow circles. These mean values show a progressive fall from near the mean value at trial 5 to a minimum at trial 25, after which the σ_k's rise markedly to relatively high levels throughout the final half of the learning.

THE APPLICATION OF THURSTONE'S DISCREPANCY AND PLOTTING TESTS TO THE PRESENT QUANTIFICATIONS

Thurstone has employed two methods for verifying the soundness of the dispersional assumptions made in the application of his method of paired comparison. One method (**35**, p. 296) is to compute back from the final scale values secured (such as the last line of Table 8) to the actual probability values from which the quantification set out (such as Table 4). This was done with the 288 relevant values involved in the 25 variables of our major quantification. Of these a single value showed a deviation more than 3σ greater than the theoretical value. A deviation as great as this is to be expected in about three cases in a thousand, which is not far from 1 in 288. The mean discrepancy was .025.

A second method employed by Thurstone to check on the dispersions involved in a given quantification (**34**,

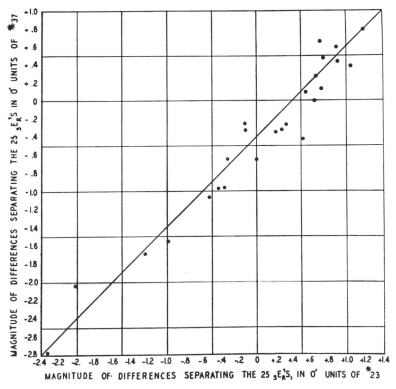

FIG. 3. Dot diagram of column having trial 37 as a common variable, plotted against the column having trial 23 as a common variable. It will be seen that these dots, despite considerable scatter, approximate a linear sequence with a slope of unity. The diagonal line drawn through the dots has a slope of exactly 1.00. The linearity as represented by zeta (**13**, p. 348) is .0371, and the calculated slope deviates from unity by .014.

PAPER

17

p. 389) is to plot against each other any two columns of such tables as Tables 5 or 7 above. He states:

"If the plot is linear it proves that the assumed normal distribution of the discriminal process is correct. If the slope is unity, it proves that the discriminal dispersions are equal."

Fifteen pairs of columns of our major quantificational project involving the 25 trials represented in Fig. 2 were thus tried out on the tables corresponding to Tables 5 and 7. It was found in general that the plots coming from the tables corresponding to Table

5 (representing Case V) were approximately linear, but their slopes deviated perceptibly from unity. However, when the same plots were made from the table corresponding to Table 7 (representing the employment of Case III), their calculated slopes were close to unity, their deviations averaging only .0248. A fairly typical plot of this type is reproduced as Fig. 3.

DISCUSSION

The scientific validity of a method of measurement or quantification is dependent in part on *a priori* considerations. One such consideration traditionally and prominently involved in the present methodology is that the distribution of momentary reaction potential differences is normal. Certain internal evidences presumably bearing on this point have been presented in the preceding section. Additional evidences of an empirical nature, the computations of which are not yet complete, will be presented in an article now in preparation (39).

Fortunately in the present situation there are other and, it is believed, more critical criteria of quantificational validity. As Bergmann and Spence remark in this connection (3, p. 23), "The actual excellence of physical measurement is entirely a matter of fact." These excellences have been found in the facts of quantitative consistency of the results of measurement with related phenomena and the great extent to which they have facilitated the simplified systematic organization of the field in which the quantifications have been employed. Similarly, the present and all other proposed methods of behavioral quantification must depend for their validation, at least in part, upon the quantitative consistencies and systematizations to which they give rise. One or two specific examples of such systematic possibilities in the present field may clarify and give point to this statement.

1. It is evident from the description of the present experiment and associated quantificational methodology that a primitive curve of learning should emerge. Now, a closely related method based on reaction thresholds in the case of conditioned winking of the type reported by Reynolds (27) should also yield a learning curve according to a published theoretical analysis (20, p. 327). With a suitable adaptation of Reynolds' experimental procedure and with more subjects available, the two methodologies should yield the same type of curve, according to present presumptions, as shown by the equations giving the best fits to them. However, owing to the difference in organisms used as subjects and other variable factors, some differences in the quantitative parameters might well be expected. If, on the other hand, quite different types of curves were yielded by the two methods, a serious question would arise as to the validity of one of the methods of quantification and possibly of both.

2. As has been pointed out, there are many different indications of reaction potential. It is probable that some forms of learning can be found which yield two or more such objective indications of the *very same* habit strength acquisition, each one of which could be used independently as reaction latency was above. It would seem that such curves of learning even though secured from quite different data should agree as to the type of best fitting equation and also, within the limits of the data sampled, as to the various constants. Such a determination may very well prove to be a critical test of the methodology.

Concrete illustrations of the scientific fertility and consistency tests of the present quantificational methodology will be presented in two other studies (11, 39). However, no single test or group of tests can completely effect such a validation. This must be left largely to the future.

SUMMARY

There is reason to believe that most, if not all, behavior is quantitatively determined by two types of internal conditions which mediate it: habit strength ($_sH_R$) and drive (D) which presumably combine in a multiplicative manner to produce reaction potential ($_sE_R$). In spite of this presumptively common basis of all behavior, there is no common method of measurement or quantification of $_sE_R$, and no common unit. This may very well account in considerable part for the present relative lack of quantitative systematization in the so-called behavior sciences.

It is probable that the major reason for the lack of a uniform quantificational methodology in the very numerous behavior studies is that reaction potential, both as habit strength and drive, is a condition hidden within the behaving organism, the existence of which is indicated, though only indirectly, by signs which are quantitatively about as various as is the behavior itself. One hopeful possibility is that while all these quantitative indicators bear different functional relations to reaction potential, it is probable that all, or nearly all, of them are monotonically related to it. On this assumption, together with certain other assumptions which are more or less common to the various psychophysical and psychological scaling methods, a sample quantification has been presented in detail for the first ten trials of a habit formation sequence. This methodology is believed to constitute a strict operational definition of $_sE_R$.

REFERENCES

1. ANREP, G. V. The irradiation of conditioned reflexes. *Proc. Royal Soc. London*, 1923, **94B**, 404–425.
2. BASS, M. J., & HULL, C. L. The irradiation of a tactile conditioned reflex in man. *J. comp. Psychol.*, 1934, **17**, 47–65.
3. BERGMANN, G., & SPENCE, K. W. The logic of psychophysical measurement. PSYCHOL, REV., 1944, **51**, 1–24.
4. CAMPBELL, N. R. *Physics: the elements.* Cambridge, England: Cambridge Univ. Press, 1920.
5. COWLES, J. T., & PENNINGTON, L. A. An improved conditioning technique for determining auditory acuity of the rat. *J. Psychol.*, 1943, **15**, 41–47.

6. EBBINGHAUS, H. *Memory* (trans. by H. A. Ruger and C. E. Bussenius). New York: Teachers College, Columbia Univ., 1913.
7. FELSINGER, J. M., GLADSTONE, A. I., YAMAGUCHI, H. G., & HULL, C. L. Reaction latency ($_st_R$) as a function of the number of reinforcements (N). *J. exp. Psychol.*, 1947, **37**, 214–228.
8. FULTON, J. F. *Muscular contraction and the reflex control of movement.* Baltimore: Williams and Wilkins Co., 1926.
9. GAGNE, R. M. External inhibition and disinhibition in a conditioned operant response. *J. exp. Psychol.*, 1941, **29**, 104–116.
10. GARVEY, C. R. A study of conditioned respiratory changes. *J. exp. Psychol.*, 1933, **16**, 471–503.
11. GLADSTONE, A. I., YAMAGUCHI, H. G., HULL, C. L., & FELSINGER, J. M. Some functional relationships of reaction potential ($_sE_R$) and related phenomena. *J. exp. Psychol.* (in press).
12. GRAHAM, C. H., & GAGNE, R. M. The acquisition, extinction, and spontaneous recovery of a conditioned operant response. *J. exp. Psychol.*, 1940, **26**, 251–280.
13. GUILFORD, J. P. *Psychometric methods.* New York: McGraw-Hill Book Co., 1936.
14. GULLIKSEN, H. A rational equation of the learning curve based on Thorndike's law of effect. *J. gen. Psychol.*, 1934, **11**, 395–434.
15. ———. Paired comparisons and the logic of measurement. PSYCHOL. REV., 1946, **53**, 199–213.
16. HERBERT, M. J. An improved technique for studying the conditioned squeak reaction in hooded rats. *J. gen. Psychol.*, 1946, **34**, 67–77.
17. HILGARD, E. R. Conditioned eyelid reactions to a light stimulus based on the reflex wink to sound. *Psychol. Monogr.*, 1931, **41**, No. 184.
18. HOVLAND, C. I. The generalization of conditioned responses: I. The sensory generalization of conditioned responses with varying frequencies of tone. *J. gen. Psychol.*, 1937, **17**, 125–148.
19. HUDGINS, C. V. Conditioning and the voluntary control of the pupillary light reflex. *J. gen. Psychol.*, 1933, 8, 3–51.
20. HULL, C. L. *Principles of behavior.* New York: D. Appleton-Century Co., Inc., 1943.
21. KAPPAUF, W. E., & SCHLOSBERG, H. Conditioned responses in the white rat. III. Conditioning as a function of the

PAPER
17

length of the period of delay. *J. genet. Psychol.*, 1937, **50**, 27–45.

22. LIDDELL, H. S., & ANDERSON, O. D. Certain characteristics of formation of conditioned reflexes in sheep. *Proc. Soc. exp. Biol. & Med.*, 1928, **26**, 81–82.

23. MAY, M. A. Ten tests of measurement. *Educ. Record*, 1939, 200–220.

24. PAVLOV, I. P. *Conditioned reflexes* (trans. by G. V. Anrep). London: Oxford Univ. Press, 1927.

25. PERIN, C. T. Behavior potentiality as a joint function of the amount of training and the degree of hunger at the time of extinction. *J. exp. Psychol.*, 1942, **30**, 93–113.

26. REESE, T. W. Application of the theory of physical measurement to the measurement of psychological magnitudes with three experimental examples. *Psychol. Monogr.*, 1943, **55**, No. 3.

27. REYNOLDS, B. The acquisition of a trace conditioned response as a function of the magnitude of the stimulus trace. *J. exp. Psychol.*, 1945, **35**, 15–30.

28. SCHLOSBERG, H., & SOLOMON, R. L. Latency of response in a choice discrimination. *J. exp. Psychol.*, 1943, **33**, 22–39.

29. SCOTT, H. D. Hypnosis and the conditioned reflex. *J. gen. Psychol.*, 1930, **4**, 113–130.

30. SOLOMON, R. L. Latency of response as a measure of learning in a 'single-door' discrimination. *Amer. J. Psychol.*, 1943, **56**, 422–432.

31. SPROW, A. J. Reactively homogeneous compound trial-and-error learning with distributed trials and terminal reinforcement. *J. exp. Psychol.*, 1947, **37**, 197–213.

32. THORNDIKE, E. L. Handwriting. *Teachers College Rec.*, 1910, **11**, No. 2.

33. THURSTONE, L. L. A law of comparative judgment. PSYCHOL. REV., 1927, **34**, 273–286.

34. ——. Psychophysical analysis. *Amer. J. Psychol.*, 1927, **38**, 368–389.

35. ——. Stimulus disperion in the method of constant stimuli. *J. exp. Psychol.*, 1932, **15**, 284–289.

36. WILLIAMS, S. B. Resistance to extinction as a function of the number of reinforcements. *J. exp. Psychol.*, 1938, **23**, 506–521.

37. WOLFLE, H. M. Time factors in conditioning finger-withdrawal. *J. gen. Psychol.*, 1930, **4**, 372–379.

38. WOODROW, H. The problem of general quantitative laws in psychology. *Psychol. Bull.*, 1942, **39**, 1–27.

39. YAMAGUCHI, H. G., HULL, C. L., FELSINGER, J. M., & GLADSTONE, A. I. Characteristics of dispersions based on momentary reaction potential $(s\dot{E}_R)$. (In prep.)

PAPER
17

CHARACTERISTICS OF DISPERSIONS BASED ON THE POOLED MOMENTARY REACTION POTENTIALS ($_s\bar{\dot{E}}_R$) OF A GROUP [1]

BY HARRY G. YAMAGUCHI, CLARK L. HULL, JOHN M. FELSINGER AND ARTHUR I. GLADSTONE

*Institute of Human Relations,
Yale University*

INTRODUCTION

In an earlier publication (**3**) we have pointed out that the soundness of a type of measurement in science is indicated jointly by (a) its fertility in yielding quantitative scientific laws and (b) the quantitative consistency of the various emerging laws and their constants among themselves and with other relevant phenomena (**1**). In any really systematic science, even such as the physics of Isaac Newton, consistency phenomena exist in profusion. A commonplace example of consistency in natural laws is seen in the operation of the primary law of falling bodies in the secondary or derived law of the ordinary pendulum. Unfortunately, in the field of behavior the number of such interlocking quantitative laws is very small and the idea that behavioral laws should show this type of consistency

[1] This is the fourth study in the series by the present authors. The experimental work, as described in the first study of the series (**2**), was performed by Mr. Felsinger, the statistical analysis was carried out by Mr. Yamaguchi and Mr. Gladstone, and Mr. Hull supervised the study as a whole and prepared the manuscript in frequent conference with the others. We are indebted to Mr. Charles B. Woodbury for the careful drawing of the several graphs which appear in the text, and to Mr. Hardy C. Wilcoxon and especially to Miss Ruth Hays for some final computations. It should be noted that the appropriateness of the words "pooled" and "of a group" in this title is reduced by the evidence reported in footnote 4, which was added just prior to publication.

is practically nonexistent. Indeed, such a validity requirement would doubtless be rejected by certain psychologists.

The earlier publication referred to above presented evidence that the power of the Thurstone psychophysical quantification technique is fertile in yielding the data from which such laws may be formulated. The objective of the present study will be, in the main, to present evidence of the consistency of this quantificational methodology and its deliverances with relevant known facts and principles.

There is generally recognized to be some uncertainty regarding the scientific status of psychological scaling methods with which the present quantificational procedure is closely allied. This is due in part to their heavy dependence upon the *a priori* assumption of the statistical 'normality' of the distribution of the differences involved, which is at the base of all psychophysical procedures. Such a dependence is demonstrated by the universal use of tables of the normal probability integral in this type of quantification. Moreover, in most scaling situations, as Thurstone long ago pointed out, there is the complication that the responses of many subjects are pooled; this may easily generate a distribution different from that of an individual subject, which alone is involved in ordinary psychophysics. This has led us to seek among other things a means to

216

test the truth of the normal probability assumption in the present experimental situation, and so the soundness of the quantification performed.

The empirical data involved in the quantification here under consideration consisted of the pooled learning latency scores of 59 albino rats. The act learned was very simple, merely the lateral movement of a straight brass tubular manipulandum which projected five-eighths inch into the animal's chamber in a sound-shielded box. One trial per day was given for a minimum of 60 successive days. In most cases the number of days was considerably more (2). The methodology employed in the quantification was an adaptation of Thurstone's psychophysical method of paired comparisons, Case III (9, 10, 11), as described in detail elsewhere (7). In general the method used in securing evidence regarding the consistency of the outcome of our quantification was based upon the fact that its application to our data yielded the empirical equation,

$$_sE_R = 2.845 \, _st_R{}^{-.483} - .599. \quad (1)$$

Here $_st_R$ is the median reaction latency of our 59 animals at a given stage of training and $_sE_R$ is the reaction potential of the same animals taken as a group, as determined by our method of quantification.

This brings us to the concept of momentary reaction latency ($_s\dot{t}_R$) as distinguished from the median reaction latency ($_st_R$). Now, by definition,

$$\text{the median } _s\dot{t}_R = _st_R. \quad (2)$$

Moreover, there is excellent reason to believe that reaction potential ($_sE_R$) is subject to momentary oscillation ($_sO_R$) or variability, exactly as reaction latency is empirically known

to be (6, pp. 304 ff.), which would naturally produce momentary reaction potential ($_s\dot{E}_R$). And since $_sE_R$ at a given stage of learning is determined from the reactions of the group as a whole, it must represent a central tendency of the $_s\dot{E}_R$'s involved, which is closely equivalent to and possibly identical with the median $_s\dot{E}_R$. As a first approximation we accordingly write the equation,

$$\text{the median } _s\dot{E}_R = _sE_R, \quad (3)$$

which parallels equation (2) in terms of reaction potential.

On these assumptions it is evident that the first members of equations (2) and (3) may be substituted for the second members in equation (1). This being the case it is tempting to assume, at least as a first approximation, that not only the medians but all the other corresponding momentary values of each equation could also be substituted in equation (1). This assumption yields the following equation,

$$_s\dot{E}_R = 2.845 \, _s\dot{t}_R{}^{-.483} - .599. \quad (4)$$

It is clear from the context that half of the latency responses at the first trial in our present learning experiment must fall below the lowest median (trial 1) involved in the derivation of equation (1), which determined the arbitrary zero value of $_sE_R$ as there expressed. It follows from an inspection of that equation that these and all momentary latencies which are longer than the longest median latency will yield negative $_s\dot{E}_R$'s. But these negative momentary reaction potentials, though small, are just as real as any; the negative sign indicates merely that they fall below the lowest median $_s\dot{E}_R$, *i.e.*, below that of the first successful trial of the group as a whole. This rela-

PAPER 18

tionship, however, is of no particular significance for our present purposes. Moreover, it is likely to be confusing. We accordingly eliminate it simply by dropping the −.599 from the right-hand member, leaving the working equation,

$$_s\dot{\bar{E}}_R = 2.845 \ _s\dot{\bar{t}}_R{}^{-.483}, \qquad (5)$$

which in effect places the zero of the scale of $_s\dot{\bar{E}}_R$'s .599 of a unit lower than does equation (1). It is evident, of course, that the soundness of equations (4) and (5) will (and must) be subject to the same quantitative consistency tests regarding soundness as are the more empirical aspects of the quantification.

With equation (5) available we should be able to (1) substitute in it any of the empirically given momentary reaction latencies, (2) calculate the corresponding momentary reaction potentials, and (3) with a large number of these available and suitably pooled and plotted determine with some directness the shape and range of the $_s\dot{\bar{E}}_R$ dispersion as derived from the behavior of pooled subjects. From these same values it should be possible by subtraction to (4) find the *differences* between momentary reaction potentials, (5) pool these differences into an appropriate distribution, (6) determine the shape and range of this difference distribution and thus determine in an objective manner the soundness of our quantificational procedure, including the assumptions underlying the writing of equations (4) and (5) above.

PAPER
18

CHARACTERISTICS OF THE DISPERSION OF POOLED $_s\dot{\bar{E}}_R$ VALUES AT THE LATENCY ASYMPTOTE

Our first task will be to examine the shape and range of the distribution of momentary reaction potential values at the latency asymptote of our data, *i.e.*, at the limit of learning. It happened that each of the 59 animals employed in the present investigation gave 10 reaction latencies at its latency asymptote and 10 more on the following 10 trials. These 20 asymptotic latencies of each animal were all converted into $_s\dot{\bar{E}}_R$'s by means of a table constructed with the aid of equation (5), yielding 20 rows of values, one for each asymptotic trial, with 59 values per row, one for each subject. An inspection of these data indicated that there was considerable oscillatory variation in these $_s\dot{\bar{E}}_R$ values, quite as would be expected from the momentary oscillation principle (6, p. 313). In addition, the first ten trials upon the whole showed a slight tendency to have larger $_s\dot{\bar{E}}_R$ values than did the second ten as a group, which presumably was caused by a slight tendency for the $_s\dot{\bar{t}}_R$'s to increase with continued training beyond the asymptote. Now, 20 rows of 59 values each comprise a total of 1180 momentary reaction potentials, enough to yield a fair indication of the function sought.

Unfortunately these data involve two independent sources of variability, (1) the oscillation function proper which appears in the responses of each organism considered by itself, and (2) the variability in the behavior of the several organisms from one another when the oscillation function is eliminated, *e.g.*, by taking the central tendency of the $_s\dot{\bar{E}}_R$'s for each individual subject. Proceeding to the isolation of the oscillation factor involved in the dispersion of the 1180 $_s\dot{\bar{E}}_R$'s, we first found the mean of the 20 asymptotic momentary reaction potential values yielded by each of the 59 animals. These means are obviously to a considerable extent free from the $_sO_R$ variability, the variability remaining being due in the main at least to the individual differences of the separate organisms. We next proceeded to eliminate so far as feasible the factor of individual differences just considered by adding to or subtracting from each set of 20 yielded by each subject an amount sufficient to make the means of the 59 groups the same. The distribution of the 1180 $_s\dot{E}_R$'s so corrected is shown in Fig. 1.

To casual inspection this dispersion bears a striking resemblance to the normal or Gaussian distribution. It has a central maximum from which it tapers off with approximate symmetry at each side, at first rapidly and then more slowly until the slope

is almost zero.   But more exact tests of normality than mere inspection are required in the present situation. For this purpose Karl Pearson has devised two rather precise quantitative functions, β_1 and β_2 (8, 14).   The indication of symmetry is given by β_1, a perfectly normal distribution yielding a value of .00.   On the other hand, β_2 gives an indication of the extent to which the distribution tends to bunch or arch in the middle, one which is strictly normal yielding a value of 3.00.   If the value of $\beta_2 > 3.00$ the distribution bunches in the middle more than is normal, and is called leptokurtic; if, on the other hand, the value of $\beta_2 < 3.00$ the dispersion tendency to bunch or arch in the middle is less than normal and is

PAPER

18

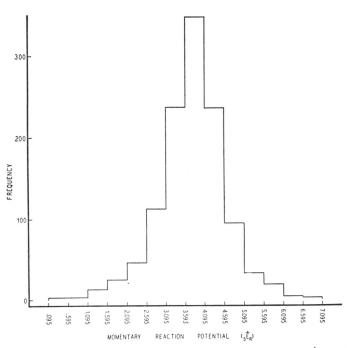

FIG. 1.   Graphic representation of the distribution of 1180 calculated $_s\dot{E}_R$ values after approximate correction for the distorting effects of the individual differences.   The unit of measurement of the values appearing at the bottom of the figure is σ' (see p. 222).

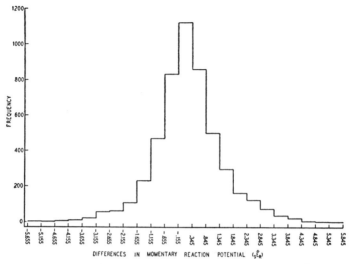

FIG. 2. Distribution of 5000 calculated momentary reaction-potential ($_s\dot{E}_R$) differences of 59 albino rats at the limit of latency reduction due to training. The unit of measurement of the values appearing at the bottom of the figure is σ' (see p. 222).

PAPER

18

called platykurtic. These values for Fig. 1 were found by appropriate computations (**14**) to be as follows:

$$\beta_1 = .1162 \ (P.E. = .097),$$
$$\beta_2 = 4.4664 \ (P.E. = 1.696).$$

The value of β_1 in comparison with its probable error indicates that if the distribution is truly skewed the asymmetry is so slight as not to be demonstrated by the number of data here available. Actually, a close inspection of Fig. 1 reveals a slightly longer tail at the left side of the distribution than at the right; the relatively large probable error suggests that this may be due to the limitations in the size of the sample. In the case of β_2 the 1.4664 excess beyond the 3.0 characteristic of the Gaussian distribution makes it clear that the distribution of Fig. 1 is leptokurtic, though the size of the probable error indicates that the present data are not sufficient to establish this as a fact in the absence of other supporting evidence.

Actually there is other supporting, though indirect, evidence which leads clearly to this interpretation. It will be presented below.

A third statistical value of some significance emerging from these data is the standard deviation of the distribution shown in Fig. 1. It was found to be .861.

CHARACTERISTICS OF THE DISPERSION OF POOLED $_s\dot{E}_R$ DIFFERENCES AT THE LATENCY ASYMPTOTE

With the 20 columns of momentary reaction potentials discussed in the preceding section available, it is evident that momentary reaction potential differences may be secured simply by subtracting the parallel values of any column from those in any other column. By this procedure the $_s\dot{E}_R$ differences secured concern only individual organisms. When these 20 columns containing 59 $_s\dot{E}_R$'s each in pairs are employed in various combinations it is evident that very large numbers of such differences may be secured.

Of the many thousands of differences thus available a systematic selection of 5000 was taken as follows. Beginning at the first asymptotic trial the $s\ddot{E}_R$ values were subtracted from those of the corresponding row of the second column, those of the second column from those of the corresponding row of the third, those of the third from those of the fourth, and so on until 500 differences were secured, the positive and negative differences being tabulated separately. Next, the $s\ddot{E}_R$'s of the first column were subtracted from those of the third, those of the second from those of the fourth, and so on (skipping one column) until 500 more differences were found. This procedure was continued in such a way as to secure more and more remote comparisons, the number of columns (*i.e.*, trials) skipped in obtaining the various sets of 500 differences being as follows:

0, 1, 2, 3, 4, 5, 6, 7, 8, and 10.

The graphic representation of this total set of differences may be seen in Fig. 2. To casual inspection this dispersion of $s\ddot{E}_R$ differences bears a striking resemblance to the normal or Gaussian distribution, much as did that of the 1180 $s\ddot{E}_R$ values shown in Fig. 1. It has a central maximum and it tapers off with approximate symmetry at each side, at first rapidly and then more slowly until the slope is almost zero. But here again more precise tests of normality are required. The β values for Fig. 2 were found by appropriate computations (14, 8) to be as follows:

$$\beta_1 = .0234 \text{ (P.E.} = .03),$$
$$\beta_2 = 3.9873 \text{ (P.E.} = .73).$$

The value of β_1, in comparison with its probable error, indicates that if the distribution is skewed the asymmetry is so slight as not to be demonstrated by this considerable number of data. In the case of β_2, the statistical indication is that the .9873 deviation beyond 3.00 has a ratio of 1.352 to its probable error, which corresponds to a probability of about 1 in 5 that it is due to the chance of sampling.

There is, however, other evidence bearing on these points. The β_1's and β_2's were calculated separately for each set of 500 differences which entered into the 5000. About half of the β_1's were in one direction and half in the other, which largely disposes of the skew evidence. On the other hand, every one of the ten sets of 500 differences showed a β_2 in excess of 3.00, as follows:

5.493, 4.203, 4.733, 4.256, 4.355,
4.263, 4.929, 4.464, 4.612, 4.553.

The probability that ten successive values would all come out in the same direction without special causation is $(1/2)^{10}$, which yields a value of only one chance in about 1024. We conclude with confidence that the distribution of $s\ddot{E}_R$ differences represented by Fig. 2 is genuinely leptokurtic in shape and by analogy that the $s\ddot{E}_R$ values represented in Fig. 1, from which Figure 2 was derived, also are distributed in a leptokurtic manner. Still further evidence supporting this conclusion is given below (pp. 230, 235).

THE CONSTRUCTION OF TWO TYPES OF EMPIRICAL LEPTOKURTIC FREQUENCY TABLE

In addition to the formal evidence that our $s\ddot{E}_R$ difference distribution is leptokurtic in form, we desired a somewhat detailed comparison of it with that of the Gaussian probability integral as represented in tables of that function. As a first step in securing such a comparison the standard deviation of the distribution of differences represented by Fig. 2 was calculated and found to be 1.2288. Next, a table was made of the frequency of the empirically obtained differences in $_s\dot{\bar{E}}_R$'s with an interval of .1 unit, the unit in question being the standard deviation of the oscillation function as employed in the quantificational method used by us (7). We shall represent this unit by the symbol σ'. An inspection of Fig. 2 will show that each interval there represented includes five such .1 σ' frequency intervals. Since the present distribution was found to be practically symmetrical, the two wings or halves of this distribution were combined, which doubled the available population for our table with the division falling at the midpoint of the modal interval. This involved the division of the middle .1 σ' of the modal set of five (Fig. 2) leaving half of the middle .1 σ' interval at the beginning of the series as such tables are ordinarily constructed. In order to make a uniform interval of a full .1 σ' throughout the series, this half interval was combined with half of the next whole .1 σ' interval for the first interval of our table, the other half of the first whole .1 σ' interval with half of the next whole .1 σ' interval, and so on throughout the entire series of 5000 differences. Incidentally this resulted in the smoothing out of a few slight irregularities in the progressive decrease in the combined frequencies (doubtless caused largely by dropped decimals) as the σ' distance increased from the middle of the original distribution.

The next step was to determine the x/σ values for our table. As already pointed out, the σ of our difference distribution was found to be 1.2288 in terms of the present σ' unit, i.e.,

$$\sigma = 1.2288 \, \sigma'.$$

Accordingly,

$$\sigma' = \frac{\sigma}{1.2288} = .8138 \, \sigma.$$

Dividing through by 10, we have

$$\frac{\sigma'}{10} = .1 \, \sigma' = .08138 \, \sigma,$$

which means that each .1 σ' interval used in our original distribution corresponds to .08138 σ.

Now, a convenient method of expressing the ordinate of an empirical distribution such as the present one is to state the number from a population of 10,000 that falls within a range of .01 σ at any given distance from the mean. In the present distribution, 468.5 of the population of 10,000 (i.e., 2 × 5000 produced by pooling the two wings of our population of differences) are found in the first interval of .08138 σ at one side of the mean. This is 8.138 times the .01 σ range customarily employed. Accordingly, 468.5 ÷ 8.138 = 57.59, which is the approximate ordinate value at the middle of the interval, i.e., at .08138 ÷ 2 = .04069 σ; or, in round numbers, at .041 σ at one side of the mean. Proceeding in this manner the next observed frequency of our data, 453.5, yields an ordinate value of 55.73, which falls in the middle of the next interval or .04069 σ + .08138 σ = .122 σ at one side of the mean. By procedures exactly analogous to those used in these two examples we secured the remaining paired entries appearing as the first two columns in Table I. By way of comparison there has been placed in

TABLE I

Ordinate values of a leptokurtic distribution with a β_2 value of 3.9873 based on a population equivalent to 10,000, with parallel values of the normal probability integral. (Taken from Guilford, 4, p. 531.)

σ distance from mean	Ordinate population for .01 σ interval on base of 10,000		σ distance from mean	Ordinate population for .01 σ interval on base of 10,000	
	leptokurtic distribution	normal distribution		leptokurtic distribution	normal distribution
.041	57.59	39.86	2.157	3.62	3.87
.122	55.73	39.61	2.238	3.69	3.25
.203	47.92	39.10	2.319	3.56	2.70
.285	44.11	38.25	2.401	3.44	2.24
.366	42.76	37.25	2.482	3.32	1.84
.448	41.90	36.05	2.563	2.83	1.51
.528	38.09	34.67	2.645	1.90	1.19
.610	33.18	33.12	2.726	1.60	.96
.692	27.46	31.44	2.808	1.41	.77
.773	24.08	29.66	2.889	1.35	.61
.854	22.30	27.80	2.970	1.23	.48
.935	20.40	25.65	3.052	1.35	.38
1.017	17.57	23.71	3.133	1.23	.30
1.099	14.75	21.79	3.215	.68	.22
1.180	12.96	19.89	3.296	.43	.17
1.261	11.43	18.04	3.377	.43	.13
1.343	11.55	16.26	3.459	.43	.10
1.424	10.14	14.56	3.540	.31	.08
1.505	7.93	12.95	3.621	.31	.06
1.587	6.76	11.27	3.702	.31	.04
1.668	5.78	9.89	3.784	.12	.031
1.750	5.71	8.65	3.865	.26	.022
1.831	5.59	7.48	3.947	.26	.016
1.912	5.22	6.44	4.028	.12	.012
1.994	4.92	5.51	4.109	.12	.009
2.075	4.06	4.59	4.191	.31	.006

PAPER
18

a parallel third column of each set of three the corresponding frequency yielded by the normal probability integral, also as based on a population of 10,000.

An examination of these two sets of ordinate values shows that adjacent to the center or mean of the distribution the leptokurtic ordinate is much greater than the normal, e.g., 57.59 versus 39.86 at the first interval. However, as the σ distance increases the leptokurtic values decrease very rapidly until at $x/\sigma = .61$ the two ordinates are practically identical. For larger values of x/σ the leptokurtic ordinates grow progressively less than the normal, then increase again, relatively, until again at $x/\sigma = 2.157$ the two ordinates have reversed their position after which the leptokurtic ordinate values remain the larger to $x/\sigma = 4.19$. This of course is generally characteristic of leptokurtic distributions (14, p. 158).

The differences between leptokurtic data and those of the normal probability integral as presented in the preceding section seemed to call for a special table constructed as are the normal probability tables now in general use. For one thing, a quantification of some leptokurtic data may be desired and we know of no appropriate table with which to do it. Accordingly, from the original difference distribution from which Table I was derived we also constructed Table II. This table is essentially a transcription of our empirical results. While it gives the main substance necessary for a table analogous to

PAPER
18

TAELE II

Table of the empirical values of a leptokurtic probability distribution whose β_2 is 3.9873. It shows the fraction of the area lying between zero and x/σ, together with the corresponding value of x/σ itself.

Area from $x/\sigma=0$	x/σ	Area from $x/\sigma=0$	x/σ
.047	.0814	.465	1.9531
.092	.1628	.469	2.0345
.131	.2441	.472	2.1159
.167	.3255	.475	2.1973
.202	.4069	.478	2.2786
.236	.4883	.481	2.3600
.267	.5697	.484	2.4414
.294	.6510	.486	2.5228
.316	.7324	.489	2.6042
.336	.8138	.490	2.6855
.354	.8952	.491	2.7669
.371	.9766	.493	2.8483
.385	1.0579	.494	2.9297
.397	1.1393	.495	3.0111
.408	1.2207	.4957	3.0924
.417	1.3021	.4968	3.1738
.426	1.3835	.4973	3.2552
.434	1.4648	.4977	3.3366
.441	1.5462	.4980	3.4180
.446	1.6276	.4984	3.4993
.451	1.7090	.4986	3.5807
.456	1.7904	.4988	3.6621
.460	1.8717	.4991	3.7435

tables of the probability integral used in psychophysical scaling, the steps are far too coarse for convenient use, especially those at the beginning, and the area intervals do not have the stepwise regularity customary in such tables. Accordingly Table III was derived from Table II by linear interpolations so that the area columns increase by equal steps of .005.

Figure 3 gives a graphic representation of the empirical leptokurtic

probability function as presented in Tables II and III, and for purposes of comparison a parallel graph of the corresponding normal probability function. It is evident from an inspection of these two tables and the graph that a rather large and systematic difference in the quantificational results must arise when an inappropriate table is applied to leptokurtic paired-comparison data in securing quantificational results, quite as already demonstrated. The next-to-last columns of Table II show that the absolute difference between the two increases as one moves away from the zero point of comparison, exactly as appears on the early portions of the graph. Even so, the *relative* size of the differences grows less from the very onset of the two curves.

THE DISTORTION OF SCALE-SEPARATION VALUES BY THE USE OF AN INAPPROPRIATE FREQUENCY TABLE

It is clear from an inspection of Tables I, II, and III together with Fig. 3 that in case a scale quantification is attempted by means of the paired-comparisons procedure as ordinarily employed, a distortion of the results secured will occur if the frequency table does not match the distribution characteristics of the data serving as the basis of the quantification. This is because the ordinate frequencies of a leptokurtic distribution which appear early in the table, i.e., which occupy positions close to the middle of the distribution, are so much greater per σ unit from the mean than is the case in a Gaussian distribution. Thus the first ordinate entry of Table I (57.59) is over 44 per cent greater than the Gaussian equivalent (39.86) at the same distance from the mean (.041 σ). This brings it about that when a per cent

PAPER

18

TABLE III

Leptokurtic distribution table derived from Table II by means of linear interpolations in such a way that the 'area' increases by steps of .005 of the total statistical population.

Area from $x/\sigma=0$	x/σ	Area from $x/\sigma=0$	x/σ	Area from $x/\sigma=0$	x/σ	Area from $x/\sigma=0$	x/σ
.005	.009	.130	.242	.255	.538	.380	1.029
.010	.017	.135	.253	.260	.551	.385	1.058
.015	.026	.140	.264	.265	.564	.390	1.092
.020	.035	.145	.276	.270	.579	.395	1.126
.025	.043	.150	.288	.275	.594	.400	1.162
.030	.052	.155	.298	.280	.609	.405	1.199
.035	.061	.160	.310	.285	.624	.410	1.239
.040	.069	.165	.321	.290	.639	.415	1.284
.045	.078	.170	.333	.295	.655	.420	1.329
.050	.087	.175	.344	.300	.673	.425	1.375
.055	.096	.180	.356	.305	.692	.430	1.424
.060	.105	.185	.367	.310	.710	.435	1.476
.065	.114	.190	.379	.315	.729	.440	1.535
.070	.123	.195	.391	.320	.749	.445	1.611
.075	.132	.200	.402	.325	.769	.450	1.693
.080	.141	.205	.414	.330	.789	.455	1.774
.085	.150	.210	.426	.335	.810	.460	1.872
.090	.159	.215	.438	.340	.832	.465	1.953
.095	.169	.220	.450	.345	.855	.470	2.062
.100	.180	.225	.462	.350	.877	.475	2.197
.105	.190	.230	.474	.355	.900	.480	2.333
.110	.200	.235	.486	.360	.924	.485	2.482
.115	.211	.240	.499	.365	.948	.490	2.686
.120	.221	.245	.512	.370	.972	.495	3.011
.125	.232	.250	.525	.375	1.000	.500	

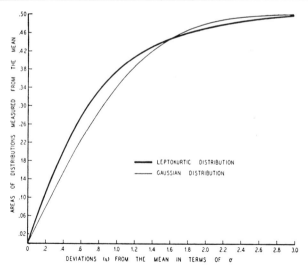

FIG. 3. Graphic representation of the empirical leptokurtic probability function given in Tables II and III and, for comparison, the corresponding values of a table of the normal probability integral.

difference in a leptokurtic comparison is not very great the σ scale value yielded by a Gaussian table may be as much as 44 per cent too large.

As suggested, this distortion is greatest where the per cent difference resulting from the comparison is small and grows progressively less as the per cent difference grows larger. A comparison of Tables II and III with a table of the normal probability integral, *e.g.*, Guilford's (4, p. 537 ff.), shows that the amount of this excess continues to decrease up to where the per cent (area) difference reaches the neighborhood of .44, after which the scale values are too small. This general relationship is shown graphically by Fig. 3.

It happens that when this sort of distortion exists its presence is revealed by a characteristic inconsistency which appears in a certain type of table utilized in the quantification technique invented by Thurstone (4, p. 228). Let it be supposed that we have a series of paired-comparison proportions with the advantage of the various items over item No. 1 as shown in the second column of values in Table IV. Assuming that the dispersion of differences involved is leptokurtic in nature with a β_2 value of approximately 4.00, we look up the scale separations corresponding to these per cent values in Table III and find them to be those shown in the

third column of Table IV. Turning to the corresponding Gaussian scale separations in Guilford's table (4, p. 537 ff.), we find that they are as appear in the fourth column of Table IV. The values in columns 3 and 4 are distinctly different from one another. The differences between the two sets of scale-separation values are shown in the fifth column of Table IV and the per cent that the Gaussian values are of the leptokurtic values appears in the last column. It will be noticed that the absolute differences *increase* as one goes down the column, whereas the per cent differences *decrease*.

In addition to the direct method of determining the amount of a given scale separation as shown in Table IV, there are several indirect methods; and if the table used is accurate and a very large number of data are involved, each of the several determinations will agree exactly with the others. Take, for example, the scale separation of items 1 and 2: the paired-comparison advantage of item 2 over item 1 amounts to .060, which our leptokurtic probability table (Table III) shows *directly* as corresponding to a scale difference of .105. Similarly, by substituting the values appearing in Table IV in the following three equations we have by indirect means three additional determinations of the same $S_2 - S_1$ value but, it will

TABLE IV

Table illustrating the origin of the scale-separation distortion arising from the use of a table of the Gaussian probability function on leptokurtic paired-comparison data.

No. of item	Advantage over S_1	Corresponding leptokurtic scale separation from S_1	Corresponding Gaussian scale separation from S_1	Absolute excess by Gaussian table	Per cent excess by Gaussian table
S_1	.000	.000	.000	.000	
S_2	.060	.105	.151	.046	44
S_3	.110	.200	.279	.079	39
S_4	.155	.298	.399	.101	34
S_5	.200	.402	.524	.122	30

be noted, *derived largely from different parts of the probability table from the portion used in the direct determination:*

By direct determination, $S_2 - S_1 = .105$. Also,

$$S_2 - S_1 = (S_3 - S_1) - (S_3 - S_2)$$
$$= (.200 - .000) - (.200 - .105)$$
$$= .200 - .095 = .105$$

and

$$S_2 - S_1 = (S_4 - S_1) - (S_4 - S_2)$$
$$= (.298 - .000) - (.298 - .105)$$
$$= .298 - .193 = .105$$

and

$$S_2 - S_1 = (S_5 - S_1) - (S_5 - S_2)$$
$$= (.402 - .000) \quad (.402 \quad .105)$$
$$= .402 - .297 = .105$$

In the case of the use of the normal probability table on the same leptokurtic paired-comparison data as those just considered, the outcome is quite different. We have already seen that the *direct determinations* of $S_2 - S_1$ by the normal probability table is definitely larger than .105, namely, .151. Secondly, we need to find the equivalent of a direct determination of the values of $S_3 - S_2$, $S_4 - S_2$, and $S_5 - S_2$. In column 3 of Table IV we see that $S_3 - S_2$ amounts to .200 - .105, or .095 σ, which corresponds (Table III) approximately to a paired-comparison advantage of .055; $S_4 - S_2$ amounts to .298 - .105, or .193 σ, which corresponds (Table III) approximately to a paired-comparison advantage of .105; $S_5 - S_2$ amounts to .402 - .105, or .297 σ, which corresponds (Table III) approximately to a paired-comparison advantage of .155; and these three per cent paired-comparison advantages correspond respectively to Gaussian scale differences (as given in Guilford's table, 4, p. 537 ff.) of .138, .266, and .399. Substituting these Gaussian values in addition to

those given in the fourth column of Table IV in the three following equations, we have:

By direct determination, $S_2 - S_1 = .151$

$$S_2 - S_1 = (S_3 - S_1) - (S_3 - S_2)$$
$$= .279 - .138 = .141$$
$$S_2 - S_1 = (S_4 - S_1) - (S_4 - S_2)$$
$$= .399 - .266 = .133$$
$$S_2 - S_1 = (S_5 - S_1) - (S_5 - S_2)$$
$$= .524 - .399 = .125$$

Thus we see that where the frequency table matches the data distribution form, the multiple determination of scale separations agrees exactly with the direct determination. On the other hand, where leptokurtic data are treated with a normal probability table (a) the value of a given scale separation as directly determined is considerably greater than are the values of those indirectly determined, *the latter decreasing in size the more remote they are from the point of direct determination.* This means that in general (b) *the longer the series of indirectly determined values, the greater this relative difference will be;* it also means that in general (c) *the directly determined value will be greater than the mean of the indirectly determined values.*

A convenient illustration and exemplary verification of the tabular distortion of the three types of scale separation just deduced appears as Table V. This is reproduced with some modifications and extensions from Guilford's well-known text (4, pp. 227, 228), the data having been taken from a classical empirical study published by Thurstone some twenty years ago (11). Naturally with a limited number of data available this table (based on the results from 239 subjects) will not display the regularity characteristic of the largely theoretical deduction just given which

PAPER

18

Table V

A table illustrating the multiple estimates of the scale separation of each item of a series from the next (4, p. 228). The directly determined (d.d.) scale separations are set in bold-faced type; the remaining values are secured by indirect determination (i.d.).

Numbers of items used in original quantification	The scale-separation estimates							
	1 from 2	2 from 3	3 from 4	4 from 5	5 from 6	6 from 7	7 from 8	8 from 9
1	*	.617	−.041	.716	−.107	.635	.000	.243
2	.589	*	.472	.595	−.021	.469	.528	*
3	.840	.366	*	.483	.726	.735	.000	.000
4	.327	.556	.282	*	−.004	.541	.184	.380
5	.448	.668	−.077	.842	*	.655	.397	.306
6	.362	−.079	.653	.511	.327	*	.255	.701
7	.528	−.345	.847	.397	.597	.385	*	.384
8	.000	.183	.663	.184	.739	.228	.412	*
9	*	*	.283	.258	.344	.545	.134	.662
Means excluding the value in bold-faced type (i.d.)	.417	.267	.400	.449	.325	.544	.209	.336
Direct (d.d.) less indirect determinations (i.d.)	.172	.099	−.118	.393	.002	−.159	.203	.326
Ratio of $\dfrac{\text{d.d.}}{\text{i.d.}}$	1.412	1.370	.705	1.875	1.006	.708	1.971	1.970

PAPER
18

* These spaces have no entries because no significant values are yielded by the original paired-comparison data.

tacitly assumes an infinite number of data. A glance shows that each of the values of the diagonal row set in bold-faced type (the directly determined scale separations) is upon the whole greater than the remaining values of its respective column. Moreover, the farther one goes down each column below the directly determined value, the smaller upon the whole become the ostensible scale separations. For example, if we take the first four columns of the table and calculate the means of the scale separations of the five diagonal rows, beginning with the directly determined row, we have:

.520, .457, .511, .350, and .235.

Thus one of our theoretical deductions (a) finds examplary verification and a lawful consistency between principles and fact is illustrated.

Similarly, the extreme of the i.d. series of values is further from the d.d. value in the same series on the first and last two columns (Table V) than on the two middle columns. Therefore the ratios of $\dfrac{\text{d.d.}}{\text{i.d.}}$ should upon the whole be larger for the four end columns than for the four middle columns. A glance at the ratios appearing at the bottom of Table V shows that this clearly tends to be the case, the means being 1.07 and 1.68 respectively, the former only 64 per cent of the latter. Thus a second theoretical deduction (b) finds exemplary verification.

Finally, the means of the indirectly determined scale separations (at the bottom of Table V) may be seen to be upon the whole less than are the results of the direct determinations (in bold-faced type), six of the eight pairs of values showing an excess in favor of the directly determined scale separations. Thus a third theoretical deduction (c) finds exemplary verification and another lawful consistency is illustrated.[2]

As our main evidence on the matter of the scale-separation distortion produced by the application of a Gaussian probability table to a leptokurtic distribution of paired-comparison data, we have the quantificational results of the present investigation which have been described in considerable detail elsewhere (2, 7). In this investigation 25 points on a learning curve (see the upper part of Fig. 4) were quantified by the use of a table of the normal probability integral. The 24 scale-difference values resulting from the direct comparisons of the 25 $_s\bar{E}_R$ items involved (and analogous to the values shown in bold-faced type in Table V) appear in the second column of Table VI (d.d.). The third column gives the parallel means of the remainder of the same columns consisting of numerous indirect determinations or estimates (i.d.) of exactly the same item separations. These values are analogous to the means at the third row from the bottom of Table V. The fourth column shows the ostensible scale-separation distortion of the several scaled items, analogous to the differences appearing in the next-to-last row of Table V.

[2] It must be noted at this point that Table V here utilized as an expository aid represents only part of the data from Thurstone's investigation. It will be shown below (Tables VII and VIII) that the mean value of the directly determined series of the entire experiment is 56 per cent greater than that of the indirectly determined series, and that the difference in question has a t statistic of 2.50 with 18 degrees of freedom, which proves it to be significant at the 2 per cent level.

Now, owing mainly to the large number of subjects used by Thurstone, very few cases of negative values appear in the columns of the directly and indirectly determined scale separations of Table V, whereas such values occur quite occasionally in Table VI. Because of the novelty of this type of table and the relationship involved we shall explain our method of calculating the distortion effects. In the case of Table V the directly determined scale-separation of items 2 and 3 is .366, while the mean of the corresponding indirectly determined scale separation is .267. The distortion obviously is $.366 - .267 = .099$. Similarly in the case of items 3 and 4 the directly determined value is .282 and the mean of the indirectly determined values is .400. The difference here also is $.282 - .400 = -.118$, *i.e.*, the difference is truly negative. But suppose that both of the $2 - 3$ values were negative? In that case both would be on the negative side of the probability distribution and the $-.366$ would indicate the same sort of scaling distortion as would obtain on the other side of a probability distribution and of exactly the same amount. However, we can *not* simply subtract,

$$-.366 - (-.267) = -.099,$$

because this would give a negative .099 which would mean the *opposite* of a distortion. Consequently we must change both signs before we subtract, thus:

$$+.366 - (+.267) = .099$$

and

$$+.282 - (+.400) = -.118.$$

Also, when the sums of the columns of direct and indirect determinations are found the signs must be ignored, though this is not the case with the

PAPER

18

TABLE VI

Columns 2, 3, and 4 of this table present the evidence concerning the scale-separation distortion due to the use of a normal probability table on leptokurtic paired-comparison data of the present study. Columns 5, 6, and 7 show parallel results from the application of an empirical leptokurtic table to the same (leptokurtic) paired-comparison data.

Trials involved in scale separation determinations	Results secured by applying a Gaussian frequency table to leptokurtic paired comparison data			Results secured by applying an empirical leptokurtic frequency table to leptokurtic paired-comparison data		
	Directly determined scale separations (d.d.)	Indirectly determined scale separation means (i.d.)	Direct determinations minus indirectly determined means	Directly determined scale separations (d.d.)	Indirectly determined scale separation means (i.d.)	Direct determinations minus indirectly determined means
(1)	(2)	(3)	(4)	(5)	(6)	(7)
1–3	.377	.320	.059	.162	.321	−.159
3–5	.700	.477	.223	.428	.379	.049
5–7	.592	.327	.265	.426	.341	.085
7–9	.483	.398	.085	.400	.291	.109
9–11	.547	.290	.257	.544	.297	.247
11–13	−.108	−.164	−.056	−.099	−.173	−.074
13–15	.157	.238	−.081	.143	.256	−.113
15–17	.428	.260	.168	.387	.260	.127
17–19	.219	.189	.030	.176	.167	.009
19–21	.025	.017	.008	.018	−.005	.023
21–23	−.204*	.211*	**	−.144	−.155	−.011
23–25	.333	.315	.018	.247	.271	−.022
25–27	.549	.210	.339	.419	.181	.238
27–29	−.156	−.334	−.178	−.106	−.328	−.222
29–31	.059	.161	−.102	.048	.210	−.162
31–34	.394	.395	−.001	.312	.342	−.030
34–37	−.384	−.347	.037	−.289	−.322	−.033
37–40	.096	.014	.082	.067	−.007	.074
40–43	.544	.533	.011	.379	.452	−.073
43–46	−.333	−.377	−.044	−.215	−.301	−.086
46–49	.301	.345	−.044	.173	.212	−.039
49–52	−.110	.020	.130	−.063*	.071*	**
52–55	.108	.046	.062	.068	.092	−.024
55–58	.135	.075	.060	.082*	−.051*	**
Sums	7.140	5.852	1.328	5.250	5.363	−.087
Means	.3104	.2544	.0577	.2386	.2438	−.00395

* Data involving cases where the direct and the indirect determinations have different signs and the latter is more than .04. In such cases the scale-separation distortion is regarded as indeterminate and is left blank with the symbol **.

fourth column which shows the distortions. By the same logic, where the indirect determination is zero the sign of the parallel direct determination is changed in case it is negative, which also gives a positive distortion result. In practice, where the indirect determination is of opposite sign yet lies within .04 of zero the differences are utilized. But otherwise where the paired values are of opposite sign the distortion effect is considered indeterminate and such values are disregarded in all computations. They are placed in the table merely in the interest of record completeness.

The third column of Table VI and

the first row of Table VIII show that the mean distortion of our own data is positive, *i.e.*, in the direction to be expected, to the amount of .0577 with a *t* statistic of 2.003. The distortion effect amounts to 22.7 per cent of the mean of the i.d. scale separation values. Since this determination has 21 degrees of freedom the difference has significance at the 6 per cent level.

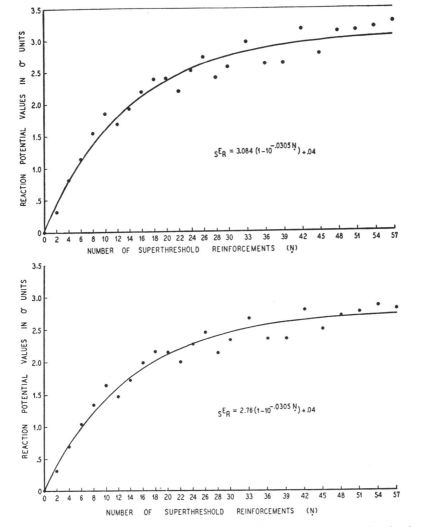

FIG. 4. Curves of learning expressing scale quantifications from the same leptokurtic paired-comparison data. The upper graph resulted from the use of a table of the normal probability integral in the quantification, the lower curve from the use of the empirical leptokurtic table. Note the detailed parallelism of the two curves.

PAPER

18

THE USE OF THE EMPIRICAL LEPTO-
KURTIC FREQUENCY TABLE IN A
SCALE QUANTIFICATION BASED
ON LEPTOKURTIC PAIRED-
COMPARISON DATA

In order to observe the results obtained from the application of the empirical leptokurtic probability table to leptokurtic data, the quantification of the 25 points of our learning curve (upper part of Fig. 4) was re-computed by means of Table III. Theoretically this procedure should yield no scale separation distortion. In order to test this deduction a treatment of the new data has been carried out in exact parallel to the outcome secured by use of the Gaussian table. The results of this procedure are presented in the last three columns of Table VI. There, quite as expected, we find the mean to be practically zero, being −.00395.

Related results of considerable significance are found in the final quantifications of the newly derived learning curve itself. These are shown as the lower graph of Fig. 4; for purposes of comparison the original learning curve derived by the use of the normal probability function (3) is presented in the upper graph to exactly the same scale of reproduction. There it may be seen by noting the irregularities in the two curves that the new table yields to a striking degree quantification values which parallel those secured by the use of the Gaussian table. When an equation was fitted to the new curve, one with exactly the same exponent found to be the best fit for the original curve also yielded the best fit for the new one. The mean square deviation of the fit to the upper curve is .0275, whereas that to the lower one is .0193. However, despite this close parallelism it is significant that the values of the new curve are slightly less than the orig-

inal values, as is characteristically indicated by the smaller coefficient of its fitted equation, 2.76, compared with the original 3.084. This means that the asymptote of the learning curve derived by the use of the leptokurtic frequency table is 10.6 per cent less than that secured by the use of the normal probability table. But the main points are that (a) in spite of the distortion resulting from the use of an inappropriate table on a set of leptokurtic paired-comparisons data, the Thurstone Case III procedure yields a practically perfectly proportioned curve of learning, and (b) the empirical table yields a quantification by means of Thurstone's Case III with the same ease as does the normal table.

DOES THE EXTENT OF $_s\ddot{E}_R$
DISPERSIONS VARY?

The question of whether the range (σ) of $_s\ddot{E}_R$ dispersions varies depending on conditions, and if so to what extent and how, is a matter of considerable technical importance because this magnitude is the natural unit for the measurement of reaction potential. In an earlier study (7) the somewhat indirect approach to this problem afforded by Thurstone's σ_k suggested rather strongly that the magnitude of the $_s\ddot{E}_R$ dispersions varies as learning progresses. It occurred to us that with the possibility of converting $_s\dot{i}_R$'s into $_s\ddot{E}_R$'s this problem could be attacked somewhat more directly and in the region of active learning, as in the former study. In order to eliminate the matter of individual differences as much as possible we decided to base our computations on the $_s\ddot{E}_R$ differences (subjects constant) between successive trials as learning progressed. In order to remove from these differences so

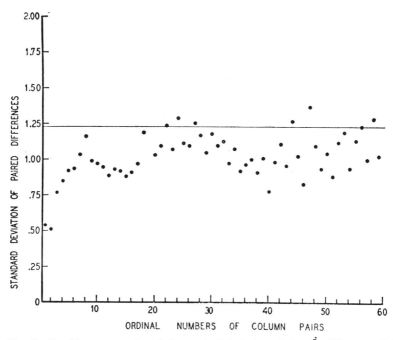

FIG. 5. Graphic representation of the standard deviations of the $_s\dot{\bar{E}}_R$ differences of 59 subjects found between the successive responses at the first 60 reinforced trials of the learning of a simple response. The light horizontal line just below 1.25 represents the standard deviation of the 5000 differences of these subjects at the limit of learning (Fig. 2).

PAPER

18

far as possible the excess due to the progressive increase in $_s\dot{\bar{E}}_R$ caused by learning as N increases, we found the mean for each column of 59 items and the difference between the means for each successive pair of columns; this amount was added to each item in the column with the smaller mean, which made the means of each of the two compared columns equal. The values of one column were then subtracted from the corresponding values of the other, the signs of the differences being retained, and the standard deviation of each set of 59 differences was calculated. Thus there was one less set of differences (and so of σ's) than there were columns of original $_s\dot{\bar{E}}_R$ values. These standard deviations are represented in Fig. 5.

An inspection of this figure shows at once that the magnitude of the several dispersions during the learning process is by no means constant, quite apart from chance variations which, incidentally, are considerable. Thus is a theoretical hypothesis (6, p. 314) definitely disproved by empirical fact. The dispersion magnitudes at first conform to a simple increasing function of N but this is soon followed by a series of undulations with crests at ordinal difference numbers 7–9; 20–24; and 55–59. This function is too complex for even approximate determination by ordinary curve-fitting procedures.

It is also noteworthy that the rise in the present series of σ values, even near the asymptote ($N = 60$),

463

does not as a whole reach the 1.2288 yielded by the 5000 differences represented in Fig. 2. This disagreement is in part due to a tendency for the standard deviations of the differences to increase with the increase in N separations on which the σ's were based. For example, the σ values for N separations from 0 to 10 (except 9, which was not determined) were, in the order of increasing separation,

1.186; 1.168; 1.188; 1.256; 1.225; 1.254; 1.220; 1.208; 1.249; 1.222.

Another factor tending to the disagreement seems to have been a gradual increase in oscillatory variability during the asymptotic trials themselves.

And, finally, there is apparent to inspection of Fig. 5 a noticeable increase in the variability of the σ's as N increases. To secure a rough quantification of this variability as distinct from presumably genuine progressive changes in σ as a function of N, we placed the data of Fig. 5 on a large-scale drawing, drew with care a smoothed curve among their central tendencies, read off the successive deviations of the individual entries from this line, and averaged these deviations in successive groups of 11 or 12 trials. These means were

.043; .088; .067; .110; and .102.

DISCUSSION

On an earlier page we referred to evidence of scale-separation distortion appearing in one of Thurstone's well-known studies of quantification based on paired comparisons mediated by a table of the normal probability integral (11). We now present the somewhat detailed evidence in the first three data columns of Table VII. This study was based on the nationality preferences, apparently, of Uni-

versity of Chicago students. A summary of the results of the part of Table VII just referred to is contained in data row 2 of Table VIII.

In order to explore somewhat further in this field, we made a similar examination of two additional published studies of the same general type. One of these was based on nationality preferences, much like the first study referred to, but of high-school children (13). The outcome of this examination is presented in some detail in the central portion of Table VII, and the final summary appears in row 3 of Table VIII. There the distortion effect is seen to be 54 per cent, or about that of the first Thurstone study, but the statistical reliability is much less. We are inclined to attribute this in part to the small number of items scaled, but also in part to the presumption that because of their lack of experience these subjects had not developed normal nationality preferences and so depended much more on mere guessing than did the more mature subjects of the other nationality preference study. The latter situation may be indicated by the relatively large number of four negative signs in the first two columns not matched by a parallel negative sign in the associated column.

The third Thurstone study which we examined was based on the judgments of 200 subjects concerning the extent to which a series of wet-dry propositions favored prohibition. The detailed data are shown as the last three columns of Table VII and the statistical outcome is presented in row 4 of Table VIII. Here again we find a per cent distortion of approximately the same size as the effects yielded by the other two Thurstone studies. The level of significance of this study and that of our own study are about the same,

TABLE VII

Summary of evidence indicating scale-separation distortion contained in three paired-comparison quantificational studies published by Thurstone. This table is constructed in a manner exactly analogous to Table IV.

Items under comparison	Nationality preferences by 239 adult human subjects (11)			Nationality preferences by 250 high-school children (13)			Wet-dry judgments by 200 subjects (12)		
	Direct determination values	Indirect determination means	Scale separation distortions	Direct determination values	Indirect determination means	Scale separation distortions	Direct determination values	Indirect determination means	Scale separation distortions
1–2	1.27	.82	.45	.28	.16	.12	1.20	.26	.94
2–3	.59	.52	.07	.11	.31	−.20	.64	.40	.24
3–4	−.08*	.07*	**	−.10	.02	.12	.36	−.02	.38
4–5	.31	.17	.14	.36	.13	.23	−.29	−.18	.11
5–6	.26	.03	.23	.25	.17	.08	2.17	2.11	.06
6–7	.45	.22	.23	.07	−.04	.11	−.16	−.23	−.07
7–8	.72	.50	.22	.39	.30	.09	.10	.02	.08
8–9	.07	.01	.06	.07	.00	.07	.58	.05	.53
9–10	.04	.09	.05	−.03*	.14*	**	−.10	.01	.11
10–11	.28	.07	.21	.10	.12	−.02	.27	.23	.04
11–12	.03	.14	−.11	.20	.08	.12	−.05	−.08	−.03
12–13	.21	.23	−.02	−.06*	.30*	**	2.17	1.55	.62
13–14	.12	.15	−.03						
14–15	.11	.03	.08						
15–16	.05	.20	−.15						
16–17	.09	.12	−.03						
17–18	.42	.10	.32						
18–19	.13	.02	.11						
19–20	.42	.31	.11						
20–21	.25	.00	.25						
Sums	5.82	3.73	2.09	1.93	1.33	.72	8.09	5.14	3.01
Means	.3063	.1963	.11	.193	.133	.072	.674	.428	.251

PAPER
18

each lacking a little of the 5 per cent level sometimes taken as the lower limit of dependability when unsupported by other evidence. Actually, the fact that all four studies sum-marized in Table VIII agree in the nature of the outcome, most of them with fair levels of significance, constitutes rather strong corroborative evidence of the genuineness of the tend-

TABLE VIII

A summary of the scale-distortion effects found in five paired-comparison quantification studies.

Study		Amount of distortion		Reliability			
Author	Reference	Absolute	Per cent of i.d.	No. of subjects	t	Degrees of freedom	Level of significance
Present	Present	.0577	22.7	59	2.003	21	6 per cent
Thurstone	11	.11	56.0	239	2.50	18	2 per cent
Thurstone	13	.072	54.0	250	1.674	9	14 per cent
Thurstone	12	.251	58.6	200	2.145	11	6 per cent
Guilford	5	.035	10.0	1	.597	5	56 per cent

ency of quantifications based on the paired comparisons of pooled subjects to yield this type of distortion.

We may also speak specifically concerning the meaning of the internal consistency encountered in the present study as being in the scientific tradition and indicating in so far the soundness of the quantification method employed and the general behavior theory which lies behind it. We have five points: (1) the characteristic leptokurtic scale-separation distortion of pooled $s\bar{E}_R$'s *indirectly* indicating that the presence of a leptokurtic distribution existed *before* the quantification was completed; (2) the *direct* determination of the leptokurtic distribution of pooled $s\bar{E}_R$'s and $s\bar{E}_R$ differences was made *after* the signs of the leptokurtic distortion were in existence; (3) since No. 1 and No. 2 were quite separate determinations, an error in either one could not have produced the other; (4) moreover, these two determinations agree in that each one demands the outcome produced by the other in the light of current theories of our quantificational procedure; (5) finally, the use of the empirical leptokurtic probability table in the quantification of the very same paired-comparison data produced a set of values which did *not* show the characteristic scale-separation distortion, as is also demanded by the theory behind our quantificational procedure.[3]

---

[3] In case the degree of leptokurtosis varies from one project to another this will present a practical difficulty. However, with modern calculating devices it should not be too laborious to compute several leptokurtic tables covering the range over which data vary according to the equation given by Pearson (8, p. lxiii):

$$y = y_0 \frac{1}{\left(1 + \dfrac{x^2}{a^2}\right)^m}.$$

Lastly we must show that the present modified procedure is not only consistent with itself and with other known facts and principles but is fertile in the sense that eight equations constituting basic laws or constants may be derived from our revised and corrected quantificational procedure. The first is

$$sE_R = 2.76 \ (1 - 10^{-.0305\dot{N}}) + .04. \quad \text{I}$$

Substituting -2 for $\dot{N}$ in the above equation (3, p. 514), we have

$$Z = 2.76 \ (1 - 10^{-.0305 \times (-2)}) + .04$$
$$= 2.76 \ (1 - 10^{.061}) + .04.$$
$$\therefore \quad Z = -.377. \quad \text{II}$$

Now (3, p. 514), Z falls $.377 + .04$ or $.417$ below the first overt superthreshold reaction. For this reason the coefficient of the new equation as based on absolute zero must be $2.76 + .417$, or 3.177, *i.e.*,

$$sE_R = 3.177 \ (1 - 10^{-.0305\dot{N}}). \quad \text{III}$$

Accordingly (3, p. 515),

$$M' = 3.177. \quad \text{IV}$$

In a similar manner (3, p. 516),

$$sL_R = 3.177 \ (1 - 10^{-.0305 \times 1.5})$$
$$= 3.177 \ (1 - 10^{-.0458})$$
$$= 3.177 \times .1.$$
$$\therefore \quad sL_R = .3177. \quad \text{V}$$

Now, substituting in the following

As a beginning, tables could perhaps be made which are based on β_2's of 3.75, 4.00, and 4.50. Meanwhile we may be able to establish a dependable rule which will enable us to estimate rather closely in advance which table will be required. If not it will be fairly easy to apply our test for scale-separation distortion, or some improved version of it, to the Thurstone Case III procedure and try the suitability of one table after another to the paired-comparison data until one is found which will yield a zero or near zero degree of distortion.

equation we have (**3**, p. 516)

$$\frac{sL_R}{M'} = \frac{.3177}{3.177} = .1.$$
$$\therefore \quad sL_R = .1 \; M'. \qquad \text{VI}$$

Also, since according to current theory the parenthetical part of the equation for reaction potential is the habit portion, we have (**3**, p. 516)

$$sH_R = 1 - 10^{-.0305\dot{N}}. \qquad \text{VII}$$

In regard to reaction latency, we have the median sE_R values from the lower curve of Fig. 4 and the corresponding median reaction latencies in **3**, p. 517. Plotting these and fitting an equation we have

$$sE_R = 2.59 \; sl_R^{-.466} - .59 \qquad \text{VIII}$$

and the mean square deviation amounts to only .0069.

SUMMARY AND CONCLUSIONS

1. Reaction latencies at the limit of learning of a group of 59 albino rats were converted into momentary reaction potentials by means of the empirical equation,

$$s\dot{\bar{E}}_R = 2.845 \; s\dot{l}_R^{-.483}.$$

2. The distribution of the $s\dot{\bar{E}}_R$'s was found directly to display a deviation from the Gaussian curve known as the leptokurtic form of kurtosis.

3. Five thousand differences between the $s\dot{\bar{E}}_R$ values from the above grouped subjects were found directly to be distributed in substantially the same leptokurtic manner, this close resemblance between two such distributions duplicating that characteristic of a pair of Gaussian distributions similarly related.[4]

[4] It happens that a number of the above individual organisms had their trials carried far beyond their learning asymptotes. The β_2's of five of these animals' $s\dot{\bar{E}}_R$ differences (median N = 2016) were calculated. They

4. The standard deviation of this $s\dot{\bar{E}}_R$ difference distribution was found to be 1.426 times that of the original $s\dot{\bar{E}}_R$ distribution, a very close approximation to the theoretical ratio for a pair of Gaussian distributions in this relationship, which is $\sqrt{2}$ or 1.414.

5. It was found possible rather easily to construct from our 5000 differences in $s\dot{\bar{E}}_R$ two types of empirical probability table, one of them analogous to the usual table of the normal probability integral used in scaling.

6. From a study of these two tables, in comparison with the corresponding types of normal probability table, a deduction was made regarding a characteristic scale-separation distortion which would appear in the process of quantifying leptokurtic paired-comparison data by means of the normal table.

7. A search revealed the presence of this distortion in our own data and also in three analogous standard published studies.

8. We found entirely feasible the use of the second form of empirical probability table, with a certain amount of interpolation, upon the original paired-comparison data of the present study for purposes of quantification by Thurstone's Case III method.

9. This yielded a quantification without the characteristic scale-separation distortion associated with the use of the normal probability table.

10. Moreover, the learning curve

were 3.0799; 3.7595; 3.8500; 4.9810; and 6.1974. These values suggest strongly that leptokurtosis may be the true basis of individual psychophysics and individual behavior theory generally, as well as of the pooled results by the Thurstone type of procedure. A repetition of Guilford's unique study (**5**) with 25 or 30 closely spaced weights and more subjects should yield a definite decision on this fundamental question.

PAPER
18

yielded by the new quantification was substantially the same as that produced by the normal table except that the coefficient of the fitted equation was 10.6 per cent smaller.

11. From this corrected learning equation it is possible to derive all of the seven or so equations regarding important behavior functions (laws and constants) originally derived from the learning equation produced by the normal probability table.

12. By using a suitable adaptation of the above procedure we found that the standard deviation of the distribution of $_s\dot{\bar{E}}_R$ differences from consecutive trials during learning gradually increased throughout the first 7 to 9 trials from about 40 to nearly 90 per cent of that at the limit of learning. Later, undulations followed but according to no simple law.

PAPER 18

13. We therefore conclude that:

A. Our data, and those of others, show that the paired comparison procedure when pooled from many subjects presents a characteristic deviation from the normal probability integral, known technically as a leptokurtic distribution.

B. The two contrasted distributions are sufficiently similar for the normal table, in conjunction with Thurstone's method of its use, to yield an empirical probability table which can be used to produce what purports to be a true quantification of momentary reaction potential $(_s\dot{\bar{E}}_R)$ from leptokurtic paired-comparison data.

C. This quantification leads to a molar law of primitive learning.

D. This law of learning, in conjunction with other empirical circumstances, leads to the quantitative statement of seven other behavior functions.

E. Thus the method of the quantification of $_s\bar{E}_R$ finally evolved is both fertile and consistent with known facts and principles.

F. The procedure followed in the present pioneering study should be applicable to the quantification of wide ranges of behavior beyond this sample.

REFERENCES

1. CAMPBELL, N. R. *Physics: the elements.* Cambridge, England: Cambridge Univ. Press, 1920.
2. FELSINGER, J. M., GLADSTONE, A. I., YAMAGUCHI, H. G., & HULL, C. L. Reaction latency $(_st_R)$ as a function of the number of reinforcements (N). *J. exp. Psychol.*, 1947, **37**, 214–228.
3. GLADSTONE, A. I., YAMAGUCHI, H. G., HULL, C. L., & FELSINGER, J. M. Some functional relationships of reaction potential $(_sE_R)$ and related phenomena. *J. exp. Psychol.*, 1947, **37**, 510–526.
4. GUILFORD, J. P. *Psychometric methods.* McGraw-Hill Book Co., 1936.
5. ——. Some empirical tests of the method of paired comparisons *J. gen. Psychol.*, 1931, **5**, 64–77.
6. HULL, C. L. *Principles of behavior.* New York: D. Appleton-Century Co., Inc., 1943.
7. ——, FELSINGER, J. M., GLADSTONE, A. I., & YAMAGUCHI, H. G. A proposed quantification of habit strength. PSYCHOL. REV., 1947, **54**, 237–254.
8. PEARSON, K. *Tables for statisticians and biometricians*, Part I. (3rd ed.) Cambridge Univ. Press, 1930.
9. THURSTONE, L. L. Psychophysical analysis. *Amer. J. Psychol.*, 1927, **38**, 368–389.
10. ——. A law of comparative judgment. PSYCHOL. REV., 1927, **34**, 273–286.
11. ——. An experimental study of nationality preferences. *J. gen. Psychol.*, 1928, **1**, 405–424.
12. ——. The measurement of opinion. *J. abn. & soc. Psychol.*, 1928, **22**, 415–530.
13. ——. Stimulus dispersions in the method of constant stimuli. *J. exp. Psychol.*, 1932, **15**, 284–297.
14. WALKER, H. M. *Elementary statistical methods.* New York: Henry Holt & Co., 1944.

Reprinted from PSYCHOLOGICAL REVIEW, Vol. 56, No. 2, March, 1949
Printed in U. S. A.

STIMULUS INTENSITY DYNAMISM (V) AND STIMULUS GENERALIZATION

BY CLARK L. HULL

Institute of Human Relations,
Yale University

INTRODUCTION

There seems little doubt that a general dynamic molar law based on stimulus intensity (i) exists and functions on a large scale. We propose to call this principle *stimulus intensity dynamism* (V). The concrete manifestations of this law have frequently been observed by experimentalists, especially in connection with the phenomenon of stimulus generalization, which explains the conjunction of the two principles in the title of the present article. We shall begin by examining some of the concrete phenomena so far reported, after which we shall attempt to arrive at a more precise though provisional formulation of the law and its joint action with stimulus intensity generalization in the determination of reaction potential magnitude.

SOME EXAMPLES OF STIMULUS INTENSITY DYNAMISM

We turn first to a stimulus-intensity generalization study carried out by Hovland (6) on human subjects. When the generalization effects of four sound intensities employed were presumably equalized, the amplitudes of

galvanic skin reactions averaged 10.1 for a stimulus of 40 decibels and 16.55 for a stimulus of 86 decibels, the number of reinforcements and everything else being constant. This greater response to a more intense stimulus is believed to involve stimulus-intensity dynamism.

J. S. Brown (1) tested the adient pull of rats to go to food which was associated with screens illuminated to the extent of .02, 5.0, and 5000.0 apparent foot candles. His report shows that when the sensory generalization effects were presumably equalized the pulling responses of his animals were 61.5 grams for .02 apparent foot candles, and 70.5 grams for 5000 foot candles. This greater response to a more intense stimulus is a clear case of stimulus-intensity dynamism. Incidentally it serves as an operational definition of the concept with which we are here primarily concerned.

Spence carried out a study (8) in which rats were trained to discriminate black from white, the two stimuli being presented simultaneously. He found that, other things equal, the rats trained to go to white made only 6.5 errors by going instead to black, whereas those trained to go to black made 19.3 errors by going instead to

PAPER

19

PAPER
19

white. This is a third case of stimulus-intensity dynamism.

At about the same time, Ruth Hays carried out in the writer's laboratory an unpublished study in which 20 rats were trained to jump against a black card for food and 20 others were trained to jump against a white card for equivalent food, the cards in this case always being presented singly. Equalizing other factors in the situation, the latencies of the jumps to white averaged 1.70 seconds, whereas those to black averaged 7.54 seconds. Since white is a stronger light stimulus than black and a reaction latency of 1.70 corresponds to a greater reaction potential than does 7.54, this is a fourth case of stimulus-intensity dynamism.

In 1886 James McKeen Cattell (2) carried out a meticulous study on two human subjects in which six different light intensities were used as the signal in a reaction-time experiment in which the hand was lifted. The means of the two subjects showed a consistent decrease in latency as the stimulus increased in intensity, the extreme mean latencies being .280 and .169 seconds, where the corresponding light intensity extremes were in the ratio of 1 to 1,000. This is accordingly regarded as a fifth case of stimulus-intensity dynamism.

More recently, Piéron (10) has reported analogous experiments with human subjects involving the effect of intensity of stimulations on reaction time in the cases of both hearing and taste. Both functions were found to be strikingly uniform and in agreement in showing that the stronger the stimulus, the shorter is the reaction latency and so the greater the reaction potential, quite as Cattell found

<hr>

[1] The two Piéron studies and that of Cattell are cited by Rashevsky (11) and by Householder and Landahl (5), where they are given a mathematico-neurological interpretation.

Finally, Hilgard and Marquis (4, p. 141 ff.) mention some conditioned-reflex studies which "demonstrate that response strength is a function of stimulus intensity, . . ."

In summary of the above facts it may be said that seven experiments appear to have uniformly found a definite tendency, other things approximately equalized, for trained responses to have a greater reaction potential ($_sE_R$) as the stimulus increases in intensity whether tested by reaction latency, amplitude, or intensity. Accordingly the principle may be considered as qualitatively well established.

There remains the problem of stating the specific quantitative law of the functional relationship. Unfortunately the evidence on this more precise but scientifically necessary aspect of the question is far less satisfactory. For example, ideal evidence on this point might be furnished by an experiment like that of Hays, described above, if a number of other squads of animals were trained, each on a different known shade of gray as well as on black and white. The asymptotes of the several learning curves as measured in $_sE_R$'s could then be expressed in a fitted equation stating the functional relationship of the several asymptotes to the associated light intensities. This would be the law of $_sE_R = V = f(i)$. In the absence of such direct evidence we must make the best shift we can with the indirect evidence at present available.

The first data bearing indirectly on the quantitative functional relationship, $V = f(i)$, are those yielded by Brown's study just mentioned. In addition to the two means secured by averaging the opposite ends of his two stimulus-generalization gradients, there is also the average of the two

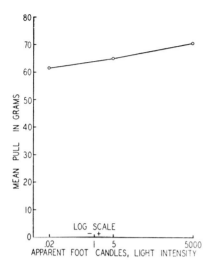

FIG. 1. Mean strength of conditioned adient pull of rats to food associated with lights of different intensity, generalization effects presumably equalized. Plotted on a logarithmic scale from values secured from Brown's data (**1**). Note that the distance on this scale from .02 to 5.0 is appreciably less than that from 5.0 to 5000.0.

approximate middles. All three values are shown graphically in Fig. 1. There it will be noticed that the relationship is nearly linear. In this connection it must be pointed out that stimulus generalization gradients of reaction potential are in general concave upward (**7**) and that averaging the middles of two such gradients will also yield a curve that is lower at its middle as related to the two ends than would be true for the undistorted relationship of stimulus-intensity dynamism to sE_R. This means that if Fig. 1 were corrected for this factor, its nearly linear shape would very probably become one of at least an appreciable convexity upward. It may be added that while strength of pull clearly is not sE_R, the two phenomena are evidently increasing functions of each other and the relationship

is presumably fairly linear throughout the main part of their ranges.

THE QUANTITATIVE LAW OF STIMU-
LUS INTENSITY DYNAMISM (*V*)
AS A FUNCTION OF STIMU-
LUS INTENSITY (*i*)

Our second indirect evidence bearing on the quantitative functional relationship of $sE_R = V = f(i)$ is somewhat more specific, though again there is some uncertainty. As already suggested, Cattell's study is believed to give positive qualitative evidence on stimulus-intensity dynamism. Here it must be noted that six intensities of light stimulus yielded six mean reaction latencies from each of two subjects. Table I shows the light intensities and the corresponding mean latencies of the two subjects on a hand-lifting response, as calculated in the writer's laboratory. The functional relationship of the two variables was found to be almost perfectly fitted by the equation,

$$st_R = .113 \times 10^{-.59 \log i} + .167. \quad (1)$$

This is presented graphically in Fig. 2.

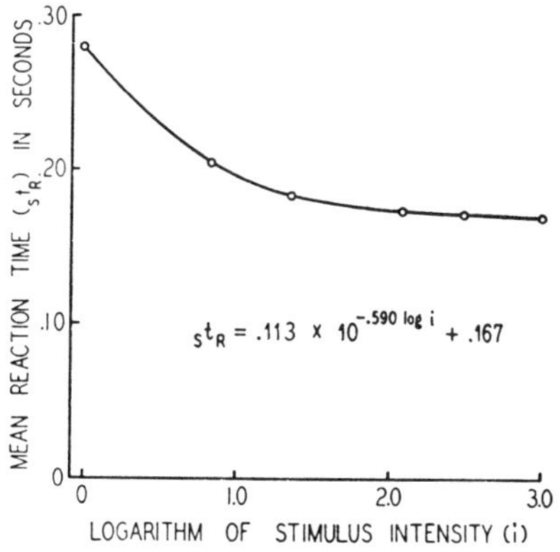

PAPER
19

$$st_R = .113 \times 10^{-.590 \log i} + .167$$

FIG. 2. Curve based on the means of the mean reaction latencies of two human subjects to light stimuli of different intensities. The original data were published by Cattell (**2**). The equation was fitted by H. C. Wilcoxon, the mean square deviation of the fit being .001.

TABLE I

Cattell's reaction-time results to various light intensities (2) with theoretically
equivalent reaction potentials as calculated by us.

Light stimulus intensities (i)	1	7	23	123	315	1000
Mean reaction latencies ($_sl_R$)	.280″	.205″	.184″	.174″	.170″	.169″
Theoretically equivalent reaction potentials ($_sE_R = V$)	.89	1.14	1.22	1.28	1.29	1.30

In our proposed interpretation of this law it is tentatively assumed that the reaction potential involved is essentially that of stimulus-intensity dynamism. Now, the incidental mediating computations are such that this equation will need to be used with an equation involving rat reaction latency, which is much slower. For that reason the equations of different origin must be adjusted so far as possible to what they would be if they were from the same origin. We have found that the medians of our rat latencies are roughly 13.6 times as long as Cattell's mean human reactions. We accordingly multiply the .113 and the .167 of equation 1 by 13.6, which yields the following equation:

$$_sl_R = 1.54 \times 10^{-.59 \log i} + 2.27. \quad (2)$$

We next note the following equation, which was fitted to some of our own empirical (rat) data (3):

$$_sE_R = 2.845(_sl_R)^{-.483} - .599. \quad (3)$$

Now, substituting in equation 3 the values of $_sl_R$ as it stands in equation 2, we have[2]

$$_sE_R = V = 2.845(1.54 \times 10^{-.59 \log i} + 2.27)^{-.483} - .599. \quad (4)$$

[2] V is an expository device employed to indicate a theoretical reaction potential ($_sE_R$) in which the quantitative influence of stimulus-intensity dynamism is explicitly included. It will serve also to indicate this particular factor which contributes to the determination of reaction potential value much as do $_sH_R$ and

Thus we have in (4) an equation which purports to express $_sE_R$ in terms of i, which we have been seeking. For example, substituting the value of $i = 7$ from Table 1 into equation 4, we have

$$V = 2.845(1.54 \times 10^{-.59 \log 7} + 2.27)^{-.483} - .599$$

$$= 2.845(1.54 \times 10^{-.59 \times .8451} + 2.27)^{-.483} - .599$$

$$= 2.845 \left(1.54 \times \frac{1}{3.152} + 2.27 \right)^{-.483} - .599$$

$$= 2.845(2.758)^{-.483} - .599.$$

$$\therefore \quad V = 1.14.$$

Performing the corresponding substitutions and computations for the remaining stimulus-intensity values, we have the bottom row of values given in Table 1.

The values in question are shown graphically in Fig. 3. There may be seen what purports to be a representation of the functional relationship of $_sE_R$, i.e., V, to i. In confirmation of our surmise based on the consideration of Brown's graph, a clearly convex-upward curve is obtained. This will be used tentatively until a more direct and dependable determination becomes available.

V. Subsequent workers will, of course, need to modify greatly the crude pioneering empirical evidence and equations here available.

Generalizing from the above considerations, we arrive at our primary principle or postulate of stimulus-intensity dynamism:

Other things constant, the magnitude of the reaction potential (sE_R, i.e., V) has an increasing monotonic relationship to the intensity (i) of the stimulus in question, the increase taking place at a progressively slower rate according to the equation

$$sE_R = V = A(1 - 10^{-b \log i}). \quad (5)$$

STIMULUS-INTENSITY DYNAMISM (V) AND STIMULUS-INTENSITY GENERALIZATION ($s\underline{E}_R$)

So far as we can now see, equations 4 or 5 and Fig. 3 represent a first approximation to the molar law of stimulus-intensity dynamism in a form relatively uncomplicated by other prin-

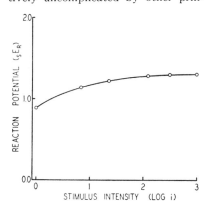

FIG. 3. Theoretical reaction potential plotted as a function of stimulus intensity on the assumption that Cattell's reaction latencies (2) represent approximately the dynamics of stimulus intensity ($sE_R = V$). Apparently the unit of stimulus intensity used by Cattell was 12.5 times as great as the subjects' stimulus threshold. Using the revised unit the curve falls to zero at a stimulus of 1 and the data are almost exactly fitted by the equation

$$sE_R = V = 1.328(1 - 10^{-.440 \log i}).$$

The fit was made by J. A. Antoinetti.

ciples. On the other hand, the results of Hovland (6), Brown (1), and Spence (8) cited above appear with equal clarity to be produced by the joint action of stimulus-intensity dynamism and stimulus generalization ($s\underline{E}_R$). This necessarily raises the question of how these two molar laws interact and the characteristic results of this interaction.

Let it be supposed that a stimulus which is subject to variability in intensity (i), such as that used by Cattell (2), is conditioned to a response at the weak extreme of its log intensity (intensity 1 = log 00, rows I and II of Table 2), with one group of subjects, and at the opposite or strong extreme of its log intensity (intensity 1000 = log 3.0) with a second group. Then let it be assumed that the stimuli are tested for generalization at the middle point (log i = 1.5, row V, Table 2), and at the opposite extreme of stimulus intensity with each group of subjects. We assume as usual (7, pp. 186, 200) that the generalization gradient values are yielded by the equation,

$$s\underline{E}_R = sE_R \times 10^{-kd}, \quad (6)$$

where sE_R is .89 at the weak intensity extreme and 1.31 at the strong intensity extreme (row III, Table 2), k is .15, and d is the difference between the log i of the point conditioned and of the point tested for generalization. In each case it follows that d is .00 at the point conditioned and 1.5 and 3.0 at the remaining two points. Substituting these three d values in equation 6 with sE_R at .89, we secure the stimulus generalization values appearing in row VI. Doing the same with sE_R at 1.31 we secure the stimulus generalization values appearing in row VII.

At this point we encounter the question of how stimulus-intensity dyna-

PAPER

19

TABLE 2

The various steps in the computations leading to the two generalization gradients as influenced by stimulus-intensity dynamism, rows VIII and IX respectively.

		1	31.62	1000
I	Stimulus intensity (i)	1	31.62	1000
II	Log i	.00	1.5	3.0
III	Equivalent reaction potential $sE_R = V$	.892	1.24	1.31
IV	V ratio (V) based on log .00	1.000	1.389	1.463
V	V ratio (V) based on log 3.0	.684	.949	1.000
VI	Simple generalization gradient starting at log i = .00	.89	.530	.316
VII	Simple generalization gradient starting at log i = 3.0	.465	.780	1.31
VIII	Row IV × row VI $s\underline{E}_R = sE_R × V$	.89	.736	.462
IX	Row V × row VII $s\underline{E}_R = sE_R × V$	.318	.74	**1.31**

mism combines with stimulus generalization on the same $S \rightarrow R$ connection. In order to expose the problem to investigation in a definite manner we propose as a first approximation to the primary molar law involved the following postulate:

When stimulus-intensity generalization and stimulus-intensity dynamism are jointly acting on the results of the same learning, they combine by the multiplication of the stimulus generalization value ($s\underline{E}_R$) by the ratio (V) of the corresponding stimulus-intensity dynamism (V) divided by the dynamism at the origin of the stimulus generalization, i.e.,

$$sE_R = s\underline{E}_R × V. \qquad (7)$$

The stimulus-intensity ratios (V) based on the origins of the respective stimulus generalizations are presented in rows IV and V of Table 2. Multiplying each of the values of row IV by

the corresponding generalization value of row VI, according to equation 7, we have the joint values given in row VIII. Similarly, multiplying the V values of row V by the generalization values in row VII, we have the joint values given in row IX. The values of rows VIII and IX are the joint results we have been seeking. The values in question are represented graphically in Fig. 4.

Generalizing on the results particularly as shown in rows VIII and IX of Table 2, and relevant considerations, we arrive immediately at five corollaries:

The middle of a gradient which is convex upward must be greater than the mean of its two ends. Therefore, by row VIII,

$$.736 > \frac{.89 + .462}{2}.$$

$$\therefore \quad .736 > .676.$$

Accordingly:

I. *When a response is conditioned to a weak stimulus and generalizes toward a fairly strong extreme of the stimulus-intensity continuum, the resulting effective gradient is convex upward.*

The middle of a gradient which is concave upward must be less than the mean of its two ends. Therefore, by row IX,

$$.74 < \frac{.318 + 1.31}{2}.$$

$$\therefore \quad .74 < .814.$$

Accordingly:

II. *When a response is conditioned to the strong extreme of the above stimulus-intensity continuum and generalizes toward the weak extreme, the resulting effective gradient is concave upward.*

By rows VIII and IX,

$$1.31 > .89.$$

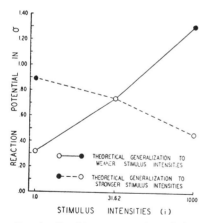

FIG. 4. Graphic representation of theoretical stimulus-intensity generalization as modified by concurrent stimulus-intensity dynamism when extending from weak toward strong stimulus intensities and from strong toward weak intensities. Solid circles represent the origins of the respective gradients.

Accordingly:

III. *The origin of the gradient originating at the stronger stimulus extreme will have a stronger reaction potential ($_sE_R$) than that originating at the weaker stimulus extreme.*

Other things equal, the more steeply a gradient slopes downward from its origin, the greater will be the quotient obtained by dividing the value of its origin by that of its termination. Therefore, by rows VIII and IX,

$$\frac{.89}{.462} < \frac{1.31}{.318}.$$

$$\therefore \quad 1.93 < 4.12.$$

Accordingly:

IV. *The general trend of the joint $_sE_R$ gradient originating at a weak stimulus intensity and generalizing toward stronger stimulus intensities has a smaller tendency to a downward slope than that extending in the opposite direction between the same stimulus intensities.*

PAPER
19

By a simple inspection of Fig. 5 it follows that,

V. *The two gradients intersect at their midpoint.*

EMPIRICAL EVIDENCE CONCERNING THE SOUNDNESS OF THE THEORETICAL COROLLARIES

We are fortunate in finding empirical evidence bearing directly on all five of our corollaries. This consists of the quantitative studies of Brown (1) and Hovland (6). Because the Cattell study, which was used to derive our equation tentatively expressing the principle of stimulus-intensity dynamism, involved motor behavior, it is possible that the corollaries based on it may in some respects be compared more appropriately with the re-

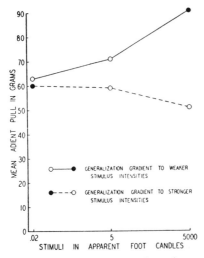

FIG. 5. Graphic representation of empirical stimulus-intensity generalization as modified by stimulus-intensity dynamism plotted to correspond roughly to Fig. 4. (Plotted from data published by Brown, 1.)

sults from Brown's study, which concerns motor reactions, than with those from Hovland's study, which concerns primarily glandular reactions. Moreover, the Cattell and Brown studies both employed light stimuli of somewhat similar magnitude. Nevertheless the results of both studies, so far as they have a bearing on our corollaries, are given—Brown's results in

Fig. 5 and Hovland's results in Table 3.

We proceed now to evaluate the two sets of empirical data by the same computational method utilized in deriving our corollaries from the numerical values contained in Table 2. The Brown values may be recognized on the graphs of Fig. 5; the parallel Hovland values have been taken from Table 3.

Brown's data present the following:

$$.59 > \frac{.60 + .51}{2}.$$

$$\therefore .59 > .555.$$

Also Hovland's data present:

$$\frac{12.98 + 14.30}{2} > \frac{11.30 + 15.75}{2}.$$

$$\therefore 13.64 > 13.53.$$

Both of the above inequalities show the respective gradients to be convex upward. It follows that, within the limits of the probable errors involved, Corollary I has empirical verification from two independent investigations.

Again, Brown's data present the following:

$$.71 < \frac{.60 + .91}{2}.$$

$$\therefore .71 < .755.$$

TABLE 3

Empirical mean generalization response amplitudes to stimuli which are the same as or weaker than the intensity of the stimulus to which the response was originally conditioned, and the corresponding values of the gradient extending in the opposite direction. The values in bold-face type are the mean amplitudes of the responses to the stimuli originally conditioned. (Compiled from Hovland's published data, 6.)

Stimulus intensities in decibels	40	60	74	86
Mean response amplitudes based on conditioning to a tone of 40 decibels' intensity	**11.30**	12.98	14.30	15.75
Mean response amplitudes based on conditioning to a tone of 86 decibels' intensity	8.90	10.94	13.37	**17.35**

Also, Hovland's data present:

$$\frac{10.94 + 13.37}{2} < \frac{8.90 + 17.35}{2}.$$

$$\therefore \quad 12.16 < 13.13.$$

Both of the above inequalities show the respective gradients to be concave upward. It follows that within the limits of the probable errors involved, Corollary II has empirical substantiation from two independent investigations.

Once more, Brown's data present the following:

$$.91 > .60.$$

Also, Hovland's data present:

$$17.35 > 11.30.$$

The above inequalities show Corollary III to be verified, within the limits of the probable errors involved, by two independent investigations.

Further, Brown's data present the following relationship:

$$\frac{.60}{.51} < \frac{.90}{.63}.$$

$$\therefore \quad 1.18 < 1.43.$$

Also, Hovland's data present:

$$\frac{11.30}{15.75} < \frac{17.35}{8.90}.$$

$$\therefore \quad .72 < 1.95.$$

The Brown data above present a conventional verification of the less slope shown by the inequality from which the corollary was derived, as may be seen by a simple inspection of Figs. 4 and 5. The Hovland data, while conforming technically to the formula, really show a marked deviation from Fig. 4 in that the gradient, supposed theoretically to slope less downward, as a matter of fact slopes upward, as shown by the decimal value of .72. Actually this probably is a verification of the logic of the basic theory, which pits stimulus generalization and stimulus-intensity dynamism against each other so far as the slope of the gradient extending from a weak stimulus intensity to a strong one is concerned. If the stimulus-intensity dynamism is very strong it will naturally reverse the downward slope which is natural to stimulus generalization operating by itself.

Finally there comes the matter of the intersection of the two gradients. Brown's gradients, as clearly shown by Fig. 5, do not intersect. On the other hand, a plot of the two Hovland gradients shows that they intersect about midway between the stimulus intensities, 74 and 86 decibels. Thus, ignoring the precise point of the intersection, one investigation substantiates Corollary V and one refutes it. Very likely the disagreement between the two empirical studies under consideration in this respect, and the failure of the corollary really to agree with both of them, depends upon the differing magnitudes in the two situations of one or more constants as yet not clearly identified.

The empirical verification of four out of five theoretical corollaries, together with a partial verification of the fifth, suggests that the postulates as a whole, including the multiplicative method of combining the $_sE_R$ and V involved, possess a considerable degree of truth but that some of them are clearly defective. As usual the nature of the defect must be sought in further research, both theoretical and empirical but primarily theoretical. As already suggested the remedy may lie in the exact determination of the magnitudes of the several constants involved, since the theoretical outcome is definitely sensitive to the variation of these magnitudes.

PAPER
19

SUMMARY

Several experimental situations have been found which seem to indicate rather clearly that reaction potential is in part a function of the stimulus intensity involved. Because no specific investigations have as yet been made of this presumptive primary molar law, its mathematical statement can at present be given only tentatively. This is that stimulus-intensity dynamism is a monotonic function, increasing at a decreasing rate, of the logarithm of stimulus intensity.

An important situation in which stimulus-intensity dynamism influences reaction potential is found where stimulus intensity is the basis of stimulus generalization. This raises the question of how the two primary molar laws combine to produce the joint effect as a secondary molar law. To secure the first approximation here utilized, we reduce stimulus-intensity dynamism to a percentage ratio based on the point of origin of the generalization gradient, and then combine the two gradients by multiplication. This procedure, together with related postulates, leads to the deduction of several quantitative corollaries, four of which agree fully with empirical fact and one of which agrees partially. The conclusion is that the theory as a whole approaches closely to a true statement of the principles involved, but is clearly lacking in some respect.

An analogous situation of considerable theoretical importance as well as complexity is found where generalization occurs on the basis of perseverative stimulus traces. This matter requires separate treatment.

PAPER
19

REFERENCES

1. BROWN, J. S. The generalization of approach responses as a function of stimulus intensity and strength of motivation. *J. comp. Psychol.*, 1942, **33**, 209–226.

2. CATTELL, J. McK. The influence of the intensity of the stimulus on the length of the reaction time. *Brain*, 1886, **8**, 512–515.

3. GLADSTONE, A. I., YAMAGUCHI, H. G., HULL, C. L., & FELSINGER, J. M. Some functional relationships of reaction potential (sE_R) and related phenomena. *J. exp. Psychol.*, 1947, **37**, 510–526.

4. HILGARD, E. R., & MARQUIS, D. G. *Conditioning and learning.* New York: D. Appleton-Century Co., 1940.

5. HOUSEHOLDER, A. S., & LANDAHL, H. D. *Mathematical biophysics of the central nervous system. Mathematical Biophysics Monograph Series*, No. 1. Bloomington, Ind.: The Principia Press, Inc., 1945.

6. HOVLAND, C. I. The generalization of conditioned responses: II. The sensory generalization of conditioned responses with varying intensities of tone. *J. genet. Psychol.*, 1937, **51**, 279–291.

7. HULL, C. L. *Principles of behavior.* New York: D. Appleton-Century Co., Inc., 1943.

8. ———. The problem of primary stimulus generalization. PSYCHOL. REV., 1947, **54**, 120–134.

9. ———. Stimulus-trace generalization, "remote" associations, and the gradient of reinforcement. (In preparation.)

10. PIÉRON, H. Nouvelles recherches sur l'analyse du temps de latence sensorielle et sur la loi qui relie le temps à l'intensité d'excitation. *L'Année psychologique*, 1920, **22**, 58–142.

11. RASHEVSKY, N. *Advances and applications of mathematical biology.* Chicago: Univ. Chicago Press, 1940.

[MS. received July 19, 1948]

Reprinted from Psychological Review. Vol. 57, No. 3, May, 1950
Printed in U. S. A.

BEHAVIOR POSTULATES AND COROLLARIES—1949

BY CLARK L. HULL

Institute of Human Relations, Yale University

The matter of isolating and formulating a set of quantitative postulates or mathematical primary principles upon which may be based a true natural-science theory, one designed to mediate the deduction of a system as complex as that concerning mammalian behavior, is a formidable undertaking. To write out the blank form of an equation such as $x = f(y)$ is quite simple, but careful planning and a certain amount of skill are often required in the determination of what the function actually is and the approximate values of the numerical constants contained in it. Moreover, suitable units of quantification must be devised. There must ordinarily be added a preliminary checking of the consistency of the formulation with known empirical facts. All this takes much time and effort. The detailed history of such a process would itself require a fair-sized volume.

Very briefly, the present writer's procedure may be described somewhat as follows. He begins with selecting two or three principles, often isolated by earlier workers, from the complex of data involving a certain class of experiments. These are generalized and quantified as tentative equations. The attempt is then made to apply the equations to a wider range of phenomena. So long as the application of these equations agrees with empirical fact they are retained. But when it seems that a given combination of formulated principles ought to mediate the deduction of an empirically known phenomenon but does not do so, the principles in question are reëxamined to the end that with the possible revision of one or more

of them they will yield the deduction sought and still mediate the true deductions already to the credit of the critical postulates.

Sometimes the deduction failure may appear to be the result of ignoring a law not yet formulated. An example of this in the present postulate set concerns the matter of stimulus-intensity dynamism (7), which appears as Postulate VI. In such a case an empirical situation is sought in the literature, where all the factors are held constant except the significant ones in question; the data which are found are plotted and an equation is fitted to these values. Usually such data are defective in one way or another, though if facilities are not available to set up a specific experiment they will be used as a first approximation. The provisional equation so secured is then tried out deductively in more general situations with other principles which presumably are also operating with it. Thus it may be seen that a large element of trial and error is involved in the process. It is to be expected that failures among such trials would be relatively more frequent in a young and fast-moving science than in an older and more stable one.

A detailed record of the theory trials made by the present writer in the behavior field is scattered through twenty-six volumes of handwritten notebooks. This series began in 1915 and extends to the present time. The system grew very slowly, especially during the early years. The first published material in the series appeared in 1929 (1). As the system took on more definite form the author began

PAPER

20

173

to present to his seminar groups from time to time somewhat formalized statements regarding special problems. These statements were made in the form of mimeographed memoranda which were later assembled and substantially bound. Four separate volumes of such bound memoranda are on deposit in the Yale University library and in the libraries of several other universities where a certain amount of interest has been manifested in such matters. The bound memoranda extend over the academic years 1936–1938, 1939–1940, 1940–1944, and 1945–1946 (8, 3, 4, 6).

From time to time during the compilation of the first three of these volumes the principles which seemed most promising at the moment were gathered together in a numbered series, sometimes accompanied by a few deductions based on the postulates in question. The dates of the chief of these series follow, with the pages of the volume where they may be found:

PAPER
20

> December 2, 1937, pp. 115–116.
> May 3, 1939, pp. 24–29.
> January 27, 1940, pp. 40–41; 45; 47–48.
> February 10, 1940, pp. 49–54.
> February 12, 1940, pp. 55–59.
> April 30, 1940, pp. 111–117.
> July 8, 1941, pp. 44–52.
> December 28, 1942, pp. 163–166.
> July 13, 1943, pp. 167–170.
> December 20, 1943, pp. 176–177.

On September 4, 1936, the writer used a much abbreviated version of an earlier set of postulates which was substantially like that listed above under date of December 2, 1937, as the basis of an address given by him as retiring president of the American Psychological Association. This was published in routine form (2) in January, 1937. The next published version of the system appeared in the joint volume, *Mathematico-Deductive Theory of Rote Learning* (9). The most recently preceding published form is presented in the bold-faced type sections scattered through the volume, *Principles of Behavior* (5).

During the years since the publication of *Principles of Behavior* numerous reasons for changes and modifications in the system as there presented have been revealed. These arose through a careful study of experimental results from Yale laboratories and from laboratories in other institutions, numerous thoughtful theoretical criticisms, and the writer's use of the postulates of the system in making concrete deductions of the systematic details of individual (non-social) behavior in connection with a book which he is now writing on this subject. As a consequence, the mathematical aspects of many of the postulates have been formulated, or reformulated, and the verbal formulation of nearly all has been modified to a certain extent. One postulate (5, p. 319) has been dropped in part as empirically erroneous, some postulates have been divided, and others have been combined; several new postulates have been added, and a number of the original postulates have been deduced from others of the present set and now appear as corollaries. The net result is an increase of from sixteen to eighteen postulates, with twelve corollaries.

The same sort of revision as that just described is certain to be necessary in the case of the present set of behavior postulates and corollaries. This is true of all natural-science theories; they must be continually checked against the growing body of empirical fact. In order to facilitate this winnowing and expanding process, the postulates and corollaries as of November, 1949, are here presented in an unbroken sequence.

Postulate I

Unlearned Stimulus-Response Connections ($_sU_R$)

Organisms at birth possess receptor-effector connections ($_sU_R$) which under combined stimulation (S) and drive (D) have the potentiality of evoking a hierarchy of responses that either individually or in combination are more likely to terminate the need than would be a random selection from the reactions resulting from other stimulus and drive combinations.

Postulate II

Molar Stimulus Traces (s') and Their Stimulus Equivalents (S')

A. When a brief stimulus (S) impinges on a suitable receptor there is initiated the recruitment phase of a self-propagating molar afferent trace impulse ($\dot{s}'$), the molar stimulus equivalent ($\dot{S}'$) of which rises as a power function of time (t) since the termination of the stimulus, i.e.,

$$\dot{S}' = At^a + 1.0,$$

$\dot{S}'$ reaching its maximum (and termination) when t equals about .450".

B. Following the maximum of the recruitment phase of the molar stimulus trace, there supervenes a more lengthy subsident phase ($\grave{s}'$), the stimulus equivalent of which descends as a power function of time (t'), i.e.,

$$\grave{S}' = B(t' + c)^{-b},$$

where $t' = t - .450''$.

C. The intensity of the molar stimulus trace (s') is a logarithmic function of the molar stimulus equivalent of the trace, i.e.,

$$s' = \log S'.$$

Postulate III

Primary Reinforcement

Whenever an effector activity (R) is closely associated with a stimulus afferent impulse or trace (s') and the conjunction is closely associated with the diminution in the receptor discharge characteristic of a need, there will result an increment to a tendency for that stimulus to evoke that response.

Corollary i

Secondary Motivation

When neutral stimuli are repeatedly and consistently associated with the evocation of a primary or secondary drive and this drive undergoes an abrupt diminution, the hitherto neutral stimuli acquire the capacity to bring about the drive stimuli (S_D) which thereby become the condition (C_D) of a secondary drive or motivation.

Corollary ii

Secondary Reinforcement

A neutral receptor impulse which occurs repeatedly and consistently in close conjunction with a reinforcing state of affairs, whether primary or secondary, will itself acquire the power of acting as a reinforcing agent.

Postulate IV

The Law of Habit Formation ($_sH_R$)

If reinforcements follow each other at evenly distributed intervals, everything else constant, the resulting habit will increase in strength as a positive growth function of the number of trials according to the equation,

$$_sH_R = 1 - 10^{-a\dot{N}}.$$

Postulate V

Primary Motivation or Drive (D) [1]

A. Primary motivation (D), at least that resulting from food privation, consists of two multiplicative components, (1) the drive proper (D') which is an increasing monotonic sig-

---

[1] This postulate, especially parts A, B, and C, is largely based on the doctoral dissertation of H. G. Yamaguchi (11). It is used here by permission of Dr. Yamaguchi.

PAPER

20

moid function of h, and (2) a negative or inanition component (ϵ) which is a positively accelerated monotonic function of h decreasing from 1.0 to zero, $i.e.$,

$$D = D' \times \epsilon.$$

B. The functional relationship of drive (D) to one drive condition (food privation) is: from $h = 0$ to about 3 hours drive rises in an approximately linear manner until the function abruptly shifts to a near horizontal, then to a concave-upward course, gradually changing to a convex-upward curve reaching a maximum of 12.3 σ at about $h = 59$, after which it gradually falls to the reaction threshold ($_sL_R$) at around $h = 100$.

C. Each drive condition (C_D) generates a characteristic drive stimulus (S_D) which is a monotonic increasing function of this state.

D. At least some drive conditions tend partially to motivate into action habits which have been set up on the basis of different drive conditions.

POSTULATE VI

Stimulus-Intensity Dynamism (V)

Other things constant, the magnitude of the stimulus-intensity component (V) of reaction potential ($_sE_R$) is a monotonic increasing logarithmic function of S, $i.e.$,

$$V = 1 - 10^{-a\log S}.$$

POSTULATE VII

Incentive Motivation (K)

The incentive function (K) is a negatively accelerated increasing monotonic function of the weight (w) of food given as reinforcement, $i.e.$,

$$K = 1 - 10^{-a\sqrt{w}}.$$

POSTULATE VIII

Delay in Reinforcement (J) [2]

The greater the delay in reinforcement, the weaker will be the resulting reaction potential, the quantitative law being,

$$J = 10^{-jt}.$$

POSTULATE IX

The Constitution of Reaction Potential ($_sE_R$)

The reaction potential ($_sE_R$) of a bit of learned behavior at any given stage of learning is determined (1) by the drive (D) operating during the learning process multiplied (2) by the dynamism of the signaling stimulus at response evocation (V_2), (3) by the incentive reinforcement (K), (4) by the gradient of delay in reinforcement (J), and (5) by the habit strength ($_sH_R$), $i.e.$,

$$_sE_R = D \times V \times K \times J \times _s\dot{H}_R.$$

where

$$_s\dot{H}_R = _sH_R \times V_1$$

and V_1 represents the stimulus intensity during the learning process.

Corollary iii

The Behavioral Summation ($\dot{+}$) of Two Reaction Potentials, $_sE_R$ and $_s\underline{E}_R$

If two stimuli, S' and S, are conditioned separately to a response (R) by $\dot{N}'$ and $\dot{N}$ reinforcements respectively, and the $_sE_R$ generalizes from S' to S in the amount of $_s\underline{E}_R$, the summation ($\dot{+}$) of the two reaction potentials at S will be the same as would result for the equiva-

[2] It is probable that this postulate ultimately will be deduced from other postulates, including II B and VI; thus it will become a corollary. In that case the phenomena represented by J would be taken over in IX by $_sH_R$, just as $_s\tilde{H}_R$ now is.

lent number of reinforcements at S, $i.e.$,

$$sE_R \dotplus s\underline{E}_R$$

$$= sE_R + s\underline{E}_R - \frac{sE_R \times s\underline{E}_R}{M},$$

where M is the asymtote of sE_R.

Corollary iv

The Withdrawal of a Smaller Reaction Potential (sE_R) from a Larger One (C)

If $C = sE_R \dotplus sE'_R$, then

$$sE_R = \frac{M(C - sE'_R)}{M - sE'_R}.$$

Corollary v

The Behavioral Summation ($\dotplus$) of Two Habit Strengths, sH_R and $s\bar{H}_R$

Since the asymptote of sH_R is 1.0,

$$sH_R \dotplus s\bar{H}_R$$

$$= sH_R + s\bar{H}_R - sH_R \times s\bar{H}_R.$$

Corollary vi

The Withdrawal of a Smaller Habit Strength (sH_R) from a Larger One (C)

If

$$C = sH_R \dotplus sH'_R,$$

then

$$sH_R = \frac{C - sH'_R}{1 - sH'_R}.$$

Corollary vii

The Problem of the Behavioral Summation ($\dotplus$) of Incentive Substances (K)

If two incentive substances, f and a, have as the exponential components of their respective functional equations $A\sqrt{w}$ and $B\sqrt{m}$, the second substance will combine ($\dotplus$) with the first in the production of the total K by taking as the exponent of the new formula: the simple addition of the units of the first substance to the product of the units of the second substance multiplied by the quotient obtained by dividing the square of the numerical portion of the second

exponent by the square of the numerical portion of the first exponent, $i.e.$, in regard to exponents,

$$w \dotplus m = w + m \times \frac{B^2}{A^2}$$

Corollary viii

The Problem of the Behavioral Summation ($\dotplus$) of Stimulus-Intensity Dynamism (V)

If two stimulus aggregates (S and S') are each scaled in terms of the absolute threshold of the stimulus in question for the subject involved, the stimulus-intensity dynamism (V) of the compound will be the simple summation of the scaled intensity values as substituted in the equation, $i.e.$,

$$V_S \dotplus V_{S'} = 1 - 10^{-v \log(S+S')}$$

POSTULATE X

Inhibitory Potential

A. Whenever a reaction (R) is evoked from an organism there is left an increment of primary negative drive (I_R) which inhibits to a degree according to its magnitude the reaction potential (sE_R) to that response.

B. With the passage of time since its formation, I_R spontaneously dissipates approximately as a simple decay function of the time (t) elapsed, $i.e.$,

$$I'_R = I_R \times 10^{-at}.$$

C. If responses (R) occur in close succession without further reinforcement, the successive increments of inhibition (ΔI_R) to these responses summate to attain appreciable amounts of I_R. These also summate with sI_R to make up an inhibitory aggregate ($\dot{I}_R$), $i.e.$,

$$\dot{I}_R = I_R \dotplus sI_R.$$

D. When experimental extinction occurs by massed practice, the $\dot{I}_R$

present at once after the successive reaction evocations is a positive growth function of the order of those responses ($\dot{n}$), i.e.,

$$\dot{I}_R = a(1 - 10^{-b\dot{n}}).$$

E. For constant values of super-threshold reaction potential ($s\bar{E}_R$) set up by massed practice, the number of unreinforced responses (n) producible by massed extinction procedure is a linear decreasing function of the magnitude of the work (W) involved in operating the manipulanda, i.e.,

$$n = A(a - bW).$$

Corollary ix

Stimuli and stimulus traces closely associated with the cessation of a given activity, and in the presence of appreciable I_R from that response, become conditioned to this particular non-activity, yielding conditioned inhibition (sI_R) which will oppose sE_R's involving this response, the amount of $\Delta_s I_R$ generated being an increasing function of the I_R present.

Corollary x

For a constant value of n, the inhibitory potential ($\dot{I}_R$) generated by the total massed extinction of reaction potentials set up by massed practice begins as a positively accelerated increasing function of the work (W) involved in operating the manipulandum, which gradually changes to a negative acceleration at around 80 grams, finally becoming asymptotic at around 110 grams.

Corollary xi

For a constant value of the work (W) involved in operating the manipulandum, the inhibitory potential ($\dot{I}_R$) generated by the massed total extinction of reaction potentials set up by massed practice is a negatively accelerated increasing function of the total number of reactions (n) required.

POSTULATE XI

Stimulus Generalization ($s\bar{H}_R$, $s\underline{E}_R$, and $s\underline{I}_R$)

A. In the case of qualitative stimuli, S_1 and S_2, the effective habit strength ($s\bar{H}_R$) generates a stimulus generalization gradient on the qualitative continuum from the simple learned attachment of S_1 to R:

$$s_2\bar{H}_R = s_1 H_R \times 10^{-ad},$$

where d represents the difference between S_1 and S_2 in j.n.d.'s, and

$$s_2\underline{E}_R = D \times V \times K \times J \times s_1\bar{H}_R,$$

where $D \times V \times K \times J$ are constant.

B. A stimulus intensity (S_1) generalizes to a second stimulus intensity (S_2) according to the equation,

$$s_2\bar{H}_R = s_1 H_R \times 10^{-bd},$$

where d represents the difference between $\log S_1$ and $\log S_2$ and

$$s_2\underline{E}_R = (s_1\bar{H}_R \times V_2)(D \times K \times J),$$

where $(D \times K \times J)$ are constant and V_2 is the stimulus-intensity dynamism of S_2.

C. In the case of qualitative stimulus differences, ordinary conditioning and extinction spontaneously generate a gradient of effective inhibitory potential (sI_R) which is a negative growth function of sI_R and d, i.e.,

$$s_2\underline{I}_R = s_1 I_R \times 10^{-ad},$$

and in the case of stimulus-intensity differences,

$$s_2\underline{I}_R = s_1 I_R \times 10^{-bd} \times V_2.$$

Corollary xii

When a habit is set up in association with a given drive intensity and its strength is tested under a different drive intensity, there will result a falling gradient of $s\bar{H}_R$ and $s\underline{E}_R$.

POSTULATE XII

Afferent Stimulus Interaction

All afferent impulses (s's) active at any given instant mutually interact, converting each other into $\bar{s}$'s which differ qualitatively from the original s's so that a reaction potential ($_sE_R$) set up on the basis of one afferent impulse (s) will show a generalization fall to $_{\bar{s}}E_R$ when the reaction (R) is evoked by the other afferent impulse (s), the amount of the change in the afferent impulses being shown by the number of j.n.d.'s separating the $_sE_R$'s involved according to the principle,

$$ d = \frac{\log \frac{_sE_R}{_{\bar{s}}E_R}}{J}. $$

POSTULATE XIII

Behavioral Oscillation

A. Reaction potential ($_sE_R$) oscillates from moment to moment, the distribution of $_sO_R$ deviating slightly from the Gaussian probability form in being leptokurtic with β_2 at about 4.0, i.e., the form of the distribution is represented by the equation,[3]

$$ y = y_0 \frac{1}{\left(1 + \frac{x^2}{a^2}\right)^m}. $$

B. The oscillation of $_sE_R$ begins with a dispersion of approximately zero at the absolute zero (Z) of $_sH_R$, this at first rising as a positive growth function of the number of subthreshold reinforcements (N) to an unsteady maximum, after which it remains relatively constant though with increasing variability.

C. The oscillations of competing reaction potentials at any given instant are asynchronous.

[3] This equation is taken from 10, p. lxiii.

POSTULATE XIV

Absolute Zero of Reaction Potential (Z) and the Reaction Threshold ($_sL_R$)

A. The reaction threshold ($_sL_R$) stands at an appreciable distance (B) above the absolute zero (Z) of reaction potential ($_sE_R$), i.e.,

$$ _sL_R = Z + B. $$

B. No reaction evocation (R) will occur unless the momentary reaction potential at the time exceeds the reaction threshold, i.e., unless,

$$ _s\dot{E}_R > {_sL_R}. $$

Corollary xiii

The Competition of Incompatible Reaction Potentials ($_s\bar{E}_R$)

When the net reaction potentials ($_s\bar{E}_R$) to two or more incompatible reactions (R) occur in an organism at the same instant, each in a magnitude greater than $_sL_R$, only that reaction whose momentary reaction potential ($_s\dot{\bar{E}}_R$) is greatest will be evoked.

POSTULATE XV

Reaction Potential ($_sE_R$) as a Function of Reaction Latency ($_st_R$)

Reaction potential ($_sE_R$) is a negatively accelerated decreasing function of the median reaction latency ($_st_R$), i.e.,

$$ _sE_R = a \, _st_R^{-b}. $$

POSTULATE XVI

Reaction Potential ($_sE_R$) as a Function of Reaction Amplitude (A)

Reaction potential ($_sE_R$) is an increasing linear function of the Tarchanoff galvanic skin reaction amplitude (A), i.e.,

$$ _sE_R = cA. $$

PAPER
20

POSTULATE XVII

Complete Experimental Extinction (n) as a Function of Reaction Potential ($_sE_R$)

A. The reaction potentials ($_sE_R$) acquired by massed reinforcements are a negatively accelerated monotonic increasing function of the median number of massed unreinforced reaction evocations (n) required to produce their experimental extinction, the work (W) involved in each operation of the manipulandum remaining constant, *i.e.*,

$$_sE_R = a(1 - 10^{-bn}) + c.$$

B. The reaction potentials ($_sE_R$) acquired by quasi-distributed reinforcements are a positively accelerated monotonic increasing function of the median number of massed unreinforced reaction evocations (n) required to produce their experimental extinction, the work (W) involved in each operation of the manipulandum remaining constant, *i.e.*,[4]

$$_sE_R = a \times 10^{bn} + c.$$

POSTULATE XVIII

Individual Differences

The "constant" numerical values appearing in equations representing primary molar behavioral laws vary from species to species, from individual to individual, and from some physiological states to others in the same individual at different times, all

---

[4] The equation of XVII B is regarded with more than usual uncertainty. Fortunately the true function can be determined by a straightforward empirical procedure.

quite apart from the factor of behavioral oscillation ($_sO_R$).

REFERENCES

1. HULL, C. L. A functional interpretation of the conditioned reflex. PSYCHOL. REV., 1929, **36**, 498–511.
2. ——. Mind, mechanism, and adaptive behavior. PSYCHOL. REV., 1937, **44**, 1–32.
3. ——. Psychological Seminar Memoranda, 1939–1940. Bound mimeographed manuscript on file in the libraries of Yale Univ., State Univ. of Iowa, and Oberlin College.
4. ——. Psychological Memoranda, 1940–1944. Bound mimeographed manuscript on file in the libraries of Yale Univ., State Univ. of Iowa, and Univ. of North Carolina.
5. ——. *Principles of behavior.* New York: D. Appleton-Century Co., Inc., 1943.
6. ——. Research Memorandum. (Concerning the empirical determination of the form of certain basic molar behavioral equations and the values of their associated constants.) 1946. Bound manuscript on file in the libraries of Yale Univ., State Univ. of Iowa, Univ. of North Carolina, and Oberlin College.
7. ——. Stimulus intensity dynamism (V) and stimulus generalization. PSYCHOL. REV., 1949, **56**, 67–76.
8. ——, & MOWRER, O. H. Hull's Psychological Seminars, 1936–1938. Bound mimeographed manuscript on file in the libraries of Yale Univ., Univ. of Chicago, and Univ. of North Carolina.
9. ——, HOVLAND, C. I., ROSS, R. T., HALL, M., PERKINS, D. T., & FITCH, F. B. *Mathematico-deductive theory of rote learning.* New Haven: Yale Univ. Press, 1940.
10. PEARSON, K. *Tables for statisticians and biometricians*, Part I (3rd ed.). Cambridge, England: Cambridge Univ. Press, 1930.
11. YAMAGUCHI, H. G. Quantification of motivation. Ph.D. thesis on file in the Yale University Library, 1949.

[MS. received November 10, 1949]

PAPER 20

Reprinted from Psychological Review, Vol. 57, No. 5, September, 1950
Printed in U. S. A.

SIMPLE QUALITATIVE DISCRIMINATION LEARNING [1]

BY CLARK L. HULL

Institute of Human Relations, Yale University

INTRODUCTION

At the outset of our consideration of the subject of simple qualitative discrimination learning it will be well to clarify our use of certain terms. It is especially important to distinguish simple discrimination learning from simple trial-and-error learning.[2]

The distinction can be made perhaps most effectively on the basis of the stimulus-response relationships involved. Let it be supposed, for example, that each of two stimuli, S_1 and S_2, has the capacity to evoke a particular reaction, R_1, as shown in Fig. 1. Because S_1 and S_2 are qualitatively equivalent in so far as the evocation of R_1 is concerned, this relationship may be said to be that of *stimulus equivalence*. Let it be supposed further that when R_1 is evoked by S_1 (S_2 being absent), the situation will be such that reinforcement will follow, but that when R_1 is evoked by S_2 (S_1 being absent) reinforcement will in no case follow. Under these conditions $S_1 \rightarrow R_1$ will be progressively strengthened by reinforcement and $S_2 \rightarrow R_1$ will be progressively weakened by experimental extinction until at length S_1 will uniformly evoke R_1 and S_2 never will; this latter constitutes the state of perfect *simple discrimination*.

In summarizing the contrast of the two types of learning just considered we may say that they are alike in that they involve the selective strengthening of one (the adaptive) receptor-effector connection, rather than some other (the unadaptive) receptor-effector connection. They are distinguished by the fact that in simple discrimination learning the receptor-effector connection selected differs on the *stimulus side* from the one eliminated, whereas in simple trial-and-error learning the receptor-effector connection selected differs on the *response side* from that which is eliminated. By extending the meaning of the word *selection* a little, we may say that *simple discrimination learning involves primarily stimulus selection, whereas simple trial-and-error learning involves primarily response selection.*

A CONCRETE EXAMPLE OF SIMPLE DISCRIMINATION LEARNING

In order that the reader may secure an appreciation of the phenomenon the theory of which we are about to

[1] The writer is indebted to Harry G. Yamaguchi for aid in the computations which led to Figs. 7 and 8, and to Ruth Hays for aid in the preparation of the manuscript and for permission to use Fig. 3, which came from an experiment performed by her.

[2] This distinction has been emphasized by Spence (**14**, pp. 429–430). The present article is essentially an elaboration of the writer's interpretation of Spence's extension and formalization (**14, 15, 16**) of Pavlov's analysis (**12**, pp. 117 ff.) of discrimination learning.

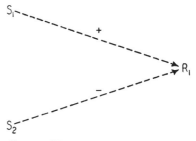

FIG. 1. Diagram showing the type of stimulus-response situation which precipitates simple discrimination learning. Because the reaction potentialities at the outset converge from S_1 and S_2 upon R_1, this is called the convergent $S \rightarrow R$ situation.

PAPER
21

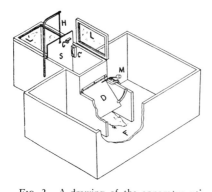

FIG. 2. A drawing of the apparatus utilized in the study of simple white-black discrimination. The albino rat is placed in the chamber beneath the transparent lid marked L', which is shown as closed. When the animal is facing the shutter (S) ready to go into the next chamber the experimenter lifts S somewhat more than enough for the animal easily to pass through into the chamber beneath the lid, L, shown as open, the shutter being suspended in this position by the hooked rod, H. Just as the shutter rises high enough for the animal to pass through, the shoulder C depresses the spring contact C', starting an electric laboratory clock recording time in hundredth seconds. Next, the animal pushes beneath the sloping cardboard door (D) to get the food, F. When the door is raised one inch the microswitch (M) stops the clock which then shows the response time of the subject. The white or black stimuli to be discriminated were placed on the side of the door faced by the rat when in the chamber beneath lid L. Reproduced from Wilcoxon, Hays, and Hull (**17**).

consider, we now present a simple concrete case of such learning.[3] This consists, first, in the associative connection of a locomotor and door-lifting response to the stimulus of a white card (S_1) which constitutes the main portion of the door (D) of Fig. 2, as seen by the animal approaching it from the chamber beneath lid L. The response to white is always followed by food reinforcement. A

[3] The fact that the example given is of quantitative discrimination makes no difference to the reader at the present stage of the theoretical analysis.

curve of this portion of the learning from its beginning approximately up to its asymptote (through days I to V) is shown in Fig. 3. The $_sE_R$ values on the graph were secured by the determination of the median response latency of a group of eight animals, and then the calculation of the equivalent reaction potential by the substitution of the $_st_R$'s in the equation,

$$_sE_R = 2.57 \ (_st_R)^{-.614}. \qquad (1)$$

Next, the training just mentioned is followed by an irregular alternation between the presentation of the white card (S_1) and of a black card (S_2). When the door-opening response (R_1) follows the presentation of the white card, food reinforcement always follows, but when R_1 follows the presentation of the black card, no food is ever given. This *differential reinforcement*, as it is called, gradually causes a differentiation in the responses to the two stimuli, as shown beginning at day 1 and continuing up through day 18. This represents the peculiarly discriminatory learning. It should be observed that on and around day 15, S_2 (black) evokes a reaction potential fairly close to zero, whereas S_1 (white) evokes a reaction potential of approximately 3.8 σ. In this connection it is notable that the reaction potential evoked by S_1 falls very markedly as differential reinforcement progresses for about six days, after which it gradually rises.

We shall now proceed to derive a theoretical account of the empirical phenomena produced by the procedure just presented.

THE SPECIAL ROLE OF INCIDENTAL STIMULI (S_3) IN DISCRIMINATION LEARNING

The most important type of discrimination learning is based on stimulus generalization (8, 5, 4). Present available evidence indicates that the gradient of stimulus generalization takes the general form graphically represented in the lower portion of Fig. 4. The phenomenon of stimulus generalization as employed by Pavlov and many other writers (12, 9, 15) is based on a continuous series of potential stimuli and for this reason this potentiality is called a *stimulus continuum*. Such a continuum could be the series of sound (pitch) vibrations varying from high to low, of colors ranging from deep red to orange, of light intensities extending from a strong illumination to one near zero in amount, or of cutaneous vibrations at a constant rate varying from a strong intensity to a weak one. The continuum utilized in the example given above was based on Munsell coated papers ranging from a white having 78.66 per cent of the reflectivity of magnesium oxide to a black having 1.21 per cent.

During learning days I to V, in the experimental situation which produced Fig. 3, it is obvious that in addition to the whiteness of S_1 (*i.e.*, of the generalization continuum), many additional or incidental stimuli presum-ably become conditioned to R_1. These include other stimuli which consistently impinge on the organism's sensorium during the repeated reinforcements. Examples of incidentally conditioned stimuli in the situation under consideration are the sound of the click when the sheet-metal shutter (S) is lifted, the lights and shadows of the chamber which the animal passes through from shutter to door (D), any odors that may be consistently present, and the infinitely complex stimuli coming from the animal's own body. We shall call these non-continuum stimulus elements the *incidental* or *static* stimuli. They will be represented as a whole by S_3. The learned attachment of S_3 to R_1 obviously sets up a separate reaction potential which operates wherever S_3 occurs, and S_3 always accompanies the generalization continuum as used in the experiment. This means that the S_3 stimuli by themselves will evoke R_1 whenever S_1 and S_2 are presented, quite apart from the latter. *Thus, so far as S_3 is concerned, this combination of circumstances may give a superficial appearance of 100 per cent generalization.*

Since both sets of stimuli, S_1 and

PAPER
21

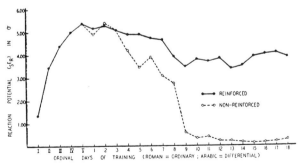

FIG. 3.   Graphic representation of the original learning (days I to V) and of the results of the differential reinforcements (days 1 to 18). Note that despite the fact that S_1 is frequently reinforced and never receives a non-reinforcement, it ends with a much lower sE_R than was displayed on day V. Graph based on data from an unpublished study performed in the writer's laboratory by Ruth Hays.

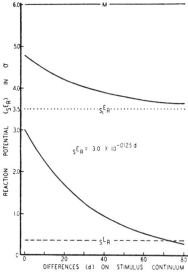

PAPER

21

FIG. 4. The lower portion of this figure shows a graphic representation of a theoretical generalization gradient on a qualitative stimulus continuum plotted in terms of j.n.d. differences. Above is shown the same gradient after it has been combined ($\dotplus$) with a reaction potential of 3.5 σ (dotted horizontal line) assumed to be caused by incidental stimuli (S_3). Note that this summation greatly distorts the generalization gradient (a) by moving it upward leaving its asymptote at the level of 3.5 σ, and (b) by greatly reducing its slope. The value of M is represented by the upper horizontal line at 6.0 σ, and that of the reaction threshold by the broken line at .355 σ.

S_3, involve the same response, their reaction potentials must combine ($\dotplus$) with each other (**9**, pp. 222 ff.). Let us assume (**11**, IV) that the irrelevant (S_3) habit strength ($_sH_R$) taken by itself amounts to .58333, whereas the habit strength of $S_1 \rightarrow R_1$ taken by itself amounts to .50. Assuming that M equals 6.0 σ and (**11**, IX) multiplying, we find that the reaction potential controlled by S_1 directly is .50 $\times$ 6.0, or 3.0 σ, and that controlled by S_3 is .5833 $\times$ 6.0, or 3.5 σ. Combining this constant incidental reaction po-

tential of 3.5 σ with each point of the generalization gradient by means of summational equation 2,

$$_{s_1}E_{R_1} \dotplus {}_{s_3}E_{R_1} = {}_{s_1}E_{R_1} + {}_{s_3}E_{R_1}$$
$$- \frac{{}_{s_1}E_{R_1} \times {}_{s_3}E_{R_1}}{M}, \quad (2)$$

we secure the displaced and distorted gradient shown above in Fig. 4.

It is important to compare these two manifestations of the same gradient. The addition of the irrelevant $_{s_3}E_R$ of 3.5 σ artificially raises the asymptote of the generalization gradient by that amount. At the same time, summation greatly flattens the gradient, though the fractional amount of fall toward the asymptote of each gradient at each increment of d is constant and exactly equal in both, in the present case approximately 56.23 per cent of the preceding point. However, if the value of M were reduced from 6.0 σ to 5.0 σ, the upper gradient would appear much less steep still, *i.e.*, it would be even more distorted, and if M were reduced to 3.6 σ the gradient would be so flat as to be practically horizontal; empirically it would hardly be detectable. At bottom this is because near the asymptote in ordinary learning (**3**) additional practice adds little to the strength of the habit.

From the preceding considerations, we arrive at our first theorem:

Theorem 1. A. *The stimulus generalization gradient as produced on a stimulus continuum by simple learning is summated with the reaction potential based on the incidental stimuli present during that learning.*

B. *This summation artificially raises the apparent asymptote of the gradient and flattens the gradient. As the incidental reaction potential approaches the magnitude of* M, *the gradient approaches the horizontal.*

Theorem 1, as illustrated by Fig. 4, finds substantial corroboration in the gradients reported by Hovland (**6, 7**). Incidentally, this may explain why Pavlov's (**12**, p. 118), Hovland's, and Brown's (**1**) generalization gradients were approximately horizontal on the first unreinforced trial utilized in the tests for generalization (see Fig. 5, first trial). As a matter of fact, practically the same thing is shown by Fig. 3 at days 1, 2, and 3, by the near equality of the white (S_1) and black (S_2) values, even though these are each based on eight differential reinforcements.

Next there arises a question of how, in case the incidental sE_R nearly equals the value of M, the generalization gradient can ever become manifest. The answer is that its appearance results from the gradual removal of the incidental sE_R by experimental extinction. Frequently, however, $S_3 \rightarrow R_1$ cannot be extinguished without the non-reinforced presentation of the stimulus continuum in some form. For example, in the

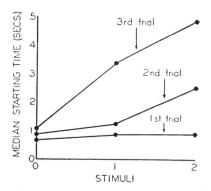

Fig. 5. Graphic representation of the gradual appearance of the stimulus generalization gradient during the process of differential reinforcement. Note that the gradient is here based on response latency and that when so represented the gradient rises, instead of falling as it does when plotted in reaction potentials. Reproduced from Brown (**1**, p. 218).

present experiment a door is required, and any door must be of some shade. Therefore, in order not to complicate the theoretical picture unduly, let us assume that when S_3 is presented for differential reinforcement, the most favorable value on the stimulus continuum to use with it is the black actually utilized in Fig. 3 as S_2, because it will presumably evoke a very weak or subthreshold sE_R. We shall accordingly neglect for the present the sE_R connected by stimulus generalization to S_2, and concentrate on the sE_R based on S_3.

At the outset of differential reinforcement, the incidental reaction potential of $S_3 \rightarrow R_1$ presumably is well along toward its asymptote (Fig. 3) from the training of days I to V. This implies that the extinction portion of the differential reinforcement training will start from near zero and presumably (**17**) will be advancing relatively rapidly. It follows that during differential reinforcement the sI_R will tend gradually to overtake the sE_R and the superthreshold portion of the $s\bar{E}_R$ will gradually approach zero, i.e., there will be a tendency toward[4]

$$s\ddot{E}_R - sI_R = 0. \qquad (3)$$

This means in effect that the effective reaction potential under the control of the incidental stimuli will for most purposes gradually become relatively neutral and unimportant in the determining of overt action. However, it may be added that many stimuli which are present nearly all the time are believed to be neutralized early in life for most responses by the process just described, and therefore do not go through the further neutralization process.[5]

[4] $s\ddot{E}_R = sE_R - sL_R$.

[5] This principle of the previous neutralization of incidental stimuli may play an important role in the transfer of training in discrimination learning.

PAPER
21

In terms of our equations as applied to Fig. 4, we simply reduce the values of the summated ($+$) but distorted gradient shown above, by 3.5 σ less the value of $_sL_R$. This is substantially a reversal of the summational procedure (equation 2) which produced it in the first place. The symbolic reversal (withdrawal, or $\div$) is performed for us by equation 4(11).

$$_{s_1}E_{R_1} = \frac{M(C - _{s_3}E_{R_1})}{M - _{s_3}E_{R_1}}, \quad (4)$$

where $C = {}_{s_1}E_{R_1} \dotplus {}_{s_3}E_{R_1}$.

This of course substantially reveals the true gradient in its proper position as represented at the bottom of the figure with which we began our analysis.

Generalizing on these considerations, we arrive at our second theorem:

Theorem 2. As the differential reinforcement trials of the discrimination learning process take place one by one, leading as they do to the practical neutralization of $S_3 \to R_1$, *the generalization gradient based on the stimulus continuum must gradually emerge with a progressively steepened gradient, standing in substantially its true form and position at the end of the process except that its level at* S_2 *must necessarily be at the reaction threshold* ($_sL_R$).

While not duplicating the conditions of the theorem, two independent studies, one by Hovland (6) and one by Brown (1) show a clear increase in the steepness of the generalization gradient as the extinction incidental to testing for the presence of the gradient progresses. The Brown results are reproduced as Fig. 5. Note the progressive increase in the slope of the gradients as the ordinal number of trials increases. Incidentally the level rises at the point conditioned, showing that $_sE_R$ is being withdrawn all along the generalization gradient.

To be wholly convincing, of course, such an experiment must remove only the $S_3 \to R_1$, whereas Brown's and Hovland's experiments, since the testing trials were not reinforced, also presumably removed a portion of $S_1 \to R_1$ as well.

DIFFERENTIAL REINFORCEMENT APPLIED TO S_1 ($+$) AND S_2 ($-$) ON THE STIMULUS CONTINUUM ONLY

With the theoretical elimination of the influence of the incidental reaction potential (S_3) by having it reduced in strength to a practical threshold value, we may now consider the effects of differential reinforcement on the stimulus continuum without this complication. This is in a sense the heart of discrimination theory.

It will be recalled that the stimulus continuum of our example was white (S_1) through the series of intervening grays down to black (S_2), the response (R_1) being originally connected to white by simple reinforced association. Now by the principle of stimulus generalization, the reaction potential of $S_1 \to R_1$ would extend in diminishing amounts toward black. Unfortunately we do not know to what low values this gradient spontaneously falls, i.e., without the influence of the extinction effects of $S_2 \to R_1$. Indeed, strictly speaking we do not know whether it spontaneously falls at all. This is because, up to the present time, when an empirical test for the gradient is made it has been done with the responses which are evoked to the various test stimuli on the continuum always non-reinforced, which would naturally introduce a certain amount of extinction all along the continuum tested for generalization. This has been considered (7, 10, p. 125) to indicate that the parts of the continuum remote from the point positively reinforced may be more susceptible to the influence of experimental extinction than are those which are closer, and that this differential resistance to extinction may be an indispensable contributing cause producing the gradient.

However this may be, one thing is clear: the conditioning of S_1 to R_1 at one point of a stimulus continuum in fact sets up the potentiality of a generalization gradient which becomes manifest either (a) by differential resistance to extinction (7, 10), or (b) by the removal of a distorting reaction potential attached to incidental stimuli (S_3). Until this uncertainty is removed by appropriate experiment the present writer is now ready to gamble that the dominant mechanism in the bringing out of the generalization gradient is the removal of the incidental $S_3 \rightarrow R_1$ reaction potential, as pointed out above. The existence of incidental stimuli in most such situations is an obvious fact. Moreover, this deduction explains at the same time the steepening of the gradient and the lowering of its asymptote. On the other hand, the hypothesis of differential resistance to experimental extinction is purely ad hoc.

The lower gradient on Fig. 6 is accordingly constructed on this hypothesis, S_1 necessarily falling on a d value of zero. The values of this gradient are calculated by means of equation 5:

$$sE_R = 4.0 \times 10^{-.0125d}. \quad (5)$$

In the differential reinforcement process in this case, the S_2 is assumed to fall at $d = 30$, which reduces the reaction potential at that point to the reaction threshold, which is taken as .355 (3). Now this reduction in reaction potential is due in the main to the accumulation of conditioned inhibition. Moreover, conditioned in-

hibition generalizes on the stimulus continuum substantially as does reaction potential (11, XI C). The slope of neither gradient is known with precision, but they presumably do not differ very much. We shall accordingly here assume them to be equal.

But in order to calculate the generalization gradient of sI_R, we must know the amount that is to be withdrawn from the sE_R at $d = 30$. Now this sE_R value is 1.6868 σ, and this withdrawal must be of the $\div$ variety which requires the use of equation 4. In this equation, therefore,

$$C = 1.6868\ \sigma,$$
$$sE_{R_1} = sL_R = .355\ \sigma,$$
$$M = 6.0\ \sigma,$$

and

$$sE_{R_2} = sI_R.$$

Substituting in equation 4, we have,

$$sI_R = \frac{M(C - sE_{R_1})}{M - sE_{R_1}},$$
$$= \frac{6.0(1.6868 - .355}{6.0 - .355},$$
$$= \frac{6.0 \times 1.3318}{5.645},$$
$$\therefore\ sI_R = 1.4156.$$

Accordingly the generalization gradient of conditioned inhibition is calculated on the equation,

$$sI_R = 1.4156^{-.0125\ d}$$

It is plotted as the shaded double-winged gradient at the bottom of the figure, inverted as it must be when plotted against the negative scale at the left.

Next, the generalized conditioned inhibition must be withdrawn ($\div$) at each point from the corresponding reaction potential by the repeated use of formula 4. A graphic representation of these differences is shown as a broken line between the two basic

PAPER

21

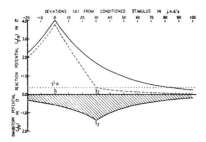

FIG. 6. Graphic representation of the theoretical interaction (÷) of the gradients of the stimulus generalization of reaction potential (upper solid curves) and of conditioned inhibition (lower solid curves) which produce the discrimination gradients (broken-line curves) between. By sighting along the section of this latter line from S_1 to S_2, it may be seen that this discrimination gradient proper still has a slight curvature remaining from the primary stimulus generalization gradient from which it was derived. Note also that its maximum ($_s\dot{E}_R$) lacks a little of the original maximum $_sE_R$. This same value appears in Fig. 7 at $d = 30$ (8, p. 25).

gradients. The portion of this difference function falling between S_1 and S_2 will be called the *discrimination gradient*. It is evident from a glance at Fig. 6, that this discriminatory gradient is much more nearly linear than an ordinary stimulus generalization gradient, and that its maximum height, the *net discriminatory potential* ($_s\dot{E}_R$), is appreciably less than the original stimulus generalization gradient above it.

Consider now the results of the application of the differential reinforcement procedure to S_1 and S_2, when the latter stands at $d = 90$. In this latter case the $_sE_R$ already stands below the reaction threshold, which means that the maximum $_sI_R$ at that point will be zero and there will be no $_sI_R$ to be withdrawn anywhere from the stimulus generalization gradient. Accordingly, on these assumptions this discrimination gradient will be the stimulus generalization gradient

without change. If S_2 is moved up to a d of 80 or 70, it is evident to inspection that the maximum amount of $_sI_R$ will be so small that its generalization will not change the stimulus generalization gradient appreciably. However, as S_2 moves up to $d = 60$ and especially to 50, it is clear that the curvature of the discrimination gradient will grow less, its slope will grow more steep, and its height ($_s\dot{E}_R$) will also grow less, ultimately becoming zero when d is 0. Various theoretical discrimination gradients of this type, as computed from the above assumptions, are represented in Fig. 7. The d value involved in each is indicated by the lowest level ($_sL_R$) reached by each.

Because of the theoretical importance of the relationship, we have also plotted the net discriminatory reaction potential ($_s\dot{E}_R$) remaining after complete differential reinforcement as a function of d. This is reproduced as Fig. 8. There it may be seen that the $_s\dot{E}_R$ begins falling very slowly as d decreases, and falls progressively more rapidly as d approaches zero.

Finally it may be stated that the ratios of $_s\dot{E}_R$ to d were calculated for the values represented in Figs. 7 and 8. They were found to increase progressively as d approaches zero.

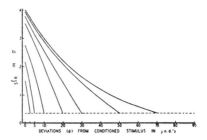

FIG. 7. Graphic representation of the theoretical discrimination gradients resulting from the differential reinforcement of discrimination learning at progressively smaller differences (d's) between S_1 and S_2.

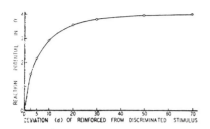

FIG. 8. Graph representing the net discriminatory reaction potential ($_s\dot{E}_R$) as the difference (d) between the reinforced and the discriminated stimulus decreases with concurrent differential reinforcement.

Generalizing on the preceding considerations, we arrive at our third theorem:

Theorem 3. A. *When differential reinforcement is applied to* S_{1+} *and* S_{2-}, *with d practically the entire range of the stimulus continuum, the gradient of* $_s E_R$ *evocable by the stimulus continuum as a whole presents a curve which is markedly concave upward with an asymptote which is the reaction threshold* ($_s L_R$).

B. *As the range of* d *is decreased, the discrimination gradient connecting* S_1 *and* S_2 *becomes less concave upward, passing into a slightly convex-upward form after* d = 30.

C. *As the range of* d *is decreased, the more nearly vertical will tend to be a straight line drawn from the reaction potentials of* S_1 *and* S_2.

D. *As the range of* d *is decreased, the smaller will be the net discriminatory reaction potential attached to* S_1, $_s \dot{E}_R$ *equalling zero when* d *equals zero.*

E. *As the range of* d *is decreased, the ratio of the* $_s \dot{E}_R$ *at* S_1 *to* d *increases with a positive acceleration.*

Up to the present time the extremely simple form of discrimination learning which has been the basis of the preceding analysis has been reported in only three published studies, those by

Frick (2), Grice (4), and Raben (13). So far as reported, none of these studies disagrees noticeably with Theorem 3. Frick (2, p. 119) presents results which tend to substantiate Theorem 3 A, and Raben reports data (13, p. 267) which are in general harmony with 3 D.

We may also take this occasion to consider the learning curves shown in Fig. 3. The curve of the first five days (I to V) is evidently the ordinary growth curve of simple learning (11, IV). With the beginning of differential reinforcement, the distinctive sort of learning characteristic of discrimination begins. The extinction effects ($_s I_R$) on S_3 and on S_2 begin to produce a fall on the non-reinforced curve. And since the reinforced curve must also gradually lose the $S_3 \rightarrow R_1$ component (Fig. 4) at the beginning of the differential reinforcement, this also should fall. In addition, the extinction effect ($_s I_R$) on S_2 generalizes to some extent to S_1, which also contributes to the fall of the reinforced curve, though not so much. But S_1 is reinforced at every response in which it is involved. It follows that the non-reinforced curve falls practically to its reaction threshold as differential reinforcement continues, whereas the reinforced curve remains fairly high. However, soon after the most rapid extinction of S_2 (and S_3) has occurred, the continual reinforcement of S_1 apparently causes a small rise in the reinforced curve, presumably because this curve had already become rather close to, though it had not quite reached, its asymptote shortly before.

AN EXPERIMENTAL PROBLEM

One of the matters which is likely to arouse a difference of opinion among serious students of behavior is the working hypothesis expressed above,

PAPER

21

that the initial empirical horizontal gradient of generalization is mainly due to the summation $(+)$ of the necessarily horizontal gradient of $_{s_3}E_{R_1}$ with the postulated curved gradient extending from $_{s_1}E_{R_1}$ to $_{s_2}E_{R_1}$. It must be admitted that the evidence in this case is at present far from clear. This situation ought not to continue in a case so fundamental for general behavior theory as this one is. Fortunately the problem would appear to be susceptible to a fairly direct experimental approach. Both time and energy fail the author to perform the task. Partly as a means of further elucidating the present theoretical approach, there are given some suggestions for a method of differentially quantifying the assumed reaction potentials of $S_1 \rightarrow R_1$ and $S_3 \rightarrow R_1$:

Let it be supposed that we wish to determine empirically the reaction potential to sound intensity of $S_1 \rightarrow R_1$, uncomplicated by $S_3 \rightarrow R_1$ values. We would begin by setting up a reinforced connection between a 100-decibel sound and the response to the apparatus such as that shown in Fig. 2, on one hundred albino rats. After this habit had reached its asymptote the median reaction latency $(_{s}t_R)$ of the group would be determined and this converted into reaction potential by equation 1 (3). This presumably would be the summation $(+)$ of the reaction potentials evoked by S_1 and S_3.

Then the 100-decibel sound stimulus component would be physically withdrawn from the stimulus complex, the median response latency noted, and this would be converted into reaction potential by equation 1. This value presumably would be the $S_3 \rightarrow R_1$ magnitude except for possible interaction effects (11, XII). It should also be appreciably less than that be-

fore the sound removal. This $S_3 \rightarrow R_1$ value withdrawn $(\div)$ from the original total reaction potential should yield the approximate value of $_{s_1}E_{R_1}$.

A useful checking approximation to the above values with the same subjects could be secured by extinguishing the $S_3 \rightarrow R_1$ reaction by massed trials. Substituting this $\dot{n}$ in an appropriate equation, $_{s}E_R = f(\dot{n})$ (11, XVII A), the equivalent, $_{s_3}E_{R_1}$ value could be secured. Then by restoring the sound and extinguishing again, substituting the new $\dot{n}$ in the equation, $_{s}E_R = f(\dot{n})$, the $_{s_1}E_{R_1}$ value (except for interaction effects) presumably would be secured.

SUMMARY

Discrimination learning in simple form is the acquisition of the power of responding differentially to stimuli, S_1 and S_2, which originally are more or less equivalent to each other in response (R_1) evocation. This process of differentiating the response-evocation potentiality of S_1 and S_2 is complicated by certain active stimuli (S_3) which are present with both S_1 and S_2. If the learning process begins by a reinforced association between the stimuli present and R_1, this necessarily sets up a similar reinforced association between S_3 and R_1 which will function both when S_1 is present and when S_2 is present, giving an appearance of generalization of the stimulus complex even if S_1 and S_2 were quite without generalization capacity.

The primary process which gives rise to the discrimination of the stimulus complex is differential reinforcement. In simple discrimination this consists in reinforcement when the correct stimulus (S_1) evokes the reaction, and in non-reinforcement when the incorrect stimulus (S_2) evokes the reaction. Since $S_3 \rightarrow R_1$

is reinforced every time $S_1 \rightarrow R_1$ occurs, and is non-reinforced every time $S_2 \rightarrow R_1$ occurs, in the course of time with an equal number of occurrences of S_1 and S_2 both $_{S_3}E_{R_1}$ and $_{S_3}I_{R_1}$ tend to approach their asymptotes, which will reduce $_SE_R$ toward its reaction threshold. Moreover, since the rates of both learnings are reduced as the asymptotes are approached, presumably S_3 also loses much of its capacity to acquire not only response R_1 but also similar responses employing the same effectors.

Along with the process of neutralizing S_3 to R_1, the differential reinforcement gradually builds up $S_1 \rightarrow R_1$. But this reaction potential generalizes to $S_2 \rightarrow R_1$, which is never reinforced, giving rise to $_{S_2}I_{R_1}$ which generalizes to $S_1 \rightarrow R_1$ and reduces the latter appreciably. The net result of this double generalization of $_SE_R$ and $_SI_R$ is the marked loss by S_2 of the power to evoke R_1 and usually the retention of a considerable though reduced power of S_1 to evoke R_1. This limitation is comparatively slight when the deviation (d) between S_1 and S_2 is great, but increases with a positive acceleration as d approaches zero.

REFERENCES

1. BROWN, J. S. The generalization of approach responses as a function of stimulus intensity and strength of motivation. *J. comp. Psychol.*, 1943, **33**, 209–226.
2. FRICK, F. C. An analysis of an operant discrimination. *J. Psychol.*, 1948, **26**, 93–123.
3. GLADSTONE, A. I., YAMAGUCHI, H. G., HULL, C. L., & FELSINGER, J. M. Some functional relationships of reaction potential ($_SE_R$) and related phenomena. *J. exp. Psychol.*, 1947, **37**, 510–526.
4. GRICE, G. R. Visual discrimination learning with simultaneous and successive presentation of stimuli. *J. comp. physiol. Psychol.*, 1949, **42**, 365–373.
5. GRICE, G. R., & SALTZ, E. The generalization of an instrumental response to stimuli varying in the size dimension (in press).
6. HOVLAND, C. I. The generalization of conditioned responses: I. The sensory generalization of conditioned responses with varying frequencies of tone. *J. gen. Psychol.*, 1937, **17**, 125–148.
7. ——. The generalization of conditioned responses: II. The sensory generalization of conditioned responses with varying intensities of tone. *J. genet. Psychol.*, 1937, **51**, 279–291.
8. HULL, C. L. The problem of stimulus equivalence in behavior theory. PSYCHOL. REV., 1939, **46**, 9–30.
9. ——. *Principles of behavior*. New York: D. Appleton-Century Co., Inc., 1943.
10. ——. The problem of primary stimulus generalization. PSYCHOL. REV., 1947, **54**, 120–134.
11. ——. Behavior postulates and corollaries—1949. PSYCHOL. REV., 1950, **57**, 173–180.
12. PAVLOV, I. P. *Conditioned reflexes* (trans. by G. V. Anrep). London: Oxford Univ. Press, 1927.
13. RABEN, M. W. The white rat's discrimination of differences in intensity of illumination measured by a running response. *J. comp. physiol. Psychol.*, 1949, **42**, 254–272.
14. SPENCE, K. W. The nature of discrimination learning in animals. PSYCHOL. REV., 1936, **43**, 427–449.
15. ——. The differential response in animals to stimuli varying within a single dimension. PSYCHOL. REV., 1937, **44**, 430–444.
16. ——. The basis of solution by chimpanzees of the intermediate size problem. *J. exp. Psychol.*, 1942, **31**, 257–271.
17. WILCOXON, H. C., HAYS, R., & HULL, C. L. A preliminary determination of the functional relationship of effective reaction potential ($_S\bar{H}_R$) and the ordinal number of Vincentized extinction reactions ($\dot{n}$). *J. exp. Psychol.*, 1950, **40**, 194–199.

[MS. received January 21, 1950]

PAPER

21

Postscript: The Decline and Lasting Influence of Clark Hull

REALITY CONSISTS of many strata of existence which come into view when different methods of investigation are employed. Each generation has its favored insight and method which in time, as it reaches a region of low diminishing returns, becomes exhausted. The history of science, with its manifold skirmishes, revolts, rebellions, and revolutions, is Nature's way of reinstating periodically a law of increasing returns. The new generation comes forward with a new method which, under optimal conditions will be in harmony with a hitherto inaccessible stratum of reality. But there is no pre-established harmony, and a generation, like a god, may fail. Each revolutionary generation moreover is destined to find that its revolution was an illusion, that its standpoint was only partial and remained circumscribed by a reality that is perhaps transgenerational. . . . No scientific standpoint proves to be valid for more than a chapter of existence, which never yields its plot's entirety. The way of wisdom is to understand how "scientific revolution," in its illusory character, is Nature's method for liberating human energies for scientific progress. Thereby we may secure from the gods their gift of serenity. (From Lewis S. Feuer, *Einstein and the Generations of Science*, p. 361.)

The "scientific revolution" that helped put Hull's theory and his influence into eclipse had two major components. First, there were the inevitable disconfirmatory findings from the experimental tests of Hull's (1943) theory, made possible by its specificity. The second, more general component consisted of changes in the intellectual climate, which, combined with the fact that the influence of Hull's theorizing had been so strong, were bound to result in reactions against it.

Difficulties with the Reinforcement Principle

We have in our commentaries identified a number of instances of the more specific experimental attacks on Hull's theory, but in the end the most serious of these were two lines of research which created difficulty for the S-R reinforcement principle, which some have taken to be the keystone of Hull's theory, and more specifically for the need- and drive-reduction hypotheses of reinforcing action that were favored by Hull and some of his followers, respectively. The first of these lines of experimentation was the incentive-contrast effect, first investigated by Elliott (1928) and later, in the context of Hull's work, by Crespi (1944) and Zeaman (1949). The second was the work of Humphreys (e.g., 1939a) on the partial reinforcement extinction effect, which we have already discussed in some detail.

Bitterman, who sees the impact of the work on incentive contrast as the most important reason for the decline of Hull's influence, writes: "It is sad that Hull and Spence themselves led the flight from the principle [of reinforcement] which has not been shown to be wrong, only insufficient, and without which there still is no reasonable account of response-selection in instrumental learning. . . ."[1]

It is true that Spence's (1956) position on the principle of reinforcement was equivocal, and was greatly affected by the experiment of Crespi. On the basis of experimental work, Spence opted for reinforcement in classical aversive conditioning and contiguity in instrumental appetitive conditioning, taking no position on the other two cells in the matrix. He frequently expressed the opinion that removal of the reinforcement principle from Hull's (1943) postulates would change nothing in the theory but the definition of N (the occurrence of a learning trial). Hull, on the other hand, was a pure reinforcement theorist to the end, although he did change his position that $S^H R$ was determined by amount and delay of reinforcement, largely on the basis of the work on incentive contrast. Number of reinforcements was now the sole determinant of $S^H R$. The *mechanism* for reinforcement was changed from need reduction in *Principles* to drive-stimulus (S_D or s_G) reduction in *A Behavior System*; this as a consequence of the third line of attack, on the special hypotheses of need and drive reduction.

Although these hypotheses as to mechanism were in no way central to a principle of reinforcement or to Hull's theory in general, they generated a variety of experiments, many of them by Hull's colleagues at Yale. F. D. Sheffield's work on the reward value of a nonnutritive reward (saccharine) (Sheffield & Roby, 1950), and copulation without ejaculation (Sheffield, Wulff, & Backer, 1951) must have influenced Hull in abandoning the need reduction hypothesis.

1. Personal communication, October 25, 1983.

SECTION 5. POSTSCRIPT

Sheffield favored a Guthrian consummatory-response hypothesis of reinforcement. The other experimental activity at Yale on the mechanisms of reinforcement was led by an experiment on a single dog in which Hull was involved (Hull, Livingston, Rouse, & Barker, 1951). Performed several years before its publication (presumably in the early 1940s, since a footnote indicates that Hull's three junior authors, who performed the experiment, were called to military service), the experiment differentiated among the reinforcing effects of true, sham, and esophageal feeding. It showed that when the dog was allowed to eat but the food did not reach the stomach (sham feeding), its feeding behavior extinguished; and that putting food directly into the stomach via an esophageal fistula served as a reinforcer relative to no feeding. This, and the results from a later, more carefully controlled series of experiments using rats as subjects, mainly by N. E. Miller and his students (e.g., Berkun, Kessen, & Miller, 1952; Kohn, 1951; Miller, Sampliner, & Woodrow, 1957), appeared to provide strong evidence against a consummatory-response position of reinforcement, certainly as strong as the evidence from Sheffield's work against a need-reduction hypothesis.[2] The drive-reduction hypothesis and drive-stimulus-reduction hypothesis, always favored by Miller (see Miller & Dollard, 1941), remained supportable, but were later subject to modification on the basis of the discovery of the Reticular Activating System (Moruzzi & Magoun, 1949) and the hypotheses of arousal and optimal arousal that followed (Berlyne, 1960; Duffy, 1962; Hebb, 1955, Lindsley, 1957; Malmo, 1959). For a complete and particularly cogent analysis of the issues surrounding the hypothesized mechanisms of reinforcement in this era, we refer the reader to Kimble (1961).

In the last version of his theory, Hull (1952) returned to his early-1930s view on the role of r_G-s_G as a factor in goal expectation, referring to this factor specifically as "incentive motivation." In a sense, then, these last writings of Hull conceptualize the function of the reinforcer in terms of both a Thorndikian "stamping-in" action and Tolman-like expectancy. On the basis of experimental work in learning in several vertebrate species, Bitterman (most recently, 1983) makes the same distinction, as does Amsel (e.g., Amsel & Stanton, 1980) on the basis of ontogenetic work. The general reinforcement principle is then still

2. Subsequent work (Chambers, 1956; Coppock & Chambers, 1954) revived the need-reduction hypothesis. It showed that a head-turning response in rats and a choice response in rabbits could be reinforced by intravenous injection of a 10 percent glucose solution. This result suggested a direct reinforcing action of a nutrient in the blood stream. The authors pointed out, however, that peripheral effects such as taste stimulation and increased temperature could result from the intravenous injection of sucrose. These might serve as secondary (learned) if not primary sources of reinforcement. The sufficient and necessary mechanisms of reinforcement had still not been isolated.

501

very much alive, at least in accounts of learning in simpler phylogenetic and ontogenetic forms. It is presumably also alive in relation to learning in more advanced forms operating at these simpler levels, for example, humans undergoing conditioning with reduced awareness of contingencies (e.g., Spence, 1966; Weiskrantz & Warrington, 1979).

At another level, we think the unresolved question of *mechanisms* of reinforcement will again come to the fore as a result of renewed interest in such problems by neuroscientists.[3] The neurobiological work is itself at two levels, neural and cellular, and we will restrict ourselves to an example of each from simple associative learning. At a neural level, recent work from Thompson's laboratory (e.g., McCormick & Thompson, 1983, 1984) has shown that tiny lesions in the cerebellum can completely eliminate the conditioned response to the CS, leaving intact the same response to the US, whereas lesions of another brain structure, the inferior olive, appear to eliminate the reinforcing function of the US. At a cellular level, the most recent work on associative learning in *Aplysia* from Kandel's laboratory (e.g., Hawkins, Abrams, Carew, & Kandel, 1983; Kandel & Schwartz, 1982) comes close to being another example of reexamining this question of mechanisms of reinforcement in a modern neurobiological context. These recent reconsiderations of the concepts and mechanisms of reinforcement in the combined contexts of phylogeny, ontogeny, and neurobiology strike us as a recent realization in biobehavioral science of Feuer's gentle assertion that "a chapter of existence [of a scientific viewpoint] . . . never yields its plot's entirety."

Changes in Intellectual Climate

Whereas the attacks on the reinforcement principle through the work on contrast, the partial reinforcement extinction effect, and need and drive reduc-

---

3. Indeed, neuroscientists who work at the level of the basic associative processes, the simplest, "unmediated" kind (Amsel, 1972), may come to find Hull's theory in *Principles* an apt counterpart at the level of behavioral constructs of the neurophysiological and neurochemical responses they observe. Though Hull's critics fault *Principles* as a "general theory of learning," Hull intended to deal in this book only with the simplest associative processes. He obviously went beyond this intention by including for analysis both classical and instrumental conditioning, and by applying the same theory to both, ignoring, as we have pointed out, his earlier "two-process" approach to instrumental learning. In the early work, the behavioral settings he had in mind for "adaptive behavior" were complex mazes, Umweg problems, and the like, whereas in *Principles* the instrumental behavior was defined almost entirely by the "Skinner box," which he conveniently (and erroneously) took to represent associative learning at its simplest level.

SECTION 5. POSTSCRIPT

tion were important factors in the decline of Hull's position. more important. we think, were changes in the intellectual climate of the 1950s and 1960s. We mention some of these in rough chronological order.

The first element in what was essentially a three-pronged attack was a rebirth of interest in physiological psychology, greatly abetted by the appearance of a book, *The Organization of Behavior* (1949), by D. O. Hebb, a student of Lashley. This was an approach that substituted for Hull's hypothetical processes and states, derived as empirical constructs from behavior, a "conceptual nervous system" to use Hebb's (1956) own later characterization. Hebb's book was nothing like Hull's *Principles;* it led to few specific predictions that could be taken directly to the laboratory as Hull's book did virtually on every page. It was, nevertheless, a stimulating and inspiring work that had a particularly important influence on research in development of sensory processes: stabilized images, effects of sensory deprivation, and the role of early experience in pattern recognition, to give a few examples. It presented in terms of constructs such as "cell assemblies" and "phase sequence" a theory of associative learning which had no use for a drivelike energizing factor. It is interesting to note that following the work, to which we have alluded, on the Reticular Activating System (Moruzzi & Magoun, 1949), Hebb (1956), in a paper titled "Drives and CNS (Conceptual Nervous System)," recanted, and theorized about a concept of arousal as important in learning. Arousal, as the title of the paper suggests, was likened to the concept of generalized drive in Hull's theory.

A second factor in the decline of Hull's influence was the reawakening of a dormant Skinnerianism, greatly stimulated by the publication in 1950 of the paper "Are theories of learning necessary?" Perhaps "dormant" in the previous sentence is not quite the right word; "overshadowed" expresses it better. Skinner's important and now classic book, *The Behavior of Organisms* (1938), with its Sherrington-style laws arrived at inductively, did appear to be overshadowed in the late 1930s and 1940s by the exciting theoretical squabbles between the followers of Hull and Tolman. These arguments were taken quickly to the laboratory. The atmosphere was heatedly partisan (the unresolved arguments are largely still with us) and Skinner's theoretical ideas were not engaged in these controversies. "Are theories of learning necessary?" was perhaps a not unnatural reaction to what Skinner and others saw as the sterility and scholasticism of these experimental outcroppings of the Hull-Tolman debates. Skinner's call to a radical positivism, followed by *Science and Human Behavior* (1953), *Schedules of Reinforcement* with Ferster (1957), and by the venture into teaching machines (1958),

503

SECTION 5. POSTSCRIPT

came at a time when many were prepared for what then appeared to be the less dogmatic "Experimental Analysis of Behavior," an approach to learning that could provide the promise of more tangible benefits—a more immediate product.

Guttman provides us with the Skinnerian view of Hull's work in the mid-1940s:

> What Hull had in his mind was the image of a certain kind of science, a style, an atmosphere, an intrinsic character. It was not to any extent an image of what this style of scientific psychology was to be used for, and what is more remarkable is that the image did not consist of any firm, experienced conception of phenomena in behavior. It was not so much an image of reality as of the proper science of these realities. No single Hullian proposition was more than tentative, and the whole was a somewhat arbitrary carrying forward of a rather obvious line of thought. . . . I remember well in 1943 sitting for many hours with B. F. Skinner and other laboratory co-workers going over the galley proofs of *Principles of Behavior,* which had been sent to Skinner for review. Our reaction, frankly, was one of amusement, for how was it possible that anyone who had any actual laboratory experience with animal behavior in a couple of species could deal with the available data so seriously, so precisely, so pontifically? . . . There seemed to us, who were Skinnerians 30-odd years ago, glaring flaws, even dangers, in Hull's appraisal of where the experimental investigation of behavior then stood and in his sentiments about how it should be advanced. Skinner's ironically titled essay "Are Theories of Learning Necessary?" (1950) was aimed at Hull. . . . (Guttman, 1977, p. 326)

The third and perhaps most decisive factor in the decline of Hullian psychology was the emergence of a new structuralism and the rebirth of Cognitive Psychology, which can be traced to information theory and the computer. The new cognitive psychology was quite different from Tolman's brand, and it addressed a subject matter for which it was a far more appropriate description than was the older one (Amsel, 1965). The subject matter was at first the idealized human adult rather than the laboratory rat. One of the main rallying points of this new structuralism turned out to be a book by Miller, Galanter, and Pribram, *Plans and the Structure of Behavior* (1960), which, despite its eventual influence, was taken less than very seriously when it first appeared. (Indeed the word "structure" could after 1960 be found in a great many titles of articles and books.) The proponents of the new cognitive structuralism could not, any more than could the physiologists or the Skinnerians, find any portion of their image reflected in the kind of Hullian theorizing that was at its most formal in *Mathematico-Deductive Theory of Rote Learning* (1940) and at its most effective in the *Principles of Behavior* (1943). Hull's theoretical papers starting in 1929 and

504

Section 5. Postscript

extending through the 1930s and later were not subject to the intensity of criticism directed at these two books, and particularly at the *Principles*. Indeed, as we showed at the outset (Table 1), "the Papers" seem to have been largely forgotten in the 1960s and 1970s and the *Principles*—and to a lesser extent *A Behavior System* (1952)—remained the main reference to Hull's work.

A metaphor from parliamentary government characterizes for us the intellectual atmosphere attending the decline in America of Hull's influence and more generally of S-R psychology, and the ascendance of cognitive psychology. Stimulus-Response Theory, previously the Government under the leadership of Hull, lost power and became the Loyal Opposition; Cognitive Theory was now clearly the Government. The previous Cognitive opposition in animal learning had been strongly and capably led by E. C. Tolman from the 1930s to the middle 1940s. The new Cognitive Government was at first (in the 1960s) in the hands of people whose main interests were and are in human memory, information processing, artificial intelligence, perception and psycholinguistics. Consequently, the arena of disagreement in the 1960s and 1970s was not as defined as it had been in the earlier Hull-versus-Tolman days of intensely partisan, but good-natured, debate.

The issues in the 1930s and 1940s were fairly clear-cut. Was learning S-S or S-R? Did learning (association-formation as opposed to performance-change) depend on a terminal state-of-affairs—reinforcement—or simply upon the contiguous presence of two stimuli (S-S)? These differences were easily reduced to rather simple experimental tests. The experiments took four major forms: latent learning, relational versus specific learning in discrimination formation, place versus response in spatial learning, and continuity versus noncontinuity. The first of these kinds of experiments addressed the necessity for reinforcement in learning; the other three were variants of the "What is learned?" question (Kendler, 1950) with the cognitive-Gestalt view in juxtaposition to the principle of simple stimulus-response modification. With some exceptions in the case of some of the transposition experiments, the experiments involved laboratory rats as subjects. With few exceptions the impetus and initiative came, as they should have come, from the Loyal Opposition: the S-R Government was under almost constant attack.

In the last decade the Cognitivists in human experimental psychology have been joined by cognitively oriented investigators of animal learning and behavior (e.g., anthologies on cognitive approaches edited by Estes, 1975; Hulse et al., 1978). Stimulus-Response is plainly the minority party. But, as we see it, the Cognitivists, particularly but not exclusively the new animal branch, have

505

SECTION 5. POSTSCRIPT

continued to act as though they were still in the minority party. Instead of leading, many of these people have continued to oppose. The impetus and initiatives to controversy still come from the Cognitivists; the new minority party has, apparently, not yet understood its role as Loyal Opposition. The attacks by the Cognitivists are not so much on some specific conceptualization of learning processes as on something more vague—Traditional Learning Theory. At times, unlike Tolman's cognitivism, the attack is also on methodological behaviorism (e.g., Dickinson, 1980). It is in connection with this kind of opposition that references to Hull have been almost entirely to the formalism of the *Principles*. The early papers, such as those with their emphasis on Pavlovian (goal expectation) mechanisms in instrumental learning ("two-process theory"), as we have seen, have been all but forgotten.

In the new cognitive leadership, the Animal Learning Ministry has been joined by psychologists who identify as ethologists and evolutionists (see Hinde & Stevenson-Hinde, 1973; Seligman & Hager, 1972). The rallying cry from these quarters is that Traditional Learning Theory has failed to consider biological-evolutionary factors and has failed to address a principle of selective association in learning. It is certainly a fair criticism of Hull that he sought to organize what was known about learning into a few general principles; but as we have seen a strong biological-adaptive emphasis was an outstanding characteristic of Hull's work, and he was criticized for that emphasis in his own time.

We must not, however, overstate the extent of decline in Hull's influence; the weight of his work is still greatly felt. A study by Myers (1970) which looked at citations in the 14 journals which were thought to be the most prestigious in psychology in a six-year period from 1962 to 1967 showed that the number of references to Clark Hull—mainly, as we have determined to *Principles* and *A Behavior System*—still placed him at the ninety-ninth percentile of those whose work was referenced at all. In terms of number of references, he ranked ninth during this period. (Kenneth Spence ranked first.) Perhaps even more telling, a study by Moore and Seberhagen (cited in Myers, 1970) in 1967, only fifteen years after Hull's death, ranked him the sixth most influential psychologist of all time after Freud, James, Wundt, Watson, and Pavlov.

Perhaps the most visible surviving part of Hull's great influence is that it continues to be attacked: it seems to be the case nowadays, particularly for the neocognitive theorists, that a book or a chapter in learning theory cannot be written without first erecting a straw man in Hull's image, and then attempting to blow it away. If imitation is one sincere form of flattery, then this kind of preoccupation, almost exclusively with the *Principles*, a 40-year-old book (and

506

SECTION 5. POSTSCRIPT

a book the younger critics of Hull seem never to have read) must certainly be another. Nothing is better evidence that Hull's influence remains than this indirect recognition by his detractors that it is still a force that could regain strength if the fashion of the moment were to fade or become less appealing.

What is most important in Hull's surviving influence is perhaps the scientific style and tradition: the willingness to provide explicit and falsifiable predictions from a set of hypotheses derived from the existing literature; the enormous body of experimental results, certainly not always confirmatory, these hypotheses have generated; the economy of a family of interrelated constructs, empirically derived; the recognition in the context of general lawfulness that if explanations are as complex (have as many degrees of freedom) as the phenomena they seek to explain, they offer no explanatory advantage; the emphasis not only on the purely associative but also the motivational processes (the latter almost completely neglected since the return of cognitive structuralism in the 1960s); the hope for and attempt at quantification in learning theory, still to this day a science of ordinal differences and interactions. If not the content— and much of this certainly survives—then the approach, the strategy, and the example of dedication are identifiable aspects of Hull's legacy. All of these qualities of the Hullian approach are in the Papers, and we have done what we can to draw attention to them in our commentaries.

It is sometimes difficult to separate out of the new, "revolutionary" approaches that which should be rendered unto Hull and that which is owed to others. To rephrase an idea from the opening passage from Feuer, not as many of the revolutionary ideas in the psychology of our generation are as inimical to Hull's as they are said to be, just as not as many of his ideas were independent of those of his precursors as he undoubtedly supposed them to be at times. "The way of wisdom" writes Feuer "is to understand how scientific revolution, in its illusory character, is Nature's method for liberating human energies for scientific progress." The wise, be they cognitive theorists, neo-Darwinian evolutionists, or whatever, will recognize that what Hull did and tried to do, what he borrowed and what he added, is part of their heritage.

References
(for nonreprinted material)

Adam, G. *Interoception and Behavior: An Experimental Study.* Budapest: Akademiai Kiado, Publishing House of the Hungarian Academy of Sciences, 1967.

Adams, D. K. Note on method. *Psychological Review* (1937), 44:212–18.

Ammons, R. B. Psychology of the scientist: IV. Passages from the "Idea Books" of Clark L. Hull. *Perceptual and Motor Skills* (1962), 15:807–82.

Amsel, A. Selective association and the anticipatory goal response mechanism as explanatory concepts in learning theory. *Journal of Experimental Psychology* (1949), 39:785–99.

——. The role of frustrative nonreward in noncontinuous reward situations. *Psychological Bulletin* (1958), 55:102–19.

—— Frustrative nonreward in partial reinforcement and discrimination learning: Some recent history and a theoretical extension. *Psychological Review* (1962), 69:306–28.

—— On inductive versus deductive approaches and neo-Hullian behaviorism. In B. Wolman & E. Nagel (eds.), *Scientific Psychology: Principles and Approaches.* New York: Basic Books, 1965.

—— Partial reinforcement effects on vigor and persistence: Advances in frustration theory derived from a variety of within-subjects experiments. In K. W. Spence & J. T. Spence (eds.), *The Psychology of Learning and Motivation,* vol. 1. New York: Academic Press, 1967.

—— Behavioral habituation, counterconditioning, and a general theory of persistence. In A. H. Black & W. F. Prokasy (eds.), *Classical Conditioning II: Current Research and Theory.* New York: Appleton-Century-Crofts, 1972.

—— Behaviorism then and now: A retrospective review of J. B. Watson's *Psychology from the Standpoint of a Behaviorist. Contemporary Psychology,* (1982), 27:343–46.

Amsel, A., & M. E. Rashotte. A perspective on S-R learning theory in America with particular reference to Clark L. Hull, his precursors and followers. In H. Zeier (ed.), *The Psychology of the 20th Century. Vol. 4. Pavlov and His Followers: From Classical Conditioning to Behavioral Therapy.* Zurich: Kindler-Verlag, 1977 (in German).

Amsel, A., & M. Stanton. Ontogeny and phylogeny of paradoxical reward effects. In J. S. Rosenblatt, R. A. Hinde, C. Beer, & M. Busnel (eds.), *Advances in the Study of Behavior.* Vol. 2. New York: Academic Press, 1980.

Anderson, J. R. *Language, Memory, and Thought.* Hillsdale, N.J.: Erlbaum, 1976.

Asratyan, E. A. Some aspects of the problem of motivation in the light of Pavlovian teaching. *Acta Physiologia Academiae Scientiarum Hungaricae* (1976), 48:323–34.

509

REFERENCES

Atkinson, R. C., G. H. Bower, & E. J. Crothers. *An Introduction to Mathematical Learning Theory*. New York: Wiley, 1965.

Baernstein, H. D., & C. L. Hull. A mechanical model of the conditioned reflex. *Journal of General Psychology* (1931):5:99–106.

Baker, T. W. Properties of compound conditioned stimuli and their components. *Psychological Bulletin* (1968), 70:611–25.

Beach, F. A. The snark was a boojum. *American Psychologist* (1950), 5:115–24.

Bekhterev, V. M. *La Psychologie Objective*. Paris, France: Alcan, 1913.

Bergmann, G., & K. W. Spence. Operationism and theory in psychology. *Psychological Review* (1941), 48:1–14.

Berkun, M. M., M. L. Kessen, & N. E. Miller. Hunger-reducing effects of food by stomach fistula versus food by mouth measured by a consummatory response. *Journal of Comparative and Physiological Psychology* (1952), 45:550–54.

Berlyne, D. E. *Conflict, Arousal, and Curiosity*. New York: McGraw-Hill, 1960.

—— *Structure and Direction in Thinking*. New York: Wiley, 1965.

Bindra, D. A unified account of classical conditioning and operant training. In A. H. Black & W. F. Prokasy (eds.), *Classical Conditioning II: Current Research and Theory*. New York: Appleton-Century-Crofts, 1972.

Bitterman, M. E. Approach-avoidance in discrimination learning. *Psychological Review* (1952), 59:172–75.

—— Toward a comparative psychology of learning. *American Psychologist* (1960), 15:704–12.

—— Phyletic differences in learning. *American Psychologist* (1965), 20:396–410.

—— Thorndike and the problem of animal intelligence. *American Psychologist* (1969), 24:444–53.

—— The comparative analysis of learning. *Science* (1975), 188:699–709.

—— Learning in man and other animals. In V. Sarris & A. Parducci (eds.), *Perspectives in Psychological Experimentation*. Hillsdale, N.J.: Erlbaum, 1983.

Boakes, R. A., M. Poli, M. J. Lockwood, & G. Goodall. A study of misbehavior: Token reinforcement in the rat. *Journal of the Experimental Analysis of Behavior* (1978), 29:115–34.

Bolles, R. C. Reinforcement, expectancy, and learning. *Psychological Review* (1972), 79:394–409.

—— *Theory of Motivation*, second edition. New York: Harper & Row, 1975.

Booth, D. A. Conditioned reactions in motivation. In F. M. Toates & T. R. Halliday (eds.), *Analysis of Motivational Processes*. London: Academic Press, 1980.

Boring, E. G. *A History of Experimental Psychology*, second edition. New York: Appleton-Century-Crofts, 1957.

Breland, K., & M. Breland. The misbehavior of organisms. *American Psychologist* (1961), 16:681–84.

Brown, J. S. The generalization of approach responses as a function of stimulus intensity and strength of motivation. *Journal of Comparative Psychology* (1942), 33:209–26. (a)

—— Factors determining conflict reactions in difficult discriminations. *Journal of Experimental Psychology* (1942), 31:272–92. (b)

Brown, J. S., & I. E. Farber. Emotions conceptualized as intervening variables—with suggestions toward a theory of frustration. *Psychological Bulletin* (1951), 48:465–95.

REFERENCES

Brown, P. L., & H. M. Jenkins. Autoshaping of the pigeon's keypeck. *Journal of the Experimental Analysis of Behavior* (1968), 11:1–8.

Brush, S. G. Should the history of science be rated X? *Science* (1974), 183:1164–72.

Burke, C. J. A theory relating momentary effective reaction potential to response latency. *Psychological Review* (1949), 56:208–23.

Burros, R. H. The application of the method of paired comparisons to the study of reaction potential. *Psychological Review* (1951), 58:60–66.

Bush, R. R., & W. K. Estes. (eds.), *Studies in Mathematical Learning Theory*. Stanford: Stanford University Press, 1959.

Bush, R. R., & F. Mosteller. A mathematical model for simple learning. *Psychological Review* (1951), 58:313–23.

——— *Stochastic Models for Learning*. New York: John Wiley, 1955.

Buzsaki, G. The "where is it?" reflex: Autoshaping the orienting response. *Journal of the Experimental Analysis of Behavior* (1982), 37:461–84.

Bykov, K. M. *The Cerebral Cortex and the Internal Organs*. New York: Chemical, 1957.

Capaldi, E. J. A sequential hypothesis of instrumental learning. In K. W. Spence & J. T. Spence (eds.), *The Psychology of Learning and Motivation*. Vol. 1. New York: Academic Press, 1967.

Chambers, R. M. Effects of intravenous glucose injections on learning, general activity, and hunger drive. *Journal of Comparative and Physiology Psychology* (1956), 45:558–64.

Coleman, S. R., & I. Gormezano. Classical conditioning and the "Law of effect": Historical and empirical assessment. *Behaviorism* (1979), 7:1–33.

Coombs, C. H., R. M. Dawes, & A. Tversky. *Mathematical Psychology*. Englewood Cliffs, N.J.: Prentice-Hall, 1970.

Coppock, H. W., & R. M. Chambers. Reinforcement of position preference by automatic intravenous injections of glucose. *Journal of Comparative and Physiological Psychology* (1954), 45:355–57.

Couvillon, P. A., & M. E. Bitterman. Some phenomena of associative learning in honeybees. *Journal of Comparative and Physiological Psychology* (1980), 94:878–85.

——— Compound conditioning in honeybees. *Journal of Comparative and Physiological Psychology* (1982), 96:192–99.

Crespi, L. P. Quantitative variation of incentive and performance in the white rat. *American Journal of Psychology* (1942), 55:467–517.

——— Amount of reinforcement and level of performance. *Psychological Review* (1944), 51:341–57.

Daly, H. B., & J. T. Daly. A mathematical model of reward and aversive nonreward: Its application in over 30 appetitive learning situations. *Journal of Experimental Psychology: General* (1982), 111:441–80.

Darwin, C. *The Origin of Species*. London: John Murray, 1859.

——— *The Expression of the Emotions in Man and Animals*. London: John Murray, 1872.

Denny, M. R. The role of secondary reinforcement in a partial reinforcement learning situation. *Journal of Experimental Psychology* (1946), 36:373–89.

Dickinson, A. Review of S. H. Hulse, H. Fowler, & W. K. Honig. *Cognitive Processes in Animal Behavior* (Hillsdale, N.J.: Erlbaum, 1978). *Quarterly Journal of Experimental Psychology* (1979), 31:551–54.

REFERENCES

—— *Contemporary Animal Learning Theory.* Cambridge: Cambridge University Press, 1980.

Dickinson, A., & R. A. Boakes. (eds.). *Mechanisms of Learning and Motivation: A Memorial Volume to Jerzy Konorski.* Hillsdale, N.J.: Erlbaum, 1979.

Dollard, J., L. W. Doob, N. E. Miller, O. H. Mowrer, & R. R. Sears. *Frustration and Aggression.* New Haven: Yale University Press, 1939.

Dollard, J., & N. E. Miller. *Personality and Psychotherapy.* New York: McGraw-Hill, 1950.

Domjan, M. Biological constraints on instrumental and classical conditioning 10 years later: Implications for general process theory. In G. H. Bower (ed.), *The Psychology of Learning and Motivation.* Vol. 17. New York: Academic Press, 1983.

Duffy, E. *Activation and Behavior.* New York: Wiley, 1962.

Dunlap, K. *Habits: Their Making and Unmaking.* New York: Liveright, 1932.

Elliott, M. H. The effect of change of reward on the maze performance of rats. *University of California Publications in Psychology* (1928), 4:19–30.

Epstein, R., R. P. Lanza, & B. F. Skinner. Symbolic communication between two pigeons. *Science* (1980), 207:543–45.

—— "Self-awareness" in the pigeon. *Science* (1981), 212:695–96.

Estes, W. K. Toward a statistical theory of learning. *Psychological Review* (1950), 57:94–107.

—— Statistical theory of spontaneous recovery and regression. *Psychological Review* (1955), 62:145–54.

—— Stimulus-response theory of drive. In M. R. Jones (ed.), *Nebraska Symposium on Motivation.* Vol. 6. Lincoln, Nebraska: University of Nebraska Press, 1958.

—— (ed). *Handbook of Learning and Cognitive Processes.* Vol. 1: Introduction to concepts and issues. Hillsdale, N.J.: Erlbaum, 1975.

Estes, W. K., & C. J. Burke. A theory of stimulus variability in learning. *Psychological Review* (1953), 60:276–86.

Estes, W. K., S. Koch, K. MacCorquodale, P. Meehl, C. G. Mueller, Jr., W. N. Schoenfeld, & W. S. Verplanck. *Modern Learning Theory.* New York: Appleton-Century-Crofts, 1954.

Fantino, E., & C. A. Logan. *The Experimental Analysis of Behavior: A Biological Perspective.* San Francisco, California: W. H. Freeman, 1979.

Felsinger, J. M., A. I. Gladstone, H. G. Yamaguchi, & C. L. Hull. Reaction latency (t) as a function of the number of reinforcements (N). *Journal of Experimental Psychology* (1947), 37:214–28.

Ferster, C. B.., & B. F. Skinner. *Schedules of Reinforcement.* New York: Appleton-Century-Crofts, 1957.

Feuer, L. S. *Einstein and the Generations of Science.* New York: Basic Books, 1974.

Feyerabend, P. K. Against method: Outline of an anarchistic theory of knowledge. In M. Radner & S. Winokur (eds.), *Minnesota Studies in the Philosophy of Science.* Vol. 4. *Analyses of Theories and Methods of Physics and Psychology.* Minneapolis: University of Minnesota Press, 1970.

Garcia, J., W. G., Hawkins. & K. W. Rusiniak. Behavioral regulation of the *milieu interne* in men and rat. *Science* (1974), 185:824–31.

Garcia, J., & R. A. Koelling. Relation of cue to consequence in avoidance learning. *Psychonomic Science* (1966), 4:123–24.

REFERENCES

Ghiselin, M. T. *The Triumph of the Darwinian Method.* Berkeley: University of California Press, 1969.

Gibbon, J., & P. Balsam. Spreading association in time. In C. M. Locurto, H. S. Terrace, & J. Gibbon (eds.), *Autoshaping and Conditioning Theory.* New York: Academic Press, 1981.

Gladstone, A. I., H. G. Yamaguchi, C. L. Hull, & J. M. Felsinger. Some functional relationships of reaction potential ($S^E R$) and related phenomena. *Journal of Experimental Psychology* (1947), 37:510–26.

Gormezano, I. Investigations of defense and reward conditioning in the rabbit. In A. H. Black & W. F. Prokasy (eds.), *Classical Conditioning II: Current Research and Theory.* New York: Appleton-Century-Crofts, 1972.

Gormezano, I., E. J. Kehoe, & B. S. Marshall. Twenty years of classical conditioning research with the rabbit. In J. M. Sprague & A. N. Epstein (eds.), *Progress in Psychobiology and Physiological Psychology.* Vol. 10. New York: Academic Press, 1983.

Gray, J. A. *Elements of a Two-process Theory of Learning.* London: Academic Press, 1975.

Grice, G. R. The relation of secondary reinforcement to delayed reward in visual discrimination learning. *Journal of Experimental Psychology* (1948), 38:1–16.

—— Stimulus intensity in response evocation. *Psychological Review* (1968), 75:359–73.

—— Information-processing dynamics of human eyelid conditioning. *Journal of Experimental Psychology: General* (1977), 106:71–93.

Grice, G. R., & J. J. Hunter. Stimulus intensity effects depend upon the type of experimental design. *Psychological Review* (1964), 71:247–56.

Grice, G. R., L. Masters, & D. L. Kohfeld, Classical conditioning without discrimination training: A test of the generalization theory of CS intensity effects. *Journal of Experimental Psychology* (1966), 72:510–13.

Gullicksen, H. A rational equation of the learning curve based on Thorndike's law of effect. *Journal of General Psychology* (1934), 11:395–434.

Guthrie, E. R., & G. P. Horton. *Cats in a Puzzle Box.* New York: Rinehart, 1946.

Guttman, N. Generalization gradients around stimuli associated with different reinforcement schedules. *Journal of Experimental Psychology* (1959), 58:335–40.

—— On Skinner and Hull: A reminiscence and projection. *American Psychologist* (1977), 32:321–28.

Guttman, N., & H. I. Kalish. Discriminability and stimulus generalization. *Journal of Experimental Psychology* (1956), 51:79–88.

Halliday, M. S. Jerzy Konorski and Western psychology. In A. Dickinson & R. A. Boakes (eds.), *Mechanisms of Learning and Motivation: A Memorial Volume to Jerzy Konorski.* Hillsdale, N.J.: Erlbaum, 1979.

Hanson, H. M. Effects of discrimination training on stimulus generalization. *Journal of Experimental Psychology* (1959), 58:321–34.

Harlow, H. F. The formation of learning sets. *Psychological Review* (1949), 56:51–65.

Hawkins, H. D., T. W. Abrams, T. J. Carew, & E. R. Kandel. A cellular mechanism of classical conditioning in Aplysia: Activity-dependent amplification of presynaptic facilitation. *Science* (1983), 219:400–5.

Hays, R. Psychology of the scientist: III. Introduction to "Passages from the 'Idea Books' of Clark L. Hull." *Perceptual and Motor Skills* (1962), 15:803–06.

REFERENCES

Hearst, E. Discrimination learning as the summation of excitation and inhibition. *Science* (1968), 162:1303–6.

Hearst, E., & H. M. Jenkins. *Sign-tracking: The Stimulus-reinforcer Relation and Directed Action.* Austin, Texas: Psychonomic Society, 1974.

Hebb, D. O. *The Organization of Behavior.* New York: Wiley, 1949.

—— Drives and the CNS (conceptual nervous system). *Psychological Review* (1955), 62:243–54.

—— The distinction between "classical" and "instrumental." *Canadian Journal of Psychology* (1956), 10:165–66.

Herrnstein, R. J. On the law of effect. *Journal of the Experimental Analysis of Behavior* (1970), 13:243–66.

Hess, E. H. Imprinting in birds. *Science* (1964), 146:1128–39.

Hilgard, E. R., & D. G. Marquis. *Conditioning and learning.* New York: Appleton-Century, 1940.

Hinde, R. A., & J. Stevenson-Hinde. *Constraints on Learning: Limitations and Predispositions.* London: Academic Press, 1973.

Hobhouse, L. T. *Mind in Evolution,* second edition. London: Macmillan, 1915.

Hollingworth, H. L. *Psychology: Its Facts and Principles.* New York: Appleton-Century, 1928.

Hollis, K. L. Pavlovian conditioning of signal-centered action patterns and autonomic behavior: A biological analysis of function. In J. S. Rosenblatt, R. A. Hinde, C. Beer, & M. C. Busnel (eds.), *Advances in the Study of Behavior.* Vol. 12. New York: Academic Press, 1982.

Honig, W. K. On the conceptual nature of cognitive terms: An initial essay. In S. H. Hulse, H. Fowler, & W. K. Honig (eds.), *Cognitive Processes in Animal Behavior.* Hillsdale, N.J.: Erlbaum, 1978.

Honig, W. K., & P. J. Urcioli. The legacy of Guttman and Kalish (1956): 25 years of research on stimulus generalization. *Journal of the Experimental Analysis of Behavior* (1981), 36:405–45.

Houston, A. Godzilla v. the creature from the black lagoon. Ethology v. psychology. In F. M. Toates & T. R. Halliday (eds.), *Analysis of Motivational Processes.* London: Academic Press, 1980.

Hovland, C. I. The generalization of conditioned responses. I. The sensory generalization of conditioned responses with varying frequencies of tone. *Journal of General Psychology* (1937), 17:125–48. (a)

—— The generalization of conditioned responses. II. The sensory generalization of conditioned responses with varying intensities of tone. *Journal of Genetic Psychology* (1937), 51:279–91. (b)

Hull, C. L. Quantitative aspects of the evolution of concepts. An experimental study. *Psychological Monographs* (1920), 28, no. 1 (whole no. 123).

—— The influence of tobacco smoking on mental and motor efficiency. *Psychological Monographs* (1924), 33, no. 3 (whole no. 150).

—— An automatic machine for making multiple aptitude forecasts. *Journal of Educational Psychology* (1925), 26:593–98. (a)

—— An automatic correlation calculating machine. *Journal of the American Statistical Association* (1925), 20:522–31. (b)

REFERENCES

—— *Aptitude Testing.* Yonkers, N.Y.: World, 1928.

—— *Hypnosis and Suggestibility. An Experimental Approach.* New York: Appleton-Century, 1933.

—— Learning: II. The factor of the conditioned reflex. In C. Murchison (ed.), *A Handbook of General Experimental Psychology.* Worcester, Mass.: Clark University Press, 1934.

—— Special review: Thorndike's *Fundamentals of Learning. Psychological Bulletin* (1935), 32:807–23.

—— *Principles of Behavior: An Introduction to Behavior Theory.* New York: Appleton-Century-Crofts, 1943.

—— Moral values, behaviorism, and the world crisis. *Transactions of the New York Academy of Sciences* (1945), 7:90–94.

—— A primary social science law. *Scientific Monthly* (1950), 71:221–28.

—— *Essentials of Behavior.* New Haven: Yale University Press, 1951.

—— *A Behavior System: An Introduction to Behavior Theory Concerning the Individual Organism.* New Haven: Yale University Press, 1952 (a).

—— Autobiography. In E. G. Boring, H. S. Langfeld, H. Werner, & R. M. Yerkes (eds.), *A History of Psychology in Autobiography.* Vol. 4. Worcester, Mass.: Clark University Press, 1952 (b).

Hull, C. L., & H. D. Baernstein. A mechanical parallel to the conditioned reflex. *Science* (1929), 70:14–15.

Hull, C. L., C. I. Hovland, R. T. Ross, M. Hall, D. T. Perkins, & F. B. Fitch. *Mathematico-deductive Theory of Rote Learning.* New Haven: Yale University Press, 1940.

Hull, C. L., & B. I. Hull. Parallel learning curves of an infant in vocabulary and in voluntary control of the bladder. *Pedagogical Seminary* (1919), 26:272–83.

Hull, C. L., J. R. Livingston, R. O. Rouse, & A. N. Barker. True, sham, and esophageal feeding as reinforcements. *Journal of Comparative and Physiological Psychology* (1951), 44:236–245.

Hulse, S. H., H. Fowler, & W. K. Honig (eds.). *Cognitive Processes in Animal Behavior.* Hillsdale, N.J.: Erlbaum, 1978.

Humphreys, L. G. The effect of random alternation of reinforcement on the acquisition and extinction of conditioned eyelid reactions. *Journal of Experimental Psychology* (1939), 25:141–58. (a)

—— Acquisition and extinction of verbal expectations in a situation analogous to conditioning. *Journal of Experimental Psychology* (1939), 25:294–301. (b)

—— Extinction of conditioned psychogalvanic responses following two conditions of reinforcement. *Journal of Experimental Psychology* (1940), 27:71–75.

—— The strength of a Thorndikian response as a function of the number of practice trials. *Journal of Comparative and Physiological Psychology* (1943), 36:101–10.

Jenkins, H. M., R. A. Barnes, & F. J. Barrera. Why autoshaping depends on trial spacing. In C. M. Locurto, H. S. Terrace, & J. Gibbon (eds.), *Autoshaping and Conditioning Theory.* New York: Academic Press, 1981.

Kamil, A. C., & T. D. Sargent (eds.). *Foraging Behavior: Ecological, Ethological, and Psychological Approaches.* New York: Garland STPM Press, 1981.

Kamin, L. J. "Attention-like" processes in classical conditioning. In M. R. Jones (ed.),

REFERENCES

Miami Symposium on the Prediction of Behavior: Aversive Stimulation. Miami: University of Miami Press, 1968.

—— Predictability, surprise, attention and conditioning. In B. A. Campbell & R. M. Church (eds.), *Punishment and Aversive Behavior.* New York: Appleton-Century-Crofts, 1969.

Kandel, E. R., & J. H. Schwartz. Molecular biology of learning: Modulation of transmitter release. *Science* (1982), 218:433–43.

Kehoe, E. J., & I. Gormezano. Configuration and combination laws in conditioning with compound stimuli. *Psychological Bulletin* (1980), 87:351–78.

Kendler, H. H. The influence of simultaneous hunger and thirst drives upon the learning of two opposed spatial responses of the white rat. *Journal of Experimental Psychology* (1946), 36:212–20.

—— "What is learned?"—A theoretical blind alley. *Psychological Review* (1952), 59:269–277.

——*Psychology: A Science in Conflict.* New York: Oxford University Press, 1981.

Kimble, G. A. *Hilgard and Marquis' Conditioning and Learning.* New York: Appleton-Century-Crofts, 1961.

Koch, S. Epilogue. In S. Koch (ed.), *Psychology: A Study of a Science.* Vol. 3. New York: McGraw-Hill, 1959.

——Clark L. Hull. In W. K. Estes, et al. (eds.), *Modern Learning Theory.* New York: Appleton-Century-Crofts, 1954.

Koffka, K. *The Growth of the Mind.* New York: Harcourt, Brace, 1925.

Kohler, W. *The Mentality of Apes.* New York: Harcourt, Brace, 1925.

—— *Gestalt Psychology.* New York: Liveright, 1929.

Kohn, M. Satiation of hunger from food injected directly into the stomach versus food ingested by mouth. *Journal of Comparative and Physiological Psychology* (1951), 44:412–22.

Konorski, J. *Integrative Activity of the Brain.* Chicago: University of Chicago Press, 1967.

Krueger, R. G., & C.L. Hull. An electro-chemical parallel to the conditioned reflex. *Journal of General Psychology* (1931), 5:262–69.

Kruse, J. M., & J. B. Overmier. Anticipation of reward omission as a cue for choice behavior. *Learning and Motivation* (1982), 13:505–25.

Kuhn, T. S. *The Structure of Scientific Revolutions.* Chicago: University of Chicago Press, 1962.

Lakatos, I., & A. Musgrave. (eds.). *Criticism and the Growth of Knowledge.* Cambridge: Cambridge University Press, 1970.

Lashley, K. S. An examination of the continuity theory as applied to discriminative learning. *Journal of General Psychology* (1942), 26:241–65.

—— The problem of serial order in behavior. In L. A. Jeffries (ed.), *Cerebral Mechanisms in Behavior.* New York: John Wiley and Sons, 1951.

Lashley, K. S., & M. Wade. The Pavlovian theory of generalization. *Psychological Review* (1946), 53:72–87.

Leeper, R. Dr. Hull's Principles of Behavior. *Journal of Genetic Psychology* (1944), 64:3–52.

REFERENCES

Levine, S. The role of irrelevant drive stimuli in learning. *Journal of Experimental Psychology* (1953), 45:410–16.

Lewin, K. Environmental forces in child behavior and development. In C. Murchison (ed.), *Handbook of Child Psychology*. Worcester, Mass.: Clark University Press, 1931.

—— *A Dynamic Theory of Personality*. Translated by D. K. Adams & K. E. Zener. New York: McGraw-Hill, 1935.

—— *Principles of Topological Psychology*. Translated by F. & G. M. Heider. New York: McGraw-Hill, 1936.

Lindsley, D. B. Psychophysiology and motivation. In M. R. Jones (ed.), *Nebraska Symposium on Motivation* (vol. 5). Lincoln, Neb.: University of Nebraska Press, 1957.

Locurto, C. M., H. S. Terrace, & J. Gibbon. *Autoshaping and Conditioning Theory*. New York: Academic Press, 1981.

Logan, F. A. A note on stimulus intensity dynamism (V). *Psychological Review* (1954), 61:77–80.

—— *Incentive. How the Conditions of Reinforcement Affect the Performance of Rats*. New Haven: Yale University Press, 1960.

—— Hybrid theory of classical conditioning. In G. H. Bower (ed.), *The Psychology of Learning and Motivation*. Vol. 11. New York: Academic Press, 1977.

—— Hybrid theory of operant conditioning. *Psychological Review* (1979), 86:507–41.

LoLordo, V. M. Classical conditioning: Compound CSs and the Rescorla-Wagner model. In M. E. Bitterman, V. M. LoLordo, J. B. Overmier, & M. E. Rashotte, *Animal Learning: Survey and Analysis*. New York: Plenum, 1979.

Lovejoy, E. *Attention in Discrimination Learning*. San Francisco: Holden-Day, 1968.

Mackintosh, N. J. *The Psychology of Animal Learning*. New York: Academic Press, 1974.

—— A theory of attention: Variations in the associability of stimuli with reinforcement. *Psychological Review* (1975), 82:276–98.

Malmo, R. B. Activation: A neurophysiological dimension. *Psychological Review* (1959), 66:367–86.

Maltzman, I. Thinking: From a behavioristic point of view. *Psychological Review* (1955), 62:275–86.

Mandler, G. From association to structure. *Psychological Review* (1962), 69:415–27.

McCormick, D. A., & R. F. Thompson. Possible neural substrate of classical conditioning within the mammalian CNS: Dentate and interpositus nuclei. *Neuroscience Abstracts*, 1983.

—— Cerebellum: Essential involvement in the classically conditioned eyelid response. *Science* (1984), 223:296–99.

Miles, W. R. On the history of research with rats and mazes: A collection of notes. *Journal of General Psychology* (1930), 3:324–37.

Miller, G. A., E. Galanter, & K. H. Pribram. *Plans and the Structure of Behavior*. New York: Holt, 1960.

Miller, N. E. A reply to "Sign-Gestalt or conditioned reflex?" *Psychological Review* (1935), 42:280–92.

—— Experimental studies in conflict. In J. McV. Hunt (ed.), *Personality and the Behavior Disorders:* Vol. 1. New York: Ronald, 1944.

REFERENCES

Miller, N. E., & J. Dollard. *Social Learning and Imitation*. New Haven: Yale University Press, 1941.

Miller, N. E., R. I. Sampliner, & P. Woodrow. Thirst-reducing effects of water by stomach fistula vs. water by mouth measured by both a consummatory and an instrumental response. *Journal of Comparative and Physiological Psychology* (1957), 50:1–5.

Morgan, C. L. *An Introduction to Comparative Psychology*. London: Walter Scott, 1894.

Morruzi, G., & H. W. Magoun. Brain stem reticular formation and activation of the EEG. *Electroencephalography and Clinical Neurophysiology* (1949), 1:455–73.

Mowrer, O. H. *Learning Theory and Behavior*. New York: Wiley, 1960(a).

—— *Learning Theory and the Symbolic Processes*. New York: Wiley, 1960(b).

Mowrer, O. H., & R. R. Lamoreaux. Conditioning and conditionality (Discrimination). *Psychological Review* (1951), 58:196–212.

Myers, C. R. Journal citations and scientific eminence in contemporary psychology. *American Psychologist* (1970), 25:1041–48.

Neisser, U. Memory: What are the important questions? In M. M. Gruneberg, P. E. Morris, & R. N. Sykes (eds.), *Practical Aspects of Memory*. London: Academic Press, 1978.

Newell, A. Production systems: Models of control structures. In W. G. Chase (ed.), *Visual Information Processing*. New York: Academic Press, 1973.

Newell, A., & H. A. Simon. *Human Problem Solving*. Englewood Cliffs, N.J.: Prentice-Hall, 1972.

Osgood, C. E. *Method and Theory in Experimental Psychology*. New York: Oxford University Press, 1953.

Overmier, J. B. Avoidance learning. In M. E. Bitterman, V. M. LoLordo, J. B. Overmier, & M. E. Rashotte, *Animal Learning: Survey and Analysis*. New York: Plenum, 1979.

Overmier, J. B., & J. A. Lawry. Pavlovian conditioning and the mediation of behavior. In G. H. Bower (ed.), *The Psychology of Learning and Motivation*. Vol. 13. New York: Academic Press, 1979.

Overmier, J. B., & M. E. P. Seligman. Effects of inescapable shock upon subsequent escape and avoidance responding. *Journal of Comparative and Physiological Psychology* (1967), 63:28–33.

Pavlov, I. P. *Conditioned Reflexes: An investigation of the Physiological Activity of the Cerebral Cortex*. Translated by G. V. Anrep. Oxford: Oxford University Press, 1927.

—— *Lectures on Conditioned Reflexes: Twenty-five Years of Objective Study of the Higher Nervous Activity (Behaviour) of Animals*. Translated by W. H. Gantt. New York: International, 1928.

—— Reply of a physiologist to psychologists. *Psychological Review* (1932), 39:91–127.

—— *Selected Works*. Moscow: Foreign Languages Publishing House, 1955.

Pearce, J. M., & G. A. Hall. A model for Pavlovian learning: Variations in the effectiveness of conditioned but not of unconditioned stimuli. *Psychological Review* (1980), 87:532–52.

Perin, C. T. Behavior potentiality as a joint function of the amount of training and degree of hunger at the time of extinction. *Journal of Experimental Psychology* (1942), 30:93–113.

518

REFERENCES

——— A quantitative investigation of the delay-of-reinforcement gradient. *Journal of Experimental Psychology* (1943), 32:37–51.

Perkins, C. C., Jr. The relation of secondary reward to gradients of reinforcement. *Journal of Experimental Psychology* (1947), 37:377–92.

——— The relation between conditioned stimulus intensity and response strength. *Journal of Experimental Psychology* (1953), 46:225–31.

Pfungst, O. *Clever Hans, the Horse of Mr. Von Osten.* Translated by Karl Rahn. New York: Holt, 1911.

Popper, K. *The Logic of Scientific Discovery.* New York: Basic Books, 1959.

——— *Conjectures and Refutations: The Growth of Scientific Knowledge.* New York: Basic Books, 1962.

——— Normal science and its dangers. In I. Lakatos & A. Musgrave (eds.), *Criticism and the Growth of Knowledge.* Cambridge: Cambridge University Press, 1970.

Rashotte, M. E. Reward training: Latent learning. In M. E. Bitterman, V. M. LoLordo, J. B. Overmier, & M. E. Rashotte, *Animal Learning: Survey and Analysis.* New York: Plenum, 1979(a).

——— Reward training: Contrast effects. In M. E. Bitterman, V. M. LoLordo, J. B. Overmier, & M. E. Rashotte, *Animal Learning: Survey and Analysis.* New York: Plenum, 1979(b).

——— Reward training: Extinction. In M. E. Bitterman, V. M. LoLordo, J. B. Overmier, & M. E. Rashotte, *Animal Learning: Survey and Analysis.* New York: Plenum, 1979(c).

Rashotte, M. E., & Amsel, A. Transfer of slow-response rituals to the extinction of a continuously rewarded response. *Journal of Comparative and Physiological Psychology* (1968), 66:432–43.

Rashotte, M. E., J. M., O'Connell, & D. L. Beidler. Associative influence on the foraging behavior of pigeons *(Columba livia). Journal of Experimental Psychology: Animal Behavior Processes* (1982), 8:142–53.

Razran, G. The observable unconscious and the inferable conscious in current Soviet psychophysiology: Interoceptive conditioning, semantic conditioning, and the orienting reflex. *Psychological Review* (1961), 68:81–147.

——— *Mind in Evolution: An East-west Synthesis of Learned Behavior and Cognition.* Boston: Houghton Mifflin, 1971.

Rescorla, R. A. Predictability and number of pairings in Pavlovian fear conditioning. *Psychonomic Science* (1966), 4:383–84.

——— Pavlovian conditioned inhibition. *Psychological Bulletin* (1969), 72:77–94.

——— Evidence for "unique stimulus" account of configural conditioning. *Journal of Comparative and Physiological Psychology* (1973), 85:331–38.

——— Some implications of a cognitive perspective on Pavlovian conditioning. In S. H. Hulse, H. Fowler, & W. J. Honig (eds.), *Cognitive Processes in Animal Behavior.* Hillsdale, N. J.: Erlbaum, 1978.

Rescorla, R. A., & P. J. Durlach. Within-event learning in Pavlovian conditioning. In N. E. Spear & R. R. Miller (eds.), *Information Processing in Animals: Memory Mechanisms.* Hillsdale, N.J.: Erlbaum, 1981.

Rescorla, R. A., & R. L. Solomon. Two-process learning theory: Relationships between

REFERENCES

Pavlovian conditioning and instrumental learning. *Psychological Review* (1967), 74:151–82.

Rescorla, R. A., & A. R. Wagner. A theory of Pavlovian conditioning: Variations in the effectiveness of reinforcement and nonreinforcement. In A. H. Black & W. F. Prokasy (eds.), *Classical Conditioning II: Current Research and Theory*. New York: Appleton-Century-Crofts, 1972.

Ritchie, B. F. Hull's treatment of learning. *Psychological Bulletin* (1944), 41:640–52.

Romanes, G. J. *Animal Intelligence*. New York: Appleton, 1883.

Ross, R. R. Positive and negative partial-reinforcement extinction effects carried through continuous reinforcement, changed motivation, and changed response. *Journal of Experimental Psychology* (1964), 68:492–502.

Rudenko, L. P. On the functional structure of conditioned reflexes to serial stimuli in dogs. *Acta Neurobiologiae Experimentalis* (1974), 34:69–79.

Seligman, M. E. P. On the generality of the laws of learning. *Psychological Review* (1970), 77:408–18.

Seligman, M. E. P., & J. L. Hager. *Biological Boundaries of Learning*. New York: Appleton-Century-Crofts, 1972.

Sheffield, F. D., & T. B. Roby. Reward value of a non-nutritive sweet taste. *Journal of Comparative and Physiological Psychology* (1950), 45:471–81.

Sheffield, F. D., J. J. Wulff, & R. Backer. Reward value of copulation without sex drive reduction. *Journal of Comparative and Physiological Psychology,* (1951), 44:3–8.

Sheffield, V. F. Extinction as a function of partial reinforcement and distribution of practice. *Journal of Experimental Psychology* (1949), 39:511–26.

Shettleworth, S. J. Constraints on learning. In D. S. Lehrman, R. A. Hinde, & E. Shaw (eds.), *Advances in the Study of Behavior*. New York: Academic Press, 1972.

—— Learning and behavioral ecology. In J. R. Krebs & N. B. Davies (eds.), *Behavioral Ecology*. Oxford: Blackwell Scientific Publications (1984).

Shipley, W. C. Indirect conditioning. *Journal of General Psychology* (1935), 12:337–57.

Simon, H. A. The behavioral and social sciences. *Science* (1980), 209:72–78.

Skinner, B. F. *The Behavior of Organisms: An Experimental Analysis*. New York: Appleton-Century-Crofts, 1938.

—— Review of Hull's *Principles of Behavior*. *American Journal of Psychology* (1944), 57:276–81.

—— Are theories of learning necessary? *Psychological Review* (1950), 57:193–216.

—— *Science and Human Behavior*. New York: Macmillan, 1953.

—— Teaching machines. *Science* (1958), 128:969–77.

—— Herrnstein and the evolution of behaviorism. *American Psychologist* (1977), 32:1006–12.

—— Pavlov's influence on psychology in America. *Journal of the History of the Behavioral Sciences* (1981), 17:242–45.

Small, W. S. An experimental study of the mental processes of the rat. *American Journal of Psychology* (1900), 11:133–65.

—— Experimental study of the mental processes of the rat. Part II. *American Journal of Psychology* (1901), 12:206–39.

REFERENCES

Smith, S., & E. R. Guthrie. *General Psychology in Terms of Behavior.* New York: Appleton, 1923.

Smith, J. C., & D. L. Roll. Trace conditioning with X-rays as the aversive stimulus. *Psychonomic Science* (1967), 9:11–12.

Sokal, M. M. The Gestalt psychologists in behaviorist America. *American Historical Review* (1984), 89, no. 5.

Solomon, R. L., & L. C. Wynne. Traumatic avoidance learning: Acquisition in normal dogs. *Psychological Monographs* (1953), 67, no. 4 (whole no. 354).

Spear, N. E., & B. A. Campbell. *Ontogeny of Learning and Memory.* Hillsdale, N.J.: Erlbaum, 1979.

Spence, K. W. The nature of discrimination learning in animals. *Psychological Review* (1936), 43:427–49.

—— The differential response in animals to stimuli varying within a single dimension. *Psychological Review* (1937), 44:430–44.

—— Gradual vs. sudden solution of discrimination problems by chimpanzees. *Journal of Comparative Psychology* (1938), 25:213–24.

—— The basis of solution by chimpanzees of the intermediate size problem. *Journal of Experimental Psychology* (1942), 31:257–71.

—— The nature of theory construction in contemporary psychology. *Psychological Review* (1944), 51:47–68.

—— The postulates and methods of "behaviorism." *Psychological Review* (1948), 55:67–78.

—— Theoretical interpretations of learning. In C. P. Stone (ed.), *Comparative Psychology.* Englewood Cliffs, N.J.: Prentice-Hall, 1951.

—— Clark Leonard Hull: 1884–1952. *American Journal of Psychology* (1952), 65:639–46.

—— Current interpretations of learning data and some recent developments in stimulus-response theory. In *Learning Theory, Personality Theory, and Clinical Research* (The Kentucky Symposium). New York: Wiley, 1954.

—— *Behavior Theory and Conditioning.* New Haven: Yale University Press, 1956.

—— *Behavior Theory and Learning. Selected Papers.* Englewood Cliffs, N.J.: Prentice Hall, 1960.

—— Discussion. In N. S. Kline (ed.), Pavlovian conference on higher nervous activity. *Annals of the New York Academy of Sciences* (1961), 92:813–1198.

—— Cognitive and drive factors in the extinction of the conditioned eye blink in human subjects. *Psychological Review* (1966), 73:445–58.

Staddon, J. E. R., & V. L. Simmelhag. The "superstition" experiment: A reexamination of its implications for the principles of adaptive behavior. *Psychological Review* (1971), 78:3–43.

Sutherland, N. S., & N. J. Mackintosh. *Mechanisms of Animal Discrimination Learning.* New York: Academic Press, 1971.

Taub, E., & A. J. Berman. Movement and learning in the absence of sensory feedback. In S. J. Freedman (ed.), *The Neuropsychology of Spatially Oriented Behavior.* Homewood, Ill.: Dorsey Press, 1968.

521

REFERENCES

Terrace, H. S. By-products of discrimination learning. In G. H. Bower (ed.), *The Psychology of Learning and Motivation*. Vol. 5. New York: Academic Press, 1972.

Terrace, H. S., J. Gibbon, L. Farrell, & M. D. Baldock. Temporal factors influencing the acquisition and maintenance of an autoshaped keypeck. *Animal Learning and Behavior* (1975), 3:53–62.

Thorndike, E. L. Animal intelligence: An experimental study of the associative processes in animals. *Psychological Monographs* (1898), 2, no. 4, (whole no. 8).

—— *Animal Intelligence: Experimental Studies*. New York: Macmillan, 1911.

—— *Educational Psychology*. Vol. 2. *The Psychology of Learning*. New York: Teachers College, Columbia University, 1913.

—— *The Fundamentals of Learning*. New York: Teachers College, Columbia University, 1932.

Thurstone, L. L. The learning curve equation. *Psychological Monographs* (1919), 26, no. 3 (whole no. 114).

—— A law of comparative judgment. *Psychological Review* (1927), 34:273–86.

—— The learning function. *Journal of Genetic Psychology* (1930), 3:469–93.

Tinklepaugh, O. L. An experimental study of representative factors in monkeys. *Journal of Comparative Psychology* (1928), 8:197–236.

Tolman, E. C. A new formula for behaviorism. *Psychological Review* (1922), 29:44–53.

—— *Purposive Behavior in Animals and Men*. New York: Century, 1932.

—— The determiners of behavior at a choice point. *Psychological Review* (1938), 45:1–41.

—— *Drives Toward War*. New York: Appleton-Century-Crofts, 1942.

Trapold, M. A., & J. B. Overmier. The second learning process in instrumental learning. In A. H. Black & W. F. Prokasy (eds.), *Classical Conditioning II: Current Research and Theory*. New York: Appleton-Century-Crofts, 1972.

Triplet, R. G. The relationship of Clark L. Hull's hypnosis research to his later learning theory: The continuity of his life's work. *Journal of the History of the Behavioral Sciences* (1982), 18:22–31.

Wagner, A. R. Priming in STM: An information-processing mechanism for self-generated or retrieval-generated depression in performance. In T. J. Tighe & R. N. Leaton (eds.), *Habituation: Perspectives from Child Development, Animal Behavior, and Neurophysiology*. Hillsdale, N.J.: Erlbaum, 1976.

—— Expectancies and the priming of STM. In S. H. Hulse, H. Fowler, & W. J. Honig (eds.), *Cognitive Processes in Animal Behavior*. Hillsdale, N.J.: Erlbaum, 1978.

—— SOP: A model of automatic memory processing in animal behavior. In N. E. Spear & R. R. Miller (eds.), *Information Processing in Animals: Memory Mechanisms*. Hillsdale, N.J.: Erlbaum, 1981.

Watson, J. B. Psychology as the behaviorist views it. *Psychological Review* (1913), 20:158–77.

—— *Behavior: An Introduction to Comparative Psychology*. New York: Holt, 1914.

—— *Psychology from the Standpoint of a Behaviorist*. Philadelphia: Lippincott, 1919.

—— *Behaviorism*. New York: Norton, 1924.

—— *Behaviorism*. New York: Norton, 1930. (Revised edition of 1924 book.)

REFERENCES

Watson, J. B., & R. Rayner. Conditioned emotional reactions. *Journal of Experimental Psychology* (1920), 3:1–14.

Weinstock, S. Resistance to extinction of a running response following partial reinforcement under widely spaced trials. *Journal of Comparative and Physiological Psychology* (1954), 47:318–22.

—— Acquisition and extinction of a partially reinforced running response at a 24-hour intertrial interval. *Journal of Experimental Psychology* (1958), 46:151–58.

Weiskrantz, L., & E. K. Warrington. Conditioning in amnesic patients. *Neuropsychologia* (1979), 17:187–94.

Wertheimer, M. Experimentelle Studien uber das Schen von Bewegungen. *Zeitschrift fur Psychologie* (1912), 61:161–265.

Wickelgren, W. A. Chunking and consolidation: A theoretical synthesis of semantic networks, configuring in conditioning, S-R versus cognitive learning, normal forgetting, the amnesic syndrome, and the hippocampal arousal system. *Psychological Review* (1979), 86:44–60.

Wickens, D. D. Compound conditioning in humans and cats. In W. F. Prokasy (ed.), *Classical Conditioning: A Symposium*. New York: Appleton-Century-Crofts, 1965.

Wilcoxon, H. C., R. Hays, & C. L. Hull. A preliminary determination of the functional relationship of effective reaction potential ($S^{\dot{E}}R$) to the ordinal number of Vicentized extinction reactions (n). *Journal of Experimental Psychology* (1950), 40:194–99.

Williams, D. R. Biconditional behavior: Conditioning without constraint. In C. M. Locurto, H. S. Terrace, & J. Gibbon (eds.), *Autoshaping and Conditioning Theory*. New York: Academic Press, 1981.

Williams, S. B. Resistance to extinction as a function of the number of reinforcements. *Journal of Experimental Psychology* (1938), 23:506–21.

Willner, J. A. Blocking of a taste aversion by prior pairings of exteroceptive stimuli with illness. *Learning and Motivation* (1978), 9:125–40.

Wilson, E. O. *Sociobiology: The New Synthesis*. Cambridge, Mass.: Belknap/Harvard, 1975.

Wilson, W., E. J. Weiss, & A. Amsel. Two tests of the Sheffield hypothesis concerning resistance to extinction, partial reinforcement, and distribution of practice. *Journal of Experimental Psychology* (1955), 50:51–60.

Woodbury, C. B. The learning of stimulus patterns by dogs. *Journal of Comparative Psychology* (1943), 35:29–40.

Yoshioka, J. G. Weber's law in the discrimination of maze distance by the white rat. *University of California Publications in Psychology* (1929), 4:155–84.

Zeaman, D. Reponse latency as a function of the amount of reinforcement. *Journal of Experimental Psychology* (1949), 39:446–83.

Name Index

525

Name Index

NAME INDEX

Hanson, H. M., 78, 513
Harlow, H. F., 89, 513
Hawkins, H. D., 502, 513
Hawkins, W. G., 30, 512
Hays, R., 87, 97, 446*n*, 470, 487*n*, 488, 489, 497, 513, 523
Hearst, E., 41, 78, 514
Hebb, D. O., 53, 501, 503, 514
Hecht, S., 271, 190
Heisenberg, W., 267
Helmholtz, H. L. F., 15
Henmon, V. A. C., 1
Herbert, M. J., 443
Herrnstein, R. J., 89, 514
Hess, E. H., 89, 514
Higginson, G. D., 212, 213, 235
Hilgard, E. R., 20, 219, 235, 389, 391, 426, 443, 470, 478, 514
Hinde, R. A., 14, 92, 506, 514
Hobbes, T., 1, 6
Hobhouse, L. T., 21, 235, 514
Hollingworth, H. L., 26, 110, 514
Hollis, K. L., 25, 30, 514
Holmes, S. J., 226, 235
Holt, E. B., 83
Honig, W. K., 11, 67, 514, 515
Honzik, C. H., 56, 221*n*, 230, 236
Horton, G. P., 89, 513
Hotelling, H., 238*n*4, 262
Householder, A. S., 470*n*, 478
Houston, A., 30 514
Hovland, C. I., 52*n*, 55, 62, 79, 323*n*1, 356-59, 374, 393, 414-17, 419-22, 425, 426, 443, 469, 473, 475-78, 486, 491, 492, 497, 514, 515
Hudgins, C. V., 443
Hull, B. I., 2, 515
Hull, C. L., 1-11, 13-15, 17, 18, 20-22, 24-55, 57, 59-90, 93-107, 140*n*, 144*n*, 160*n*, 164*n*, 165*n*, 166*n*, 181*n*, 235, 262, 290, 319*n*, 350, 356, 360*n*, 374, 382, 390-93, 400, 409, 413*n*, 414, 415, 419, 421, 425, 426, 427*n*, 443, 444, 446*n*, 468, 478, 486, 488, 497, 499, 500, 501, 502*n*, 503-7, 510, 513-16, 523
Hulse, S. H., 11, 505, 515
Hume, D., 1, 6
Humphrey, G., 401, 410
Humphreys, L. G., 40, 103, 104, 500, 515

Hunter, J. J., 68, 513
Hunter, W. S., 16, 400
Hutchins, R. M., 5

Ivanov Smolensky, A. G., 115

James, W., 171*n*, 375, 401, 506
Jastrow, J., 1
Jenkins, H. M., 41, 77, 89, 94, 511, 514, 515
Johnson, H. M., 235
Joule, J. P., 424

Kalish, H. I., 67, 513
Kamil, A. C., 30, 515
Kamin, L. J., 38, 77, 515, 516
Kampf, B., 175
Kandel, E. R., 66, 502, 516
Kant, I., 1, 6
Kantor, J. R., 83
Kappauf, W. E., 443
Katona, G., 265*n*
Kehoe, E. J., 39, 89, 513, 516
Kelley, T. L., 238*n*4, 263
Kendler, H. H., 13, 93, 103, 505, 516
Kessen, M. L., 501, 510
Kimble, G. A., 48, 501, 516
Koch, S., 7, 32, 66, 97, 99*n*, 512, 5 6
Koelling, R. A., 92, 512
Koffka, K., 20, 21, 32, 136, 235, 516
Kohfeld, D. L., 68, 513
Kohler, W., 3, 20-23, 32, 52, 69, 71, 136, 252, 263, 350, 404, 406*n*, 410, 516
Kohn, M., 501, 510
Konorski, J., 40, 78, 516
Krechevsky, I., 57
Krim, N. B., 263
Krueger, R. G., 33, 263, 319*n*, 516
Krueger, W. C. F., 290
Kruse, J. M., 51, 516
Kuhn, T. S., 61, 91, 516

Lakatos, I., 61, 516
Lamoreaux, R. R., 68, 518
Landahl, H. D., 470*n*, 478
Langfeld, H. S., 83, 87, 105
Lanza, R. P., 44, 512
Lashley, K. S., 39, 64, 66, 67, 235, 418-23, 425, 426, 503, 516
Lawry, J. A., 40, 41, 518

527

Subject Index

531

Subject Index

Gestalt Theory: and "stimulus," 69, 71, 74-75, 404n4; early influence on Hull, 3, 20-21; Kohler's reaction to Hull-Spence theory (1941), 22-23; Lewin's influence on Hull, 52, 52n, 338-39, 388-92; vs. deductive S-R theory, 32-33, 46, 47, 52, 55-59, 136-38, 245-46, 252-53, 339n17, 323-50, 353-74, 388-92, 409, 505; Wertheimer's view of Hull-Spence theory (1939), 57-59; *see also* Tolman

Goal Attraction and Directing Ideas, 34-44, 107, 157-76, 173n

Goal Gradient Hypothesis, 47-48, 177-78, 206n, 323n2, 323-50; applied to maze learning, 178-95, 222; relation to gradient of reinforcement, 48, 323n2, 324n5

Habit Family Hierarchy, 49-50, 52-53, 197-205

Hull, Clark: agreement (1934), to write *Principles*, 57; at Yale's Institute of Human Relations, 5; biographical sketch, 1-7; citations of papers and books in learning (1970–79), 9-10, 506; legacy to psychology, 507; plans for 3-volume "magnum opus", 5-7; relation of Papers to other works, 7-11, 70, 81, 479-80

Hullian Neo-Behaviorism: Amsel's view, 43-44, 62-63

Incentive Motivation, 40-41, 105-7, 175-76, 304n, 316-17, 500-2; *see also* Fractional Anticipatory Goal Response

Inhibition: alleged neglect in American learning theory, 78-79; as a corrective process in adaptive behavior, 26-27, 111-21; disinhibition, 212-16; external, 214-16, 408; generalization of, 334-35, 368-70, 405-6, 493-94; *see also* Extinction; Discrimination Learning

Knowledge and Purpose, 34-44, 50, 107, 141-55, 205

Machines: and artificial intelligence, 33, 50, 140, 237-38, 319n; and cognitive science, 33, 43-44; influence on Hull's thinking, 2-5, 6, 7, 31, 33, 86, 139-40, 140n, 249, 262

Mathematical Learning Theory, 99-102

Maze Learning: 37, 47-51, 127-35, 157-58, 167-70, 177-95, 197-216, 218-35, 324-38, 502n

Miller, Neal: analysis of foresight, 32, 55; mechanisms of reinforcement, 501; public discussion with Tolman (1934), 55-56; role in Institute of Human Relations, 5, 18; *see also* Conflict Theory

Misbehavior of Organisms: and autoshaping, 94-95; and constraints on learning, 93; Skinner's report of Hull's comment on (1937), 42; relation to r_G-s_G, 41-42, 161

Motivation: directive effects of drive stimuli, 75; *see also* Incentive Motivation

Neural Basis of Learning, 19, 66, 69, 82-85, 502

Neuroscience, 502, 502n

Partial Reinforcement Effect: Hull's reaction to Humphreys' work, 103-4; *see also* Extinction; Frustration Theory

Pavlov I. P.: influence on Hull, 3, 7, 18-20, 25-30, 31, 36, 41, 42, 51, 66-67, 70, 74, 356, 373, 375, 399, 402, 406, 409, 412-13, 487n2, 502n

Pavlovian and Trial-and-Error Learning: relationship between, 19-20, 25, 28-29, 31, 106, 121n, 168n, 214-16, 245n, 301, 307-8, 344, 502n

Physiological Psychology, 85; as a factor in the decline of Hullian influence, 503; relation to Gestalt theory, 71

Problem Solving: novel solutions in, 50-53, 209-12, 237-63, 317-18; S-R analysis of, 37, 39, 246-52, 256-61

Pure Stimulus Act, 35, 145-49; functional significance of, 146-47, 154, 160; organic basis of symbolism, 147, 154, 175, 244

Psychologists: academic training of, 400

Quantification in Learning Theory, 47, 61, 82, 96, 97-102, 271-72, 325n7, 360n, 384n, 400, 427-43, 446-68, 496; application of Thurstone's scaling technique, 98-99, 99n, 425, 440, 446, 464; Skinner's reaction to quantification in *Principles*, 98-99; subsequent work by Hull's followers, 99-100; *see also* Signal Detection Theory

Redintegration, 110-4, 143, 153, 159, 160, 166; and "within-compound" associations, 26